BINDING CORPORATE RULES

Binding Corporate Rules

Corporate Self-Regulation of Global Data Transfers

LOKKE MOEREL

OXFORD
UNIVERSITY PRESS

OXFORD
UNIVERSITY PRESS

Great Clarendon Street, Oxford, OX2 6DP
United Kingdom

Oxford University Press is a department of the University of Oxford. It furthers the University's objective of excellence in research, scholarship, and education by publishing worldwide. Oxford is a registered trade mark of Oxford University Press in the UK and in certain other countries

First Edition published in 2012

Impression: 1

British Library Cataloguing in Publication Data
Data available

Library of Congress Cataloging in Publication Data
Library of Congress Control Number: 2012939876

ISBN 978–0–19–966291–3

Printed in Great Britain by
CPI Group (UK) Ltd, Croydon, CR0 4YY

Acknowledgements

In performing the research for this book I have had help in many forms. I obviously benefited from all discussions on Binding Corporate Rules with the Dutch Data Protection Authority and the members of the BCR working group, the advice and input we received from their foreign group companies, as well as US and other external foreign counsel. My thanks further go to my firm De Brauw Blackstone Westbroek for again granting me the space to pursue my academic interests and facilitated practical support, provided by Stephen Machon, who edited my English and Mieke Merkelijn, who provided research assistance and edited many footnotes. I am further indebted to The Hague Institute for International Law for launching the HiiL Research Program 'Private Actors and Self-regulation', into the legitimacy, effectiveness, enforcement, and quality of different forms of transnational private regulation. My participation in the HiiL Program brought me into contact with the European experts on transnational private regulation and their invaluable work products as part of this programme, from which I greatly benefited. This book is based on Part II of my dissertation 'BCR–Fixing the Regulatory Patchwork of Data Protection', which I publicly defended at Tilburg University on 11 September 2011. In writing my dissertation I greatly benefited from the constructive comments of my PhD supervisor Corien Prins, and those of the members of my Review Committee, Christopher Millard, Martijn Polak, Linda Senden, and Colin Scott.

Contents

Table of Cases

Table of Instruments, International Agreements, and Guidelines

Abbreviations

ADR	Alternative Dispute Resolution
A-G	Advocate General
APEC	Asia-Pacific Economic Cooperation
APPI	Act on the Protection of Personal Information
BEREC	Body of European Regulators for Electronic Communication
BEUC	Bureau Européen des Unions de Consommateurs/The European Consumers' Organization
BCR	Binding Corporate Rules
BGC	Binding Global Codes
BR	Better Regulation
BRIC	Brazil, Russia, India, and China
CBPR	Cross Border Privacy Rules
CIPL	Centre for Information Policy Leadership
CNIL	La Commission nationale de l'informatique et des libertés
COPPA	Children's Online Privacy Protection Act
CPA	Certified Public Accountant
CRM	Customer Relationship Management
CSR	Corporate Social Responsibility
CTLR	Computer Technology Law Report
CWC	Central Works Council
DCFR	Draft Common Frames of Reference
DG	Directorate-General
DPA	Data Protection Authority
DPD	Data Protection Directive
EC	European Community
EC	European Commission
ECHR	European Convention for the Protection of Human Rights and Fundamental Freedoms
ECJ	European Court of Justice
ECR	European Court Report
ECSC	European Community of Coal and Steel
EDPB	European Data Protection Board
EDPS	European Data Protection Supervisor
EEA	European Economic Area
EFTA	European Free Trade Association
ESAs	European Supervisory Authorities
EU	European Union
EWC	European Works Council
FAQ	Frequently Asked Questions
FEDMA	Federation of European and Interactive Marketing
FSA	Financial Services Authority
FTC Act	Federal Trade Commission Act
FTSE	Financial Times Stock Exchange

GAAP	Generally Accepted Accounting Principles
GAF	Global Accountancy Framework
GLBA	Gramm-Leach-Bliley Act
HiiL	The Hague Institute for the Internationalisation of Law
HIPPAA	Health Insurance Portability and Accountability Act
HITECH	Health Information Technology for Economic and Clinical Health Act
HR	Human Resources
ICC	International Chamber of Commerce
ICCPR	International Covenant on Civil and Political Rights
ICT	Information and Communication Technologies
IFRS	International Financial Reporting Standards
ILO	International Labour Organization
IOSCO	International Organization of Securities Commission
ISAs	Independent Supervisory Authorities
IT	Information Technologies
ITU	International Telecommunication Union
LSE	London School of Economics
MNC(s)	Multinational Corporation(s)
MNE(s)	Multinational Enterprise(s)
MRP	Mutual Recognition Procedure
NGOs	Non-governmental Organizations
NYSE	New York Stock Exchange
OECD	Organisation for Economic Co-operation and Development
OFAC	Office of Foreign Assets Controls
OJ	Official Journal of the European Union
OPTA	Onafhankelijke Post en Telecommunicatie Authoriteit (Dutch Supervisory Authority on Telecom Operators)
P&I	Privacy & Informatie
PIAs	Privacy Impact Assessments
PIL	Private International Law
PIPEDA	Canadian Personal Information Protection and Electronic Document Act
PNR	Passenger Name Records
Pub.L.	Public Law
RSCAS	Robert Schuman Centre for Advanced Studies
SAS 70	Statement on Auditing Standards No 70
SBN	Security Breach Notification
SCC	Specialist Computer Centres
SEC	US Securities and Exchange Commission
SWIFT	Society for Worldwide Interbank Financial Telecommunication
TNC(s)	Transnational Corporation(s)
TPR	Transnational Private Regulation
TFEU	Treaty on the Functioning of the European Union
UN	United Nations
USC	United States Code
WC	Works Council
WP 29	Art 29 Data Protection Working Party
WPNR	Weekblad voor Privaatrecht, Notariaat en Registratie
WPPJ	Working Party on Police and Justice
WSIS	World Summit on the Information Society

1

Introduction

1.1 Background

In 1999, a major US bank implemented an IT system in the US, in which it centralized its processing of employee and customer data (including data of consumers) of all its establishments around the world. The group companies obtained access on a remote basis to the data in the central IT system. This access was not limited to a group company's own employee and customer data, but also to certain data from other group companies for purposes of management information. As the US bank had establishments in most European Union (*EU)* Member States, the transfer of the employee and customer data of these EU establishments to the US and other non-EU countries triggered the EU data protection laws of these Member States. The law firm in London I worked for at the time was tasked with ensuring that these data transfers were in compliance with the EU data transfer rules. At that time this required coordination of (i) entering into the EU Standard Contractual Clauses between each of the EU data exporters (ie the EU group companies) and each of the non-EU data importers (ie the US group company that centrally processed the data as well as all other group companies established in non-EU countries that were not considered by the European Commission as providing an adequate level of data protection), and (ii) meeting all formal permit and notification requirements in these Member States. After four years we had to conclude that despite our efforts, at major cost to the client, we had not succeeded in our mission to meet all formalities in the Member States. In certain Member States, the data protection authorities, in spite of many reminders, never issued the required permits, and some never replied at all. Even worse, after four years, we had to establish that the central data processing operation had substantially changed over time, additional data categories had been added, additional central applications had been implemented (such as online performance evaluation), security measures had changed, and more. As a result, the myriad of EU Standard Contractual Clauses entered into between all group companies had become outdated, and a repeat exercise was indicated. I remember telling the client at the time, as well as my own thoughts that if I were the client, I would not repeat the exercise. Despite major efforts and costs, the compliance effort had not resulted in the desired formal compliance. But more importantly, the exercise had not brought any material data protection in practice to the employees and customers. The exercise had been performed by a network of external counsel, completely without the involvement of the company itself. If anything, it just constituted paper compliance, shuffling contracts and permits, put in a drawer never to be looked at again. Though the contracts contained broad third-party beneficiary rights and remedies of employees and customers, the chances that these third parties would be aware of these rights and remedies were minimal (there being no requirement to publish such contracts), and if aware, the chances that employees or customers would act on these rights against the company in a foreign jurisdiction were even less.

In the same years, we regularly received instructions of multinationals, especially from outside the EU, to review their global privacy policies for compliance with EU data protection laws. These policies contained processing instructions to employees on how to process personal data of employees and customers in the performance of their tasks, and also provided for a complaints procedure if things went amiss. These reviews led to many changes in these policies, especially regarding the purposes allowed for data processing, requirements for consent and data retention, etc. These reviews did lead to actual changes in the data processing practices of the relevant multinational, and this on a global basis. Further, enquiries taught us that introduction of the internal complaints procedures led to an increase in complaints, which I took as a positive sign rather than negative, it being likely that prior to introduction of these codes, complaints were not being pursued at all rather than their not being there. My conclusion at the time was that introduction of these global privacy policies brought substantial additional material data protection to employees and customers in practice, while the administrative burden on the companies to comply with formal requirements was minimal. Money spent on external counsel was a fraction, as this concerned marking up companies' data protection policies rather than coordinating the entering into a network of formal contracts and notification and permit procedures.

Combining the two experiences led to the thought that implementation of a global privacy policy would actually prove a better tool to regulate the intercompany data transfers of multinationals than would ever be achieved by the entering into a contractual network of EU Standard Contractual Clauses. I floated the idea at some international conferences, and finally in a more public manner in the *Financieele Dagblad* of 3 April 2003:

> **Boundless Privacy**
> The Dutch Data Protection Act requires that for any exchange of personal data between group companies outside the EU, contracts need to be in place between all the group companies concerned. With a company that is even slightly multinational, this can quickly lead to hundreds of contracts. Madness.
>
> A few examples. A company implements a human resources system which contains the data of employees worldwide and which is accessible to the management of all group companies. A car manufacturer with offices over the entire world exchanges customer data with its subsidiaries in order to coordinate which clients will receive Wimbledon tickets.
>
> They should be able to do that, or so you think. All regular acts performed in the normal course of business should be acceptable and permissible. Who thinks that is thinking outside the Personal Data Protection Act. Transferring personal data, such as

employee data and data of customers of the car manufacturer, is prohibited to those countries outside the European Economic Area (EEA) that do not offer an adequate level of protection of personal data. Transferring personal data to an own group company in these countries also falls under this prohibition.

Should you forget to notify this transfer to the Dutch Data Protection Authority, then you yourself – without the approval of the customer – hang a criminal law sanction above your head. Intentional violation – you are now warned! – can lead to your doing time for six months.

Thankfully there are a few exceptions to the prohibition on transfers. But not to the duty to notify the Authority. Data transfers to group companies via a central HR system is in certain instances permissible, the most important of which are if (1) the employees concerned have provided their informed consent for the transfer, or (2) the Minister of Justice has granted a permit. Consent may be refused, and via this route it is practically not viable to transfer the complete employee processing to the group company operating the central database.

If the centralisation of the database is for management information purposes, this is only worthwhile when indeed all employee data are included. The most practical solution is to request a permit. The permit can be granted when 'adequate safeguards' to protect personal data are offered. What are adequate safeguards?

The European Commission has drafted model contracts. When the exporter of the data has concluded such model contract with the importer of the data outside the EEA, the company will receive a permit on this basis. That sounds reasonable. But how does this work out in the example of the worldwide accessible HR database? The Dutch group company then exchanges data with all its establishments outside the EEA, the French company with all establishments outside the EEA, and so on. This leads to hundreds of intercompany contracts.

It is a good thing that personal data are not, just like that, transferred to countries where there is no control over the further processing of the data. But influencing such further processing is certainly possible within a group of companies. Instead of concluding hundreds of contracts between group companies, an internal code of conduct, which all group companies adhere to, imposing strict rules for the processing of personal data, would lead to the same result. This code of conduct could provide, among other things, that the individual employees and customers involved will obtain the legal rights and remedies against the foreign group companies that they would have under their own national law.

Many companies have already implemented this type of worldwide code of conduct. Not because this was legally required, but because in a global company, all concerned have an interest in streamlining the internal procedures for data exchange. Pushing back frontiers. And now to await a model code of conduct from the European Commission.

The day after this publication, the Dutch Data Protection Commissioner (at the time Peter Hustinx), invited my (by that time Dutch) law firm and five of our multinational clients[1] to a meeting to discuss the possibility of a corporate privacy code as an alternative to the EU Standard Contractual Clauses. A working group

[1] The initial working group consisted of Philips, Shell, AkzoNobel, Sara Lee, and Heineken, at a later stage other multinationals joined such as Schlumberger, DSM, and AEGON.

was established which met regularly for the next year. In June of that year the advisory committee to the European Commission on data protection (*Working Party 29*)[2] issued the first (of a series of six) opinions on corporate privacy codes as an alternative tool for data transfers, which corporate codes it labelled 'Binding Corporate Rules' (*BCR*). Though the first opinion discussed the possibility of BCR in very general terms only, the fact that the Working Party 29 also thought the concept possible was helpful in moving the discussions in the BCR working group forward. In June 2004, the meetings and discussions resulted in a template form of BCR for employee data, which could be subsequently adapted by multinationals to their specific requirements. The discussions were based on the understanding between the Dutch data protection authority (*Dutch DPA*) and the multinationals that, while the working group was in the process of discussing how to translate the data protection requirements under the Data Protection Directive into a practical data protection compliance programme to be embodied in BCR, the Dutch DPA would not pursue these multinationals based on non-compliance in respect of their intercompany data transfers. This enabled the multinationals to spend their time and efforts on developing the compliance tools required for a data protection compliance programme, such as development of an audit programme, training modules for employees and the privacy officers, and privacy impact assessment tools. The experiences of the multinationals when developing these compliance tools, the feedback they received on the draft template BCR from their group companies around the world and review of the draft BCR by external US and other non-EU counsel, led in their turn to changes in the template BCR. Experiences were also shared with DPAs of other Member States receptive to the concept of BCR, most notably in the so-called Berlin meeting,[3] where the DPAs of a limited number of Member States and a representative of the European Commission, together with three multinationals (and their outside counsel) shared experiences in a closed meeting. The results of these discussions were fed back to the Working Party 29 and led, in turn, to the Working Party 29's five subsequent opinions on BCR. The crystallization of the BCR regime further led to the introduction of the

[2] The Working Party 29 was established as an advisory body to the European Commission under Art 29 Data Protection Directive. The Working Party 29 has advisory status only and acts independently, see Art 29(2) Data Protection Directive. Members are representatives of each of the data protection authorities (*DPAs*), the European Data Protection Supervisor and the European Commission. The tasks of the Working Party 29 are clearly formulated and are publicly available. It issues opinions to 'contribute to the uniform application of the Data Protection Directive and advises on proposals for EU legislation having an impact of data protection'. See the Document '"Tasks of the Article 29 Data Protection Working Party', as published at <http://www.ec.europa.eu>. Though the opinions of the Working Party 29 are non-binding, they are often followed in practice by the DPAs and, as such, often set the rules de facto for application of the Data Protection Directive. The DPAs are, however, not obliged to do so and on specific topics (in particular on BCR) some DPAs follow their own course. See in more detail Chapter 6, paragraph 6.5, in particular n 51. For more detail on the Working Party 29, its tasks and procedural rules see Chapter 10, para 10.7.2–10.7.4.

[3] The meeting took place on 27 and 28 May 2004. Participants were representatives of the DPAs of Austria, Germany, Hungary, Poland, the UK, and the Netherlands, the European Commission and further GE, Philips, and DaimlerChrysler, (the multinationals at that time being most advanced in their BCR project).

mutual recognition procedure, whereby a number of DPAs agreed to mutually recognize each other's BCR authorizations.

As such, the joint development of the BCR template by the Dutch DPA and the working group of multinationals showed similarities with what my research later demonstrated to be 'learning-based meta-regulation', where legislators that aim to regulate self-regulation do so in cooperation with the companies that wish (or have to) introduce the self-regulation, based on a number of learning cycles.

My research made me realize that the development of the BCR regime constitutes a remarkable example of the emergence of a form of transnational meta-regulation (ie 'regulation of self-regulation'), whereby transnational effect is achieved not so much by transnational public regulation and transnational approvals, but by mutual recognition among national regulators of their respective publicly recognized private codes.

Another topic which attracted my attention in that period was the scope of the applicability regime of the Data Protection Directive. When advising on cross-border data processing operations, the first question to be answered is whether, and if so which of, the data protection laws of the Member States are applicable. Two trends became visible in the opinions of the Working Party 29 on the applicability regime of the Directive. Both were from a practical perspective understandable and even desirable, but were incompatible with each other and both contrary to the (legislative history of the) Data Protection Directive.

The applicability regime of the Data Protection Directive is based on the principle of cumulation of applicable laws. In the highly visible SWIFT case, SWIFT was headquartered in Belgium and had a number of establishments in the EU. Based on the cumulation principle, the central data processing operations of SWIFT in principle attract the laws of all Member States where SWIFT has an establishment. As this apparently (also in the eyes of the Working Party 29) was not desirable, the Working Party 29 applied only the law of SWIFT's headquarters (ie Belgian law) to all data processing operations of SWIFT in the EU.

On the other hand, with the increased access of EU citizens to the internet, there was an increasing number of foreign-based websites that processed data of EU citizens by means of cookies. As these foreign websites often have no establishments in the EU and do not otherwise use equipment in the EU, the protection of the Data Protection Directive does not, in principle, extend to the processing of EU data via these websites. The Working Party 29, however, qualified the computers of the users on which the cookies were placed as the 'use of equipment' in the EU and thus applied EU data protection law.

These opinions led in practice to companies filing notifications and requesting permits for data transfers which were returned by DPAs since, in their opinion, the law of their respective Member State did not apply, or conversely to a lack of compliance with EU data protection requirements as companies operating foreign websites never even thought of the possibility that the Data Protection Directive could be applicable. This widespread confusion was the trigger for my research into the applicability regime of the Data Protection Directive, which led to a number of publications and papers with recommendations for changes to the applicability regime.[4/5] In December 2009, the Working Party 29 subsequently acknowledged for the first time that the scope of applicability of the Directive was indeed confusing, and announced it would issue a further opinion on the topic.[6] Shortly thereafter, the European Commission issued its Communication on the revision of the Data Protection Directive and announced it would indeed revise the applicability regime thereof. In December 2010, the Working Party 29 issued its further opinion on the applicability regime[7], which deviates in many instances from its earlier opinions and recommends amending the applicability regime very much along the lines as suggested in my publications.[8] At the time this book went to print the status on the thinking of the European Commission on the applicability and jurisdiction regime of the Data Protection Directive is reflected in the proposal on a new EU regulation on data protection[9] which was communicated by the European Commission on 25 January 2012[10] (*Proposed Regulation*). By choosing the form of an EU regulation as a legislative instrument instead of an EU directive, the issue of cumulation of applicable laws within the EU is to a large extent[11] solved as there will only be one data protection law that is applicable in all Member States. As to applicability of the Proposed Regulation to data processing by, for instance, foreign-based websites, the Proposed Regulation covers this as it applies to data

[4] Lokke Moerel, 'The long arm reach of EU data protection law: Does the Data Protection Directive apply to processing of personal data of EU citizens by websites worldwide?' [2011] 1 *International Data Privacy Law*, at 28–46. This publication at its turn was based on a paper presented at the 2009 ESIL-ASIL Research Forum 'Changing Futures? Science and International Law', held in Helsinki, Finland, October 2009.

[5] Lokke Moerel, 'Back to basics: when does EU data protection law apply?' [2011] 2 *International Data Privacy Law*, at 92–110. This publication in its turn draws on two earlier publications in Dutch on the interpretation by the Dutch DPA of Art 4 of the Dutch Data Protection Act, 'Back to Basics: wanneer is de Wet bescherming Persoonsgegevens van toepassing?' (2008/3) *Computerrecht*, at 81 and '"Art. 4 Wbp revisited"; naschrift De nieuwe WP Opinie inzake Search Engines' (2008/6) *Computerrecht*, at 290.

[6] See WP 168, The Future of Privacy, Joint contribution to the Consultation of the European Commission on the legal framework for the fundamental right to protection of personal data, as adopted on 1 December 2009 (*WP Contribution on The Future of Privacy*), at paras 26–8.

[7] Article 29 Data Protection Working Party, Opinion 8/2010 on applicable law, adopted on 16 December 2010, 0836/10/EN WP (*WP Opinion on applicable law*).

[8] My publications in n 4 and n 5 have formed the basis for Chapters 2 and 3 of my dissertation *Binding Corporate Rules—Fixing the Regulatory Patchwork of Data Protection* (Amsterdam 2011), which I publicly defended on 19 September 2011 at Tilburg University. These chapters include the opinion of the Working Party 29 as set out in the WP Opinion on applicable law, n 7, on the respective issues.

[9] European Commission, 'Proposal for a Regulation of the European Parliament and of the Council on the protection of individuals with regard to the processing of personal data and on the free movement of such data' (*General Data Protection Regulation*), COM(2012) 11 final, to be found at <http://ec.europa.eu/justice/newsroom/data-protection/news/120125_en.htm>.

[10] European Commission, Communication of the Commission to the European Council, the European Economical and Social Committee of the Regions, Safeguarding Privacy in a Connected World. A European Data Protection Framework for the 21st Century, COM(2012) 9 final (25 January 2012).

[11] The Proposed Regulation leaves the regulation of certain topics to the Member States. Examples are the regulation of exemptions for data processing purposes of journalistic, artistic, or literary expression (Art 80); the regulation of data processing for health purposes (Art 81) and in the context of employment (Art 82). As a result the laws of the Member States will still deviate in certain respects. Further, the applicability regime as included in the Proposed Regulation will still lead to cumulation of these applicable national laws.

processing related to the offering of goods and services to data subjects in the EU as well as to the monitoring of their behaviour.[12]

Though much has been achieved on the topics of BCR and the applicability regime of the Directive since 2003, this is not the end of it, though. If anything it became clear in my research into the applicability regime, that the EU (like all legislators in the area of data protection) tries to use the scope of its laws to keep a grip on data when transferred across borders. By applying its law also when data are transferred abroad, the data remain protected. It also became clear to me that this is an attempt which is doomed to fail from the start. Territoriality is, and will remain, a key factor for applicable law, jurisdiction and enforcement regimes. Applicability, jurisdiction, and enforcement regimes are therefore inherently delineated and cannot be instrumental in filling the gaps in the protection of personal data and subsequent enforcement. This automatically also applies to the data transfer regimes in these laws, as these are only triggered if the relevant data protection law is applicable in the first place.

This would not pose a problem if all countries in the world were to have adequate data protection laws and enforcement. Cross-border cooperation would then be a solution to achieving protection of EU originated data. The current data protection landscape is, however, still a far cry from a proper global network of data protection laws and a global data protection standard is generally not considered achievable in the coming 10 years. This is not meant to say that we then just have to accept that control is inevitably lost over data after they have been transferred or made part of the cloud. To the contrary, it is meant to say that we have to be more creative in trying to achieve the desired cross-border protection.

When discussing and negotiating the template BCR in the BCR working group with the Dutch DPA, it became clear to me that a possible alternative for the cross-border enforcement issues inherent to the patchwork of national legislation is a choice of law and forum in BCR. Such choice of law and forum may drastically improve the data protection and the access to remedies for the individuals covered by the BCR. If a breach occurs, rather than pursuing rights through traditional judicial means, the individual affected will be able to file a complaint with the group company with which s/he has a relationship, regardless of where the breach occurred or which of the group companies was responsible for the breach. The individual will, therefore, not have to prove which of the group companies was at fault, which is one of the obstacles in practice to bringing and succeeding in a claim. There is also no issue as to which law applies and whether the relevant law provides for data protection since the breach is governed by the BCR. The complaint may be filed by the individual in her/his own language. The group company that received the complaint will be responsible for ensuring that the complaint is processed through the complaints procedure of the multinational and will ensure provision of the required translations. If the complaints procedure does not lead to a satisfying result for the individual, the group company will facilitate the filing of the complaint with the DPA

[12] Article 3(2) Proposed Regulation.

or the courts of the DPA of the chosen forum. This procedure will lead to enforceable rights even in jurisdictions where no (adequate) data protection laws are in place or where insufficient enforcement (infrastructure) is available. It further overcomes language issues and time zones and minimizes cost.

During the discussions in the BCR working group on a template form of BCR, many questions came up which were jointly solved and led to changes in the template BCR, including how to ensure that unilateral undertakings in BCR can be enforced by the beneficiaries of BCR (ie the employees and customers of the multinational). However, other questions also came up which were not easily solved and obviously required further research. One of them is whether indeed a choice of law and forum in BCR is possible or whether this contravenes the mandatory applicability and jurisdiction regime of the Data Protection Directive and/or the employee and consumer protection regimes under European rules of private international law. Further, since multinationals are not necessarily limited to the EU, recognition of BCR in the EU is not sufficient. For BCR to operate on a global basis, recognition of BCR is required also in non-EU countries for outbound data transfers from their respective countries. This requires further research whether, and if so, under which conditions, a private law instrument like BCR may be acceptable also by such non-EU countries. This is in the belief that in the present age of 'big data', cross-border solutions will not be achieved by national legislation while it is in the interest of governments, multinationals, and individuals alike to protect personal data ubiquitously.

1.2 Subject Matter and Aim of this Book

> The digital era is characterized by an unprecedented continuous worldwide flow of data both within multinational companies as well as with their external service providers. While large corporations operate internationally, state governments legislate nationally. Besides leaving gaps in the patchwork of national data protection regulations, this situation also leads to overlaps in applicable national rules that often deviate or outright conflict. These conflicts make it impossible for multinational corporations to comply fully and consistently as to their many forms of cross-border data processing. Further, the traditional territory-based enforcement tools are not adequate for states to force compliance. This legal landscape provides a challenging background to test whether transnational private regulation[13] of data protection can provide solutions where legislation fails to.

[13] The term 'private regulation' is used here in the broad sense, covering both pure self-regulation and regulated self-regulation. Pure self-regulation refers to regulation processes where the state has no involvement. To describe self-regulation when it is combined with laws enacted by the state, various terms are used, such as regulated self-regulation, co-regulation, enforced self-regulation, and audited self-regulation. For a discussion on these various types, see Wolfgang Schulz and Thorsten Held, *Regulated self-regulation as a form of modern government. An analysis of case studies from media and telecommunications law* (University of Luton Press 2004), at 7.

1.2.1 Background

In the digital age, data protection is of increasing concern for governments, individuals and companies alike. While many multinational companies fully act on a seamless worldwide basis, states remain bound to their respective territories. The maturing of the internet especially led to a vast increase in cross-border flows of personal data both within and between groups of companies. Though all countries face essentially the same dilemma of how to regulate these vast flows of personal information, their governments have chosen substantially different solutions to do so. Within the EU the protection of individuals prevailed and the rights of individuals in respect of the processing of their personal data became a fundamental right and freedom. The desire to avoid gaps in the protection of personal data and to prevent circumvention of the Data Protection Directive led EU legislators to provide for a very broad scope of applicability of the Data Protection Directive ('long arm reach'). The wish to regulate the outbound transnational data streams from the EU resulted in another 'long arm' provision in the Data Protection Directive, where it prohibited data transfers to countries outside the EU without an adequate level of protection (*EU data transfer rules*). This extraterritorial provision prompted many countries outside the EU to follow suit in adopting comprehensive data protection legislation to facilitate ongoing access by their multinationals to the EU market. These states also struggled to regulate their outbound transnational data streams which resulted in many states adopting equally 'long arm reach' data protection laws and multiple instances of 'overregulation' (ie where rules are made so generally applicable that they apply prima facie to processing of personal data of their nationals wherever processed around the world). In addition, many of these countries have imposed restrictions on the outbound transfer of personal data from their respective countries. Such outbound data transfer requirements are considered necessary by most countries as there are still many countries with no data protection laws at all as well as countries (most notably the US) with a limited regime, where public regulation is targeted at certain sensitive industries and data categories only. As a consequence the worldwide data protection regulatory landscape at present consists of at best a patchwork of very diverse national data protection laws, which laws often deviate or even outright conflict.

A specific challenge for data protection regulators across the world is posed by the fact that enforcement of data protection legislation is based on a jurisdictional approach. In the international environment this leads to many long arm reach data protection laws having no hope of enforcement in practice if the relevant company is also not established in the relevant jurisdiction. Further, the concepts of applicable law and jurisdiction are embedded in a long tradition of private international law, where laws that over-extend their jurisdictional reach are considered an unacceptable form of 'hyper-regulation' if they apply so indiscriminately that there is no hope of enforcement. Applicability regimes are therefore inherently delineated and cannot be instrumental in solving the present gaps in the protection of personal data and the enforcement thereof.

At present the data protection regulators aim to solve the cross-border enforcement issues by a 'network approach', where data protection authorities of different jurisdictions cooperate in the event of cross-border violations. Until the time all jurisdictions have adequate data protection laws and supervision thereof, this network approach cannot adequately solve the enforcement issues presently faced by data protection regulators. Though there is a persistent call for a legally binding global standard for data protection and there are some concrete initiatives in this respect, it is not expected, however, that a global standard will indeed be realized within the coming 10 years. The present regulatory landscape is still too diverse for such a standard to be acceptable for adoption on a global level. In any event the adoption of a global standard should not be taken as the holy grail for all international jurisdiction and enforcement issues as presently seen in the data protection field. Even if global standards exist, differences in enforcement between countries will remain as in practice regulatory enforcement at the national level proves patchy, whether this is due to lack of resources or the prioritization by national governments of national commercial or other interests above regulatory enforcement. Solutions may therefore only be forthcoming if some form of central enforcement could be implemented by, for instance, the DPA and courts of the jurisdiction where the multinational company has its headquarters.

The existing overlap and conflicts in applicable data protection laws makes a 100 per cent worldwide compliance for multinational companies a practical impossibility. Compliance would require multinational companies not only to track and comply with the material data protection rules of each jurisdiction but also to track and comply with all requirements relating to data transfers between specific countries. Further, multinational companies largely ignore the EU data transfer rules as these lead to impossible administrative burdens. Rather than strive for compliance with the national laws on a country-by-country basis, many multinational companies implement worldwide self-regulation (by introducing corporate privacy policies). These company-wide data protection rules provide for an adequate level of data protection, and ignore possible stricter national provisions. The foregoing significantly affects the capacity of EU DPAs to enforce compliance by multinational companies in the area of data protection. The introduction of corporate privacy policies by multinational companies has created a bottom-up pressure on national legal orders. This is reflected in how third-party beneficiaries of such policies invoke them before national courts (so far mainly in the US), and the pressure exerted on the EU DPAs to recognize these corporate privacy policies as instruments to ensure an adequate level of data protection throughout the group of companies, justifying the international transfers of data between the individual group companies, wherever located. The Working Party 29[14] recognizes the added value of transnational private regulation (*TPR*) in the data protection area in light of the gaps and deficiencies of the present EU data transfer regime. The Working Party 29 set criteria for this TPR to provide for a minimum level of protection for

[14] See on the Working Party 29 n 2.

the processing of data by a multinational on a worldwide basis. With BCR, the Working Party 29 introduced a complex hybrid system of self-regulation (corporate privacy policies) with public arrangements (the DPAs validating such corporate privacy policies and providing support in the area of enforcement). The BCR regime established by the Working Party 29 introduces the possibility of worldwide central enforcement of such BCR by the DPA and courts of the EU headquarters of the multinationals.

The regulatory environment described above, and the deficiencies in protection and enforcement make a challenging background to research whether any gaps and deficiencies in the present applicability and jurisdiction regime of the Data Protection Directive may be addressed by transnational self-regulation, rather than by long arm jurisdiction-based legislation and jurisdiction-based enforcement. Of special interest in that context are the relative merits of central enforcement of BCR through one lead DPA (this lead DPA taking over the enforcement from other DPAs in their respective territories) over the present reliance on enforcement on a network basis (whereby DPAs cooperate in the enforcement in order to enable each DPA to enforce on its own territory).

1.2.2 Aim of this book

Assessment of the suitability and relative merits of corporate self-regulation of data protection as an instrument to regulate global data transfers

In the recent past a vast body of research has been conducted into:

(i) the legitimacy of TPR to regulate corporate conduct in a globalized society;
(ii) how TPR can be aligned with principles of private international law (*PIL*)
(iii) how TPR can be used to implement the 'principle of accountability' in respect of compliance with the relevant legal requirements; and
(iv) the area of corporate social responsibility (*CSR*), where multinationals also implement TPR to overcome differences in regulations and regulatory approaches between countries and as part of their global reputation management.

None of the research above addresses specifically that of TPR regulating data protection in an international environment. Also, the Working Party 29 and the DPAs have little experience with TPR as a tool to regulate cross-border data compliance. Though the Working Party 29 has recently approved the concept of BCR, some DPAs still struggle with the requirements under which these BCR can be recognized and enforced. Similar uncertainty exists as how to fit the BCR concept with the regulatory data protection regimes of other countries or regions like the APEC Privacy Framework. Given this lack of experience, I assess the BCR regime in light of the findings of existing general research into the legal arenas above. Two main topics I address are to what extent data protection may be regulated by TPR and whether a choice of law and forum is allowed under PIL so that indeed central enforcement of BCR is possible. This book results in proposals for improvement of the BCR regime as well as proposals as to how to fit this hybrid system with other existing data protection regimes across the world (especially in the US) and new regulatory regimes in development today (especially by the APEC countries). The objective is to investigate how to further the acceptance of BCR as a mainstream global solution to regulate global corporate conduct in the area of data protection. BCR may then indeed provide a private solution to solve the gaps in protection and enforcement as presented by the current patchwork of national data protection laws and jurisdiction based enforcement thereof.

Part of this assessment will also be to test the following hypotheses:

(i) BCR as an instance of TPR can do better than the present territory-based state regulation of data protection in terms of:
   (a) avoiding gaps in protection and enforcement as presented by the current patchwork of national data protection laws and state-based enforcement; and
   (b) regulating transborder data flows.

(ii) The BCR regime as currently developed by the Working Party 29 does not sufficiently incorporate or is not sufficiently aligned with principles of PIL, best practices when implementing the principle of accountability, generally accepted legitimacy demands made of TPR, and best practices as to CSR, in order for BCR to be acceptable on a global basis as a form of TPR to regulate global corporate conduct in the area of data protection (societal relevance).

1.2.3 Relevance and recommendations

With this book, I intend to (i) contribute to the academic debate on these topics; (ii) further the acceptance of BCR as a mainstream global solution to regulate global corporate conduct in the area of data protection (societal relevance); and (iii) provide concrete suggestions to EU legislators on how to improve these regimes.

Re (i) Academic relevance

The academic relevance of my research has already been addressed in the previous paragraphs. In addition, I mention that the assessment of the BCR concept in particular in light of the findings of the existing research into the legitimacy of TPR to regulate corporate conduct in a globalized society, adds an interesting concrete example in practice to test the merits of these findings. This is particularly relevant as under EU law data protection qualifies as a human right,[15] and the existing literature is divided on the issue whether human rights are indeed fit to be regulated by TPR (and in particular CSR codes) and the existing research has until now not

[15] See in detail Chapter 3, n 3.

been extended to the role of self-regulation in the data protection field.[16] The BCR regime constitutes further a remarkable example of the emergence of a form of transnational meta-regulation (ie 'regulation of self-regulation'), whereby transnational effect is achieved not so much by transnational public regulation and transnational approvals, but by mutual recognition among national regulators of their respective publicly recognized private codes.

Re (ii) Further acceptance of BCR as mainstream solution (societal relevance)

The substantial efforts and cost for multinationals to embark on a worldwide BCR programme without having certainty (i) whether the BCR concept will work on an EU wide basis; and (ii) about the time frame within which EU-wide approval of BCR may ultimately be achieved, prove an obstacle in practice for multinationals to decide on the adoption of BCR within their group of companies. Multinationals will benefit if the uncertainties as to the validity and enforcement of BCR are solved and the BCR authorization procedure is streamlined. Given the present non-compliance by multinationals with the EU data transfer rules and the cross-border enforcement issues encountered by individuals in the enforcement of their rights, individuals may equally benefit.

The assessment of the BCR regime in light of the findings of existing research on TPR, PIL, CSR, and the accountability principle, will accelerate the acceptance and credibility of BCR as the mainstream global solution. This is not only beneficial to multinationals, but at the same time will also enhance the protection afforded to individuals of one of their fundamental rights and freedoms.

Re (iii) Recommendations to EU legislators

My suggestions to EU legislators for improvement are not made collectively at the end, but rather throughout the text where indicated and are placed in a framework. An overview of my recommendations can be found in Chapter 12 and further in Annex I, which also provides a matrix listing for each recommendation which of the disciplines led to such recommendation, as well as whether such recommendation overlaps with those made for revision of the Data Protection Directive by the Rand Report, the Working Party 29, the European Data Protection Supervisor, the Centre for Information Policy Leadership, and/or the European Commission.

1.2.4 Prior research and publications

This book has already been published as Part II of my dissertation *BCR—Fixing the Regulatory Patchwork of Data Protection*,[17] which I publicly defended at Tilburg University on 11 September 2011. Changes to the text have been limited to attune

[16] Several case studies in respect of TPR of human rights (including BCR) are presently performed as part of the HiiL Program (see on the HiiL Program para 1.2.4).

[17] See n 8.

the text to the fact that I have left out Part I of my dissertation on the applicability and jurisdiction regime of the Data Protection Directive. Further, I have included new text and footnotes to show the changes to EU data protection law as proposed in the Proposed Regulation.[18] Though I left out Part I of my dissertation, the current text in many aspects relies on the prior research on the applicability and jurisdiction regime of the Data Protection Directive.[19]

For this book I have further made use of my desk research[20] performed as part of the HiiL Research Program 'Private Actors and Self-Regulation', into the legitimacy, effectiveness, enforcement, and quality of different forms of TPR (*HiiL Program*).[21] As part of the HiiL Program, I carry out a case study into the legitimacy, effectiveness, enforcement, and quality of BCR as a form of TPR of data protection. The empirical research in respect of the effectiveness of BCR in providing material data protection to individuals is outside the scope of this publication, but is currently being conducted as part of the HiiL Program, and will be published at a later stage.[22]

[18] See n 9.

[19] See n 4, n 5 and further Part I of my dissertation (n 8).

[20] In particular my paper 'Transnational Private Regulation of Data Protection' prepared for the 2010 HiiL Annual Conference on Transnational Private Regulation, June 2010, Dublin, to be found at <http://www.privateregulation.eu>.

[21] For the scope of the HiiL Program's research, see HiiL 2008, 'The Added Value of Private Regulation in an International world? Towards a Model of the Legitimacy, Effectiveness, Enforcement and Quality of Private Regulation' and the 'Draft Inventory Report', both dated May 2008 and to be found at <http://www.hagueppgnetwork.org/towards-the-hppgn/>. The central research questions of the HiiL Program are set out in the Draft Inventory Report, at para 2.5:

1. Is regulation with a transnational dimension, drafted by private actors, more successful than formal, state-regulation in regulating the conduct of corporations active in the global market?
2. If so, to what extent, under what conditions and with respect to which areas does private regulation have a—positive or negative—impact upon the effective and efficient functioning of national legal orders?
3. The main objective of the research is to formulate a model (or a number of models), which could be of use to governments and to private actors, in which these questions come together and be answered.

The HiiL Program will, on a theoretical level, research the following topics:

- What are the transnational constitutional foundations of private regulation;
- What are the differences between private regulation at national and transnational level: what contrasting modes of acquiring legitimacy and effectiveness are adopted;
- What is the role of private regulation as an alternative or a complement to public regulation (are there common principles that can be identified?);
- What factors or principles are—or should be—relevant/decisive in making regulatory choices from the point of view of effectiveness (including learning), enforcement, legitimacy, and quality? (normative determinants);
- What are the unintended (and potentially counterproductive) effects associated with the emergence of a plurality of legal regimes at transnational level in terms both of effectiveness and legitimacy?
- What is the role of regulatory impact assessment concerning the choice between public and private regulation and the principle of proportionality?

[22] The final report of the HiiL Program is expected in December 2012.

1.2.5 Scope

This book does not concern itself with the desirability of data protection legislation per se or the relative merits of the different regulatory systems set up by legislators across the world. Multinationals have to operate in the present regulatory landscape and for this book this is taken as a given.

I further concentrate on the topic of cross-border data protection and enforcement in the private sector. This concerns cross-border flows of personal data both within groups of companies and between groups of companies. Though many types of cross-border data flows are carried out between public authorities and further between companies and public authorities (especially for law enforcement purposes), these types of data flows give rise to special issues and are outside the scope of this book.

The point of departure for this book is that data protection regulation should be designed and evaluated based on whether rules provide for material data protection for individuals in practice rather than whether they provide for rights and remedies in theory.[23]

This book is current up to 1 February 2012, and all hyperlinks were valid on that date.

1.3 Outline

Chapter 2 contains an introduction to the concept of Binding Corporate Rules and the topics discussed in this book.

Chapter 3 gives an introduction to the worldwide data protection regulatory landscape and the different types of regulatory systems. An overview is given of the basic principles of the Data Protection Directive (and the changes envisaged by the Proposed Regulation), as knowledge of these principles is required for a proper understanding of the BCR regime. The APEC Privacy Framework is also discussed as a representative of a data protection system based on an organizational approach rather than a territorial approach.

Chapter 4 discusses some trends and developments in the regulatory landscape, such as the increasing tensions between the different regulatory systems, the prospects of the growing call for a global data protection standard, and the cross-border enforcement issues presently encountered by DPAs and individuals alike. The chapter concludes with a discussion of possible alternative solutions to improve the position of individuals in case of cross-border data protection violations. One of

[23] In July 2010, the Working Party 29 explicitly embraced this perspective of 'law in action' as opposed to 'law in theory': see WP 173, Opinion 3/2010 on the principle of accountability adopted on 13 July 2010 (*WP Opinion on the principle of accountability*) at 3: 'Data protection must move from "theory to practice". Legal requirements must be translated into real data protection measures. (. . .) In its document on The Future of Privacy (WP 168) of December 2009, the Article 29 Working Party expressed the view that the present legal framework has not been successful in ensuring that data protection requirements translate into effective mechanisms that deliver real protection.'

these solutions requires the introduction by multinationals of global corporate self-regulation backed up by government enforcement. By introducing the possibility for multinationals to make a choice of law and forum in these self-regulatory codes, it would be possible to have these codes supervised and enforced on a worldwide basis by one 'lead' DPA (*Lead DPA*) only, preferably the authority of the place of establishment of the headquarters of such multinational.

Chapter 5 discusses a number of practical developments encountered by multinationals, which result in the data processing operations of multinationals being governed by a myriad of national data protection laws. It is subsequently discussed why and how multinationals mitigate their global data protection risks by means of a global corporate privacy code.

Chapter 6 introduces the BCR regime as developed by the Working Party 29, recognizing corporate self-regulation as an alternative method for multinationals to comply with the EU data transfer rules. The European BCR approval procedure is discussed as well as its shortcomings. It is further discussed in which non-EU countries BCR are (potentially) recognized as a valid data transfer tool also for data transfers from these non-EU countries. Recommendations are made to recognize BCR as a valid tool for data transfers when revising the Directive and to streamline the BCR authorization procedure.

Chapter 7 discusses some contractual issues in light of the requirement that BCR should be internally binding on the group companies and employees of the multinational and externally binding for the benefit of the beneficiaries of BCR. The latter requires discussion of the enforceability of unilateral undertakings by the beneficiaries of BCR. TPR is further often effectuated through contractual 'supply chain management', a solution which is also part of the BCR regime. Also supply chain management raises issues of enforceability by the beneficiaries of these contracts, which are of equal relevance to BCR. How the various supply chain issues can be best addressed in BCR is also discussed.

Chapter 8 discusses the interaction of BCR with rules of PIL, which is twofold. First there is the traditional function of PIL, where for instance a choice of law and forum made in BCR has to comply with rules of PIL. This requires answering the questions of (i) which instruments of PIL are in scope?; do the rules of PIL take precedence over the applicability and jurisdiction regime of the Directive?; and (iii) is a choice of law possible under the Directive? It is further discussed how the BCR applicability and enforcement regime can be best set up to avoid the current pitfalls under the employee and consumer protection regimes of PIL. The second function of PIL is as a potential source of 'meta-norms' for BCR. It is discussed how the BCR applicability and enforcement regime can be best aligned with the underlying policy choices behind PIL instruments and doctrines in order to be able to achieve universal acceptance of BCR.

Chapter 9 discusses BCR in the wider context of the introduction of the 'accountability principle' in the area of data protection and in other fields of law. Specific attention is devoted as to how regulators can provide companies with incentives and tools to use their own inherent 'regulatory capacities'. Separately discussed are the merits and the relevance for BCR of the proposal by the Working

Party 29 to introduce in the revised Directive a provision that controllers will remain accountable for the protection of their data even after these data have been transferred to a third party.

Chapter 10 evaluates BCR as a form of TPR. This concerns the issue of what the optimal form of meta-regulation is when choosing TPR. The discipline of how best to regulate (the rules for rule-making, the search for meta-norms) has in the EU become known under the label 'Better Regulation' (*BR*). In this chapter BCR are evaluated from the perspective of BR as to (i) whether the norm-setting as to BCR meets the basic requirements for EU law-making, for instance as to requirements of participation and transparency; and (ii) whether BCR (qualifying as co-regulation) concern an area of law for which EU legislators consider co- or self-regulation appropriate. Proposals are made to bring the BCR norm-setting, evaluation/monitoring, and enforcement in line with the body of thought on BR.

Chapter 11 addresses BCR as a form of CSR. It is discussed to what extent data protection is covered by international soft law instruments setting guidelines for CSR, and if so, whether this has any repercussions for the BCR regime. This requires (again) a discussion of regulating human rights, not so much in the context of whether these may be regulated by self-regulation, but whether the international instruments on CSR require that fundamental rights held by individuals should be viewed as imposing duties directly on multinationals, even for activities of these multinationals in countries that do not recognize such human rights.

Chapter 12 presents my overall conclusions and recommendations and gives an evaluation of the research objectives and hypotheses.

2

Binding Corporate Rules: An Overview

2.1 Data Here, Data There, Data Everywhere[1]

At the time of adoption of the European Data Protection Directive (1995) (*Directive*)[2] the expectation was that the establishment and functioning of the European internal market[3] would lead to a substantial increase in cross-border flows of personal data between all those involved in economic activity *within* the EU Member States.[4] To facilitate a free flow of these personal data within the EU, the object of the Directive was to achieve full harmonization of data protection laws within the EU.[5] The wish to protect European data even if transferred outside of the EU resulted in a prohibition of data transfers to non-EU countries[6] without an

[1] 'The Data Deluge: Businesses, governments and society are only starting to tap its vast potential' *The Economist*, 25 February 2010. *The Economist* reports that the world is currently undergoing an unprecedented 'information explosion', which transforms our society into a 'data centred economy'. This phenomenon is coined by scientists and computer engineers as 'big data': 'Everywhere you look, the quantity of information in the world is soaring. According to one estimate, mankind created 150 exabytes (billion gigabytes) of data in 2005. This year, it will create 1,200 exabytes. Merely keeping up with this flood, and storing the bits that might be useful, is difficult enough. Analysing it, to spot patterns and extract useful information, is harder still. Even so, the data deluge is already starting to transform business, government, science and everyday life (...). It has great potential for good—as long as consumers, companies and governments make the right choices about when to restrict the flow of data, and when to encourage it.'

[2] Directive 95/46/EC of the European Parliament and the Council of 24 October 1995 on the protection of individuals with regard to the processing of personal data and on the free movement of such data, [1995] OJ L281/31 (*Data Protection Directive*).

[3] The legal basis for the Data Protection Directive is Art 95 (formerly 100a) of the Consolidated Version of the Treaty establishing the European Community, [2002] OJ C325/1 (*EC Treaty*). See further Recitals 1–9 of the Data Protection Directive. The EC Treaty has been replaced by the Consolidated Version of the Treaty on the Functioning of the European Union [2010] OJ C83/49 (*TFEU*). Article 95 EC Treaty is now Art 114 TFEU.

[4] Recitals 5 and 6 of the Directive. The Directive also foresaw an increase in the exchange of personal data between companies as a result of the increase in scientific and technical cooperation and the introduction of new telecommunication networks in the Community, which would necessitate and facilitate the cross-border flow of personal data, see Recital 5 Directive.

[5] See Recital 8 Directive, indicating that the purpose of the Directive was full harmonization with the exception of specific discretionary powers in a limited number of areas (for instance it is left to the individual Member States to provide in which cases controllers are authorized to process sensitive data). See also Case C-101/01 *Bodil Lindqvist* [2003] ECR I-12971, at paras 95–6.

[6] The three countries of the European Free Trade Association (EFTA) (Iceland, Liechtenstein, and Norway) have ratified the Data Protection Directive in the EEA agreement (cf Decision of the EEA Joint Committee No 83/1999 of 25 June 1999 amending Protocol 37 and Annex XI (Telecommunication services) to the EEA Agreement, OJ L 296/41, of 23 November 2000). The free flow of

adequate level of data protection.[7] It is clear that the EU data transfer rules date from the time the internet was not yet widely used. The EU transfer rules were devised when transborder data flows were still typically point-to-point transfers, for instance if a company transferred an employee abroad to another group company and provided the employee's file and other employee records to such other group company or in the case of a cross-border takeover.[8]

The EU transfer rules prompted many non-EU countries to follow suit in adopting comprehensive data protection legislation in order for their companies to maintain access to the EU market.[9] Though these laws all regulate more or less the same subject matter, their governments have chosen substantially different solutions to do so. In the EU the rights of individuals in respect of processing of their personal data became a fundamental human right and freedom,[10] but in many other jurisdictions another form of protection was chosen. Also, there are still many

information extends to these countries. References to the EU should be understood to include the EFTA countries, ie they also concern the European Economic Area (*EEA*).

[7] Recitals 56 and 57 of the Directive. See also European Commission, Amended Proposal for a Council Directive on the protection of individuals with regard to the processing of personal data and on the free movement of such data, COM(92) 422 final, 15 October 1992, at 34, indicating that without restrictions on international data transfers, 'the Community's efforts to guarantee a high level of protection for individuals could be nullified by transfers to other countries in which the protection provided is inadequate'. See Ulrich Dammann and Spiros Simitis, *EG-Datenschutzrichtlinie* (Nomos 1997), at 270 (translation by the author): 'The corresponding regulations have to guarantee that the protection guaranteed within the territory of the EU will not be nullified by a transfer to a territory, where there is no or no equivalent level of data protection.'

[8] Christopher Kuner, *Regulation of Transborder Data Flows under Data Protection and Privacy Law: Past, Present and Future* TILT Law & Technology Working Paper No 016/2010, October 2010, Version 1.0, at 10, to be found at <http://papers.ssrn.com/sol3/papers.cfm?abstract_id=1689483>. See also Opinion 1/2010 on the concepts of 'controller' and 'processor' (WP 169), at para II.2, pointing out that 'when Directive 95/46/EC was adopted, the context of data processing was still relatively clear and straightforward, but that is no longer the case' due to a growing tendency towards organizational differentiation, development of Information and Communication Technologies (ICTs), and globalization. See further *Vodafone, Privacy—an evolving challenge*, to be found at <http://www.vodafone.com/content/dam/vodafone/about/public_policy/future_ofprivacy/privacy_an_evolving_challenge_update.pdf>, at 2: 'Back in 1995, when the Data Protection Directive was adopted, only 18 per cent of Europeans had access to a PC, and the percentage of people with a mobile phone in Europe was 4 per cent. Only 1 per cent had access to the internet and, even within industry, IT use was relatively basic. People didn't have "online profiles"; indeed when it came to the use of personal information the individual was essentially passive. Large organizations, like banks, hospitals, government departments, were the only bodies with the capacity to process large amounts of information. This information was seldom shared as it was, in general, kept in discrete segregated silos on local servers'.

[9] This puts the situation in a positive light. However, at the time of introduction of the Directive, it was clear that the EU dictated its standard on the rest of the world based on the concept of reciprocity: EU personal data may only be transferred to a country that provides equivalent protection. Representatives from outside the EU argued that the Directive thus had an improper extraterritorial effect and was protectionist. The complaints however did not stick and the export of the EU model has been very successful. Even the U.S. capitulated by agreeing to implement the Safe Harbor Framework (see n 71 below). See also Corien Prins 'Should ICT Regulation Be Undertaken at an International Level?', in Bert-Jaap Koops et al (eds.), *Starting Points for ICT Regulation. Deconstructing Prevalent Policy One-Liners* (TCM Asser Press 2006), at 172.

[10] See eg Art 16 TFEU and Art 8 EU Charter of Fundamental Rights (annexed to the TFEU and legally binding for EU Member States since December 2009), both recognizing the right to data protection.

countries with no data protection laws at all as well as countries (most notably the US) with a limited regime, where public regulation of data processing in the private sector is targeted at certain sensitive industries and further provides for data breach notification obligations in respect of specific categories of personal data only.[11] The result at present is a worldwide data protection regulatory landscape consisting of at best a patchwork of very diverse national data protection laws.

Though the Directive foresaw an increase in data flows within the EU, the digital era has resulted in an unprecedented continuous *worldwide* flow of data both within multinational companies[12] as well as with their external outsourcing service providers. Multinationals process personal data in the course of business.[13] Employee data are processed, for instance, for purposes of execution of the employment agreement (salary payment, performance evaluation, succession planning). Multinationals selling consumer products further process personal data of their customers. But multinationals involved in business-to-business transactions also process personal data of the contact persons within their suppliers, corporate customers, and other business partners. Specific industries like the pharmaceutical sector may in addition process specific categories of personal data for instance in the course of performing scientific research involving patients. Due to the globalization of the activities of these multinationals, these data are not relevant to one group company only (for instance, the group company employing the relevant employee), but are relevant also to other group companies. An example is performance evaluations and succession planning. Most multinationals have a matrix organization, which entails that their business is managed not so much on a country-by-country basis but per business unit, which may extend over many countries. It is therefore possible that the manager of an employee is not located in his own country. Evaluation of the employee's performance will then require a transfer of

[11] See on limited regimes Chapter 3, para 3.3 and further on data breach notification legislation in the U.S. Chapter 5, para 5.3.

[12] The term 'multinational company' refers to corporate enterprises with establishments across the world (typically in several or all continents). In literature, many acronyms are used such as MNCs (Multinational Corporations), MNEs (Multinational Enterprises), or TNCs (Transnational Corporations). For readability, I use only the term multinational.

[13] For a description of the magnitude of the recent worldwide explosion of data collection and sharing, see 'A special report on managing information: Data, data everywhere. Information has gone from scarce to superabundant. That brings huge new benefits, but also big headaches' *The Economist*, 25 January 2010, stating that: 'Wal-Mart, a retail giant, handles more than 1m customer transactions every hour, feeding databases estimated at more than 2.5 petabytes—the equivalent of 167 times the books in America's Library of Congress (...). Facebook, a social-networking website, is home to 40 billion photos. And decoding the human genome involves analysing 3 billion base pairs—which took ten years the first time it was done, in 2003, but can now be achieved in one week. All these examples tell the same story: that the world contains an unimaginably vast amount of digital information which is getting ever vaster ever more rapidly. This makes it possible to do many things that previously could not be done: spot business trends, prevent diseases, combat crime and so on. Managed well, the data can be used to unlock new sources of economic value, provide fresh insights into science and hold governments to account. But they are also creating a host of new problems. Despite the abundance of tools to capture, process and share all this information—sensors, computers, mobile phones and the like—it already exceeds the available storage space (see chart 1). Moreover, ensuring data security and protecting privacy is becoming harder as the information multiplies and is shared ever more widely around the world.'

his performance data to the country of his manager and ultimately to central management of his business unit, which may be located yet somewhere else. The same applies to supplier data. Multinationals more and more centralize their purchasing to achieve cost savings. This requires the centralization of their supplier data which are subsequently shared with other group companies.

Another development is that these transfers are no longer point-to-point (via fixed telecommunication lines) but between multiple computers communicating through a private network or the internet. Multinationals have further started to integrate their various local IT systems and now process their employee and customer data in central IT systems, which entails a continuous worldwide transfer of data between their group companies. These central IT systems may subsequently be outsourced to third-party service providers.[14] For cost reasons these service providers often provide their services from offshore locations outside the EU.[15] Such offshoring may involve transfers of the data of the multinational to all service centres of the outsourcing supplier in the countries involved. Transfers of data within the multinational and offshoring to third countries may be subject to a multitude of applicable data protection laws. The data transfer issues are further multiplied by recent technical developments such as dynamic routing[16] and cloud computing.[17] As a result of these developments it is no longer predictable how data will be routed over the internet and where the data will be ultimately stored. This proliferation of transborder data flows has triggered the application of the EU transfer rules on an unprecedented scale. Multinationals (whether with headquarters within or outside the EU) find compliance with all applicable national data protection laws[18] a 'challenge' as the present regulatory environment features many overlaps of applicable laws, which laws often vary or are even in outright conflict.[19] Many countries[20] have followed the EU in imposing restrictions on the outbound transfer of personal data from their territories. These restrictions require

[14] For instance with server management, the outsourcing supplier hosts the servers of a customer on which the customer's IT applications operate (varying from HR to CRM applications).

[15] Favourites include the 'BRIC' countries (Brazil, Russia, India, and China).

[16] Dynamic routing is the opposite of static routing, where data are processed through a network by a fixed path. With dynamic routing it cannot be predicted how data will be routed over the internet.

[17] Cloud computing is defined by The National Institute of Standards and Technology (NIST) as: 'a model for enabling convenient, on-demand network access to a shared pool of configurable computing resources (e.g., networks, servers, storage, applications, and services) that can be rapidly provisioned and released with minimal management effort or service provider interaction.' <http://en.wikipedia.org/wiki/Cloud_computing-cite_note-5#cite_note-5>. The key characteristic of cloud computing is that the computing is 'in the cloud' ie the processing and the related data are not in a specified, known, or static place. This is in contrast to a model in which the processing takes place in one or more specific servers that are known.

[18] Kuner estimates that of the 192 Member States of the United Nations about 50–60 currently have a legal framework for data protection. See Christopher Kuner, 'An International Legal Framework for Data Protection: Issues and Prospects' [2009] *Computer Law and Security Review*, at 307, para III.

[19] Even in the EU, where data protection laws are harmonized such conflicts do present themselves. For instance, in Germany it is required for employers to register the religious faith of employees (as employers pay church tax on behalf of employees), while in most other countries it is expressly prohibited to process the religious faith of an employee.

[20] About 60 countries have some form of data transfer restriction. See for a comprehensive overview Kuner (n 8), at 55–89.

multinationals to track and comply not only with the material data protection rules of each jurisdiction but also with all requirements relating to data transfers between specific countries.

The existing regulatory minefield in the data protection area has led many multinationals to implement worldwide corporate privacy policies.[21] These company-wide data protection rules aim to provide for a uniform adequate[22] level of data protection throughout the relevant group of companies rather than strive for compliance by the multinational on a country-by-country basis. The multinationals accept the risk of possible non-compliance with any stricter rules at the national level. Furthermore, given the administrative burden involved with complying with the various national transfer rules[23], most multinationals just ignore these transfer rules insofar as their intra-company transfers of personal data are concerned. They may also ignore the data transfer rules in the case of offshoring and the use of cloud computing.[24]

Data protection authorities in the various EU Member States (*DPAs*)[25] are well aware of the fact that multinationals exchange personal data on a worldwide basis and outsource their IT to countries without an adequate system of data protection.[26] Practice shows that the enforcement tools of the DPAs are at present not sufficient to force compliance, whether due to lack of cooperation between national states, lack of enforcement tools at the disposal of the DPAs, lack of resources, or the sheer volume of non-compliance.[27]

[21] This is based on my observations as a practitioner advising multinationals on their worldwide data protection compliance. Part of the HiiL Program is to perform empirical research in this respect.

[22] The term 'adequate' is not used in the meaning of Art 25(1) Directive, but is here used to express that the multinational does not attempt to make the global policy compliant with all applicable national data protection laws in order to ensure compliance on a worldwide basis. This would entail that the strictest provisions of all national laws would be cumulatively applicable throughout the world. The multinational therefore makes choices between different features of different systems to come to an overall adequate level of protection.

[23] For the EU administrative requirements, see Chapter 3, para 3.1.1 below, which include in many Member States authorization of such transfers by the DPAs of the Member States from which the data are exported and notification of the data processing to the DPAs.

[24] This is not only my own observation as a practitioner, but is confirmed by research performed on behalf of the European Commission: see n 26 and n 27.

[25] References to the DPAs should be understood to include data protection authorities of the EEA countries: see n 6.

[26] See Commission of the European Communities, First Report on the Implementation of the Data Protection Directive (95/46/EC), 15 March 2003, COM/2003/265 final (*First Report on the Directive*), at 19. National DPAs are supposed to notify the Commission when they authorize a transfer under Art 26(2) Directive. The Commission notes that it has received only a 'derisory number of notifications compared with what might reasonably be expected'. The Commission further notes that 'combined with other evidence pointing in the same direction, this suggests that many unauthorized and possibly illegal transfers are being made to destinations or recipients not guaranteeing adequate protection'.

[27] Rand Europe, Review of the European Data Protection Directive, Technical Report dated May 2009 (*Rand Report*), at 35. Douwe Korff, *EC Study on implementation of the Data Protection Directive, Comparative study of national laws*, September 2002, Human Rights Centre University of Essex, at 209, to be found at <http://papers.ssrn.com>, notes that 'the powers now vested in the data protection authorities, as currently exercised, have *not been able to counter continuing widespread disregard for the data protection laws in the Member States'.* See further Omer Teme, 'For Privacy, The European Commission Must Be Innovative' *Center for Democracy & Technology*, 28 February 2011, to be

The complications with the EU data transfer rules in particular have led multinationals to put pressure on the DPAs to recognize their corporate privacy policies as providing an adequate level of protection for the processing of personal data throughout their groups of companies. Insofar as such processing involves transfers of personal data to a group company in a country without an adequate level of data protection, 'adequate safeguards' are provided for by the corporate privacy policy.[28] The advisory committee to the European Commission on data protection (*Working Party 29*)[29] recognizes the added value of such transnational private regulation in the data protection area in light of the gaps and deficiencies of the present EU data transfer regime. The Working Party 29 has set criteria for these corporate privacy policies in order to ensure a minimum level of protection for the processing of personal data throughout the group of companies. One of these requirements is that these privacy policies should be 'internally binding' within the organization (on all group companies and employees) and 'externally binding' for the benefit of individuals (ie must create third-party beneficiary rights for the individuals).[30] To express this binding character of these corporate privacy policies the Working Party 29 labels them 'Binding Corporate Rules' (*BCR*). The BCR regime set by the Working Party 29 introduces the possibility of central supervision of worldwide compliance with such BCR by one of the DPAs of the EU Member States. With BCR, the Working Party 29 introduced a complex hybrid system of regulation of cross-border data transfers combining transnational self-regulation (corporate privacy policies) with public arrangements (the DPAs validating such corporate privacy policies and providing supervision and enforcement). Despite the opinions issued by the Working Party 29 on the concept of BCR, some DPAs still do not agree to these requirements and refuse to recognize BCR or set additional requirements in this respect.[31] In any event uncertainty exists as to whether BCR will also be accepted as a valid data transfer tool by non-EU jurisdictions that have their own data transfer restrictions. As a consequence it is at present still uncertain whether

found at <http://www.cdt.org/blogs/privacy-european-commission-must-be-innovative>: 'Enforcement is a sore issue for the EU DPD. It is an open secret that the framework is largely not enforced. Indeed, implementation of the EU DPD is probably highest among U.S. based multinationals, which implement strict compliance programs for risk management purposes and as part of overall corporate governance schemes'; and Commentary in Response to the European Commission's Communication on 'A comprehensive approach to personal data protection'. Centre for Information Policy Leadership, January 2011, to be found at <http://www.huntonfiles.com> (*Opinion on the Communication of the Commission on the revision of the Directive*), at 12: 'Articles 25 and 26 of the existing Directive have been simultaneously its most controversial and most burdensome provisions. It is also arguable that they have been the least effective if full account is taken of current volumes of international transfers. (. . .). The result is the paradox that substantial resources are expended by some organisations to try "to get it right" whilst there is an unmeasured non-compliance by other organisations which ignore the requirements.'

[28] As required for the transfer of data to countries without adequate protection, pursuant to Art 26 (2) Directive.

[29] See on the Working Party 29, Chapter 1, n 2 and on its tasks and procedural rules in more detail Chapter 10, paras 10.7.2–10.7.4.

[30] See on these requirements in detail Chapter 7, para 7.2–7.3.

[31] See for examples n 40 and n 43 below.

the BCR concept will work on an EU-wide basis, let alone at a global level, and the time frame within which this may ultimately be achieved.[32]

The Working Party 29 acknowledges the shortcomings of the EU data transfer rules and of the present BCR regime and has advised the European Commission (Commission) to address these in the upcoming revision of the Directive[33] which was launched by the Commission on 1 July 2009. Subsequently, the Commission in its Communication of November 2010 on the revision of the Directive[34] announced that it will indeed 'improve and streamline the current procedures for international data transfers, including (. . .) Binding Corporate Rules'.[35] On 25 January 2012, the Commission communicated[36] its proposal for a new EU regulation on data protection[37] (*Proposed Regulation*). The Proposed Regulation indeed provides that BCR are one of the standard tools for intercompany data transfers and further provides for an EU-wide authorization procedure (see further Chapter 3, paragraph 3.1).

2.2 Relevance of BCR as a Data Transfer Tool at Global Level

For a number of reasons the introduction of the BCR regime is an important development and is expected to gain further relevance in the coming years.[38]

[32] See in more detail Chapter 6, para 6.5.

[33] See WP Contribution on The Future of Privacy (Chapter 1, n 6), at para 38, listing as recommendations: 'Recognising BCR as appropriate tool to provide adequate safeguards'; and 'Defining the main substantive and procedural elements of BCRs, following the WP29 Opinions on the subject'. What is noteworthy here is that the Working Party 29 (apparently) is not even sure that BCR can indeed be a tool for the transfer of data to countries without adequate protection under Art 26(2) of the Directive. See further the WP Opinion on the principle of accountability (Chapter 1, n 23), at para 56.

[34] See European Commission, 'Communication from the Commission to the European Parliament, the Council, the Economic and Social Committee and the Committee of the Regions, A comprehensive approach on personal data protection in the European Union,' COM(2010) 609/3 (4 November 2010), at paras 2.2.1 and 2.2.3 (*EC Communication on the revision of the Directive*).

[35] EC Communication on the revision of the Directive (n 34), at 16; Viviane Reding, 'The Upcoming Data Protection Reform for the European Union' [2011] 1 *International Data Privacy Law*, at 5. This was already the recommendation in the First Implementation Report (see First Report on the Directive (n 26), at 18), and is further in line with the recommendations of the Rand Report (see Rand Report (n 27), at 42) and of the European Data Protection Supervisor, see Opinion of the European Data Protection Supervisor on the Communication from the Commission to the European Parliament, the Council, the Economic and Social Committee and the Committee of the Regions—'A comprehensive approach on personal data protection in the European Union' (*EDPS Opinion on the revision of the Directive*), at para 127. See in detail Chapter 6, para 6.6.

[36] Communication of the Commission to the European Council, the European Economical and Social Committee of the Regions, Safeguarding Privacy in a Connected World A European Data Protection Framework for the 21st Century, see Chapter 1, n 10.

[37] European Commission, 'Proposal for a Regulation of the European Parliament and of the Council on the protection of individuals with regard to the processing of personal data and on the free movement of such data' (*General Data Protection Regulation*); see Chapter 1, n 9.

[38] See also Kuner (n 8), at 24.

2.2.1 No global standard

International data transfers are generally considered essential to the advancement of global trade[39] and the economic and social development of individual countries.[40] At the same time, concerns about data processing risks in certain countries have led many countries to introduce restrictions on outbound data transfers.[41] Recently, these concerns have increased due to certain countries expanding their state policing powers to access data of foreign citizens.[42] The growing number of incidents recently where foreign governments use their state control powers and demand access to foreign data[43] only strengthens the data protection concerns of

[39] As already acknowledged at the time the Directive was enacted, see Recital 56: 'Whereas cross-border flows of personal data are necessary to the expansion of international trade (. . .)'. See also Kuner (n 8), at 34–5, however, also concluding that more 'hard research has to be done to confirm the effects of transborder data flows'.

[40] See recommendation of the OECD Council Concerning Guidelines Governing the Protection of Privacy and Transborder flows of Personal Data (23 September 1980) (*OECD Privacy Guidelines*), preamble, to be found at <http://www.oecd.org> and *APEC Privacy Framework (2005)*, to be found at <http://www.apec.org>, preamble at para 2; Kuner (n 8), at 8 and 34. At 8, Kuner indicates that the economic, legal, and social importance of transborder data flow is at present not adequately recognized at the highest levels of government, and that more research has to be undertaken to measure the economic benefits and costs of regulation of trans-border data flows.

[41] See for a comprehensive overview of the various perceived risks that underlie regulation of transborder data flows: Kuner (n 8), at 30–3.

[42] The U.S. Patriot Act (see Chapter 4, para 4.1 below) is an example of a recent expansion of state control powers which triggered data transfer restrictions in other countries. See Kuner (n 8), at 31–2, giving the example that Canadian provinces have enacted a restriction of the outsourcing of data of Canadian public bodies based on concerns about access to such data by the U.S. government under the U.S. Patriot Act. The increase in surveillance is not limited to the U.S. This is also an issue within the EU. For an overview of the EU security data exchange policies and the data protection implications, see Tenth Annual Report of the Article 29 Working Party on Data Protection, at 7–8 (to be found at <http://ec.europa.eu/justice/policies/privacy/workinggroup/wpdocs/index_en.htm>). In 2004, the EU and U.S. finally entered into an agreement on the much debated data transfers to the U.S. Department of Homeland Security of 'passenger name records (*PNR*) of air passengers' travelling from Europe. Until this point, these transfers lacked a legal basis under the Directive. Another source of tension was the revelation in 2006 that, since 2001, U.S. authorities repeatedly enforced the disclosure of payment transaction data processed by SWIFT (Society for Worldwide Interbank Financial Telecommunication) for the purpose of fighting terrorism, based on government subpoenas, in violation of the EU transfer rules. To avoid further violations of data protection, SWIFT transferred its data processing facilities from the U.S. to Switzerland. The violation has been recently remedied in the Agreement between the European Union and the United States of America on the processing and transfer of Financial Messaging Data from the European Union to the United States for purposes of the Terrorist Finance Tracking Program, [2010] OJ L8/11, as approved on behalf of the Union by the Council Decision 2010/412/EU of 13 July 2010 OJ L195/3. This approval followed the proposal from the European Commission, and gained the consent of the European Parliament (European Parliament legislative resolution of 8 July 2010 on the draft Council decision on the conclusion of the Agreement between the European Union and the United States of America on the processing and transfer of Financial Messaging Data from the European Union to the United States for the purposes of the Terrorist Finance Tracking Program (11222/1/2010/REV 1 and COR 1 – C7-0158/2010 – 2010/0178(NLE) (*Agreement on Transfer of Financial Messaging Data*)).

[43] Examples are the refusal of India to allow Blackberry handheld devices because the data are encrypted, demanding that entities offering communication services in India should also maintain communications equipment there, facilitating real-time access to corporate messages. See Daniel Emery, 'India threatens to suspend Blackberry by 31 August,' *BBC News Online*, 13 August 2010, available online at <http://www.bbc.co.uk/news/technology-10951607>. Another example is China,

countries that underlie their data transfer rules.[44] As a result we may expect that increasingly more countries will introduce data protection legislation[45], which in most cases will also include outbound data transfer rules. It is only when data protection laws are harmonized on a global basis that the need to adopt data transfer rules will be eliminated.[46] Although there is a persistent call for a legally binding global standard for data protection and there are some concrete initiatives in this respect, it is not expected that such a global standard will indeed be realized within the coming 10 years.[47] The present regulatory landscape is still too diverse for such a standard to be adopted on a global level. Therefore, at least for the near future, the existence of data transfer rules is a given and even on the increase. Data transfer instruments such as BCR therefore are expected to gain importance as instruments in facilitating cross-border data transfers.

2.2.2 Bridging function of BCR between different legal systems

Governments choose very different rationales for their data protection legislation: EU legislation is based on protecting fundamental rights and freedoms whereas, for instance, the APEC Privacy Framework is aimed at securing economic benefits of e-commerce.[48] The rationales underlying the regulation of outbound data transfers are also very different. Broadly speaking, there are two approaches to data transfer rules to be distinguished: territory-based rules and organization-based rules.[49] The EU data transfer rules are an example of the first approach and allow data transfers when the country of destination provides for 'adequate' data protection.[50] The

which requires service providers doing business in China to reveal data to Chinese law enforcement authorities. eg in January 2010 Google threatened to withdraw from China referring to China-based cyber attacks on its databases and the e-mail accounts of some users, and China's attempts to 'limit free speech on the Web', as the reasons for its decision. See *The New York Times* Google Inc. profile at <http://topics.nytimes.com/top/news/business/companies/google_inc/index.html?scp=2&sq=china%20google%20yahoo&st=cse>. Another example is a U.S. court order from 14 December 2010, demanding release of details about the accounts of WikiLeaks founder Julian Assange and other WikiLeaks activists, including Birgitta Jonsdottir, an Icelandic parliamentarian (see <http://www.bbc.co.uk/news/world-us-canada-12141530>).

[44] As a practitioner, I see a trend for multinationals to avoid having data processing facilities in countries with excessive state control powers. After introduction of the U.S. Patriot Act, many multinationals relocated their central IT facilities (which were initially transferred to the U.S. mainly for cost reasons) back to the EU. A public example is the Society for Worldwide Interbank Financial Communications (*SWIFT*), which relocated its central processing facilities in the U.S. to Switzerland for reasons of U.S. state control powers under the U.S. Patriot Act. See press release of 4 October 2007 to be found at <www.swift.com> and n 42 above.

[45] Kuner (n 8), at 42.

[46] See Spiros Simitis (ed.), *Bundesdatengeschutzgesetz* (Nomos 2006), at 123.

[47] See in detail Chapter 4, para 4.2.

[48] APEC Privacy Framework (n 40), at 3: 'APEC economies realise that a key part of efforts to improve consumer confidence and ensure growth of electronic commerce must be cooperation to balance and promote both effective information privacy protection and the free flow of information in the Asia Pacific region.' See also Kuner (n 8), at 27.

[49] See for this categorization Kuner (n 8), at 28.

[50] Another example is Art 2(1) Additional Protocol to the Convention for the protection of individuals with regard to the automatic processing of personal data regarding Supervisory Authorities and transborder data flows, 8 November 2001 (*Additional Protocol to Convention 108*), to be found

APEC Privacy Framework is an example of the second approach, and holds organizations accountable for the protection of personal data also after they transfer such data to other organizations (wherever located).[51] Though the starting points of these two approaches may seem very different, in practice the two systems in their application to a large extent converge. For instance, the Directive also facilitates 'organizational based' data transfer tools, legitimizing data transfers between organizations if the EU Standard Contractual Clauses are used or if US companies have adhered to the US Safe Harbor Framework.[52] Introduction in the EU of the BCR regime, making a multinational an adequate 'safe haven' for data protection purposes wherever its group companies are located, is a further prime example of an 'organizational based' tool for data transfers. APEC through its Privacy Framework also intends to facilitate a similar organizational tool, providing that Member Economies shall endeavour to ensure that organizations adopt 'Cross Border Privacy Rules' (*CBPR*) as a manner to facilitate their cross-border data transfers.[53]

The APEC Privacy Framework at its turn also incorporates elements of the territory-based approach, where it encourages Member Economies to develop cooperative bilateral or multinational arrangements so that the participating countries will cooperate in the investigation and enforcement of data protection violations. The APEC Privacy Framework explicitly provides that such cooperation may be declined or limited by a Member Economy where cooperation would lead to violation of the national laws or policies of a Member Economy. Thus, if the laws of the counterpart are not considered 'equivalent' to a country's national law, cooperation may be declined; a result very similar to the EU adequacy rule.[54] Though it is expected that the EU and APEC systems of data transfer rules will converge further,[55] it is clear that BCR and CBPR will be an important common

at<http://conventions.coe.int/Treaty/Commun/QueVoulezVous.asp?NT=181&CM=1&CL=ENG>, which provides that each party shall allow transfers of personal data to a non-party only if an 'adequate level of protection is assured'. Other examples (although here the starting point is reversed in the sense that transfers are in principle allowed but may be blocked or restricted in certain circumstances) are: the OECD Privacy Guidelines, which allow restriction of outbound data transfers in case the country of destiny does not provide for 'equivalent protection', see OECD Privacy Guidelines (n 40), at para 17; the UN Guidelines concerning Computerized Personal Files of 14 December 1990 (UN Doc E/CN.4/1990/72), at para 9, allowing restrictions in case the other territory does not provide for 'reciprocal safeguards'; and Art 12 of Convention 108 which allows restrictions 'except where the regulations of the other party provide an equivalent protection'.

[51] See Chapter 3, para 3.4 on the APEC Privacy Framework, and in particular for the accountability rule in respect of data transfers.

[52] See on the Safe Harbor Framework n 71.

[53] APEC Privacy Framework (n 40), at III Cooperative Development of Cross Border privacy Rules, at para 46–8.

[54] See also Kuner (n 8), at 30.

[55] Kuner (n 8), at 40 concludes that neither the geographical nor the organizational approach is inherently better than the other, each having advantages and disadvantages. What is needed is for the two approaches to co-exist, whereby the solution selected by a country should be accompanied by measures to avoid its inherent disadvantages, as otherwise the first approach will tend to be excessively bureaucratic and the second too reactive. A solution is also to mix the two approaches. Examples given are Canada, where for the decision whether a company has implemented sufficient organizational and contractual measures as part of its accountability obligations, the location to which the data are to be

factor of the two systems.[56] BCR will thus fulfil a bridging function between the two systems facilitating international data transfers even where (in this case) the EU and the APEC Member Economies cannot agree on what the appropriate universal level of data protection should be.[57]

2.2.3 Limitations of state legislative and enforcement powers

Territoriality is a key factor for the applicability and enforcement regimes of the data protection laws across the world.[58] However, in a globalized society where companies operate on a cross-border basis and technology facilitates seamless cross-border data flows, reliance on territoriality as an organizing principle to regulate these data flows is inherently flawed.[59] Most state regulation is aimed solely at protecting individuals in a relevant state territory, whether the offensive acts are performed in the territory or aimed at the citizens in the relevant territory (think of media and advertising laws). Specific to data protection is that protection of data of an individual in the territory itself is not sufficient as data of individuals may also flow outside the territory. As a result, data protection is one of the few legal fields that aims to protect individuals outside their territory as well,[60] when their data are

transferred is taken into account. See Christopher Kuner, 'Developing an adequate legal framework for international data transfers', in Serge Gutwirth et al (eds.), *Reinventing Data Protection?* (Springer 2009), at 271. The Australian Government, Australian Privacy Principles, Exposure Draft of 24 June 2010, at 15–17, to be found at <http://www.aph.gov.au/binaries/senate/committee/fapa_ctte/priv_exp_drafts/guide/exposure_draft.pdf>(Draft Australian Privacy Principles) also seek to combine the geographical and organizational approach.

[56] In general it is the expectation that private sector instruments will likely assume increasing importance in coming years. See Kuner (n 8) at 24; and Prins (n 9), at 173: 'A final remark is that the case of personal data protection is also a fine illustration of the role that soft law (codes of conduct, privacy policies, corporate rules, privacy seals and trust marks) and the actors involved therein can play in establishing a certain degree of international protection.'

[57] For a critique of the 'adequacy' of data protection expected to be provided by the APEC Privacy Framework, see Chapter 3, para 3.4, n 161.

[58] See Moerel (Chapter 1, n 8), at para 2.3.6 and 3.2–3.2.1. See further Kuner (n 8), at 11 and 41.

[59] See Moerel (Chapter 1, n 8), at para 3.11: 'The underlying principle of territoriality whereby a physical connection is required to a territory is no longer suited to be applied in the current day reality'; or as phrased by Stephen J. Kobrin, *The Trans-Atlantic Data Privacy Dispute, Territorial Jurisdiction and Global Governance*, Working Paper Series, The Wharton School (November 2002), at 23: 'Extraterritorial reach not only becomes the norm, the concept itself loses meaning as the distinction between domestic and international affairs blurs to the point where it is no longer meaningful and territoriality becomes problematic as the organizing principle underlying the international political system.' See also Kobrin (above), at 28: 'Transnational integration, however, is increasingly relational rather than geographic; the new political space from which effective and legitimate governance must emerge takes the form of relational networks rather than territory, a "space of flows" rather than a "space of spaces"'.

[60] A parallel can be made with export control regulations, where the export of technology that may endanger state security (as it may enable foreign governments in developing weapons etc) is restricted. Though not identical, parallels can also be found with corporate social responsibility regulation. This aims to protect citizens in a territory against products that are manufactured in ways which violate human rights abroad. In the criminal arena, a parallel may be made with the 'passive personality principle' of public international law. This principle allows a sovereign state, in limited cases, to claim jurisdiction to try foreign nationals for offences committed abroad on the basis that the crime affects their own nationals. On this concept, see Alina Kaczorowska, *Public International Law* (4th edn

transferred abroad (and such other country does not provide for protection of such data). This is the main motivation for the introduction of data transfer rules. In addition to data transfer rules, many countries have tried to protect the data of their citizens when transferred abroad by expanding the long arm reach of their data protection laws (ie by expanding the scope of their applicability regimes).[61] This poses many questions under private international law (*PIL*). Though data protection regulations may be of relatively recent times, the concepts of applicable law, jurisdiction, and enforcement are embedded in a long tradition of PIL, whereby laws that over-extend their jurisdictional reach are considered to be an unacceptable form of 'hyper-regulation' if they apply so indiscriminately that there is no hope of enforcement.[62] Enforcement powers of states and the jurisdiction of their courts are also subject to limitations set by PIL.[63] Applicability and enforcement regimes are therefore inherently delineated and cannot be instrumental in filling the gaps in the protection of personal data and the enforcement of protection.[64] At present, the main tool available to the authorities to try to solve any gaps in the international patchwork of applicable laws and enforcement is seeking cooperation with other DPAs in the event of cross-border data protection violations (the 'network approach', where each DPA enforces its own rules in its own territory).[65] In practice,

(Routledge 2010), at 322: 'According to the passive personality principle a State has jurisdiction to punish aliens for harmful acts committed abroad against its nationals;' and Tim Hillier, *Sourcebook on Public International Law* (Cavendish 1998), at 279: 'Under this principle, jurisdiction is claimed on the basis of the nationality of the actual or potential victim. In other words, a state may assert jurisdiction over activities which, although committed abroad by foreign nationals, have affected or will affect nationals of the state.' The passive personality principle has been rejected as a ground of jurisdiction by the International Court of Justice in the SS Lotus case (*France v Turkey* 1927 P.C.I.J. (ser. A) No 10 (7 Sept)) and has been described as 'the most difficult principle to justify in theory' (Kaczorowska, at 322, see also Hillier, at 279). Of this principle, it has also been said that 'while many civil law countries claim jurisdiction on this ground, others such as the UK and the U.S., tend to regard it as contrary to international law so far as ordinary torts and crimes are concerned but not in respect of terrorist killings and the taking of hostages etc' (see Kaczorowaka, at 322).

[61] Kuner (n 8), at 7 comments that the rules of applicable law and data transfer are often intertwined, whereby countries use rules on applicable law to protect data across their borders, 'thus using applicable law to serve the same purpose as regulation of transborder data flows'.

[62] An example is the interpretation by the Working Party 29 of Art 4(1)(c) Directive, as a result of which the Directive applies if a non-EU website uses cookies to process personal data of EU citizens, by taking the position that the sending by a non-EU based website of cookies to the computers of internet users in the EU constitutes the use of 'equipment' in the EU, triggering the applicability rule of Art 4(1)(c). See Working Document on determining the international application of EU data protection law to personal data processed on the Internet by non-EU based websites (WP 56, 30 May 2002) (*Working Document on Non-EU Based Websites*), at 11. See Moerel (Chapter 1, n 8), at para 3.7.3, in particular fn 64.

[63] See Christopher Kuner, *European Data Protection Law: Corporate Compliance and Regulation* (Oxford University Press 2007), at 125 and Kuner (n 55), at 271.

[64] See Moerel (Chapter 1, n 8), at Chapters 2 and 3 where I discussed the delineations of the present applicability and jurisdictional regime of the Directive, and Christopher Kuner, 'Data Protection Law and International Jurisdiction on the Internet (Part 1)' [2010] *International Journal of Law and Information Technology*, at 183.

[65] Pursuant to Art 28(6) and (7) Directive, DPAs are required to cooperate with one another, exchange useful information, and may be requested to exercise their powers by a DPA of another Member State (ie enforcement is based on a 'network approach'). See for the APEC Privacy Framework (Chapter 3, para 3.4, n 162). See further Chapter 4, para 4.3.

seeking such cooperation is increasingly common.[66] However, until such time as all jurisdictions have adequate data protection laws and supervision of these laws, this network approach cannot adequately solve all gaps in applicable laws and enforcement issues presently faced by data protection regulators.

At first glance the absence of a global data protection regime may seem to be to the advantage of multinationals, being able to benefit from any gaps in protection and avoid liability for doing so. This is, however, not the case. As multinationals benefited from harmonization of the data protection laws in the EU by the introduction of the Directive[67] and will benefit from further approximation of the EU data protection laws in the upcoming revision of the Directive,[68] multinationals operating on a global basis would also benefit from global norms and central supervision and related enforcement. This would enable them to streamline their data processing operations not only on an EU-wide basis but also globally and further ensure a consistent and predictable interpretation and application of the data protection rules. As this is not yet achievable by global public regulation, BCR may play a role here. If it is possible to make a choice of law and forum in BCR, it would be possible to have BCR supervised and enforced by one 'Lead' DPA only, preferably the authority of the place of establishment of the headquarters of such multinational. BCR may thus function as a private regulatory response to the inherent limitations of rules on applicable law and jurisdiction.

[66] Kuner (n 8), at 32 and 42.

[67] Prior to the adoption of the Directive, the data protection laws in the Member States were very diverse with France, Germany, and Sweden having comprehensive data protection laws and, on the other hand, Spain, Italy, Portugal, Greece, and Belgium having no data protection laws at all. According to Recital 7 of the Directive, the main consideration for introduction of the Directive was 'the existence of a wide variety of national laws, regulations and administrative provisions' which were considered to 'constitute an obstacle to the pursuit of a number of economic activities at Community level, distort competition and impede authorities in the discharge of their responsibilities under Community law'. See further Recital 8: 'whereas, in order to remove the obstacles to flows of personal data, the level of [data protection] must be equivalent in all Member States.' See on the economic and social benefits of free cross-border data flows, Kuner, (n 8), noting (at 6) that '[p] ersonal data are now crucial raw materials of the global economy'; and (at 9) that 'confidence in data processing and privacy protection have become important factors to enable the acceptance of electronic commerce', while at the same time noting (at 8) that the 'economic, legal and social importance of transborder data flows is not adequately recognised at the highest levels of government' and that 'important research remains to be done in areas such as measuring the economic effects of transborder data flows'.

[68] It is generally acknowledged that the main shortcoming of the Directive is that the level of harmonization under the current framework is unsatisfactory due to (i) the fact that the Directive leaves the Member States too much discretion in implementing the provisions thereof (see Recital 9 Directive) and (ii) the many instances of incorrect implementation by the Member States. This was already the conclusion of the First Implementation Report on the Directive (n 26), at 11 and action point 6 at 24. See for the same conclusions the WP Contribution on the Future of Privacy (Chapter 1, n 6), at paras 18–21; the EC Communication on the revision of the Directive (n 34), at 10; and the EDPS Opinion on the revision of the Directive (n 35), at 7 and 12. See para 5.3 of the EDPS Opinion on the revision of the Directive for areas that according to the EDPS require further harmonization.

2.2.4 Stepping stone to further harmonization

The application of BCR by multinationals to group companies in countries where no (or less) data protection exists may have an important example function in those countries, as their nationals also benefit from this protection.[69] Though no hard research has been carried out in this respect, in general it can be said that transnational private regulation (*TPR*) that is based on non-binding 'soft law' is often a stepping stone to hard law.[70] A similar influence may be expected of implementation of BCR on a large scale. This being said, it should be noted that at the time the Safe Harbor Framework[71] was introduced in the US, it was the expectation that this would ultimately lead to elevation of the overall level of data

[69] Kuner, (n 8), at 6 indicates that this is a benefit of data transfer rules.

[70] Application of TPR on a worldwide basis has the potential to import the rule of law and developed countries' business norms into the world of emerging economies, which in itself may be a bottom up driver for the ultimate acceptability of an international standard. For such an effect of TPR, see John M. Conley and Cynthia A. Williams, *Global Banks as Global Sustainability Regulators: the Equator Principles*, at 5, available at <http://www.hill.org>, and literature therein referred to. See further Fabrizio Cafaggi, *New Foundations of Transnational Private Regulation*, EUI Working papers RSCAS 2010/53, at 15; Deirdre Curtin and Linda Senden, 'Public accountability of Transnational Private Regulation' [2011] 38 *Journal of Law and Society*, at 185; and Bert-Jaap Koops, Miriam Lips, Sjaak Nouwt, Corien Prins, Maurice Schellekens, 'Should Self-Regulation Be The Starting Point?', in Bert-Jaap Koops et al (eds.), *Starting Points for ICT Regulation. Deconstructing Prevalent Policy One-Liners* (TCM Asser Press 2006), Chapter 5, at 140. Cafaggi (above), at 17 signals that if soft law is in place TPR also 'operates as a vehicle to harden soft law, providing binding force' and 'confers higher legitimacy' to such soft law. This is based on the conclusion of Cafaggi (at 1) that TPR is generally voluntary, but after it has been adopted it becomes binding: 'Parties who wish to join the regulatory bodies participating to the regime are free to do so, however, once they are in, they are legally bound and violation of the rules is subject to legal sanctions.'

[71] See for the Commission's adequacy decision regarding data protection in the U.S.: European Commission Decision 2000/520 of 26 July 2000 pursuant to Directive 95/46 of the European Parliament and of the Council on the adequacy of the protection provided by the Safe Harbor privacy principles and related frequently asked questions and answers issued by the U.S. Department of Commerce, [2000] OJ L215/7. The U.S. Safe Harbor Framework further consists of the exchange of letters between the U.S. Department of Commerce and the European Commission, and letters from the Department of Transportation and Federal Trade Commission on their enforcement powers (*U.S. Safe Harbor Framework*). As explained in the Safe Harbor Privacy Principles issued by the U.S. Department of Commerce on 21 July 2000, (ANNEX I to 2000/520/EC Commission Decision of 26 July 2000 on the adequacy of the protection provided by the Safe Harbor privacy principles), the principles are intended for the purpose of qualifying for the Safe Harbor and the presumption of 'adequacy' it creates. To qualify for the Safe Harbor scheme, an organization must comply with a set of seven privacy principles:

1) notice (inform an individual as to the purpose of processing, contact information of the organization and complaint procedure, etc);
2) choice (opt-out regarding disclosure to a third party or use incompatible with the purpose for which the data was initially collected, and opt-in regarding sensitive information);
3) onward transfer (permitted only if the notice and choice requirements are respected; an organization must ensure that its agent complies with these principles, the Directive, or another adequacy finding);
4) security (reasonable precautions must be taken to ensure data security);
5) data integrity (data should be reliable, accurate, complete, and current and processing is not excessive with regard to the purposes for which the data was collected);
6) access (an organization must ensure individual access rights); and

protection in the US. It seems that this expectation has not (fully) materialized.[72] Rather than increasing the overall level of data protection, introduction of the Safe Harbor Framework often led in practice to US companies introducing a higher standard only for EU customers.[73]

2.3 Evaluation of the BCR Regime from Different Dimensions

In light of the above it is worth looking at the BCR regime as introduced by the Working Party 29 in more detail in order to determine whether this co-regulatory[74] tool is indeed suitable to achieve protection of one of the fundamental rights and

7) enforcement ('mechanisms for assuring compliance with the Principles, recourse for individuals to whom the data relate affected by non-compliance with the Principles, and consequences for the organization when the Principles are not followed').

[72] See Duncan H. Brown and Jeffrey Layne Blevins, 'The Safe Harbor Agreement between the United States and Europe: A Missed Opportunity to balance the Interests of E-Commerce and Privacy On-Line' (2002) *Journal of Broadcasting and Electronic Media* 46(4) available online at <http://www.allbusiness.com/legal/laws/384290-1.html>. Brown and Blevins are of the opinion that the Safe Harbor Framework did not live up to its potential to elevate the level of U.S. data protection: 'The "ratcheting up of national standards" for personal data privacy protection in the U.S. (...) might happen in response to the safe-harbor provisions did not transpire. (... S)everal years before (...) a number of analysts (...) had believed that the proposed Data Protection Directive "might open a 'policy window' leading to the strengthening of privacy laws in the United States and the establishment of some form of commission" (...). In the earlier case, there was certainly no change, and it now appears likely that the status quo will again be maintained in the U.S. despite the existence of the safe harbor.' See, however, Peter P. Swire, 'Elephants and Mice Revisited: Law and Choice of Law on the Internet' (2005) *University of Pennsylvania Law Review*, vol 153, at 1987: 'the Safe Harbor has been fairly successful at meeting two strategic goals: avoiding a trans-Atlantic trade war and providing a reasonable baseline for privacy protection in transborder activities (...). Agreement on the Safe Harbor can also be defended as a "soft" harmonization of privacy law. Both for organizations who have formally enrolled in the Safe Harbor, and for the larger group of organizations who are aware of the Safe Harbor, the Safe Harbor principles give a widely known set of rules for what is considered appropriate corporate action. Even though most companies will never face an enforcement action or a privacy audit, any organization that deviates substantially from the Safe Harbor principles runs the risk of exposure and enforcement. The potential number of choice-of-law cases involving privacy is greatly reduced under this soft version of harmonization that gives notice to organizations about key, expected privacy protections.'

[73] See Vera Bergelson (2003), 'It's Personal But is it Mine? Toward Property Rights in Personal Information' U.C. Davis Law Review 37: 379, at 396. Bergelson, acknowledges the role of the Safe Harbor Framework as 'an important step in establishing a data protection regime in this country', but considers the framework 'just an emergency measure designed to deal with the ultimatum issued by the EU to the United States' and states that 'the "Safe Harbor" approach creates an incentive for U.S. participants to maintain two privacy standards—the higher one for European consumers and the lower one for the domestic consumers' (this referring to Robert Gellman, *Privacy, Consumers, and Costs: How the Lack of Privacy Costs Consumers and Why Business Studies of Privacy Costs are Biased and Incomplete*, available at <http://www.epic.org/reports/dmfprivacy.html#2> (March 2002)).

[74] Co-regulation is 'the mechanism whereby a Community legislative act entrusts the attainment of the objectives defined by the legislative authority to parties which are recognised in the field (such as economic operators, the social partners, non-governmental organisations, or associations)'. See the 2003 Inter-Institutional Agreement on Better Lawmaking concluded between the European Parliament, the EU Council of Ministers and the European Commission of 16 December 2003 (2003/C321/01), [2003] OJ C321/1, in particular Article 18 (*Inter-Institutional Agreement on Better Law Making*).

freedoms of EU nationals in a transnational environment. For that purpose the BCR regime may be seen and evaluated in the context of a number of different dimensions:

2.3.1 Evaluation of BCR as a form of transnational private regulation

Legislators (including EU legislators) that wish to regulate global corporate conduct opt for 'regulating' TPR rather than introducing public regulation with its inherent limitations as to jurisdictional and authoritative scope of state competence.[75] The discipline of how to best regulate (the rules for rule-making, the search for meta-norms) has come to be known in the EU as 'Better Regulation' (*BR*). In the substantial body of research concerning the concept of BR and TPR, questions are raised as to:

- the suitability of TPR to regulate human rights;[76]
- how to best regulate TPR, which of the different forms of regulation would be most suitable to regulate TPR;
- the legitimacy of TPR as compared to public regulation;
- how to align TPR with conventional principles of contract law (TPR raises questions of enforceability by third-party beneficiaries of such TPR)
- TPR is often effectuated through contractual 'supply chain management', which solution is also part of the BCR regime. Supply chain management also raises issues of enforceability by the beneficiaries of these contracts, which are of equal relevance to BCR; and
- TPR further raise several questions of PIL if the third-party beneficiaries are employees and consumers. The European rules of PIL entail that a choice of law and forum in the BCR may not affect the substantive rights and remedies or the dispute settlement procedures which are available to EU employees or EU consumers.

2.3.2 Evaluation of BCR as implementation of corporate accountability

In some areas of law legislators (including the Commission) introduce the 'principle of accountability' in respect of compliance with the relevant legal requirements. The main purpose of 'accountability' is to use the law to hold businesses accountable for taking their responsibilities seriously by using various mechanisms to encourage or force businesses to put internal governance structures and

[75] See for EU legislators: European Commission, White Paper on European Governance (2001) COM 428 final (*White Paper on European Governance*), at 21; and the 2003 Inter-Institutional Agreement on 'Better Lawmaking' (n 74). See further Chapter 4, n 34 and para 4.4.1.

[76] Also the Commission seems to be of the opinion that TPR is not suitable to regulate human rights. See White Paper on European Governance (n 75), at 21 and the Inter-Institutional Agreement on Better Lawmaking (n 74), at 3. See for a critical discussion of the position of the Commission and the other EU institutions, Chapter 10, para 10.5.

management systems in place. The Working Party 29 has proposed that the accountability principle be included in the revised Directive. The Commission communicated[77] that it intends to include the accountability principle in the revised Directive and indeed included a provision on accountability of the controller in the Proposed Regulation.[78] This will entail that in addition to the obligation to comply with the EU data protection requirements, an independent obligation will be introduced to implement a proper data protection compliance programme. The BCR regime is mentioned by the Working Party 29 as the prime example where the principle of accountability has been embodied. This being said, the BCR regime should be evaluated against:

- the proposal of the Working Party 29 to introduce the accountability principle;
- other data protection legislation that incorporates the accountability principle; and
- the general body of research in respect of the principle of accountability as introduced in other fields of law.

2.3.3 Evaluation of BCR in the context of corporate social responsibility

Many multinationals voluntarily adopt 'Corporate Social Responsibility' (*CSR*) codes to overcome differences in regulations and regulatory approaches between countries and as part of their global reputation management. Typically, CSR codes involve a commitment by multinationals (usually in their Code of Ethics or Business Principles) to respect human and civil rights, to protect the environment, to oppose bribery and corruption, and to commit to fairness to their customers and suppliers. The range of issues brought under the umbrella of CSR is constantly expanding and often now also includes a commitment to protect the privacy of employees and customers. Various topics concerning CSR are also of relevance to BCR. In the substantial body of research concerning CSR, similar issues are raised as set out above in respect of TPR (CSR being a form of TPR). Additional issues that are raised which equally apply to BCR are:

- Various international non-governmental and intergovernmental organizations have issued instruments with guidelines for CSR codes (so-called soft law). Relevant for BCR is to what extent the right to data protection of the stakeholders of a company is covered by these soft law instruments and whether this has any repercussions for the BCR regime as it presently stands.
- CSR codes are voluntarily unilateral undertakings, but global legal practice shows how the law is being used to hold multinationals legally accountable for application of their CSR codes, which is of relevance to BCR as well.

[77] EC Communication on the revision of the Directive (n 34), at 11–12.
[78] See Art 19 Proposed Regulation (Chapter 1, n 10).

2.4 The Quest for Meta-norms for BCR

As TPR operates in a plurality of public and private normative orders and with a plurality of actors, TPR has to function within many different spheres.[79] For TPR to be acceptable, TPR has to 'construct relationships of recognition with the different public and private orders it comes into contact with'.[80] This will not be different for BCR. Also BCR have to operate within many different spheres: the national jurisdiction where the multinational has its primary establishment, the national jurisdictions where the multinational has secondary establishments, the contractual relationships the multinational has with its employees, its customers, its suppliers, its sub-contractors, and many supra-national spheres (at the EU, APEC, global level, etc). For BCR to be acceptable in all different public and private spheres it touches upon, it must be aligned with the existing legal disciplines and other bodies of thought it interacts with.[81] This is not so much to say that BCR, for instance, should be in compliance with rules of PIL or that BCR should observe rules of contract law, though these obviously cannot be ignored.[82] The different disciplines (or perspectives) from which BCR may be evaluated, however, also potentially provide a source of 'meta-norms' for BCR.[83] 'Meta-norms', are defined by one author as 'norm[s] to which parties can commit without betraying their loyalty to their own legal systems'.[84] BCR will also have to accommodate this duality. Multinationals implementing BCR cannot ignore the national rules of the jurisdictions in which they operate, but they also have to operate on a global level which sets its own demands. For BCR (operating at the global level) to be acceptable at the national level, BCR will have to 'build on the assumption of common reference points'[85] between national jurisdictions and different disciplines. For example if BCR are reviewed from the perspective of the discipline of 'ethics' of law, we have to look for:

> the set of social norms commonly accepted on the basis of agreements and conventions, and therefore sustained by rational choices of multiple agents. Once those norms have passed the universalizability test, which is what meta-ethically distinguishes them from rules of mere prudence or from social norms not susceptible to moral meaning,

[79] Jacco Bomhoff and Anne Meuwese, 'The Meta-Regulation of Transnational Private Regulation' *Journal of Law and Society* 38(1), March 2011, at 160.

[80] Bomhoff and Meuwese (n 79), at 160.

[81] Bomhoff and Meuwese (n 79), at 170 and 172.

[82] This is also called the function of PIL as a 'mechanism' or the 'touch down' function thereof, as due to rules of PIL, state law becomes relevant again for TPR (for instance as to questions of whether a choice of law may be made in TPR, enforcement of TPR etc). See Bomhoff and Meuwese (n 79), at 171.

[83] Especially as to the socio-economic and political implications behind PIL instruments and doctrines. See Bomhoff and Meuwese (n 79), at 172.

[84] Bomhoff and Meuwese (n 79), at 164 (citing C. Joerges, 'Constitutionalism in Postnational Constellations: Contrasting Social Regulation in the EU and in the WTO', in C. Joerges and E.-U. Petersmann (eds.), *Constitutionalism, Multilevel Trade Governance and Social Regulation* (Hart Publishing 2006)).

[85] Bomhoff and Meuwese (n 79), at 165.

> they are effective by dint of their social function of solving cooperation and coordination problems.[86]

The quest for universality of BCR seems a bit daunting, but a first attempt at identifying common reference points (meta-norms) for BCR is undertaken in this book by evaluating the concept of BCR from the different dimensions and perspectives set out above. Perhaps not so surprisingly, such evaluation will indeed show many common denominators across the disciplines. Though at present there are no hard and fast rules against which TPR (let alone BCR) should be evaluated, I will take these common denominators of the different disciplines as meta-norms for evaluating BCR. On this basis I will make suggestions for improvements of the BCR regime, as well as suggestions how to fit the BCR concept into the regulatory data protection regimes of other countries or regions like the APEC Privacy Framework. The objective is to achieve that BCR can be accepted as a mainstream global solution to regulate global corporate conduct in the area of data protection, also in countries where at present no (or insufficient) data protection is afforded. BCR may then indeed provide a solution to avoid the present gaps in protection and enforcement as presented by the current patchwork of national data protection laws.

[86] Lorenzo Sacconi, 'Corporate Social Responsibility (CSR) as a Model of "extended" Corporate Governance: an Explanation Based on the Economic Theories of Social Contract, Reputation', in Fabrizio Cafaggi, *Reframing Self-Regulation in European Private Law* (Kluwer Law International 2006), Chapter 12, at 294.

3

The Worldwide Data Protection Regulatory Landscape

In the digital age, data protection is of increasing concern to governments, individuals, and companies alike. All advanced industrial societies face essentially the same dilemma of how to regulate these vast flows of personal information, but their governments have chosen substantially different solutions to do so.[1/2] Any government regulation in the area of data protection needs to balance the interests of organizations that use personal data against the potential harm such use could cause individuals.

3.1 EU Data Protection Regime

Within the EU the protection of individuals prevailed and the rights of individuals in respect of processing of their personal data became a fundamental human right and freedom.[3] Despite the fierce resistance of many interest groups

[1] See Joel Reidenberg, 'Resolving Conflicting International Data Privacy Rules in Cyberspace' [2000] *Stanford Law Review*, at 1315, 1318.

[2] For a comprehensive overview of different data protection regimes, see Abraham L. Newman, *Protectors of Privacy, Regulating Personal Data in the Global Economy* (Cornell University Press 2008). The distinction between 'comprehensive regimes' and 'limited regimes' as used here was initially introduced by Newman. See also Prins (Chapter 2, n 9), at para 6.4.3.

[3] The Council of Europe recognized (certain aspects) of data protection as a fundamental human right in Art 8 of the European Convention for the Protection of Human Rights and Fundamental Freedoms of 4 November 1950 (*ECHR*) as further specified in Convention 108 for the Protection of Individuals with Regard to the Automatic Processing of Personal Data of 28 January 1981 (*Convention 108*), both to be found at <http://www.conventions.coe.int>. According to its Recital 11, the Directive gives substance to and amplifies the data protection principles of Convention 108, which was considered not specific enough to provide for sufficient protection. After adoption of the Directive, an additional protocol to Convention 108 was considered necessary as it was thought there were missing elements which Convention 108 did not provide for, such as (i) a data protection supervisory system and (ii) restrictions on data transfer to countries not party to it (see Additional Protocol to Convention 108 (Chapter 2, n 50). See further Art 8 of the Charter of Fundamental Rights of the European Union (Chapter 2, n 10) where the right to data protection was recognized as a separate right (alongside the right of respect for private and family life laid down in Art 7). In *Promusicae* (Case C-275/06 *Promusicae* [2008] ECR I-271), the ECJ acknowledged this status of 'a further fundamental right', namely the 'right that guarantees protection of personal data and hence of private life'. According to the ECJ, 'this right is however not absolute but must be balanced against other

across the industry[4], the EU subsequently adopted the Directive.[5] Further in this chapter I will discuss the main elements of the Directive, which forms the main building block of data protection law in the EU. As indicated in paragraph 1.1, the Commission has launched a revision of the Directive, the latest status of which is reflected in the Proposed Regulation as issued in January 2012.[6] My original dissertation was available to the Commission when drafting this Proposal, and I have inserted additional text and footnotes in these Chapters to reflect the changes as envisaged by the Commission in this Proposed Regulation. Though these changes may seem extensive, many of these concern codifications of the interpretations given by the Working Party 29 in its many opinions on the various topics since the adoption of the Directive and therefore are less of a landslide than would appear from the face of the Proposed Regulation.

fundamental rights', see at paras 63, 65, and 68. The status of data protection as a fundamental right and freedom is given a legally binding basis in the recently adopted TFEU (Chapter 2, n 3). The TFEU abolishes the pillar structure and introduces, in Art 16, a provision on data protection with general application, which means that all areas of EU law are covered (ie also the second and third pillars which are presently excluded from the scope of the Directive pursuant to Art 3(2) thereof). Article 16 TFEU is designed to be the central source of data protection within the EU. It mirrors Art 8 Charter of the Fundamental Rights of the European Union. The constitutional character of data protection therefore now has been made part of the legal framework of the EU. On the development of data protection as a constitutional right in the EU, see P. De Hert and S. Gutwirth, 'Data Protection in the Case Law of Strasbourg and Luxembourg: Constitutionalism in Action', in Serge Gutwirth et al (eds.), *Reinventing Data Protection?* (Springer 2009), Chapter 1, at para 1.1.2.

4 See Newman (n 2), at 13, reporting that companies expected at the time that the implementation of comprehensive processing rules would have serious financial implications. Further, nationally oriented companies that relied on information exchange (insurance providers and direct marketers) expected to lose from a reduction in data sharing and to benefit little from the free data transfers which would be created within the EU by harmonization of the various national laws. Also, multinationals opposed the new laws as they feared that the data exchange between their EU and non-EU companies would be hindered. Non-EU multinationals feared exclusion from the EU market.

5 Hereafter I will discuss the Directive, which forms the main building block of data protection law within the EU. The Directive is, however, not the only directive that regulates data protection in the EU. Other EU legislative instruments for regulating data protection are:

- Regulation (EC) No 45/2001 of the European Parliament and of the Council of 18 December 2000 on the protection of individuals with regard to the processing of personal data by the Community institutions and bodies and on the free movement of such data, OJ 2001, L 8;
- Directive 2002/58/EC of the European Parliament and of the Council of 12 July 2002 concerning the processing of personal data and the protection of privacy in the electronic communications sector (Directive on privacy and electronic communications), OJ 2002 L 201, as revised by Directive 2009/136/EC of the European Parliament and of the Council of 25 November 2009 (*e-Privacy Directive*); and
- Council Framework Decision 2008/977/JHA of 27 November 2008 on the protection of personal data processed in the framework of police and judicial cooperation in criminal matters OJ 2008 L 350.

6 See Chapter 1, n 10.

3.1.1 Material processing principles

The Directive provides for comprehensive data processing rules governing both the private and (part of) the public[7] sector throughout the EU. The Directive imposes requirements on the 'controller' of a data processing.[8] Any processing of personal data has to comply with certain material processing requirements. Though the recitals of the Directive do not indicate so, the processing requirements of the Directive are clearly inspired by the privacy principles of the OECD Privacy Guidelines.[9] Personal data must be processed fairly and lawfully,[10] collected for specified and legitimate purposes only,[11] and the processing of these data must be

[7] Pursuant to Art 3(2) Directive, processing operations concerning public safety, defence, state security, and the activities of the state in areas of criminal law, are excluded from the scope of the Directive. The TFEU abolishes the pillar structure and in Art 16 introduces a provision on data protection with general application (see n 3). The Proposed Regulation still has more or less the same scope (see in particular Art 2(2)(a) and (e)), where activities concerning national security and processing by competent authorities for the purposes of prevention, investigation, detection or prosecution of criminal offences, or the execution of criminal penalties are excluded. These data processings will be governed by the separate proposal for a new directive issued by the European Commission at the same date as the Proposed Regulation, see European Commission, 'Proposal for a Directive of the European Parliament and of the Council on the protection of individuals with regard to the processing of personal data by competent authorities for the purposes of prevention, investigation, detection or prosecution of criminal offences or the execution of criminal penalties, and the free movement of such data', COM(2012) 10 final, to be found at <http://ec.europa.eu/justice/newsroom/data-protection/news/120125_en.htm>.

[8] Controller means the '(legal) person, public authority, agency or other body who alone or jointly with others, determines the purposes and means of the processing of personal data' (Art 2(d) Directive). From the definition it follows that it is possible to have multiple controllers for the same processing. See in detail on the concepts of 'controller' and 'processor' WP 169 Opinion 1/2010 on the concepts of 'controller' and 'processor', 16 February 2010 (WP Opinion on controller and processor). The Proposed Regulation defines 'controller' slightly differently: 'the natural or legal person, public authority, agency or any other body which alone or jointly with others, determines the purposes, conditions and means of the processing of personal data' (Art 4(5) Proposed Regulation). What is also new is a specific rule that is introduced in Art 24 Proposed Regulation, providing that joint controllers may determine their respective responsibilities by means of an arrangement between them.

[9] OECD Privacy Guidelines (Chapter 2, n 40). The Guidelines prescribe that: collection of data should be limited, lawful, and fair, with knowledge or consent of a data subject (para 7); data collected should be relevant to the purposes of collection, accurate, complete, and up-to-date (para 8); the purposes of collection should be specified at the time of or prior to data collection and subsequent use should not go beyond declared purposes (para 9); data should not be disclosed, made available, or used for purposes other than those specified unless there is a data subject consent or a requirement of law (para 10); reasonable security safeguards should be taken against loss or unauthorized access, destruction, use, modification, or disclosure of data (para 11); developments, practices and policies with respect to personal data should be open; establishing the existence and nature of personal data, and the main purposes of their use, the identity and usual residence of the data controller should be facilitated (para 12); an individual should have the right to obtain a confirmation from a controller in an accessible manner whether or not the data controller has data relating to him; challenge data related to him, and have it corrected, erased, rectified, completed, or amended (para 13); the data controller should be accountable for compliance with the data protection measures (para 14).

[10] Article 6(1)(a) Directive, cf Art 5 Proposed Regulation. The criteria for lawful processing of personal data are specified in Art 7 Directive (cf Art 6 Proposed Regulation). Article 8 Directive provides for the general prohibition on processing special categories of personal data (ie 'sensitive data') as well as the exceptions from this general rule (cf Art 9 Proposed Regulation).

[11] Article 6(1)(b) Directive (cf Art 5(b) Proposed Regulation).

adequate, relevant, and not excessive in relation to the purposes for which the data were collected or further processed.[12]

Proposed Regulation The main changes envisaged in the Proposed Regulation are that certain requirements will also be directly imposed on a 'processor'[13] of personal data,[14] and further that joint controllers may divide the controller responsibilities between them.[15] This concerns their internal liability only, as externally joint controllers will remain jointly and severally liable for the entire amount of damages.[16] The Proposed Regulation further provides for similar material processing principles[17] but adds three: (i) a transparency principle (personal data shall be processed in a transparent manner in relation to the data subject);[18] (ii) a data minimization principle (personal data processed shall only be processed if, and as long as, the purposes cannot be fulfilled by processing data that do not permit identification);[19] and (iii) the establishment of a comprehensive responsibility and liability of the controller.[20]

3.1.2 Other fundamental obligations

Other fundamental obligations of the controller under the Directive are that personal data must be adequately secured[21] and that data processing operations need to be notified to the national data protection authority (*DPA*).[22]

Proposed Regulation The Proposed Regulation brings some fundamental changes. The security obligation is also imposed directly on processors.[23] The general notification obligation is no longer part of the Proposed Regulation, but

12 Article 6(1)(c) Directive (cf Art 5(c) Proposed Regulation).

13 Article 2(e) Directive defines a processor as 'a (legal) person, public authority, agency or any other body that processes personal data on behalf of the controller'. The definition in Art 4(6) Proposed Regulation is nearly identical.

14 Direct obligations of a processor under the Proposed Regulation are eg the obligation of the processor (i) not to process personal data except on instructions from the controller or if required to do so by EU or Member State law (Art 27); (ii) maintain documentation of all processing operations under its responsibility and to make these available on request to the supervisory authority (Art 28); to cooperate with the supervisory authority (Art 29); to implement appropriate technical and organizational security measures (Art 30); to obtain a prior authorization of the supervisory authority or to consult the supervisory authority in specific cases (Art 34); to designate a data protection officer (a) if the processor is a public authority or body or a large enterprise; and (b) if the processing operations require regular and systematic monitoring (Art 35); and to transfer personal data to a third country only if the processor has adduced additional safeguards (Art 42).

15 Article 24 Proposed Regulation.

16 Article 77(2) Proposed Regulation.

17 Article 5(1)(a), (b), (c), and (d) Proposed Regulation.

18 Article 5(1)(a) Proposed Regulation.

19 Article 5(1)(c) and (e) Proposed Regulation. The data minimization principle seems an alternative manner of expressing the proportionality and subsidiarity principle and seems further to have been implemented in the new obligation of the controller of data protection by design and default as provided in Art 23 Proposed Regulation.

20 Article 5(1)(f) Proposed Regulation, which seems an expression of the accountability principle (see on the accountability principle extensively Chapter 9).

21 Article 17 Directive. cf Art 30 Proposed Regulation.

22 Articles 18–19 Directive.

23 Article 30 Proposed Regulation.

replaced by the requirements for controllers (i) to maintain documentation of the processing operations under its responsibility;[24] (ii) the requirement to carry out a data protection impact assessment prior to risky processing operations;[25] and (iii) to consult the DPA in case the data protection impact assessment at sub-paragraph (ii) indicates a high degree of specific risks.[26] The Proposed Regulation further adds a number of other general obligations of the controller (and in certain cases of the processor)[27] (i) an 'accountability' obligation (ie the responsibility of the controller to comply with the Regulation and to demonstrate this compliance, including by way of adoption of internal policies and mechanisms for ensuring such compliance);[28] (ii) to establish procedures to inform individuals and for the exercise of their rights;[29] (iii) to implement principles of data protection by design and by default;[30] (iv) to cooperate with the DPA;[31] (v) to notify personal data breaches to the DPA and individuals;[32] and (vi) to appoint a data protection officer for large enterprises or where the core activities of the controller consist of processing operations which require regular and systematic monitoring.[33]

3.1.3 Rights of data subjects

Under the Directive individuals should be informed about processing of their data,[34] and individuals should be granted rights of access, rectification and objection to processing.[35]

Proposed Regulation The Proposed Regulation provides for similar rights, but adds the right of individuals (i) to be forgotten;[36] (ii) not to be subject to a measure based on profiling;[37] and (iii) to data portability.[38]

3.1.4 Scope of applicability

The Directive harmonized various national data protection laws already in force in some EU Member States.[39] The aim of the Directive was to work as a single market

[24] Article 28 Proposed Regulation. See on this further Chapter 9, para 9.3.4, in particular n 86.
[25] Article 33(2) Proposed Regulation.
[26] Article 34 Proposed Regulation.
[27] See n 14.
[28] Article 22 Proposed Regulation. See also Art11(1) Proposed Regulation.
[29] Article 12 Proposed Regulation.
[30] Article 23 Proposed Regulation.
[31] Article 29 Proposed Regulation.
[32] Article 31 and 32 Proposed Regulation.
[33] Article 35 Proposed Regulation.
[34] Article 10 Directive. cf Arts 11 and Art 14 Proposed Regulation.
[35] Article 12 and 14 Directive. cf Arts 15, 16, 17, and 19 Proposed Regulation.
[36] Article 17 Proposed Regulation.
[37] Article 20 Proposed Regulation.
[38] Article 18 Proposed Regulation.
[39] See Chapter 2, n 67.

measure to facilitate the free flow of data within the EU.[40] The wish to avoid gaps in the protection of personal data and to prevent circumvention of the protection of the Directive has led EU legislators to provide for a very broad scope of applicability of the Directive ('long arm reach'). The main applicability rule of the Directive[41] prescribes that the national data protection laws apply in the event a controller processes data 'in the context of the activities of an establishment (of such controller) in the EU'. For applicability of the national data protection laws it is not required that the controller itself is established within a Member State. To avoid the circumvention of the protection of the Directive, a second applicability rule[42] was introduced, which provides that the national data protection laws also apply if the controller has no establishment in a Member State, but 'makes use of equipment located within the EU for the processing of data', unless such equipment is used for mere transit purposes only.

Proposed Regulation Under the Proposed Regulation, the issue of which national data protection laws apply is to a large extent solved, by choosing the form of an EU regulation as a legislative instrument instead of an EU directive. As EU regulations are directly applicable in all Member States, there will only be one data protection law that is applicable in all Member States.[43] As to the applicability rules themselves, the Proposed Regulation follows to a large extent the proposal of the Working Party 29,[44] whereby the first applicability rule remains that the Regulation applies to the processing of personal data in the context of the activities of an establishment of a controller or processor in the EU;[45] and the second applicability rule is replaced by the rule that the Regulation will also apply to the processing of personal data of data subjects residing in the EU by a controller not established in the EU, where the processing activities are related to: (i) the offering of goods or services to such data subjects in the EU; or (ii) the monitoring of their behaviour.[46]

[40] The legal basis for the Directive is Art 95 (formerly 100a) EC Treaty (Chapter 2, n 3). See further Recitals 1–9 of the Directive.

[41] Article 4(1)(a) Directive. See on the scope of this applicability rule, and proposals for improvement Moerel (Chapter 1, n 8), at Chapter 2.

[42] Article 4(1)(c) Directive. See on the scope of this applicability rule, and proposals for improvement Moerel (Chapter 1, n 8), at Chapter 3.

[43] See Chapter 1, n 11.

[44] See WP Contribution on The Future of Privacy (Chapter 1, n 6), at paras 37–9.

[45] Article 3(1) Proposed Regulation. This provision also provides that the Regulation applies if data are processed in the context of the activities of a processor in the EU. The reason for including processors in this provision is that the Proposed Regulation also includes direct obligations of processors which should be triggered independently whether the Regulation applies to the controller or not. It is questionable whether this provision will do the trick. Under the current thinking of the Working Party 29, processors process data on behalf of controllers, and based thereon the Working Party 29 considers that these data are (therefore) not processed also in the context of the activities of the processor. I have already debated this starting point, as in my opinion the activities of the data processor are the processing of data, which is an activity in itself (what activity would processors then have, none?). I assume that the Proposed Regulation embraces this new starting point, otherwise the applicability rule of Art 3(1) would never lead to applicability of the Regulation to processors. See on this Moerel, (Chapter 1, n 8), at paras 2.4 and 2.10.2.

[46] Article 3(2) Proposed Regulation.

3.1.5 EU transfer rules

The wish to also regulate the trans-European data streams has resulted in a further extension of applicability of the Directive, where it prohibits data transfers from the EU to countries outside the EU without an adequate level of protection[47] (*EU transfer rules*).[48] The EU transfer rules are not considered to be one of the material processing principles (listed in paragraph 3.1.1. above), as the transfer rules are a mechanism to ensure that these material processing principles will be observed, rather than being a fundamental processing principle itself.[49] This being said, the transfer rules are crucial in their own right to guarantee the protection provided by the Directive and therefore are a key cornerstone of the Directive.[50] The Directive contains only a limited number of derogations from the EU transfer rules.[51] The Commission can issue a finding that a certain country provides for an adequate level of protection as a result of which the EU transfer rules do not apply to such country (*adequacy finding*).[52] In practice only a limited number of countries have obtained such an adequacy finding.[53] As multinationals typically transfer data

[47] Article 25(1) Directive.

[48] Given the equivalent protection in the Member States resulting from implementation of the Directive, the EU transfer rules were not made applicable to transfers of personal data within the EU. See Recital 9 of the Directive.

[49] This is evidenced by the fact that in the Directive the EU transfer rules are not included in chapter II (The General Rules on the Lawfulness of the Processing of Personal Data), but in a separate chapter IV (Transfer of Personal Data to Third Countries). For a similar separation of the basic principles and the transfer rules see the Joint Proposal for a Draft of International Standards on the Protection of Privacy with regard to the processing of Personal Data (*Madrid Draft Proposal for International Standards*), as adopted on 5 November 2009 at The International Conference of Data Protection and Privacy Commissioners in Madrid by the participating data protection authorities, to be found at <http://www.agpd.es>, where the transfer rules are included in Part III, section 15 and the basic principles of data protection in Part II. See also the OECD Guidelines (Chapter 2, n 40), where the rules on transborder data transfer are included in Part III ('Basic principles of international application: free flow and legitimate restrictions') and the basic principles in Part II ('Basic principles of national application'). See also Kuner (Chapter 2, n 8), at 27.

[50] See WP 12, Working Document on Transfers of personal data to third countries: Applying Arts 25 and 26 Directive, 24 July 1998 (WP 12), at 6, where the Working Party 29 lists 'six content principles' of which the sixth is: 'restrictions on onward transfers—further transfers of the personal data by the recipient of the original data transfer should be permitted only where the second recipient (ie the recipient of the onward transfer) is also subject to rules affording an adequate level of protection. The only exceptions permitted should be in line with Article 26(1) of the directive.' Since a restriction on onward transfers was at the time missing from Convention 108, the Working Party 29 considered the protection provided by the countries that had at the time ratified Convention 108 was insufficient (see WP 12, at 8). This led to adoption of a transfer rule similar to that in the Directive in Art 2 Additional Protocol to Convention 108 (Chapter 2, n 50).

[51] For the derogations to the EU transfer rules, see Arts 25–26 Directive.

[52] Articles 25(6) and 31(2) Directive.

[53] For the countries that have obtained an adequacy finding, see<http://ec.europa.eu/justice/policies/privacy/thridcountries/index_en.htm>. These are presently: Argentina; Canadian organizations subject to the Canadian Personal Information Protection and Electronic Documents Act (*PIPED Act*); Switzerland; the Bailiwick of Guernsey; the Bailiwick of Jersey; the Isle of Man; Israel; and Andorra. The Working Party 29 issued an Opinion that it considers New Zealand as providing for an adequate level of protection. See Opinion 11/2011 on the level of protection of personal data in New Zealand dated 4 April 2011 (WP 182). The European Commission decision confirming this has not been issued yet.

worldwide, this derogation is therefore of limited relevance only. The Commission has further approved specific mechanisms for the regulation of data flows between the EU and the US. For instance, the Commission has approved data transfers from the EU to the US when an organization in the US has voluntarily adhered to the US Safe Harbor Framework.[54]

Another ground for allowing a data transfer is obtaining the consent of the individual for such transfer.[55] For consent to be valid it should be 'freely given'.[56] This requirement entails that an individual should be able to refuse his consent or withdraw it any time.[57] In the case of cross-border transfers of employee data between group companies, obtaining consent is hardly ever an option because employee consent is presumed not to be 'freely given' as it is given in the context of a relationship of authority.[58] Also in the consumer context, the validity of consent can be questioned in case of repeated or even structural transfers or if the transfer in question is disproportionate.[59] More generally, there is a growing concern that

[54] See Chapter 2, n 71. Other examples are the agreement between the EU and the U.S. regarding transfers of air passenger name records data (Council Decision 2007/551/CFSP/JHA of 23 July 2007), and the Agreement on Transfer of Financial Messaging Data, (Chapter 2, n 42).

[55] Article 26(1)(a) Directive.

[56] Article 2(h) Directive defines consent as 'any freely, given specific and informed indication of his or her wishes by which the data subject signifies his agreement to personal data relating to him being processed'. Consent implies that the data controller has given the relevant information about the purposes and extent of the data processing for which consent is given.

[57] See WP Opinion 8/2001 on the processing of personal data in the employment context adopted on 13 September 2001 (WP 48), at 23: 'Consent must at all times be freely given. Thus a worker must be able to withdraw consent without prejudice.' That data subjects have the right to withdraw consent is further generally assumed in literature: see Waltraut Kotschy, 'Directive 95/46/EC, General Rules on the Lawfulness of the Processing of Personal Data', in A. Bullesbach, Y. Poullet, and Corien Prins (eds.), *Concise European IT law* (Kluwer Law International 2006), at 47. In some Member States, the right to withdraw consent has been provided for in the national law. For instance, see Art 5 (1) para 2 of the Dutch Data Protection Act: 'The data subjects or their legal representative may withdraw consent at any time.' Along the same lines, in respect of consent of consumers, see Opinion 2/2010 on online behavioural advertising, adopted on 22 June 2010 (WP 171), at 21: 'If/when an individual asks for a deletion of his/her profile or if he/she exercises his/her right to withdraw the consent, these actions require the ad network provider to erase or delete promptly the data subject's information insofar as the ad network provider ceases to have the necessary legal grounds (ie the consent) allowing the processing.'; Liam Curren and Jane Kaye, 'Revoking consent: A "blind spot" in data protection law?' (2010) *Computer Law & Security Review* 26(3), at 278 acknowledge that 'it is generally assumed that individuals have a right to withdraw, or revoke, their consent to the processing of their personal data by others', but indicate that there are arguments that the Directive may not include such a right. At 282, Curren and Kayne indicate that the UK DPA (the ICO) also interprets the right to withdraw consent narrowly, stating that the latest data protection guide provides that it is possible for consent to be withdrawn 'depending on the nature of the consent given and the circumstances in which [the data controller is] collecting or using the information'. However, their subsequent conclusion is that data subjects should have the right to revoke consent, as the lack of such a right 'could amount to a major shortcoming if individuals should actually be empowered to exercise control of their privacy in a meaningful way' (at 279 et seq).

[58] See WP 48 (n 57), at 23: 'Where as a necessary and unavoidable consequence of the employment relationship an employer has to process personal information, it is misleading if an employer seeks to legitimize this processing through consent. Reliance on consent should therefore be confined to cases where the worker has a genuine free choice and is subsequently able to withdraw the consent without detriment.'

[59] See WP 114 Working document on a common interpretation of Article 26(1) Directive 95/46/EC of 24 October 1995, 25 November 2005 (WP 114), at 11: 'Consent is unlikely to provide an

individuals may not understand what they are consenting to,[60] that there is no meaningful default option available if they do not wish to provide consent,[61] and that the granting of consent becomes a mechanical matter of 'ticking the box', ie becomes subject to 'routinization' and therefore meaningless.[62] Consent as a

adequate long-term framework for data controllers in cases of repeated or even structural transfers for the processing in question. In fact, particularly if the transfer forms an intrinsic part of the main processing (eg centralisation of a world database of human resources, which needs to be fed by continual and systematic data transfers to be operational), the data controllers could find themselves in insoluble situations if just one data subject subsequently decided to withdraw his consent. Strictly speaking, the data relating to a person who had withdrawn his consent could no longer be transferred; failing this, the transfer would continue to be partially based on the data subject's consent, but an alternative solution (a contract, BCR, etc.) would have to be found for data relating to subjects who had withdrawn their consent. Relying on consent may therefore prove to be a "false good solution", simple at first glance but in reality complex and cumbersome.' Further, even if consent is obtained, the processing by a controller still has to meet the proportionality principle. Though the proportionality principle is not included in the material processing principles (see para 3.1.1 above), this principle is considered to be inherent in the bulk of these principles (especially in the requirements of Art 6(1) Directive that data have to be processed fairly, collected for legitimate purposes only, and must be adequate, relevant, and not excessive). Consent may be considered invalid if the processing for which consent is requested is disproportionate. On how the fundamental right to data protection safeguards data subjects and leads to the conclusion that consent has (and should have) a limited value as an independent legal ground for data processing, see Antoinette Rouvroy and Yves Poullet, 'The right to Informational Self-Determination and the Value of Self-Development. Reassessing the Importance of Privacy for Democracy', in Serge Gutwirth et al (eds.), *Reinventing Data Protection?* (Springer 2009), Chapter 2, at 72–6; and Lee A. Bygrave and Dag Wiese Schartum, 'Consent, Proportionality and Collective Power', in: Serge Gutwirth et al (eds.), *Reinventing Data Protection?* (Springer 2009), at paras 9.3 and 9.4. The Working Party 29 in its WP Contribution on The Future of Privacy (Chapter 1, n 6), at 17, recommends to the Commission to specify the requirements of consent taking into account inter alia the following observations: 'There are many cases in which consent cannot be freely given, especially when there is a clear unbalance between the data subject and the data controller (for example in the employment context or when data must be provided to public authorities). In addition, the requirement that consent has to be informed starts from the assumption that it needs to be fully understandable to the data subject what will happen if he decides to consent to the processing of his data. However, the complexity of data collection practices, business models, vendor relationships and technological applications in many cases outstrips the individual's ability or willingness to make decisions to control the use and sharing of information through active choice' (this is in reference to 'Data Protection Accountability: The essential Elements—A Document for Discussion', Centre for Information Policy Leadership, as Secretariat to the Galway Project, October 2009, at 4). This recommendation is repeated in a further Opinion of the Working Party 29 on the requirements of consent, see Article 29 Data Protection Working Party, Opinion 15/2011 on the definition of consent, adopted on 13 July 2011, 01197/11/EN (WP 187 WP Opinion on consent), in particular at 13–16. In its turn, the Commission announced that the controls of consent will indeed be strengthened in the revised Directive. See EC Communication on the revision of the Directive (Chapter 2, n 34), at 6 and 9. The European Data Protection Supervisor (*EDPS*) supports this position of the Commission, see EDPS opinion on revision of the Directive (Chapter 2, n 35), at para 82 at 18. In the Proposed Regulation, the requirements of consent are codified in Art 7, which explicitly provides that consent does not provide a valid legal ground where the individual has no genuine and free choice and is subsequently not able to refuse or withdraw consent without detriment, especially where there is a clear imbalance between the data subject and the controller (Art 7(4)) and further that consent in any event does not provide a valid legal ground for processing in the public or employment sector (Art 7(5)).

[60] See citation Working Party 29 in n 59 and Roger Brownsword, 'Consent in Data protection Law', in Serge Gutwirth et al (eds.), *Reinventing Data Protection?* (Springer 2009), Chapter 2, at 90, rightfully notes that 'until background rights, including the background informational rights have been established, consent has no reference point'.

[61] Kuner (Chapter 2, n 8), at 20 and 30.

[62] On the risks of routinization of consent, see Roger Brownsword (n 60), Chapter 2, at 90.

structural basis for data transfers within a multinational group of companies is therefore often not feasible.

The main other derogation to the EU transfer rules is that a Member State may authorize a certain transfer of data to a third country which does not provide for an adequate level of data protection, if the controller 'adduces adequate safeguards with respect to the protection of personal data'.[63] The Commission has approved the use of EU standard contractual clauses (*EU Standard Contractual Clauses*)[64] for this purpose, which have to be entered into between the EU data exporting company and the non-EU data importing company.

Proposed Regulation The Proposed Regulation contains some major changes to the current EU data transfer regime.[65] The EU transfer rules are also directly applicable to data processors.[66] The Proposed Regulation further contains a 'general principle for transfers' which provides that data transfers by controllers and processors may only take place if the provisions on data transfer of the Proposed Regulation are complied with 'including for onward transfers of personal data from the third country or an international organization to another third country or to another international organization'.[67] This seems to imply that controllers and processors will be responsible not only to ensure that a valid ground is present when transferring data to a third party recipient, but also to regulate onward data transfers by such data recipient. It is not clear what type of measures will be required of controllers and processors to ensure this obligation is met. I will discuss this requirement further in Chapter 9, paragraph 9.5.1 as part of accountability for onward data transfers. The Proposed Regulation further sets out the criteria, conditions, and procedures for the adoption of an adequacy decision by the Commission, which were missing in the Directive.[68]

The data transfer regime under the Proposed Regulation is still 'territory based' (ie transfers are only allowed when the country of destiny provides for 'adequate' data protection), but the inflexibility of the data transfer regime under the Directive is mitigated for instance by providing that adequacy decisions may also relate to a territory or a processing sector within a third country.[69] The Proposed Regulation allows further more 'organizational based' data transfer solutions. In addition to the EU Standard Contractual Clauses 'appropriate safeguards' may also be adduced by (i) binding corporate rules; (ii) standard data protection clauses adopted by a DPA, provided these are declared generally valid by the Commission; and (iii) entering into of contractual clauses between controller or processor and the recipient of the

[63] Article 26(2) Directive.

[64] The approved EU Standard Contractual Clauses may be found at <http://ec.europa.eu/justice_home/fsj/privacy/modelcontracts/index_en.htm>.

[65] Articles 40–44 Proposed Regulation.

[66] See Art 40 Proposed Regulation.

[67] Article 40 Proposed Regulation.

[68] Article 41 Proposed Regulation. The criteria for the Commission's assessment of an adequate or not adequate level of protection include expressly the rule of law, judicial redress, and independent supervision; see Art 40(2) Proposed Regulation.

[69] Article 41(1) Proposed Regulation.

data, provided these contractual clauses obtained the prior authorization of the DPA.[70]

An improvement is further that (under limited circumstances) the 'legitimate interest' of the controller can serve as a legal basis for data transfer.[71] The Proposed Regulation confirms that consent does not provide a valid legal ground for data transfers where there is a significant imbalance between the position of the data subject and the controller.[72] This seems a codification of the earlier Opinions of the Working Party 29, that in the case of cross-border transfers of employee data between group companies, obtaining consent is hardly ever an option because employee consent is presumed not to be 'freely given'.[73]

3.1.6 Third-party processors

If a controller involves a processor[74] to process personal data on its behalf, the controller has to enter into a written[75] data processing agreement with the processor and impose a number of mandatory processing conditions:[76]

(i) the processor may only act on instructions from the controller;

(ii) the processor must implement appropriate technical and organizational security measures as defined by the law in which the data processor is established;[77] and

(iii) the controller must be entitled to review the security measures taken by the processor and the processor must submit its data processing facilities to audits conducted by the controller in connection therewith.[78]

If a controller in the EU transfers data to a processor in a non-EU country, the EU transfer rules apply. For these transfers the Commission has approved specific controller-to-processor EU Standard Contractual Clauses.[79]

[70] Article 42 Proposed Regulation. See Art 43 Proposed Regulation for the requirements for transfers by way of BCR. See on these criteria in detail Chapter 6, n 69.

[71] Article 44(1)(h) Proposed Regulation.

[72] See Art 7(4) and (5) Proposed Regulation.

[73] See n 58 and 59.

[74] See for definition n 13.

[75] Or other equivalent form. See Art 17(4) Directive.

[76] Article 17(2) and (3) Directive.

[77] Article 17(3) Directive.

[78] This is an implementation of the requirement in Art 17(2) Directive that the controller must ensure compliance by the processor with the security measures.

[79] The approved EU Standard Contractual Clauses for controller-to-processor transfers are to be found at <http://ec.europa.eu/justice_home/fsj/privacy/modelcontracts/index_en.htm>. The latest EU Standard Contractual Clauses for controller-to-processor entered into force on 15 May 2010 and now also facilitate the onward transfer by the non-EU based processor to non-EU based sub-processors (*EU Standard Contractual Clauses for Processors*). On these new EU Standard Contractual Clauses, see Christopher Kuner, 'The New EU Standard Contractual Clauses For International Data Transfers to Data Processors' *Privacy & Security Law Report,* 19 April 2010, at 1–7.

Proposed Regulation The Proposed Regulation provides for a similar regime, but adds some mandatory processing provisions to be included in the processor agreement:[80]

(i) employ only staff who have committed themselves to confidentiality or are under a statutory obligation of confidentiality;
(ii) enlist another processor only with the prior permission of the controller;
(iii) provisions to ensure the necessary technical and organizational requirements to enable the controller to respond to requests for exercising the data subject's rights;
(iv) assist the controller in ensuring compliance with the general controller obligations;
(v) hand over all results to the controller after the end of the processing and not process the personal data otherwise; and
(vi) make available to the controller and the DPA all information necessary to verify compliance with the foregoing obligations.

Another new addition is that a processor who processes personal data other than as instructed by the controller, shall be considered to be a controller in respect of that processing and shall be subject to the rules on joint controllers.[81] See on the merits of this provision Chapter 9, paragraph 9.6.

3.1.7 Jurisdiction and enforcement

Each of the Member States has established a DPA to monitor and enforce compliance with its national data protection law.[82] The DPAs exercise their function with complete independence.[83] The Directive has further ensured that each of these DPAs has been endowed with: investigative powers, effective powers of intervention, and the power to engage in legal proceedings.[84]

Proposed Regulation The Proposed Regulation provides for a similar regime. Additional elements are: (i) an express codification of the conditions for the independence of the DPAs and its members, implementing the case law of the ECJ;[85] and (ii) additional powers, most notably the power (and in specific cases, the obligation) to impose fines for administrative offences.[86]

[80] Article 26(2) Proposed Regulation.
[81] Article 26(4) Proposed Regulation.
[82] Article 28(1) Directive. cf Art 45 Proposed Regulation.
[83] Recital 62 and Article 28(1) Directive. See further Art 8(3) TFEU. See in more detail on the requirement of independence of DPAs (and the lack thereof in some Member States), Chapter 10, para 10.7.5.
[84] Article 28(3) Directive.
[85] Articles 47 and 48 Proposed Regulation clarify the conditions for the independence of the DPAs and its members, implementing Case C-518/07 *Commission v Germany* [2010] ECR 2010 p I-1885.
[86] Article 53 Proposed Regulation. See further Art 79 Proposed Regulation obliging DPAs to sanction specific administrative offences by imposing fines between specified minimum and maximum amounts, with due regard to the circumstances of each individual case.

Jurisdiction to hear claims

'Any person' who wishes to file a claim concerning his rights under the Directive may do so with any DPA, regardless of his nationality and regardless of which of the data protection laws of the Member States is applicable.[87] Complaints about violations of the Directive can therefore never be rejected based on lack of jurisdiction of a DPA.[88] The jurisdiction regime for DPAs to hear claims is therefore very broad indeed and has a strong protective element.[89] If the relevant DPA requires the assistance of another DPA to decide on the claim (for instance as the claim is governed by the law of another Member State or if the actual processing takes place in another Member State), such other DPA has to provide all relevant information and assistance.[90] Claims may also be lodged by 'an association representing that person'. This is not the equivalent of the traditional concept of a 'class action' where damages may also be claimed, as DPAs do not have the right to award damages,[91] but in other respects its effect may be similar.[92] It entails that organizations such as civil liberties organizations, consumer associations, trade unions, or privacy activist groups may lodge a complaint with the DPA on behalf of an

[87] Article 28(4) Directive. That it is not a requirement that the own law of the DPA applies can be derived from Art 28(6) Directive: 'Each supervisory authority is competent, whatever the national law applicable to the processing in question'. With 'national law' reference is made to one of the data protection laws of another Member State rather than any other foreign law. This can be derived from the fact that the Directive contains many other provisions, which contain references to 'applicable national law', which all refer to the laws of the Member States only. This can also be derived from the commentary of Ulrich Dammann and Spiros Simitis, *EG-Datenschutzrichtlinie* (Nomos Verlagsgesellschaft 1997), at 313. cf Art 73(1) Proposed Regulation. As the Proposed Regulation is in the form of a regulation which is directly applicable in all Member States, DPAs will only in a limited number of cases have to apply foreign law, see on this Chapter 4, para 4.4.3.

[88] Dammann and Simitis (n 87), at 313.

[89] It is difficult to classify the jurisdictional basis of Art 28(4) Directive (or Art 73(1) Proposed Regulation) in a distinct category. In any event the jurisdictional basis is not the territoriality principle since the jurisdiction of the DPA is not dependent on the fact that the data processing takes place within its country or that the controller is established in its country. The jurisdictional basis is also not the personality principle as the claimant may also be a non-national. The jurisdictional basis which shows the most connection is the 'effects doctrine', which is concerned with protection of the nationals in that state's territory. The difference here, however, is that the protection is not only afforded to the nationals in the territory, but to all individuals regardless of their nationality. This is considered justified as the Directive provides for protection of a fundamental right which should be afforded not only to own nationals. It can be debated whether this constitutes a too far-reaching basis for jurisdiction; see Moerel (Chapter 1, n 8), at para 4.11.

[90] Article 28(6) Directive: 'The supervisory authorities shall cooperate with one another to the extent necessary for the performance of their duties, in particular by exchanging all useful information.' cf Arts 55–56 Proposed Regulation.

[91] The right to award damages is not included in the powers the DPAs are to be endowed with pursuant to Art 28(3) Directive (see also Art 53 Proposed Regulation). Article 22 Directive ensures that individuals may bring a claim for damages through the courts, see further Art 77 Proposed Regulation.

[92] Douwe Korff, *New Challenges to Data Protection Study—Working Paper No. 2: Data Protection Laws in the EU: The Difficulties in Meeting the Challenges Posed by Global Social and Technical Developments* (15 January 2010), European Commission DG Justice, Freedom and Security Report, available at SSRN: <http://ssrn.com/abstract=1638949>, at 99.

individual or groups of individuals.[93] The DPA will then be able to exercise its enforcement powers. Decisions by the DPAs may be appealed before the courts.[94] *Proposed Regulation* The Proposed Regulation provides for a similar regime.[95] However, broader rights are granted to bodies, organizations, or associations where they can also lodge a complaint with the DPA on their own behalf in case of a violation by a controller of its data breach notification requirements.[96]

Jurisdiction to enforce

Concerning the enforcement powers of the DPA, the rule of jurisdiction is based on the territoriality principle: each DPA has jurisdiction in its own territory. Conversely, DPAs cannot enforce their powers outside their territory. The Directive provides jurisdiction regardless of the applicable national law.[97] This is relevant as the applicability regime of the Directive (see paragraph 3.1.4 above) may well lead to the applicability of the laws of another Member State than the Member State where the data processing takes place.[98] As a result, whenever these powers may be exercised (ie because a processing takes place in the relevant territory or if a controller is established in the relevant territory), the DPA of the relevant Member State has jurisdiction. By this provision the Directive ensures that there is always one DPA that can actually exercise its powers. Otherwise the DPA where the individual has filed his claim cannot exercise its powers as, for instance, the relevant processing or assets are not in its territory. By ensuring that such DPA can request the assistance of the DPA that can exercise its powers,[99] effective enforcement is ensured throughout the EU (ie enforcement is based on a 'network approach').

Proposed Regulation The Proposed Regulation provides for a similar regime of competence of a DPA on the territory of its own Member State, but complements this general rule by the new competence of one authority in the case that a controller or processor is established in several Member States (ie the 'country of origin principle' for jurisdiction).[100] The competent DPA will be the DPA of the

[93] Article 28(4) Directive; see also Korff (n92), at 99. cf Art 73(2) Proposed Regulation.

[94] Article 28(3) Directive. cf Art 74(1) Proposed Regulation. Article 74(3) Proposed Regulation provides that proceedings against a DPA have to be brought before the courts of the DPA.

[95] See for references to relevant provisions of the Proposed Regulation, the previous footnotes.

[96] Article 73(3) Proposed Regulation. See for the data breach notification requirements Arts 31 and 32 Proposed Regulation.

[97] See n 88. Article 28(6) Directive: 'Each supervisory authority is competent, whatever the national law applicable to the processing in question, to exercise, on the territory of its own Member State, the powers conferred on it in accordance with para 3. Each authority may be requested to exercise their powers by an authority of another Member State.' cf Art 51(1) Proposed Regulation. As the Proposed Regulation is in the form of a regulation, which is directly applicable in all Member States, DPAs will only in a limited number of cases have to apply foreign law, see on this Chapter 4, para 4.4.3.

[98] For instance, if the controller is established in one Member State and involves a processor in another Member State to process data on its behalf.

[99] Article 28(6), last sentence, Directive.

[100] Article 51(2) of the Proposed Regulation.

main establishment of the controller or processor.[101] Other DPAs will have to provide assistance and cooperation to the competent DPA.[102] I note that this central competence of one DPA relates to jurisdiction to enforce only. The other DPAs keep their jurisdiction to hear claims.

Redress to the courts of the Member States

The Directive has further ensured that all Member States allow for the possibility of individuals to seek judicial redress through the courts.[103] The Directive does not prescribe which court; this is left to be decided by the Member States.[104] The Directive also does not describe which remedies. General opinion, however, is that a judicial remedy does not only concern a ruling on whether the breach occurred, but also includes the possibility to obtain mandatory or prohibitive injunctions (the former to order a defendant to do something; the latter to refrain from doing something, or to cease doing it).[105] The Directive stipulates that the rights

[101] Recitals 27 and 28 to the Proposed Regulation provide for guidance as to how to determine the 'main establishment of a controller':

> (27) The main establishment of a controller in the Union should be determined according to objective criteria and should imply the effective and real exercise of management activities determining the main decisions as to the purposes, conditions and means of processing through stable arrangements. This criterion should not depend whether the processing of personal data is actually carried out at that location; the presence and use of technical means and technologies for processing personal data or processing activities do not, in themselves, constitute such main establishment and are therefore no determining criteria for a main establishment. The main establishment of the processor should be the place of its central administration in the Union.
>
> (28) A group of undertakings should cover a controlling undertaking and its controlled undertakings, whereby the controlling undertaking should be the undertaking which can exercise a dominant influence over the other undertakings by virtue, for example, of ownership, financial participation or the rules which govern it or the power to have personal data protection rules implemented.

[102] Mutual assistance and cooperation has to be provided in accordance with Arts 55–56 Proposed Regulation. See on the country of origin rule for jurisdiction Chapter 4, para 4.4.3.

[103] Article 22 Directive: '(. . .) Member States shall provide for the right of every person to a judicial remedy for any breach of the rights guaranteed to him by the national law applicable to the processing in question.' The reference to a 'judicial remedy' indicates that a claim may be filed through a 'court' of the Member States. The German language version of the Directive is more explicit in this respect where it requires that 'every person can file a claim *through the court*' ('jede Person (. . .) bei Gericht einen Rechtsbehelf einlegen kann'). See further Dammann and Simitis (n 87), at 260. cf Arts 74–75 Proposed Regulation.

[104] Dammann and Simitis (n 87), at 260: 'Which type of court and which court should be chosen in the different cases, is to the discretion of the national law. The Directive just requires that a judicial remedy is available through a court.' The Proposed Regulation also does not specify which type of court or which court.

[105] Dammann and Simitis (n 87), at 260 (para 5), come to this conclusion based on the fact that Art 22 Directive 'entails that *effective* remedies must be provided'. Korff (n 92), at 96, notes that there is no specific guidance in the Directive and by the Working Party 29 on the precise form (or forms) that the remedy should take, but indicates that 'in this respect it is instructive to look at the clarification issued by the EU on the somewhat weaker but still similar requirement in the "Safe Harbor" principle on enforcement, that there must be an "independent recourse mechanism" available to data subjects. In the Frequently Asked Questions (FAQs) on this principle, it is made clear that the mechanism must be

individuals enjoy are those of 'the national law applicable'.[106] The Directive ensured further a right to compensation for any damage suffered by the individual as a result of an unlawful processing operation also under 'applicable national law.'[107] As indicated before, the applicable national law may be a different law from the law of the court.[108] Owing to the discretionary powers of the Member States in the implementation of the Directive, there are many different ways in which Member States have chosen to implement the requirement to provide for judicial redress and the right to damages.[109] However, under most national implementation laws, claims for damages have to be brought before the civil courts (either based on tort or on enforcement of a right *sui generis*)[110] and questions of when and which remedies, such as injunctions or damages, are to be awarded are

able, in so far as feasible, to "reverse or correct" any effects of non-compliance, to ensure that future processing will be in conformity with the Safe Harbor principles, and where appropriate, that processing of the personal data of the individual who has brought the complaint will cease (FAQ 11). Clearly, mutatis mutandis these should also be the minimum requirements for effective judicial remedies under the Directive. They imply that courts, apart from awarding compensation, should also be able to issue injunctions in the relevant proceedings, ordering controllers to either take specific action or to refrain from certain matters (injunctions are indeed expressly mentioned in Safe Harbor FAQ 11).' cf Art 76(5) Proposed Regulation, which provides that the Member States shall ensure that 'court actions available under national law allow for the rapid adoption of measures including interim measures, designed to terminate any alleged infringement and to prevent any further impairment of the interests involved'.

106 Article 22 Directive. cf Art 76(5) Proposed Regulation.

107 Article 23 Directive. According to Korff (n 92), at 96, also 'the right to compensation under Article 23 (...) is to be granted under the "applicable law". This (...) is important, because (...) the laws in the Member States differ in this respect'. cf Art 77(1) Proposed Regulation, which provides for the right to compensation of damages per se, and not insofar as these are available under applicable national law.

108 Korff (n 92), at 95–6, notes that this is relevant as these rights (and the exceptions and derogations from those rights) differ per Member State. At 96, Korff further notes that Member States '(at least in the opinion of the Article 29 Working Party) (...) are not entirely free to determine what kind of damage may provide a cause of action. This is again made clear in an assessment of the appropriateness of safeguards in the context of transborder data flows, specifically in its comments on the adequacy of sectoral codes of conduct in this regard. On this, the Working Party 29 writes that: "If the self-regulatory code is shown to have been breached, a remedy should be available to the data subject. This remedy must put right the problem (e.g. correct or delete any inaccurate data, ensure that processing for incompatible purposes ceases) and, if damage to the data subject has resulted, allow for the payment of appropriate compensation. It should be borne in mind that 'damage' in the sense of the data protection directive includes not only physical damage and financial loss, but also any psychological or moral harm caused (known as 'distress' under UK and US law)". (...) If this applies in that context, it should also apply to the implementation of the right to compensation in the national laws of the Member States', referring to Article 29 Working Party, Working Document on Transfers of personal data to third countries: Applying Articles 25 and 26 EU data protection directive (WP12 of 24 July 1998), 13). cf again Art 77(1) Proposed Regulation, which provides for the right to compensation of damages per se, and not insofar as these are available under applicable national law.

109 For an overview of the different manners in which the Directive is implemented in the national laws of the Member States, see Douwe Korff, *EC Study on implementation of the Data Protection Directive, Comparative Study of National Laws*, September 2002, Human Rights Centre University of Essex, at 209, to be found at <http://papers.ssrn.com>.

110 Korff (n 109), at Chapter 13, discussing the different legal bases on which damages can be claimed, varying from the ordinary rules on civil and administrative liability rules in a country (as in Finland, France, and Luxembourg) to liability in tort (as in Ireland and the Netherlands). As the Proposed Regulation will be directly applicable in the Member States, this will be the legal basis for claiming damages.

left to the national law on administrative or civil liability.[111] As to jurisdiction, most Member States have left it to their courts to decide jurisdiction based on their own rules of civil or administrative procedure[112] and the courts further apply their own procedural law.

The Directive further ensured that the Member States have laid down the sanctions to be imposed in case of infringement of the provisions adopted pursuant

[111] Korff (n 92), at 96. See, however, Bing, 'Data protection, jurisdiction and the choice of law' [1999] *Privacy Law and Policy Reporter* 65, at 9: 'According to Art 23, the Member States are obliged to "provide that any person who has suffered damage as a result of an unlawful processing operation or of any act incompatible with the national provisions adopted pursuant to this Directive is entitled to receive compensation from the controller for the damage suffered". This is, therefore, an obligation under the Directive to include liability provisions for data protection violations, and in this way such provisions may be seen as being "pursuant" to the Directive. This is, however, a somewhat formal argument. Clauses on liability for data protection violations are related to those applying to the invasion of privacy, which will often have, in national law, a sufficiently broad scope to include violations of the provisions introduced pursuant to the Directive. In my opinion, it may be somewhat artificial to construe such traditional provisions as being introduced pursuant to the Directive, and also apply the "proper law of data protection" for the choice of law with respect to liability. But this is certainly one possibility for the interpretation of the Directive which should not be omitted.' Bing, at 10, further points out 'that the law relating to liability might vary to a great extent between different countries. The European Directive Art 23 requires that member countries implement provisions granting compensation for violations of the data protection provisions following the Directive. It is, however, unclear whether this requires member countries to ensure that there is compensation for non-economic loss, and the co-ordination is limited to this general requirement. There is diversity among countries in the law relating to liability, especially with respect to non-economic damage, which is the probable damage in privacy cases. For instance, many European countries require statutory authorisation to award such damages, while the Common Law countries have a less strict doctrine.' Bing, at 23, warns that 'there may be an advantage in forum shopping in such instances'. cf Art 76(5) Proposed Regulation, which also leaves the question when and which judicial remedies are available to the laws of the Member States, provided that 'court actions available under national law allow for the rapid adoption of measures including interim measures, designed to terminate any alleged infringement and to prevent any further impairment of the interests involved'.

[112] In data protection cases this means that the courts of the Member States will apply EC Regulation 44/2001 of 22 December 2000 on jurisdiction and enforcement [2001] OJ L12/1 (*Brussels I Regulation*) to decide their jurisdiction. Kuner (Chapter 2, n 63), at 112; Bing (n 110), at 7. See also WP Opinion on applicable law (Chapter 1, n 7), at 10: 'The provisions of the Directive also determine the scope of applicability of the national laws of the Member States, but they do not affect the jurisdiction of national courts to decide relevant cases before them'. See for the French courts: Douwe Korff (ed.), (2010) *Comparative study on different approaches to new privacy challenges, in particular in the light of technological developments: Country Study A.3—France*, available at: <http://ssrn.com/abstract=1638955>, at 34. The French courts follow the general rules of the law of administrative and civil procedure in data protection cases. From the case study by Korff it appears that '[a]s far as non-criminal judicial remedies are concerned, the Law itself is largely silent [...] simply because in France, anyone whose rights or interests are or may be affected by unlawful action, such as processing in contravention of the data protection law, can in any case appeal to the courts for redress and/or compensation, also and in particular in speedy interlocutory proceedings (en référé). The "relevant judge" (the judge with competence to rule on the matter) differs according to the controller: Matters relating to processing by public bodies will be decided by the administrative courts; matters relating to processing by private sector bodies or individuals by the civil courts.' The Proposed Regulation does provide for specific jurisdiction rules.

to the Directive.[113] These judicial remedies are without prejudice to the sanction and enforcement powers of the DPAs discussed before.[114]

Proposed Regulation The Proposed Regulation provides for a similar regime of redress to the courts. Additional judicial remedies are (i) a judicial remedy for obliging the DPA to act on a complaint;[115] (ii) that the judicial remedies may also be brought to court by bodies, organizations, or associations on behalf of one or more data subjects;[116] and (iii) that the DPAs may bring an action to court to enforce the provisions of the Regulation.[117] Further, rather than relying on the national jurisdiction regimes of the civil courts of the Member States, the Proposed Regulation provides that proceedings against the DPA (obliging the DPA to act on a complaint) must be brought before the courts of the DPA.[118] Proceedings against the controller or processor must be brought either before the court of the Member State of the defendant (ie the controller/processor) or before the court of the Member State in which the data subject is residing.[119]

3.1.8 Working Party 29

The Working Party 29 was established as an advisory body to the Commission under Article 29 of the Directive. The Working Party 29 has advisory status only and acts independently.[120] Members are representatives of each of the DPAs, of the European Data Protection Supervisor, and of the Commission. The tasks of the Working Party 29 are to issue Opinions to 'contribute to the uniform application of the Directive and [to] advise (. . .) on proposals for EU legislation having an impact on data protection'.[121] The Working Party 29 further coordinates and facilitates cross-border enforcement actions by the DPAs, but has no enforcement powers itself. Though the opinions of the Working Party 29 are non-binding, they are followed in practice by the DPAs and de facto set the rules for application of the Directive. See on the role of the Working Party 29 in more detail Chapter 6, paragraph 6.6.6, and on its tasks and procedural rules Chapter 10, paragraphs 10.7.2–10.7.4.

113 Article 24 Directive. Dammann and Simitis (n 87), at 266 (para 3), indicate that this provision also relates to the judicial remedies prescribed by Arts 22 and 23. cf Art 78 Proposed Regulation.

114 Article 22 Directive. Dammann and Simitis (n 87), at 260, comment that this element is included in Art 22 to make clear that the Member States 'must offer both possibilities concurrently'. They further note 'that the Directive does not elaborate on how the procedural architecture should be. It does for example not forbid to restrict the access to the court if not first an administrative procedure has been completed, for instance the complaints procedure with the DPA. Relevant is only that the judicial remedy is available'. The element that judicial remedies are without prejudice to the sanction and enforcement powers of the DPA is left out of the Proposed Regulation, probably as it is obvious.

115 Article 74(2) Proposed Regulation.

116 Article 76(1) Proposed Regulation.

117 Article 76(2) Proposed Regulation.

118 Article 74(3) Proposed Regulation.

119 Article 75(2) Proposed Regulation.

120 Article 29(1) Directive. See Chapter 10, para 10.7.3 on the (lack of) independence of the Working Party 29.

121 See the Document 'Tasks of the Working Party 29', as published at <http://www.ec.europa.eu>.

Proposed Regulation Under the Proposed Regulation the Working Party 29 will be replaced by an European Data Protection Board (*EDPB*),[122] with a similar independent[123] and advisory status.[124] Additional elements are: (i) an express codification of some conditions for the independence of the EDPB, such as the fact that the Commission is no longer a member of the EDPB[125] but has the right to participate and to be represented,[126] and (ii) the secretariat of the EDPB will now be hosted by the European Data Protection Supervisor (*EDPS*) (instead of by the Commission, as is the case now).[127] The tasks of the EDPB are similar to those of the Working Party 29, but provide for additional elements where the scope of activities has been broadened. An example is the role of the EDPB in the newly introduced consistency mechanism.[128] The consistency mechanism is a procedure to ensure the unity of application of the Regulation in transborder data processing operations. Pursuant to the consistency mechanism, DPAs are required to submit certain draft measures that are intended to produce legal effects for opinion to the EDPB:[129] (i) measures relating to processing activities which are related to the offering of goods or services to data subjects in several Member States or to the monitoring of their behaviour; (ii) processing activities which may substantially affect the free movement of personal data within the EU; (iii) adopting a list of the processing operations subject to prior consultation of a DPA;[130] (iv) determining standard data protection clauses;[131] (v) authorization of individual contractual clauses between controllers or processors and recipients of data;[132] and (vi) approvals of BCR.[133] If the DPA, after having received the opinion of the EDPB, intends to maintain its draft measure, it will inform the EDPB thereof, after which the Commission may also issue an opinion.[134] If the DPA, after having received the opinion of the Commission, still maintains its draft measure, the Commission may adopt a reasoned decision requiring the DPA to suspend the adoption of the draft measure, which may remain in force for a period of maximum 12 months.[135]

122 Article 64 Proposed Regulation
123 Article 65 Proposed Regulation.
124 Article 66 Proposed Regulation.
125 Article 64(2) Proposed Regulation. cf Art 29(2) Directive, pursuant to which the Commission is a member of the Working Party 29.
126 Article 64(4) Proposed Regulation.
127 Article 71(1) Proposed Regulation.
128 Article 57–63 Proposed Regulation.
129 Article 58(2) Proposed Regulation.
130 Article 34(5) Proposed Regulation.
131 Article 42(2)(c) Proposed Regulation.
132 Article 42(2)(d) Proposed Regulation.
133 Article 43 Proposed Regulation.
134 Articles 58(8) and 59(1) Proposed Regulation.
135 Article 60 Proposed Regulation.

3.1.9 Self- and co-regulation

The Directive explicitly encourages the drawing up of codes of conduct as a useful instrument to contribute to the proper implementation of the national data protection provisions, taking into account the specific features of the various sectors.[136] As some of the material processing principles in the Directive are of a general nature, the EU legislators consider it desirable that such general principles are further detailed when applied to the data processing as part of the services of a specific sector. To ensure compliance of such codes of conduct with the Directive, trade associations, and other bodies representing groups of controllers may submit their codes to the opinion of their national DPA. The DPA may seek the views of the beneficiaries of these codes or their representatives.[137] Union codes of conduct may be submitted to the Working Party 29 for opinion and also the Working Party 29 may seek the views of the beneficiaries or their representatives.[138] Though the use of codes of conduct is encouraged by EU legislators and the Working Party 29, the number of codes actually adopted is at this time very limited and—with two exceptions[139]—are at Member State level only.[140]

Proposed Regulation Under the Proposed Regulation, codes of conduct are equally encouraged.[141] The differences are that as to national codes of conduct, DPAs are required to consult data subjects on the draft codes[142] and that Union codes may be submitted to the Commission[143] rather than the (successor of the) Working Party 29. The Commission can adopt an implementing act deciding that such Union code has general validity.[144] The Commission has to consult stakeholders during the preparatory work.[145] The Commission further has to follow the

[136] See Recital 61 and Art 27 Directive.

[137] Article 27(2) Directive.

[138] Article 27(3) Directive.

[139] The two organizations that achieved European validation of their codes of conduct so far are: the Federation of European and Interactive Marketing (FEDMA) and the International Air Transportation Association.

[140] On the lack of uptake of self-regulatory codes, see Sjaak Nouwt, 'Towards a Common Approach to Data Protection', in Serge Gutwirth et al (eds.), *Reinventing Data Protection?* (Springer 2009), Chapter 17, at para 17.5.

[141] Article 38 Proposed Regulation.

[142] Article 38(2) Proposed Regulation. Under Art 27(2) Directive, consultation of data subjects is voluntary.

[143] Article 38(3) Proposed Regulation.

[144] Article 38(4) Proposed Regulation. The Commission will have delegated powers under Art 86 (2) Proposed Regulation and has to notify the delegated act to the European Parliament and to the Council on the basis of Art 86(4) Proposed Regulation. Such delegated act will enter into force if no objection has been expressed by the European Parliament or the Council within two months after notification or if, before the expiry of that period, they have informed the Commission that they will not object conform Art 86(5) Proposed Regulation.

[145] See Recital 129 to the Proposed Regulation which states in respect of delegated acts: 'It is of particular importance that the Commission carry out appropriate consultations during its preparatory work, including at expert level'. See further Communication from the Commission to the EP and the Council—COM(2009) 673 final, para 4.2. (Preparatory work for the adoption of delegated acts): 'In addition, and where necessary, the Commission will conduct any research, analysis, hearings and consultations required, in the form best suited to the fields in question and the time limits that have been laid down.'

examination procedure.[146] The Proposed Regulation requires that any Union code of conduct will have to provide for out-of-court proceedings and other dispute resolution procedures for resolving disputes between controllers and data subjects, this without prejudice to the rights of the data subjects under the Regulation.[147]

3.2 Other Comprehensive Regimes

The EU transfer rules have prompted many non-EU countries to follow suit in adopting comprehensive data protection legislation[148] to ensure that their multinational companies retain access to the EU market.[149] Some of the countries that have introduced comprehensive data protection laws have explicitly chosen the EU regulatory system as a starting point.[150]

The states that have introduced a comprehensive system all struggle to regulate transnational data flows, which results in many of these states adopting a similar 'long arm reach' as the Directive. In addition, many of these countries have imposed similar restrictions on the outbound transfer of personal data from their countries to countries that do not provide an adequate level of data protection.[151]

146 Article 38(4) Proposed Regulation. See for the examination procedure Art 87(2) Proposed Regulation and Art 5 Regulation (EU) 182/2011 of the European Parliament and of the Council of 16 February 2011 laying down the rules and general principles concerning mechanisms for control by Member States of the Commission's exercise of implementing powers. The examination procedure should ensure that implementing acts cannot be adopted by the Commission if they are not in accordance with the opinion of a committee composed of representatives of the Member States and chaired by the Commission.

147 Article 38(1)(h) Proposed Regulation.

148 Presently about 60 countries have comprehensive data protection legislation (including the majority of the OECD countries), see <http://www.privacyinternational.org> and <http://www.mofoprivacy.com>. Kuner (Chapter 2, n 18), at para III, estimates that of the 192 Member States of the United Nations about 50–60 currently have a legal framework for data protection. For a comprehensive overview of about 60 countries that have data protection laws, see Miriam Wugmeister, Karin Retzer, Cynthia Rich, 'Global solution for cross-border data transfers: making the case for corporate privacy rules' [2007] *Georgetown Journal of International Law*, vol 38, at 449–98. On the process of how the EU influenced other countries in adopting EU-based data protection laws, resulting in a shift towards the comprehensive system, see Newman (n 2), at Chapters 4–5.

149 T. Büthe and W. Mattli, *The New Global Rulers: The Privatization of Regulation in the World Economy* (Princeton University Press 2011), at 34 (and literature referred to in fn 53): 'In the realm of data protection for e-commerce, regional standards developed in Europe at the EU level, largely won out over U.S. standards as the global standards after a period of (...) competition among public regulators, because firms that are engaged in transnational e-commerce were ultimately more concerned with adopting a single set of privacy standards for their increasingly global operations. United States databases with consumer information whose commercial use was illegal under EU standards thus lost most of their value.'

150 This applies especially to countries in South America.

151 Countries with outbound transfer requirements include: Australia; Switzerland; Argentina; Mauritius; Russia; Singapore; South Korea; Hong Kong; Iceland; Israel; Taiwan; Thailand; Tunisia, the United Arab Emirates and (per 22 December 2011) Mexico. Canada and Japan also de facto impose cross-border transfer rules as under their laws the party transferring personal data to a third party (wherever located) remains accountable for the processing of the data. As a consequence, the party transferring the data will normally have to impose contractual data protection obligations on the third party to guarantee that such third party will provide the required level of protection. For a

3.3 Limited Regimes

Other countries (including the US and many countries in Asia) have taken a limited approach to data protection.[152] The limited regimes[153] mostly focus on the public sector (shaping the processing and transfer of personal data among governmental agencies) and a select number of sensitive industries (most notably healthcare and telecommunications). These limited systems generally permit the processing and transfer of personal data and rely on market mechanisms to check inappropriate processing activities. In these countries the protection of personal data is left to be driven by consumer demand and by industry self-regulation,[154] with patchy results at best. Under the EU transfer rules, these limited regimes are not considered as providing an adequate level of protection for the processing of personal data in those countries and a transfer of personal data from the EU to those countries constitutes a violation of the Directive.

3.4 APEC Privacy Framework

In 2005, the APEC Member Economies (which include Australia, Canada, China, Japan, and the US)[155] adopted the APEC Privacy Framework.[156] The APEC

comprehensive overview of countries with data transfer requirements, see Kuner (Chapter 2, n 8), at Annex I at 55 and Wugmeister, Retzer and Rich (n 148), at para II sub C.

152 During the 1970s and 1980s, the comprehensive systems and limited systems were in relative parity. Countries which initially took a limited approach but have now moved to comprehensive systems are: Australia, Canada, Japan, Czech Republic, Switzerland, Lithuania, New Zealand, and Slovakia. Countries considering legislative reform based on the Directive include Hong Kong and several jurisdictions in Latin America, such as Chile and Ecuador. Limited systems are still in place in the US, Korea and Thailand. For a comprehensive description of systems with a comprehensive approach and systems with a limited approach, see Newman (n 2), Chapter 2. For a further comprehensive overview of the 60 countries that have data protection laws, see Wugmeister, Retzer, Rich (n 148), at para II A.

153 Many (further) categorizations are possible. See for instance Cécile De Terwangne, 'Is a Global Data Protection Regulatory Model Possible?', in Serge Gutwirth et al (eds.), *Reinventing Data Protection?* (Springer 2009), Chapter 10, at para 10.3, using a further categorization of the limited systems alongside the comprehensive model (the piecemeal model, the sector-oriented model, and the risk-burden balance model).

154 Newman (n 2), at 24. For a comprehensive overview of the U.S. on the 'patchwork of privacy regulation and the lack of a dedicated privacy enforcement agency', see Kenneth A. Bamberger and Deirdre K. Mulligan, 'Privacy on the Books and on the Ground' *Stanford Law Review* Vol 63, January 2011; UC Berkeley Public Law Research Paper No. 1568385, available at SSRN: <http://ssrn.com/abstract=1568385, at 103–14>. Also in the U.S. is a strong call for adopting 'omnibus privacy statutes' based on the model adopted throughout Europe, see Bamberger and Mulligan, at 104. For further reading on the U.S. approach of relying on a combination of sectoral law, market forces, and self-regulation, reporting that the Department of Commerce and the Federal Trade Commission expressly favor a self-regulatory approach, see Ira Rubinstein, *Privacy and Regulatory Innovation: Moving Beyond Voluntary Codes* (1 March 2010), NYU School of Law, Public Law Research Paper No 10-16. Available at SSRN: <http://ssrn.com/abstract=1510275>, at 2.

155 APEC is the Asia-Pacific Economic Cooperation, which is an intergovernmental forum in the Asia-Pacific region. At present 21 countries are Member Economies.

156 APEC Privacy Framework (Chapter 2, n 40).

Privacy Framework provides for similar material processing principles[157] as the Directive. However, for a number of reasons the APEC Privacy Framework is not expected to lead to an adequate level of protection as required by the Directive. First of all, the APEC Privacy Framework is voluntary[158] and it is unclear how many Member Economies will indeed implement it. The APEC Privacy Framework further explicitly recognizes that in view of differences in social, economic, and legal backgrounds of Member Economies, the principles may be implemented in different ways. At present many APEC Member Economies already have their own data protection laws which are very diverse in nature. This divergence is likely to be continued.[159] The APEC Privacy Framework may be implemented through self-regulation[160] and the APEC principles are subject to derogation by mandatory rules of national law (for instance, the state control powers of such country).[161] It is therefore not to be expected that in the near future the APEC Privacy Framework will provide an adequate uniform level of data protection throughout the APEC region.[162]

The data transfer rules in the APEC Privacy Framework merit specific discussion. These are based on the 'accountability principle'. Principle 26 of the APEC Privacy Framework provides that if a controller transfers personal data to third parties, the controller remains accountable for taking reasonable steps to ensure that the relevant third party will protect the information consistently with the APEC principles. As a consequence, some form of central enforcement is introduced. Data subjects can address the original controller for breach of this obligation rather than the third-party recipient for a breach by such third party, which de facto results in centralizing enforcement to a certain extent.[163] A more or less similar result is achieved under Japanese law[164] and the Canadian PIPED Act.[165] The data protection laws in Japan and Canada do not distinguish between domestic and cross-border transfers to third parties. They apply the same rules, regardless of the

[157] The main APEC Privacy Principles are: (I) preventing harm; (II) notice, providing for the information rights of individuals; (III) collection limitation, similar to the data minimization principle; (IV) uses of personal information, combining purpose limitation and lawfulness principles; (V) choice, expressing the principle of self-determination; (IV) integrity of personal information; (VII) security safeguards; (VIII) the right of access and correction; and (IX) accountability.

[158] See APEC Privacy Framework, preamble para 4, where it is noteworthy that the APEC Privacy Framework carefully avoids the word 'right'.

[159] Kuner (Chapter 2, n 8), at 21.

[160] APEC Privacy Framework (Chapter 2, n 40), at 34.

[161] APEC Privacy Framework (Chapter 2, n 40), at 8.

[162] Chris Pounder, 'Why the APEC Privacy Framework is unlikely to protect privacy,' to be found at <http://www.out-law.com>; Lee Bygrave, 'International Agreements to Protect Personal Data', in James B. Rule and Graham Greenleaf, *Global Privacy Protection: The First Generation* (Edward Elgar Publishing 2009), at 44–5; Kuner (Chapter 2, n 8), at 22–3; De Terwangne (n 153), at 181 and 183, gives a good overview of all critiques about the weaknesses of the APEC Privacy Framework.

[163] Otherwise, enforcement under the APEC Privacy Framework (Chapter 2, n 40) is also based on the principle of cross-border cooperation between national data protection supervisors rather than central supervision, see Annex B sub II and III of the APEC Privacy Framework.

[164] Kojin Joho Hogo Ho (Act on the Protection of Personal information), Law No 57 of 2003, unofficial translation to be found at <http://www.cas.go.jp/jp/seisaku/hourei/data/APPI.pdf>.

[165] Canadian Personal Information Protection and Electronic Documents Act (*PIPED Act*), to be found at <http://laws.justice.gc.ca/eng/P-8.6/page-1.html>.

location of the third party. These laws require that organizations remain accountable for information that is in their possession or custody, also after this information has been transferred to a third party.[166] At first sight, this seems to provide for a more extensive accountability of the original controller (ie for the outcome) than under the APEC Privacy Framework (where the original controller is only accountable for taking reasonable steps to ensure protection). However, case law indicates that also under the PIPED Act the original controller is only accountable for ensuring that adequate contractual or other means are in place (rather than for the outcome itself).[167] Also in Japan, organizations must establish contracts with service providers and other third parties that contain certain specific data security provisions.[168] A similar approach is chosen in the draft Australian Privacy Principles.[169]

[166] See PIPED Act (n 165), at s 5, 4.1.3 first sentence: 'An organization is responsible for personal information in its possession or custody, including information that has been transferred to a third party for processing.'

[167] See PIPED Act (n 165), at s 5, 4.1.3, second sentence: 'The organization shall use contractual or other means to provide a comparable level of protection while the information is processed by a third party.' See further the Decision of the Office of the Privacy Commissioner of Canada of 02 April 2007 on the complaint of Ms Philippa Lawson (available at <http://www.cippic.ca/documents/privacy/pipeda-complaints/OPCC_Letter_re_National.pdf>). This Decision illustrates that under Principle 4.1.3 of Schedule 1 of the PIPED Act, the Canadian exporter of personal data is only responsible for the measures it takes to ensure 'a comparable level' of data protection, rather than for the actual outcome. The complaint was filed against National Bank of Canada that transferred personal information to SWIFT, established in the U.S. for processing of monetary transfers, which, in turn, disclosed some information pertaining to Canadian citizens to the U.S. government for counter-terrorism purposes without seeking consent of those individuals or informing them. The Office of the Privacy Commissioner stated that 'the banks did not disclose the information, SWIFT did. The contractual language between the banks and SWIFT clearly places responsibility for responding to such subpoenas in the hands of SWIFT; the banks notify their customers of the possibility of such disclosures by way of their respective privacy policies. Given that SWIFT was responsible for the disclosures, not the banks, the issues of the purpose for the disclosures and of the lack of consent are dealt with in the Commissioner-initiated complaint against SWIFT (...).' (at 13). Therefore, National Bank of Canada was not found responsible for the outcome of transfer of personal data. The Office of the Privacy Commissioner did, however, examine the measures the bank took to secure 'a comparable level of protection' (at 3–13). In particular, the Office of Privacy Commissioner finds that the bank 'has in place a contract with its third-party service provider that provides guarantees of confidentiality and security of personal information. The contract allows for oversight, monitoring, and an audit of the service being provided' (at 13). The Office points out that 'at the very least, a company in Canada that outsources information processing to a company that operates in the U.S. should notify its customers that the information may be available to the U.S. government or its agencies under a lawful order made in that country, National Bank has clear language in its Confidentiality Policy, which informs customers [of such a possibility.]' (at 12). The Office concludes that what the Act demands is that when outsourcing data processing to service providers in other countries, 'organizations be transparent about their personal information handling practices and protect customer personal information in the hands of third-party service providers to the extent possible by contractual means' (at 13). In the case at hand, the National Bank did meet those requirements.

[168] Article 22 Act on the Protection of Personal Information (n 164).

[169] See the Draft Australian Privacy Principles (Chapter 2, n 55). Also the Draft introduces a general accountability principle and makes clear that this also applies in case the data are transferred abroad. See Part B, s 19 of the Draft: 'This Act extends to an act done, or practice engaged in, outside Australia by an agency. This Act and an approved privacy code extend to an act done, or practice engaged in, outside Australia by an organisation that has an Australian link.'

4

Trends and Developments in the Legal Landscape

4.1 Increasing Tension between Different Regulatory Systems

With the increased data exchange inherent to the digital era, the diverse national regulatory systems are increasingly in contact with one another and the differences in approach have become an increased source of economic and security disputes between nations.[1] The economic debate concentrates on the limited regimes claiming that the future of e-commerce depends on the free flow of data and the comprehensive regimes claiming that the future of e-commerce depends on individuals being prepared to participate in e-commerce activities only if their privacy has been guaranteed against business and government surveillance.[2] After 9/11 this economic debate has transformed into a security debate about the information requirements of the *war on terrorism*. Tension between the US and the EU came to a height when the US introduced the Patriot Act, expanding the state policing powers to counter terrorism. As a result of heightened security concerns, the US government has used its expanded powers to claim access to increasing amounts of data processed about foreign citizens.[3] This increasingly presents multinationals with catch-22 situations where (especially) US government institutions require transfers of personal data of EU citizens while these transfers are outright violations of EU transfer rules.[4] A very public example is the SWIFT case. Following several press reports in June 2006,[5] it was revealed that the US Department of the Treasury

[1] For the recent increase in surveillance across countries, see the study by Privacy International, 'European Privacy and Human Rights 2010', to be found at <http://www.privacyinternational.org/ephr>.

[2] Newman (Chapter 3, n 2), at 12–14.

[3] This increase in surveillance is not limited to the U.S. This is also an issue in the EU. For an overview of the EU security data exchange policies and the data protection implications, see the Tenth Annual Report of the Article 29 Working Party on Data Protection, at 7–8 (to be found at <http://ec.europa.eu/justice/policies/privacy/workinggroup/wpdocs/index_en.htm>). In 2004, the EU and U.S. finally entered into an agreement on the much debated transfers to the U.S. Department of Homeland Security of 'passenger name records of air passengers' travelling from Europe (Chapter 3, n 54). Until then these transfers lacked a legal basis under the Directive.

[4] On these data protection issues, see Lokke Moerel, Jeroen Koeter, and Nani Jansen, 'U. S. Subpoenas and European Data Protection Legislation' *US Privacy & Data Security Law Journal*, July 2009, at 649–59.

[5] 'U.S. Secretly Tracks Global Bank Data' *Los Angeles Times*, 23 June 2006; 'Bank Data is Sifted by U.S. in Secret to Block Terror' *New York Times*, 23 June 2006.

had served administrative subpoenas on the Society for Worldwide Interbank Financial Telecommunication (*SWIFT*) in order to transfer personal data located on SWIFT's server in the US for counter-terrorism purposes. SWIFT is a cooperative society under Belgian law that is owned by European financial institutions. It operates a worldwide financial messaging system in relation to financial transfers between financial institutions. The information processed by SWIFT concerns messages on the financial transactions of EU citizens, amounting to more than 12 million messages on a daily basis. These messages contain without question personal data of EU citizens. The Working Party 29 issued an opinion on the transfers of personal data by SWIFT based on the subpoenas issued by the US Treasury Department.[6] The Working Party 29 concluded that SWIFT and the financial institutions that use SWIFT's services had breached European data protection laws by transferring the personal data to the US without ensuring adequate protection of such data and by failing to inform the individuals concerned about how their personal data were being (subsequently) processed. In hindsight, it is clear that SWIFT found itself in a conflict-of-law position between applicable US laws (granting US authorities certain powers to seize data) and European data protection requirements. To avoid further violations of data protection, SWIFT transferred its data processing facilities from the US to Switzerland. In 2010, the violation was remedied in the Agreement between the EU and the US on the processing and transfer of Financial Messaging Data from the EU to the US for purposes of the Terrorist Finance Tracking Program.[7]

As indicated, the catch-22 situation SWIFT found itself in is not unique. To date, many EU-based companies have encountered similar situations where US supervisory authorities such as the SEC, FTC, OFAC, the US Department of Justice, or the US Department of the Treasury request information from their US group company, whether on a voluntary basis prior to such authority deciding whether to institute an official investigation, based on a criminal or administrative subpoena, or on the grounds of various specific statutes.[8] Often, the information requested may involve handing over e-mail correspondence between the US group company and its EU parent company, whose e-mail correspondence is often (centrally) stored on a server located at the parent company. EU data protection laws apply to such data and do not provide for a valid legal ground for transfer of such data.[9] A company may also find itself facing similar dilemmas outside the realm of criminal or government investigations. This could be the case when a civil suit is filed in the US and data originating from the EU has to be presented for

[6] Article 29 Working Party Opinion 10/2006 on the processing of personal data by the Security for Worldwide Interbank Financial Telecommunication (SWIFT) adopted on 22 November 2006, 01935/06/EN (WP 128).

[7] See Chapter 2, n 42.

[8] A subpoena could be issued on the grounds of various statutes, including the Patriot Act, Foreign Intelligence Surveillance Act, the Stored Communications Act, or on the basis of National Security Letters.

[9] See for an extensive discussion of all possible grounds Moerel, Koeter, and Jansen, n 4.

pre-trial discovery.[10] Incidents are not limited to the EU and the US. More in general, there are a growing number of incidents where foreign governments use their state control powers and demand access to foreign data. China, for example, requires service providers doing business in China to reveal data to Chinese law enforcement authorities and India has refused to allow BlackBerry handheld communication devices as the data are encrypted, demanding that entities offering communication services in India also maintain communications equipment in India facilitating real-time access to corporate messages by the Indian government.[11]

4.2 Towards a Global Standard for Data Protection?

At present there is no treaty, convention, or other instrument that is legally binding and which regulates data protection on a global basis.[12] The only global data protection instruments issued to date take the form of non-binding guidance documents.[13] Although there is a persistent call for a binding international global standard for data protection[14] and there are some concrete initiatives in this

[10] The Hague Evidence Convention provides a standard procedure through which the court of one country can request assistance from the designated central authority of another in obtaining relevant information in civil and commercial matters. It should be noted that not all EU Member States are a party to The Hague Evidence Convention and some contracting Member States (like France, Spain, the Netherlands, and Germany) have filed a reservation under Art 23 thereof, with the effect that pre-trial discovery of any information is not allowed in relation to foreign legislation. There are no multilateral treaties that regulate the cross-border exchange of information in regard to the type of subpoenas that fall within the scope of this chapter. However, arrangements can be made per sector. For example, the Dutch Financial Supervision Act allows for the Dutch National Bank to provide information on possible violations of certain U.S. and other laws to its U.S. counterparts.

[11] See the *BBC* article and the *New York Times* Google Inc. profile mentioned in Chapter 2, n 43.

[12] The conventions that contain a binding right to data protection are on a regional rather than global basis, such as the European Convention for the Protection of Human Rights and Fundamental Freedoms of 4 November 1950, as further specified in Convention 108 for the Protection of Individuals with Regard to the Automatic processing of Personal Data of 28 January 1981 (both to be found at <http://www.conventions.coe.int>), which Convention 108 has been completed 10 years later by the Additional Protocol to Convention 108 (Chapter 2, n 50). Convention 108 has been ratified by 43 countries mainly in Europe and the Additional Protocol to Convention 108 by 30 countries. This is the state per January 2011, see the statistics of ratification of or accession to the Convention 108 at <http://conventions.coe.int/Treaty/Commun/ChercheSig.asp?NT=108&CM=1&DF=18/02/2011&CL=ENG> and to the Additional Protocol at <http://conventions.coe.int/Treaty/Commun/ChercheSig.asp?NT=181&CM=3&DF=14/01/2011&CL=ENG>. Also the Charter of Fundamental Rights of the European Union of 12 December 2000, [2000] OJ C364/01 (to be found at <http://www.europarl.europa.eu>) has become binding after TFEU came into force in December 2009.

[13] OECD Guidelines on the Protection of Privacy and Transborder Flows of Personal Data (1981) (Chapter 2, n 40); the UN Guidelines concerning Computerized Personal Data Files of 14 December 1990 (Chapter 2, n 50).

[14] On the desirability of introducing a global legal framework for data protection and the initiatives in respect thereto and prospects thereof, see Kuner (Chapter 2, n 8), at 307. The first initiative of relevance dates from 2005, when the 27th International Conference of Data Protection and Privacy Commissioners issued the 'Montreux declaration' which appealed to the United Nations to prepare a binding legal instrument detailing the right to data protection and privacy as enforceable human rights, to be found at <http://www.privacyconference2005.org>. This appeal was repeated at the

respect[15], it is generally not expected that such a global standard will be realized within the coming 10 years. The present regulatory landscape is considered still too diverse for such a standard to be acceptable for adoption on a global level.[16] It is clear that the many instances of 'soft law' in the data protection area show a large number of common denominators[17] which is typically a stepping stone to hard

2008 conference, to be found at <http://www.privacyconference2008.org>. See further the Recommendation on Cross-Border Co-operation in the Enforcement of Laws Protecting Privacy, adopted by the OECD Council on 12 June 2007, at 4–5, which also stresses the need to reach a common protection of personal data throughout the world, to be found at <http://www.oecd.org>. Much attention was further received by the call for global privacy standards for online privacy worldwide by Peter Fleisscher (the Chief Privacy Officer of Google) in his blog of 14 September 2007. Many commentators doubted the true intentions of Google. See Nouwt (Chapter 3, n 140), at 286 and 291. See for an overview of the criticisms: De Terwangne (Chapter 3, n 153), at 175. See further for an overview of the various calls for international harmonization and international standards wherever possible in respect of the broader context of the online environment, which also included calls for global standards in respect of the free flow of information while protecting the privacy thereof: Prins (Chapter 2, n 9), at Chapter 6, at para 6.2. The first call for global principles in EU context seems to have been at the EU Ministerial Conference 'Global Information networks: Realising the Potential', where Ministers of 29 EU Member States agreed on Recommendation 46: 'Ministers agree to work together towards global principles on the free flow of information whilst protecting the privacy and personal and business data, building on the work undertaken by the EU, the Council of Europe, the OECD and the UN', to be found at <http://ec.europa.eu/archives/ISPO/policy/isf/documents/declarations/Bonn-Ministerial-Declaration.htm>. See recently (4 May 2010) The Stockholm Program, 'An open and secure Europe serving and protecting citizens', OJ C115, 04/05/2010, at para 2.5 at 11, where the European Council recommended that 'the Union must be a driving force behind the development and promotion of international standards for personal data protection, based on relevant Union instruments on data protection and the 1981 Council of Europe Convention on the Protection of Personal Data, and in the conclusion of appropriate bi-lateral instruments'.

15 See the Madrid Draft Proposal for International Standards (Chapter 3, n 49). At the same time, there are also discussions in relation to the future revision of Convention 108 of the Council of Europe and of the OECD Privacy Guidelines. See EDPS Opinion on the revision of the Directive (Chapter 2, n 35), at 6.

16 Bygrave (Chapter 3, n 162), at 48–9. See also (citing Bygrave) Kuner (Chapter 2, n 18), at para IV; and Prins (Chapter 2, n 9), at 173. At 196–9, Prins further identifies a number of criteria based on which it can be evaluated whether a certain area is suitable for regulation at an international level. Based on her analysis the question is justified whether data protection is inherently suitable for issuing global standards at all. The EDPS seems more optimistic as to a global standard, see EDPS Opinion on the revision of the Directive (Chapter 2, n 35), at 6 and 25 recommending the Commission to facilitate the achievement of such Madrid International Standards and to ensure consistency with initiatives to revise Convention 108 and the OECD Privacy Guidelines (see Chapter 2, n 40).

17 See De Terwangne (Chapter 3, n 153), at para 10.5 for an overview of the existing international and regional standards and at para 10.5.2 for a listing of the 'admitted core data protection principles' that are part of universal data protection standards:

- collection limitation principle;
- data quality principle;
- purpose specification and limitation/use limitation principle;
- non-discrimination (sensitive data);
- security principle;
- openness principle;
- individual participation principle (right of access and of correction);
- responsibility/accountability principle; and
- proper level of protection in case of transborder data flows.

See also the Opinion on the Communication of the Commission on the revision of the Directive (Chapter 2, n 27), at 4: 'Beneath some different language, there is in fact a surprising amount of common ground across the issues raised in the Communication and reforms now under active

law.[18] The international consensus, however, seems more to be focused on the objectives (ie the data protection to be achieved) than on the means to achieve such protection, on which the views differ widely.[19] The way forward is therefore first and foremost 'to work towards achieving "policy operability" at the international level': 'That is, agreeing on goals a policy should achieve, while recognising that nations may adopt somewhat different policy means to implement the goals'.[20] The OECD takes this view also in a guidance document on privacy in the online environment issued in 2003:[21]

> There is a broad consensus on the important role of privacy protection in building trust in the online environment. Effectively protecting privacy online and ensuring the continued transborder flow of personal data are shared objectives. The means by which those objectives may be achieved are viewed differently in member countries. There is agreement however, that there is no uniform solution. A mix of regulatory and self-regulatory approaches blending legal, technical and educational solutions that suit the legal, cultural and societal context in which they operate holds the promise to provide effective solutions that, beyond the objective of building bridges, go to the actual integration of different elements into viable solutions.

In line with these OECD guidelines, the expectation is that private sector instruments (like BCR under the Directive and CBPR under the APEC Privacy Framework) will assume increasing importance in the coming years.[22] In Chapter 2, paragraph 2.2, I discussed that the organizational-based data transfer tools BCR and CBPR are an important common factor of the Directive and the APEC Privacy Framework and are therefore expected to fulfil an important bridging function between these two systems in the near future.

While a global standard is not yet to be expected, a global standard should in any event not be taken as the Holy Grail for all international jurisdiction and enforcement issues as presently seen in the data protection field.[23] The limitations of law as

discussion in the USA, notably in response to thinking within the Federal Trade Commission and the Department of Commerce and at Congressional level.'

18 See Chapter 2, n 70.

19 See eg the comment in the Welcome Speech of the Australian Federal Privacy Commissioner Malcolm Crompton at the 25th international Conference of Data Protection and Privacy Commissioners (10–12 September 2003) in Sydney: 'If we look around the world we can see the different ways that countries are seeking to meet this dynamic challenge [ie effective privacy protection], taking into account their particular culture and history (. . .) we must be prepared to explore a number of possible ways in which privacy can be respected'.

20 See Prins (Chapter 2, n 9), at 194, and especially fn 156. See also the Opinion on the Communication of the Commission on the revision of the Directive (Chapter 2, n 27), at 3 and 8: 'The Centre certainly agrees that higher priority should go on harmonising regulatory approaches in practice than on substantive laws.'

21 *Privacy Online. OECD Guidance on Policy and Practice* (OECD Publishing 2003), at 4, to be found at <http://www.oecdbookshop.org>.

22 See Kuner (Chapter 2, n 8) at 24; and Prins (Chapter 2, n 8), at 173: 'A final remark is that the case of personal data protection is also a fine illustration of the role that soft law (codes of conduct, privacy policies, corporate rules, privacy seals and trust marks) and the actors involved therein can play in establishing a certain degree of international protection.'

23 See Prins (Chapter 2, n 9), at para 6.5, for a comprehensive discussion of the standard arguments used to justify the quest for international regulation in the online world (including data protection).

a means of controlling international business are much more endemic than calls for global standards imply.[24] The chances of effective enforcement of global standards are limited if at the national level regulatory enforcement proves patchy, whether this is due to lack of effective institutional means, lack of resources, penalties that are treated as a business cost or a licence to be paid rather than a deterrent,[25] or due to the fact that damages are difficult to quantify or too small to be bothered with on an individual scale.[26] At the international level additional complicating factors play a role, such as cultural differences and the prioritization by national governments of national commercial or other interests above regulatory enforcement of global standards.[27] The latter factor is, however, not expected to play a major role in the data protection arena, in the sense that data processing industries would transfer to 'data havens' where enforcement would have no priority.[28] Even today, when there are many jurisdictions with lax or no privacy safeguards at all, there is little hard evidence of a widespread transfer of data processing industries to such data havens.[29] To the contrary, jurisdictions with lax data protection laws often also have excessive state control powers. Multinationals, when having to decide in which jurisdiction to locate their central data processing facilities, in practice tend to avoid these countries.[30]

[24] See Doreen McBarnet, 'Corporate social responsibility beyond law, through law, for law: the new corporate accountability' in McBarnet, Voiculescu, Campbell (eds.), *The New Corporate Accountability, Corporate Social Responsibility and the Law* (Cambridge University Press 2007), at 44–5. This is even the case in the EU, see the Rand Report (Chapter 2, n 27), at 35. See also Charles Raab and Bert-Jaap Koops, 'Privacy Actors, Performances and the Future of privacy Protection', in Serge Gutwirth et al (eds.), *Reinventing Data Protection?* (Springer 2009), at 216; Wugmeister, Retzer, Rich (Chapter 3, n 148), at 470.

[25] In my experience, many companies see threats of potential data protection violations as a possible cost rather than a deterrent. It is therefore not surprising that the Working Party 29 recommends to include in the revised Directive a uniform approach as to the sanctions the Member States are to implement to ensure that all DPAs will have the necessary powers, including the power to impose financial sanctions, see WP Contribution on The Future of Privacy (Chapter 1, n 6), at para 90.

[26] Colin David Scott, *Enforcing Consumer Protection Laws* (30 July 2009), UCD Working Papers in Law, Criminology & Socio-Legal Studies Research Paper No 15/2009, available at SSRN: <http://ssrn.com/abstract=1441256>, at 4, also published in: Geraint Howells, Iain Ramsay, and Thomas Wilhelmsson (eds.), *Handbook of International Consumer Law and Policy* (Edward Elgar 2010). This is also the main cause identified for the lack of enforcement of data protection, see in more detail para 4.3, in particular the citations from the Rand Report in n 47.

[27] McBarnet (n 24), at 45–6.

[28] This is a fear expressed in the First Report on the Directive (Chapter 2, n 26), at 19: 'An overly lax attitude in some Member States (. . .) risks weakening protection in the EU as a whole, because with the free movement guaranteed by the Directive, data flows are likely to switch to the "least burdensome" point of export.'

[29] Kuner (Chapter 2, n 8), at 31; and Prins (Chapter 2, n 9), at 181, both referring to Colin J. Bennett and Charles D. Raab, *The Governance of Privacy* (MIT Press 2006), at 279.

[30] This is based on my experience as a practitioner when advising multinationals on how to structure their worldwide data processing facilities. About 10 years ago, many EU-based multinationals transferred their central data processing operations to the U.S., mainly for cost reasons (cheap electricity). Due to the enactment of the U.S. Patriot Act, granting the U.S. government authorities the right also to request transfer of data of foreign citizens, many EU based multinationals transferred critical data processing facilities back to the EU. The highest profile example is SWIFT, see (Chapter 2, n 42). See also Burk (n 31), at 266 and fn 20: 'The certainty offered by a well-developed body of relevant law may in many instances offer greater business value than would relaxed regulation of information distribution.' See on the phenomenon of a regulatory 'race to the top' whereby more

Further, a well-known downside of international/global regulation as opposed to national regulation is that it excludes any competition between national regulations which curtails regulatory innovations, this while there is an increasing need to continuously adapt existing rules in view of rapidly changing circumstances and views.[31] For instance, if the EU data transfer rules had been universally adopted around the globe, the alternative solution of accountability for data transfers (as adopted under the APEC Privacy Framework) would not have come into existence. The latter system may well prove in practice to be the better solution (see on this Chapter 9, paragraph 9.5). Any global standard should therefore in any event be limited to setting general principles, leaving any detailed rules to secondary regulation which can be amended more quickly, if changing circumstances so require.[32] From this perspective, the present 'common ground' on 'core data protection principles'[33] may therefore already be sufficient for a global standard to materialize.[34]

stringent national or regional regulatory standards become the de facto global standard (with a permanent divergence by a small group of countries with weak domestic political and legal institutions and little concern for their international reputation), Büthe and Mattli (Chapter 3, n 149), at 24, in particular the research referred to in fn 16.

[31] Prins (Chapter 2, n 9), at para 6.6; Dan L. Burk, 'Comment on "Should ICT Regulation be Undertaken at an International Level?"', in Bert-Jaap Koops et al (eds.), *Starting Points for ICT Regulation. Deconstructing Prevalent Policy One-Liners* (TCM Asser Press 2006), at para 9.3, at 266–7: '(...) an international agreement forces international business to operate in a world where "one size fits all". Opportunities for jurisdictional experimentation and innovation are curtailed' and concluding that the international inefficiencies resulting from an international agreement 'may be no less serious than the inefficiencies resulting from a lack of co-ordination'. For a similar observation in the context of company law, see The Report of the High Level Group of Company Law Experts on a Modern Regulatory Framework for Company Law in Europe, Brussels, 4 November 2002, to be found at <http://ec.europa.eu/internal_market/company/modern/index_en.htm>, at para 2, observing that the system in the EU of harmonizing company law 'may have led to a certain "petrification" of the law', while 'simultaneously there is a growing need to continuously adapt existing rules in view of rapidly changing circumstances and views. The "shelf life" of law tends to become more limited as society changes more rapidly, and company law is no exception'.

[32] For a similar observation in the context of company law, see The Report of the High Level Group of Company Law Experts on a Modern Regulatory Framework for Company Law in Europe (n 31), at para 2: 'Fixed rules in primary legislation may offer the benefits of certainty, democratic legitimacy and usually strong possibilities of enforcement. But this comes at a cost of little or no flexibility, and disability of keeping pace with changing circumstances.'

[33] See n 19.

[34] I note that such a global standard itself need not necessary itself be binding at the global level. Global standards can also be developed by private institutions whereafter bindingness can subsequently be achieved by national or regional governments adopting such standards in their respective national laws. This indirect manner of achieving global harmonization is a much observed phenomenon in the global arena. See on this shift from *national public* regulation to *global private* rule-making: Büthe and Mattli (Chapter 3, n 149), at Chapter 1 'The Rise of Private Regulation in the World Economy'. See in particular at 5: where Büthe and Mattli observe as a trend: 'the delegation of regulatory authority from governments to a single international private-sector body that, for its area of expertise, is viewed by both public and private actors as the obvious forum for global regulation. (...) This simultaneous privatization and internationalization of governance is driven, in part, by governments' lack of requisite technical expertise, financial resources, or flexibility to deal expeditiously with ever more complex and urgent regulatory tasks'. Büthe and Mattli give as a striking example of both (i) norm-setting in general principles only and (ii) privatization and internationalization of norm-setting the landmark decision of the SEC in August 2008, to switch the U.S. accounting standards (at that time the U.S. Generally Accepted Accounting Principles (GAAP)) to the International Financial Reporting Standards (IFRS), produced by the International Accounting Standards Board, a private-sector regulator based in

In light of the 'data explosion' the world is presently experiencing,[35] data protection issues have become so vast and urgent that they can no longer be ignored by governments and multinationals alike.[36] In face of the huge challenge to regulate a global phenomenon that is already a reality and a moving target at that, my prediction is that agreement on the basic data protection principles in a global standard may prove less of a hurdle than past experiences with attempts to come to a global standard would suggest.[37]

4.3 Cross-border Enforcement Issues

Applicability, jurisdiction, and enforcement of data protection legislation are generally based on a jurisdictional approach.[38] These concepts are subject to limitations set by private international law (*PIL*).[39] This is due to the fact that a

London; see SEC 'Roadmap to IFRS Adoption, Federal Register,' 14 November 2008. At 2, Büthe and Mattli indicate that the implications of this switch are momentous as 'GAAP are highly detailed and address a vast range of specific situations (. . .) and the IFRS, by contrast, have traditionally been principle-based. They lay-out key objectives of sound reporting and offer general guidance instead of detailed rules' as a result of which 'twenty-five thousand pages of complex U.S. accounting rules become obsolete, replaced by some twenty-five hundred pages of IFRS'. Earlier the EU already made the use of IFRS mandatory for companies with publicly traded financial securities, by including a reference to IFRS in EU legislation'; see Büthe and Mattli, at 4 and at 99 (discussing the adoption for the EU of IFRS 8 (specifying what information a corporation must disclose in its consolidated financial statements), by Commission Regulation 1358/2007 of 21 November 2007, OJ L 304/9.

35 See *The Economist*, 'The Data Deluge: Businesses, governments and society are only starting to tap its vast potential' (Chapter 2, n 1).

36 And indeed are not ignored, as evidenced by the flurry of legislative action in the area of data protection and security around the world. See for an overview Kuner (Chapter 2, n 8), at addendum D.

37 This is already evidenced by recent rapprochement between the U.S.–EU views on data protection: see eg a publication 'Google, Internet Companies Face Too Many Privacy Rules, U. S. Official Says', dated 25 March 2011, to be found at <http://www.bloomberg.com>, reporting that 'Google and other U.S. Internet companies may be hampered by a multiplicity of data protection rules in Europe and beyond that are "potential barriers to the free flow of information," a U.S. official said. Daniel Weitzner, an Internet policy official in the U.S. Commerce Department, said regulators don't always recognize companies' efforts to set basic data protection standards that are adequate to stem abuses of privacy. (. . .) "It's awfully difficult to adapt privacy practices for a hundred or more different" jurisdictions, Weitzner told reporters in Brussels the day after a meeting with Viviane Reding, the European Union's justice commissioner. "That is a substantial barrier today." (. . .) Cooperation between the EU and the U.S. may promote global standards for data privacy, Reding said in a speech today. Planned changes to data protection rules in both regions "seem to be quite convergent," she said. "Our cooperation has a good chance to be the first step towards the development and promotion of international legal standards," Reding said.'

38 Also the APEC Privacy Framework 2005 (Chapter 2, n 40) is based on the principle of cross-border cooperation between national data protection supervisors, see Annex B sub II and III of the APEC Privacy Framework. Some form of central enforcement is however realized by the accountability principle for data transfers. See Chapter 3, para 3.4 and in more detail para 4.4.4.

39 See Kuner (Chapter 2, n 55), at 27 and Kuner (Chapter 2, n 63), at 125: 'With regard to the ability of the EU Member States to enforce their own data protection law on foreign websites outside their borders, the answer is clear that this would be in violation of international law', referring to F.A. Mann, 'The doctrine of jurisdiction in international law' (1964) 111 *Recueil des Cours* 9, 145–6: '[I]s it open to a State to have resort to its own legal system and, in particular, its own courts for the purpose of making the conduct of foreigners in foreign countries conform to its own commands? . . . It would seem that the answers to the above questions must be in the negative. Any other result would be

key concept of determining the limits of state regulation is 'sovereignty'. The concept of sovereignty is founded on the very existence of territory: 'the principle where a state is deemed to exercise exclusive power over its territory can be considered [to be] the fundamental axiom of classical international law'.[40] Cross-border data flows inherently challenge such sovereignty. In order to seek regulation of these cross-border data flows, states gave their laws a long arm reach (both in terms of scope of applicability of their laws and adopting outbound data transfer rules). Though data protection regulations may be of relatively recent times, the concepts of applicable law and jurisdiction are embedded in a long tradition of PIL, where laws that over-extend their jurisdictional reach are considered an unacceptable form of 'hyper-regulation' if they apply so indiscriminately that there is no hope of enforcement.[41] Applicability regimes are therefore inherently delineated and cannot be instrumental in solving the present gaps in the protection of personal data and its enforcement.[42] This automatically also applies to data transfer regimes, as these are only triggered if the relevant data protection laws are applicable in the first place.[43]

From a practical perspective, the jurisdictional approach to enforcement leads to many long arm reach data protection laws having no hope of enforcement if the relevant multinational is not established in the relevant jurisdiction or if the data processing operation is not physically located there.[44] This challenge is not specific to data protection. Similar issues are encountered in case of enforcement of any national right due to the fact that there is no global convention for the enforcement of a national right in other jurisdictions or for recognition and enforcement of court decisions in other jurisdictions.[45] Cross-border enforcement issues proliferate if

repugnant to one's commonsense and the dictates of justice, to that distribution of State jurisdiction and to that idea of international forbearance without which the present international order cannot continue.'

[40] Prins (Chapter 2, n 9), at 191, especially fn 164.

[41] Moerel (Chapter 1, n 8), at Chapter 3.

[42] See Moerel (Chapter 1, n 8), at para 3.11, where I discussed the delineations of the present applicability and jurisdictional regime of the Directive. See also Kuner (Chapter 2, n 64), at 183.

[43] Kuner (Chapter 2, n 8), at 7, 15, and 31 indicates that regulation of transborder data flows in the EU was originally designed to prevent circumvention of data protection law. Kuner's position is, however, not substantiated by the legislative history, of the Directive (see Chapter 2, n 2). Based on the legislative history, the conclusion seems to be that the EU data transfer rules are designed to prevent that the protection afforded by the Directive from being nullified if data are subsequently transferred abroad. As indicated in the text, data transfer rules are only triggered if the relevant data protection law is applicable in the first place. Any circumvention of protection can therefore only be addressed by the applicability regime in the Directive and not by the data transfer rules (as Kuner implicates).

[44] Article 29 Working Party Opinion 7/2001 on the Draft Commission Decision (version 31 August 2001) on Standard Contractual Clauses for the Transfer of personal Data to Data Processors Established in Third Countries under Article 26(4) of Directive 95/46 (WP 47, 13 September 2001), at 3 says that 'the physical location of the data in third countries makes the enforcement of the contract or the decisions taken by Supervisory Authorities considerably more difficult'. See Kuner (Chapter 2, n 55), at 271 and Moerel (Chapter 1, n 8), at para 3.5.

[45] Illustrative of this is the fact that The Hague Conference (a treaty drafting body with 62 Member States) has (after more than a decade of work) ceased working on a new Convention on Jurisdiction and the Recognition and Enforcement of Foreign Judgements in Civil and Commercial Matters. For the relevant texts and status', see <http://www.hcch.net>. Kuner (Chapter 2, n 8), at 43 comments that it

(as with data protection) the laws are highly varied across the globe or even lacking (as is often the case in developing countries).[46] As a result questions arise as to the enforceability in an international context, for instance whether supervisory authorities of a country are entitled (or obliged) to provide assistance to another supervisory authority in respect of a breach of such authorities' national law while this would not constitute a breach in the country of the authority whose assistance is requested. Similar questions arise in respect of investigation powers and recognition or enforcement of foreign judgments, etc.[47] This may entail that supervisory authorities have to obtain information on alleged breaches via the internet rather than rely on investigations performed in the relevant other jurisdictions.

From the perspective of individuals whose data are processed, the present jurisdictional approach does not provide effective protection. This is not for a lack of rights and remedies of individuals. For instance, the Directive provides for quite broad remedies and liabilities and in principle allows individuals ample opportunity to ensure that a breach is remedied and compensation is obtained. However, to effectuate these rights and remedies through traditional judicial means is not viable in practice for a number of reasons. Data protection breaches in most cases involve relatively small levels of economic damages for individuals where it would be more costly to pursue a case through traditional judicial means.[48] Due to

is unrealistic to expect such cross-border enforcement treaties to be forthcoming in the area of data protection as countries recently refused opportunities to enact global legal instruments protecting consumers in electronic commerce. See also Prins (n 9), at 15. Also, in the data protection area no progress in this respect has been made whatsoever. See for the status in respect of data protection: Hague Conference on Private International Law, Cross-Border Data Flows and Protection of Privacy, Note submitted by the Permanent Bureau (13 March 2010), to be found at <http://www.hcch.net/upload/wop/genaff2010pd13e.pdf>.

46 See in respect of consumer protection laws, Scott, n 26, at 1. See on the parallel between cross-border enforcement issues between data protection and consumer protection para 4.4.2.

47 See Prins (Chapter 2, n 9), at 173.

48 The Rand Report (Chapter 2, n 27), at 35: 'Enforcing the Directive can be difficult because the damages suffered are often intangible (or sometimes not evident in the short term), it is difficult to assign a value to any damages, and determining responsibilities is complex'. The Rand Report indicates that, though remedies and liabilities in the Directive are quite broad, and in principle allow ample opportunity for data subjects to obtain compensation for damages, this approach does not function in practice if damages are not immediate, are difficult to quantify or are too small to be bothered with on an individual scale. The Rand Report indicates that the approach chosen in the Directive 'does not function in practice for a number of reasons, including:

- There may not be any immediate damages, such as when confidential data, eg credit card numbers, are leaked. As long as the data has not yet been abused, it may be difficult to obtain any compensation, even if negligence on the data controller's part has created a substantial security and privacy risk.
- The extent of damages may be difficult to quantify. To continue the example above: suppose a credit card is abused, but the bank rectifies the problem by refunding the injured party and by issuing a new card. The data subject must still obtain a new card, cancel any payments linked to the old number, notify service providers of changed payment info, etc. Clearly, this loss of time and effort has a cost, but how can it be calculated fairly?
- Damages are typically too small to bother with on an individual scale. If 20,000 credit cards must be revoked because a data controller has been careless, 20,000 individuals will have to go through

the networked economy, even relatively simple breaches of data protection further present complicated cross-border jurisdictional and enforcement issues. The example below is for clarification.

> A US consumer purchases a product over the internet from a Dutch company. The Dutch company involves one of its group companies in India for customer service purposes (help desk for installation of the product). The Dutch company has a privacy policy informing the consumer that his data are shared with the Indian group company for helpdesk services and the consumer provides his consent for this. The data of the consumer are hacked and the consumer becomes subject of identity theft. Here, as in all other cases, the consumer has to determine: (i) who is at fault; (ii) what laws apply; (iii) what are his rights under the applicable law(s); (iv) what are his damages; and (iv) where to seek redress. Even in this relatively straightforward case answering of each of these questions proves problematic and leads to the consumer effectively having no recourse.
>
> *Re (i) Who is at fault?* In this case it will be difficult to establish which company is at fault (ie the Dutch or the Indian company) as in practice it is often impossible to determine at which point in a network a hacker found entry. As a consequence it will be impossible to prove for the consumer which of the two companies actually did not secure the data properly, in the absence of which each company can avoid liability.
>
> *Re (ii) What laws apply?* The Federal Trade Commission Act (*FTC Act*) does not apply to a Dutch company doing business from the Netherlands and the FTC has no jurisdiction.[49] Dutch data protection law applies in respect of the data processing by the Dutch company. Supposing that the consumer can prove the security breach occurred in the systems of the Dutch company, the consumer can file a complaint with the Dutch DPA. Chances are slim that the Dutch DPA will take action based on

> the aforementioned steps. The collective damage is clearly substantial, but it is quite unlikely that any of the individuals involved will undertake any action, since any compensation is likely to be dwarfed by the extra effort and expenditure required to obtain it. The risk of sanctions for the data controller responsible for such an incident therefore remains limited.'

The Rand Report concludes with: 'If errors are unlikely to have serious consequences, there is no incentive for data controllers to comply with data protection provisions. Enforcement is also perceived to be hampered by the fact that DPAs are poorly funded and overloaded with cases.' See Scott (n 26), at 4, presenting a similar observation in respect of consumer protection laws. Douwe Korff, *New Challenges to Data Protection Study* Working Paper No 2: Data Protection Laws in the EU: The Difficulties in Meeting the Challenges Posed by Global Social and Technical Developments (15 January 2010), European Commission DG Justice, Freedom and Security Report, available at SSRN: <http://ssrn.com/abstract=1638949>, at 98 notes: 'Indeed, and we may end this sub-section on this, it appears that litigation in the courts by ordinary citizens is extremely rare. In the UK, the case of Naomi Campbell, briefly set out in section 2.3(b) above, was the first case ever in which compensation was awarded for breaches of data protection law, but this remains a very rare instance. In other countries there may be more actions, but in most, the cost and effort of formal court proceedings deter most potential claimants. In our Final Report, we will examine if this can be changed and ought to change. We believe that, especially in the light of the weakness of enforcement by the data protection authorities (as noted in the next sub-sections), possibilities for empowering ordinary citizens should be further explored. We will examine why class actions are still extremely rare in Europe, also on data protection issues, and whether other, non-EU countries have more effective systems of this kind in place.'

[49] See s 5 FTC Act (15 USC 45). The Act generally does not apply to foreign trade with a limited number of exceptions, for instance in case of 'practices involving foreign commerce that (i) cause or are likely to cause reasonably foreseeable injury within the United States; or (ii) involve material conduct occurring within the United States' (s 5(4)(A)).

an individual complaint of a US consumer in an isolated case. Instigating civil action in the Netherlands is too costly and not justified in light of the damages (if any) suffered by the US consumer. Language issues and time differences may also prove an impediment. If the consumer can prove that the security breach occurred in India, chances are that the Indian company did not breach any provision of Indian law, as a result of which no recourse is available at all.

Re (iii) What are his rights?/Re (iv) Proof of damages.

As long as the relevant identity theft has not led (yet) to any actual damages (like abuse of the credit card number of the US consumer), it will be difficult for the US consumer to prove actual damages and to establish whether these are recoverable under Dutch law.

From this example it may be clear that even if the questions can be answered, in practice still no effective resources may be available. The Working Party 29, the EDPS, and the Commission are well aware of the lack of access to justice of data subjects and have proposed to address this (to some extent) in the upcoming revision of the Directive.[50] The Working Party 29 has proposed the introduction of the possibility of class actions and the introduction of an obligation of data controllers to provide for complaints procedures that are more accessible, effective, and affordable. If these do not resolve the dispute, the data subject should (besides access to the courts) be able to turn to alternative dispute resolution provided for by the industry.[51] This is also the advice of the EDPS.[52] The Commission has indicated it intends to adopt the proposal to facilitate class actions, which should according to the Commission be extended 'to DPAs and to civil society organisations as well as other associations representing data subjects' interests'.[53] These possibilities for class actions are indeed included in the recently published Proposed

[50] See Chapter 2, n 26 and n 27 for an overview of the official EU documents showing the knowledge of the lack of enforcement of data protection laws in the EU. See for the lack of access to justice of data subjects EDPS Opinion on the revision of the Directive (Chapter 2, n 35), at para 96:

> In cases with smaller impact, it is unlikely that the victims of a breach of data protection rules would bring individual actions against the controllers, given the costs, delays, uncertainties, risks and burdens they would be exposed to.

[51] WP Contribution on The Future of Privacy (Chapter 1, n 6), at para 62, at 16. See also the Rand Report (Chapter 2, n 27), at 55: 'Alternative Dispute Resolution (ADR)—ADR measures are regarded as a useful means of permitting consumers/citizens to exercise their rights more easily. The principle is that they permit easier access to justice without having to go through the complex, time consuming and uncertain judicial system. They may be particularly useful in consumer contexts where relatively small levels of economic damage are being considered and where it would be more costly to pursue a case through traditional judicial means.'

[52] EDPS Opinion on the revision of the Directive (Chapter 2, n 35), at para 96: 'These difficulties could be overcome or substantially alleviated if a system of collective redress were in place, empowering the victims of breaches to bundle their individual claims in a single action. (...) The EDPS would also favour the empowerment of qualified entities, such as consumer associations or public bodies, to bring actions for damages on behalf of victims of data protection breaches. These actions should be without prejudice to the right of data subject to bring individual actions. The EDPS would also favour the empowerment of qualified entities, such as consumer associations or public bodies, to bring actions for damages on behalf of victims of data protection breaches.'

[53] EC Communication on the revision of the Directive (Chapter 2, n 34), at 9.

Regulation.[54] The Proposed Regulation, however, does not provide for an obligation of controllers to provide for complaints procedures.[55] From the example given it may be clear that the introduction of the possibility of class actions alone will not address the cross-border issues encountered by individuals.[56]

At first glance the absence of effective enforcement of data protection may seem to be to the advantage of multinationals processing data, who can avoid potential liabilities. This is, however, not necessarily the case. As will be discussed in Chapter 5, paragraphs 5.3 and 5.4, there are compelling reasons for multinationals to implement their own global privacy policies to be able to ensure (to a certain extent) uniform data processing rules throughout their group of companies and to ensure central supervision and enforcement by one Lead DPA and the courts of one of the Member States. This would avoid the present patchwork of local and cross-border privacy rules in about as many as 60 different jurisdictions in the world.[57]

In areas of law where substantial harmonization has already taken place, initiatives to ensure cross-border enforcement do exist and in isolated cases uniform procedures have been established.[58] This is, however, not yet the case in the area of data protection. At present, the main tool applied by DPAs to try to solve gaps in applicable data protection laws and enforcement is by seeking cooperation with other DPAs in the event of cross-border data protection violations (ie a network approach, each authority in its own territory).[59] In order to ensure that each authority may indeed play its role in such cooperation, there is a clear call for enforcing the positions and powers of DPAs around the world and further for

[54] See Chapter 3, para 3.1.7.

[55] Other than as part of codes of conduct, see Art 38(1)(h) Proposed Regulation.

[56] See Scott (n 26), at 4 reporting that class actions are valuable in the category of cases where damage to consumers is extensive, but less so where damages are diffuse or small.

[57] See Chapter 3, n 148.

[58] Mostly in the area of criminal law. Prins (Chapter 2, n 9), at 175 and 186. An example is the adoption of the Council of Europe's Cybercrime Treaty to be found at <http://conventions.coe.int/treaty/en/treaties/html/185.htm>.

[59] Pursuant to Art 28(6) and (7) Directive, the DPAs are required to cooperate with one another, exchange useful information and may be requested to exercise their powers by the DPA of another Member State (ie enforcement is based on a 'network approach'). See for the APEC Privacy Framework (Chapter 2, n 40). See further the Recommendation on Cross-Border Co-operation in the Enforcement of Laws Protecting Privacy, adopted by the OECD Council on 12 June 2007, at Point 2 of the Annex: this Recommendation is intended to foster international cooperation among Privacy Enforcement Authorities in order to address the challenges of protecting the personal information of individuals wherever the information or individuals may be located. It reflects a commitment by member countries to improve their enforcement systems and laws where needed to increase their effectiveness in protecting privacy, that also stresses the need to reach a common protection of personal data throughout the world', to be found at <http://www.oecd.org>. Since November 2006 the DPAs share best practices in the context of the 'London Initiative'. See P. Hustinx, 'The Role of Data Protection Authorities', in Serge Gutwirth et al (eds.), *Reinventing Data Protection?* (Springer 2009), at para 7.5 and Prins (Chapter 2, n 9), at 190. The Proposed Regulation codifies the foregoing by explicitly providing in Art 45 for international cooperation mechanisms for the protection of personal data between the Commission and the supervisory authorities of third countries, in particular those considered offering an adequate level of protection, taking into account the Recommendation by the Organization for Economic Co-operation and Development (OECD) on cross-border cooperation in the enforcement of laws protecting privacy of 12 June 2007, see the Explanatory Memorandum to the Proposed Regulation (Chapter 1, n 9), at 12.

aligning and coordinating enforcement policies.[60] In practice DPAs increasingly seek such cooperation.[61] However, until such time as all jurisdictions have adequate data protection laws and supervision of these laws, this network approach cannot adequately solve all gaps in applicable laws and enforcement issues faced by DPAs. Further, as discussed in Chapter 4, paragraph 4.2 concerning global standards, even if international regulation of data protection including enforcement were forthcoming, experiences in other areas of law show that the actual enforcement activity often proves very different per jurisdiction.[62]

4.4 Thinking about Alternative Solutions for Enforcement

4.4.1 Self-regulation backed up by governmental enforcement tools

When looking at other forms of international ICT regulation on cross-border enforcement, these show few ideas about a more integral approach to enforcement.[63] Initially, ICT regulators both at the national and the international level seemed to be united in their opinion that industry self-regulation and alternative dispute resolution (*ADR*) would prove a better alternative to solve enforcement issues in an international context than the traditional forms of jurisdiction-based government regulation, dispute resolution, and enforcement mechanisms.[64] However, as ICT law developed over the years, by now a preference can be discerned for co-regulation above pure self-regulation.[65] The prevailing current thinking is that

[60] See Recommendation on Cross-Border Co-operation in the Enforcement of Laws Protecting Privacy (n 35) and the WP Contribution on the Future of Privacy (Chapter 1, n 6), at para 7, advising the Commission to strengthen and clarify the roles for DPAs and their cooperation within the EU and further at para 36, advising the Commission 'to encourage the cooperation between international data protection authorities, for example on a transatlantic level'. The Commission announced in its Communication on the revision of the Directive (Chapter 2, n 34), at para 2.5 to examine how to 'strengthen, clarify and harmonise the status and the powers of the national Data Protection Authorities and ways to improve the cooperation and cooperation between DPAs'. See also the EDPS Opinion on the revision of the Directive (Chapter 2, n 35), at para 140. See further the Declaration of Civil Society Organizations, adopted on 25 September in Montreal, stating that 'stronger and more aggressive action by privacy commissioners is required', finding them uniquely positioned to defend our society's core values and rights of privacy, to be found at <http://www.privacyconference2007.gc.ca/Terra_Incognita_resolutions_ngo_E.html>. The Proposed Regulation indeed strengthens the enforcement powers of the DPAs by adding the power (and the obligation) to impose sanctions for administrative offences (Arts 51 and 79 Proposed Regulation) and extensive mutual assistance obligation (Arts 55–56) and a consistency mechanism to ensure a consistent application of the regulation throughout the EU (Arts 57–60). See further Chapter 3, para 3.1.7.

[61] Kuner (Chapter 2, n 8), at 32 and 42.

[62] See Chapter 4, para 4.2 in particular n 24.

[63] Prins (Chapter 2, n 9), at 187.

[64] See Miriam Lips, 'Inventory of General ICT Regulatory Starting Points', in Bert-Jaap Koops et al (eds.), *Starting Points for ICT Regulation. Deconstructing Prevalent Policy One-Liners* (TCM Asser Press 2006), at Chapter 2, para 2.6; WP Contribution on the Future of Privacy (Chapter 1, n 6), at 8.

[65] See for a comprehensive overview of the developments: Koops, Lips, Nouwt, Prins, and Schellekens (Chapter 2, n 70), at 123 and Yves Poullet, 'ICT and Co-Regulation: Towards a New Regulatory Approach?', in Bert-Jaap Koops et al (eds.), *Starting Points for ICT Regulation. Deconstructing Prevalent Policy One-Liners* (TCM Asser Press 2006), at 247. For the preference for co-regulation as to data protection, see the Opinion on the Communication of the Commission on the revision of the

enforcement, in particular, cannot be left to industry alone; self-regulation should be backed up by governmental enforcement tools. This can only be achieved by means of co-regulation rather than by self-regulation and ADR.[66] See in the same vein the OECD, which considers that the most effective online privacy protection will be delivered through a mix of regulatory and self-regulatory approaches,[67] whereby, according to the OECD, self-regulation will be more effective when it is backed up with appropriate legislation and effective government enforcement tools.[68]

4.4.2 Parallel with enforcement of consumer protection laws

In the absence of more in-depth studies on cross-border enforcement of data protection, reference may be made to the general literature in respect of cross-border

Directive (Chapter 2, n 27), at 12: 'We prefer the approach of "Co-regulation", where there is a clear and binding framework of principle which both requires and encourages companies to decide and demonstrate how they have achieved the desired outcomes in their own way. At domestic and international level, this is one of the main attractions of the Accountability principle—minimum imposed burden and maximum effectiveness in practice.' See for the preference in broader context: EC White Paper on European Governance (Chapter 2, n 75), at 20–1. See further Fabrizio Cafaggi, 'Private Law-making and European Integration: Where Do They Meet, When Do They Conflict', in Dawn Oliver, Tony Prosser, and Richard Rawlings (eds.) *The Regulatory State* (Oxford University Press, 2011) at 212, who notes that the Commission shows a clear preference for co-regulation, but that 'the Parliament has displayed scepticism, if not opposition to the use of (...) alternatives to legislation on the basis primarily of legitimacy arguments'. At 225, Cafaggi indicates that for TPR to work, 'strong and effective public institutions are needed' as TPR complements rather than substitutes public law-making. See further at 227: 'I have distinguished the constitutional foundations of self-regulation from co-regulation emphasising the importance of public intervention to ensure legitimacy and binding effects'. See also Cafaggi (Chapter 2, n 70), at 3.

66 See for a definition of co-regulation the EC White Paper on European Governance (Chapter 2, n 75), at 21: 'Co-regulation implies that a framework of overall objectives, basic rights, enforcement and appeal mechanisms, and conditions for monitoring is set in the legislation'. The Inter-Institutional Agreement on 'Better Lawmaking' (Chapter 2, n 74) gives a somewhat different definition of co-regulation in Art 18: 'the mechanism whereby a Community legislative act entrusts the attainment of the objectives defined by the legislative authority to parties which are recognised in the field (such as economic operators, the social partners, non-governmental organisations, or associations).' This definition makes a clear divide whereby the legislators have to identify the essential public policy objectives and whereby the means, by which these public policy objectives have to be met, are established by the public and private sector together. This partitioning of responsibilities is also advocated by Art 49 of the 'WSIS Declaration of Principles', as adopted at the World Summit on the Information Society (*WSIS*) which was organized by the International Telecommunication Union (ITU) and took place in Geneva on 10–12 December 2003. The Declaration of Principles is to be found at the ITU website <http://www.itu.int> (ref. WSIS-03/GENEVA/DOC/0004).

67 See Privacy On-Line, OECD Guidance (n 21), at 28. See also Maurice Schellekens, Bert-Jaap Koops, and Corien Prins, *Conclusion*, in Bert-Jaap Koops et al (eds.), *Starting Points for ICT Regulation. Deconstructing Prevalent Policy One-Liners* (TCM Asser Press 2006), Chapter 8, at 233 and Poullet (n 64), at 248.

68 Privacy On-Line, OECD Guidance (n 21), at 28. It has to be noted however that until now, practice has not shown many examples of effective governmental enforcement in the international context. It is often the private sector or non-governmental organizations that take the lead in realizing successful international cooperation on enforcement. See Prins (Chapter 2, n 9), at 187, giving as an isolated example of an effective international enforcement system, the international approach of combating child pornography, for which an international network of hotlines is at work, see <http://www.inhope.org>.

enforcement of consumer protection laws, which is shaped by ideas about what generally works in regulatory enforcement.[69] Many parallels can be identified between enforcement of data protection and consumer rights. And like data protection laws, consumer protection laws are highly varied across the globe and in some countries (especially in developing countries) even lacking. Styles of enforcement in countries differ widely, with the increased access of consumers to the internet, and where consumers are increasingly faced with cross-border enforcement against foreign suppliers, there is a similar problem of widely diffused small losses which makes private enforcement unrealistic. To counterbalance the lack of private enforcement, many countries have set up public agencies tasked with monitoring and enforcement of consumer laws (very similar to the role and powers of DPAs). Technical developments in e-commerce increasingly give satisfied and dissatisfied consumers a voice, which developments do not so much give consumers redress potential, but enable future customers to assess the risk of default by its counterparty;[70] a parallel here with data protection are the 'naming and shaming' sites publishing data security breaches, and websites ranking the worst privacy violators, etc.[71]

Summarizing the developments in the policy thinking about enforcement of consumer protection laws, these show three stages in the regulatory response to the rise of the consumer society. Initially, enforcement was left to procedures in private law. The second stage in the 1960s and 1970s comprised a legislative response under which public agencies were empowered to take a more active approach to consumer protection. The third stage is labelled by some as the 'post-interventionist phase', 'in which the state is accorded a more modest role in stimulating market and community governance forms which are targeted at weaknesses in the state's capacity to deliver'.[72] The general assumption of the third stage is that traditional forms of private enforcement complemented by agency enforcement (ie which is the current status under the Directive) are inadequate to force compliance, and that it is helpful to understand 'the conditions under which businesses comply with their responsibilities',[73] that the 'knowledge and capacity for effective controls lies with industry, NGOs, companies and consumers' (rather than the state),[74] and 'to adopt a wider conception of enforcement which embraces both formal and informal mechanisms through which agencies (and others) seek to promote compliance'.[75] 'Then the challenge for government is how to harness that capacity and steer it, for example through promoting the development and exchange of information, and changing incentives, such that it delivers on public objectives for consumer law regimes with both a degree of effectiveness matched by

[69] This paragraph draws on Scott (n 26), at 1–2.3.
[70] Scott (n 26), at 6.
[71] See further Chapter 5, para 5.3 and in particular n 28.
[72] Scott (n 26), at 16 and 17, referring to Norbert Reich, 'Diverse Approaches to Consumer Protection Philosophy' *Journal of Consumer Policy* [1992], 14: 257–92.
[73] Scott (n 26), at 3.
[74] Scott (n 26), at 17.
[75] Scott (n 26), at 3.

sufficiency of legitimacy.'[76] Translating this into practical measures leads to the following. In cases where damage to individuals is extensive, the introduction of the possibility of class actions appears to be an adequate response.[77] In cases where damages are diffused and small, novel forms of enforcement are indicated, which can take many forms.[78] Examples given are as diverse as:

- introduction of new remedies for consumers which do not require formal enforcement. An example is the right of a cooling off period, provided for instance in the EU Distance Selling Directive,[79] typically accompanied by an obligation of the company to notify customers of this right and how it may be exercised;[80]
- imposing strict liability on companies as a solution to overcome the difficulty of consumers to prove wilfulness on the part of the company;
- empowering consumer organizations to enforce consumer protection laws;[81]
- enforcement not against companies violating the consumer protection law, but via 'gate keepers', for instance by imposing a charge back obligation on credit card issuers where companies do not meet their consumer contract obligations';[82]
- imposing disclosure and information obligations on companies on the basis of which consumers can make purchase decisions and NGOs can organize boycotts of products that they consider below standards or harmful, or 'buycotts' of products that they consider as particularly worthy of support;[83] and
- stimulating accreditation and monitoring schemes, so consumers can make informed purchase decisions.[84]

More radical approaches suggest that 'there is a value in seeking to stimulate self-regulatory measures by businesses which can then be monitored and steered by public agencies'.[85] An interesting parallel in this context is that (contrary to the expectations in the early days of internet), there are very few court cases dealing with cross-border consumer disputes.[86] One of the mechanisms that prevents these

[76] Scott (n 26), at 17.

[77] Scott (n 26), at 4.

[78] The examples are based on examples discussed in Scott (n 26).

[79] Article 6 and 4(1)(f) Directive 97/7/EC of the European Parliament and of the Council of 20 May 1997 on the protection of consumers in respect of distance contracts, [1997] OJ L144/19 (*Distance Selling Directive*).

[80] Scott (n 26), at 5.

[81] Scott (n 26), at 8–9.

[82] Scott (n 26), at 9. Another example in the internet context is imposing an obligation on banks to block payments to illegal online gambling sites provided by companies established in gambling paradises.

[83] Scott (n 26), at 3.

[84] Scott (n 26), at 17.

[85] Scott (n 26), at 15 referring to Christine Parker and John Braithwaite, 'Regulation', in Peter Cane and Mark Tushnet (eds.), *The Oxford Handbook of Legal Studies* (Oxford University Press 2003).

[86] Swire (Chapter 2, n 72), notes that despite the fact that 'every encounter in cyberspace (...) raises the possibility that diverse laws will apply' and that the 'rules for choosing among diverse laws

disputes is 'the existence of self-regulatory and other systems'.[87] Examples are the use of credit cards for online payments which bring their own dispute resolution system[88] and the emergence of large intermediaries like e-Bay, which was at first just regulated by the ratings and review consumers could post, but later introduced full-fledged dispute resolution.[89] Regulating the 'self-regulation' by such key players may be more effective than issuing further material rules.

It is outside the scope of this book to evaluate the optimal mix of enforcement measures for data protection. There are, however, a number of reasons why this general literature is relevant for this book. The main one is the realization that the (by now) traditional forms of private enforcement complemented by agency enforcement (as is the current status under the Directive) are inadequate to force compliance, and that introduction of the possibility of class actions will not be sufficient to address the cross-border enforcement issues in the data protection arena. More creativity is required and the general literature in both the international ICT and the consumer protection areas point in the direction of self-regulation backed up with governmental enforcement. Further, self-regulation does not materialize just like that and some of the alternative enforcement measures in the consumer protection arena are intended to work as an incentive for just that purpose. For instance, the imposition of disclosure obligations on companies has

(...) thus appear uniquely important for cyberspace. Surprisingly, however, the number of actual cases addressing choice of law on the Internet is far, far lower than the initial analysis would suggest. Although there is the possibility of diverse national laws in every Internet encounter, some mysterious mechanisms are reducing the actual conflicts to a handful of cases'.

[87] Swire (Chapter 2, n 72), at 1976.

[88] Swire (Chapter 2, n 72), at 1990, gives this as the main reason for the fact that there are so few court cases involving online consumer purchases: 'e-cash systems have failed to become widespread. Instead, credit card purchases (and systems such as PayPal that are based on credit and debit card accounts) have become the dominant means of payment over the Internet.' As a result '[s]ellers and buyers are subject to the elaborate rules of the credit card payment system, and so there is relatively little recourse to national courts. Credit cards have two decisive consumer protections compared with e-cash systems. If there is unauthorized use of the credit or debit card, the individual's loss is limited by U.S. statute, usually to $50.47. In addition, the credit card brings with it an already-functioning dispute resolution system. If a merchant claims that a customer has spent $200 on software, and the customer disagrees, then the customer is not charged for the $200 while the dispute is in process. With these ready-made ways to protect customers against unauthorized use and to resolve disputes, the credit card system inspires trust in consumers, creates effective dispute resolution mechanisms, and avoids the need for recourse to national courts.'

[89] Swire (Chapter 2, n 72), at 1991–2: 'The third early prediction about e-commerce was that search engines and the global reach of the Internet would eliminate the need for wholesalers and other intermediaries. Consumers can feel that it is very risky, however, to buy from a website they have never heard of, in a country far away. One major cure for this problem has been the phenomenal growth of auction sites, especially the Internet intermediary eBay (...). Although it was likely not a major goal of eBay's managers to avoid conflict-of-laws disputes, that has been one effect of the business model. Initially, trust in eBay was supposed to result from feedback ratings that customers gave to each other. Over time, however, eBay has created an entire legal system that accompanies each sale. The system contains at least a dozen consumer protections, including fraud protection for the buyer, an escrow service so that buyers can examine an item before payment goes to the seller, a verified identity programme, and a system for fraud enforcement including referrals if necessary for criminal activity. (...) Although eBay initially became famous for small purchases, such as hobbyist collectibles, today's eBay includes numerous auctions for valuable items such as diamonds. Even these large consumer transactions appear to be conducted without recourse to national courts, avoiding judicial pronouncements.'

proven a stronger incentive for companies to achieve compliance (often by introducing self-regulatory policies) than the introduction of material rules. I discuss this element and its relevance for data protection in Chapter 9, paragraphs 9.2.1–9.3.3. Also, in the chapters where I discuss specific enforcement issues of data protection (for instance, in the context of supply-chain management in Chapter 7, paragraphs 7.5–7.6), I will draw on the empirical research and the general literature on enforcement of consumer protection laws. Thirdly, and more generally, what I found instructive myself in this literature is that at first glance, the possibility of self-regulation and this particularly in an international context has a flavour of 'leniency', of a soft approach to compliance and that in an area where human rights are at stake. The first thought is 'who is going to monitor and enforce compliance?' It is instructive to realize that empirical research shows that government regulation and enforcement will not do the trick in a cross-border environment unless such governmental regulation aims at regulating private regulation and some form of governmental enforcement of such private regulation. This concerns the concept of 'meta-regulation', which has two elements. The first concerns how regulators can provide companies with incentives and tools to use their own inherent regulatory capacity. This I discuss in Chapter 9 in the wider context of introduction of the 'principle of accountability'. The second element concerns the optimal form of meta-regulation for governments to choose to regulate corporate self-regulation. I discuss the question 'how best to regulate' in Chapter 10.

To set the background for this book I discuss below three (partial) solutions which may contribute to the thinking on how to improve the position of individuals in case of cross-border data protection violations.[90] One of these solutions requires the introduction of self-regulation backed up by government enforcement. This is not meant to imply that this is thus the best of the three solutions. The solutions are totally different in nature, and in this book I will show that these options can be combined and also have to be combined to achieve hopefully a better final result than we are presented with today. The underlying goal of all three solutions is to try to achieve some form of *integral* enforcement of cross-border data protection. By integral, I do not mean the network approach where each supervisory authority enforces in its own territory and the relevant supervisory authorities work together.[91] By an integral approach,

[90] Kuner (Chapter 8, n 16), looks at this issue from a jurisdictional perspective and concludes that the increasing jurisdictional conflicts on the internet involving data protection law cannot be solved merely by changes to jurisdictional rules, but that other measures should also be considered. See at 24–30, for Kuner's suggestions: (i) achieve greater harmonization of the law; (ii) technical solutions (such as geolocation, whereby the internet can be 'zoned' geographically and thus making it easier to limit jurisdictional risk); (iii) development of a theory of comity or reasonableness (whereby jurisdiction is not to be asserted even when technically it could be); and (iv) greater interaction between the jurisdiction and data protection worlds (by improving interaction between scholars, international organizations, regulators, and others working on international jurisdiction, and those working on data protection). Though all good suggestions, my assessment is that more creative solutions are indicated to achieve some form of meaningful redress for individuals.

[91] In the EU such cooperation in respect of enforcement of consumer protection laws is made mandatory by Regulation 2006/2004/EC of the European Parliament and the Council on cooperation between national authorities responsible for the enforcement of consumer protection laws.

I mean that enforcement is somehow centralized, one supervisory authority being able to enforce on a cross-border basis. This would solve some of the problems discussed above, most notably the potential requirement to address different courts under application of different laws. The starting point of each of these solutions is that, given the sovereignty of states, any such form of central enforcement will involve the relinquishing by a state of enforcement powers of such state in cross-border situations, in return for central enforcement powers in other cases. As long as the instances where central enforcement powers are obtained are of more relevance to a regulator than the instances in which enforcement powers are relinquished, this would seem a viable option. Taking this as a starting point, the three alternative mechanisms that can be identified to achieve some form of central enforcement are:

(i) the country of origin approach;
(ii) the accountability approach; and
(iii) choice of law and forum in TPR.

4.4.3 Country of origin approach

Central supervision may (at least for the EU) be achieved by introducing the country of origin principle.[92] European legislators already have introduced the country of origin principle for certain areas of law, most notably for cross-border television broadcasting services[93] and e-commerce services.[94/95] According to the country of origin principle, each Member State applies its own law to the services provided by service providers established in its territory (ie these services are governed by the law of their 'country of origin'). The other countries must allow these services to be provided within their jurisdiction and may not apply additional

[92] See also Lips (n 64), at 49; and Prins (Chapter 2, n 9), at 195.

[93] Directive 89/552/EEC of the European Parliament and of the Council of 3 October 1989 on the coordination of certain provisions laid down by law, regulation or administrative action in Member States concerning the provision of audiovisual media services, [1989] OJ L 298/ 23 (*Television without Frontiers Directive*) as amended by Directive 2007/65/EC of the European Parliament and of the Council of 11 December 2007 (renaming the Television without Frontiers Directive into *Audiovisual Media Services Directive*).

[94] Directive 2000/31/EC of the European Parliament and of the Council of 8 June 2000 on certain legal aspects of information society services, in particular electronic commerce, in the Internal Market, [2000] OJ L 178/1 (*E-commerce Directive*). See E.M.L. Moerel, 'The country of origin principle in the E-commerce Directive: the expected "one stop shop"?' [2001] CTLR, at 184.

[95] Another example is the 'passporting' of the approval of a prospectus required by a company for an offer of securities to the public, or the admission to the trading on a regulated market for securities, by the regulator of the 'home Member State' of the company for the whole of the EU. See Art 17 and Recitals 14 and 45 Directive 2003/71/EC of the European Parliament and of the Council of 4 November 2003 on the prospectus to be published when securities are offered to the public or admitted to trading and amending Directive 2001/34/EC (*Prospectus Directive*). See in particular Recital 14: 'The grant to the issuer of a single passport, valid throughout the Community, and the application of the country of origin principle require the identification of the home Member State as the one best placed to regulate the issuer for the purposes of this Directive.'

regulations.[96] This prevents the cumulative application of the different national laws to cross-border services within the relevant region. Application of the country of origin principle is considered justified in a European context if a certain area of law has been extensively harmonized within the EU. Given the purpose of the Directive (full harmonization of data protection law within the EU),[97] introduction of the country of origin principle also for data protection law would have been the obvious choice, but this was at the time apparently not yet feasible.[98] Recently, the Working Party 29 and the EDPS have recommended adoption of the country of origin principle also for data protection when revising the Directive.[99] According to the country of origin principle, the Member States would each apply their own law to data processing by controllers who are 'established' in their territory (ie such data processing is governed by the law of their 'country of origin'). What is relevant here is that application of the country of origin principle results in no more than one place of establishment of the controller in respect of the data processing involved. For instance, the E-commerce Directive provides that if the service provider of e-commerce services has more than one place of business in the EU (ie more than one establishment), such provider is considered 'established' for purposes of application of the country of origin principle, in the Member State where the service provider has 'its centre of activities' for that particular service.[100] The same applies to broadcasting services. The Television without Frontiers Directive provides a set of factors to determine which of multiple establishments involved in a certain broadcasting service should be considered to have 'effective control' over the relevant service (ie should be considered the 'primary establishment' for purposes of application of the country of origin principle).[101] In the data protection context this would mean that if a parent company processes the employee data of all of its group companies in a central HR system located in a Member State, the 'centre of activities' regarding this central processing and the 'effective control' over such

[96] See Arts 2 and 2a and Recitals 10–14 Television without Frontiers Directive and Art 3 and Recital 5 E-commerce Directive.

[97] See Recital 8 Directive, indicating that the purpose of the Directive was full harmonization with the exception of specific discretionary powers in a limited number of areas. See also Case C-101/01 *Bodil Lindqvist* [2003] ECR I-12971, at para 95–6.

[98] See Moerel (Chapter 1, n 8), at 48.

[99] WP Opinion on applicable law (Chapter 1, n 7), at 31: 'The change envisaged in order to simplify the rules for determining applicable law would consist of a shift back to the country of origin principle: all establishments of a controller within the EU would then apply the same law regardless of the territory in which they are located. In this perspective, the location of the main establishment of the controller would be the first criterion to be applied. The fact that several establishments exist within the EU would not trigger a distributed application of national laws.' See further the EDPS Opinion on revision of the Directive (n 58), at 125: 'If some significant margin of manoeuvre is kept in the new instrument, the EDPS would support the suggestion from the Working Party for a shift from a distributive application of different national laws to a centralised application of a single legislation in all Member States where a controller has establishments.' See also Moerel (Chapter 1, n 8), at paras 2.10.5–2.11, where I propose to introduce the country of origin principle in the Directive.

[100] See Recital 13 of the E-commerce Directive.

[101] Article 2(3) Television without Frontiers Directive. See for an overview of the case law: Oliver Castendyk, Egbert Dommering, Alexander Scheuer, *European Media Law* (Kluwer International 2008), at 847–66.

central processing is with the parent company in that Member State. Under the E-commerce Directive and the Television without Frontiers Directive, the country of origin principle applies *to a specific service*. If a multinational, for instance, provides different e-commerce services, then for each of these services the 'centre of activities' has to be determined and these may therefore differ. As a consequence, the different e-commerce services of a multinational in the EU may still be subject to the laws of different Member States. As for data protection, I propose not to link the country of origin principle to specific data processing operations, as these will in practice be very difficult to discern. The reason for this is that by now the data processing operations of a multinational are in most cases so intertwined (and in any event connected) that it becomes very difficult to identify the separate processing operations and decide what is their centre of activities. And as the systems in most cases feed into each other, keeping track of applicable law per data feed is a practical impossibility. Instead the proposal is to apply one law to all data processing activities of a multinational which are covered by the Directive (the multinational qualifying as a controller in this respect).[102] This would preferably be the law of the EU Headquarters of the multinational (the company having control in the EU of all data processing operations of such multinational).

As a consequence the DPA of the EU Headquarters will have central supervision powers and the other DPAs must assist the DPA and courts of the country of origin.[103] This is a form of integral enforcement which will require that the DPA of the country of origin has supervisory powers to the detriment of other DPAs (ie such other DPAs will have to relinquish their supervisory powers as to the secondary establishments in their respective territories). In return such other DPAs obtain central enforcement in respect of the processing activities of multinationals that have their primary establishment in such DPAs' respective territories. To avoid uncertainty in respect of the effect of the introduction of the country of origin principle also on jurisdiction of the DPAs, I recommend that EU legislators, when revising the Directive, make explicit that introduction of the country of origin principle also leads to central jurisdiction of the DPA of the country of origin.

Taking it one step further, I cannot see any justified objection against extending the country of origin principle also to those countries that have obtained an adequacy finding.[104] If it is considered safe to transfer data from the EU to those countries, this implies that we can rely on the enforcement systems of those countries to protect these EU-originated data. Also in those cases the 'trade off'

102 The EDPS proposes to apply 'a single legislation in all Member States where a controller has establishments'. This seems mistaken. However, it may well be possible that the single law has to apply also to data processing operations in Member States other than the Member States where the multinational has an establishment (or non-EU countries for that matter). For application of the Directive the connecting factor is not the Member States where the multinational has an establishment, but rather 'whether the processing takes place *in the context* of the activities of an establishment of the controller in a Member State'. The data processing operation itself may take place in another Member State or even outside the EU. See Moerel (Chapter 1, n 8), at paras 2.3.6–2.3.7.

103 See also Art 19 E-commerce Directive.

104 See on adequacy findings Chapter 3, para 3.1.5 and especially n 52.

in enforcement powers referred to above seems to work out in a positive manner. The benefits of obtaining central enforcement in respect of an EU-based multinational that has the centre of its processing activities in the EU seems to outweigh any national enforcement powers of Member States in respect of an EU group company that is co-controller to part of a central database only operated by the parent company outside the EU.

However, even if introduction of the country of origin principle were forthcoming at the EU level (and could possibly be extended to adequate countries), it is not expected that this will be feasible on a truly international scale. Introduction of the country of origin principle will therefore be only a partial solution of cross-border enforcement issues. However, this being said, introduction of the country of origin principle would be a clear improvement to the present enforcement system in the EU, which can be extended to countries that have obtained an adequacy ruling. In my earlier research on the applicability and jurisdiction regime of the Directive, I have recommended the introduction of the country of origin principle to prevent the accumulation of applicable laws of the Member States and to achieve central enforcement.[105] I repeat this recommendation here, with the addition that I recommend extending the country of origin principle also to countries that have obtained an adequacy ruling.

Further thought has to be given to whether introduction of a country of origin principle should also apply to the rights of data subjects, or that data subjects would keep their rights under their national law (as suggested by one author).[106] This is a moot point if the rights of data subjects are properly harmonized and a proper cooperation is ensured between the DPAs in the event of complaints (see the end of this section 4.4.3). This will provide a better solution than excluding the rights of data subjects from applicability of the country of origin principle altogether.

I note that the country of origin principle will to a large extent become superfluous if the Directive were to be replaced by an EU regulation[107] in the upcoming revision of the Directive (as per my *Recommendation 6* in Chapter 6, paragraph 6.6.6).[108] As EU regulations are directly applicable in the Member States and do not require implementation into national law, the issue of cumulation of applicable laws within the EU is to a large extent resolved, as there will only be one data protection law that is applicable in all Member States. I say to a large extent, as even if the Directive is replaced by a regulation, topics will remain to be regulated

105 Moerel (Chapter 1, n 8), at para 2.11.

106 See J.H.J Terstegge, 'Home Country Control—Improving Privacy Compliance and Supervision' [2002] *P&I*, at 258: 'However, not all legal requirements should be exported to other member states. The rights of the data subjects should at all times be addressed under the national law of the subsidiary which collected the personal data or which is responsible for managing the relationship between the company and the data subject.'

107 Article 288 TFEU defines a regulation as follows: 'A regulation shall have general application. It shall be binding in its entirety and directly applicable in all Member States.' Whereas 'A directive shall be binding, as to the result to be achieved, upon each Member State to which it is addressed, but shall leave to the national authorities the choice of form and methods.'

108 Which the European legislators are empowered to do pursuant to Art 291(1) Consolidated Version of the Treaty on the Functioning of the European Union [2010] OJ C83/49 (*TFEU*).

by the Member States themselves.[109] For these topics, the country of origin principle will remain relevant to avoid cumulation of applicable laws.[110] I further note, that so far as *jurisdiction* of the DPAs is concerned, the country of origin rule will in any event remain relevant (ie also if the Directive were to be replaced by a regulation). Multinationals with more establishments in the EU will still have an interest in, for instance, being able to comply with notification or permit requirements under EU data protection law in their country of origin only. The same applies for the possibility of central enforcement in respect of the data processing operations of such multinationals. *Recommendation 1* will therefore also have relevance if the Directive were to be replaced by an EU regulation.

Proposed Regulation I note that the Commission has chosen to replace the Directive by an EU regulation as a result of which the issue of the accumulation of applicable laws is to a large extent resolved. As predicted, the Proposed Regulation further leaves the regulation of certain topics to the Member States.[111] For these topics the country of origin principle for applicable law remains relevant, but this is not included in the Proposed Regulation. The Proposed Regulation, however, does provide for the country of origin principle for jurisdiction to enforce.[112] The Lead DPA will be the DPA of the Member State in which the main establishment of the controller is located. Other DPAs will have to provide assistance and cooperation to the Lead DPA. This central competence of the Lead DPA relates to jurisdiction to enforce only, other DPAs keep their jurisdiction to hear claims. As redress of individuals to the courts is concerned, individuals may bring proceedings against controllers or processors also before the courts of the Member State where the individual has his habitual residence.[113] This system therefore does not lead to full central supervision for a multinational as more DPAs and courts may have competence. The country of origin principle I envisage would lead to full central supervision of the data operations of a multinational by the DPA and courts of the main place of establishment of the controller. If this is too far-reaching, an alternative (achieving the same result) could be a provision that if other DPAs or courts are addressed than the Lead DPA, these will refer the complaints and claims to the Lead DPA (or the courts of the Lead DPA) and coordinate the communications with the individual in this respect.

Recommendation 1

Introduce the country of origin principle both for applicable law and jurisdiction and extend this principle also to countries having obtained an adequacy ruling under Article 25(6) Directive.

[109] See Chapter 1, n 11.

[110] The applicability regime as provided by Art 2(1) and (2) Proposed Regulation will in these cases lead to cumulation of applicable laws. The Proposed Regulation currently does not provide for a country of origin principle for applicable law.

[111] See for an overview Chapter 1, n 11.

[112] Article 51(2) Proposed Regulation, see further Chapter 3, para 3.1.7.

[113] See on jurisdiction of the DPAs and of the courts under the Proposed Regulation Chapter 3, para 3.1.7.

4.4.4 Accountability approach

Though enforcement of the APEC Privacy Framework is also based on cooperation between Member Economies,[114] some form of central enforcement is achieved by Principle 26 of the APEC Privacy Framework (see Chapter 3, paragraph 3.4). This principle provides that if a controller transfers personal data to third parties, the controller remains accountable for taking reasonable steps to ensure that the relevant third party will protect the information consistent with the APEC Principles. As a consequence, individuals can address the original controller for breach of this obligation in addition to addressing the third-party recipient for a breach by such third party. This results de facto in partially centralizing enforcement. Even if multiple onward transfers have taken place, enforcement may still take place against the original controller. What is relevant here is that application of the accountability rule leads to more parties that can be addressed for a specific breach, but not to one party being responsible for the whole processing. There are often more parties responsible for various parts of one processing (each being controller of a part of the processing only). These joint controllers may not necessarily be established in the same country. All these controllers will remain accountable for their respective parts of the processing also after transfer if the data processing is subsequently transferred to a third party. In case of a breach, the DPAs and the data subjects can now enforce also against the original joint controllers rather than just against the data importer. Assuming that in many cases the original controller will be established in the country of the data subject, this may be considered an improvement, but will it also lead to more effective enforcement? If the DPAs and data subjects in all countries concerned have to take enforcement action to achieve full enforcement in respect of a data processing activity, enforcement is still not efficient. This would only be achieved if the accountability principle could lead to central accountability for the processing activity as a whole. This result, however, will only be achieved by implementing the country of origin principle rather than an accountability principle for data transfers. The following example is provided as clarification:

A multinational has set up a separate group company as a shared service centre for the data processing of all its group companies. The individual group companies transfer their data to the shared service centre which processes the data on behalf of such group companies (ie acts as a data processor on behalf of its group companies). The shared service centre transfers all data to a third party outside the EU. The accountability principle would make each individual group company accountable for all subsequent transfers of the data of that group company (ie these group companies each being the original controller of their data). However, efficient enforcement would be best served with accountability of the parent having the effective control over the central processing including all data transfers.

[114] Otherwise, the APEC Privacy Framework (Chapter 2, n 40) is also based on the principle of cross-border cooperation between national data protection supervisors rather than central supervision; see Annex B sub II and III of the APEC Privacy Framework.

In addition to introduction of the country of origin principle the Working Party 29 seems to be in favour of introduction of an accountability rule for data transfers in the revised Directive (though this seems to be in addition to the present data transfer rules rather than as a replacement thereof).[115] I discuss the merits of this proposal in Chapter 9, paragraph 9.7.

4.4.5 Private choice of law and forum in transnational private regulation

Central supervision and enforcement might also be achieved if companies were able to regulate their data protection in transnational private regulation (*TPR*) and make a choice of forum for central supervision and enforcement by one 'Lead' DPA and the courts of the country of such Lead DPA.[116] This would preferably be the authority of the place of establishment of the EU Headquarters of such multinational. If a cross-border breach occurs, such Lead DPA (and its courts) would be able to enforce on a cross-border basis. If this form of central enforcement is at the same time accompanied by an obligation of the multinational to facilitate cross-border enforcement within their group of companies, the beneficiaries of the TPR would also be better off. If a breach occurs, the individual will be able to file a complaint with the group company with which he has a relationship, regardless of where the breach occurred or which of the group companies was responsible for the breach. The complaint may be filed by the individual in his own language. The group company that received the complaint will be responsible for ensuring that the complaint is processed through the complaints procedure of the multinational and will ensure the required translations. If the complaints procedure does not lead to a satisfying result for the individual, the group company will facilitate the filing of the complaint with the Lead DPA or the courts of the Lead DPA. This procedure would lead to enforceable rights even in jurisdictions where no (adequate) data protection laws are in place or where insufficient enforcement (infrastructure) is available. It further overcomes language issues and time zones and minimizes cost.

Looking at the three alternatives discussed above, the conclusion from an enforcement perspective is that introduction of the country of origin principle is in any event to be recommended as this would lead to central enforcement throughout the EU, possibly extended to the countries that obtained an adequacy ruling. However, looking at a global scale, a choice of law and forum through TPR would seem to be a promising alternative.

To what extent data protection may be regulated by TPR and whether any choice of law and forum is allowed under PIL so that central supervision and enforcement are indeed possible, are two main topics of this book and are evaluated in Chapter 9 and Chapter 8, respectively.

[115] WP Contribution on The Future of Privacy (Chapter 1, n 6), at para 39.

[116] This option is also mentioned by Prins (Chapter 2, n 9), at 178, noting however: (i) that restrictions may apply under the PIL of the home country of the relevant company adopting the TPR; and (ii) that the applicability of the rules of PIL do not provide legal certainty when applied to online situations. See also Wugmeister, Retzer, Rich (Chapter 3, n 148), at 477 and Cafaggi (n 65), at 227.

5

Trends and Developments in Multinational Corporate Practice

5.1 Increase in International Data Transfers within and between Multinationals

As indicated in the Introduction, the digital era shows an unprecedented continuous worldwide flow of data both within multinational companies as well as with their external service providers. These transfers are facilitated by the maturing of internet technology, but three specific factors in particular play a pivotal role:

- *Centralization of ICT.* Multinationals recently have begun to use enhanced technology to streamline their ICT on a worldwide basis, facilitating central storage of personal data of their employees and customers (including consumers) and having these data accessible on a worldwide basis. Internet technology also increasingly facilitates central e-commerce and e-procurement solutions, involving central processing of consumer and vendor data. Multinationals consider the efficient worldwide intercompany flow of employee and customer information and the enhanced management information generated by these central systems, to be critical for the management and competitive functioning of their operations.[1]
- *Outsourcing and offshoring.* Another trend is that multinationals outsource their ICT (helpdesk services, server management, and application services) to third parties, mostly for cost reasons. As part of these services such third-party service provider processes the personal data of employees and customers of the multinational.[2] To save costs, most outsourcing suppliers subsequently offshore these helpdesk and server management services to countries outside the EU.[3] Often a 'follow the sun principle' is followed to ensure 24–7 helpdesk services against the lowest costs (ie by making use of the regular working hours of the different time zones). Such offshoring involves the transfer of the

[1] This book does not concern itself with the desirability of this policy of companies, but takes it as a given. In my experience, multinationals rarely take data protection considerations into account when implementing new technologies. The task for their legal departments is to address the data protection implications after the decisions to implement new (cost-saving) technologies have been made.

[2] For instance with server management, the outsourcing supplier hosts the servers of the customer on which all such customer's IT applications operate (varying from HR to CRM applications).

[3] Favourites are the 'BRIC' countries (Brazil, Russia, India, and China).

employee and customer data to all service centres of these outsourcing suppliers in the countries involved.

- *Dynamic routing and cloud computing.* A third trend is that for the transfers of data both by multinationals and their service providers increasing use is made of technology, that leaves uncertain how the data will ultimately be routed (use is made of 'dynamic routing'). Further, for storage purposes, increasing use is made of 'cloud computing',[4] where it is not always foreseeable where the data will ultimately be stored[5] as use is made of unused storage capacity around the globe as it presents itself at a given moment in time.

5.2 Multiple Jurisdictions

As a consequence of these trends, the central data processing and storage by multinationals with establishments around the world and related offshoring to third countries attracts a multitude of applicable national data protection laws.[6] Some federal countries also have data protection laws that vary per state and in many cases data protection is not regulated in one comprehensive data protection law, but is found in many sectoral laws.[7] Multinationals (whether with headquarters within or outside the EU) find compliance with all applicable national laws a 'challenge' for a host of reasons:

- As many provisions of the various national data protection laws diverge or conflict outright[8] 100 per cent worldwide compliance by a multinational is a practical impossibility. This is especially a problem if a multinational has implemented a central system for the processing of its employee or customer data. For instance, many laws impose an obligation to ensure that personal data are protected from loss and corruption. Some countries have even issued specific technical requirements. In the event of a central system, however, it will only be possible to implement *one set of security standards*; local variations

[4] See for the data protection implications of cloud computing, Lieneke Viergever, 'Privacy in the Clouds' [2010] *Tijdschrift voor Internetrecht*, at 78–86.

[5] I note that by now some cloud service providers do localize their services to a certain jurisdiction or regional zone, see Simon Bradshaw, Christopher Millard, and Ian Walden, *Contracts for Clouds: Comparison and Analysis of the Terms and Conditions of Cloud Computing Services* Queen Mary School of Law Legal Studies Research Paper No 63/2010. Available at SSRN: <http://ssrn.com/abstract=1662374>, at 5 and at para 4.10.

[6] If in a central system data are processed of EU subsidiaries, such central processing will in any event have to comply with all EU data protection laws. Also, the transfer of such data to the offshoring countries will be subject to the EU data transfer rules. Other national data protection laws have a similar extensive scope.

[7] Examples are the federal states of Germany and the provinces of Canada. Often data protection rules are not comprehensively enacted in a single data protection act, but rather enacted in different sectoral laws. This is even to a certain extent the case for the EU, where data protection regulations for the private sector can also be found in the e-Privacy Directive (Chapter 3, n 5).

[8] An example is Germany, where it is required for employers to register the religious faith of employees. The processing of religious data is, however, prohibited in other Member States (see Chapter 2, n 19).

will not be possible.[9] If requirements are set in technical standards, only one can be followed leading to automatic non-compliance in all other cases.

- As many national data protection laws are based on a long arm reach (to avoid gaps in the protection of personal data or to prevent circumvention of their data protection laws), it has become difficult for multinationals to track and comply with all applicable laws. This especially poses an obstacle in the event of unforeseen situations, such as a data security breach. Due to central storage and cloud computing, a single security incident may involve data of a host of individuals residing in countries around the world, which may trigger as many national notification requirements. It is difficult for multinationals to predict where a security incident will occur and whether, and if so, which types of personal data will be involved and where the individuals reside whose data are compromised. As a consequence it may be difficult to comply with security breach legislation in the event such breach actually occurs. For instance, in the US more than 45 states have imposed notification obligations on organizations that discover (or are notified about) a data security breach.[10] While there are some similarities, these state laws have different scopes (some apply to computerized data only, others also apply to other media), different definitions of personal information, different harm thresholds, different timing requirements for notification to individuals, different requirements for notifying state agencies and credit agencies, different requirements for substitute notification, etc. Some laws even contain conflicting requirements.[11] In addition, the US has several federal laws regulating security breaches involving medical and health data.[12] At federal level specific data breach notification requirements also apply to financial institutions.[13] Besides the US, there are 13 other countries regulating data security breaches of which eight have mandatory breach notification obligations.[14] In the EU a data security breach notification

[9] Even in the EU, the security requirements are not sufficiently harmonized. The Directive just requires Member States to implement 'adequate safety measures'. Each EU country has subsequently decided for itself what it considers to be 'adequate safety measures'. In Italy and Spain, the security requirements are even set in technical specifications which are difficult to combine. See Annex B ('Disciplinare Tecnico') to the Italian Data Protection Act, English translation to be found at <http://www.mofoprivacy.com>. See further the IT security measures introduced in Spain by Royal Decree 1720/2007 of 21 December 2007, unofficial translation to be found on the website of the Spanish DPA <http://www.agpd.es>. In addition there are many other laws that regulate data security, especially in relation to sensitive data such as health data, like the US HIPPAA and HITECH, see n 12.

[10] These state security breach notification laws are understood to be modelled on the California Security Breach Notification Act, which came into force in July 2007 (Cal. Civ. Code § 1798.82 (LEXIS through 2007, ch 12, 7 June 2007)).

[11] An example is the law of the State of Massachusetts. This law does not allow description of the incident, while several other U.S. states require such description.

[12] Health Insurance Portability and Accountability Act (*HIPAA*) of 1996 (Pub.L.104–91) and the Health Information Technology for Economic and Clinical Health Act (*HITECH*), enacted as part of the American Recovery and Reinvestment Act of 2009 (Pub.L. 111–15).

[13] Under the Gramm-Leach-Bliley Act (GLBA), also known as the Financial Services Modernization Act of 1999 (Pub.L. 106–102).

[14] See for a summary overview Karin Retzer and Joanna Łopatowska, 'Dealing with Data Breaches in Europe and Beyond', *PLC Cross-border Data Protection Handbook 2011/12*.

requirement has recently been imposed on the providers of electronic communication services.[15] The expectation is that this notification obligation will be extended to all data controllers in the revised Directive.[16] Further, Mexico has introduced and South Africa is presently in the process of introducing, notification requirements in the event of a data security breach.[17] As a consequence of this myriad of rules, companies can only issue instructions on *how to proceed* in the event of a security incident rather than instructions on *how to comply* with all the laws in the event of an incident.[18]

- The transfer of data between EU companies and non-EU companies of the same group triggers the application of the EU transfer rules (see Chapter 3, paragraph 3.1.5 above). In practice the only option[19] for most multinationals to comply with these transfer rules is to introduce adequate safeguards for the protection of personal data by entering into EU Standard Contractual Clauses between (each of their) EU data exporting companies and (each of their) data importing companies. This is not a workable solution for multinationals that exchange numerous data between all group companies around the world as part of their daily routine. This would lead to hundreds (and sometimes thousands) of agreements to be concluded between group companies. As the data processing operations of a multinational are subject to continuous change, these contracts would require frequent updating as well.[20] The same

[15] See Art 2(4)(c) e-Privacy Directive (Chapter 3, n 5). The deadline for transposing the e-Privacy Directive into national laws was 25 May 2011.

[16] WP Contribution on the Future of Privacy (Chapter 1, n 6), at 16; EC Communication on the revision of the Directive (Chapter 2, n 34), at 6–7; EDPS Opinion on the revision of the Directive (Chapter 2, n 35), at para 75. Member States that did not await EU legislation and had already introduced a general data security breach notification requirement are Germany and Austria (notification to individuals) and Ireland (notification to the DPA, which in its turn decides on notification to individuals). Member States that have voluntary guidelines prescribing notification are the UK (notification to the DPA) and Denmark (notification to individuals). cf Art 31 and Art 32 Proposed Regulation.

[17] Mexico: Federal Law on the Protection of Personal Data Held by Private Parties (*Ley federal de protección de datos personales en posesión de los particulares*) published on 5 July 2010, took effect on 6 July 2010. Available at <http://www.dof.gob.mx/nota_detalle.php?codigo=5150631&fecha=05/07/2010> (in Spanish). South Africa: Art 21 of the Protection of Personal Information Bill (still in legislative process) available at <http://www.pmg.org.za/files/bills/090825b9-09.pdf>.

[18] Thus a security breach in a central data storage facility of a multinational may trigger a host of different obligations: for instance notification obligations to Californian nationals (if data of nationals from California are involved), an obligation to offer a public apology (if data of Japanese nationals are involved), or (within the near future) an obligation to notify the breach to the EU DPAs and EU nationals (if the EU data protection laws are applicable to the processing).

[19] As multinationals transfer data on a truly worldwide basis, the other derogations of the Directive are not of practical use. The countries that obtained an adequacy ruling are only very limited in number (and will therefore not facilitate a worldwide solution). The option to obtain consent of the individuals for the transfers is in practice not possible if the data concerned are employee data. Employee consent may not be considered 'freely given' as employees are in a relationship of authority. See for a discussion of the options (and their pros and cons) available to multinationals to facilitate cross-border intercompany transfers of data: Wugmeister, Retzer, Rich (Chapter 3, n 148), at Chapter III.

[20] The Rand Report (Chapter 2, n 27) identifies six main weaknesses of the Directive, of which two concern the EU data transfer rules (outmoded) and the EU data transfer tools (cumbersome). See also ICC Report on binding corporate rules for international transfer of 28 October 2004 (*ICC Report on BCR*), at 11, to be found at <http://www.iccwbo.org> Doc.373-22/115, where as a benefit of

applies if such multinational outsources its IT to a third-party service provider with establishments in non-adequate countries. In most cases the countries involved in offshoring are *not* considered by the Commission to provide for an adequate level of data protection (ie do not qualify for an adequacy finding). As a result, the transfer of personal data to these countries requires each of the EU subsidiaries of the multinational to enter into EU Standard Contractual Clauses with each of the subsidiaries of the service provider involved in providing the services.

- A complicating factor is that certain countries following suit with European legislators have also imposed restrictions on the transfer of personal data from their respective countries to countries that are (by such countries) not considered to provide an adequate level of data protection (see Chapter 3, paragraph 3.2 above). These data transfer regulations exist not only at the national level, but also at the state level in some federal countries,[21] and may take the form of practical requirements like notification to the DPAs who may subsequently block transfers or impose conditions on them.[22] It is a serious obstacle for multinationals to have to comply not only with the material data protection rules of each jurisdiction, but also to track and comply with all requirements relating to data transfers *between specific countries*.

5.3 Corporate Mitigation of Data Protection Risks

In order to mitigate worldwide data protection risks[23] throughout their group of companies, many multinationals have introduced some form of global corporate privacy policy. These companies have chosen a top-down approach (central instructions to their group companies) rather than trying to achieve bottom-up data protection compliance on a country-by-country basis. For the reasons set out in paragraph 5.2, these multinationals, when setting up their corporate privacy policies, have set their own worldwide rules for what they consider to be an

introducing BCR is listed, 'the company does not need to conclude (and keep track of) thousands of contracts between its corporate members'. See also Wugmeister, Retzer, Rich (Chapter 3, n 147), Chapter IV and V, at 475: 'Managing the contracts among affiliated entities or obtaining workers' consents imposes an enormous administrative burden on companies. Any given organisation may need to manage hundreds or thousands of contracts depending on how many affiliates the organisation has at the time. In addition, anytime there is an organisational change among the parties to the contract (. . .), new contracts will need to be negotiated', and at 749: 'From a business perspective, Corporate Privacy Rules are attractive because they would enable organisations to implement uniform privacy policies and practices on a regional or global basis without the administrative, legal, and organisational complexities of contracts.'

[21] This is, for instance, the case in the German federal states and in some Canadian provinces. See Kuner (Chapter 2, n 8), at Annex B.

[22] See Kuner (Chapter 2, n 8), at 22.

[23] 'Risks' is used in a broad sense and from the perspective of the multinational. Risks include the risk of non-compliance with applicable national laws, risks of security breaches which may trigger applicable national data security breach notification requirements, as well as the risk to the reputation of the company.

adequate protection for their employees and customers based on general principles of data protection expressed by the OECD Privacy Guidelines and as *underlying* the Directive. Furthermore, given the administrative burdens, most multinationals ignore the EU data transfer rules and transfer their data to all group companies worldwide.[24] The same applies to the EU data transfer rules in the event of offshoring. The EU data transfer requirements are considered to create an obstacle to offshoring of services and in practice are ignored by many outsourcing service providers and multinationals alike. Although many DPAs have an arsenal of enforcement tools (both administrative and criminal) and cooperate amongst themselves in relation to enforcement,[25] most companies consider reputational risk to be their single greatest concern, which motivates their privacy compliance in practice.[26] Another strong driver for companies to adopt global data privacy and security policies has been the introduction of the many (especially US) data security breach notification laws (see paragraph 5.2 above), which forces companies to notify data subjects in cases where their data are exposed due to a security breach.[27] This may lead to headlines in newspapers about such security breaches. Privacy rights' advocacy organizations collect data on major security breach notifications and ensure instant worldwide publicity by publishing the collective results on their websites and providing a forum for instant criticism and debate.[28] In that sense, it is

[24] See Chapter 2, n 26 and 27.

[25] Sanctions for non-compliance with local EU privacy laws vary from country to country, but often involve criminal liability in the event of transfer of data to countries outside the EU, criminal or administrative fines in the event of a failure to comply with registration obligations of the relevant data processing with the national DPAs, and in some cases also criminal liability for directors is in place. Most DPAs can apply administrative enforcement, in which case the controller will be given a set period to comply with the local data protection laws. If the controller does not comply, the authority may remedy the violation itself. This especially poses a threat for databases that are accessible worldwide as it will be difficult to bring these into compliance with all applicable privacy laws on very short notice (the option remaining for a multinational to close down the central database, which is obviously not viable). For an overview of possible sanctions and the enforcement policies of the DPAs, see the report 'Privacy Protected 2008' at <http://www.linklaters.com>.

[26] This is my experience in practice advising many multinationals on their worldwide compliance. See further McBarnet (Chapter 4, n 24), at 17, referring to research by assurance company AON, which showed that the top 2000 private and public sector organizations regard damage to their reputation as their biggest risk, under Aon Insurance Group, 2000, reported in SustainAbility, *The changing landscape of liability* (Sustainability 2004), at 17. See also the Opinion on the Communication of the Commission on the revision of the Directive (Chapter 2, n 27), at 4: 'There has been a transformation since the Directive was adopted in 1995, with the majority of commercial organisations now driven by reputational, financial and other reasons for *wanting* to process personal data properly.'

[27] Bamberger and Mulligan (Chapter 3, n 154), at 106, report their results of empirical research in the U.S. which shows that introduction of the U.S. data breach notification laws has been a main driver for what he calls substantial 'privacy on the ground' compliance by U.S. companies: 'While individual U.S. sectoral statutes and the EU Data Protection Directive were credited in some instances for firms' initial commitment of resources and personnel, and for the establishment of a regulatory floor, the path these professionals would take was influenced by two other regulatory developments, notably: the rise of the Federal Trade Commission's role as an "activist privacy regulator" advancing an evolving consumer-oriented understanding of privacy; and the passage of state Security Breach Notification (SBN) laws as a means for binding corporate performance on privacy to reputation capital.'

[28] For an overview of worldwide data security breaches, see <http://www.privacyrights.org> and <http://www.attrition.org> (reporting 850 major data breaches since 2001). Many more may be found by simply searching for 'data breach security'.

frequently commented that there is no 'hiding place' for multinationals.[29] As 'brand value' is an increasing component of the market value of a company, so too is reputation.[30] Outsourcing does not diminish this reputational exposure[31] as in practice any mistakes made by sub-contractors are attributed in the press to well-known brand holders, as they are easy targets for criticism (a phenomenon which has been labelled the 'brand boomerang').[32] The classic case here is Nike. Nike, like many other multinationals, has its products manufactured in cheap labour countries by independent suppliers. Nike in fact at the time was only its designs and the brand. In 1998 *the Guardian*[33] reported that manufacturers of Nike products seriously violated human rights (using child labour and working hours above and against wages below, what even local laws allowed). Nike's code and local law were broken, but not by Nike (as the CEO of Nike was the first to point out). However, Nike was held to account by civil society campaigners, demonstrations, 'shoe-ins' (publicly throwing away of Nike trainers), public rejection of sponsorships, a flood of publications and cartoons in newspapers, and a substantial fall in profits.[34] Ultimately, Nike also lost a court case in the US based on unfair competition and false advertising.[35] The Nike case illustrates what can happen if companies stick to a legal notion of corporate responsibility only. An example of this in the data protection field is the resignation in August 2010 by the CEO of a Hong Kong cashless payment operator due to intense criticism of the handling of data protection issues at the company, which admitted to selling personal data of nearly two million customers to business partners. The company did not violate any applicable laws or regulations, but the CEO decided to step down 'as the

[29] See on the phenomenon that due to new technology there is no hiding place for multinationals as to corporate responsibility, McBarnet (Chapter 4, n 24), at 15.

[30] McBarnet (Chapter 4, n 24), at 16, referring to the analysis of FTSE 100 companies in 2005, which found that 60 per cent of the companies' market value had to be categorized as 'intangible' and 53 per cent under U.S. Fortune 500 in 2006. An interesting perspective on the value of reputation of a company is provided by Sacconi (Chapter 2, n 86), at 317, who explains the crucial role the reputation mechanism plays in economic theories, in particular the 'trust game': 'Reputation is one of the most valuable, albeit intangible, of the firm's assets. It is reputation that induces the stakeholders to trust the firm and consequently to cooperate with it, so that transactions come about at low costs of control or bargaining.' See Sacconi (Chapter 2, n 86), at 18 for an explanation of how the trust game functions as to CSR which includes privacy. See further Chapter 11, para 11.2.10.

[31] I note that in the case of outsourcing data processing operations, data security offered by the outsourcing supplier is often better than when the company itself processed the data (in my experience as a practitioner, this is often one of the reasons to outsource). In that sense, outsourcing may not create additional exposure for the company.

[32] An example is the public attack on H&M and C&A in the Dutch newspapers (*Volkskrant*, 3 September 2010) for breaching human rights when it was revealed that a manufacturer they both use in India violates the rights of (all female) textile workers by not offering an employment contract and prohibiting contact with labour unions. The women are de facto locked up in housing on the walled manufacturing property, 25 per cent of their wages are withheld for their dowry to be paid only after three years of service and payment of a wedding, which will only induce workers to work extremely long hours. Additionally, the manufacturer only pays overtime after three years of employment. For some other examples see McBarnet (Chapter 4, n 24), at 16.

[33] 13 June 1998.

[34] McBarnet (Chapter 4, n 24), at 16.

[35] See Supreme Court of California, *re Marc Kasky v Nike, et al*, 2 Cal. Daily Op. Serv. 3790, 2002 Daily Journal D.A.R. 4757.

company works to regain public trust and confidence'.[36] Research shows that even in case of data leaks in respect of which the multinational is not to blame whatsoever (for instance if criminal hackers have stolen data), data breach notifications in respect of confidential data (like credit card data) are shown to have a serious impact on the stock prices of listed companies.[37] This reputational exposure of multinationals for data protection and security breaches has had a strong impact on the compliance efforts of companies in an effort to try to prevent data protection and security breaches rather than address these after the fact. Given the global nature of these companies and their suppliers these efforts have necessarily also extended to countries that do not have data protection and security laws.

5.4 Other Drivers for Corporate Privacy Policies

Other factors appear to play a role in inducing multinationals to introduce corporate privacy policies. The factors discussed below are based on my experience in assisting EU-based multinationals in deciding on the introduction of BCR. Part of my research under the HiiL Program will be to perform empirical research to verify whether these factors do indeed play a role and/or whether other factors are also relevant. It is possible that this empirical research will show that the factors I encounter in practice are 'EU centric' and that the factors may vary from region to region (ie 'national or regional narratives' may apply). This empirical research into the 'driving forces' behind BCR (also labelled 'practical determinants') is part of the HiiL Program in order to be able to evaluate why a particular type of regulation has been resorted to (in particular private or co-regulation). My study of existing research into practical determinants influencing the emergence of new TPR in other areas of law showed a remarkable overlap with the practical determinants I have encountered for BCR. For readability purposes I have included the practical determinants, as identified in this existing research regarding TPR in other areas, in the footnotes.[38]

[36] See *Wall Street Journal*, 4 August 2010 <http://www.wsj.com>. It is clear in any event that, notwithstanding consumers' lack of understanding about how companies collect and use consumer data, consumers care about their privacy. See on this topic extensively Preliminary FTC Staff Report, *Protecting Consumer Privacy in an Era of Rapid Change, A proposed Framework for Business and Policymakers*, December 2010, at 28. The FTC provides some illustrative facts and figures, such as that 35 per cent of Facebook's 350 million users customized their privacy settings when Facebook released new privacy controls in December 2009; and the fact that 77 million Mozilla Firefox users downloaded NoScript, a privacy and security-enhancing tool that blocks Javascript commands.

[37] Katherine Campbell, Lawrence A. Gordon, Martin P. Loeb and Lei Zhou, 'The economic cost of publicly announced information security breaches: empirical evidence from the stock market' (2003) *Journal of Computer Security* 11, at 443–5, which reports that they 'find a highly significant negative reaction [on stock prices] for those breaches that relate to violations of confidentiality'; and L. Murphy Smith and Jacob L. Smith, 'Cyber Crimes Aimed at Publicly Traded Companies: Is Stock Price Affected?' Texas A&M University, at 12, to be found at <http://www.tamu.edu/>: 'Results suggest that costs of cyber crime go beyond stolen assets, lost business, and company reputation, but also include a negative impact on the company's stock price, at least in the short run.' See further Annex 6 for a table with effect on stock prices in 10 cases.

[38] See for an overview of practical determinants that play a role in emergence of TPR in other areas of law, Cafaggi (Chapter 2, n 70) at 4–8, who lists as the main factors:

Based on my experience in practice, I believe that the following practical determinants have played a role in the decision-making of multinationals to introduce corporate privacy policies:

(i) *Need for international harmonization.* The main driver is the need to overcome normative fragmentation of market regulation, often associated with divergent state legislation.

(ii) *Weakness of states as global rule-makers.* It has proven difficult for states to regulate markets that operate across boundaries. The main driver for TPR is the need for harmonization at the global level of regulatory standards or at least for strong coordination by way of mutual recognition. Failure to reach political consensus over treaty-based solutions triggers TPR.

(iii) *Weaknesses of state regulation in monitoring compliance with international standards.* Often domestic monitoring brings about conflicting results which are contrary to the rationale of the international standard.

(iv) *Weakness of public international law.* The accountability of international organizations is still mainly ensured by states. This intermediate role hampers the rule making by non-state actors and international public entities which triggers TPR.

(v) *Technology.* New technologies and in particular the internet have redistributed rule-making power from national to transnational and public to private.

(vi) *Distributional effects.* TPR enables a shift in cost of compliance from states to private actors but also from developed economies to developing economies (where the TPR is implemented and monitored). Cost may then be partly transferred to suppliers upstream and ultimately consumers. TPR may increase the power and market share of big suppliers and impose a threshold for market entry which may be a trigger for adopting TPR).

For an overview of practical determinants specifically for CSR codes (labelled by McBarnet 'contextual drivers'), see McBarnet (Chapter 4, n 24), at 13–22, which also shows a remarkable overlap. Some *additional* 'contextual drivers' are identified which may be caused by the fact that CSR codes have a longer presence in the market. Examples are:

- What McBarnet calls 'concerned consumption', whereby consumers avoid products and services of companies that they consider as having questionable ethics (eg the public is prepared to pay more for fair trade goods). As far as I am aware there has been no empirical research performed into whether data protection compliance has an influence on spending patterns of consumers. In practice I have encountered the situation where a multinational hesitated to implement privacy notices and consent for data processing in connection with the sale of software based on the assumption that sales would go down. After the implementation, the multinational reported that against all expectations, sales had gone up notably after implementation of the data protection requirements. Practice has shown similar experiences with implementation of online opt-in requirements for direct e-mail where prior opt-out requirements applied. If the opt-in opportunity was given with a possibility for consumers to select their areas of interest from among a number of options, response was larger than expected (and resulted in many consumers opting in who would have otherwise opted out). This is obviously an area of interest for further empirical research.
- What McBarnet calls a 'socially responsible investment', where investment funds and investment companies and banks screen companies based on their ethical values and compliance. For that purpose for instance the FTSE (Financial Times Stock Exchange Index) introduced in 2001 the FTSE4Good index using criteria based on CSR and the Dow Jones has the Sustainability Index. If privacy compliance is also included in CSR codes and reporting on privacy in annual accounts will be required in a prescribed format, it is not unthinkable that privacy will be included in the criteria for these indices. In certain business areas that are sensitive to privacy issues, a privacy ranking is published by the veteran international privacy watchdog Privacy International. For a ranking of the major internet service providers, see the report 'A race to the Bottom—Privacy Ranks of Internet Service Providers', to be found at <http://www.privacy.international.org>.
- McBarnet finally reports on the self-enhancing or self-serving function of what he calls the CSR industry (CSR consultants, lawyers, accountants specialized in advising on CSR policies, offering training and writing codes of conduct; CSR standard-setting organizations; CSR reporting certification firms; CSR magazines; CSR conference organizers, etc). All these businesses have invested

- Given the diverging (and in many instances conflicting) national data protection rules, 100 per cent worldwide compliance is practically impossible.[39] In respect of central systems and applications, therefore many *policy decisions* have to be taken in respect of data security and data processing rules on the basis of what such company considers as offering *adequate protection* rather than full compliance with all relevant national laws. These strategic decisions have obviously to be taken on a central level and then imposed on the various group companies. This is generally effectuated by means of implementing a corporate privacy code.
- As data from central ICT systems may also be processed by employees in countries where no (adequate) data protection law applies, such employees have to be instructed on how to process the relevant data stored in the central systems, which is also done by means of a corporate privacy policy.
- But even if a country does provide for an adequate level of protection, a privacy policy is generally required. For instance, the EU data protection rules concern general processing principles, which have to be 'translated' into practical guidelines for employees involved in the processing of the data. One of the processing principles is that data may be processed 'for specified and legitimate purposes only'. This requires a specification tailored to the operations of the multinational of which categories of data may be processed, for which purposes, by which categories of employees, and for how long such

in CSR, with the result that CSR has become a business and a market factor itself. This is fuelled by the fact that many working in this area are CSR 'enthusiasts' and have a personal interest in keeping up CSR momentum. A clear parallel with the data protection area can be seen here. The recent past shows many new privacy right advocacy organizations, privacy seal organizations, and specialist privacy consultancy firms, and within my experience equal enthusiasm is apparent as in the CSR sector.

The empirical research to be performed in respect of contextual drivers for BCR as part of the HiiL Program will show whether the additional contextual drivers as identified by McBarnet indeed also play a role for BCR. However, as Neil Gunningham notes in respect of corporate environmental responsibility, the general conclusion will probably be that many contextual drivers play a role varying from law and social and economic pressures; see Neil Gunningham, 'Corporate environmental responsibility: the law and the limits of voluntarism', in McBarnet, Voiculescu, Campbell, *The New Corporate Accountability, Corporate Social Responsibility and the Law* (Cambridge University Press 2007), at 500. See on the rise of private regulation in the world economy: Büthe and Mattli (Chapter 3, n 149), at Chapter 1 'The Rise of Private Regulation in the World Economy', in particular at 5: 'This simultaneous privatization and internationalization of governance is driven, in part, by governments' lack of requisite technical expertise, financial resources, or flexibility to deal expeditiously with ever more complex and urgent regulatory tasks, Firms and other private actors also often push for private governance, which they see as leading to more cost-effective rules more efficiently than government regulation'. See further at 25, where Büthe and Mattli note as a main driver for TPR the 'excruciatingly slow pace of standards production' of public regulators.

[39] Implementation of all national laws would de facto imply that the strictest national law applies to a multinational on a worldwide basis. For most companies this is understandably not an acceptable starting point. The DPAs have in practice recognized this by accepting BCR that provide for an adequate level of protection rather than only authorizing BCR which comply with all applicable national requirements.

data may be subsequently stored. The use of open norms is one of the reasons that the Directive explicitly encourages the introduction of privacy codes for sectors of industry, as it is understood that the general norms may require specification for specific industry sectors.[40]

- Multinationals apply a risk-based approach to regulatory compliance, including data protection compliance.[41] Priorities are identified in the roll-out of compliance measures, whereby priority is given to high-risk data processing systems (such as sensitive or financial data) and to systems that have the largest security risks (such as cross-border systems). This is in line with the approach to data protection compliance taken from the start by the Working Party 29.[42] These strategic decisions based on a risk assessment can only be taken at a central level (mostly by the parent company) and then imposed on the group companies. This risk-based approach to data protection is compatible with the broader trend of introducing the 'principle of accountability' for data protec-

[40] Recital 61 Directive.

[41] This is based on my experience assisting multinationals with their data protection compliance. Risk assessments of data processing systems are generally performed by multinationals by means of 'Privacy Impact Assessments' (*PIAs*). In most cases, firstly a quick scan will be made to assess the risk category of each system. After this, the high risk, cross-border systems will be subject to the most extensive PIA and certain local-for-local paper-based filing systems with low risk will not be subjected to further review. On the risk-based approach of multinationals in relation to their supply chain management, see in particular Doreen McBarnet and Marina Kurkchiyan, 'Corporate social responsibility through contractual control? Global supply chains and other regulation', in McBarnet, Voiculescu, Campbell, *The New Corporate Accountability, Corporate Social Responsibility and the Law* (Cambridge University Press 2007), at 63: 'The supply chain is becoming increasingly recognised as an area of reputational—and indeed insurance—risk, with a number of companies beginning to develop a "risk-based approach to supplier engagement" and "systems to identify higher risk suppliers"' (referring to Vodafone's Corporate Social Responsibility Report for 2004–05, at 24 and other examples listed).

[42] The Working Party 29 applied from the start a risk-based approach to data protection compliance, indicating as the first (of three) objectives of the Directive 'to deliver a good level of compliance', acknowledging that a 100 per cent compliance is not achievable in practice. See WP 12 (Chapter 3, n 50), at 7: 'The objectives of a data protection system are essentially threefold: 1) to deliver a good level of compliance with the rules. (No system can guarantee 100 per cent compliance, but some are better than others). A good system is generally characterized by a high degree of awareness among data controllers of their obligations, and among data subjects of their rights and the means of exercising them.' The Working Party 29 further applied from the start a risk-based approach as to the content of data protection obligations (ie requiring stricter security measures in case of a transfer of sensitive data, etc), as well as to identifying priorities in enforcement for the DPAs. See WP 12 (Chapter 3, n 50), at 28. Such a risk-based approach is further in line with the first recommendation for amendment of the Directive made in the Rand Report (Chapter 2, n 27) at 42: 'Encourage the use of a risk based approach to the application of the rules, focusing on acts of data processing where harm can reasonably be expected.' See further at 50, where the Rand Report recommends the introduction of the accountability principle and recommends that all compliance tools (like privacy policies, PIAs, training programmes) will be drafted on a risk-based approach, reflecting the scale of the data processing (amount of data, cross-border environment) privacy-sensitive nature (health data), and the field of activity of the data controller (financial sector, healthcare). The Rand Report, at 57, recommends introduction of a risk-based sanction system. The EDPS proposes a risk-based notification system, by proposing to limit the obligation to notify to specific kinds of processing that entail specific risks, stating that 'these notifications could trigger further steps such as prior checking of the processing'. This is without prejudice to the prior-checking requirement also imposed on the basis of specific risks, such as large-scale information systems (EDPS Opinion on the revision of the Directive, (Chapter 2, n 35), at paras 62, 63 at 15).

tion (see Chapter 9), which is also risk-based and fits in with the trend where legislators focus on achieving desired outcomes through regulating corporate governance processes. This signifies a decisive move in the direction of abandoning traditional 'command and control' state regulatory schemes in favour of 'responsive regulation', which is supposed to facilitate self-regulation programmes.[43] Introduction of the accountability principle in the revised Directive is in conformance with the recommendation of the Working Party 29 to the Commission for the revision of the Directive and the Rand Report[44], and has been incorporated by the Commission in the Proposed Regulation.[45] Introduction of the accountability principle will mean that multinationals will have to implement a data protection compliance programme, which in any event will require a corporate privacy policy setting the data protection standard for such company (see for the implications of the introduction of the accountability principle in the revised Directive Chapter 9 below).

- Enforcement action by DPAs customarily starts with a regulatory investigation (privacy audit). In order to be able to show (initial) privacy compliance, the multinational subject of an investigatory audit will have to have readily at hand (i) the internal data processing instructions (ie the corporate privacy policy) and (ii) the results of its internal privacy audits (auditing compliance against the corporate privacy policy). Experience shows that DPAs realize that 100 per cent privacy compliance is not achievable, but accept this as long as a company takes a structured approach to its privacy compliance.
- Last, but not least, the introduction of corporate privacy policies fits within the broader trend of corporate social responsibility (*CSR*) where multinationals adopt CSR codes to express their commitment to human and civil rights, the environment, opposition to bribery and corruption, and fairness to their customers and suppliers. The range of issues is constantly expanding[46] and many CSR codes[47] by now also contain a commitment to protect the privacy

[43] For instance in respect of achieving desired CSR outcomes, see Christine Parker, 'Meta-regulation: legal accountability for corporate social responsibility', in McBarnet, Voiculescu, Campbell, *The New Corporate Accountability, Corporate Social Responsibility and the Law* (Cambridge University Press 2007), at 228: 'To the extent that scholars and policy makers focus on achieving CSR through corporate governance processes (i.e., meta-regulation), it signifies a decisive move in the direction of abandoning traditional "command and control" state regulatory schemes in favour of "responsive regulation", which is supposed to facilitate—yet not enforce and dictate—self-regulation programmes and "compliance-oriented" regulation, which is carried out through corporate consent and voluntary organizational processes of reflexive learning.' For more detail on risk-based regulation, see Chapter 9, para 9.3.

[44] See WP Contribution on The Future of Privacy (Chapter 1, n 6), para 37–9 and for a more detailed opinion on the accountability principle itself, see WP Opinion on the principle of accountability (Chapter 1, n 7), at 10.

[45] Article 22 Proposed Regulation.

[46] See on CSR for instance Sacconi (Chapter 2, n 86), at 289–344. See further the research listed in *The added value of private regulation in an international world? Towards a model of the legitimacy, effectiveness, enforcement and quality of private regulation* HiiL 2007–08, at 8–10, to be found at <http://www.hiil.org>.

[47] Often called: 'Company Ethics Code', 'Company Business Values', or 'Company Business Principles'.

of employees and customers.[48] At first, for some multinationals, adoption of privacy commitments was part of a strategy to achieve competitive advantage in an industry sector.[49] Practice has shown that, for instance, licence revenues increase if proper privacy policies are implemented.[50] By now, however, adoption of privacy commitments no longer seems to be an advantage but non-adoption a disadvantage.[51] See Chapter 11 for an evaluation of BCR in the context of CSR.

It is on account of these drivers that some multinationals introduced corporate privacy policies and, having introduced these policies, asked the DPAs to recognize these policies as an alternative means to comply with the EU data transfer rules. The underlying thought is that as their policies introduce an adequate level of protection within their group of companies, this company group constitutes a 'safe haven' for the processing of personal data, as a result of which data may flow freely between the companies within the group. In the next chapter I discuss the EU authorization procedure and the conditions under which a global privacy policy of a multinational may be recognized as Binding Corporate Rules, constituting an alternative method of complying with the EU data transfer rules.

48 See eg the CSR codes of Philips, Shell, and Sara Lee.

49 This certainly applies to adoption of CSR codes (see McBarnet (Chapter 4, n 24), at 21), but in my experience also applies (to a lesser extent) to adoption of privacy commitments. For instance the Dutch ISP XS4All made it a distinguishing factor in its advertising campaign for paid ISP services, where it depicted under the heading 'Everything has a cost', the privacy provisions in the general terms and conditions of its main competitors providing free ISP services, allowing such competitor to sell the personal data of its subscribers to third parties for advertising purposes.

50 See n 38.

51 This is a common feature with general experiences with CSR. See Conley and Williams (Chapter 2, n 70), at 21.

6

The BCR Regime

6.1 Introduction

The complications with the EU transfer rules have led multinationals to put pressure on the data protection authorities (*DPAs*) to recognize their corporate privacy policies as equivalent to the EU Standard Contractual Clauses for the purpose of facilitating their intercompany transfers of personal data.[1] As their corporate privacy policies are based on the general processing principles of the OECD Privacy Guidelines and of the Directive (see paragraph 3.1.1), it can be argued that they establish an 'adequate level' of protection of personal data within their group of companies (a 'safe haven'). Insofar as such processing involves data transfers to group companies in a non-adequate country, the policy provides for the 'adequate safeguards' as required pursuant to Article 26(2) Directive.[2]

The Working Party 29 and the DPAs are well aware of the fact that multinationals exchange personal data on a worldwide basis (through their central systems) and outsource their ICT to non-adequate countries and realize that the traditional jurisdiction-based enforcement tools are not adequate to force compliance.[3] The Working Party 29 has recognized the added value of transnational corporate self-regulation in the data protection area in light of the deficiencies of the present enforcement regime of the Directive and has recognized corporate self-regulation as an alternative method of complying with the data transfer rules of the Directive.[4] Thus the Working Party 29 has in fact

[1] See on this Chapter 1, para 1.1.

[2] As required for the transfer of data to non-adequate countries pursuant to Art 26(2) Directive. This exercise is different from the approval of codes of conduct provided for in Art 27 Directive, which codes are aimed at the practical application of the relevant applicable national data protection law in a specific sector. These codes of conduct therefore have to be fully compliant with the relevant national law. For BCR it is sufficient that they provide for an adequate level of protection which may be in some respects different from or stricter than applicable data protection laws of the Member States. Note that the BCR do not set aside any applicable national requirements; the company will remain bound by law. These national requirements, however, do not need to be included in the BCR. See WP 74 Transfer of Personal Data to Third Countries: Applying Article 26(2) of the EU Data Protection Directive to Binding Corporate Rules for International Data Transfers, adopted on 3 June 2003, at 7 (WP 74). A common denominator of BCR and codes of conduct under Art 27 Directive is that both are supposed to overcome the level of abstraction of the data protection processing principles. See WP 74, at 14.

[3] See Chapter 2, n 26.

[4] See WP 74 (n 2), at 6. See for a comprehensive overview of benefits of BCR for individuals and businesses: Wugmeister, Retzer, Rich (Chapter 3, n 148), Chapter V.

approved a voluntary system of a combination of self-regulation with public validation and enforcement. For the paragraphs hereafter, it is relevant to know that the Working Party 29 has advisory status only.[5] Though the opinions of the Working Party 29 are followed in practice by the individual DPAs, they are not obliged to do so and (in relation to Binding Corporate Rules) some DPAs follow their own course.[6]

6.2 BCR Requirements

To date, the Working Party 29 has issued seven Opinions[7] (*WP Opinions*) setting out criteria that a corporate privacy policy should meet before it can be approved as 'Binding Corporate Rules' (*BCR*). The WP Opinions make clear that recognition by DPAs of BCR as a valid tool for data transfers is voluntary.[8] As BCR are not recognized in the Directive, it is up to the DPAs in the national approval procedures whether to recognize BCR as a valid tool for data transfers or not.[9] The Working Party 29 has issued a checklist with the elements that the Working Party 29 recommends being incorporated in BCR and considered by the national DPAs in their assessment of adequacy.[10] The Working Party 29 has announced that the requirements are not carved in stone and may be revisited.[11] Indeed, the Working Party 29 has held a consultation[12] and a public hearing[13] on the first of the WP Opinions, the input from which was taken into consideration when developing its subsequent WP Opinions. Some DPAs (eg of the UK and Austria) have published further national guidance clarifying issues a company must

[5] See Chapter 2, n 29.

[6] See n 53 below.

[7] WP 74 (n 2); WP 107, Working Document Setting Forth a Co-Operation Procedure for Issuing Common Opinions on Adequate Safeguards Resulting from 'Binding Corporate Rules', adopted on 14 April 2005 (WP 107); WP 108, Working Document Establishing a Model Checklist Application for Approval of Binding Corporate Rules adopted on 14 April 2005 (WP 108); WP 153, Working Document Setting Up a Table with the Elements and Principles to be found in Binding Corporate Rules adopted on 24 June 2008 (WP 153); WP 154, Working Document Setting Up a Framework for the Structure of Binding Corporate Rules adopted on 24 June 2008 (WP 154); WP 155 Working Document on Frequently Asked Questions (FAQs) related to Binding Corporate Rules adopted on 24 June 2008 (WP 155); and WP 133, Recommendation 1/2007 on the Standard Application for Approval of Binding Corporate Rules for the Transfer of Personal Data adopted on 10 January 2007 (WP 133). For a general discussion of the BCR requirements see Kuner (Chapter 4, n 39), at paras 4.120–153.

[8] WP 108 (n 7), at 2.

[9] BCR are subsequently not recognized by all DPAs, see further below at n 53.

[10] See for the latest checklist WP 153 (n 7).

[11] This was announced in WP 74 (n 2) and in practice the later WP documents issued by the Working Party do indeed deviate in certain respects from the requirements initially listed in WP 74.

[12] For which a number of multinationals and industry groups were invited to submit their input. See for their contributions <http://www.ec.europa.eu>.

[13] See the official summary of the public hearing on internal codes of conduct for multinationals drafted by the Dutch DPA, to be found at <http://www.ec.europa.eu>. The public hearing was attended by 30 representatives of the business community and one consumer organization.

address in its BCR.[14] The main requirements set by the Working Party 29 for BCR are the following:

(i) If the headquarters of the multinational are not established within the EU, the multinational should appoint an EU group company to have delegated data protection responsibilities (*Delegated EU Headquarters*).[15]

(ii) BCR should be submitted for approval to the DPA of the Member State where the relevant multinational has its headquarters (*EU Headquarters*). If the multinational does not have its headquarters in the EU (or it is not clear where the ultimate parent company is established), the application must be submitted to the 'most appropriate' DPA, which will in most cases be the DPA of the Delegated EU Headquarters (*Lead DPA*).[16]

(iii) The geographical and material scope of BCR should make clear whether BCR apply worldwide or to EU-originated data only[17/18], which data are covered, the categories of individuals covered, the countries covered, etc.

[14] For the UK: 'Transfers of Personal Data to Third Countries: Applying Article 26(2) of the EU Data Protection Directive to Binding Corporate Rules for International Data Transfers: Putting the concept into practice in the United Kingdom', Information Commissioner, 11 February 2004, to be found at <http://www.ico.gov.uk>. For Austria: 'Required Contents of Submission for Approval of "Binding Corporate Rules" to the information Commissioner', Information Commissioner, SR/HR/BCR Checklist 11/2/2004, at 1, to be found at <http://www.dsk.gv.at>.

[15] See for this requirement WP 74 (n 2), at 18.

[16] See WP 107 (n 7) for relevant criteria to decide which DPA is the most appropriate.

[17] The Working Party 29 accepts that the scope of BCR is limited to EU-originated data only. In practice most companies opt for applicability of their BCR to all data processed by the company. Various factors play a role in this decision. The most important factor is that companies find it hard to explain to their employees and customers why protection is afforded to some and not to others, which is often experienced as an unjustifiable discrimination between individuals. This is especially the case with multinationals headquartered in the EU, where adherence to data protection rules is by now part of their regular compliance and has been integrated in their corporate culture, as a consequence of which the limitation of these rights to EU-originated data based only on the argument that other countries do not require that protection, seems against the ethical sensibilities of the managers. For a similar effect of other forms of TPR, see Conley and Williams (Chapter 2, n 70), at 15, and literature therein referred to. More practical determinants are: (i) the fact that it is difficult to 'tag' EU-originated data in such a manner that compliance with the BCR can be ensured even if these data are further transferred to other databases within the company (this is a common occurrence as often local databases are 'fed' with data stored in the central HR or CRM database); and (ii) the fact that the employees who process data often process both data of EU origin and non-EU-originated data, and would have to receive different sets of instructions for the different types of data even while these often coincide in the same databases. Compliance with the BCR for EU-originated data can then only be ensured by imposing the stricter BCR processing regime.

[18] Examples of BCR that have introduced some form of limitation as to scope are the BCR of DaimlerChrysler (which applies only to personal data that are subject to data transfer restrictions) and those of GE (these BCR apply to all data processing worldwide, but do not provide for an 'adequate' level of data protection according to EU standards. For EU-originated data, GE has added an addendum to its BCR that provides for additional requirements for the processing of EU-originated data, which ensures the required adequate level to obtain the required permit for data transfers. Other options to limit the scope of BCR to a certain extent are for instance: (i) to apply the material processing principles of the BCR on a worldwide basis regardless of the origin of the personal data and the location of the processing, but restrict the BCR for transfers to third parties (outside the group of companies) to EU-originated data only; and (ii) to exclude from the transfer rules any local-for-local transfers.

(iv) BCR should describe the *nature* of the data processed (i.e. categories of data and sensitivity thereof), the *purposes* for which they are processed,[19] and the extent of the international *data transfers* within the group.[20]

(v) BCR should incorporate the material data processing principles (transparency, fairness, purpose limitation, data quality, rights of individuals, and security) (see Chapter 3, paragraph 3.1.1 above) and the restrictions on onward transfers to third parties outside the group (see also Chapter 3, paragraph 3.1.5).[21]

(vi) BCR should be *internally* binding within the organization (on all group companies and on employees) and *externally* binding for the benefit of individuals (ie must create third-party beneficiary rights for individuals).[22]

(vii) BCR should provide for a network of privacy officers for handling complaints and ensuring compliance with the rules.[23]

[19] The categories of data and purposes for which they are processed can only be described in a very general manner. The data processing operations of a multinational change on a daily bases (where systems are replaced or added) and any specific description of the data processed would be outdated the moment the inventory would have been made. I have attached as Annex II an example of a BCR for employee data and as Annex III a BCR for customer data. In Art 2 of these BCR a generic description can be found of categories of data and legitimate business purposes for which these are processed. In Art 4 of these template BCR a generic description can be found of categories of sensitive data and legitimate business purposes for which they may processed. These descriptions have been approved by various Lead DPAs.

[20] As data are transferred on a continuous basis within a multinational group of companies it is difficult (if not impossible) to include in BCR information on 'the extent of the data transfers within the group'. This is solved in practice by providing to the Lead DPA an overview of the IT infrastructure of the multinational, ie an overview of the main IT systems of the multinational and the locations where they are hosted, which provides a general idea of how the data flow within the group.

[21] See WP 154 (n 7) on how these general processing principles can be 'translated' into practical requirements in BCR. See further the template BCR in Annex II and Annex III: Arts 5–6 (Quantity and Quality of Data); Arts 6–7 (Information Requirements); Arts 7–8 (Individual Rights of Access and Rectification); Arts 8–9 (Security and Confidentiality Requirements); Arts 9–10 (Automated Decision-making); Arts 10–11 (Transfer of Data to Third Parties).

[22] For how internal and external bindingness may be achieved in practice see paras 7.2 and 7.3 respectively.

[23] See for an example of a privacy governance structure Arts 12–13 of the template BCR in Annex II and III. A frequently asked question is whether the privacy governance structure must be stand-alone or whether the existing compliance officers' network of a multinational may be tasked also with privacy compliance. The BCR regime does not require that the network of privacy officers is stand-alone and as the privacy officer's compliance function is often not a full-time job, it may from a cost perspective be advisable to link up as much as possible with existing structures. This being said, it is not always the most logical step to task the compliance officers with privacy compliance tasks as well. For instance, in the case of BCR for employee data, an HR manager may sometimes be better placed than a compliance officer to respond to data access requests and complaints. Practice further shows that it is not advisable to task the legal department with the privacy compliance function. The business must feel completely free to come to the legal department to ask for advice in respect of data protection compliance, without feeling threatened that they are being reported on. Combining these different tasks may entail that compliance questions are kept from the legal department, which is undesirable. As to how the network should be created, multinationals are free to choose the basis for creating the network, as long as the network created adequately covers the entirety of the organization. For instance, privacy officers can be appointed on a geographical basis (for each group company, country, or region), on a functional basis (eg all HR personnel worldwide), or per business unit (eg extending to all personnel worldwide

(viii) There should be an internal complaint handling process.[24]

(ix) Compliance with BCR should be enforceable by the individuals via the DPA and the courts in the Member State of (i) the EU group company at the origin of the transfer *or* (ii) the EU Headquarters or the Delegated EU Headquarters.[25]

(x) The (Delegated) EU Headquarters should accept liability for paying compensation and remedying breaches of BCR.[26]

(xi) The burden of proof with respect to an alleged breach of BCR should rest with the (Delegated) EU Headquarters and not with the individual.[27]

(xii) The group companies should have a duty to cooperate with the DPAs, to abide by their advice regarding BCR, and to submit to their audits.[28]

(xiii) BCR should provide for an auditing programme covering all aspects of BCR, including methods of ensuring that corrective actions have taken place. The audits have to take place on a regular basis (by either internal or external accredited auditors) or on specific request from the corporate privacy function. BCR must provide that the results of the audit will be communicated to the privacy function and the ultimate parent's board. The DPAs must have the right of access to the results of such audits.[29]

working for a specific business line). In practice often a combination is made whereby privacy officers are in principle appointed on a geographical basis, but where certain business units have specific privacy issues (eg perform scientific research involving health data of patients), a specific privacy officer for such business unit is appointed.

[24] See for a proper complaints procedure with the possibility for appeal Arts 16–17 of the template BCR in Annexes II and III.

[25] In the template BCR in Annexes II and II, the second option is chosen, whereby the BCR are enforceable via the DPA and courts of the EU headquarters of the multinational only. This is the DPA who has reviewed and authorized the BCR under the applicability of the DPA's own law. This ensures for the multinational a consistent and predictable interpretation and application of the BCR. Some DPAs have the position that this requirement does not provide an option for the multinational to choose from, but requires BCR to provide both options to the individuals to choose from.

[26] The WP Opinions do not specify according to what law this liability should be considered. In the template BCR in Annexes II and II, it is therefore provided that individuals shall only be entitled to remedies available under the laws of the EU Headquarters of the multinational; this to ensure that the competent DPA (and courts of the DPA) can apply their own laws. The template BCR in Annexes II and III further limit liability of the multinational to direct damages suffered by the individual. This limitation of liability has been accepted by a number of Lead DPAs.

[27] This requirement has been criticized by companies applying for BCR. The main criticism is that the full reversal of the burden of proof entices frivolous and unfounded complaints by data subjects, which are difficult to disprove by the company (it being impossible to prove a 'negative'). In practice the Lead DPAs accept the following provision: 'Where data subjects can demonstrate that they have suffered damages and establish facts which show it is plausible that the damage has occurred because of the breach of the BCR, it will be for the EU headquarters to prove that the damages suffered by the individual due to a violation of the BCR are not attributable to the relevant group company.'

[28] This requirement has also been criticized by companies applying for BCR. Not all DPAs have audit rights under their national law and would now acquire such rights just because a company opts for BCR. In practice, Lead DPAs accept that the right to have access to the audit results and the audit right is granted to the Lead DPA only. Other DPAs keep their own access rights and audit rights to the extent they have these under their own laws.

[29] See Arts 15–16 template BCR.

(xiv) The individuals concerned should have easy access to BCR, and in particular easy access to the information about their rights.[30]

(xv) There must be a suitable training of the employees who process the data.[31]

(xvi) There should be a process for updating BCR and a mechanism for reporting changes in BCR to the Lead DPA.[32]

(xvii) The group companies should be obliged to be 'transparent' if applicable national law prevents the group from complying with BCR, to take an informed decision about what action to take, and to consult with the Lead DPA in case of doubt.[33]

6.3 Different Types of BCR

6.3.1 BCR for controllers

The BCR regime as developed by the Working Party 29 addresses the data processing obligations of *data controllers*.[34] This is logical as the requirements of the Directive are directed at controllers of personal data only. The Directive does not (directly) impose obligations on data processors.[35] Instead, the Directive imposes an obligation on controllers, when they involve a data processor to process data on their behalf, to impose certain mandatory requirements on that processor. In paragraph 2.1, I discussed how multinationals in the course of their business activities process different types of data, the main categories being (i) employee data; (ii) personal data of customers, suppliers, and other business partners; and (iii) specific categories of data. An example mentioned of the last category is the processing by the pharmaceutical industry of large quantities of patient data as part of their scientific research. Here a patient is neither employee nor customer or business partner. In respect of all these categories, the multinational processes these data in its capacity of data controller. However, it is possible that group companies in certain cases also act in a capacity of data processor on behalf of other group companies. This is, for instance, the case if a multinational has centralized certain

[30] See Art 1.6 of the template BCR. Note that BCR for employee data need only be published on the company intranet for employees to be aware of BCR and their rights. It is advisable not to publish BCR for employee data on the company's website as well, as this may trigger authority of for instance the US Federal Trade Commission (FTC). See Chapter 7, paragraph 7.3.4 on the authority of the FTC to take action against companies that misrepresent their privacy practices in their corporate privacy codes.

[31] See Arts 14–15 of the template BCRs.

[32] In practice the Lead DPAs accept that significant changes only require the approval of the Lead DPA and may be reported to the Lead DPA on a yearly basis. See also Arts 20.1–21.1 of the template BCR.

[33] These are not the only conflicts between BCR and applicable local law which may occur; see Arts 19–20 of the template BCR for the different conflicts and safeguards how to address these.

[34] See for definition Chapter 3, n 13.

[35] See Chapter 3, para 3.1.1.

data processing operations in a shared service centre. In that case the shared service centre processes data on behalf of the other group companies (ie in a capacity of data processor). Such data processing will still be covered by BCR for data controllers as in that case other group companies of the multinational qualify as controller (as a result of which the processing activities are still covered by the BCR). This is no longer the case if a group company starts processing data on behalf of a third party outside the multinational group of companies. These activities would not be covered by a BCR for controllers. See however paragraph 6.3.3 for the possibility of BCR for processors.

6.3.2 BCR for employee data vs BCR for customer data

Though in theory one comprehensive corporate privacy policy would be feasible setting out the data controller obligations for the processing by a multinational of all different categories of data, in practice multinationals regulate these different types of data by separate BCR. The reason is first and foremost the clarity of the relevant policies and the resulting processing instructions for the employees who process the different types of data. By adopting different policies for the separate categories of data, the instructions can be more tailored to the processing at hand. This is desirable because the applicable data protection rules vary according to the data processed. For instance, direct marketing rules are of relevance only for customer data, and not for employee data. Also, the consent rules vary on whether consent is requested of a customer or of an employee. Yet different rules apply if specific categories of data are processed, like the patient data for research purposes as mentioned before. From a practical perspective, these different types of data are mostly also processed by different departments within a multinational; customer data are mostly processed by the marketing department, employee data mostly by the HR department, and patient data by the R&D department. Also for this reason separate sets of instructions are indicated. To illustrate the differences and how these work out in concrete examples of BCR, I attach as Annex II an example of a BCR for employee data and as Annex III a BCR for customer data. These template forms incorporate the relevant requirements and have been approved by a number of DPAs.[36]

6.3.3 BCR for processors

If a multinational processes personal data on behalf of its customers, these activities fall outside the BCR for controllers. This is the case if, for instance, the business

[36] In April 2011, the Working Party 29 started publishing the names of the companies whose BCR have been approved, to be found at <http://ec.europa.eu/justice/policies/privacy/binding_rules/bcr_cooperation_en.htm>. The website (which since its launch has not been updated) indicates that the BCR of 15 multinationals have been approved by five Lead DPAs (UK, France, Luxembourg, the Netherlands, and Germany). Some of these BCR are for employee data, others for customer data, and others for both. In January 2011, the Dutch DPA informally communicated that 46 BCR applications were in the pipeline throughout the EU.

activities of a multinational consist of the provision of data processing services to other companies (eg payroll processing on behalf of a customer). Such customer data are then processed by the relevant multinational in a capacity as data processor. Until now the BCR regime has been applied to data processing obligations of controllers only.

However, there are no convincing reasons why BCR for processors would not also be conceivable.[37] As already discussed in paragraph 5.1, if a multinational with establishments in the EU outsources data processing services to a third-party service provider with establishments in non-adequate countries, this also triggers the application of the EU transfer rules. As a result, the transfer of personal data to these countries requires each of the EU subsidiaries of the multinational to enter into EU Standard Contractual Clauses with each of the group companies of the service provider involved in providing the outsourcing services. A solution for the requirement of these numerous EU Standard Contractual Clauses may be that the outsourcing provider also adopts BCR to regulate its data processor obligations. The BCR would then consist of a privacy policy which applies to all group companies of the service provider introducing company-wide processor obligations (especially as to the company-wide security requirements), together with general commitments in respect of training, auditing, etc. If the multinational being the controller of the data has BCR for controllers in place and the outsourcing service provider being the data processor has BCR for processors in place, a free exchange of data would also be facilitated between these two multinationals. The concept of an organizational tool to govern the involvement of a data processor is already embodied in the EU Standard Contractual Clauses for controller-to-processor relations and further exists under the Safe Harbor Framework, where companies can either adhere to the controller regime or the processor regime.[38] A first draft BCR for processors has been submitted to the Dutch DPA, which has referred the request to the Working Party 29 for opinion.

Proposed Regulation BCR for processors are facilitated by the Proposed Regulation. The data transfer rules in the Proposed Regulation also apply directly to data processors,[39] and appropriate safeguards can be provided for both controllers and processors by BCR.[40]

Since the introduction of a potential regime for BCR for processors is outside the scope of this book, I will refrain from elaborating further.

[37] I first suggested the possibility of BCR for processors at the Conference on international transfers of personal data, co-organized by the Commission, the Working Party 29, and the US Department of Commerce, Brussels (23–24 October 2006), and further by Eduardo Usteran at several other data protection conferences. See Binding Safe Processor Rules, at <http://www.youtube.com>.

[38] <http://www.export.gov/safeharbor>.

[39] See Art 42(1) Proposed Regulation.

[40] See Art 42(2) Proposed Regulation.

6.4 EU BCR Approval Procedure

In principle a multinational requires the approval of its BCR in all Member States[41] where it has an establishment and from where personal data are transferred outside the EU. To facilitate the approval procedures, the Working Party 29 initially introduced the 'EU Cooperation Procedure' (*CP*).[42] The multinational had to introduce the CP by approaching the most appropriate DPA,[43] which was then appointed as 'lead' DPA (*Lead DPA*). The Lead DPA subsequently coordinated the comments of the other DPAs whose approval was required, which led to a final draft which was subsequently circulated again by the Lead DPA to the other DPAs for final approval. After the first experiences with the CP had been positive, the DPAs of (by now) 19 Member States joined the 'Mutual Recognition Procedure' (*MRP*), which entails that these DPAs will mutually recognize each other's adequacy findings in respect of BCR without further review of the draft BCR involved.[44] Like the CP, the MRP requires that one of the DPAs is appointed Lead DPA. This Lead DPA will be assisted by one or two other DPAs to co-review the BCR (*Co-Leads*). The Co-Leads should be the DPAs of a Member State where the relevant multinational has 'a strong presence'. The steps to be taken are as follows: the multinational submits its BCR application to the DPA it considers suited to act as Lead DPA and lists the Member States in which the multinational has a presence. This DPA will subsequently contact the other DPAs involved to solicit their consent that it indeed may act as Lead DPA. After it has been established that the relevant DPA can indeed act as Lead DPA, the Co-Leads will be selected and contacted by the Lead DPA. Then the consultation phase starts where the BCR are reviewed by the Lead DPA and discussed with the multinational, which may lead to amendments to the BCR (see paragraph 6.5 for the sequence of steps of this consultation phase). After the consultation phase has ended, the BCR will be informally approved by the Lead DPA. The Lead DPA will then solicit the input of the Co-Leads. Apparently there are informal agreements between the DPAs that are part of the MRP to respond to the request of the Lead DPA for input within one month.[45] The comments of the Co-Leads may lead to further consultations with

[41] This is except for the UK where submission is voluntary. See Information Commissioner, 'Transfers of Personal Data to Third Countries: Applying Article 26(2) of the EU Data Protection Directive to Binding Corporate Rules for International Data Transfers: Putting the concept into practice in the United Kingdom', 11 February 2004, to be found at <http://www.ico.gov.uk>.

[42] See for a description of the coordinated procedure WP 107 (n 7).

[43] See WP 107 (n 7), at 2 for the relevant criteria to decide which DPA is the most appropriate to act as Lead DPA.

[44] See for a first press release Working Party 29 on 2 October 2008. At present, the following countries have joined the Mutual Recognition Procedure: Austria, Belgium, Bulgaria, Cyprus, Czech Republic, France, Germany, Iceland, Ireland, Italy, Latvia, Liechtenstein, Luxembourg, Malta, the Netherlands, Norway, Slovak Republic, Spain, and the United Kingdom. Some DPAs (like the Danish DPA) have not officially adhered to the MRP, but in practice automatically approve applications for BCR that have been approved in the MRP.

[45] This is according to informal information provided by the Dutch DPA. At present, the experience in practice is that these timelines are not observed by the Co-Leads.

the multinational and possible changes to the BCR. The so-finalized BCR will then have to be formally adopted by the ultimate parent of the multinational. After having been formally adopted by the multinational, the BCR will be submitted for formal approval by the Lead DPA. Upon formal approval by the Lead DPA, the BCR will automatically be recognized by the other DPAs that are part of the MRP. For those Member States that are not part of the MRP and in respect of which the multinational therefore still requires an approval, the Lead DPA will initiate the CP to obtain the approval by these DPAs.

6.4.1 How to align the MRP with EU works council requirements?

Multinationals introducing BCR and starting up the MRP have to make sure that these procedures are in accordance with EU works council consultation and approval requirements. A multinational with subsidiaries in two or more Member States can be obliged to set up a European works council (*EWC*).[46] The rights of the EWC are generally limited to information and consultation with regard to matters with an EU dimension which are of common interest to the entire group, or to at least two group companies in different Member States. As a rule of thumb, adoption of BCR is a matter that falls within the scope of the rights of the EWC. The EWC—if established—must therefore be informed of and consulted on this matter.

Multinationals with establishments in the EU will further have to comply with specific works council requirements in the Member States in which they have establishments.[47] In some Member States they will be obliged to set up a national works council (*WC*) and (if more group companies are established in a Member State) also a central works council (*CWC*). Matters which are of common interest to the majority of the group companies in a Member State will be dealt with by the CWC (in most Member States to the detriment of the rights of the WC). The specific rights to which a national WC/CWC is entitled must, however, be determined on the basis of national legislation. As a rule of thumb, the intended decision to introduce BCR requires in most Member States at least the prior information and consultation of the WC/CWC and in some Member States, their prior consent.[48] Further, the actual decision to adopt BCR can also require the consent of the WC/CWC. The rights of the WC/CWC apply next to those of the EWC (unless explicitly agreed otherwise).

Multinationals have to ensure that they comply with the works council requirements as part of the MRP. This will mostly entail that as soon as a company decides to embark on a BCR project (ie before a DPA is contacted to act as Lead DPA), the local WC/CWC in each Member State and the EWC should be informally consulted. For that purpose, the company has to inform the EWC/WC/CWC:

46 Pursuant to Directive 1994/45/EC of 22 September 1994.

47 As a result of Directive 2002/14/EC of 11 March 2002.

48 See eg Art 27 para 1 under k Dutch Works Councils Act.

(i) that draft BCR are being drawn up;
(ii) that the draft BCR will be drawn up in consultation with the Lead DPA;
(iii) that the local WC/CWC will be consulted when the draft BCR has the *informal* approval of the Lead DPA; and
(iv) of the time frame in which all the above will take place.

Once the Lead DPA has given its *informal* approval, the formal consent procedure or advisory proceedings (depending on the applicable national rules) with the WC/CWC are instituted. As the EWC has already been consulted, it is sufficient to inform the EWC of the final result.

To enable a multinational submitting BCR to the MRP to meet these works council requirements, the most logical sequence of steps in the consultation phase is as follows:[49]

(i) the multinational submits its draft BCR for review and informal approval by the Lead DPA;
(ii) after the informal approval from the Lead DPA is obtained, the company institutes the formal works council consent or advisory proceedings (this depending on the applicable national rules);
(iii) when the consent of the works council is obtained (or the works council consultation procedure is completed), the company formally adopts the BCR (which in most cases takes adoption of the BCR by the board of management of the parent company of the multinational); and
(iv) the company submits the adopted BCR for formal approval by the Lead DPA.

The sequence above is the most opportune for various reasons. Formal approval by the Lead DPA will only be given by the Lead DPA for BCR that have been formally adopted by the company (to avoid the risk that the MRP has to be reopened in case of changes). The company in its turn will only formally adopt BCR after it has obtained the comfort of the Lead DPA that what it adopts will be acceptable to the Lead DPA (ie after informal approval is obtained).[50]

Further, the company can only formally approve BCR after it has obtained the approval by the works council (or after the consultation process has been completed). In any event the company will want to avoid that the works council is consulted about BCR that may not be acceptable to the Lead DPA. The reason for this is that multinationals in most cases have establishments in a large number of Member States. The (coordination of) the formal works council consent and consultation procedures involves as many countries

[49] These are the steps agreed with the Dutch DPA if it acts as Lead DPA in a BCR approval process.

[50] Another practical issue is that the board of management of the parent company of a large multinational may have a very strict policy as to which topics may be discussed at board level, and at which frequency. If a policy is submitted for approval and is approved, such policy may not be resubmitted for approval until the next round of discussion of the relevant topic is scheduled. These boards have so many topics to discuss and policies to adopt that repeated submission is not an option.

and may take many months. Any changes to BCR will yet have to be resubmitted to the works council procedures, which would lead to unnecessary delays. Another reason is that the works council in its turn in practice heavily relies on the informal confirmation by the Lead DPA, that the BCR in question indeed provide for an adequate level of protection (and thus meet the criteria of Article 26(2) Directive).

6.5 Shortcomings of the BCR Approval Procedure

Though the present system of the MRP (possibly supplemented by the CP) is obviously a substantial improvement as compared to just the CP, the situation is still unnecessarily cumbersome and requires further streamlining. It is unworkable in practice that, despite the position of the Working Party 29 on BCR, some DPAs still refuse to authorize BCR or apply other limitations.[51] This is possible because the WP Opinions of the Working Party are not binding[52] and BCR are not recognized as an alternative tool for data transfers in the Directive or any other form of binding EU regulation or decision. As a consequence the Member States have discretion whether to accept BCR as an adequate tool or not. Apparently the Working Party 29 has not been able to convince all DPAs of the usefulness of BCR as an alternative tool for data transfers[53] or of the advantages of joining the MRP (at present 19 out of 26 Member States have joined). Other unnecessary obstacles in the BCR approval procedure are the

[51] At the moment, Hungary, Estonia, the Slovak Republic, and Romania still refuse to recognize BCR as a valid basis for transfers. In Estonia the DPA announced an intention to issue data transfer guidelines in the autumn of 2011, which were expected to be more favourable for BCR. However, other than the statement that the EU Standard Contractual Clauses are not the only means to achieve 'adequate safeguards' no reference is made to BCR in the transfer guidelines, see the site of the Estonian DPA at <http://www.aki.ee/eng/?part=html&id=103>. Portugal refuses to become part of the MRP as 'it is unable to rely on a decision determining data protection adequacy by another EU DPA' and has further stated that 'unilateral declarations are not valid for international data transfers'. A contract, in the form of an intra-group agreement, would still be necessary between group companies to facilitate any international data transfers to third countries which do not meet European data protection adequacy standards. Such agreements must be notified to the Portuguese DPA (see *Privacy Laws & Business Newsletter* 2 December 2010, at 1 and 3). Another limitation is that certain Member States consider BCR to authorize specific existing transfers, but not future transfers.

[52] See Chapter 2, n 29.

[53] The Working Party 29 itself is also of the opinion that this approval procedure requires streamlining. See WP Opinion on the principle of accountability (Chapter 1, n 23), at para 5, where in the context of BCR it is explicitly mentioned that 'it is also relevant to discuss the mechanisms to streamline the current system based on authorisations of data transfers by national authorities'. Also the Rand Report (Chapter 2, n 27) identifies one of the main weaknesses of the Directive (see at 26 and 35) as being that 'the length of time and effort to get [. . .] Binding Corporate Rules approved is excessive. Uneven practices of approval and authorisation; too little coordination between the Member States'. It recommends (see Recommendation 2, at 43) that the use of alternatives to the adequacy rule (such as BCR), should be facilitated as a priority in any Member State. See also the ICC Report on BCR (Chapter 5, n 20), at 12; Wugmeister, Retzer, Rich (Chapter 3, n 148), at 481; and EDPS Opinion on the revision of the Directive (Chapter 2, n 35), at para 8.4.

many additional national requirements imposed by the various Member States (which apply on top of the requirements set by the Working Party 29). These additional national requirements are very diverse (and sometimes even highly unusual) in nature and seriously undermine the benefits for multinationals of adopting BCR in the first place.[54] No comprehensive overview of such national requirements is available for multinationals,[55] which in practice leads to much unnecessary delay in identifying and completing all national formalities. Though in practice the Working Party 29 has made efforts to put pressure on individual DPAs to eliminate such additional national requirements, the Working Party 29 is not able to enforce this in any way.

Separate discussion requires the position of some DPAs that multinationals that have BCR in place, still have to put in place intra-group data processor agreements if certain group companies process data on behalf of others. This seems to be mistaken. If group companies process data on behalf of other group companies, in respect of those processing operations there is always a controller within the group of companies. In other words, the BCR will always apply to the relevant data processing and all group companies (whether in their capacity of controller or processor) will have to abide by the BCR. Intra-company data processor agreements will not add anything to these obligations, as these obligations are already embodied in the BCR (which have to be both internally and externally binding to be eligible for authorization). The conclusion is that multinationals having BCR are no longer required to put intra-group data processor agreements in place as these obligations are covered by the BCR. It would be helpful if the Working Party 29 could confirm this in one of its Opinions, or, if it does not agree, indicate which additional data processor provisions should be included in BCR to ensure that the mandatory data processor provisions are met for intra-group data processor activities.

[54] National requirements vary: most Member States (except Ireland, United Kingdom, Norway, and Slovenia) require that on top of the MRP/CO procedure, an individual authorization with the relevant DPA is obtained by the national legal entity (or entities) that transfer data from the relevant Member State; local translation requirements apply in Austria, Belgium, Czeck Republic, France, Poland, Spain, Lithuania, Italy, Greece, Luxembourg, Sweden, and some federal states of Germany; Belgium still requires incorporation of the BCR in a Royal Decree signed by the King, though the procedure to issue the Decree has recently been simplified; Germany requires review of the BCR both by the Berlin DPA and the federal state where the main processing takes place, and other federal states (most notably Hamburg and Niedersachsen) require that, in addition to the BCR, EU Standard Contractual Clauses and (in case the importer of data is a data processor) data processor agreements must be entered into for data transfers from that state, while the wish to avoid entering into such model contracts and data processor agreements was the reason why multinationals adopted BCR in the first place! See further examples given in n 51.

[55] In April 2011, the Working Party 29 published a table with an overview of the national filing requirements for authorization of transfers on the basis of BCR: <http://ec.europa.eu/justice/policies/privacy/docs/binding-rules/table_national_administrative_requirements_14_04_11_en.pdf>, but this overview is not complete and in many instances incorrect.

6.6 How to Address Shortcomings in the BCR Regime and the BCR Approval Procedure?

Below I will discuss the main shortcomings of the BCR regime and in particular the MRP and make proposals for improvement to European legislators. At the end of each paragraph, I have inserted additional text and footnotes to reflect to what extent my proposals are incorporated by the Commission in the Proposed Regulation.

6.6.1 Recognize BCR, define main BCR requirements, and impose the Mutual Recognition Procedure

European legislators would be well advised to address the shortcomings of the BCR approval procedure in the upcoming revision of the Directive by (i) recognizing BCR in the revised Directive as an appropriate tool to provide adequate safeguards, including defining the main substantive requirements and (ii) defining and imposing the MRP on all Member States. This would fit in with Article 27 Directive that encourages self- and co-regulatory approaches to data protection through codes of conduct. This is also the recommendation in the First Report on the Directive of the Commission,[56] in line with the recommendations in the Rand Report,[57] the advice of the Working Party 29 itself in its WP Contribution on the Future of Privacy,[58] and the EDPS in its Opinion on revision of the Directive.[59] The Commission in its recent communication on the revised Directive of

[56] See First Report on the Directive (Chapter 2, n 26), at 18.

[57] See Rand Report (Chapter 2, n 27), at 42, where it is recommended to 'ensure that BCR can be more easily used to ensure the legitimacy of personal data transfers to third countries. This could be achieved by formalizing the measures currently being developed by certain supervisory bodies, with associated guidance as to their common understanding, and should be designed so as to maximize common acceptability across Member States. Care should be taken to maintain incentives for the private sector. The current attempts to introduce a system of mutual recognition between Member States are partly successful but run into problems, notably because some of the national transpositions have not included a sufficient legal basis for adopting such a system. Member States should be persuaded to amend their national personal data protection law accordingly to allow such systems to operate in practice'.

[58] See WP Contribution on The Future of Privacy (Chapter 1, n 6), at para 38, where it recommends including a provision on BCR in the new legal framework to serve the following purposes:

- Recognising BCR as [an] appropriate tool to provide adequate safeguards;
- Defining the main substantive and procedural elements of BCR, following the WP29 Opinions on the subject.

Noteworthy here is that the Working Party (apparently) is not even sure that BCR can indeed be a tool for the transfer of data to non-adequate countries under Art 26(2) Directive. See WP Opinion on the principle of accountability (Chapter 1, n 23), at para 56.

[59] EDPS Opinion on the revision of the Directive (Chapter 2, n 35), at para 127:

> The EDPS recommends addressing conditions for BCR in an explicit way in the new legal instrument, by:
>
> - 'recognizing explicitly BCR as tools that provide adequate safeguards;
> - providing for the main elements/conditions for the adoption of BCR;

November 2010 announced that it will indeed 'improve and streamline the current procedures for international data transfers, including (...) Binding Corporate Rules'.[60] When revising the MRP, EU legislators are well advised to take into account the fact that at present, the Lead DPAs already lack the resources to process the current number of BCR applications causing a backlog of BCR applications.[61] Though in absolute terms the number of BCR applications is very small, considering BCR applications is time-consuming and the BCR applications are concentrated within a very limited number of Lead DPAs.[62] If the uptake of BCR increases, staffing of BCR applications for such DPAs will become even more problematic, if not impossible.[63] A simple streamlining of the MRP will therefore not be sufficient. One solution is that DPAs could appoint third-party certifying agencies to certify BCR on their behalf.[64] A more radical solution recently suggested by the Centre for Information Policy Leadership is to have multinationals self-certify their BCR.[65] This recommendation is in line with the general empirical

- setting forth cooperation procedures for the adoption of BCR, including criteria for the selection of a leading supervisory authority (one stop shop).'

60 EC Communication on the revision of the Directive (Chapter 2, n 34), at 16; Viviane Reding (Chapter 2, n 35), at 3–5.

61 This is based on my experience as a practitioner. The BCR applications are concentrated up until this point with five Lead DPAs (see n 36), where a backlog of BCR applications has already accrued. Those authorities are limited in expanding their resources. See also Centre for Information Policy Leadership, 'A New Approach to International Transfers in Response to the European Commission's Communication on "A comprehensive approach to personal data protection"' (January 2011), to be found at <http://www.huntonfiles.com> (*CIPL New Approach to International Transfers*), at 4.

62 The DPAs of the UK, Germany, France, and the Netherlands.

63 CIPL New Approach to International Transfers (n 61) at 4: 'A 2003 Yale study conservatively estimates that there are some 63.000 multinational corporations, with 821,000 subsidiaries. They directly employ 90 million people and produce 25 per cent of the world's gross product. It can be asserted with confidence that every single multinational corporation now transfers personal data internationally. Beyond that, there are countless SMEs and other organisations which are not multinationals, but which are nevertheless involved daily in international transfers of personal data, often of highly sensitive nature. In short, it is inconceivable that the BCR approach—without improvement—could meet the potential underlying demand.'

64 This in line with the intention of the Commission to explore the creation of EU certification schemes for privacy compliant products and services. See EC Communication on revision of the Directive (Chapter 2, n 34), para 2.2.5 at 12. The EDPS supports this and suggests including a provision in the revised Directive 'providing for their creation and possible effect across the EU'. See EDPS Opinion on the revision of the Directive (Chapter 2, n 35), at para 7.4. See on the possibility of introducing certification schemes also WP Contribution on the Future of Privacy (Chapter 1, n 6), at para 58 at 15; The Stockholm Program (Chapter 4, n 14), at para 3.5 at 11; and the Rand Report (Chapter 2, n 27), at 53, also lists certification as one of the possible tools to implement data protection principles: 'Standards provide additional support for accountability, by permitting a regular review of whether those that have agreed to abide by certain rules do so. This is only possible, however, if organisations become compliant (i.e. get certified) against a standard, rather than merely implementing the best practice.'

65 The New Approach to International Transfers on (n 61), at 7: 'Organisations would self-certify their own Code without the need for prior DPA approval, which is simply not practicable with the scale of the challenge' and 'if self-certification is considered too radical, there are other options for the initial adoption or approval of a Binding Global Code to ensure that minimum requirements are in fact met. These include certification by an independent Third Party (Accountability Agent) appointed by a DPA at the expense of the business or certification by a Third Party approved by the DPA'. The suggestion of self-certification or, if this is not acceptable, certification by a DPA, has also been suggested by Wugmeister, Retzer, Rich (Chapter 3, n 147), at 485.

and theoretical public policy literature, which suggests that the long-term attention that 'regulating self-regulation' requires is too costly and difficult to maintain if regulators do not 'prompt organisations' rigorous self-evaluation and investment in the search for appropriate solutions to regulatory problems'.[66]

Proposed Regulation The Proposed Regulation indeed clarifies that BCR are an appropriate tool to adduce 'appropriate safeguards'. By choosing the form of an EU regulation (instead of a directive) which is directly applicable in all Member States, BCR will be available as a tool for data transfers in all Member States, without further national authorization. What is new is that BCR for processors will become possible. The data transfer rules under the Proposed Regulation also apply directly to data processors,[67] and appropriate safeguards can be provided by BCR for both controllers and processors.[68] The Proposed Regulation further (quite comprehensively) codifies the current BCR regime set by the Working Party 29.[69] Changes

[66] Sharon Gilad, 'It runs in the family: meta-regulation and its siblings' (2010) *Regulation & Governance* 4, at 502.

[67] See Art 40 Proposed Regulation.

[68] See Arts 42(1) and (2) and 43(1)(a) and (3) Proposed Regulation. This was still under discussion at the time of writing. See para 6.3.3

[69] See the Explanatory Memorandum to the Proposed Regulation, Chapter 1, n 9, at 12. See for the BCR requirements Art 43 Proposed Regulation:

1. A supervisory authority shall in accordance with the consistency mechanism set out in Article 58 approve binding corporate rules, provided that they
   - (a) are legally binding and apply to and are enforced by every member within the controller's or processor's group of undertakings, and include their employees;
   - (b) expressly confer enforceable rights on data subjects;
   - (c) fulfil the requirements laid down in paragraph 2.
2. The binding corporate rules shall at least specify:
   - (a) the structure and contact details of the group of undertakings and its members;
   - (b) the data transfers or set of transfers, including the categories of personal data, the type of processing and its purposes, the type of data subjects affected and the identification of the third country or countries in question;
   - (c) their legally binding nature, both internally and externally;
   - (d) the general data protection principles, in particular purpose limitation, data quality, legal basis for the processing, processing of sensitive personal data; measures to ensure data security; and the requirements for onward transfers to organisations which are not bound by the policies;
   - (e) the rights of data subjects and the means to exercise these rights, including the right not to be subject to a measure based on profiling in accordance with Article 20, the right to lodge a complaint before the competent supervisory authority and before the competent courts of the Member States in accordance with Article 75, and to obtain redress and, where appropriate, compensation for a breach of the binding corporate rules;
   - (f) the acceptance by the controller or processor established on the territory of a Member State of liability for any breaches of the binding corporate rules by any member of the group of undertakings not established in the Union; the controller or the processor may only be exempted from this liability, in whole or in part, if he proves that that member is not responsible for the event giving rise to the damage;
   - (g) how the information on the binding corporate rules, in particular on the provisions referred to in points (d), (e) and (f) of this paragraph is provided to the data subjects in accordance with Article 11;
   - (h) the tasks of the data protection officer designated in accordance with Article 35, including monitoring within the group of undertakings the compliance with the binding corporate rules, as well as monitoring the training and complaint handling;

seem to be limited to reflect other changes brought by the Proposed Regulation. An example is that it is no longer a BCR requirement that if the headquarters of the multinational are not established within the EU, the multinational should appoint an EU group company to have delegated data protection responsibilities (see BCR requirement (i)). The reason is that the Proposed Regulation provides for the country of origin principle for jurisdiction, which entails that if a multinational is established within more than one Member State, the DPA of the main establishment of the multinational shall have competence for the supervision of the processing activities of the multinational in all Member States. In other words, the multinational will no longer have to appoint the group company with delegated responsibility, as the responsible group company is already defined by the Proposed Regulation. Further, by having one lead supervising DPA only, the MRP procedure has in fact become superfluous. Authorization will be the task of the DPA of the main establishment of the multinational. To ensure that the DPAs are aligned when one of them acts as the Lead DPA, the Proposed Regulation introduces the so-called consistency mechanism.[70] The consistency mechanism is a procedure to ensure the unity of application of the Regulation (inter alia) in respect of authorizations of BCR.[71] Pursuant to the consistency mechanism the Lead DPA is required to submit its draft approval of BCR for opinion to (the successor of the Working Party 29) the European Data Protection Board (*EDPB*). If the Lead DPA, after having received the opinion of the EDPB, intends to maintain its draft authorization, it will have to inform the EDPB thereof, after which the Commission may also issue an opinion.[72] If the lead DPA, after having received the opinion of the Commission, still maintains its draft BCR authorization, the Commission may adopt a reasoned decision requiring the DPA to suspend the adoption of the draft measure.[73] I note that by introducing the consistency mechanism, BCR will no longer have to be reviewed by the Co-Leads, which will reduce the workload of the DPAs. Instead the workload of the EDPB will increase substantially. Though the Proposed Regulation introduces the possibility of establishment of data protection certification mechanisms,[74] these seem to be intended only to allow individuals to verify for instance compliance of companies with their BCR rather than to replace BCR authorizations themselves.

(i) the mechanisms within the group of undertakings aiming at ensuring the verification of compliance with the binding corporate rules.
(j) the mechanisms for reporting and recording changes to the policies and reporting these changes to the supervisory authority;
(k) the co-operation mechanism with the supervisory authority to ensure compliance by any member of the group of undertakings, in particular by making available to the supervisory authority the results of the verifications of the measures referred to in point (i) of this paragraph.

[70] Article 57–63 Proposed Regulation. See for the draft decisions to be submitted to the EDPB Chapter 3, para 3.1.8.

[71] Article 58(2)(f) Proposed Regulation.

[72] Article 59(1) Proposed Regulation.

[73] Article 60(1) Proposed Regulation.

[74] Article 39 Proposed Regulation.

6.6.2 Define BCR requirements in general principles

The recommendation that the revised Directive should 'define the main substantive requirements' for BCR does not imply that these should be defined in detail. In order for the revised Directive to remain 'future proof', the norm-setting in the revised Directive should be in general terms only: eg BCR should provide for an adequate level of protection, should provide for internal complaints procedures, etc. Detailed norm-setting can and should be delegated to the Commission in accordance with recently introduced Articles 290[75] and 291 TFEU[76] in order to ensure that the relevant norms remain more adaptable to changing circumstances and insights.[77] This is not a new insight, but has also been the trend in other areas of law, like company and financial markets law.[78] In the words of the High Level Group of Company Law Experts in its 2002 Report on a Modern Regulatory Framework for Company Law in Europe:[79]

> We noted that the system of harmonising company law through Directives – that have to be implemented by Member states – may have led to a certain 'petrifaction'. Once Member States have agreed to an approach in an area of company law and have implemented a Directive accordingly, it becomes very hard to change the Directive and the underlying approach. Simultaneously however, there is a growing need to continuously adapt existing rules in view of rapidly changing circumstances and views. The 'shelf life' of law tends to become more limited as society changes more rapidly, and company law is no exception. Fixed rules in primary legislation may offer the benefits of certainty, democratic legitimacy and usually strong possibilities of enforcement. But this comes at a cost of little or no flexibility, and disability of keeping pace with changing circumstances. EU Directives are in practice even more inflexible than primary legislation. We can see a movement in Member States to use alternatives for primary legislation by government and parliament, which allow for greater flexibility. Such alternatives include:
>
> Secondary regulation by the government, based on primary legislation in which broad objectives and principles are laid down; the secondary regulation can be amended more quickly when circumstances require change. (This process also often enables more effective consultation and reflection of an expert consensus).

[75] Article 290(1) TFEU provides that EU legislative acts may 'delegate to the Commission the power to adopt non-legislative acts of general application to supplement or amend certain non-essential elements of the legislative act' (ie 'delegated acts').

[76] Article 291(2) TFEU provides that EU legislative acts may 'confer implementing powers on the Commission', 'where uniform conditions for implementing legally binding Union acts are needed' (ie 'implementing acts').

[77] The EDPS in its Opinion on the revision of the Directive (Chapter 2, n 35), at paras 106 and 114, recommends to delegate specific tasks to the Commission in order to supplement the basic criteria on for instance accountability, privacy by design, etc.

[78] A striking example of the trend to move from detailed rules to principle-based standards is the switch by the SEC from the highly detailed U.S. accounting standards (GAAP) to the principle-based IFRS, see in more detail Chapter 4, n 34.

[79] The Report of the High Level Group of Company Law Experts on a Modern Regulatory Framework for Company Law in Europe, Brussels, 4 November 2002 (Chapter 4, n 31), at para 2.

Proposed Regulation The Proposed Regulation provides for a quite literal codification of the BCR requirements as defined by the Working Party 29 (see paragraph 6.2). My earlier comments that some of these requirements are too detailed, therefore also apply to the requirements in the Proposed Regulation (see again paragraph 6.2, where I inserted my comments in the footnotes). The Proposed Regulation does, however, delegate to the Commission the power to adopt detailed norms for BCR in the form of delegated acts in accordance with Article 290 TFEU.[80]

6.6.3 Adequate level of protection

When setting the main substantive requirements for BCR, European legislators should also provide that the BCR should ensure an adequate level of protection (only) rather than a level equivalent to that of the Directive. The Rand Report[81] rightly observes that the present: 'pass-porting of the BCR is regarded as counter productive, since the regulators review them more stringently than SCCs [Standard Contractual Clauses] because, if approved, they will be valid in several countries.' This has also been the experience of multinationals in the BCR approval procedures. Also, more generally, the experience is that whenever self-regulation is attempted and submitted for review to DPAs, this leads to an 'enhancement rather than a substitute means of making data protection legislative requirements more effective and legitimate'.[82] The criteria for review of BCR became yet even stricter the moment the DPAs agreed on the MRP, when instead of review by the Lead DPA the two Co-Leads were added to the review process.[83] By insisting on an equivalent level of protection and sometimes even superseding protection,[84] rather than an adequate level, the baby is thrown out with the bathwater. Multinationals, when applying for BCR, experience this as being punished rather than being encouraged to embark on a BCR implementation and authorization project, which may be an explanation for the current low uptake of BCR.[85] This seems a disadvantage to all concerned, including the EU citizens the Working Party 29 and DPAs try so hard to protect. In this borderless world only global solutions will truly result in an increase in compliance and privacy protection for everyone

80 Articles 43(3) and 86 Proposed Regulation.

81 Rand Report (Chapter 2, n 27), at para 3.3.4.

82 See in respect of privacy policies in the area of electronic communications, where the conclusion was that the low uptake was possibly due to a perception that they are an 'enhancement rather than a substitute means of making data protection legislative requirements more effective and legitimate'. See reference in the Rand Report (Chapter 2, n 27), at 10 to the Report of WIK-Consult and Rand Europe: Comparison of Privacy and Trust policies in the Area of Electronic Communications—Final Report, European Commission 2007, at 10, to be found at <http://www.ec.europa.eu>.

83 This is based on my experience assisting multinationals in their BCR applications.

84 In n 27 and n 28 some examples are given of where DPAs have been trying to obtain rights and remedies or additional protection for data subjects via BCR that DPAs and data subjects do not have under their national laws. This may seem a good result in the short term, but is counterproductive in the long.

85 See n 82.

concerned.[86] If European legislators wish to increase the current low uptake of BCR, the advice is to set the requirement for BCR at an adequate level rather than accumulating all national requirements.[87] It seems that the Commission is aware of the fact that at present it is insufficiently clear what the required level for protection is when data are transferred outside of the EU. In its EC Communication on the revision of the Directive, it announced that it will examine how to improve the current data transfer regime by examining how 'to clarify the Commission's adequacy procedure and better specify the criteria and requirements for assessing the level of data protection in a third country or an international organisation' as well as 'to define core EU data protection elements, which could be used for all types of international agreements'.[88]

Proposed Regulation The Proposed Regulation indeed sets out some high-level criteria to be taken into account by the Commission for the assessment of the adequacy of the level of data protection.[89] These, however, do not provide guidance for BCR requirements. Further, the Proposed Regulation does not provide for 'core EU data protection elements' which could be used for all types of international agreements, and also these can therefore not provide guidance for BCR.

6.6.4 Harmonize the powers of DPAs

It is in any event advisable to harmonize the enforcement powers of the DPAs at the right level. At present certain DPAs lack certain enforcement rights which they try to obtain via the BCR regime.[90] If the enforcement regime were properly harmonized at the right level, this would no longer be necessary. As equal enforcement powers do not also guarantee a harmonized enforcement strategy, I further recommend developing a common enforcement strategy for the Lead DPAs to ensure a common approach. These recommendations in respect of enforcement are in line with the recommendations of the Rand Report, the Working Party 29, the EDPS, and the Commission itself.[91]

[86] Wugmeister, Retzer, Rich (Chapter 3, n 148), at 497: 'Once a practical global solution is developed, compliance will increase, thus increasing privacy protection for everyone concerned, and greater economic benefits will flow to the countries that permit businesses to utilize a global solution for their cross-border data transfers.'

[87] The Opinion on the Communication of the Commission on the revision of the Directive (Chapter 2, n 27), at 3 states: 'Harmonisation must be based on common principles and objectives, avoiding both highest and lowest common denominators. Harmonising regulatory approaches, including robust education programmes, is as important as the substance of the law itself.'

[88] EC Communication on the revision of the Directive (Chapter 2, n 34), at 16.

[89] The high-level criteria for the Commission's assessment of an adequate or not adequate level of protection include the rule of law, judicial redress, independent supervision, and international commitments made, see Art 41(2) Proposed Regulation.

[90] See examples in n 27 and n 28.

[91] See the Rand Report (Chapter 2, n 27), at x and xiv and 57–8. See in particular at 44: '*Recommendation 4: Develop common enforcement strategies*. The London Initiative of DPAs should develop a common enforcement strategy for independent supervisory authorities, crystallised in an instrument such as a non-binding Memorandum of Understanding. This should be published and endorsed by the EDPS so that the standards used to judge the regulated are clear. This strategy should take into account legal and cultural traditions and contexts across the Member States and use these

Proposed Regulation The Proposed Regulation indeed provides for the required harmonization of powers of DPAs at the right level. Further the Proposed Regulation provides for extensive provisions on mutual assistance and cooperation. For a discussion of the powers of the DPAs and mutual assistance, see Chapter 3, paragraph 3.1.7.

6.6.5 Replace Directive by an EU regulation

Given the fact that many of the obstacles in the MRP and CP are caused by differences between the various national implementation laws in the Member States and differences in enforcement powers of the DPAs,[92] I recommend that, rather than trying to ensure a proper implementation of the Directive and further harmonize certain requirements, European legislators choose the form of an EU regulation[93] as a legislative instrument rather than an EU directive to regulate data protection. This is also the recommendation of the EDPS.[94] As EU regulations are directly applicable in all Member States, and do not require further implementation in national legislation (which always leads to variations in the implementation provisions), uniformity between the laws of the Member States will be ensured to a much greater extent.[95] Also if the form of an EU regulation is chosen, I recommend

differences to its advantage.' See also the WP Contribution on the Future of Privacy (Chapter 1, n 6), at para 7 at 22, where the Working Party 29 advises the Commission to strengthen and clarify the roles of DPAs and their cooperation within the EU. The Commission announced in its Communication on the revision of the Directive (Chapter 2, n 34), at para 2.5 to examine how to 'strengthen, clarify and harmonise the status and the powers of the national Data Protection Authorities and ways to improve the cooperation and coordination between DPAs'. This is also the opinion of the EDPS, see the EDPS Opinion on the revision of the Directive (Chapter 2, n 35), at paras 59 and 140. See further the Declaration of Civil Society Organizations, adopted on 25 September in Montreal, stating that 'stronger and more aggressive action by privacy commissioners is required', finding them uniquely positioned to defend our society's core values and rights of privacy, to be found at <http://www.privacyconference2007.gc.ca/Terra_Incognita_resolutions_ngo_E.html>

[92] It is generally acknowledged that the main shortcoming of the Directive is that the level of harmonization under the current framework is unsatisfactory, see Chapter 2, n 68 and see further n 91 and n 94.

[93] Article 288 TFEU defines a regulation as follows: 'A regulation shall have general application. It shall be binding in its entirety and directly applicable in all Member States.' Whereas 'A directive shall be binding, as to the result to be achieved, upon each Member State to which it is addressed, but shall leave to the national authorities the choice of form and methods'.

[94] EDPS Opinion on the revision of the Directive (Chapter 2, n 35) at para 5.5: 'A Regulation would reduce room for contradictory interpretations and for unjustified differences in the implementation and the application of the law. It would also reduce the importance of determining the law applicable to processing operations within the EU, which is one of the most controversial aspects of the present system.' See further at Chapter 8, para 8.5.

[95] European legislators are free to choose the relevant legislative instrument when implementing the right to data protection under Art 16 TFEU. The TFEU prescribes in a number of cases whether European legislators should act by means of a regulation or directive. However, in numerous other cases, including in respect of the implementation of Art 16 TFEU, the relevant article does not specify a particular kind of secondary law to be used, but uses a neutral wording such as 'rules', 'measures', etc. In those cases European legislators are free to choose the appropriate Community instrument (ie directive, regulation, or decision), provided the principle of proportionality is observed. See Art 296 TFEU: 'Where the Treaties do not specify the type of act to be adopted, the institutions shall select it

that detailed norm-setting can and should be delegated to the Commission in accordance with recently introduced Articles 290 and 291 TFEU.[96]

Proposed Regulation The Commission has indeed chosen the form of an EU regulation as a legislative instrument rather than an EU directive to regulate data protection and further delegates to the Commission the power to adopt specific delegated and implementing acts in accordance with Articles 290 and 291 TFEU.[97]

6.6.6 Role of the Working Party 29

As European legislators (with delegation to the Commission) will not be able to specify all BCR requirements in full detail, the Working Party 29 will continue to play an important role in *providing guidelines* in respect of these requirements. The (informal or de facto) delegation of norm-setting in respect of BCR to the Working Party 29 (as has been the case to date) seems contrary to the new rules on delegation, which are limited to delegation to the Commission only.[98] The Working Party 29 seems to realize this where it, rather than suggesting that its opinions become binding, suggests that the Commission insists 'on a strong commitment by the members of the Working Party 29 to implement the views of the Working Party 29 into national practice'.[99] Also, the EDPS proposes to 'make the opinions more authoritative' by including an obligation for the DPAs and the Commission 'to take utmost account of opinions'.[100] The EDPS puts a caveat against introducing stronger measures, such as giving binding force to Working Party 29 positions, as this 'would have consequences as for instance

on a case-by-case basis, in compliance with the applicable procedures and with the principle of proportionality.' See also: Bruno de Witte, 'Legal Instruments and Law-Making in the Lisbon Treaty', in Stefan Griller and Jacques Ziller (eds.), *The Lisbon Treaty: EU Constitutionalism without a Constitutional Treaty?* (Springer 2008), at 96 and 97; Jacques Ziller, 'Constitutional Boundaries of Self-Regulation', in Fabrizio Cafaggi (ed.), *Reframing Self-Regulation in European Private Law* (Kluwer Law International 2006), at 157. Kuner (Chapter 2, n 63), at 44, points out that 'so far no data protection instruments of direct relevance to business have been implemented by way of regulation, but this may change in the future'.

96 See n 75 and n 76.

97 See Art 86 Proposed Regulation for a comprehensive overview of all powers of the Commission to adopt delegated acts. See Art 62 Proposed Regulation for a number of the powers of the Commission to adopt implementing acts and further many specific provisions in the Proposed Regulation.

98 See n 75 and n 76.

99 WP Contribution on The Future of Privacy (Chapter 1, n 6), para 99. See also Wugmeister, Retzer and Rich (Chapter 3, n 148), at 492.

100 EDPS opinion on the revision of the Directive (Chapter 2, n 35), at 146: 'The EDPS recomends solutions which would make opinions of the Working Party more authoritative without modifying substantially its way of functioning. The EDPS suggests including an obligation for the DPAs and the Commission to take utmost account of opinions and common positions adopted by the Working Party, based on the model adopted for the positions of the Body of European Regulators for Electronic Communications (BEREC). Furthermore, the new legal instrument could give the Working Party the explicit task to adopt 'interpretative recommendations.' These alternative solutions would give the positions of the Working Party a stronger role, also before the courts. For the position of the BEREC: Regulation (EC) No 1211/2009 of the European Parliament and of the Council of 25 November 2009 establishing the Body of European Regulators for Electronic Communications (BEREC) and the Office, OJ L337, 9 18.12.200, p 1.

transparency and redress requirements'.[101] Given the fact that (as is now also already the case) the intention of both the Working Party 29 and the EDPS is that the opinions will be more than just guidelines, but policy rules de facto setting norms for DPAs and controllers, the conclusion should rather be that 'legitimacy' requirements like transparency and redress should already also apply to such de facto norm-setting. This issue is discussed in Chapter 10, in particular paragraph 10.7.3.

As to the enforcement function of the Working Party 29, the Working Party 29 at present coordinates and facilitates cross-border enforcement actions, but has no enforcement powers itself. It may be clear that increasingly more cases require coordination of enforcement on a cross-border basis. Illustrative examples are the fact that at present the Working Party 29 already fills a coordinating role in respect of enforcement of the national data protection laws of the Member States against a number of (inherently cross-border) ad network providers, browser providers, search engine operators, and social networking site providers.[102] The EDPS also signals the fact that such coordination on an EU-wide basis will be indicated more and more, but does not propose to solve this by granting the Working Party 29 decision-making and enforcement powers[103] (as the EDPS itself has in respect of data protection compliance of the EU institutions[104]). Given the fact that cross-border data protection violations will increasingly be the rule rather than the exception, it is worth considering whether central enforcement should be considered by creating a pan-European DPA that will take over some of the powers and responsibilities of the national DPAs, similar to that which is presently agreed in

101 EDPS Opinion on the revision of the Directive (Chapter 2, n 35), at para 151: 'The EDPS would put a caveat against introducing stronger measures, such as giving binding force to WP 29 positions. This would undermine the independent status of individual DPAs, which has to be guaranteed by the Member States under national law. Would the Working Party decisions have a direct impact on third parties such as data controllers, new procedures should be foreseen including safeguards such as transparency and redress, including possibly appeal before the European Court of Justice.'

102 All dating from 2010 and to be found at <http://ec.europa.eu/justice/policies/privacy/workinggroup/wpdocs/2010-others_en.htm>.

103 EDPS Opinion on the revision of the Directive (Chapter 2, n 35), at para 148–9: 'Some cases have a strategic dimension which should be addressed in a centralised way. The Article 29 Working Party facilitates coordination and enforcement actions between DPAs in major data protection issues with such international implications. This was the case with social networks and search engines, as well as with regard to coordinated inspections conducted in different Member States on telecommunication and health insurance issues. There are however limits to the enforcement actions that the Working Party can undertake under the present framework. Common positions can be taken by the Working Party, but there is no instrument to ensure that these positions are effectively implemented in practice.'

104 The EDPS itself, alongside its advisory functions, possesses extensive enforcement powers. According to the Regulation (EC) No 45/2001 of the European Parliament and of the Council of 18 December 2000 on the protection of individuals with regard to the processing of personal data by the Community institutions and bodies and on the free movement of such data, the EDPS is given powers to 'monitor and ensure' respect of data protection principles by the European bodies and institutions (Art 46(c)); keep a register of processing operations (Art 46(i)); execute prior checks of the notified processing (Art 46(j)); order the institutions' compliance with the requests to exercise data subjects' rights (Art 47(1)(c)); warn or admonish the controller (Art 47(1)(d)); ban processing (Art 47(1)(f)); refer the matter to the ECJ (Art 47(1)(h)) and intervene in the ongoing ECJ proceedings (Art 47(1)(j)). Article 47(2) gives the EDPS the right to access all information necessary to fulfil its duties and, with reasonable grounds, access to premises.

respect of the supervision of the European financial markets.[105] The same applies to the authorization and subsequent supervision and enforcement of BCR. As BCR have EU-wide application, the most logical set-up would be to task such pan-European DPA with central authorization, supervision, and enforcement of BCR. Given the number of multinationals with establishments in the EU, this may prove too much of a burden. Though from a theoretical perspective tasking a pan-European DPA with BCR approvals etc, seems optimal, I note that the Lead DPA of the EU headquarters of the multinational is in fact well-placed to authorize, supervise, and enforce. It seems more a matter to ensure that such Lead DPA applies EU norms rather than sets these and cannot be influenced by national interests. An acceptable in-between solution is reflected in the Proposed Regulation, which is discussed below. In any event it is clear that based on existing case law[106] and literature[107] many questions can be posed as to

[105] On 22 September 2010, the European Parliament voted for a new supervisory framework for financial regulations that came into force in January 2011. Part of this new framework will be the replacement of the existing financial committees with advisory powers only, by three pan-European Supervisory Authorities to which certain national powers are transferred. For an overview of the reforms, see <http://www.ec.europa.eu> under 'financial supervision.'

[106] This case law still dates from the 1950s when the ECJ first considered the question of legality of delegation to an agency in the *Meroni* cases: Case 9/56, *Meroni & Co Industrie Metallurgiche SpA v High Authority* [1958] ECR 133 and Case 10/56 *Meroni & Co Industrie Metallurgiche SAS v High Authority of the European Coal and Steel Community* [1958] ECR. The cases are based on similar facts, decisions were rendered on the same day, and the conclusions and reasoning of the ECJ largely coincide. On the facts of the cases, Meroni filed for annulment of a decision of the High Authority of the European Community of Coal and Steel (ECSC) ordering Meroni to pay a sum of money to the Imported Ferrous Scrap Equalization Fund. The Fund was a voluntary body of large steel companies that received authorization of the High Authority of ECSC to exercise powers on the common ferrous scrap market. The ECJ found the decision of the High Authority regarding Meroni null and void. To achieve this conclusion the ECJ, among others, had to examine if the authorization of the High Authority constituted delegation of powers and if such delegation was lawful. The ECJ found that delegation took place, and that such a delegation constituted a violation of the EC Treaty. However, the Court did not rule out delegation completely. The Meroni test (Case 9/56 at 151–2) is the following:

- in general, an EU institution cannot delegate more or broader powers than it has itself under the Treaty;
- within the scope of the institution's own powers, only clearly defined executive powers may be delegated to another body, whereas, discretionary powers implying a wide margin of discretion which may make possible the execution of actual economic policy, cannot be delegated;
- the delegated powers are subject to the same conditions to which the EU institutions would have been subject if they had exercised them directly, such as the obligation to state reasons, publish annual reports, and judicial control;
- the powers delegated remain subject to conditions determined by the delegating EU institution and subject to its continuing supervision; and
- the institutional balance between the EC institutions must not be distorted.

[107] On the issues relating to the legal basis for the delegation of supervisory and enforcement powers to European Supervisory Authorities, see Luc Verhey and Tom Zwart, *Agencies in European and Comparative Perspective* (Intersentia 2003); Ronald van Ooik, 'The Growing Importance of Agencies in the EU: Shifting Governance and the Institutional Balance' in D.M. Curtin and R.A. Wessel (eds.), *Good governance and the European Union: Reflections on Concepts, Institutions and Substance,* (Intersentia 2005), at 151–2). Verhey and Zwart at 130 and Ooik at 151–2, offer an alternative reading of the *Meroni* doctrine, which justifies the creation of the EU agencies with powers broader than pure managerial or technical tasks, provided that the institutional balance is respected. Van Ooik at 152, continues that as the balance 'emerged from the E(E)C Treaty itself, [t]reaty legislator itself [...] may change the institutional balance [...] by giving an explicit and clear Treaty basis to a certain body'. Alternatively,

the legal basis for such delegation of powers to an EU supervisory authority. Indeed, the position of EU and national independent regulatory authorities has been subject to academic and political debate in the Member States ever since their foundation.[108] This being said, in its 2001 White Paper on European Governance, the Commission noted that there were already 12 pan-European regulatory agencies and communicated its intent to create more of these and listed the conditions on which it considers this possible.[109] These conditions are clearly inspired by the requirements for delegation set by the ECJ in the *Meroni* cases.[110] The Commission subsequently issued an operating framework for such EU agencies[111] and in 2010 communicated its substantiation of the legal basis for setting up the new EU financial supervisory authorities and the powers of the latter to take legally binding decisions.[112] Whether the views of the

creation of effective system of supervision and control 'may mitigate objections against a far-reaching delegation of powers to independent agencies'. See further H. van Meerten and A. Ottow, 'The proposals for the European Supervisory Authorities: the right (legal) way forward?' [2010] *Tijdschrift voor Financieel Recht*, vol 1; available at SSRN: <http://ssrn.com/abstract=1517371>. Van Meerten and Ottow observe at 37, that acting under Art 291 TFEU, Member States may, by adopting a legislative act, delegate implementation to a European agency. On this, they say that 'delegating decision making power from one competent national authority to another is already recognized and embedded in EU law. If this is possible, Member States can via primary and secondary EU law certainly delegate these powers to an agency. And to be perfectly clear: ultimately only the Court can determine a breach of EU law'.

108 Annetje Ottow and Saskia Lavrijssen, 'The legality of independent regulatory authorities', in L. Besselink, F. Pennings and A. Prechal (eds.), *The Eclipse of Legality* (Kluwer Law International 2010), Chapter 5, at 73, and especially the literature listed in fn 1.

109 White Paper on European Governance (Chapter 2, n 75), at 24: 'The creation of further autonomous EU regulatory agencies in clearly defined areas will improve the way rules are applied and enforced across the Union. Such agencies should be granted the power to take individual decisions in application of regulatory measures. They should operate with a degree of independence and within a clear framework established by the legislature. The regulation creating each agency should set out the limits of their activities and powers, their responsibilities and requirements for openness.' The Commission further set the following conditions for the creation of regulatory agencies at EU level:

- The Treaties allow some responsibilities to be granted directly to agencies. This should be done in a way that respects the balance of powers between the Institutions and does not impinge on their respective roles and powers. This implies the following conditions:
- Agencies can be granted the power to take individual decisions in specific areas but cannot adopt general regulatory measures. In particular, they can be granted decision making power in areas where a single public interest predominates and the tasks to be carried out require particular technical expertise (eg air safety).
- Agencies cannot be given responsibilities for which the Treaty has conferred a direct power of decision on the Commission (for example, in the area of competition policy).
- Agencies cannot be granted decision-making power in areas in which they would have to arbitrate between conflicting public interests, exercise political discretion or carry out complex economic assessments.
- Agencies must be subject to an effective system of supervision and control.

110 See n 106.

111 Commission Communication, 'The operating framework for the European Regulatory Agencies', COM (2002) 718.

112 On 11 November 2009, the Second Chamber of the Dutch Parliament sent a request to the European Commission as to the proposals of the European Commission for Regulations concerning the reinforcement of the Financial Supervision in the EU—COM(2009)499, COM(2009)501, COM (2009)502, and COM(2009)503, requiring the Commission to further substantiate the relationship between the legal basis for setting up the new European Supervisory Authorities (ESAs) and the powers of the latter to take legally binding decisions. The European Commission in its reply dated 5 February

Commission are indeed in conformity with the requirements of TFEU is ultimately the decision of the ECJ. However, based on the position of the Commission, it seems possible to also establish an EU supervisory authority for data protection to which certain decision and enforcement powers are delegated. I note that granting such central enforcement powers to the Working Party 29 would have as a consequence that the Working Party 29 would have to combine its advisory tasks with enforcement, which is generally considered to be a difficult combination (the first task interfering with the required freedom to execute the second) and further contrary to concepts of 'separation of powers', as it involves a mixing of (quasi) norm-setting and adjudicative tasks.[113] In any event this requires further research which is outside the scope of this book. It will suffice here by my recommending to European legislators that they investigate whether (and to what extent) it is indicated to establish a pan-European DPA to which certain supervisory and enforcement powers are delegated in case of data processing operations with an EU dimension.

Proposed Regulation Under the Proposed Regulation authorization of BCR will remain with the Lead DPA (as the DPA where the multinational has its main

2010, to be found at<http://ec.europa.eu/dgs/secretariat_general/relations/relations_other/npo/docs/netherlands/2009/com20090499_500_501_502_503/com20090499_500_501_502_503_tweede-kamer_reply_en.pdf>, gives the following justification: 'Regarding the first issue, the Court of Justice has acknowledged [See CJCE, C-217/04, pt 44] that Article 95 of the Treaty relating to the adoption of measures for the approximation of legislation for the establishment and functioning of the internal market provides an appropriate legal basis for setting up a "Community body responsible for contributing to the implementation of a process of harmonisation", when the tasks conferred on such a body are closely related to the subject matter of the acts approximating the national legislations. The purpose and tasks of the ESAs—assisting competent national supervisory authorities in the consistent interpretation and application of Community rules and contributing to financial stability necessary for financial integration—are closely linked to the objectives of the Community acquis concerning the internal market for financial services. It was therefore decided to establish the ESAs on the basis of Article 95 of the Treaty. Concerning the powers of the proposed ESAs, it should be stressed that while Article 95 of the Treaty is clear about the objective of such Community bodies, it does not specify their precise powers. However, case law has recognised the possibility for Community institutions to delegate binding powers to these bodies, in so far as the delegation relates only to clearly defined executive competences, meaning that the delegated powers cannot consist of "a discretionary power implying a wide margin of discretion which may, according to the use which is made of it, make possible the execution of actual economic policy". Moreover, the delegating authority cannot grant to the ESAs more powers than those that it holds from the Treaty. This entails that it is possible for a legislative measure to grant to an agency an independent power to adopt binding decisions, provided that such a power is contained within a precise legal framework and is limited in its scope. Moreover, the power entrusted to such Community bodies should be limited to executive tasks, and must therefore be confined to the adoption of individual decisions.'

[113] This criticism is also voiced in respect of the present combination of tasks of some DPAs. See eg the study into the competences of the Dutch DPA conducted by the Commission Brouwer-Korf, *Gewoon Doen. Beschermen van veiligheid en persoonlijke levenssfeer, Rapport aan de ministers van Justitie en Binnenlandse zaken* (The Hague, 2009), at para 3.7, at 63–4, to be found at <http://www.rijksoverheid.nl/documenten-en-publicaties/rapporten/2009/01/22/rapport-gewoon-doen-beschermen-van-veiligheid-en-persoonlijke-levenssfeer.html>. The Commission concluded that the mixture of the various roles of the Dutch DPA and in particular the combination of, on the one hand, advising organizations on data protection compliance and approving self-regulatory codes and, on the other hand, enforcement thereof is inappropriate, as the first role limits the freedom of the DPA in its enforcement role. Further the Commission notes that it is strange that organizations have to address the same authority for advice while this authority can subsequently use such information to enforce. See further J.E.J. Prins, *Burgers en Hun Privacy: Over Verhouding En Houding Tot Een Ongemakkelijk Bezit,* (NJCM 2010), at 11; and the Report *i-Overheid* of the Wetenschappelijk Raad voor het Regeringsbeleid, at para 7.1.2, at 174–5, to be found at <http://www.binnenlandsbestuur.nl/Uploads/Files/Document/Ioverheid.pdf>.

establishment). To ensure that the DPAs are aligned when acting as the Lead DPA, the Lead DPA is required to submit its draft approval of BCR for opinion to the European Data Protection Board (*EDPB*), the successor of the Working Party 29[114] (see on the EDPB and its tasks in more detail Chapter 3, paragraph 3.1.8). Though no enforcement powers are granted to the EDPB, its role has been substantially strengthened by the newly introduced consistency mechanism.[115] The consistency mechanism is a procedure to ensure the unity of application of the Regulation in transborder data processing operations. Pursuant to the consistency mechanism DPAs are required to submit certain draft measures or authorizations (which include draft authorizations of BCR) for opinion to the EDPB.[116] If the DPA, after having received the opinion of the EDPB, intends to maintain its draft measure, the Commission may also issue an opinion[117] and ultimately adopt a reasoned decision requiring the DPA to suspend the adoption of the draft measure, which may remain in force for a period of maximum 12 months.[118] Further, the Proposed Regulation improves the coordination of enforcement in cross-border cases by requiring the competent DPA in such cases to invite other DPAs if individuals in the Member States of these DPAs are likely to be effected by a processing operation.[119] All in all, under the Proposed Regulation, the position of the successor of the Working Party 29 is substantially strengthened by the 'back up' suspension power of the Commission and further the delegation to the Commission to adopt implementing acts in relation to the matters to be submitted to the EDPS for opinion (which include draft BCR authorizations).[120] This being said, the proposed system achieves the desired results in an indirect manner, and I here repeat my recommendation to European legislators that they investigate whether (and to what extent) it is possible to establish a true pan-European DPA to which certain decision-making and enforcement powers are delegated in the case of data processing operations with an EU dimension.

In summary, the above leads to the following recommendations to European legislators:

Recommendation 2

Recognize BCR as an appropriate tool to provide adequate safeguards for the transfer of data and define the main substantive requirements for BCR:

- to be defined in general principles;
- to be set at an adequate level;
- taking into account the specific comments in this paragraph,

and to delegate the further norm-setting to the Commission pursuant to Article 290 and 291 TFEU.

[114] Articles 43(1) and 58(2)(f) Proposed Regulation.
[115] Article 57–63 Proposed Regulation.
[116] See on the measures to be submitted Chapter 3, para 3.1.8.
[117] Articles 58(8) and 59(1) Proposed Regulation.
[118] Article 60 Proposed Regulation.
[119] Article 56 Proposed Regulation.
[120] Article 62 Proposed Regulation.

Recommendation 3
Define the MRP and impose the MRP on all Member States.

Recommendation 4
Investigate whether it is indicated to establish a pan-European Data Protection Supervisory Authority, to which certain decision-making and enforcement powers are delegated in case of data processing operations with an EU dimension.

Recommendation 5
Provide for equal enforcement powers for DPAs and develop a common enforcement strategy for the DPAs to ensure equal enforcement.

Recommendation 6
Replace the Directive by an EU regulation when revising the Directive.

6.7 Recognition of BCR in Other Countries

A substantial number of non-EU countries have data transfer restrictions (see Chapter 3, paragraph 3.2). For multinationals to also comply with the data transfer rules from those countries, it is crucial that these countries recognize BCR also as a tool to facilitate data transfers from their countries. At the moment, the EEA countries and Switzerland acknowledge BCR as a tool for data transfers (Norway is even part of the MRP).[121] Further, the Additional Protocol to Convention 108[122] provides for data transfer rules similar to the Directive and should also be able to facilitate BCR. The Additional Protocol to Convention 108 has been ratified or acceded to by 30 countries of which a number are non-EEA countries,[123] and which countries therefore (should be able to) recognize BCR. The APEC Privacy Framework intends to facilitate a similar organizational tool, where it provides that Member Economies shall endeavour to facilitate that organizations adopt 'Cross Border Privacy Rules' (*CBPR*) as a manner to facilitate their cross-

[121] In Switzerland BCR are recognized as an appropriate tool pursuant to para 6(2) of the Swiss Data Protection Act. BCR have to be notified to the federal DPA and are then valid without any further review.
[122] See Chapter 2, n 50.
[123] Albania, Andorra, Bosnia and Herzegovina, Croatia, the former Yugoslav Republic of Macedonia, Monaco, Montenegro, Serbia, Switzerland, and Ukraine. This is the state as per January 2011; to see the statistics of ratification of or accession to the Additional Protocol visit <http://conventions.coe.int/Treaty/Commun/ChercheSig.asp?NT=181&CM=3&DF=14/01/2011&CL=ENG>.

border data transfers.[124] In countries that have introduced the accountability approach (also for) data transfers, eg Canada and Japan, organizational measures like introducing CBPR are already a requirement (see Chapter 3, paragraph 3.4). For these countries, recognition of BCR may be more or less assumed. This will also apply if the proposed Australian Privacy Principles become law.[125] In the US there are also proposals to introduce a co-regulatory approach for regulating privacy in the US, which is very similar to the BCR regime, where companies create a privacy safe harbour and enjoy considerable scope in shaping self-regulatory guidelines, while government retains general oversight authority to approve and enforce these guidelines.[126] All in all, given the fact that the EU has a high level of data protection, the expectation is justified that if BCR are recognized by the EU as providing an adequate level of protection for data transfers, BCR will also be recognized by other countries. A pre-condition for this is that countries do recognize self-regulatory tools rather than public regulation or contractual tools as an instrument to regulate transborder transfers. Again, the expectation is that in most countries this will not pose problems or if this does pose problems, countries are willing to address these. As early as 1985, the OECD published the Declaration on Transborder Data Flows,[127] in which the OECD expressed the intention to 'develop common approaches for dealing with issues related to transborder data flows and, when appropriate, develop harmonised solutions'. Also the Madrid Draft Proposal for International Standards provides that data transfers may be carried out if tools like BCR are implemented.[128] From the above is clear, however, that in respect of

124 The APEC member economies have explicitly agreed:

- To endeavour to support the development and recognition or acceptance of organizations' cross-border privacy rules across the APEC region, recognizing that organizations would still be responsible for complying with the local data protection requirements, as well as with all applicable laws. Such cross-border privacy rules should adhere to the APEC Privacy Principles.
- To give effect to such cross-border privacy rules, Member Economies will endeavour to work with appropriate stakeholders to develop frameworks or mechanisms for the mutual recognition or acceptance of such cross-border privacy rules between and among the economies.
- To endeavour to ensure that such cross-border privacy rules and recognition or acceptance mechanisms facilitate responsible and accountable cross-border data transfers and effective privacy protections without creating unnecessary barriers to cross-border information flows, including unnecessary administrative and bureaucratic burdens for businesses and consumers.

See APEC Privacy Framework (Chapter 2, n 40), Part B, Section III, Cooperative Development of Cross-border Privacy Rules, Principles 46–8. See also the CIPL New Approach to International Transfers (Chapter 6, n 61), at 8: 'The BGC approach has the potential to align with equivalent provisions in the APEC Privacy Framework to achieve a genuinely global solution, but perhaps with the robust substance which would flow from European leadership.'

125 See on the Australian Privacy Principles (Chapter 2, n 55).

126 Rubinstein (Chapter 3, n 153), at 47.

127 11 April 1985. Available at <http://www.oecd.org>.

128 Madrid Draft Proposal for International Standards (Chapter 3, n 49), at para 15(2).

recognition of BCR as a tool for outbound data transfers from non-EU countries, a lot of 'work' still has to be done. It is recommended that this work be undertaken by the Commission, rather than it being left to individual companies to obtain recognition of their individual BCR in such countries. The optimal solution would obviously be that these countries not only recognize BCR as a tool for data transfers also from their country, but that the Commission also comes to an agreement for mutual recognition of BCR and central enforcement.[129] By central enforcement I mean that all supervisory authorities involved in supervision of a certain multinational group of companies accept that in respect of the BCR of such company one Lead DPA (and the courts of such Lead DPA) have central supervision and enforcement powers. The Lead DPA should preferably be the DPA of the country of establishment of the headquarters of the multinational, to ensure such company can indeed effectuate compliance throughout its group of companies. In any event, EU legislators should improve the cross-border cooperation both between the DPAs and with DPAs outside the EU, in the enforcement of data protection laws.[130]

Proposed Regulation The Proposed Regulation provides for an explicit obligation of the Commission and the DPAs, in particular in respect of countries that have obtained an adequacy finding,[131] to take appropriate steps to (i) develop effective international cooperation mechanisms to facilitate the enforcement of legislation for the protection of personal data; and (ii) provide international mutual assistance in the enforcement of data protection legislation.[132] I assume this is sufficiently broad to extend also to ensuring the recognition of BCR as a tool for outbound data transfers by third countries and central enforcement in respect thereof.

Recommendation 7

Engage with non-EU countries in mutual recognition and enforcement of BCR as a tool for cross-border data transfers.

[129] See for more or less similar recommendations: Wugmeister, Retzer, Rich (Chapter 3, n 148), at 494; the Rand Report (Chapter 2, n 27), at 57; and the CIPL New Approach to International Transfers, (Chapter 6, n 61), at 7.

[130] A good basis therefore seems to be the OECD 2007 Recommendation on Cross Border Co-operation in the Enforcement of Laws Protecting Privacy, to be found at <http://www.oecd.org>. See Chapter 4, para 4.3, especially n 58. See further The Stockholm Program (Chapter 4, n 14), 1–38, at para 2.5 at 10: 'The Union must secure a comprehensive strategy to protect data within the Union and in its relations with other countries.' See also the EDPS Opinion on the revision of the Directive (Chapter 2, n 35), at para 166 and 185; and the EC Communication on the revision of the Directive (Chapter 2, n 34), at para 2.4.2 at 17.

[131] Article 45(2) Proposed Regulation.

[132] Article 45(1) Proposed Regulation.

6.8 Conclusion

In this chapter I have evaluated the BCR regime, including the MRP, and my conclusion is that already based on an evaluation of the regime itself, without evaluation from other disciplines, a number of improvements are possible to address the shortcomings of the regime. In the following chapters I will evaluate the BCR regime from different disciplines, starting with general principles of contract law, to evaluate whether this should lead to further recommendations.

7

BCR and Contract Law

7.1 Introduction

In the introduction to this book, I indicated that the emergence of BCR is part of a wider trend where legislators who wish to regulate global corporate conduct opt for 'regulating' transnational private regulation (*TPR*) rather than introducing public regulation with its inherent jurisdictional limitations. There is by now a vast body of research concerning the concept of TPR.[1] As also indicated in the introduction to this book, the main questions raised in this research in respect of TPR,[2] and which are of equal relevance to BCR, are the following:

- TPR raises questions of private international law (*PIL*) as to the validity of a choice of law and forum in TPR;
- the suitability of TPR for regulating human rights;
- how to best regulate TPR, ie which of the different forms of regulation would be most suitable to regulate TPR;
- the legitimacy of TPR as compared to public regulation;
- the alignment of TPR with conventional principles of contract law (TPR raises questions of enforceability by the third-party beneficiaries of such TPR);
- the enforceability of contractual 'supply chain management' as a mechanism to effectuate TPR, which solution is also part of the BCR regime.

I will discuss the questions above in the following chapters. In this chapter I will start with the contractual issues (the questions of enforceability by third-party beneficiaries and supply chain management issues) as these are of prime relevance to the BCR regime. The first requirement set by the Working Party 29 in respect of BCR is that BCR should be 'internally binding' within the organization (ie on all group companies and on employees) and 'externally binding' for the benefit of individuals (ie must create third-party beneficiary rights for the individuals).

The questions under PIL are subsequently discussed in Chapter 8. An evaluation of BCR as a form of TPR is given in Chapter 9.

[1] For an inventory of prior research, see the 'Survey of Research Programmes', Annex 2 to *The added value of private regulation in an international world? Towards a model of the legitimacy, effectiveness, enforcement and quality of private regulation*, HiiL 2007–08, at 1–21, to be found at <http://www.hiil.org>.

[2] These research questions will also be addressed in the HiiL Program, see Chapter 1, n 21.

7.2 Internally Binding

In practice BCR are made internally binding on group companies and on employees.

7.2.1 Binding on group companies

The BCR will bind the party that adopts the BCR, ie the (Delegated) EU Headquarters. The group companies would not be bound unless they are signatories to the BCR or if the (Delegated) EU Headquarters has adopted the BCR also on their behalf (and was duly authorized to do so). However, as one of the requirements of the Working Party 29 is that the (Delegated) EU Headquarters has to accept liability for paying compensation and remedying breaches of the BCR by all group companies, this is irrelevant. The (Delegated) EU Headquarters will subsequently have to seek redress for any breaches of the BCR by a group company from such group company. For those purposes some multinationals have intra-company arrangements in place. If a multinational wishes to make the BCR legally binding on all individual group companies, various possibilities exist. The most obvious is to back up the BCR with intra-group agreements, either in a multi-party agreement in which all group companies participate, or each group company has a separate identical contract with the parent.[3]

7.2.2 Binding on employees

The requirement in the WP Opinions that BCR should be internally binding on employees is in practice complied with by means of a clause in the individual employment contracts, that all company codes (as amended from time to time) should be complied with.[4]

7.3 Externally Binding

7.3.1 Enforceability of unilateral undertakings

BCR are in principle a unilateral undertaking by the multinational and not a contract.[5] Most, but not all, Member States seem to take the view that rights

[3] See ICC Report on BCR (Chapter 5, n 20), at 18–22 on possible structures to achieve that BCR are binding on all group companies.

[4] See ICC Report on BCR (Chapter 5, n 20), at 23, reporting that in all countries researched (Belgium, Denmark, Germany, the Netherlands, the UK, Spain, Hong Kong, Japan, Switzerland, and the US), inclusion of a contractual clause in employment agreements is valid. Another possibility reported is linking observance of the BCR with disciplinary procedures. This may improve adherence to the BCR, but would not make BCR legally binding on employees.

[5] This holds true unless specific contractual measures are implemented, see further para 7.3.5.

may be granted to third parties by means of unilateral undertakings.[6] For instance, under Dutch law unilateral undertakings are considered valid and binding on the party giving the undertaking[7] and all provisions of Dutch contract law will apply *mutatis mutandis* to such unilateral undertaking.[8] The Dutch Civil Code further contains an express provision to ensure that any such undertakings may be enforced before Dutch courts.[9]

7.3.2 Other grounds of enforcement

Even if certain jurisdictions do not consider unilateral undertakings to have binding effect, such legal orders will to varying extents recognize the protection of reliance on promises.[10] Where in a business context one party makes a promise which induces reliance by another party, such other party must be protected by law. The key element is whether there is 'self-binding behaviour that gives the impression of being serious'.[11] In BCR this self-binding behaviour is a given, as otherwise the BCR will not be eligible for approval by the Lead DPA. An important parallel here is the enforcement of unilateral undertakings made by companies in their CSR codes. For a long time many companies and lawyers thought these promises constituted moral obligations at best but had no legal effect. However, in many jurisdictions creative legal bases have been developed to enforce CSR codes against the parent company for human rights violations by their group companies or manufacturers in developing countries.[12] Some are very specific to the relevant

[6] See WP 133, part 2: Background Paper, fn 10 (Chapter 6, n 7), where it is mentioned that according to the civil law of some jurisdictions (eg Italy and Spain) unilateral declarations or unilateral undertakings do not have binding effect. See further ICC Report on BCR (Chapter 5, n 20), at 24, where an overview is provided of countries in which unilateral undertakings by the parent company are enforceable (Belgium, Denmark, Germany, the Netherlands, the UK, and Hong Kong); countries where they are not enforceable (Spain, Japan), and countries where possibly problems exist (Switzerland and the U.S.).

[7] Asser/Hartkamp & Sieburg 6-III 2010, no 101, at 79, and the literature and case law therein referred to. This is in line with EU developments. See eg Art 2:107 Principles of European Contract Law: 'A promise which is intended to be legally binding without acceptance is binding.' See also Art 3.20 Unidroit Principles of International Commercial Contracts 2004 and Art II-1:103 Draft Common Frames of Reference (*DCFR*).

[8] Asser/Hartkamp & Sieburg 6-III 2009, No 101 (n 7), at 81, and literature and case law therein referred to.

[9] Article 3:296 Dutch Civil Code.

[10] This para draws on Carola Glinski, 'Corporate codes of conduct: moral or legal obligation?', in McBarnet, Voiculescu, Campbell, *The New Corporate Accountability, Corporate Social Responsibility and the Law* (Cambridge University Press 2007), at 119–47.

[11] Glinski (n 10), at 123.

[12] For a comprehensive overview of legal basis found for enforcement of CSR codes, see Doreen McBarnet and Patrick Schmidt, 'Corporate accountability through creative enforcement: human rights, the Alien Torts Claims act and the limits of legal impunity', in McBarnet, Voiculescu, Campbell, *The New Corporate Accountability, Corporate Social Responsibility and the Law* (Cambridge University Press 2007), at 148–76. For further reading on the enforcement of unilateral undertakings in the EU and outside, see Wugmeister, Retzer, Rich (Chapter 3, n 148), at 491–4. On the Dutch situation, see A.J.A.J. Eijsbouts, 'Elementaire beginselen van Maatschappelijk Verantwoord Ondernemen', in A.J.A.J. Eijsbouts et al, *Maatschappelijk Verantwoord Ondernemen en het Recht*, Preadviezen NJV 2010–1 (Kluwer 2010), at Chapter 2, at paras 5, 6, and 7.

jurisdictions and I will refrain from discussing these here.[13] Below I summarize briefly the main grounds of enforcement in the EU that may be applied to enforce unilateral undertakings in corporate codes of conduct in general and further a specific example of enforcement of corporate privacy codes in the US.

7.3.3 Grounds of enforcement in the EU

For codes of conduct that are made public (as will be BCR for customer data[14]), various grounds of enforcement can be construed under EU law: non-compliance with the code may constitute (i) a violation of the law on misleading advertising;[15] (ii) an unfair commercial practice;[16] or (iii) a violation of the principles of conformity of goods under contracts of sale.[17]

Companies can also be held liable if they violate their own (internal) technical norms even if these internal standards exceed what is legally required in general.[18] Parent companies may further be liable based on tort law if a code of conduct was set at a level that was too low or if the code of conduct implies a control over subsidiaries based on which the parent has a duty of care to ensure that group companies comply.[19] Some of the legal grounds listed above do not provide for adequate remedies for the individual third-party beneficiaries. For instance, the traditional remedy in unfair competition law is an injunction, which generally can only be invoked by consumer associations rather than individuals[20] and

[13] See also Chapter 11, para 11.1 for the enforceability of CSR codes.

[14] BCR have to be made known to the data subjects concerned. In case of BCR for employee data, this involves publishing the BCR on, for instance, the company intranet rather than on the internet. This therefore does not entail making the BCR available to the general public.

[15] See Directive 84/450/EEC relating to the approximation of the laws, regulations and administrative provisions of the Member States concerning misleading advertising, [1984] OJ 1984 L250/17. Pursuant to Art 2, 'advertising' means the making of a representation in any form in connection with a business in order to promote the supply of goods or services; and 'misleading advertising' includes advertising which deceives or is likely to deceive the persons to whom it is addressed, or whom it reaches, and which, by reason of its deceptive nature, are likely to be affected in their economic behaviour. BCR for consumers could qualify as such.

[16] See Directive 2005/29/EC on unfair commercial practices, [2005] OJ L149/22. Article 6(2)(b) provides that a commercial practice shall be regarded as misleading in cases of 'non-compliance by the trader with commitments contained in codes of conduct by which the trader has undertaken to be bound, where (i) the commitment is not aspirational but is firm and is capable of being verified; and (ii) the trader indicates in a commercial practice that he is bound by the code'. Article 2(d) requires that the act by the trader was directly connected with the promotion, sale, or supply of a product. From the perspective of BCR, this may be the case if the conditions of sale contains a privacy provision which contain a reference to these BCR.

[17] See Directive 1999/44/EC on certain aspects of the sale of consumer goods and associated guarantees, [1991] OJ L171/12. Pursuant to Art 2(2)(d), the concept of conformity includes conformity with public statements on the specific characteristics made about products not only by the seller, but also by the producer or his representative, particularly in advertising or on labelling. BCR may constitute such relevant statement as well.

[18] Glinski (n 10), at 135.

[19] Glinski (n 10), at 141–6.

[20] A notable exception is Spanish law. The Directive on unfair commercial practices does not require the introduction of individual rights, but does not prohibit them either (see Recital 9).

only in some jurisdictions may consumer associations also sue for damages (eg Germany).[21]

7.3.4 Enforcement of corporate data protection policies in the US

For the enforcement of data protection policies, the enforcement action of the US Federal Trade Commission (*FTC*) is particularly relevant. In the past 10 years the FTC has used its authority under section 5 FTC Act, which prohibits unfair or deceptive trade practices, to take action against companies that misrepresent their privacy practices to consumers.[22] The FTC also enforces a number of sector-specific statutes that include data protection provisions, including the Fair Credit Reporting Act, the Gramm-Leach-Bliley Act, the Children's Online Privacy Protection Act (COPPA), the CAN-SPAM Act, and the Telemarketing and Consumer Fraud and Abuse Prevention Act (Do Not Call Rule).[23] Some highlights in the FTC's enforcement action include the charges it issued against Google, stating that Google had used deceptive tactics and violated its own privacy promises to consumers when it launched its social network, Google Buzz, in 2010. On 30 March 2011, the FTC announced[24] that Google accepted the FTC settlement order barring the company from future privacy misrepresentations, requiring it to implement a comprehensive privacy programme, with regular, independent privacy

[21] Paragraph 8 of the Law against Unfair Competition (*Gesetz gegen den unlauteren Wettbewerb-UWG*) of 3 July 2004. This will change under the Proposed Regulation, see Chapter 3, para 3.1.7.

[22] An overview of FTC enforcement cases in respect of data protection policies can be found at <http://www.ftc.gov>. This is an example where a public agency is not only tasked with enforcement of administrative or criminal legislation but also tasked with monitoring and enforcement of businesses to act consistently with their private law obligations, see Scott (Chapter 4, n 26), at 7.

[23] The Fair Credit Reporting Act, 15 U.S.C. para 1681 (2010) (regulating the reporting on consumer credit history); Gramm-Leach-Bliley Act, 15 U.S.C. paras 6801–6809 (2010) (regulating consumer financial data); COPPA, 15 U.S.C. paras 6501–6506 (2010) (regulating information about children); CAN-SPAM Act, 15 U.S.C. paras 7701–7713 (2010) (regulating unsolicited electronic messages); and Do Not Call Rule, U.S.C. paras 6101–6108 (2010) (regulating telemarketing calls).

[24] See press release dated 30 March 2011 'FTC Charges Deceptive Privacy Practices in Google's Rollout of Its Buzz Social Network. Google Agrees to Implement Comprehensive Privacy Program to Protect Consumer Data', to be found at <http://ftc.gov/opa/2011/03/google.shtm>. The FTC announced that Google agreed to settle charges that it used deceptive tactics and violated its own privacy promises to consumers when it launched its social network, Google Buzz, in 2010. According to the FTC's complaint (i) Google led Gmail users to believe that they could choose whether or not they wanted to join Google Buzz, while the options for declining or leaving Google Buzz were ineffective; (ii) for those who joined Google Buzz, the controls for limiting the sharing of their personal information were difficult to locate and confusing; (iii) Google violated its privacy policies by using information provided for Gmail for another purpose—social networking—without obtaining consumers' permission in advance; (iv) Google misrepresented that it was treating personal information from the EU in accordance with the U.S. Safe Harbor Framework because it failed to give consumers notice and choice before using their information for a different purpose from that for which it was collected. The settlement requires Google (i) to obtain consumers' consent before sharing their information with third parties if Google modifies its sharing practices; (ii) to establish and maintain a comprehensive privacy programme that is reasonably designed to: (a) address privacy risks related to the development and management of new and existing products and services for consumers, and (b) protect the privacy and confidentiality of covered information; and (c) to obtain initial and biennial assessments for 20 years from an independent auditor to ensure that it is following the required comprehensive privacy programme.

audits for the next 20 years. The settlement with Google marked the first time that the FTC required a company to implement a comprehensive privacy programme to protect the privacy of consumers' information (as opposed to a comprehensive security programme), and that the FTC alleged violations of the substantive privacy requirements of the US Safe Harbor Framework. As multinationals will publish their BCR for customer data on the internet (in order to comply with BCR requirement (xiv)),[25] the FTC has authority to take action if a multinational subsequently does not comply with its BCR. Although the FTC Act applies to consumers only, the FTC claims[26] that it has the authority to also prosecute employee privacy codes (as they are also private individuals). This seems questionable as employee privacy codes apply to individuals in their capacity of employee and not in their capacity of consumer and are in most cases not published on the internet, but on the multinational's *intranet* only. As a result it is difficult to see why this could constitute an unfair or deceptive trade practice.

7.3.5 Solutions to ensure that BCR are externally binding

If Lead DPAs in certain countries have doubts[27] about whether BCR are externally binding (ie legally enforceable) in their respective jurisdictions, a solution is to put a contract in place between the (Delegated) EU Headquarters and, for instance, the group company in the jurisdiction of the DPA. In any event it is possible in all Member States to grant third-party beneficiary rights in a contract.[28] However, rather than having to resort to such legal solutions, it would simplify matters considerably if European legislators could provide in the revised Directive that BCR can be enforced as unilateral undertakings by the third-party beneficiaries. This issue of external bindingness is not particular to BCR. In the literature regarding TPR, authors comment that the conventional principles of contract law are not adequate to cater for enforceability of TPR by the beneficiaries of TPR and that the law needs to be reformed to accommodate this.[29] As such general reform of the law to facilitate enforcement by third-party beneficiaries of unilateral undertakings (such as TPR) is outside the scope of this book, I will limit my

[25] The multinational will have to make its BCR 'easily accessible to the individuals concerned'. In the case of BCR for customer data (ie consumers), this may be achieved by the multinational by publishing the BCR on its corporate website.

[26] To date the FTC has not taken action against a company for false or deceptive trade practices with respect to employee data, and it is an open question whether it indeed may do so. See Wugmeister, Retzer, Rich (Chapter 3, n 148), at 489 in particular fn 81.

[27] In my experience, the Lead DPAs of the UK, France, Germany, and the Netherlands accept that BCR, being unilateral undertakings, are externally binding.

[28] WP 74 (Chapter 6, n 2), at 12, fn 11 and WP 133, part 2: Background Paper, fn 10 (Chapter 6, n 7), where it is mentioned that 'in the lack of specific legislative provision for the bindingness of such declarations, only a contract with third party beneficiary clauses between the members of the group may give proof of bindingness'. See the ICC Report on BCR (Chapter 5, n 20), at 25, for an overview of countries where BCR can be made binding for data subjects by making them third-party beneficiaries under a contract (yes in: Belgium, Denmark, the Netherlands, Germany, Spain, the UK, Switzerland); no: Japan and Hong Kong; possibly in: the U.S.).

[29] This is discussed in para 7.4, see in particular n 34.

recommendation to enforceability of BCR. This recommendation is of paramount importance as the enforceability of BCR will be shown to be a requirement under all disciplines against which BCR will be evaluated in this book. These all require that BCR provide for 'sufficient possibilities of redress for the beneficiaries'.[30] The enforceability of BCR as unilateral undertakings is a prerequisite for any such form of redress. I will not repeat this recommendation in the following chapters, but it equally applies there.

Proposed Regulation The issue of BCR being externally binding has not been solved in the Proposed Regulation. It is still left to the multinational adopting BCR to ensure that their BCR are externally binding.[31]

Recommendation 8

Provide that BCR can be enforced as unilateral undertakings by the beneficiaries of BCR.

7.4 Contractual 'Supply Chain Management'

Similar limitations under contract law are presented when TPR are imposed by a party on other parties in the supply chain, through contractual provisions in their supply chain contracts.[32] To a certain extent the BCR regime also relies on supply chain management to ensure protection of the employee and consumer data governed by BCR. If a multinational contracts with a third party in the context of which personal data of employees or consumers are transferred to such third party, contractual safeguards to protect these data should be put in place. Examples are when a multinational contracts with a third party to arrange all travel of its employees, or to manage its car fleet, corporate credit cards, or employee communication devices. Compliance with the material data processing principles under BCR will only be possible if the multinational imposes on its external supplier sufficient safeguards for the data protection interests of the employees and consumers. To achieve this, the BCR regime requires that BCR provide for the obligation of the multinational to enter into written agreements with its external suppliers, which have to meet the following requirements:[33]

[30] See for evaluation of BCR from perspective of PIL: Chapter 8, para 8.3.3; from perspective of accountability: Chapter 9, para 9.2; from perspective of legitimacy of TPR: Chapter 10, para 10.6.3; and from perspective of CSR: Chapter 11, para 11.2.9.

[31] Article 43(2)(c) Proposed Regulation.

[32] As is often done with food standards, environmental standards, CSR codes, etc. On contractual supply chain management in respect of CSR, see McBarnet and Kurkchiyan (Chapter 5, n 41). See further on supply chain management as to food safety requirements, Fabrizio Cafaggi, *Private Regulation, Supply Chain and Contractual Networks: The case of Food Safety*, EUI Working Papers RSCAS 2010/10.

[33] See BCR requirement (v) in Chapter 6, para 6.2.

- in the case of an external data controller: the written contract should impose the relevant material BCR principles on the supplier;
- in the case of an external processor: the written contract should impose the mandatory processor obligations on such external processor (see Chapter 3, paragraph 3.1.6 above);
- if the external controller or processor is located outside the EU: the data transfer rules in BCR also have to be complied with, for instance by making use of the EU Standard Contractual Clauses (see Chapter 3, paragraph 3.1.5 above).

In the general literature regarding contractual supply chain management of TPR, there are two issues identified, which are of equal relevance to the contractual safeguards imposed by the multinational on its external suppliers. The first is that the present third-party beneficiary doctrine (in the absence of a specific clause thereto) in most cases does not provide for the possibility for the beneficiaries of TPR to enforce their rights under the TPR also against the third-party supplier.[34] The second issue is that, even in case the contract with the third-party supplier contains a third-party beneficiary clause, enforcement by the beneficiaries against such third-party supplier is not very realistic, suppliers being often located in countries where contractual enforcement is not easy.[35] A third more general issue raised in the literature regarding contractual supply management of TPR, is the inherent weakness of a chain of contracts along the supply chain replicating the required contractual clauses. The chain is as strong as the first link and therefore dependent on the contracting power of the parties to the main contract.[36] This is also a feature of IT outsourcing arrangements, since in most cases the main outsourcing supplier not only involves many of its group companies as a sub-processor, but also third parties not part of its group of companies as sub-processor. As a backdrop to the discussion of these three issues, it is important to realize that (maybe surprisingly) at present supply chain management, especially in the

[34] See Cafaggi (Chapter 2, n 93), at 31, under reference (see fn 173) to *Doe v Wal-Mart* 572 F.3d 677 (9th Circ. 2009), where the court denied workers of a supplier of Wal-Mart the status of third-party beneficiaries, arguing that the clause incorporated in the contract between Wal-Mart and the supplier did not constitute a promise on behalf of Wal-Mart towards the workers, since this would have been necessary in order to establish third-party beneficiary rights. In the eyes of the court, 'the requirement that the suppliers were to provide sufficient working conditions and the clause that gave Wal-Mart the right to conduct inspections of the working si[t]e whether those requirements were kept, concerned purely the relationship between the two contracting parties but had no beneficial effect to the workers themselves'. See also Cafaggi (n 32), at 25: 'Neither individual consumers nor consumer associations are technically part of these contracts, which makes it difficult to enforce them if violations occur. Legal systems define different ways in which these contracts can be directly enforced by consumers and/or their associations: (1) "*action directe*" by the consumer against the supplier, (2) require unequivocal statements that their contracts are for the benefit of third parties, (3) allow enforcement using implied terms of consumer contracts, (4) grant individual or class remedies under civil liability, (5) qualify violations as unfair commercial practices.'

[35] See Cafaggi (Chapter 2, n 70), at 32 and further, para 4.3.

[36] Cafaggi (n 32), at 13.

consumer protection area, is arguably the strongest tool to achieve consumer protection in practice. As one author puts it:[37]

> It is through the contracts between manufacturers and their component suppliers and between retailers and distributors and manufacturers that many of the norms governing standards which can be expected of consumer products are set. A key contemporary example is the power of major supermarkets to set and enforce their standards for such matters as food safety. In many service sectors too contracts have a central role in defining standards. A key example is where service providers operate as a franchise (. . .).

This is despite the fact that contractual control of the supply chain rarely results in enforcement through the courts and in effectuating the agreed remedies for breach. Rather the contracts and contractual remedies provide a framework within which exchange occurs and matters are solved not so much by the terms of the contract but by adjustment of continuing relations.[38] Given the fact that by nowadays data processing is increasingly performed in networks whether within multinationals, between multinationals, or between multinationals and individual customers (ie internet users), the participants in such networks manage the risks: they accept them, try to limit or minimize them, or transfer them to co-contractors or other partners.[39] Based hereon the conclusion is justified that (as with consumer protection) supply chain management will become increasingly important, if not decisive, in achieving data protection in practice.

7.5 How to Address the Contractual Supply Chain Management Issues in BCR?

7.5.1 Enforceability against the external supplier

The WP Opinions do not require imposing a third-party beneficiary clause in contracts the multinational enters into with its external suppliers. However, if the external supplier is established in a non-adequate country, the multinational will have to 'adduce additional safeguards with respect to the protection of personal

[37] Scott (Chapter 4, n 26), at 6.

[38] Scott (Chapter 4, n 26), at 6 (under reference to Stuart Macaulay, 'Non-Contractual Relations in Business: A Preliminary Study' (1963) *American Sociological Review* 28: 55–83; Hugh Beale and Tony Dugdale, 'Contracts Between Businessmen' (1975) *British Journal of Law and Society* 2: 45–60) reports that 'sociological research both in the UK and the United States suggests that where problems do emerge within contractual settings, businesspeople may not be inclined to rely on the letter of their contractual entitlements to pursue litigation. Rather contracts provide a framework within which exchange occurs, but the response to the contract is not dictated by the contract'.

[39] Pierre Trudel, 'Privacy Protection on the Internet', in Serge Gutwirth et al (eds.), *Reinventing Data Protection?* (Springer 2009), Chapter 19, at 332–4. See Raab and Koops (Chapter 4, n 24), at 220, who have attempted to map the landscape of privacy actors in the online data protection arena 'showing a remarkable range of diverse and versatile actors with many potential interconnections and interrelationships'.

data',[40] which will in most cases be achieved by the multinational and the external supplier entering into the EU Standard Contractual Clauses. The EU Standard Contractual Clauses contain specific third-party beneficiary clauses which (under certain circumstances) enable data subjects to bring an action against the external supplier in case of a data protection breach.[41] As indicated, the WP Opinions do not require imposing an equivalent third-party beneficiary clause in contracts the multinational enters into with external suppliers established in the EU or other adequate countries. The underlying reasoning for this is probably that such third-party supplier is directly subject to the data protection laws of the EU or such adequate country which provide for sufficient protection of data. However, this is not automatically the case. One example is provided to clarify this.

BCR for employee data often contain a clause that employee data will not be used for direct marketing purposes. The multinational enters into a framework agreement for health insurance for its employees. Individual employees can enter into an individual insurance agreement with the insurance company under this framework agreement. The multinational correctly imposes the terms of the BCR on the insurance company. Under the current EU law, the insurance company (being a controller in its own right) is in principle authorized to use the data of its customers (ie the employees) for direct marketing purposes on an opt-out basis.[42] If the insurance company, despite its contractual restrictions, uses the employee data for direct marketing, the employees will have an interest in being able to act directly against the insurance company.

The only way to address this would be to make a third-party beneficiary clause mandatory in all contractual arrangements of the multinational with its external suppliers in the context of which personal data are transferred. This being said, I seriously doubt whether this suggestion would indeed lead to better enforceability of data protection by individuals in practice. Individual data subjects will not sue third-party suppliers, if only for cost reasons which will in most, if not in all, cases outweigh the damages suffered by the individual.[43] I will therefore not recommend that this requirement should be made part of the BCR regime. Rather, my conclusion is that the third-party beneficiary clause in the EU Standard Contractual Clauses—though looking good on paper—does not offer any meaningful form of redress for the third-party beneficiaries.[44] Worse, since the EU Standard Contractual Clauses may not be deviated from and the rights of the third-party beneficiaries are prescribed in detail, multinationals contracting with their external suppliers will

[40] See Chapter 3, para 3.1.5, n 63.

[41] See Art 11(2) of the EU Standard Contractual Clauses for processors and Arts I(e) and III of the EU Standard Contractual Clauses for controllers.

[42] See for the opt-out possibility for sending direct email to existing customers: Art 13(2) Directive 2002/58/EC of the European Parliament and of the Council of 12 July 2002 concerning the processing of personal data and the protection of privacy in the electronic communications sector, OJ 2002 L201, 37; as revised by Directive 2009/136/EC of the European Parliament and of the Council of 25 November 2009 (*e-Privacy Directive*).

[43] See Chapter 4, para 4.3 for enforcement issues in respect data protection leading to a lack of enforcement in practice.

[44] Kuner (Chapter 2, n 55), at 271.

not consider improving on these, even though they certainly would have (or better: are the only ones that have) the bargaining power to do so. That multinationals are here the party best positioned to ensure better rights for the beneficiaries is not a new insight, but a fact well known in other areas of law. This is one of the reasons for states to resort to TPR as the contracting parties have more power to enforce compliance than does the threat of traditional judicial means. As one author (in the context of supply chain management in respect of food safety) puts it:[45]

> States are weak enforcers of rules concerning transnational supply chains, so resorting to private regulation is an implicit delegation to industry, in particular retailers, of the task of devising compliance mechanisms to be applied in suppliers' countries. Market accountability through self-enforcing contracts, by threatening contract termination or lack of renewal, may offer better incentives to comply than legal accountability before domestic courts. Litigation in importing countries represents only a last resort mechanism; self-enforcing contracts, based on asymmetric contractual powers and market-share, often provide more effective enforcement mechanisms.

The recommendation to EU legislators concerning BCR is therefore not to focus on traditional judicial legal rights and remedies of individuals, but concentrate on means of redress that actually achieve compliance in practice.[46] If any new requirements are to be formulated to address a potential lack of redress by the beneficiaries of TPR, a practical solution would be that the internal complaints procedure that is required under BCR is made open also for complaints of beneficiaries as to the processing of their data by the external suppliers of the multinational complemented by an obligation of the multinational to follow these up with its external suppliers. This suggestion will be part of my combined recommendations in Chapter 9, paragraph 9.7, in the context of introducing the accountability principle for data transfers.

7.5.2 Enforceability against the multinational

Rather than relying on *ex post* enforcement, a second solution suggested in the literature to improve compliance throughout the supply chain with contractually imposed TPR obligations, is to impose a monitoring obligation on the multinational having adopted the TPR.[47] Most supply contracts already contain a provision regarding monitoring by the multinational of compliance of the external supplier, but a *right* to do so only.[48] This is the same in the context of data protection. Most outsourcing contracts under which a multinational transfers personal data to a supplier will include such monitoring and auditing provisions. Since in outsourcing relations many of the data processing operations of a supplier are similar for different customers, the parties often agree that the data processing operations of a supplier are certified by an external auditor for the benefit of all

[45] Cafaggi (n 32), at 9.
[46] As is also the recommendation of the Working Party 29, see Chapter 1, n 23.
[47] Cafaggi (Chapter 2, n 70), at 32 and Cafaggi (n 32), at 15.
[48] Cafaggi (Chapter 2, n 70), at 32; McBarnet and Kurkchiyan (Chapter 5, n 41), at 75.

customers, saving costs and time for all involved. Rather than the multinational monitoring and auditing the operations of the supplier, the supplier will yearly submit a 'Third Party Memorandum', a statement of the external auditor, describing the data processing operations of the supplier, the applicable control mechanisms and a certification that the data processing operations of the supplier are compliant.[49] The right to audit is further one of the mandatory processor provisions which have to be included in all data processing agreements the multinational enters into with a data processor.[50] The question is whether the *right* of multinationals to monitor and audit compliance should be replaced by an *obligation* to do so. In short, I would not be in favour of introducing this obligation in the BCR regime. Large multinationals have thousands of suppliers and introducing ongoing monitoring and auditing obligations in respect of external suppliers involves a disproportionate increase in effort and costs. As indicated before, since it is in their own interest that the data transferred to a third party are properly processed, multinationals mostly put proper safeguards in place, including the right to monitor or audit compliance of the third-party supplier, if so deemed necessary. If critical data processing operations are outsourced, multinationals require periodic audit statements on compliance with security and other requirements under the outsourcing contract. It should be left to the multinationals to assess based on a risk assessment if, and if so, which monitoring and auditing measures are indicated.[51] This approach is very much part of an 'accountability principle' for data transfers, and will be further discussed in Chapter 9, paragraph 9.3.2.

A second solution suggested in the literature to improve compliance with contractually imposed TPR obligations, is to require that TPR contain a provision allowing the pursuit of remedies against the multinational in case it has not

[49] If a multinational is listed in the U.S., and the outsourcing can influence the content and reliability of the annual accounts, such a Third Party Memorandum has to meet requirements under s 404 of the Sarbanes-Oxley Act and the rules of the U.S. Securities and Exchange Commission. This requires a statement to conform to the auditing rules of the U.S. accounting organization, the 'Statement on Auditing Standards No. 70: Service organisations' (in practice often referred to as '*SAS 70*' statement). See Lokke Moerel and Bart van Reeken e.a., *Outsourcing, een juridische gids voor de praktijk* (3rd edn Kluwer May 2009), at para 9.3.8.

[50] See on the mandatory processor provisions Chapter 3, para 3.1.6.

[51] McBarnet and Kurkchiyan (Chapter 6, n 41), at 63 note: 'The supply chain is becoming increasingly recognised as an area of reputational—and indeed insurance—risk, with a number of companies beginning to develop a "risk-based approach to supplier engagement" and "systems to identify higher risk suppliers"' (this referring to Vodafone Corporate Social Responsibility Report for 2004–05, at 24 and other examples listed). McBarnet and Kurkchiyan (Chapter 6, n 41), at 75, further note that 'in line with the partnership model, however, the enforcement approach [of multinationals against their suppliers] is not punitive but follows the "compliance model" approach. [The] policy is more about bringing their suppliers into compliance over time than immediately resorting to penalties. Best practice involves on-site monitoring of all suppliers at the outset, to check whether they meet the requirements, identifying and reporting shortcomings and carrying out follow-up assessments of progress towards rectifying them, usually over an agreed period of time. There will also be a "continuous improvement" programme and continued periodic audits'. See further at 79: 'In terms of legal consequences, non-compliance with the contract is highly unlikely to ever result in a court case (...) As is usual in business contracts more generally, any sanction for non-compliance normally consists of economic leverage rather than legal procedure. (...) perhaps the most persuasive and effective non-legal sanction comprises a refusal to deal with the other party in the future.'

imposed proper contractual protections on the external supplier as required by the TPR.[52] This requirement seems to be already implied in the present BCR regime. The BCR regime requires that the multinational imposes contractual data protection provisions on its external suppliers. If the multinational fails to do so, the beneficiaries of the BCR can act against the multinational. Explicitly providing so in the BCR will make no difference. Reading the suggestion made in the general literature regarding TPR, it comes very close to introducing the accountability approach[53] to data transfers as included in the APEC Privacy Framework and the countries that have already introduced this principle (see Chapter 3, paragraph 3.4). I will discuss the merits of the accountability approach to data transfers in Chapter 9, paragraph 9.5 and will refrain here from making recommendations conforming to this suggestion.

7.5.3 From 'supply chain' to 'network'

Simply put, the contractual chain (whereby a party to a contract involves a subcontractor, who, in turn, involves a sub-sub contractor, etc) is as strong as the first link and the outcome for beneficiaries is therefore very much dependent on the contracting power of the parties to the main contract. Another weakness of a chain of identical obligations is that the various parties involved in the chain may be responsible for different parts of the services and it will not be clear with which party the respective obligations as to the beneficiaries may lie. A suggestion in the literature relating to TPR is to approach the supply chain as a contractual network rather than a chain.[54] Effective supply management is achieved when the risk of non-compliance is minimized at the source of the risk. Rather than imposing requirements on all subsequent parties in the network, a more productive exercise may be to first identify the risks, their source, and then allocate responsibilities accordingly. Different solutions are suggested in the literature to incentivize the parties to a 'network' to ensure the optimal allocation of the responsibilities over the parties involved. Legislative measures suggested to achieve this are: (i) allocating strict liability with the party with the best negotiation powers (who will use this power to allocate responsibilities); (ii) imposing 'network' liability (ie all parties are jointly and severally liable for the compliance of the network as a whole);[55] and imposing joint and several liability on 'gate keepers'.[56] In the context of online data protection potential gate keepers may be ISPs, being intermediaries between

52 Cafaggi (n 32), at 25.

53 Cafaggi (n 32), at 25: 'This tension may be solved in different ways: by imposing the primacy of a liability driven network, or by disentangling the contractual form of the network from the liability regime. In the latter case, enterprises along the chain will be able to arrange their own internal organisational structure which will be affected by the liability regime but not necessarily entirely shaped by it.'

54 Cafaggi (n 32), at 13 and 17 and further para 8.

55 Cafaggi (n 32), at 17 and 25.

56 Scott (Chapter 4, n 26), at 9, gives as an example credit card companies having the capacity to issue charge backs to companies breaching consumer contracts. Another example is banks having the capacity to block payments to illegal gambling sites.

individuals and companies as online data processing is concerned and having the capacity to block websites. I will discuss the merits of these suggestions in Chapter 9, paragraph 9.5.3, as again, these are very much part of an 'accountability' requirement in respect of data transfers.

7.6 Conclusion as to Contractual Issues of BCR

In this chapter I discussed the contractual issues of BCR, which concern the question of enforceability of BCR by third-party beneficiaries and supply chain management issues under BCR. My conclusion is that the enforceability issue of BCR by third-party beneficiaries may and should be solved. The supply chain management issues of BCR are not that easily solved or optimized. Supply chain management is not new and the existing literature on supply chain management of other forms of TPR provides a host of ideas on how to optimize such management. Given the fact that data processing is performed in networks rather than in neat one-to-one relationships, contractual supply chain management will become correspondingly important, and may prove ultimately the strongest tool to achieve data protection in practice. The options I discussed for improving supply chain management have not led to specific recommendations as the merits of these will be further discussed in Chapter 9 as part of introducing the accountability principle for data transfers.

8

BCR and EU Rules of Private International Law

8.1 Introduction

BCR, like most transnational private regulation (*TPR*), have to function within many different public and private spheres. For BCR to be acceptable in all different spheres they touch on, they must be aligned with the existing disciplines they interact with.[1] The main discipline BCR touches on is that of private international law (*PIL*). As one author puts it, PIL is the 'queen mother of all transnational legal thought'.[2] The interaction with PIL is twofold. First there is the traditional function of PIL where, for instance, a choice of law and forum made in BCR has to comply with rules of PIL. This is also called the function of PIL as a 'mechanism' or the 'touch down' function.[3] Owing to these rules of PIL, state law becomes relevant, again, for instance as a choice of law and forum leads to the competence of the courts and questions arise as to enforcement of judgments of such courts.[4] The second function of PIL is that of a potential source of 'meta-norms' for BCR.[5] For BCR (operating at the global level) to be acceptable at the national level, BCR will have to 'build on the assumption of common reference points' between national jurisdictions.[6] Sidelining, for instance, the underlying policy choices behind PIL instruments and doctrines will not achieve universal acceptance.[7]

Assessing the role of PIL in respect of BCR has been surprisingly difficult for a number of reasons. As to PIL's role as a mechanism, it is surprising how little interest the disciplines of TPR and PIL show in each other's fields. As one author from the TPR discipline recently put it 'standard treatments of transnational regulation (...) rarely devote sustained attention to discussion of PIL matters'.[8] This lack of interest is reciprocal, as I have not come across any substantive

[1] See Chapter 2, n 81.

[2] C. Joerges, *Rethinking European Law's Supremacy*, EUI Working Papers 2005/12 (2005), at 7.

[3] See Bomhoff and Meuwese (Chapter 2, n 79), at 172.

[4] See Bomhoff and Meuwese (Chapter 2, n 79), at 171.

[5] Especially as to the socio-economic and political implications behind PIL instruments and doctrines. See Bomhoff and Meuwese (Chapter 2, n 79), at 172.

[6] Bomhoff and Meuwese (Chapter 2, n 79), at 165. See in more detail Chapter 2, para 2.4.

[7] Bomhoff and Meuwese (Chapter 2, n 79), at 172.

[8] Bomhoff and Meuwese (Chapter 2, n 79), at 172. Noteworthy is that the authors themselves also do not discuss the PIL issues relating to TPR.

discussion of the role of PIL as to TPR in standard treatments of PIL either. As to the second function of PIL as a potential source of meta-norms, it is relevant that PIL traditionally does not incorporate a regulatory perspective, in the sense that it is intended to achieve a certain desired outcome. Rather it is based on 'substantive neutrality' (as to the law applicable) which is traditionally considered the appropriate basis for the main starting point for EU rules of PIL, being choice of law.[9] This being said, underlying meta-norms can be discerned especially in relation to the exceptions to the main principle of choice of law and forum that were considered necessary in instruments of PIL and which are relevant to BCR as well.

8.1.1 PIL as a mechanism

The introduction by a multinational of BCR raises several questions of PIL. Though most of the WP Opinions do not explicitly state so, the WP Opinions seem to be based on the assumption that BCR will apply to the relevant processing of personal data by a multinational, *unless* in a certain jurisdiction stricter national requirements apply. In this case such stricter national requirements must be met in the relevant jurisdiction, ie the BCR should provide for a *minimum level of protection* for the processing of personal data by the multinational, setting aside the national data protection laws at least for the relevant minimum level.[10] Further, the WP Opinions require that BCR provide for the possibility of enforcement of BCR via the forum of either (i) the EU group company at the origin of the transfer or (ii) the (Delegated) EU Headquarters,[11] setting aside the jurisdiction that the courts of other Member States may have under applicable rules of PIL.[12] These requirements of the Working Party 29 pose problems with (i) the mandatory nature of the applicability and enforcement regime of the Directive and (ii) the EU rules of PIL (and also non-EU rules of PIL for that matter). As to rules of PIL, an additional problem is posed by the fact that the main personal data processed by multinationals under BCR concern personal data of their employees and those of their customers, who are in many cases consumers. As far as employee and consumer contracts are concerned, the rules of PIL create a mandatory regime—both in terms of applicable substantive law and in terms of dispute resolution mechanisms—which may not be set aside to the detriment of the employee or the consumer by a choice of law or forum.

[9] This concept is still the main principle of the EU rules of PIL. Bomhoff and Meuwese (Chapter 2, n 79), at 174.

[10] See for instance WP 153 (Chapter 6, n 7), at 11, where is stated that it is advisable that the BCR state that 'where the local legislation, for instance EU legislation, requires a higher level of protection for personal data it takes precedence over the BCR'.

[11] WP 74 (Chapter 6, n 2), at 19.

[12] Also Art 43(2)(f) Proposed Regulation seems to require that the controller or processor 'established on the territory of a Member State [accepts] liability for any breaches of the binding corporate rules by any member of the group of undertakings not established in the Union'. Based on Art 51(2) Proposed Regulation, this seems to refer to the main establishment of the multinational in the EU, see also Chapter 6, para 6.6.1.

8.1.2 Preferences of multinationals

Another problem posed under PIL is due to the fact that multinationals introducing BCR have a strong interest in including a choice of law and forum clause in their BCR. The main reason for this is that it is in the interest of the multinational that all complaints under the BCR are ultimately dealt with by the Lead DPA (and the courts of the Lead DPA) as this DPA negotiated the provisions of the BCR under the applicability of the Lead DPAs own law (ie the law under which the provisions of the BCR were drafted). This ensures for the multinational a consistent and predictable interpretation and application of the BCR. For the same reason the multinational has an interest in the Lead DPA having central supervision over the BCR.[13] Again, as under BCR mainly employee and consumer data are processed, this poses problems as to (i) the mandatory nature of the applicability and enforcement regime of the Directive and (ii) EU rules of PIL.

8.1.3 Preferences of beneficiaries of BCR?

The background of both the mandatory rules of the Directive and the consumer and employee protection regimes under PIL is the protection of weaker parties (ie employees and consumers). The question, however, is whether in this case the interests of the employees and consumers are indeed best served by not allowing a choice of law and forum for the jurisdiction of the Lead DPA. In Chapter 4, paragraph 4.3, I discussed that though individuals have proper rights and remedies under the Directive, these are difficult to effectuate in practice. I also discussed some alternative options that offer more realistic hope of redress for individuals. One possible alternative I put forward is a choice of law and forum in TPR (in this case BCR). Such choice of law and forum will drastically improve the data protection and the access to remedies for the individuals covered by the BCR. This would work out as follows.

The BCR regime requires that the multinational implements a complaint procedure. If a breach occurs, the individual affected will be able to file a complaint with the group company with which he has a relationship, regardless of where the breach occurred or which of the group companies was responsible for the breach. The individual will therefore not have to prove which of the group companies was at fault (which is one of the obstacles in practice to bringing and succeeding in a claim). There is also no issue as to which law applies and whether the relevant law provides for data protection. The complaint may be filed by the individual in his own language. The group company that received the complaint will be responsible for ensuring that the complaint is processed through the complaints procedure of the multinational and for ensuring the required translations are provided. If the complaints procedure does not lead to a satisfying result for the individual, the

[13] The WP Opinions require an obligation of the group companies to cooperate with all DPAs, to abide by their advice in respect of the BCR, and to accept to be audited by the DPAs.

group company will facilitate the filing of the complaint with the Lead DPA or the courts of the Lead DPA. This procedure will lead to enforceable rights even in jurisdictions where no (adequate) data protection laws are in place or where insufficient enforcement (infrastructure) is available. It further overcomes language issues and time zones and minimizes costs. None of the cross-border enforcement issues discussed in Chapter 4, paragraph 4.3 apply.

The fact that employees and consumers may actually be best served with a choice of law and forum in BCR, is a factor to be taken into account when evaluating the PIL issues in respect of BCR.

Proposed Regulation I note that the changes envisaged in the Proposed Regulation in respect of applicability, jurisdiction, and enforcement of the Regulation have very little impact on the PIL issues in respect of BCR as discussed in this chapter. For a discussion of the envisaged changes to the applicability, jurisdiction, and enforcement regime in the Proposed Regulation, I refer to Chapter 3, paragraphs 3.1.4 and 3.1.7. Where the Proposed Regulation will bring about changes, these will be indicated in the footnotes.

8.2 Applicability, Jurisdiction, and Enforcement

In this chapter, I will discuss how the applicability, jurisdiction, and enforcement regime of BCR can be best set up in light of the combined requirements of the Working Party 29 and the multinational's preferences as discussed above and the requirements of PIL. For that purpose a number of questions will be discussed:

- *Which instruments of PIL are relevant?* This requires first a discussion of how the data protection regime under the Directive should be qualified, as public or private. For instance the Brussels I Regulation[14] applies to civil and commercial matters only (Chapter 3, paragraph 3.1.1).

The conclusion will be that the EU data protection regime is clearly a combination of private and public law, the logical consequence of which is that the different parts should be treated accordingly.

- *Do the rules of PIL take precedence over the applicability and jurisdiction regime of the Directive?* This depends on whether the applicability and enforcement regime of the Directive is considered to provide 'conflict rules' and as such take precedence over the general conflict rules of PIL (paragraph 8.3.2).

The conclusion here will be that the applicability and jurisdiction regime of the Directive takes precedence over the relevant rules of PIL.

- *Is a choice of law and forum possible under the Directive?* The next question is whether a multinational can make a choice of law and forum in BCR which

[14] EC Regulation 44/2001 of 22 December 2000 on jurisdiction and enforcement [2001] OJ L12/1 (*Brussels I Regulation*).

deviates from the applicability and enforcement regime of the Directive. This depends on whether the applicability and enforcement regime of the Directive is of a mandatory nature (in which case parties cannot deviate from this regime by making a choice of law and forum in a contract) (paragraph 8.3.3).

The answer will be that the applicability and enforcement regime is of a mandatory nature and that a choice of law and forum is as a rule not possible. There are, however, good arguments that this rule may find exception if in BCR the law and forum of another Member State are chosen. In light of the uncertainty of whether a choice of law and forum may be made in BCR, the conclusion will be that multinationals are advised to set up the applicability and enforcement regime of BCR in such a manner that the pitfall of deviation from the mandatory applicability and jurisdiction regime of the Directive is avoided.

- *How may the applicability and enforceability regime of BCR be set up?* The recommendation is that BCR should be set up in such a manner that they do not provide for a *minimum* level of protection, but rather provide for *supplemental* protection. As all national rights and remedies of individuals thus remain in place, BCR do not contravene the mandatory applicability and enforcement regime of the Directive. In this set up a choice of law and forum in BCR (as to the supplemental rights and remedies provided) seems to be an option (paragraph 8.4).
- *What are PIL issues as to the proposed BCR applicability and enforcement regime?* PIL questions that have to be answered in respect of the proposed BCR applicability and enforcement regime are:
  (i) whether Rome I and Brussels I Regulation apply to this choice of law and forum made in BCR (paragraph 8.6);
  (ii) and if so, whether such choice of law and forum is in conformity with the EU employee and consumer protection regimes of PIL (paragraph 8.8); and
  (iii) whether the choice of law and forum clause in BCR meets the requirements *as to form* under PIL (paragraph 8.9).

My overall conclusions and recommendations are presented in paragraph 8.11.

8.3 Role Left for EU Rules of PIL?

8.3.1 Qualification of data protection law

To determine which instruments of PIL may be in scope, it is relevant whether data protection law should be qualified as private law, public law, or a combination of these. For instance, the Brussels I Regulation[15] applies to civil and commercial matters only. Further, if data protection is to be considered public law, a court or

[15] Article 1 Brussels I Regulation.

DPA would always have to apply its own law and never a foreign data protection law.[16] The Directive does not provide for a classification (ie private or public) nor does it prescribe how the Member States must implement the Directive in their national law (ie as constitutional rules, mandatory rules, or regulatory rules).[17] As a consequence there are many different ways in which Member States have chosen to implement the Directive in their national legislation.[18] Also, by studying these national laws it is impossible to come to a preponderant classification of EU data protection law in one single category (ie either private or public). As the right to data protection is a fundamental human right and freedom,[19] and the basis for the Directive is to implement these rights and ensure a high level of protection,[20] a number of Member States have chosen the constitutional approach to implementation of the Directive[21] or have otherwise provided that their data protection laws are of a mandatory nature.[22] The courts and DPAs of these countries will in all probability apply their own rules as *ordre publique* which will be applied regardless of the applicable law.[23] In any event the rules in the Directive regarding the DPAs and their duties, powers and decisions are typically of a public nature. This being said, the Directive provides that consent can be given by an individual for a data processing activity (that would otherwise be in violation of the provisions of the Directive), and that data processing is allowed to the extent necessary for the

[16] See Jon Bing, *Data protection, jurisdiction and the Choice of Law*, paper delivered at the 21st International Conference on Privacy and Data Protection, Hong Kong, 14 September 1999, at 2, to be found at <http://www.pcpd.org>. See also Christopher Kuner, 'Internet Jurisdiction and Data Protection Law: An International Legal Analysis (Part 1)' (1 October 2010), *International Journal of Law and Information Technology*, Vol 18, p 176. Available at SSRN: <http://ssrn.com/abstract=1496847>, at 10, also referring to Bing and further to Maria Veronica Perez Asinari, 'International Aspects of Personal Data Protection: Quo Vadis EU?', in Maria Veronica Perez Asinari and Pablo Palazzi (eds.), *Challenges of Privacy and Data Protection Law* (31 Cahiers du CRID) (Bruylant 2008), at 381, 405, stating that Art 4 of the EU Directive 'could be considered, in principle, as a mandatory rule', but adding that 'the nature of this Article has not been extensively studied'.

[17] C.M.K.C. Cuijpers, *Privacyrecht of privaatrecht. Een privaatrechtelijk alternatief voor de implementatie van de Europese Privacy richtlijn* (diss. Tilburg) (Wolf Legal Publishers 2004), at para 6.4, in particular at 222; Colette Cuijpers, 'A Private Law Approach to Privacy; Mandatory Law Obliged?' [2007] *SCRIPT-ed*, doi: 10.2966/scrip.040407.304, at para 3. The Commission when revising the Directive has opted for an EU regulation as a legislative instrument. Regulations are directly applicable in all Member States and therefore will no longer require national implementation.

[18] For an overview of the different ways in which the Directive is implemented in the national laws of the Member States, see Korff (Chapter 2, n 27). In para 3.4, an overview is given of the different status the various Member States have given to data protection rights (varying from a constitutional status overriding any other national laws (as in Germany) to a status whereby other laws override the data protection laws (as in Sweden)). See further at Chapter 13, discussing the different legal bases on which damages can be claimed, varying from the ordinary rules on civil and administrative liability rules in a country (as in Finland, France and Luxembourg) to liability in tort (as in Ireland and the Netherlands).

[19] See Chapter 3, n 3.

[20] See Recitals 10 and 11 of the Directive. cf Recitals 1–3 Draft Regulation.

[21] See Korff (Chapter 2, n 27). Korff lists the Member States (most notably Germany, Spain, Greece, Italy, Portugal, and Austria) that have chosen the constitutional approach to implementation of the Directive.

[22] See eg the legislative history to the Dutch Data Protection Act, Kamerstukken II 1997/98, 25 892, no 3, at 10.

[23] Bing (n 16), at 3; Kuner (Chapter 2, n 8), at 11; and Kuner (n 16), at 10.

performance of a contract to which the data subject is a party, which are both typically of a private nature.[24] The Directive further provides for the possibility that a DPA takes enforcement action even if the law of another Member State is applicable to the relevant processing (which also suggests that the object matter is not of a public nature).[25] Finally, under most national implementation laws, claims for damages have to be brought before the civil courts (either based on tort or on enforcement of a right *sui generis*),[26] which is also typical for private law. The conclusion is that EU data protection law is clearly a combination of the two categories, the logical consequence of which is that the different regimes (public vs private) should be applied concurrently depending on the relevant category.[27]

8.3.2 Do the conflict rules of the Directive take precedence over PIL?

Given the mixed nature of EU data protection law, the question is whether the applicability and enforcement regime of the Directive (the 'conflict rules') take precedence over the general conflict rules of EU PIL or whether they are intended to supplement these.[28] EU rules of PIL provide that conflict rules in relation to specific matters which are contained in Community instruments or in national

[24] See Arts 7(a) and (b) Directive.

[25] See Art 28(6) Directive: 'each supervisory authority is competent, whatever the national law applicable to the processing in question, to exercise, on the territory of its own Member State, the powers conferred on it in accordance with para. 3 (. . .)'. These powers include the right to engage in legal proceedings where the national provisions have been violated. cf Art 51(1) Proposed Regulation. As the Proposed Regulation is in the form of a regulation which is directly applicable in all Member States, DPAs will only in a limited number of cases have to apply foreign law, see on this Chapter 4, para 4.4.3.

[26] Korff (Chapter 2, n 27), at Chapter 13, discussing the different legal bases on which damages can be claimed, varying from the ordinary rules on civil and administrative liability rules in a country (as in Finland, France, and Luxembourg) to liability in tort (as in Ireland and the Netherlands). The Proposed Regulation provides for a similar regime of redress to the courts, see Chapter 3, para 3.1.7.

[27] See Bing (n 16), at 3: 'Data protection legislation will typically contain provisions of a public law nature, relating to an authority and its duties and decisions. But the law will also often include civil law provisions, typically on liability for data protection violations. The provisions of data protection legislation may therefore have to be qualified as belonging to different areas of law, to which different relevant connection criteria are assigned. Following the traditional method, different aspects of one case may then have to be decided by different *lex causae*, which easily may lead to distortions as the legislation is conceived as an organic whole where the different provisions support an appropriate solution.' See also Kuner (n 16), at 10: 'It thus seems preferable to conclude that data protection law should not be considered to be solely public law or private law, but that its characterization should depend on the specific activity or issue in question. Thus, if an action is taken by a data protection authority (for example, an enforcement action such as an audit), then this should be considered to be a matter of public law, but if action is taken by a private actor (such as signing a data transfer agreement with another private party), then it should be considered one of private law (albeit it with a strong regulatory element). There will be many situations when the public and private nature of data protection law become intertwined, and it may be difficult to distinguish between them in a particular case.' Also under the Proposed Regulation, no explicit choice is made whether EU data protection law is to be qualified as public or private.

[28] The scope of a European directive is determined by a one-sided applicability rule, ie a conflict rule that solely indicates the scope of the directive itself and does not provide a rule about the relation to possible applicability of other rules, see C.A. Joustra, 'Europese richtlijnen en Internationaal privaatrecht' (European Directives and Private International Law) [1999] *WPNR* 6369, at 666, and references to other literature.

legislation harmonized pursuant to such instruments, take priority over the conflict rules under PIL.[29] The conflict rules of the Directive are 'one-sided' to the extent that they provide the scope of the Directive as to when the Directive applies and when the DPAs and courts have jurisdiction, rather than true conflict rules as to which regime takes precedence.[30] However, given that the purpose of the Directive is maximum harmonization of data protection law within the EU,[31] the conclusion is justified that the applicability and jurisdiction regime of the Directive should be considered to be conflict rules that take precedence over those in PIL.[32] The fact that the Directive itself does not explicitly provide for this is not considered to be decisive in this respect.[33]

8.3.3 Choice of law and forum

The next question is whether the multinational can make a choice of law and forum in BCR which deviates from the applicability and jurisdiction regime of the

[29] See Art 23 Rome I, and in particular recital 40 thereto and Art 67 Brussels I Regulation. See also L. Strikwerda, *Inleiding tot het Nederlands Internationaal privaatrecht* (Kluwer 2008), at 69, in respect of the predecessor of Rome I. According to Strikwerda, one-sided scope rules take precedence over general conflict-of-law rules as the national court addressed will apply the rules within scope, regardless of the applicable law. See also Cheshire, North, and Fawcett, *Private International Law* (Oxford University Press 2008), at 737 (in particular fn 621) and at 762 and Joustra (n 28), at 666.

[30] The applicability and enforcement regime of the Proposed Regulation is set up in a similar manner, see Chapter 3, paras 3.1.4 and 3.1.7.

[31] See Recital 8 Directive, indicating that the purpose of the Directive is full harmonization with the exception of specific discretionary powers in a limited number of areas. See further Joined Cases C-465/00, C-138, C-139/01 *Österreichischer Rundfunk/Neukomm* [2003] ECR I-04989, at para 100 and Case C-101/01 *Bodil Lindqvist* [2003] ECR I-12971, at paras 95–6. See further the EC Communication on the revision of the Directive (Chapter 2, n 34), at para 2.12.1, where the Commission announces it will 'examine the means to achieve further harmonization of data protection rules at EU level'. As the Proposed Regulation is in the form of a regulation that will be directly applicable in all Member States, full harmonization will be achieved, except for certain selected topics which are left to be regulated by the Member States, see Chapter 1, n 11.

[32] See also P.H. Blok, 'Privacybescherming in alle staten' (Privacy protection; a problem everywhere) [2005] *Computerrecht*, at 302–3. This is also the opinion of the Working Party 29, see Working Document on Non-EU Based Websites (Chapter 2, n 62), at 6: 'as the directive addresses the issue of applicable law and establishes a criterion for determining the law on substance that should provide the solution to a case, the directive itself fulfils the role of so-called "rule of conflict" and no recourse to other existing criteria of international private law is necessary.' See further Peter Swire, 'Of Elephants, Mice, and Privacy: International Choice of Law and the Internet' (1998) 32 *International Lawyer* 991, at 994: 'Conflict of law rules in such legislation [the Directive] take precedence over national rules' and 'the [Rome] Convention does not take precedence over choice of law rules that are included in European Union legislation.'

[33] See Blok (n 32), at 302–3; and Joustra (n 28), at 666 (and further literature therein referred to). An example of an EU directive that provides for a conflict-of-law rule that is considered to take precedence over those in PIL, but that does not explicitly provides so, is Directive 96/71/EC of the European Parliament and of the Council of 16 December 1996 concerning the posting of workers in the framework of the provision of services, OJ L 018, 1. The original proposal for Rome I explicitly acknowledged this Directive as one that contains a conflict-of-law rule which takes precedence over the conflict rules of Rome I, ie falls within the scope of Art 23 Rome I. See Art 22(a) original proposal Rome I and Annex I thereof, which was omitted in the final version. See Cheshire, North, and Fawcett (n 29), at 762. Also the Proposed Regulation does not provide that its applicability and enforcement regime takes precedence over rules of PIL, but also this will not be considered decisive in this respect.

Directive. The answer to this question depends on whether the Directive should be considered to impose rules of mandatory law (or not). If the provisions (including the applicability and jurisdiction provisions) of the Directive are of a mandatory nature, these cannot be deviated from by contract. Given the status of data protection as a fundamental human right and freedom,[34] the (sometimes silent) assumption in the literature is that the Directive is indeed of a mandatory nature.[35] The fact that the Directive itself does not provide that its provisions are of a mandatory nature is (again) not considered to be decisive in this respect.[36] Despite some (isolated) criticism of the mandatory nature of data protection,[37] it is not expected that this will change in the future. The status of data protection as a fundamental right and freedom has been strengthened by its implementation in the recently adopted Treaty on the Functioning of the European Union (*TFEU*).[38]

[34] See Chapter 3, n 3. The constitutional character of the right to data protection as opposed to the right to privacy is challenged by Peter Blok, *Het recht op privacy.Een onderzoek naar de betekenis van het begrip 'privacy' in het Nederlandse en Amerikaanse recht* (Boom Juridische Uitgevers 2002), in particular Chapter 3 and 5; see also Cuijpers (referring to Blok) (n 17), at 312.

[35] The scarce literature that does explicitly discuss the issue predominantly confirms the mandatory nature of the Directive: Blok (n 32), at 303; Lucas Bergkamp, *European community Law for the New Economy* (Intersentia 2003), at 123; Stefano Rodotà, 'Data Protection as a Fundamental Right', in: Serge Gutwirth et al (eds.), *Reinventing Data Protection?* (Springer 2009), Chapter 3; Nadezhda Purtova, *Property Rights in Personal Data: a European Perspective*, diss. TILT (Boxpress, Oisterwijk), at 196–208. See also Colette Cuijpers, 'A Private Law Approach to Privacy: Mandatory Law Obliged?' [2007] *SCRIPT-ed* 4(4), at 306, which acknowledges that the general assumption in literature is that the Directive is of a mandatory nature. The arguments presented by Cuijpers to dispute this are each discussed and (convincingly) rejected by Purtova (above), at 197 et seq. The main argument of Cuijpers (at 311), is that the Directive cannot be of a mandatory nature as it facilitates the freedom to contract, eg where it provides that consent can be given by a data subject for a data processing and where it allows data processing to the extent necessary for the performance of a contract to which the data subject is a party. Cuijpers ignores that this 'contractual' legal basis for processing is strictly safeguarded by the Directive (ie is a 'controlled' legal basis for processing) and remains subject to the other protection provisions of the Directive like the principle of proportionality (see Chapter 3, n 59). Further, Cuijpers ignores that 'consent' is a fundamental element of a rights-based approach to data protection. Consent comes into play if any act would otherwise be in violation of the consenting party's right. As Brownsword puts it: 'Where a data protection regime is underwritten by an ethic of rights and where (as I take it) the ethic is based on a choice (or will) theory of rights, there is no escaping the fact that consent must be central to this regime. This is because, quite simply, consent is an integral dynamic within such rights-based approach.' See Brownsword (Chapter 3, n 60), Chapter 3, at para 4.2 ('The Centrality of Consent'). Further, on how the fundamental right to data protection safeguards data subjects and leads to the conclusion that consent has (and should have) a limited value as an independent legal ground for data processing, see Rouvroy and Poullet (Chapter 3, n 59), at 72–6.

[36] See Blok (n 32), at 303. This refers to EU directives that cannot be deviated from by contract, but whereby the Directive itself does not explicitly provide so. Examples listed by Blok are the Directive 2003/33/EC, [2003] OJ L152 (tobacco), and Directive 2001/83/EC, [2001] OJ L311 (advertising of pharmaceuticals). Again, for a different viewpoint, see Cuijpers (n 17), at 221–2 and Cuijpers (n 17), at 304, where Cuijpers argues that the Directive does not impose mandatory rules of law based inter alia on the absence of a clause in the Directive prescribing mandatory law, this (*a contrario*) referring to a number of directives which do contain clauses requiring the mandatory character of one or more of its provisions. That *a contrario* arguments are often unreliable is evidenced by the foregoing examples given by Blok of directives that do not contain a clause requiring the mandatory character and yet do have a mandatory character. Also the Proposed Regulation does not provide that its provisions are of a mandatory nature, but also this will not considered to be decisive in this respect.

[37] Cuijpers (n 17), at 222–3; Cuijpers, (n 17), at 304.

[38] See Chapter 3, n 3.

Also, the recent EC Communication on the revision of the Directive[39] indicates that the Commission 'building on these new legal possibilities [ie in TFEU] will give the highest priority to ensuring respect for the fundamental right to data protection throughout the Union'.[40] This EC Communication on the revision of the Directive further points strongly in the direction of further approximation of EU data protection laws and this at the highest level of the equation.[41] This is also reflected in the recently published Proposed Regulation.[42] Data protection being a fundamental human right, the question is whether there is any room left for the freedom to contract, which is (also) a European fundamental right and freedom.[43] It is clear that according to the European Court of Justice (*ECJ*) the right to data protection 'is (...) not absolute but must be balanced against other fundamental rights'.[44] According to the ECJ such balancing is in the first place made in the Directive itself and further by the adoption of the implementation laws by the Member States and their application by the national authorities.[45] The Commission also indicates in the EC Communication on revision of the Directive that 'other relevant fundamental rights enshrined in the Charter (...) have to be taken fully into account while ensuring the fundamental right to the protection of personal data'.[46] It is not clear whether the ECJ and the Commission intend to imply that (as these other fundamental rights are already taken into account when drafting the Directive and the implementation laws itself) there is little room left for (a further) balancing of the right to data protection against other fundamental rights,[47] or intend to indicate that in all cases a further balancing should be

[39] See EC Communication on the revision of the Directive (Chapter 2, n 34), at paras 2.2.1. and 2.2.3.

[40] The new legal basis for adoption of the Proposed Regulation is Art 16 TFEU, see Explanatory Memorandum, to the Proposed Regulation (Chapter 1, n 9), at 5 and the heading of the Proposed Regulation.

[41] See EC Communication on revision of the Directive (Chapter 2, n 34), at para 2.1, where the Commission states that it intends to strengthen the individuals' rights, by inter alia increasing transparency for data subjects, enhancing control over one's own data, strengthening the principle of data minimization, and improving the modalities of exercise of the rights of access, rectification, erasure or blocking of data, and ensuring informed and free consent.

[42] By choosing the form of a regulation with direct applicability in all Member States, full harmonization will be achieved (with the exception of selected topics which are left to be regulated by the Member States, see Chapter 1, n 11). That the Proposed Regulation intends to strengthen the protection provided to individuals is reflected in Recital 9 of the Proposed Regulation.

[43] See eg Joined Cases C-90/90 and C-91/90 *Jean Neu* [1991] ECR I-3617, at para 13.

[44] See Case C-275/06 *Promusicae* [2008] ECR I-271, at paras 63, 65, and 68. See also Case C-101/01 *Bodil Lindqvist* [2003] ECR I-12971, at para 79.

[45] Case *Bodil Lindqvist* (n 44), at para 82: 'The mechanisms allowing those different rights and interests to be balanced are contained, first in Directive 95/46 itself, in that it provides for rules which determine in what circumstances and to what extent the processing of personal data is lawful and what safeguards must be provided for. Second, they result from the adoption, by the Member States, of national provisions implementing that directive and their application by the national authorities.'

[46] See EC Communication on the revision of the Directive (n 34), at 4.

[47] See Rodotà (n 35), Chapter 3, at 80: '2. Being aimed at affording a strong protection to individuals, the right to data protection may not be considered as subordinate to other rights. It means we have to go beyond the simple balancing test technique, because the very nature of data protection as "fundamental right" (Y. Poullet). 3. Accordingly, restrictions or limitations are only admissible if certain specific conditions are fulfilled, rather than merely on the basis of the balancing of

undertaken.[48] The Proposed Regulation is more explicit in this respect where it lists the other fundamental rights that have indeed been taken into account when drafting the Proposed Regulation, which will leave very little room for (a further) balancing of the right to data protection under the Proposed Regulation against these other fundamental rights.[49] In any event it is clear that the conclusion should not be that the freedom to contract should have priority over the right to data protection, as being the 'more important' right.[50] Rather the conclusion seems to be that the rights under the Directive cannot be contracted away. At the most, in a specific case, the right to data protection has to be balanced against the freedom to contract and in weighing the interests in the particular case involved, priority may be given to one over the other. Applying this conclusion to the question of whether a choice of law and forum in BCR is possible, the outcome is that this is not possible if this in any way diminishes the rights and remedies of individuals under the Directive. Only if such choice were not in any manner to lead to diminished protection, is there room for balancing the right to data protection against the freedom to contract. This requirement seems only to be met if a choice of the law of another Member State were made (than would apply pursuant to the regime of the Directive).[51] Due to the maximum harmonization of the laws of the Member States, such choice would not in any way diminish the protection afforded by the Directive to data subjects. Balancing the two fundamental rights here could weigh in favour of the freedom to contract.[52]

interests. Article 8 of the Convention for the protection of human rights provides that "there shall be no interference by a public authority with the exercise of these rights except such as is in accordance with the law and is necessary in a *democratic* society".'

48 As seems to be implied by Purtova (n 35), at 203.

49 See Recital 139 Proposed Regulation, which explicitly reflects that the Regulation: 'In view of the fact that, as underlined by the Court of Justice of the European Union, the right to the protection of personal data is not an absolute right, but must be considered in relation to its function in society and be balanced with other fundamental rights, in accordance with the principle of proportionality, this Regulation respects all fundamental rights and observes the principles recognized in the Charter of Fundamental Rights of the European Union as enshrined in the Treaties, notably the right to respect for private and family life, home and communications, the right to the protection of personal data, the freedom of thought, conscience and religion, the freedom of expression and information, the freedom to conduct a business, the right to an effective remedy and to a fair trial as well as cultural, religious and linguistic diversity'.

50 See Rodotà (n 35), at 80: 'Being aimed at affording a strong protection to individuals, the right to data protection may not be considered as subordinate to other rights. It means we have to go beyond the simple balancing test technique, because the very nature of data protection as "fundamental right" (Y. Poullet)'; Purtova (n 35), at 203; Olha Cherednychenko, 'EU Fundamental Rights, EC Fundamental Freedoms and Private Law' (2006) *European Review of Private Law* 1, at 36. Differently, see Cuijpers (n 11), at 306 and 317 who advocates that the freedom to contract takes priority over the right to data protection.

51 This is assuming that the Directive does indeed provide for the highest level of data protection overall. Under the Proposed Regulation a choice of law will have limited relevance only. As the Proposed Regulation will be directly applicable in all Member States, there will be only one data protection law. The Proposed Regulation, however, leaves some selected topics to be regulated by the Member States, see Chapter 1, n 11. In respect of those topics, a choice of law would remain relevant. See also Chapter 4, para 4.4.3.

52 Blok (n 32), at 303 is of the opinion that due to the mandatory nature of the Directive, a choice of law is not possible, but in general comments that the outcome could be different if the law chosen to

A similar balancing may be made in case the *forum* of another Member State is chosen. Again, given the high level of harmonization, the data protection afforded to individuals should not be diminished if another DPA were competent. As all DPAs have a duty to cooperate in the enforcement, this entails only a shift in which DPA takes the lead in enforcement. As to jurisdiction of the courts of the Member States in data protection cases, the Directive leaves it to the Member States to provide for the jurisdiction rules of their courts and most Member States have not enacted special rules, but rely on their civil procedural law (which are primarily determined by EU rules of PIL).[53] Under these rules a choice of forum is in principle possible.[54] Again, as with a choice of law, it seems that the protection afforded to data subjects would not be diminished if a choice of forum could be made for the DPA and the courts of another Member State. It should be noted that even if a choice of law and forum is possible, such agreement will be valid only between the parties that have agreed. As DPAs are not a party to such agreement, DPAs may therefore ignore the choice of another DPA. Further, any obligation the controller has vis-à-vis the DPA will remain in place (such as notification duties, the obligation to appoint a representative in EEA territory if the controller is established outside the EEA, permit requirements, etc).[55]

Further, any such choice of law and forum will be subject to general rules of PIL. For instance, Article 3(4) of Rome I provides that if the law of a non-Member State is chosen (eg to avoid the protection afforded by the Directive), while all other elements relevant to the situation at the time the choice is made are located in one or more Member States, 'the parties' choice of applicable law other than that of a Member State shall not prejudice the application of provisions of Community law (...), which cannot be derogated from by agreement.'[56] In other words,

apply is the law of another Member State, since in that case the data protection afforded to the data subject should not be diminished given the full harmonization of data protection law across the EU. Cuijpers (n 17), at 317, also comes to the conclusion that a choice of law is possible, but this is based on the starting point that the Directive is not of a mandatory nature and that therefore deviation by a choice of law should as a rule be possible.

[53] Rather than relying on the national jurisdiction regimes of the civil courts of the Member States, Art 74(3) Proposed Regulation provides that proceedings against a DPA have to be brought before the courts of the DPA and Art 75(2) Proposed Regulation provides that proceedings against the controller or processor must be brought either before the court of the Member State of the defendant (ie of the DPA or the controller/processor) or before the court of the Member State in which the data subject is residing. See further Chapter 3, para 3.1.7.

[54] See Art 23 Brussels I Regulation. This freedom is not unlimited. Specific requirements apply for contracts with weaker parties, such as employees and consumers and further requirements apply as to form. These are discussed in para 8.6 below. As the Proposed Regulation provides for jurisdiction rules for the courts (see n 53), there does not seem to remain room for applying EU rules of PIL. At the most, as with a choice of law, in a specific case, the right to data protection has to be balanced against the freedom to contract and in weighing the interests in the particular case involved, priority may be given to one over the other. The outcome of this assessment under the Proposed Regulation would then be the same as indicated under the Directive.

[55] Blok (n 32), at 303; and Cuijpers (n 17), at para 6.6.5.

[56] Article 3(3) Rome I further provides that if the law of one country is chosen, while all other elements relevant to the situation at the time of choice are located in a different country, the choice of the parties shall not prejudice the application of the law of that other country. This provision is less

according to PIL a choice of law will be possible, but does not set aside mandatory provisions of Community law.[57]

Based on the above, the conclusion is that there are good arguments that a choice of law and forum should be possible in respect of data protection, provided the law and forum of another Member State are chosen. This conclusion seems to be in line with rules of PIL 'as a mechanism' as well as with the underlying choices in the European PIL instruments (whereby a choice of law of another state is possible as long as the protection provided for by Community law is not set aside). In the context of BCR the law chosen should preferably be the law of the Lead DPA, this being the law under which the BCR are drawn up. As to forum, this should preferably also be the Lead DPA and the courts of the country of the Lead DPA. Besides the fact that this DPA reviewed and approved the BCR (which ensures a uniform interpretation of the BCR also in future disputes), the (EU) Delegated Headquarters is also established in that country, which will ensure optimal enforceability of the BCR.

Given the identified uncertainties as to whether indeed a valid choice of law and forum can be made in respect of data protection (even if limited to the rights and remedies of a private nature and limited to a choice of law and forum of one of the Member States), I recommend that European legislators ensure that in BCR such choice of law and forum may be made for the laws and courts of the Member State of the Lead DPA and further that the Lead DPA will have central supervision in respect of such BCR, and may involve other DPAs if so required for enforcement in the territories of the other Member States. If European legislators were to introduce the country of origin principle also for data protection (as per *Recommendation 1)*,[58] it would seem that the possibility of a choice of law and forum would no longer be necessary as in that case the data processing operations of the multinational would already be governed by the data protection laws of the Member State of origin of the multinational and the DPA and courts of such country of origin would have sole competence. However, as BCR apply to the data processing operations of the multinational on a worldwide basis (ie also to data processing operations not governed by the EU data protection laws), the possibility of a choice of law and forum remains relevant for such non-EU data processing operations.

Proposed Regulation Though the Proposed Regulation is in the form of a regulation and therefore has direct applicability in the Member States, there still remain topics which will be regulated by the national laws of the Member States for which a choice of law will remain relevant. Though the Proposed Regulation further provides for the country of origin principle for jurisdiction to enforce,

relevant to the processing of data by multinationals, as such processing will in most cases be of a cross-border nature and therefore involve more countries.

[57] Article 3(4) Rome I, is a codification of case law of the ECJ. For an overview of prior case law, see Cheshire, North, and Fawcett (n 29), at 737. See further Strikwerda (n 29), at 67. Such a choice of law and forum would further have to comply with the employee and consumer protection regime of Rome I and the Brussels I Regulation, see para 8.6 below.

[58] See Chapter 4, para 4.4.3.

individuals may still bring complaints or proceedings to other DPAs and courts than the Lead DPA and its courts. Also under the Proposed Regulation therefore, the recommendation below will continue to be relevant.

Recommendation 9

Provide that in BCR a choice of law and forum may be made for the laws and courts of the Member State of the Lead DPA and further that the Lead DPA will have central supervision in respect of such BCR, and may involve other DPAs if so required for enforcement in the territories of the other Member States.

If this Recommendation is followed, a multinational having BCR would have to comply with the data protection law of one Member State only. This is certainly an improvement compared to the present situation in which the applicability regime of the Directive is based on an accumulation of applicable data protection laws of the Member States.[59] However, ultimately multinationals would be best served if they could apply one uniform data processing regime on a global basis. In other words, they would be best served if they could apply the BCR regime on a global basis, *including in the EU*. I do not see any convincing reason why this would not be acceptable to EU legislators. At present, the multinational applies the laws of the Member States in the EU and the BCR outside the EU. If data originating from the EU are transferred to a non-adequate country, the protection such data obtain is that of the adequate level provided for by the BCR. If it is acceptable that EU data obtain an adequate level of protection outside the EU, this adequate level of protection should also be acceptable for protection of EU data within the EU. It is more a matter of setting the right level for adequacy, and in that sense the general assumption that the level of data protection provided by the Directive is the highest (or in any event higher than an 'adequate level' of a protection) is something of a myth. The material processing rules under the Directive and those of countries that obtained an adequacy ruling are in most cases approximately the same. If the Directive is considered stricter, this often concerns more formal requirements like time frames for responding to requests of individuals, notification and permit requirements, etc. Multinationals implementing IT systems processing data on a cross-border basis verify compliance with these material data processing rules. The actual protection afforded to individuals is in the tuning of these systems (what data are processed, access controls, decisions on security). Subsequent notification of these processing operations to the DPAs, or a 10-day instead of a 4-week period to reply to access requests, do not provide additional material protection to individuals. These are 'national hurdles' to take. Some of this thinking can be recognized in the various opinions and recommendations made in respect of the

[59] See Moerel (Chapter 1, n 8), at para 2.3.6.

revision of the Directive. These all focus on 'privacy by design',[60] on enforcement *ex post* to the detriment of requirements *ex ante* like notification and permit requirements,[61] and 'specify the criteria and requirements for assessing the level of data protection in a third country or an international organisation' and further 'to define core EU data protection elements, which could be used for all types of international agreements'.[62] If the protection in BCR is indeed set at the required adequacy level (and includes all core EU data protection elements), there are no objections to applying the provisions of BCR also within the EU instead of the data protection laws of the Member States.[63]

Recommendation 10

Provide that if multinationals adopt BCR, the BCR apply instead of the national data protection laws of the Member States.

8.4 The Applicability, Supervision, and Enforcement Regime of BCR: How It May Work

At this time it is uncertain whether a choice of law and forum may be made in BCR (hence *Recommendation 9*), and further whether in the EU the BCR rules may be applied instead of the national laws of the Member States (hence *Recommendation 10*). Hereafter, I discuss how the applicability and enforcement regime of BCR may currently be best set up (ie in the situation that these recommendations are not implemented). At present, multinationals are best advised to set up the applicability and enforcement regime of BCR in such a manner that the pitfall of deviation from the mandatory applicability and enforcement regime of the Directive is avoided. However, even if the applicability and enforcement regime is set up in such a

[60] See the Rand Report (Chapter 2, n 27), at 44 and the WP Contribution on the Future of Privacy (Chapter 2, n 33), at para 4 at 12 et seq, urging the Commission to introduce 'privacy by design' as a new principle in the revised Directive. The EC Communication on the revision of the Directive (Chapter 2, n 34), at 12, states the Commission's intent to 'further promot[e] the use of PETs and the possibilities for the concrete implementation of the concept of "Privacy by Design"'; and the EDPS Opinion on the revision of the Directive (Chapter 2, n 35), at paras 108–15 et seq.

[61] The Rand Report (Chapter 2, n 27), at para 3.3.2 at 28, concludes that the *ex ante* measures to ensure transparency of processing via information and notification requirements are largely ineffective. See also the WP Contribution on the Future of Privacy (Chapter 2, n 33), at 21, where the Working Party 29 advocates a simplification or reduction of the notification requirements, also because the accountability principle would achieve the same purposes. The EC Communication on revision of the Directive (Chapter 2, n 34), at 10, pleads for 'simplification' of the current notification regime. In a recent speech, Neelie Kroes, the Vice-President of the European Commission responsible for the Digital Agenda, compares the notification requirement to a 'formality', see 'Towards a European Cloud Computing Strategy', speech for World Economic Forum Davos, 27 January 2011, available at <http://europa.eu>). The EDPS Opinion on the revision of the Directive (Chapter 2, n 35), at para 62 at 15, supports the initiative to restrict application of the notification obligation to processing operations that are expected to bear more risk of violation.

[62] EC Communication on the revision of the Directive (Chapter 2, n 34), at 16.

[63] See in detail on the new provisions of the Proposed Regulation, including the provision containing the requirements for assessing adequacy, Chapter 3, para 3.1.5.

manner, some PIL issues remain. Below I first discuss how the applicability and enforcement regime may be best set up (paragraphs 8.4.1–8.4.3) and thereafter I discuss whether this applicability and enforcement regime (if drafted as suggested), is indeed valid and binding under rules of PIL and in particular the employee and consumer protection regime thereof (paragraphs 8.5–8.10).

8.4.1 How should the applicable law regime be set up under BCR?

The BCR should not provide for a *minimum* protection where the applicable national data protection rules apply only if they provide for *more data protection,* but rather the reverse. The BCR should provide that any processing by the multinational of personal data will remain governed by applicable national law and that the BCR provide for *supplemental* protection only. In other words, the BCR apply only if the BCR contain rights or remedies that go beyond those provided by applicable national law. If rights and remedies are equal under national law and the BCR, national law prevails. The BCR therewith does not provide for a minimum protection, but provides a 'top on' protection until an adequate level of data protection is achieved. The scope of applicability of BCR is illustrated by the following examples (Figures 8.1–8.4).

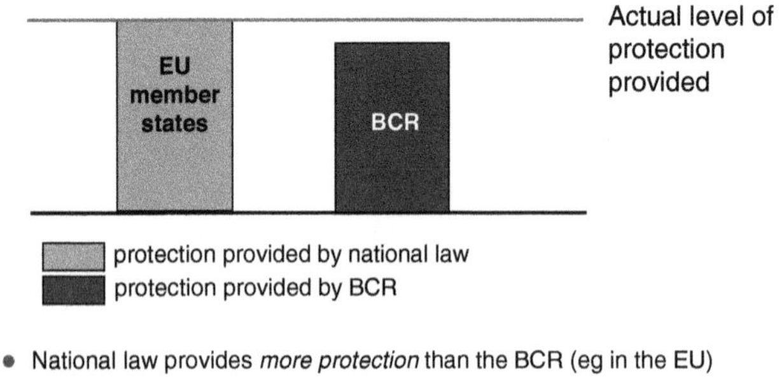

Figure 8.1 National law provides more protection than the BCR

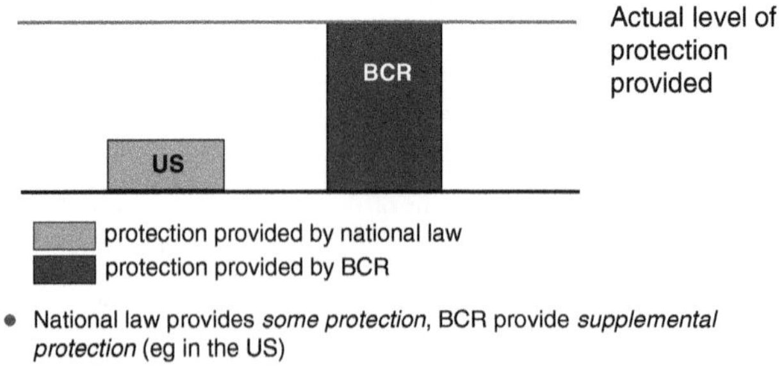

Figure 8.2 National law provides some protection, BCR provide supplemental protection

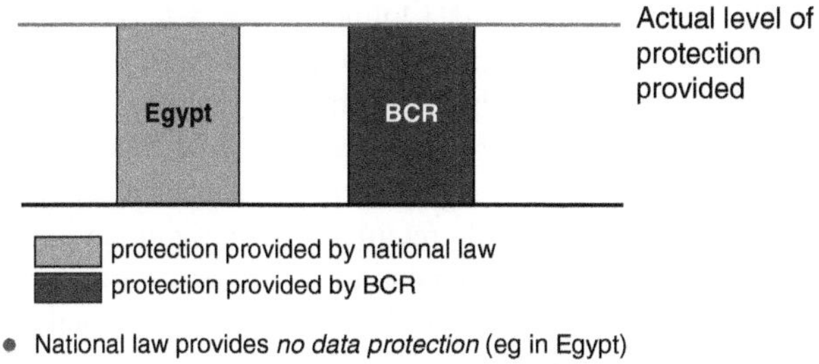

Figure 8.3 National law provides no data protection

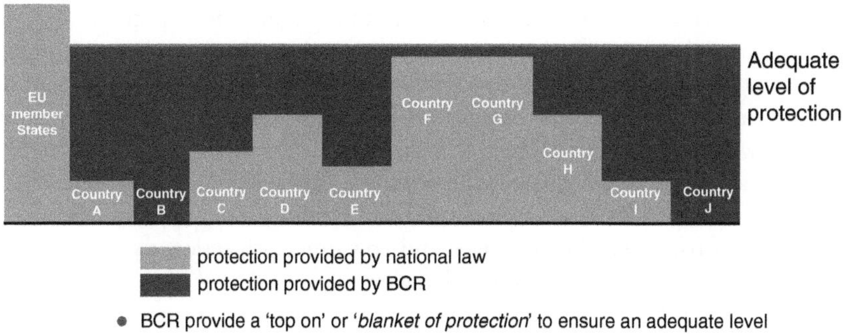

Figure 8.4 BCR provide a 'top on' or 'blanket of protection' to ensure an adequate level

As the BCR do not contravene the applicability regime of the Directive, since it provides for supplemental rights in jurisdictions only (which are not governed by the Directive), a choice of law in respect of this supplemental protection would seem to be a valid option.

8.4.2 How should the enforcement regime for BCR be set up?

In line with the choice of the law of the Lead DPA, a choice should also be made for the forum of the Lead DPA. As a consequence any complaints and claims of an individual concerning any *supplemental* rights granted under the BCR may be brought by the individual against the (Delegated) EU Headquarters. Again, as under BCR individuals keep their own rights and remedies, the BCR do not contravene the enforcement regime of the Directive and a choice of forum would seem to be a valid option.

8.4.3 How should supervision of BCR be set up?

To ensure central supervision by the Lead DPA, the BCR could provide that the BCR will be supervised by the Lead DPA only. This is a clear deviation from the requirements listed in the WP Opinions (see Chapter 6 above), which prescribe that in respect of the BCR, all group companies should have a duty to cooperate with all DPAs and abide by their advice regarding the BCR and submit to their audits.[64] There is no valid reason for the Working Party 29 to require that indeed all DPAs have rights of supervision and auditing in respect of BCR. After all, as the individuals retain all their rights and remedies under applicable national law, BCR do not take away any existing jurisdiction, supervision, or enforcement powers from the DPAs. This requirement of the Working Party 29 seems to be inspired more by the wish of certain DPAs currently not having audit rights under their national law,[65] to remedy that inadequacy, rather than by a legitimate concern for proper supervision of BCR. Such supervision is adequately addressed by granting the Lead DPA central supervisory and enforcement powers (including full audit rights) in respect of BCR (as per *Recommendation 9*).[66] As it is the expectation that the lack of proper harmonization of enforcement powers of the DPAs will be addressed in the revised Directive[67] (see *Recommendation 5*), this requirement of the Working Party 29 will probably solve itself.

If BCR are drafted as suggested, the question arises whether such choice of law and forum clauses in BCR are indeed valid and binding under applicable EU rules of PIL and in particular the employee and consumer protection regimes of these rules. First a short overview is given of the relevant provisions of EU PIL concerning choice of law and forum clauses in employee and consumer contracts.

8.5 Choice of Law and Forum

8.5.1 Employee contracts

Insofar as applicable law is concerned, Article 8(1) of EC Regulation 593/2008 of 17 June 2008 on the law applicable to contractual obligations (*Rome I*)[68] provides that an individual employment contract will be governed by the law chosen by the parties. However, such choice of law may not have the result of depriving the employee of the protection afforded to him by the mandatory rules of the labour law which would be applicable in the absence of a choice of law clause (being the mandatory provisions of the labour law of the place where he habitually carries out his work). A choice of another law in the employment contract cannot set aside these mandatory provisions to the detriment of the employee.

As far as a choice of forum is concerned, Article 21(2) of EC Regulation 44/2001 of 22 December 2000 on jurisdiction and enforcement (*Brussels I Regulation*)[69]

[64] See BCR requirement (xii).

[65] Which is, for instance, the case in the UK.

[66] The Dutch DPA (acting as Lead DPA) has approved BCR that contain central supervision (including auditing) by the Lead DPA only.

[67] See Chapter 6, para 6.6.

[68] [2008] OJ L177/6.

[69] [2001] OJ L12/1.

provides that a choice of forum clause is valid only if it *allows* the employee to bring proceedings before a court or courts other than those indicated in Article 19 Brussels I Regulation (being the courts of the place where the group company is domiciled or the courts of the place where the employee habitually carries out his work). In other words, choice of forum clauses in employee contracts may only *add* a competent court and any agreement to the contrary will have no legal force.[70]

8.5.2 Consumer contracts

For consumer contracts, more or less similar rules apply as to employee contracts. As to a choice of law clause in a consumer contract, Article 6(2) Rome I provides that the consumer may always rely on the mandatory rules of the law of his habitual residence, and to that extent set aside a choice of law clause referring to another law. Further, pursuant to Article 17(2) Brussels I Regulation a choice of forum clause in a consumer contract is also valid only if it *allows* the consumer to bring proceedings before another court than those indicated in Article 16(1) Brussels I Regulation (being the courts of the place where the group company is domiciled or the courts of the place where the consumer is domiciled). Also in consumer contracts a choice of forum clause may therefore only *add* a competent court and any agreement to the contrary will have no legal force.[71]

A prerequisite for applying the above rules is that the contract is entered into by the company while it (i) pursues its commercial activities in the Member State where the consumer has his habitual residence or (ii) directs such activities (also) to that Member State, in both cases provided the contract falls within the scope of such activity.[72]

A general requirement for all choice of forum clauses is that an 'agreement conferring jurisdiction' must be either in writing or evidenced in writing (Article 23(1)(a) Brussels I Regulation).

8.6 Relevance of Rome I and the Brussels I Regulation for BCR

The limitations in respect of choice of law and forum clauses in employee and consumer contracts as set out above, may well be of relevance to the choice of law and forum clauses in BCR.

BCR for employee data The requirement in the WP Opinions that BCR be internally binding within the organization of the multinational (ie on all group companies and on employees) and externally binding for the benefit of the employees (must create rights for employees) will in many cases be complied with by the multinational by making BCR binding on employees. In this case there is little

[70] Article 23(5) Brussels I Regulation.
[71] Article 23(5) Brussels I Regulation.
[72] Article 6(1) Rome I and Art 15(1)(c) Brussels I Regulation.

doubt that the employee protection regimes of Article 8(1) Rome I and Articles 19 and 21(2) Brussels I Regulation apply (*employee protection regime*).

BCR for customer data The requirement in the WP Opinions that the BCR be externally binding for the benefit of the consumers may be complied with by the multinational making BCR part of the individual consumer contracts by including a clause to that effect. Also in that case, there is little doubt that the consumer protection regimes of Article 6(2) Rome I and Articles 16 and 17(2) Brussels I Regulation apply (*consumer protection regime*).

However, also if BCR are *not made part* of the individual employee or consumer contracts, it cannot be excluded that the employee and consumer protection regime may be of relevance. Even if BCR are *not made part* of the individual contracts, BCR will in most cases still be closely connected to these employee or consumer contracts, if only for the reason that the data processed under BCR are (in most cases) processed by the multinational in the context of the performance of these contracts. Employee data will be processed for salary payment purposes or for employee performance evaluation purposes; consumer data are processed for administering the purchase orders, delivery and payment under the consumer contracts, etc. This entails the risk that these data will be considered processed (also) as part of the individual employment or consumer contract and that any choice of law or forum clause in this respect (though being part of the BCR) should be subject to the employee and consumer protection regimes (*assumption 1*).

Multinationals under their BCR also process data of individuals with whom they have not (yet) entered into an employee or consumer contract. Examples are data processed by the multinational of job applicants and prospective customers. Most companies have a database with current and potential job applicants and further extensive marketing databases with data of potential customers. With all these individuals no employee or consumer agreement is in place. The marketing databases further contain the data of their existing customers, which data are not necessarily just processed in the performance of the respective consumer contracts but will also be processed to market other products or services of the multinational. However, in those cases too, the processing of data still seems to be very closely connected with the (potential) contracts to be concluded (ie data of job applicants are processed with a view to entering into an employment agreement and data of prospective customers are processed with a view to entering into a consumer agreement). From a protection perspective[73] it may be argued that it is logical to apply the employee and consumer protection regimes to these cases as well (*assumption 2*).

Below I will evaluate whether these assumptions are correct. In summary, an evaluation of the case law of the ECJ does not per se support assumption 1 and in any event does not support assumption 2. Taking as a starting point that the employee and consumer protection regimes should be interpreted restrictively,[74] the conclusion will be that these regimes should not apply to BCR. First however,

[73] The protection element is explicitly expressed in Recital 13 Brussels I Regulation and Recitals 23 and 24 Rome I.

[74] See n 82.

the requirements for applicability of the employee and consumer protection regimes will be discussed.

For applicability of both the employee and the consumer protection regimes under both Rome I and the Brussels I Regulation, it is required that a 'contract is concluded' with the employee or consumer or that it is 'a matter relating to such contract'. These requirements are extensively dealt with by the ECJ in its case law concerning the consumer protection regime in respect of forum clauses under the Brussels I Regulation. As the substantive scope and the provisions of Rome I, Rome II, and the Brussels I Regulation are intended to be aligned to ensure consistency, this case law is also of relevance to choice of law clauses under Rome I.[75]

8.6.1 Contract concluded

The ECJ ruled that applicability of the consumer protection regime under the Brussels Convention[76] (the predecessor of the Brussels I Regulation)[77] requires a 'contract concluded' by a consumer 'for the supply of goods or a contract for the

[75] Recital 7 Rome I provides that the substantive scope and provisions Rome I should be consistent with the Brussels I Regulation and Rome II. Recital 7 Rome II contains a similar statement. Recital 24 Rome I further indicates that the conditions for applying the consumer protection rule are brought in line with those of the Brussels Convention to ensure consistency, and Recital 24 Rome I states that for Art 15(1) Rome I to be applicable, since 'it is not sufficient for an undertaking to target its activities to the Member State of the consumer's residence or at a number of Member States including that Member State; a contract must also be concluded within the framework of its activities'. For the reverse situation, see Case 9/87 *Arcado* [1988] ECR 1988 01539, at para 15, where the ECJ, in a judgment concerning the interpretation of Art 5(1) Brussels Convention, in its turn refers to the scope of Art 10 (of the predecessor of) Rome I ([1980] OJ L266/1). The fact that the concepts under Rome I, Rome II, and the Brussels I Regulation should be aligned does not mean that they are by definition identical in all cases. Concepts in all PIL instruments should be understood autonomously. It has been repeatedly held by the ECJ that the concepts used in the Brussels Convention—and in particular those featured in Art 5(1) and (3) and Art 13—must be interpreted independently, by reference principally to the system and objectives of this regulation, in order to ensure that it is uniformly applied in all contracting states. On this, see in particular: Case C-27/02 *Engler* [2005] ECR I-481, at para 33; Case 150/77 *Bertrand* [1978] ECR 1431, at paras 14, 15, and 16; Case C-89/91 *Shearson Lehman Hutton* [1993] ECR I-139, at para 13; Case C-269/95 *Benincasa* [1997] ECR I-3767, at para 12; Case C-99/96 *Mietz* [1999] ECR I-2277, at para 26; and Case C-96/00 *Gabriel* ECR I-6367, at para 37). Further, Recital 11 Rome II states that the concept of a non-contractual obligation varies from one Member State to another and that therefore this concept should be understood to be autonomous. Rome I and II must be construed together so that the scope of each other excludes the other. An obligation is either contractual (and covered by Rome I) or non-contractual (and covered by Rome II): see John Ahern and William Binchy, *The Rome II Regulation on the Law Applicable to Non-contractual Obligations: a new international litigation regime* (Martinus Nijhoff Publishers 2009), at 60 (-Chapter 'The Scope of "Non-Contractual Obligations"' by Andrew Scott). If the concept of non-contractual obligations under Rome II is to be construed autonomously, this will by definition also apply to the concept of contractual obligations under Rome I.

[76] See Art 13(3) Brussels Convention on Jurisdiction and the Enforcement of Judgments in Civil and Commercial Matters, [1972] OJ L299/31 at 32, as amended by Conventions on the Accession of the New Member States to that Convention, consolidated text [1998] OJ C27/1.

[77] See Art 16 Brussels I Regulation. The Brussels I Regulation should be interpreted in the light of the case law decided under the Brussels Convention, see the opinion of the A-G Leger in Case C-281/02 *Owusu* [2005] ECR I-1383.

supply of services' (*Engler*).[78] The ECJ further ruled that the specific rules for jurisdiction in consumer and employee contracts in the Brussels Convention[79] constitute *a derogation* from the basic rule of the Brussels Convention,[80] which confers jurisdiction on the courts of the contracting state in which the defendant is domiciled. According to the ECJ (referring to its settled case law),[81] these specific rules of jurisdiction must give rise to a *strict interpretation* which cannot go beyond the cases envisaged by the Brussels Convention *and in all cases require a contract concluded by the consumer or employee.*[82]

In *Engler*, a professional vendor sent a letter on its own initiative to the consumer's domicile, without any request by her, designating her by name as the winner of a prize. Though the letter included a catalogue and order form, no contract was concluded. The ECJ held:

> Although it is indisputable that in a situation of that kind the claimant in the main proceedings is a consumer covered by the first paragraph of Article 13 of the Brussels Convention and that the vendor made contact with the consumer in the manner provided for in point 3(a) of that provision, by sending her a personalised letter containing a prize notification together with a catalogue and an order form for the sale of its goods in the Contracting State where she resides in order to induce her to take up the vendor's offer, the fact remains that in this case the vendor's initiative was not followed by the conclusion of a contract between the consumer and the vendor for one of the purposes referred to in that provision and in the course of which the parties assumed reciprocal obligations. It is common ground that, in the case in the main proceedings, the award of the prize allegedly won by the consumer was not subject to the condition that she orders goods from Janus Versand and no order was in fact placed by Ms Engler. Furthermore, it does not appear anywhere in the file that, by claiming the award of the promised 'prize', Ms Engler assumed any obligation towards that company, even by incurring an expense in order to obtain the award of the prize. In those circumstances, an action such as that brought by Ms Engler in the case in the main proceedings cannot be regarded as being contractual in nature for the purposes of Article 13, first paragraph, point 3, of the Brussels Convention. Contrary to the submissions of Ms Engler and the Austrian Government, that finding is not invalidated by the objective underlying that provision, namely to ensure adequate protection for the consumer as the party deemed to be economically weaker, or by the fact that, in this case, the letter was sent by Janus Versand to the consumer in person accompanied by a claim form entitled 'request for trial without obligation' and clearly intended to induce her to place an order for goods sold by that company. As is apparent from its

[78] Case C-27/02 *Engler* [2005] ECR I-481. This case concerned a letter personally addressed to an Austrian national (Ms Engler) and sent by a German mail order company, which gave Ms Engler the impression that she had won a prize.

[79] As provided for in Arts 13–15 Brussels Convention, currently Arts 16 and 19 Brussels I Regulation.

[80] Article 2 first para Brussels Convention.

[81] See, in particular, Case 150/77 *Bertrand* [1978] ECR 1431, at para 17; Case C-89/91 *Shearson Lehman Hutton* [1993] ECR I-139, at paras 14 to 16; Case C-269/95 *Benincasa* [1997] ECR I-3767, at para 13; and Case C-99/96 *Mietz* [1999] ECR I-2277, at para 27.

[82] Case C-27/02 *Engler* [2005] ECR I-481, at para 43.

wording, Article 13 clearly covers a 'contract concluded' by a consumer 'for the supply of goods or a contract for the supply of services'.

In 2009, the ECJ expanded on this ruling in respect of the consumer protection regime under the Brussels I Regulation (*Ilsinger*).[83] The facts in *Ilsinger* were identical to those in *Engler*, but for the fact that the consumer had in fact placed an order for goods with the vendor although this was not a condition for being awarded the prize. The ECJ explicitly held that its earlier case law in respect of Article 13 Brussels Convention was still valid as the clauses (Article 13 Brussels Convention and Article 15 Brussels I Regulation) both contain a similar requirement for the conclusion of a consumer contract. The ECJ, however, subsequently held that Article 15 Brussels Convention did apply in the case at hand as now the requirement of a consumer contract was being met (as evidenced by the placement of the order by the consumer).[84] The consumer could rely on the protection regime and initiate proceedings before the court of her own country. This is noteworthy as the promise of the prize by the vendor was a *unilateral undertaking* which was not tied in with a requirement for the ordering of the goods.

8.6.2 Matters relating to a contract

The employee and consumer protection regimes further apply 'in matters relating to' an employee or consumer contract. According to the ECJ 'matters relating to a contract' means that the claim must be contractual in nature but extends to claims 'which are so closely linked to the employee or consumer contract as to be indivisible'.[85]

8.6.3 Application of ECJ case law to BCR

Based on the case law above, it may well be argued that even if BCR for customer data are not made part of the individual consumer contracts, the consumer protection regime is applicable to BCR. Though BCR are in that case a unilateral undertaking independent from a consumer contract, it may be argued that the protection regime would apply from the moment the company indeed enters into a consumer contract with a consumer (however, still not in case no contract is entered into with the consumer). A similar argument can be made as to BCR for employee data. Even if BCR are not made part of an employment agreement, it may be argued that the employee protection regime applies from the moment the company indeed enters into an employment agreement. Further, if indeed an individual employment contract or consumer contract is concluded, it can easily be argued that the processing of data of the relevant employee or consumer is 'a matter relating' to such contract.

[83] Now in respect of Art 15 Brussels I Regulation, the successor to Art 13 Brussels Convention. See Case C-180/06 *Ilsinger*, [2009] OJ C153/3, at para 58.

[84] See Case C-180/06 *Ilsinger*, [2009] OJ C153/3, at para 59.

[85] Cheshire, North, and Fawcett (n 29), at 268 and ECJ case law listed in fn 268.

The arguments against this conclusion are that the data protection rights under the Directive are to be enforced under national data protection law (or tort law)[86] and therefore are in themselves not contractual in nature. Further, the BCR do not relate to the individual employee or consumer contract as the BCR apply *irrespective* of whether an employee or consumer contract is concluded. The BCR contain general undertakings by a multinational to process data of *any individual* the company has dealings with. As indicated, besides employees and consumers with whom the multinational has actually entered into a contract, the BCR also apply to the processing of data of job applicants, ex-employees, independent contractors, contact persons of corporate customers of company, its suppliers or other business contacts, as well as of individuals who take part in research projects or pilots undertaken by the company and to marketing data of consumers who may be interested in products or services of the company.

Further, the distinction that can be made with *Ilsinger* is that there the promise by the vendor to the consumer was made on an *individual basis* and was closely connected with the contract entered into (was intended to entice the consumer into entering into the relevant contract). At first glance this seems an artificial distinction, but in future case law of the ECJ this may well prove to be decisive. BCR are not directed specifically to an individual consumer to entice that consumer into a contract. That this may be a relevant distinction is supported by the employee protection regime which specifies explicitly that it applies to *individual* (as opposed to collective) employee contracts only.[87] The general opinion is that agreements between employer and employee representatives do not qualify as such nor collective employment contracts and also not employee regulations and collective regulations (even if made on behalf of or for the benefit of the employees), unless these are made a part of the individual contracts.[88]

Taking as a starting point that the employee and consumer protection regimes should be interpreted restrictively, the conclusion should be that these regimes do not apply to BCR. This conclusion is further supported by the fact that BCR (providing for supplemental protection only) do not take away any rights or remedies related to the employee and consumer contracts. All rights and remedies of employees and consumers under applicable law remain in place. The choice of forum clause in the BCR is meant to provide a forum to enforce *additional* rights and remedies (above any existing national rights and remedies) which the BCR may grant. Since this forum clause is not meant to *take away* any dispute settlement

[86] The legal basis for enforcement of data protection rights varies per Member State. See Chapter 4, n 24.

[87] Article 18 Brussels I Regulation. The element 'individual' is not included in the provision in respect of the consumer protection regime. However, the text of Art 15 Brussels I Regulation clearly applies to individual consumer agreements 'in matters related to a contract concluded by a person, the consumer, (. . .)'. The specific insertion of the element 'individual' in the provision of the employee protection clause functions to make it clear that collective employment agreements are excluded, which inclusion is not required in the consumer protection clause as there is no equivalent concept for consumer contracts.

[88] Report Jenard/Moller, [1990] OJ C189/77, at para 60. P.H.L.M. Kuypers, *Forumkeuze in het Nederlands internationaal privaatrecht* (Kluwer 2008), at 468.

mechanisms which are available under applicable national law, the choice of forum clause does not seem to run contrary to the underlying protection objectives of the PIL regimes for employment and consumer relationships. In fact such choice of law and forum may well lead to improved redress.

It is clear that this is still an open issue which ultimately has to be decided by the ECJ. It is therefore recommended that European legislators provide that in BCR (as to the supplemental protection provided by the BCR) a choice of law and forum may be made. As this is already a (sub) part of *Recommendation 9*, this does not lead to a separate recommendation here.

8.6.4 Relevance of Rome II?

If the consumer and employee protection regimes of Rome I do not apply as there is no employee or consumer contract, the question may arise whether the choice of law clause in BCR should then be decided based on EC Regulation 864/2007 of 11 July 2007 on the law applicable to non-contractual obligations (*Rome II*).[89] Rome II also contains employee and consumer protection regimes as to a choice of law in respect of non-contractual obligations vis-à-vis employees or consumers. At first sight Rome II may seem applicable as in many jurisdictions a breach of data protection qualifies as a tort. However, in this event too a choice of law in BCR will be decided based on Rome I, this to the detriment of Rome II.[90] Again, a parallel should be sought with the case law of the ECJ in respect of the employee and consumer protection regime under the Brussels Convention (the predecessor of the Brussels I Regulation). In *Engler*, the ECJ held that the consumer protection regime was not applicable as there was no contract concluded, but subsequently ruled that this did not automatically entail that the action is not contractual in nature for purposes of Article 5(1) Brussels Convention. In *Engler* the ECJ had to decide whether the claim for the prize promised in the letter sent by the vendor should subsequently be considered as being *contractual in nature* for the purposes of Article 5(1) or as being *tortuous for purposes* of Article 5(3) Brussels Convention:

> It follows that the finding made in paragraphs 38 and 44 of the present judgment that the legal action brought in the main proceedings is not contractual in nature for the purposes of the first paragraph of Article 13 of the Brussels Convention does not in itself prevent that action from relating to a contract for the purposes of Article 5(1). In order to determine whether such is the case in the main proceedings, it must be observed that it is clear from the case-law, first, that although Article 5(1) of the Brussels Convention *does not require* the conclusion of a contract (...).

From this case and other case law of the ECJ it may be derived that the ECJ gives a very broad meaning to what constitutes a 'contractual obligation' under Article 5(1) Brussels I Regulation. For Article 5(1) Brussels I Regulation to apply, 'the establishment of a legal obligation freely consented to by one person towards another

[89] [2007] OJ L 99/40.

[90] Rome I and Rome II must be construed together, see n 75.

and on which the claimant's action is based' is sufficient.[91] It is therefore *not* required that a contract be concluded; an obligation freely assumed by one party towards another is sufficient.[92] An example of a unilateral undertaking that the ECJ considers qualifying as an 'obligation freely assumed' is *Engler*, which concerned the letter sent by the professional vendor on its own initiative to the consumer's domicile, without any request by her, designating her by name as the winner of a prize. The ECJ decided that such a letter, sent to addressees and by the means chosen by the sender solely on its own initiative, constituted an obligation 'freely assumed'. The ECJ further held that:

> as the addressee of the letter expressly accepted the prize notification made out in her favour by requesting payment of the prize, at least from that moment, the intentional act of a professional vendor in circumstances such as those in the main proceedings must be regarded as an act capable of constituting an obligation which binds its author as in a matter relating to a contract.

In line with the above case law, there seems little doubt that the unilateral undertakings contained in BCR qualify as 'freely assumed' and will constitute contractual obligations, this at least from the moment that the BCR are enforced by an employee or consumer, as this will constitute acceptance. The consequence is that a choice of law made by the multinational in BCR should be assessed based on Rome I rather than Rome II.[93]

8.7 Summary Conclusion: Applicability of Employee and Consumer Protection Regimes

In summary, the conclusion is that the employee and consumer protection regimes in Rome I and the Brussels I Regulation will apply in those cases where the BCR are made part of the employee or the consumer contract by including a clause to that effect. Insofar as a company processes employee and consumer data under BCR without making BCR part of the individual consumer and employee contracts, the conclusion is that the employee and consumer protection regimes in Rome I and the Brussels I Regulation should not apply. However, from the above it is clear that the latter is still an open issue which should be ultimately decided by the ECJ. In the meantime, multinationals are well advised to draft their BCR in such a manner that these regimes are (as much as possible) complied with. Below, I will evaluate

[91] Case C-27/02 *Engler* [2005] ECR I-481, at para 51; Case C-26/91 *Handte* [1992] ECR I-3967, at para 15; Case C-51/97 *Réunion européenne and Others* [1998] ECR I-6534, at para 17; Case C-334/00 *Tacconi* [2002] ECR I-7357, at para 23; and Case C-265/02 *Frahuil* [2004] ECR I-0000, at para 24.

[92] Case C-334/00 *Tacconi* [2002] ECR I-7357, at para 22.

[93] For a similar conclusion based on an analysis of the various definitions of contractual obligations in the contracting states prior to the above ECJ case law, see Richard Plender, *The European Contracts Convention, The Rome Convention on the Choice of Law for Contracts* (Sweet & Maxwell 1991), at 51 and fn 11. Plender also concludes that an obligation may be contractual for the purposes of the Rome Convention, although the forum characterizes the appropriate remedy as one in tort (at 52).

such choice of law and forum clause in BCR against the employee and consumer protection regimes under PIL.

8.8 Are the Choice of Law and Forum Clauses Validly Entered Into?

Pursuant to Article 10 of Rome I, the existence and validity of a contract or any term thereof (including the choice of law and forum clauses) must be determined by the law which would govern the contract if the contract or term were valid. This provision also applies to unilateral undertakings which fall within the scope of the employee or consumer protection regime of Rome I.[94] The law chosen to apply to BCR therefore decides whether BCR are binding and whether the choice of law clause made therein is valid. As discussed in Chapter 7, paragraph 7.3.1, most Member States consider that rights may be granted to third parties by means of unilateral undertakings.[95] In that case the choice of law and forum clauses will also be validly made. If a Member State does not consider that third-party beneficiary rights may be granted by a unilateral undertaking, the contractual solutions should be followed as explained in Chapter 7, paragraph 7.3.5.

8.9 Are the Choice of Law and Forum Clauses Themselves Valid and Binding?

Assuming that the choice of law and forum clauses are validly *made*, the question arises whether the choice of law and forum clauses *themselves* are valid and binding. From paragraph 8.5, it follows that the choice of law clause cannot set aside the mandatory provisions of (i) the labour law of the place where the employee habitually carries out his work or (ii) the consumer law of the place where the consumer is domiciled. As BCR only apply if they provide additional rights and remedies in favour of the employee or the consumer, the choice of law clause is not in violation of the provisions of Rome I. From paragraph 8.6.3 it follows that the choice of forum clause cannot set aside the jurisdiction of the courts indicated by

94 See also Strikwerda (n 29) in respect of the predecessor of Rome I, at 166. Article 11(3) Rome I is not of relevance here as it relates to a 'unilateral act intended to have legal effect relating to an existing or contemplated contract'. Unilateral acts that are intended to have legal effect and that relate to an existing or contemplated contract, are for instance an offer, remission of a debt, declaration of rescission or notice of termination. See Cheshire, North, and Fawcett (n 29), at 748 and the *Report on the Convention on the law applicable to contractual obligations* by Mario Giuliano, Professor, University of Milan, and Paul Lagarde, Professor, University of Paris I, [1980] OJ C282, at 29. BCR are independent unilateral undertakings rather than unilateral acts and are not in relation to a contemplated or existing agreement. For purposes of Rome I, they should rather be considered as a 'contractual obligation' within the scope of Art 5(1) Rome I itself, rather than a unilateral act relating to such contractual obligation.

95 See WP 133, part 2: background to Paper fn 10 (Chapter 6, n 7), where it is mentioned that according to the civil law of some jurisdictions (eg Italy and Spain), unilateral declarations or unilateral undertakings do not have binding effect.

the Brussels I Regulation. The forum clause in BCR can therefore only create *additional forums* in favour of the employee or the consumer. This is clearly a broader protection provided to the employee or consumer than the choice of law clause (which is in principle valid, as are any mandatory provisions of the labour law of the employee or the consumer law of the consumer). If the employee and consumer protection regime were indeed to apply to BCR, the conclusion should then be that the choice of forum clause would not hold as the choice of forum in BCR is meant as an *exclusive forum* for the additional rights granted to the employees and consumers and not as an *alternative forum*. As a side note I mention that in practice this does not pose much of a problem. The benefits for individuals provided by the complaints procedure in BCR (as supported by enforcement by the Lead DPA and the courts of the Lead DPA) entail in practice that individuals prefer to follow this procedure rather than addressing their own court. This being said, it would obviously be welcomed if European legislators were to provide that a valid choice of forum clause could be made in BCR. This is already part of *Recommendation 9*.

8.10 Choice of Forum should be (Evidenced) in Writing

8.10.1 BCR as unilateral undertakings

The next[96] problem is that Article 23(1)(a) Brussels I Regulation requires that an agreement conferring jurisdiction be '*either in writing or evidenced in writing*'. This requirement should also be interpreted in an autonomous manner.[97] Specific requirements under applicable national law should be ignored.[98] The ECJ interprets Article 23 Brussels I Regulation in a strict manner.[99] Case law of the ECJ shows that the 'in writing' requirement is satisfied only when there is a *written contract* which contains a choice of jurisdiction and that any variant on this causes problems.[100] Case law further shows that the alternative '*evidenced* in writing' is foremost designed to deal with the situation where there is an oral contract which is confirmed in writing.[101] When applying this case law to BCR, it seems difficult to conclude that the forum clause is made in writing (as BCR are unilateral undertakings only) or is evidenced in writing (as in respect of BCR, there is no oral contract which is confirmed in writing). Rather the reverse, BCR contain an offer in writing and if there is acceptance, this is a tacit acceptance by the employee or

[96] The requirements of Art 23 Brussels I Regulation also apply in the case of a choice of forum clause in employee and consumer contracts. See for an overview of literature and case law, see P.H.L. M. Kuypers (n 88), at 490. See further Cheshire, North, and Fawcett (n 29), at 271 and 275. The use of jurisdiction clauses in consumer cases must not infringe the Unfair Terms in Consumer Contracts Regulations 1999 (SI 1999/3159), pursuant to which jurisdiction clauses that have not been individually negotiated and exclude or hinder the consumer's right to take legal action (like confer exclusive jurisdiction on the seller's place of business) must be regarded as unfair.

[97] See case law ECJ in n 75.

[98] Case C 159/97 *Castelletti* [1999] ECR I-1597, at para 39.

[99] Cheshire, North, and Fawcett (n 29), at 291.

[100] Cheshire, North, and Fawcett (n 29), at 291.

[101] Cheshire, North, and Fawcett (n 29), at 292 and case law referred to in fn 759.

consumer which is not confirmed in writing. This leads to the conclusion that the choice of forum clause in BCR does not meet the requirements as to form. This entails that employees or consumers may enforce the additional rights and remedies granted in BCR against the company, but that the company in its turn may not invoke the choice of forum clause against the employees or consumers (as this forum clause does not meet the stricter requirement that such clause has been concluded in writing or evidenced in writing). This seems a very undesirable outcome. National case law in some Member States shows that national courts under circumstances honour a choice of forum clause, which is contained in a written offer which has been tacitly agreed by the other party.[102] Tacit acceptance may for instance be concluded if a plaintiff bases its claim on BCR with a choice of forum clause, without indicating that he does *not* accept the choice of forum.[103] However, this does not add much as the same result would also be achieved by Article 24 Brussels I Regulation, pursuant to which the court of a Member State before which a defendant appears will have jurisdiction. If the employee or consumer addresses the forum chosen in BCR and the multinational appears in court, such court will have jurisdiction.[104] However, if the employee or consumer addresses *its own court*, the multinational will not be able to invoke the forum clause against the employee or consumer.

8.10.2 Contractual solution

In Chapter 8, paragraph 7.3.5, I discussed that a solution to solve the issue that in certain countries unilateral undertakings cannot be considered to confer rights on third parties, is to have the (Delegated) EU Headquarters enter into a contract with one of its other group companies containing a third-party beneficiary clause for the benefit of the employee or consumer. The question is then whether the requirements as to form (ie the forum clause should be in writing or evidenced in writing) also apply in relation to the third-party beneficiaries. Case law makes clear that a third-party beneficiary may invoke a choice of forum clause which is made on his behalf even though the third party has not satisfied the requirements as to form.[105] Case law, however, does not seem to support the reverse situation. The choice of forum clause cannot be invoked *against* a third-party beneficiary who has not separately consented to the choice of forum clause.[106] Again, to solve all issues

[102] P.H.L.M. Kuypers (n 88), at 318.

[103] P.H.L.M. Kuypers (n 88), at 319.

[104] Cheshire, North, and Fawcett (n 29), at 296.

[105] See eg Case 201/82 *Gerling* [1983] ECR 2503, where the ECJ decided that a choice of forum clause in an insurance contract, which was made for the benefit of the policy beneficiary, could be invoked by the beneficiary even if he had not signed the insurance contract.

[106] If a third party succeeds to the rights and obligations of an original party under a contract that complies with the requirements of Art 23 Brussels I Regulation, the third party cannot avoid the obligations in respect of jurisdiction by arguing that he did not (separately) consent to the jurisdiction clause. See Case 71/83 *Tilly Russ* [1984] ECR 2417, which concerned a bill of lading and the binding effect of a choice of forum clause as against the (third-party) holder of the bill of lading who, under the applicable national law, had become a party to the transportation agreement. The choice of forum

identified above as to the form requirements for a choice of forum, it would be welcomed if European legislators provided that a valid choice of forum clause may be made in BCR (as per *Recommendation 10*).

8.11 Conclusions: How the Applicability, Supervision, and Enforcement Regime of BCR May Work

As indicated at the beginning of this chapter, it is in the interest of the multinational that all complaints under its BCR are ultimately dealt with by the Lead DPA (and the courts of the Member State of such DPA) that negotiated the provisions of the BCR under applicability of the DPA's own law (ie the law under which the provisions of the BCR were drafted). This ensures for the multinational a consistent and predictable interpretation of the BCR. For the same reason the multinational has an interest in the Lead DPA having central supervision over the BCR. It is clear that even if BCR are drafted as recommended and provide for supplemental protection only, many PIL issues arise in respect of a choice of law and forum clause in BCR. This is the case, despite such choice of law and forum not being contrary to the underlying policy choices of the consumer and employee protection regimes of Rome I and the Brussels I Regulation. To the contrary, such choice of law and forum would drastically improve the data protection and the access to remedies for the individuals covered by BCR.

could be invoked vis-à-vis such a third party. If a third party is not a successor to the rights and obligations of one of the original parties to the agreement, the choice of forum clause can be invoked vis-à-vis him only if he has accepted the jurisdiction clause in the original agreement as per the requirements of Art 23 Brussels I Regulation. See, Case C-387/98 *Coreck Maritime* [2000] ECR I-9337.

9

BCR and the 'Accountability Principle'

9.1 The Accountability Principle in the Field of Data Protection

In December 2009, the Working Party 29 together with the Working Party on Police and Justice (*WPPJ*) issued a joint paper 'The Future of Privacy'[1] in which they expressed the view that the present European legal framework for data protection has not been successful in ensuring that the data protection requirements translate into effective mechanisms that deliver real protection.[2] To improve this situation, the Working Party 29 and the WPPJ proposed to the Commission to include the 'principle of accountability' in the revised Directive.[3] With the acknowledgement that 'accountability' may have different meanings in different languages and legal systems,[4] the Working Party 29 and WPPJ proceeded with describing the measures which 'accountability' requires (rather than focusing on a definition). In short, this principle entails that the controller is required:

(i) to implement appropriate and effective measures to put the material processing principles of the Directive into effect; and
(ii) to demonstrate these measures to the DPA on its request.

The European Data Protection Supervisor (*EDPS*) supports the proposal of the Working Party 29.[5] In its turn the Commission in its EC Communication on revision of the Directive indicated that it 'will explore ways of ensuring that data controllers put in place effective policies and mechanisms to ensure compliance with data protection rules. In doing so, it will take into account the current debate

[1] See Chapter 1, n 6.

[2] WP Contribution on The Future of Privacy (Chapter 1, n 6), para 8 at 6: '[T]he main principles of data protection are still valid despite these important challenges. The level of data protection in the EU can benefit from a better application of the existing data protection principles in practice.' Also at para 78 at 10: 'In practice Article 17 (1) has not been successful in making data protection sufficiently effective in organizations, also due to different approaches taken in the national implementing measures.'

[3] WP Contribution on The Future of Privacy (Chapter 1, n 6), at para 79.

[4] WP Contribution on The Future of Privacy (Chapter 1, n 6), at para 21 at 7: 'The term "accountability" comes from the Anglo-Saxon world where it is in common use and where there is a broadly shared understanding of its meaning—even though defining what exactly accountability means is complex. In general terms though, its emphasis is on showing how responsibility is exercised and making this verifiable. Responsibility and accountability are two sides of the same coin and both essential elements of good governance. Only when responsibility is demonstrated as working effectively in practice can sufficient trust be developed.'

[5] EDPS Opinion on the revision of the Directive (Chapter 2, n 35), at para 7.2.

on the possible introduction of an "accountability" principle'.[6] The current status is that the Commission indeed included a provision on accountability of the controller in the Proposed Regulation.[7]

The principle of accountability is not new and is already applied in some other fields of law.[8] The principle has also from the start been applied in the field of data protection. The accountability principle is one of the main principles in the OECD Privacy Guidelines,[9] the APEC Privacy Framework,[10] the Canadian PIPED Act,[11] and also of the more recent Madrid Draft Proposal for International Standards,[12] the ISO draft standard 29100 setting a privacy

[6] EC Communication on the revision of the Directive (Chapter 2, n 34), at 11–12.

[7] See Art 22 Proposed Regulation: 'The controller shall adopt policies and implement appropriate measures to ensure and be able to demonstrate that the processing of personal data is performed in compliance with this Regulation, including the assignment of responsibilities, and the training of staff involved in the processing operations.'

[8] For instance the Securities and Exchange Commission requires that companies implement a code of ethics and show evidence of effective implementation procedures. See <http://www.sec.gov/about/laws/secrulesregs.htm>. For other examples, see para 9.2 below. Under EU law, investment managers have to show sufficient and proper administrative organization in order to obtain authorization (see eg Art 5 Directive 2004/39/EC of the European Parliament and of the Council of 21 April 2004 on markets in financial instruments amending Council Directives 85/611/EEC and 93/6/EEC and Directive 2000/12/EC of the European Parliament and of the Council and repealing Council Directive 93/22/EEC).

[9] See Chapter 2, n 40, at 14: 'A data controller should be accountable for complying with measures which give effect to the principles stated above.' The principles 'stated above' concern the material processing principles.

[10] See Chapter 2, n 40, Principle 26: 'A personal information controller should be accountable for complying with measures that give effect to the Principles stated above. When personal information is to be transferred to another person or organization, whether domestically or internationally, the personal information controller should obtain the consent of the individual or exercise due diligence and take reasonable steps to ensure that the recipient person or organization will protect the information consistently with these Principles.'

[11] Personal Information Protection and Electronic Documents Act, 200, C.5, to be found at <http://www.laws.justice.gc.ca>. See Sch I, s 4.1, where the first Principle requires developing and implementing policies and practices to uphold the 10 fair information principles, including implementing procedures for protecting personal information and establishing procedures for receiving and responding to complaints and inquiries:

> Principle 1—Accountability
>
> An organization is responsible for personal information under its control and shall designate an individual or individuals who are accountable for the organization's compliance with the following principles.
>
> 4.1.1 Accountability for the organization's compliance with the principles rests with the designated individual(s), even though other individuals within the organization may be responsible for the day-to-day collection and processing of personal information. In addition, other individuals within the organization may be delegated to act on behalf of the designated individual(s).
>
> 4.1.2 The identity of the individual(s) designated by the organization to oversee the organization's compliance with the principles shall be made known upon request.
>
> 4.1.3 An organization is responsible for personal information in its possession or custody, including information that has been transferred to a third party for processing. The organization shall use contractual or other means to provide a comparable level of protection while the information is being processed by a third party.

[12] See Madrid Draft Proposal for International Standards (Chapter 3, n 49), Art 11: '[T]he responsible person shall: a. take all the necessary measures to observe the principles and obligations set out in this Document and in the applicable national legislation; and b. have the necessary internal mechanisms in place for demonstrating such observance both to data subjects and to the supervisory authorities in the exercise of their powers, as established in para. 23.'

framework,[13] the draft Australian Privacy Principles,[14] the FTC Proposed Framework for Consumer Privacy,[15] and the Kerry-McCain Commercial Privacy Bill of Rights Act of 2011.[16]

[13] As issued by the Centre for Information Policy Leadership, to be found at <http://www.informationpolicycentre.com>. The Centre is also engaged in an initiative to explore the effects of the principle of accountability in respect of data protection.

[14] Australian Government, Australian Privacy Principles (Chapter 2, n 55). The Exposure Draft does not use the word 'accountability', but contains provisions that are close in content to the twofold structure of the accountability principle as envisaged by the Working Party 29 and the Commission. This requires that a controller must: (i) take organizational and technological measures to comply with the data protection rules; and (ii) be able to demonstrate compliance in case of an audit. Principle I(2) of the Australian Privacy Principles, on 'open and transparent management of personal information', requires that:

> an entity must take such steps as are reasonable in the circumstances to implement practices, procedures and systems relating to the entity's functions and activities that:
>
> (a) will ensure that the entity complies with the Australian Privacy Principles; and
>
> (b) will enable the entity to deal with inquiries or complaints from individuals about the entity's compliance with the Australian Privacy Principles.
>
> (3) An entity must have a clearly expressed and up-to-date policy (the privacy policy) about the management of personal information by the entity.
>
> (4) Without limiting subparagraph (3), the privacy policy must contain the following information:
>
> (a) the kinds of personal information that the entity collects and holds;
>
> (b) how the entity collects and holds personal information;
>
> (c) the purposes for which the entity collects, holds, uses and discloses personal information;
>
> (d) how an individual may access personal information about the individual that is held by the entity and seek the correction of such information;
>
> (e) how an individual may complain about an interference with the privacy of the individual and how the entity will deal with such a complaint;
>
> (f) whether the entity is likely to disclose personal information to overseas recipients;
>
> (g) if the entity is likely to disclose personal information to overseas recipients-the countries in which such recipients are likely to be located if it is practicable to specify those countries in the privacy policy.

Pursuant to Part B, paragraph 19 of the Exposure Draft, the same requirement applies in case of the transborder data transfers: 'This Act extends to an act done, or practice engaged in, outside Australia by an agency. This Act and an approved privacy code extend to an act done, or practice engaged in, outside Australia by an organisation that has an Australian link.'

[15] The FTC does not use the term accountability, but principle 1 of the FTC Proposed Framework for Consumer Privacy (Chapter 5, n 36), at 1, requires companies to have comprehensive data management procedures in place:

> • Companies should promote consumer privacy throughout their organisations and at every stage of the development of their products and services.
>
> • Companies should incorporate substantive privacy protections into their practices, such as data security, reasonable collection limits, sound retention practices, and data accuracy.
>
> • Companies should maintain comprehensive data management procedures throughout the life cycle of their products and services.

Confusingly, the FTC labels this principle 'Privacy by Default', which term has a different meaning under EU law, see EC Communication on the revision of the Directive (Chapter 2, n 34), para 2.2.4, at 12.

[16] Sections 102 (Accountability) and 103 (Privacy by Design) Kerry-McCain Commercial Privacy Bill of Rights Act of 2011:

9.2 The Accountability Principle According to General Literature

According to the extensive literature on accountability in the public policy literature and fields of law other than data protection, the main purpose of 'accountability' is to use the law to hold businesses accountable 'for taking their responsibilities seriously by using various mechanisms to encourage or enforce businesses to put in place internal governance structures, management practices and corporate cultures aimed at achieving responsible outcomes'.[17] The law attempts to constitute corporate consciences 'to want to do what they should do' and not just to produce legally compliant outputs.[18] The regulatory initiatives to seek to do this are often called 'meta-regulation', ie the regulation of internal self-regulation.[19] The underlying

> SEC. 102. ACCOUNTABILITY.
>
> Each covered entity shall, in a manner proportional to the size, type, and nature of the covered information it collects—
>
> (1) have managerial accountability, proportional to the size and structure of the covered entity, for the adoption and implementation of policies consistent with this Act;
>
> (2) have a process to respond to non-frivolous inquiries from individuals regarding the collection, use, transfer, or storage of covered information relating to such individuals; and
>
> (3) describe the means of compliance of the covered entity with the requirements of this Act upon request from—(A) the Commission; or
>
> (B) an appropriate safe harbor program established under section 501.
>
> SEC. 103. PRIVACY BY DESIGN.
>
> Each covered entity shall, in a manner proportional to the size, type, and nature of the covered information that it collects, implement a comprehensive information privacy program by—
>
> incorporating necessary development processes and practices throughout the product life cycle that are designed to safeguard the personally identifiable information that is covered information of individuals based on—
>
> (A) the reasonable expectations of such individuals regarding privacy; and
>
> (B) the relevant threats that need to be guarded against in meeting those expectations; and
>
> (2) maintaining appropriate management processes and practices throughout the data life cycle that are designed to ensure that information systems comply with—
>
> (A) the provisions of this Act;
>
> (B) the privacy policies of a covered entity; and
>
> (C) the privacy preferences of individuals that are consistent with the consent choices and related mechanisms of individual participation as described in section 202.

[17] Parker (Chapter 5, n 43), at 207.

[18] Parker (Chapter 5, n 43), at 208.

[19] Many other terms are used in this context. See for an enumeration Gilad (Chapter 6, n 66), at 485: 'system-based regulation, enforced self-regulation, management-based regulation, principles-based regulation.' Another label is 'horizontal supervision' (whereby actions are adjusted by the supervisory authority and the supervised entity in cooperation) as opposed to vertical supervision, which is the traditional *command and control* model, whereby any actions of the supervised entity are corrected top down by the supervisory authority. See A.T. Ottow, *De Markt Meester? De zoektocht naar nieuwe vormen van toezicht* (Boom Juridische Uitgevers 2009) in particular para 2.1. On the expansion of regulation from government to governance, see Ramses Wessel and Jan Wouters, 'The Phenomenon of Multilevel Regulation: Interactions between Global, EU and National Regulatory Spheres', in Andreas Follesdal,

assumption is that organizations, not being individuals, can only be responsible by building responsibility into their practice and structure. Accountability is part of risk-based regulation,[20] where companies themselves prioritize and tailor their compliance efforts dependent on the level of risk involved. Meta-regulation is expected to be able to achieve more sustainable compliance with traditional regulatory goals 'because it latches onto companies' inherent capacity to manage themselves'.[21] The aim of meta-regulation therefore is to make sure the relevant values are 'built into the practice and structure of the company'.[22] In order to achieve these objectives, meta-regulation requires companies 'to put in place formal governance structures and management systems that help to produce a responsible culture and management in practice',[23] while recognizing that regulators may not know exactly what the right processes and even the results would look like in each situation and further that these may change over time.[24] More fundamental, one of the underlying drivers for meta-regulation is the recognition in the general policy literature that prescriptive regulation (where regulators prescribe the desired behaviour) has 'inherent limitations to achieve the underlying regulatory objectives due to "regulators" imperfect access to factual information and to theoretical knowledge (eg of the solutions that could most effectively and efficiently mitigate risks to regulatory objectives). More fundamental, prescriptive regulation is an inherently limited tool for managing complex, heterogeneous, and dynamic social realities, which leads to both excessive and insufficient regulation'.[25]

Ramses A. Wessel, and Jan Wouters (eds.), *Multilevel regulation and the EU, The interplay between global, European and national normative processes* (Martinus Nijhof Publishers 2008), at 22–47.

[20] McBarnet (Chapter 4, n 24), at 34–6. For risk-based regulation in respect of CSR see Parker (Chapter 5, n 43), at 228: 'To the extent that scholars and policy makers focus on achieving CSR through corporate governance processes (ie, meta-regulation), it signifies a decisive move in the direction of abandoning traditional "command and control" state regulatory schemes in favour of "responsive regulation", which is supposed to facilitate—yet not enforce and dictate—self-regulation programmes and "compliance-oriented" regulation, which is carried out through corporate consent and voluntary organizational processes of reflexive learning.' As to risk-management by multinationals of their supply chain, see McBarnet and Kurkchiyan (Chapter 5, n 41), at 63 cited in n 41. See further Julia Black, 'The Emergence of Risk Based Regulation and the New Public Management in the UK' [2005] *Public Law*, at 512–49.

[21] Parker (Chapter 5, n 43), at 212. The fact that meta-regulation 'latches onto companies' inherent capacity to manage themselves' is at the same time seen by many as the main weakness of meta-regulation. See for instance Black (n 20), at 512–49: 'the firm's internal controls will be directed at ensuring the firm achieves the objectives it sets for itself: namely profits and market share. Whilst proponents of meta-regulation are correct to argue that its strength lies in the ability to leverage off a firm's own systems of internal control, and indeed regulators should fashion their own regulatory processes on those controls, this difference in objectives means that regulators can never rely on a firm's own systems without some modifications. The problem then arises, however, of locating those differences and ensuring both regulator and regulated understand them.' See for an overview of studies that have assessed the impact on compliance of introduction of regulation based on accountability Gilad (Chapter 6, n 66), at para 3, at 491–2, concluding that 'on the whole, the above studies seem to point to the positive impact of process-oriented regulatory institutions on firms' performance'.

[22] Parker (Chapter 5, n 43), at 215.

[23] Parker (Chapter 5, n 43), at 216.

[24] Parker (Chapter 5, n 43), at 217.

[25] Gilad (Chapter 6, n 66), at 493, referring to C. Sunstein, 'Problems with Rules' [1995] *California Law Review* 83, 953–1026; and J. Black, *Rules and Regulators* (Clarendon Press 1997).

According to the extensive literature on what it takes for organizations to be internally committed to legal compliance, this requires at least:[26]

- high-level policies setting out the legal and ethical obligations the company wishes to adhere to;
- institutionalization of these policies within management and employee accountability and performance measurement systems and the company's standard operating procedures;
- clear communication and training in programmes for raising awareness of the existence and the substance of policies;
- internal reporting and monitoring systems;
- complaint procedures and a possibility of whistle-blowing;
- internal and external reviews or audits of the performance of the compliance system, which feed back to the highest level; and
- external disclosure in the annual reports in a comparable format.

9.2.1 External disclosure requirement

The requirement of external disclosure in a comparable format is increasingly being discussed in the literature as a necessity to ensure that external stakeholders have access to information on the relevant compliance efforts of the company and any related shortcomings and remedial efforts. Reporting in a standard format further facilitates comparison between companies and inclusion of performance in indices, which appears to be a strong incentive to enforce compliance.[27] This is also advocated in the law and economics approach, according to which 'the law should be concerned with promoting efficient solutions within market transactions, for example by improving the flow of information on the basis of which consumers make market decisions'.[28] Especially in areas where companies are concerned with reputational damage, this may provide a stronger ability of consumers to secure remedies than the law.[29] This is also the view of the High Level Group of Company Law Experts on a Modern Regulatory Framework for Company Law in Europe:[30]

[26] Parker (Chapter 5, n 43), at 216.

[27] See: Kevin Campbell and Douglas Vick, 'Disclosure law and the market for corporate social responsibility', at 241–78; and Peter Muchlinski, 'Corporate social responsibility and international law: the case of human rights and multinational enterprises', at 453, both in: McBarnet, Voiculescu, Campbell, *The New Corporate Accountability, Corporate Social Responsibility and the Law* (Cambridge University Press 2007). Also Gunningham (Chapter 5, n 38), at 495. Recent illustrations that reporting and indices are influential are to be found in the Dutch newspapers of September 2010, where Royal Shell was dropped from the Sustainability index. The previous year, the bonus programme of Shell was made dependent on this ranking ('Shell uit duurzaamheid index gezet' *Financieele Dagblad* 10 September 2010; 'Shell geschrapt van lijst schone bedrijven' *Volkskrant* 9 September 2010).

[28] Scott (Chapter 4, n 26), at 1.

[29] Scott (Chapter 4, n 26), at 4.

[30] Report of the High Level Group of Company Law Experts on a Modern Regulatory Framework for Company Law in Europe, Brussels, 4 November 2002 (Chapter 4, n 31), at para 3 at 961–2 (*Disclosure of Information as a Regulatory Tool*).

Requiring disclosure of information can be a powerful regulatory tool in company law. It enhances the accountability for and the transparency of the company's governance and its affairs. The mere fact that for example governance structures or particular actions or facts have to be disclosed, and therefore will have to be explained, creates an incentive to renounce structures outside what is considered to be best practice and to avoid actions that are in breach of fiduciary duties or regulatory requirements or could be criticised as being outside best practice. For those who participate in companies or do business with companies, information is a necessary element in order to be able to assess their position and respond to changes which are relevant to them. High quality, relevant information is an indispensable adjunct to the effective exercise of governance powers. (. . .) Disclosure requirements can sometimes provide a more efficient regulatory tool than substantive regulation through more or less detailed rules. Such disclosure creates a lighter regulatory environment and allows for greater flexibility and adaptability. Although the regulatory effect may in theory be more indirect and remote than with substantive rules, in practice enforcement of disclosure requirements as such is normally easier.

9.2.2 Learning-oriented approach

The latest empirical and theoretical research in the public policy arena[31] suggests that a specific innovative form of meta-regulation is best placed to overcome some of the weaknesses of the prevalent forms of regulation based on the accountability principle. In cases where the regulator knows the result it is trying to achieve, but does not know the means for achieving it, or if circumstances are likely to change in ways that the regulator cannot predict, or when the regulator does not know the precise result that it desires, research shows that prescriptive regulation will be ineffective.[32] In those cases a more open-ended learning-oriented approach has been shown to produce better compliance results.[33] In such a learning-oriented approach, regulators set broadly defined goals and companies are encouraged to experiment with more efficient and effective means to achieve these goals. The companies are expected to continuously evaluate their efforts in light of the regulatory goals and implement potential improvements (also labelled 'double

[31] This paragraph draws on Gilad (Chapter 6, n 66), at 486–506, which gives a good overview of the empirical and theoretical research in the public policy arena and further identifies the topics which require further empirical research.

[32] Gilad (Chapter 6, n 66), at 485 and 489, citing C.L. Ford, 'New Governance, Compliance, and Principles-based Securities Regulation' [2008] *American Business Law Journal*, 45, 1–60: 'open-ended, learning systems are preferable . . . where the regulator knows the result it is trying to achieve but does not know the means for achieving it, when circumstances are likely to change in ways that the [regulator] cannot predict, or when the [regulator] does not even know the precise result that [it] desires.'

[33] Gilad (Chapter 6, n 66), at 485. At 503, Gilad notes that the empirical research has shown 'that organizational complexity hinders corporations' capacity for compliance and learning from failures. (. . .) The empirical question, which remains to be answered, is whether a meta-regulatory approach, which holds regulatees accountable for continuous improvement and provides them with examples of how other organizations cope with internal complexity, can support organizations' capacity building'.

loop learning').[34] The companies have to feed their self-evaluations to the regulators.[35] The regulators subsequently assess and benchmark the companies' relative performance and disseminate examples of successful solutions (also labelled 'triple loop learning').[36] The regulators therefore do not evaluate the systems and controls *ex ante*, but 'rather make their judgements based on the basis of organisations' ongoing evaluation of the (...) outcomes of the changes that they introduce'.[37]

The empirical research also indicates that the learning-oriented approach is also best placed if a regulator is faced with an industry that is impervious to regulatory prescription because of widespread business resistance or lack of commitment or capacity for compliance.[38] In short, the learning-oriented approach is more likely to enhance an organization's self-regulatory capacity and overcome regulatory resistance[39] by enhancing the internal awareness of the risks involved, implementing proper governance including centres of expertise, providing managers with additional sources of information and control, thus driving managers to constantly improve their risk-detection and mitigation processes.[40]

Extensive elaboration on data protection compliance by multinationals is unnecessary, as all elements that are indicative for applying the 'learning-oriented approach' are present. The technical developments in the digital era proceed at such a fast pace and are so varied and unpredictable that their impact on data protection is impossible to predict, as a result of which any attempt of regulators (even if

[34] The first loop of learning being the development and implementation of the first set of compliance measures. See for a description of the double and triple loop learning cycle: Gilad (Chapter 6, n 66), at 488, referring to C. Parker, *The Open Corporation: Effective Self-regulation and Democracy* (Cambridge University Press, 2001) 'Meta-regulation expects organisations to not only identify risks and devise internal control systems, but also to continuously evaluate the efficacy of their internal systems and incrementally improve them in light of this evaluation (ie double loop learning). (...) Regulators should consciously engage in learning about the industries and the problems they are trying to manage, assess the impact of their strategies, and continuously improve their regulatory strategies accordingly (ie triple loop learning).'

[35] Gilad (Chapter 6, n 66), at 493.

[36] Gilad (Chapter 6, n 66), at 487–98 and 499. Gilad at 489 provides as an example of this incremental learning model the 'Treating Customers Fairly' initiative as launched by the UK Financial Services Authority (FSA), to be found at<http://www.fsa.gov.uk/pages/Doing/Regulated/tcf/library/index.shtml>. The initiative required firms to evaluate their corporate culture against the duty 'to treat its customers fairly', set up appropriate systems and controls, consistently measure their performance, and provide evidence that the solutions that they were implementing were resulting in change to outcomes. Based on the review of the evidence provided, the FSA subsequently issued over the years informal guidance to the industry, gradually developing analytic frameworks to guide firms' self-evaluation process and provided firms with 'good' and 'bad' examples.

[37] Gilad (Chapter 6, n 66), at 493, under reference to J. Black, ;Forms and Paradoxes of Principles-based Regulation' [2008] *Capital Markets Law Review* 3, 425–57 and Ford (n 32).

[38] Gilad (Chapter 6, n 66), at 485.

[39] Gilad (Chapter 6, n 66), at 502. Empirical research has shown that there are many other relevant factors to drive transformative change to the practices of an organization, such as the hurdle that 'the regulatory goals need to be embraced by senior managers', and further that the 'managers' commitment to regulatory goals and the internal compliance programme has to be communicated and internalized beyond the upper echelons of [the] organizations—all the way down to front-level employees across the organization', see Gilad (Chapter 6, n 66), at 500.

[40] Gilad (Chapter 6, n 66), at 498 and 502, referring to R.A. Kagan and J.T. Scholz, 'The Criminology of the Corporation and Regulatory Enforcement Strategies', in K. Hawkins and John Thomas (eds.), *Enforcing Regulation* Kluwer-Nijhoff 1984), at 67–97.

assisted by the organisations themselves) to issue prescriptive regulation is doomed to failure. Similar uncertainty exists as to the most appropriate means to enhance data protection compliance. As discussed, there is further a widespread and pervasive non-compliance of multinationals with, especially, the EU data transfer rules.[41] The relevance of the learning-oriented approach to BCR is evaluated in paragraph 9.3.2. In that context, the findings of existing research on this type of meta-regulation are taken into account.

The learning-oriented approach calls for a combination of regulators with a high capacity for data collection and analysis, a stable regulatory agenda, and sufficient funding[42] so as to provide the latitude for the regulator to pass through the various learning cycles of a long-term incremental learning process.[43] To engage companies in the incremental learning process, regulators will further have to establish a relationship of trust with the regulated companies. To inspire trust, for instance, that regulators will not use the information gained about such companies during the incremental learning process and then later formally prosecute such company.[44]

As indicated, part and parcel of this form of meta-regulation is the regulatory dissemination of good practice examples. This may have as a consequence that for 'high performers' in the industry there is 'less potential for competitive advantage from innovation', as regulatory innovations are shared by the regulators with other companies.[45] Advantage for high performers however may come in intangible forms, such as being recognized as an industry leader, good relations with regulators, and market recognition.[46] For those lagging behind, the dissemination of good practice obviously reduces costs of devising compliance tools which may lower the threshold for entry into the self-regulatory system. Despite such 'recycling' of regulatory innovations, the overall implementation cost of this form of meta-regulation is more expensive for all companies than compliance with prescriptive regulation, 'as it demands constant improvement rather than one-off planning and implementation'.[47]

[41] See Chapter 2, n 26 and n 27.

[42] From the regulators' perspective, regulatory assessment costs are likely to be high as regulators are required to engage with the regulatees in discussions about organization-specific risks and the merits of possibly novel solutions and controls, see Gilad (Chapter 6, n 66), at 496.

[43] Gilad (Chapter 6, n 66), at 498: this requires 'high regulatory capacity for data collection and analysis and a stable regulatory agenda that would enable regulators and regulatees to engage in incremental learning. The latter, in turn, requires that regulators and regulatees enjoy mutual trust and external political and public support, which would provide them with latitude for short term experimentation in pursuit of long-term improvements'.

[44] Gilad (Chapter 6, n 66), at 497: 'This may mean that in the early stages regulators should not involve formal assessments of regulatees' performance as long as they are seen to cooperate with the self-improvement process.' See further at 497, referring to Black (n 37): 'for regulatees to engage in experimentation, regulators will need to establish a relationship of trust with the industry so that organisations feel confident that regulators are not simply trying to shift to them the blame for future failure.'

[45] Gilad (Chapter 6, n 66), at 499 however notes that 'high performers may value the status of industry leaders and the credit they could gain from that in their interaction with regulators, colleagues, and the public'.

[46] See n 45.

[47] Gilad (Chapter 6, n 66), at 499. Gilad, however, also notes that empirical research shows that companies cognitively experience the efforts and cost involved with the incremental improvement of their own compliance systems and controls as less onerous than the efforts and cost involved with the implementation of *ex ante* devised regulatory systems and controls, as these often result in organisations

The main risks identified in respect of the learning-oriented approach are that the incremental learning process (i) will result in a deadlock, where the companies await regulatory guidance and assurance that the proposed systems and controls are acceptable, whereas regulators will feel unable to make a judgment;[48] (ii) will lead to the systems and controls of the companies not meeting regulatory goals due to the fact that regulators are not able to identify flaws in companies' programmes; and (iii) will lead to regulators pursuing a 'tick-box' approach to assessing organizations' compliance. This drives companies to treat non-binding advice as if it were compulsory, which may lead companies to implement extensive and expensive, albeit ineffective, internal compliance programmes.[49]

9.2.3 Sticks and carrots

Further, a common denominator in the literature on the accountability principle in other fields of law is that introduction of this principle should be accompanied by clear incentives for companies to implement robust compliance programmes, and in particular that sanctions will be mitigated if a proper compliance programme was in place.[50] As one author put it: 'the sanctioning practice in relation to risk-based regulation should also be risk-based.'[51] Other authors are more pragmatic and note that the move to a risk-based sanctioning practice is often driven by concerns of regulators to reduce regulatory burdens through the adoption of proportionality in enforcement.[52]

Regulatory practice shows that legislators in other fields of law have found many ways to incentivize companies to implement compliance programmes. Regulators of financial institutions (like the SEC, NASDAQ, and the NYSE) have, in particular, shown great creativity in this respect by:[53]

- requiring a code of business conduct and ethics and evidence of effective implementation procedures;[54]

having to implement 'extensive and expensive, albeit ineffective, internal compliance programs'. See Gilad (Chapter 6, n 66), at 497, referring to K.D. Krawiec, 'Cosmetic Compliance and the Failure of Negotiated Governance' [2003] *Washington University Law Review* 81, at 487–544.

48 Gilad (Chapter 6, n 66), at 496.

49 Gilad (Chapter 6, n 66), at 496–7.

50 McBarnet (Chapter 4, n 24), at 36–7, Parker (Chapter 5, n 43), at 218–23 and Ottow (n 19), at para 3.2, in particular at 31.

51 Ottow (n 19), at 31; see further McBarnet (Chapter 4, n 24), at 36.

52 Scott (Chapter 4, n 26), at 2 noting that the enforcement practice in consumer protection cases, which 'might lead the observer to think that [this] would be shaped by ideas that work in regulatory enforcement generally', is in fact 'in many jurisdictions, qualified by recent concerns to reduce regulatory burdens through the adoption of proportionality in enforcement'. See Scott (Chapter 4, n 26), at 16, giving as an example the UK, where an analysis was issued of how regulatory goals might be pursued with the least burdensome necessary measures, referring to: Better Regulation Taskforce, *Alternatives to State Regulation* (Cabinet Office 2002); and Philip Hampton, *Reducing Administrative Burdens: Effective Inspection and Enforcement* (HM Treasury, 2005).

53 This draws on examples listed in: McBarnet (Chapter 4, n 24) at 36–7, Parker (Chapter 5, n 43), at 218–23 and Ottow (n 19), at para 3.2.

54 See s 406(c) Sarbanes-Oxley Act which contains a comply or explain requirement for a Company Code of Ethics, to be found at <http://www.sec.gov/rules/final/33-8177.htm> and (since 4 November 2003) the NASD Rule 4350(n), which requires a Code of Business Conduct and the New York Stock

- requiring whistle-blower policies (protecting whistle-blowers) be put in place,[55] which fosters a culture of compliance with the internal codes;
- introducing 'comply or explain' requirements: disclosure requirements as to how companies have complied with certain principles of good governance and when they choose not to, explain why they did so;[56]
- considering a compliance programme as an important aspect in determining liability or penalties;[57]
- considering the robustness of a company's internal systems for managing operational risk as a factor in deciding their capital adequacy ratios;[58]
- using discretionary powers to make informal settlements requiring implementation of compliance systems or considering an effective compliance system a factor in deciding whether to prosecute or not;[59]
- treating companies that have a proper compliance programme with more trust and subjecting them to less regulatory inspection;[60]
- making the existence of a compliance programme a condition of licence or permits required before a company can engage in a certain business; examples

Exchange Corporate Governance Rules, para 303A of the NYSE Listed Company Manual, requiring Corporate Governance Guidelines and a Code of Business Conduct and Ethics, both to be found at <http://www.sec.gov/rules/sro/34-48745.htm>.

[55] As required by the Sarbanes-Oxley Act (2002), Pub.L.No. 107–204, and also by many corporate governance codes in Europe. See for an overview of the corporate governance codes in the EU: <http://www.ecgi.org/codes/index.php>.

[56] By requiring a company to publish its compliance efforts, an incentive is provided to actually implement those measures. As the well known IT consultancy firm Gartner puts it, 'you get what you inspect'. France was the first country to make reporting on the 'social consequences of a company's activities' (both at a group level and internationally) mandatory for publicly listed companies in their annual reports. See Aurora Voiculescu, 'Green paper to new uses of human rights instruments', in McBarnet, Voiculescu, Campbell, *The New Corporate Accountability, Corporate Social Responsibility and the Law* (Cambridge University Press 2007), at 376. This 'comply or explain' principle has been introduced in many corporate governance codes in and outside Europe. For an overview of all such codes, see <http://www.ecgi.org/codes/index.php>. For an explanatory memorandum of the EU Corporate Governance Forum on the 'comply or explain' principle, a statement dated 6 March 2006, can be found at: <http://ec.europa.eu/internal_market/company/ecgforum/index_en.htm>. On the effect of disclosure requirements (especially if they are in a comparable format), see Campbell and Vick (n 27), at 241–78.

[57] Examples are the U.S. Federal Sentencing Guidelines for Organizations, which state that the existence of an effective compliance system will provide companies or individuals with a reduction of penalty, and the sanction guidelines of the Dutch supervisory authority on telecom operators (OPTA), Stcrt, 11 March 2008, no 50, at 27.

[58] See the Committee on Banking Supervision, *Basel II: International Convergence of Capital Measurement and Capital Standards: A Revised Framework* (June 2004), available at <http://www.bis.org>, which is a voluntary agreement between G10 nations to harmonize standards for national banking regulation.

[59] This is common practice of regulators both in the UK and the Commonwealth countries (see Parker (Chapter 5, n 43), at 219), as well as for instance in the Netherlands. See Ottow (n 19), at 29–31.

[60] See McBarnet (Chapter 4, n 24), at 36: 'A similar use of enforcement policies has been mooted in the United Kingdom, where companies that demonstrated themselves to be "responsible", would be treated with more trust and less regulatory inspection,' (referring to the 'Hampton Review', P. Hampton, *Reducing Administrative Burdens, Effective Implementation and Enforcement* (HM Treasury 2004).

are the licence requirements for financial services firms that include broad-ranging internal systems for ensuring integrity of funds;[61]

- fast-tracking the granting of licences or permits; scheduling inspections less frequently; and
- making government procurement decisions conditional on implementation of proper compliance systems.

9.2.4 The 'right' regulatory response

Empirical research in respect of enforcement of consumer protection laws suggests that the 'right' regulatory response to violations also depends on the type of business involved and should be tailored to (i) businesses which fundamentally seek to be compliant as one of their operating values; (ii) amoral calculators which operate on a cost–benefit basis and who will comply where it makes sense from a cost–benefit perspective; and (iii) incompetents who, whatever their intent, lack the capacity to organize themselves to comply with regulatory requirements.[62] With the compliant organizations, it is suggested that low-level enforcement approaches based on education and advice and a more cooperative (rather than adversarial) regulatory style is indicated, where the regulator and company negotiate over responses to violations rather than go to court over them.[63] With the amoral calculators it is suggested that a pyramid of sanctions should be available for regulators ranging between education and advice, through warnings and penalties, to prosecution and ultimately licence revocation. Incompetents are beyond help and their licences should be revoked.[64]

9.3 Review of the BCR Regime against Accountability Requirements in the General Literature

9.3.1 Good fit with data protection

My first observation is that on all accounts the 'accountability principle' does seem to be a good fit with EU data protection law. As indicated, 'accountability' is part of risk-based regulation, where companies themselves prioritize and tailor their compliance efforts dependent on the level of risk involved. This fits well with many provisions in the Directive, requiring for instance 'appropriate' security measures, 'adequate' data protection safeguards, etc. As to these concepts, the Working Party

[61] See for examples Parker (Chapter 5, n 43), at 220.

[62] Scott (Chapter 4, n 26), at 15, referring to Robert Kagan and John Scholz, 'The "Criminology of the Corporation" and Regulatory Enforcement Strategies', in Keith Hawkins and John Thomas (eds.), *Enforcing Regulation* (Kluwer-Nijhoff 1984).

[63] See on the different styles of enforcement: Scott (Chapter 4, n 26), at para 3.3. This process is also labelled 'bargaining in the shadow of the law'.

[64] Scott (Chapter 4, n 26), at 15, referring to Ian Ayres and John Braithwaite, *Responsive Regulation: Transcending the Deregulation Debate* (Oxford 1992).

29 from the start has applied a risk-based approach, indicating as the first (of three) objectives of the Directive 'to deliver a good level of compliance', acknowledging that a 100 per cent compliance is not achievable in practice.[65] The Working Party 29 further has applied from the start a risk-based approach to the content of data protection obligations (ie requiring stricter security measures in the case of a transfer of sensitive data, etc) as well as identifying priorities in enforcement for the DPAs.[66] This risk-based approach is also how multinationals manage their data protection in practice.[67] In the digital society, data flows in networks, whether within multinationals, between multinationals, or between multinationals and individual customers (ie internet users). The participants in such networks manage risks: they accept them, try to limit or minimize them, or transfer them to co-contractors or other partners whether through supply chain management or otherwise (see Chapter 7, paragraph 7.4 above).[68] In practice therefore, data protection is regulated through risk management. Because in the data protection context so many partners and actors are involved,[69] it seems impossible for regulators to regulate the data streams in any meaningful way without indeed 'latching onto companies' inherent capacity to manage their risks'. As already indicated in

[65] WP 12 (Chapter 3, n 50), at 7: 'The objectives of a data protection system are essentially threefold: 1) to deliver a good level of compliance with the rules. (No system can guarantee 100 per cent compliance, but some are better than others). A good system is generally characterised by a high degree of awareness among data controllers of their obligations, and among data subjects of their rights and the means of exercising them.'

[66] WP 12 (Chapter 3, n 50), at 28 where the Working Party instructs DPAs to take a risk-based approach as to data transfers:

> It would constitute guidance regarding which cases of data transfer should be considered as 'priority cases' for examination or even investigation, and thereby allow the resources available to be directed towards those transfers which raise the greatest concerns in terms of the protection of data subjects.
>
> - The Working Party considers that among those categories of transfer which pose particular risks to privacy and therefore merit particular attention are the following:
> - those transfers involving certain sensitive categories of data as defined by Article 8 of the directive;
> - transfers which carry the risk of financial loss (e.g. credit card payments over the Internet);
> - transfers carrying a risk to personal safety;
> - transfers made for the purposes of making a decision which significantly affects the individual (such as recruitment or promotion decisions, the granting of credit, etc.);
> - transfers which carry a risk of serious embarrassment or tarnishing of an individual's reputation;
> - transfers which may result in specific actions which constitute a significant intrusion into an individual's private life, such as unsolicited telephone calls;
> - repetitive transfers involving massive volumes of data (such as transactional data processed over telecommunications networks, the Internet etc.);
> - transfers involving the collection of data using new technologies, which, for instance could be undertaken in a particularly covert or clandestine manner (e.g. Internet cookies).

[67] See Chapter 5, para 5.4, especially n 41.

[68] In particular n 39. As to risk-management of the supply chain, see McBarnet and Kurkchiyan (Chapter 5, n 41), at 63.

[69] See Chapter 7, n 39.

Chapter 7, paragraph 7.5.3, this is not a new insight, but a fact well-known in other areas of law and a reason for states to resort to TPR since the contracting parties have more power to enforce compliance in transnational situations than does the threat of traditional judicial means.[70]

Further, the general nature of the material data processing principles in the Directive requires that these principles are 'translated' into practical instructions for employees on how to process personal data. Employees will have to receive training, compliance has to be monitored, etc. This has led multinationals to introduce corporate privacy policies and compliance programmes long before the introduction of the accountability principle was considered (see Chapter 5, paragraph 5.4).

Multinationals introducing BCR can further be categorized as type (a) businesses (see paragraph 9.2.4), which concern companies that fundamentally seek to be compliant as one of their operating values. For type (a) companies, the right regulatory response is 'a cooperative regulatory style, based on education and advice and where the regulator and multinational negotiate over responses to violations rather than go to court over them'.[71] For type (a) companies, introduction of a self-regulatory regime such as BCR therefore seems the indicated regulatory approach.

9.3.2 Learning-oriented approach

Based on the general policy research and literature, meta-regulation based on the 'learning-oriented approach' seems to be indicated for data protection compliance by multinationals (see paragraph 9.2.2). In fact this has very much been the manner in which the BCR requirements came into existence. The multinationals approached the DPAs to discuss their BCR (see paragraph 1.1). The information obtained by the relevant DPAs in these initial discussions with the multinationals, and the documents developed between the multinationals and these DPAs in that context (such as privacy impact assessments) were subsequently fed back to the Working Party 29 and found their way into the WP Opinions (achieving initial 'triple loop learning'). Reviewing the BCR regime against the findings of the research into the learning-oriented approach, the 'second loop learning' (whereby companies evaluate their own systems and controls and incrementally improve these) is missing. This is relevant as it is safe to say that data protection compliance programmes are still in development,[72] where further innovations are possible and best practices have therefore not yet crystallized. My conclusion is that the chances of effectiveness of the BCR regime will be improved if companies would have to not only identify data protection risks and devise internal control systems, but also achieve double loop learning by evaluating the efficacy of their internal systems and incrementally improve them in light of this evaluation. Such incremental learning

[70] Cafaggi (Chapter 7, n 32), at 9.

[71] See para 9.2.4.

[72] As evidenced by the recent efforts to identify data protection accountability requirements by the Working Party 29, the Centre for Information Policy Leadership, the worldwide data protection supervisors in the Madrid Draft Proposal for International Standards, and the Commission, see para 9.4.3.

will also foster the self-regulatory capacity within the multinational and overcome (remaining) regulatory resistance. This element can be addressed by introducing as a BCR requirement that multinationals 'are to periodically review the totality of their BCR accountability programme to determine whether modification is necessary'. This requirement is also one of the 'common fundamentals' of the accountability requirements as defined by the Centre for Information Policy Leadership (*CIPL*)[73] and will be part of the recommendations to be made in paragraph 9.4.3. This requirement is also included in the Proposed Regulation.[74]

Another element that is missing in the present regime is how the Commission and the Working Party 29 may become engaged in this ongoing learning process of multinationals and the problems they are trying to manage in order for them to be able to improve their regulatory strategies accordingly (achieve ongoing triple loop learning). Part of this learning process can be achieved by the Commission organizing working groups which can be tasked with defining, for instance, the accountability requirements for data transfers by multinationals to third parties outside their group of companies. I discuss this further in paragraph 9.4.4. Another matter entirely is whether it is useful to include in the BCR regime a more structural feedback by multinationals of the evaluation of their BCR compliance programmes to, for instance, the Lead DPA. With this I do not refer to the results of the periodic audits of their BCR compliance, but rather to the results of periodic verifications of the overall effectiveness of the compliance programme in its entirety. For a number of reasons I do not think this is advisable. The Lead DPA is already entitled to receive such evaluation reports upon its request (see for an overview of the *passive* information in the BCR requirements of the multinational towards the Lead DPA Chapter 10, paragraph 10.7.6). In light of the strong *passive* information requirements towards the Lead DPA, introduction of additional *active* information obligations of the multinational towards the Lead DPA does not seem effective. This will just increase administrative burdens on multinationals, while leading to an information overload with the Lead DPA. This may lead to expectations of review of such information by the Lead DPA, which seems unrealistic[75] and will therefore just work counterproductively. And if the Lead DPAs were indeed to review some of the evaluations, chances are that due to time pressure this would result in a 'tick-boxing' of requirements, which often leads to a semi-prescriptive regime which has a freezing effect on innovations (see paragraph 9.2.2). Further, many multinationals consider that providing auditing and evaluation reports to the Lead DPA may have a counterproductive effect by stifling the open manner in which internal audits and evaluations are performed if the participants are aware that the results will be reported to the Lead DPA.[76] My recommendation is that other manners should

[73] See para 9.4.4.

[74] See Art 22(3) Proposed Regulation (Chapter 1, n 10): 'The controller shall implement mechanisms to ensure the verification of the effectiveness of the measures referred to in paragraphs 1 and 2. If proportionate, this verification shall be carried out by independent internal or external auditors.'

[75] See for the workload of the Lead DPAs para 6.6.1 in particular n 63.

[76] See also Chapter 6, para 6.6.3.

be found to engage EU legislators in the learning process of the multinationals as to data protection compliance. This is further discussed in paragraph 9.5.3.

9.3.3 External disclosure requirement

Review of the BCR regime against the accountability requirements in the general literature as to other fields of law shows a nearly complete overlap. The exception, so far, is the requirement of transparency: the requirement of a company to publicly report on (in this case) data protection compliance in a comparable format. Given the fact that reputation is a key driver for data protection compliance (see Chapter 5, paragraph 5.3) and further for reasons to be discussed as part of the evaluation of BCR as a form of TPR and CSR, I recommend including this publication requirement in the BCR criteria. This is also the recommendation of the Rand Report and the Working Party 29.[77] Though the Commission included a publication requirement in an earlier draft,[78] this publication requirement did not make it to the Proposed Regulation. This recommendation will be included in the recommendations to be made in Chapter 9, paragraph 9.4.3.

9.3.4 Sticks and carrots

The general literature further makes abundantly clear that the introduction of the accountability principle should be accompanied by both sticks and carrots (ie should provide for clear incentives for companies to implement robust compliance programmes and disincentives if they don't). This is also the recommendation of the Rand Report,[79] the Working Party 29,[80] the CIPL,[81]

[77] The Rand Report (Chapter 2, n 27), at 53 and WP Contribution on the Future of Privacy (n 1, n 6), at 20: 'The effectiveness of the provisions of Directive 95/46/EC is dependent on data controllers' effort towards achieving these objectives. This requires the following proactive measures (...) Transparency of these adopted measures vis-à-vis the data subjects and the public in general. Transparency requirements contribute to the accountability of data controllers (e.g. publication of privacy policies on the internet, transparency in regard to internal complaints procedures, and publication in annual reports).'

[78] See Art 19(4) draft Proposed Regulation, version 56 (29 November 2011), which was leaked to the press on 7 December 2011: 'Wherever the controller publishes or is required by law to publish a regular report of its activities, such report shall contain the controller's policies in relation to the protection of personal data, the risks linked to the data processing by the controller and the measures taken to mitigate such risks', to be found at <http://www.statewatch.org/news/2011/dec/eu-com-draft-dp-reg-inter-service-consultation.pdf>.

[79] Rand Report (Chapter 2, n 27) at 42: 'Ensure that BCR can be more easily used to ensure the legitimacy of personal data transfers to third countries, rather than relying on determining the adequacy of entire countries. This could be achieved by formalising the measures currently being developed by certain supervisory bodies, with associated guidance as to their common understanding, and should be designed so as to maximise common acceptability across Member States. Care should be taken to maintain incentives for the private sector.'

[80] WP Contribution on the Future of Privacy (Chapter 1, n 6), at para 81 at 20: 'A built-in reward structure could be foreseen in law to induce organisations to implement them [ie the accountability measures].'

[81] See the Opinion on the Communication of the Commission on the revision of the Directive (Chapter 2, n 27), at 13: 'A multinational organisation which adopts and implements an acceptable

and the EDPS.[82] The question is what the above means in the BCR setting. It is clear that the present 'carrot' for introducing BCR (ie authorization of intra-company data transfers) apparently doesn't provide a strong enough incentive as evidenced by the very low pick up of BCR (see Chapter 6, paragraph 6.5 above). Other incentives will have to be thought of.[83] Obvious other incentives for introduction of BCR could be to:

- introduce risk-based sanctions for companies that have introduced BCR, where implementation of a compliance programme is a substantial mitigating factor;[84]

Binding Global Code would accept responsibility for its fulfilment and for ensuring delivery of fundamental rights. In return—and for as long that remains true—it would be treated as satisfying EU and other requirements for international data transfers.' See further the CIPL New Approach to International Standards, Chapter 6, n 61), at 7: the main 'carrot' presented by the Centre is that the multinational introducing a Binding Global Code, may 'self-certify their own Code without the need for prior DPA approval, which is simply not practicable with the scale of the challenge' and 'if self-certification is considered too radical, there are other options for the initial adoption or approval of a Binding Global Code to ensure that minimum requirements are in fact met. These include certification by an independent Third Party (Accountability Agent) appointed by a DPA at the expense of the business or certification by a Third Party approved by the DPA.'

[82] EDPS Opinion on the revision of the Directive (Chapter 2, n 35), at para 177 at 22.

[83] Rubinstein (Chapter 3, n 154), at 47, proposes for the U.S. a co-regulatory approach for regulating privacy which is very similar to the BCR regime whereby companies create a privacy safe harbour and enjoy considerable scope in shaping self-regulatory guidelines, while government retains general oversight authority to approve and enforce these guidelines. The basic idea underlying his proposal is that such a co-regulatory approach could more effectively use 'both sticks and carrots as incentives.'

As 'sticks' are suggested

- that privacy legislation would allow civil actions and liquidated damages awards against firms that do not participate in an approved safe harbour programme;
- broader opt-in requirements;
- external and independent audits of regulatory compliance and mandatory reporting to the FTC; and
- stricter requirements in respect of behavioural marketing (ie ban on use of sensitive information and data retention limit of one month).

As 'carrots' are suggested:

- exemption from civil actions and liquidated damages;
- cost savings such as compliance reviews based on self-assessment, rather than external audits by an independent third party;
- government recognition of better performing firms (FTC 'seal of approval');
- government procurement preferences for products or services of participating firms; and
- regulatory flexibility for specific business models such as online behavioural marketing.

[84] Article 79(2) Proposed Regulation (Chapter 1, n 10), provides to a certain extent for risk-based levying of sanctions: 'The administrative sanction shall be in each individual case effective, proportionate and dissuasive. The amount of the administrative fine shall be fixed with due regard to the nature, gravity and duration of the breach, the intentional or negligent character of the infringement, the degree of responsibility of the natural or legal person and of previous breaches by this person, *the technical and organisational measures and procedures implemented pursuant to Article 23 [ie privacy by the design]* and the degree of co-operation with the supervisory authority in order to remedy the breach.'

- provide that if a multinational adopts BCR, the BCR apply instead of the national data protection laws of the Member States (as per *Recommendation 10*);
- introduce the possibility that in BCR a choice of law and forum may be made for the laws and courts of the Member State of the Lead DPA, releasing a multinational of the burden of complying with other possible applicable EU data protection laws (as per *Recommendation 9*);[85]
- abolish the notification requirements for multinationals with BCR or, as next best alternative, provide for the possibility of central notification of all data processing operations of a multinational to the Lead DPA;[86]
- (to the extent required, see Chapter 6, paragraph 6.5) provide that multinationals having BCR do not have to have intra-group data processor agreements in place if group companies process personal data on behalf of other group companies; and
- provide that multinationals having BCR in place may in respect of onward data transfers to third parties have their EU (Delegated) Headquarters enter into EU Standard Contractual Clauses with such third party on behalf of all group companies.

What is lacking in the Proposed Regulation is a reference also to the general accountability measures for which the controller is responsible pursuant to Art 22 Proposed Regulation (see for citation n 7).

[85] *Recommendation 9* is to a large extent superfluous if the country of origin principle is introduced in the revised Directive or if the Directive is to be replaced by an EU regulation as a legislative instrument. In those cases the issue of cumulation of applicable laws within the EU is to a large extent solved, but not completely. Also in these cases *Recommendation 9* will remain relevant, see on this extensively Chapter 4, para. 4.4.3 and Chapter 8, para 8.3.3.

[86] See also the Rand Report (Chapter 2, n 27) at 42, recommending to 'reduce the burden of the notification obligation, by making non-notification the general rule rather than the exception,' whereby 'notification should be required only in cases of notable risk or harm, or when transparency cannot be adequately ensured via other means'. The Opinion on the Communication of the Commission on the revision of the Directive (Chapter 2, n 27), at 9, suggest abolishing the notification requirements and replacing them by a registration of controllers of their 'basic details of corporate identity'. The EDPS in its Opinion on the revision of the Directive (Chapter 2, n 35), at para 172, recommends simplifying and/or reducing the scope of the notification requirements by: (i) limiting the obligation to notify to specific kinds of processing operations entailing specific risks; (ii) introducing a registration requirement of controllers; (iii) introducing a pan-European notification form. See further EC Communication on revision of the Directive (Chapter 2, n 34), at 2.2.2, at 10. These good intentions have not materialized in the Proposed Regulation. Instead of general notification to the DPAs required by Arts 18(1) and 19 Directive, Art 28 Proposed Regulation, introduces the obligation for controllers to maintain documentation of the processing operations under their responsibility. Given the extensiveness of the documentation obligation under the Proposed Regulation not much seems to be gained by the abolishment of the notification obligation. Further, Art 34 Proposed Regulation introduces cases where consultation of the DPAs is mandatory prior to starting a new processing operation. Consultation will, for example, be mandatory whenever the privacy impact assessment (as required pursuant to Art 33 Proposed Regulation) indicates that processing operations are by virtue of their nature, their scope, or their purposes, likely to present a high degree of specific risks. Given the global nature of data processing operations of multinationals, it may be expected that many of their data processing operations will qualify for such prior consultation which may well prove more of an administrative burden than the general notification requirements under the current Directive. An incentive for multinationals adopting BCR would obviously be that multinationals would be exempted from such prior consultation requirements if their processing operations meet the material provisions of their BCR.

Recommendation 11

Introduce incentives for multinationals to adopt BCR, such as:

- risk-based sanctions for a violation of data protection by multinationals that have implemented BCR (where the implementation of a proper compliance programme is a mitigating factor);
- provide that if multinationals adopt BCR, the BCR apply instead of the national data protection laws of the Member States (as per *Recommendation 10*);
- provide that in BCR a choice of law and forum may be made for the laws and courts of the Member State of the Lead DPA (see *Recommendation 9*);
- abolish the notification requirements, or, as next best alternative, provide for the possibility of central notification of all data processing of a multinational to the Lead DPA;
- provide that multinationals having BCR do not have to have intra-group data processor agreements in place if group companies process personal data on behalf of other group companies;
- provide that multinationals having BCR in place may in respect of onward data transfers to third parties have their EU (Delegated) Headquarters enter into EU Standard Contractual Clauses with such third party on behalf of all group companies; and
- exempt multinationals that have BCR in place from the *ex ante* consultation or authorization requirements as included in the Proposed Regulation.

9.4 The Accountability Principle in the Field of Data Protection

Three main sources for accountability requirements as to data protection are the compliance measures as defined by (i) the Working Party 29, (ii) the Madrid Draft Proposal for International Standards, and (iii) the Centre for Information Policy Leadership. Recently, the Commission in its Proposed Regulation also provided for an accountability provision.[87] However, rather than subsequently listing the main required accountability measures, the Proposed Regulation refers to a number of other provisions in the Proposed Regulation. This makes it more difficult to derive what the Commission exactly considers to constitute a comprehensive data protection compliance programme for companies.

I will first discuss the accountability requirements defined by the Working Party 29, as these are the most comprehensive. Where indicated I will make references to the Proposed Regulation. Thereafter I will—briefly—discuss any additional requirements under the Proposed Regulation and the Madrid Draft Proposal for International Standards. My overall conclusion will be that the accountability

[87] Article 22 Proposed Regulation.

requirements as defined by the Working Party 29, the Madrid Draft Proposal for International Standards, and the Proposed Regulation are in many cases too specific and may prove even counterproductive to achieving optimal data protection compliance by companies. I will then discuss the 'common fundamentals' for accountability as defined by the Centre for Information Policy Leadership (*CIPL*). These common fundamentals show a near complete overlap with those defined by the Working Party 29 and the Madrid Draft Proposal for International Standards, which is not surprising as these were already available at the time of drafting the common fundamentals. The added value of these common fundamentals, however, is that the accountability requirements are set in more general obligations (while still describing in the explanatory notes to the requirements what is understood under the relevant general heading) which are far better suited to serve as a basis for accountability as part of the BCR regime. The added value of these fundamentals is further that they set out the collection of requirements in a more logical grouping of requirements and this all in a terminology which is (more) familiar to companies. My conclusion and recommendation will therefore be that EU legislators, when setting the main requirements for the BCR regime, will adopt those defined by the CIPL and disregard those defined by the Working Party 29 and the Madrid Draft Proposal for International Standards, which seem to have formed the basis for the accountability provision in the Proposed Regulation. For those interested in the outcome of the analysis, I refer to paragraph 9.4.4 on the common fundamentals.

An issue to be discussed separately is that the BCR regime reflects the accountability approach to regulate *intercompany* data transfers only. As soon as the multinational with BCR transfers data outside the company group to a third party in a non-adequate country, however, the regular EU data transfer rules have to be complied with (ie the EU Standard Contractual Clauses, consent of data subjects, etc). The question is whether this system for *onward transfers* in the BCR regime should be replaced by a system based on accountability as well. My conclusion will be that this would indeed be advisable and I will discuss what these accountability requirements as to onward transfers should look like in paragraph 9.5.

I will now first discuss the accountability requirements defined by the Working Party 29, the Proposed Regulation, and the Madrid Draft Proposal for International Standards, and whether these are different or provide for additional requirements as compared to the BCR regime.

9.4.1 Working Party 29 accountability requirements

As a follow-up to its WP Contribution on The Future of Privacy, recommending the introduction of the accountability principle in the revised Directive, the Working Party 29 issued an Opinion on the accountability principle,[88] elaborating on the implications of the accountability principle in practice. The Working Party 29 proposed the following concrete provision:

[88] WP Opinion on the principle of accountability (Chapter 1, n 23), at 10.

Article X—Implementation of data protection principles

1. The controller shall implement appropriate and effective measures to ensure that the principles and obligations set out in the Directive are complied with.
2. The controller shall demonstrate compliance with paragraph 1 to the supervisory authority on its request.

In its Opinion on the accountability principle, the Working Party 29 stressed that introduction of this provision in the Directive does *not* constitute additional requirements,[89] as 'most of the requirements set out in this provision actually already exist, albeit less explicitly, under existing laws' and that to comply with these existing legal requirements, it is already 'intrinsically necessary to set up, and possibly verify, data protection related procedures. (...)In summary, the new provision does not aim at subjecting data controllers to new principles but rather at ensuring de facto, effective compliance with existing ones'.[90] As to the consequences of compliance with the accountability principle, the Working Party 29:

> highlights that fulfilling the accountability principle does not necessarily mean that a controller is in compliance with the substantive principles [...], i.e., it does not offer a legal presumption of compliance nor does it replace any of those principles. [...] In practice however, companies with a robust compliance program are according to the Working Party 29 more likely to be in compliance with the law.[91] (*Sic*)

More important is the remark of the Working Party 29 that compliance with the accountability principle may play a role in assessing sanctions by the DPAs related to violation of the substantive principles.[92] This is also in line with the Rand Report that recommends a risk-based approach to sanctions, where also the compliance measures that were in place are a factor for the sanction to be imposed.[93] Another important observation of the Working Party 29 is that introduction of the accountability principle justifies that the role of the DPAs can be more *ex post* rather than *ex ante*, justifying that certain administrative requirements (like prior notification requirements) be replaced or diminished.[94] This is also the recommendation of the

[89] The Working Party 29 also tries to substantiate that elements of the accountability principle are already introduced in European data protection law. The examples which the Working Party 29 give are, however, very limited and cannot veil the fact that introduction of the accountability principle would be a *novum* in European data protection law.

[90] The EDPS is more realistic in its view that the Directive contains elements of accountability, but that these have limited scope only. See the EDPS Opinion on the revision of the Directive (n 35), at para 102: 'This type of provision is not entirely new. Article 6(2) of the Directive 95/46 refers to the principles relating to data quality and mentions that "It shall be for the controller to ensure that para. 1 is complied with." Equally, Article 17 (1) requires data controllers to implement measures, of both a technical and organisational nature. However, these provisions have a limited scope. Inserting a general provision on accountability would stimulate controllers to put into place proactive measures in order to be able to comply with all the elements of data protection law.'

[91] WP Opinion on the principle of accountability (Chapter 1, n 23), at 11.

[92] WP Opinion on the principle of accountability (Chapter 1, n 23), at 11.

[93] Where criteria are taken into account such as the: (i) egregiousness of the conduct (was the breach the result of carelessness; what were the measures in place to protect personal data, etc); (ii) the number of data subjects affected; (iii) monetary loss; etc. See Rand Report (Chapter 2, n 27), at 57.

[94] WP Opinion on the principle of accountability (Chapter 1, n 23), paras 54 and 63.

Rand Report encouraging a risk-based approach, 'making non-notification the general rule rather than the exception'[95] and further that in respect of BCR 'care should be taken to ensure incentives for the private sector'.[96] A similar comment is made by the Working Party 29 in its Opinion on the Future of Privacy:[97] 'A built-in reward structure could be foreseen in law to induce organizations to implement them [ie the accountability measures].' The above recommendations are in line with the general literature on the principle of accountability (see *Recommendation 11* above).

Proposed Regulation These recommendations are not fully adopted in the Proposed Regulation. For instance the Proposed Regulation does adopt a risk-based approach for sanctioning, but takes into account only the extent to which a company has implemented principles of privacy by design and default, rather than compliance with the accountability principle in general.[98] The Proposed Regulation further seems indeed to abolish general notification to the DPAs under the Directive, but instead introduces the obligation for controllers to maintain extensive documentation of their processing operations[99] and further an *ex ante* consultation requirement for data processing operations of which the (mandatory) privacy impact assessment indicates that these are 'by virtue of their nature, their scope or their purposes, likely to present a high degree of specific risks'.[100] These prior consultation requirements may well prove more burdensome to multinationals than the general notification requirements under the current Directive.

The Working Party 29 subsequently gave a non-exhaustive list of common accountability measures:[101]

(i) establishing internal procedures prior to the creation of new personal data processing operations (internal review, assessment, etc);

(ii) setting up written and binding data protection policies to be considered and applied to new data processing operations (eg, compliance with data quality, notice, security principles, access, etc), which should be available to data subjects;

(iii) mapping of procedures to ensure proper identification of all data processing operations and maintenance of an inventory of data processing operations;

95 The Rand Report (Chapter 2, n 27), at x and 42.

96 The Rand Report (n Chapter 2, n 27), at 42.

97 WP Opinion on the principle of accountability (Chapter 1, n 23), at 20.

98 See Art 79(2) Proposed Regulation. See on this further para 9.4.2.

99 See Art 28 Proposed Regulation. See further n 105.

100 See more extensively n 86.

101 As a complementary approach, the Working Party 29 suggests including not only the general accountability principle as cited above, but also the measures cited above as an illustrative list of measures that could be encouraged at a national level (see WP Opinion on the principle of accountability (Chapter 1, n 23), at 12).

(iv) appointing a data protection officer and other individuals with responsibility for data protection;

(v) offering adequate data protection, training and education to staff members. This should include those processing (or responsible for) the personal data (such as human resources directors) but also IT managers, developers, and directors of business units. Sufficient resources should be allocated for privacy management, etc;

(vi) setting up procedures to manage access, correction and deletion requests which should be transparent to data subjects;

(vii) establishing an internal complaints handling mechanism;

(viii) setting up internal procedures for the effective management and reporting of security breaches;

(ix) performing privacy impact assessments in specific circumstances; and

(x) implementing and supervising verification procedures to ensure that all the measures not only exist on paper but that they are implemented and work in practice (internal or external audits, etc).

The Working Party 29 further notes that 'transparency is an integral part of the accountability measures, both vis-à-vis the data subjects and the public in general'. Examples of transparency measures that increase accountability include

(xi) publishing privacy policies on the internet, by providing transparency in regard to internal complaints procedures and through publication in annual reports.[102]

Comparison of Working Party 29 requirements with the BCR regime

Review of the Working Party 29 accountability requirements shows a nearly complete overlap with the requirements the Working Party 29 set for BCR (see Chapter 6, paragraph 6.2 above). In its Opinion on the accountability principle, the Working Party 29 also explicitly notes that the BCR regime already reflects the accountability principle: 'Indeed BCR are codes of practice, which multinational organisations draw up and follow, containing internal measures designed to put data protection principles into effect (such as audit, training programmes, network of privacy officers, handling complaint system)'.[103] Reviewing the WP Opinion on the accountability principle, it seems to have been rather the other way around; the work on BCR by the Working Party 29 seems to have been the basis for the listing of the accountability measures in its Opinion on accountability. Compared to the BCR requirements, the WP Opinion on the accountability principle provides for three more explicit and five additional requirements. I discuss these requirements below.

[102] WP Opinion on the principle of accountability (Chapter 1, n 23), para 48.

[103] WP Opinion on the principle of accountability (Chapter 1, n 23), at 7, 10, 15, and 16, and Wugmeister, Retzer, Rich (Chapter 3, n 148), at 450.

More explicit requirements identified by the Working Party 29 are:

(i) establishing internal procedures prior to the creation of new personal data processing operations;

(iii) mapping procedures to ensure proper identification of all data processing operations and maintenance of an inventory of data processing operations; and

(ix) performing privacy impact assessments in specific circumstances.

There is little discussion that the elements above should indeed be present for a multinational to be able to be 'in control' of its data processing operations.

Proposed Regulation Similar additional requirements are also provided by the Proposed Regulation, where controllers are required to:

- implement, both at the time of the determination of the means for processing and at the time of the processing itself, appropriate technical and organizational measures and procedures in such a way that the processing will meet the requirements of the Regulation;[104]
- document all data processing operations and provide these on request to the DPA;[105]
- perform a privacy impact assessment prior to implementation of a data processing operation if such processing is likely to present specific risks to the rights and freedoms of data subjects by virtue of their nature, their scope, or their purposes.[106]

[104] See the principle of data protection by design and by default as implemented in Art 23 Proposed Regulation.

[105] See Article 28(1) Proposed Regulation. Article 28(2) subsequently provides which information such documentation will have to contain:

(a) the name and contact details of the controller, or any joint controller or processor, and of the representative, if any;

(b) the name and contact details of the data protection officer, if any;

(c) the purposes of the processing, including the legitimate interests pursued by the controller where the processing is based on point (f) of Article 6(1);

(d) a description of the categories of data subjects and of the categories of personal data relating to them;

(e) the recipients or categories of recipients of the personal data, including the controllers to whom personal data are disclosed for the legitimate interest pursued by them;

(f) where applicable, transfers of data to a third country or an international organisation, including the identification of that third country or international organisation and, in case of transfers referred to in point (h) of Article 44(1), the documentation of appropriate safeguards;

(g) a general indication of the time limits for erasure of the different categories of data; (h) the description of the mechanisms referred to in Article 22(3).

[106] See Art 33 Proposed Regulation.

Although till now not explicitly included as such in the current BCR requirements, in practice multinationals indeed comply with these requirements.

At present the BCR regime requires a 'detailed description of the data processed and the data flows'. For large multinationals this is not doable in the BCR itself, due to the number of data processing operations in such multinationals (easily over 10,000) and the pace of changes, replacements, and additions. For multinationals to be able to be 'in control' of their data processing operations (in the sense that they are able to know which systems they operate and whether these are data protection compliant), multinationals perform 'privacy impact assessments' (*PIAs*) at the time of implementation of a new data processing system (or material changes to existing systems). The PIAs are a questionnaire filled out by the manager(s) responsible for the relevant data processing system, listing all relevant details (such as the system owner, the data processed, purposes of processing, level of data security, recipients of the data, etc). This PIA is subsequently verified for data protection and security compliance by the responsible privacy officer. If the privacy officer detects a violation of the BCR, the data processing system will be adapted, the PIA adapted accordingly and resubmitted for approval to the relevant privacy officer. To ensure continued compliance, changes to a data processing system may only be made after the PIA has been adapted accordingly and resubmitted for approval by the responsible privacy officer. The multinational has oversight over its collective data processing operations by including the individual PIAs together in an inventory.

I do not dispute that these three requirements listed by the Working Party 29 (and also to be found in the Proposed Regulation) should be part of a data protection compliance programme, but I do not recommend including these requirements in their present form in the BCR regime. The main reason for this is that the requirements are too specific and have as an inherent danger working as a 'tick box' list for compliance measures regardless of their actual impact on compliance.[107] Rather, accountability rules should be formulated as overall framework rules to 'latch onto the inherent capacity of the multinational to organise itself' in order to achieve that multinationals take responsibility for the *outcome* of their compliance efforts. An example is provided as an illustration.

As indicated, the first WP Opinion on BCR requires that BCR provide for a 'detailed description of the data processed and the data flows' (as is now also included as a general requirement for all companies under the Proposed Regulation). This was practically not viable, not least because by the time such description was given by the multinational it would already be outdated. In the first discussions about BCR with for instance the Dutch DPA, the DPA acknowledged this impossibility and instead requested a 'blueprint' of two

[107] J.W. Winter, 'Geen regels maar best practices', in K.M. van Hassel and M.P. Nieuwe Weme (eds.), *Willems' wegen, Opstellen aangeboden aan prof.mr. J.H.M. Willems* (Kluwer, 2010), at 464.

cross-border IT systems of the multinational to verify whether the multinational had indeed brought these systems into compliance with the BCR requirements. As the system documentation of a large cross-border IT system of a multinational may well entail many binders of technical information, the multinational proposed instead to provide an overview of the information relevant to verify data protection compliance of those IT systems (which we called 'privacy impact assessments'). At the time these were paper questionnaires filled out to include the relevant information. Now we see that the Opinion on accountability prescribes that in certain cases PIAs have to be performed and that an inventory is kept of the data processing operations. However, many multinationals have now moved on and PIAs are no longer performed by means of hardcopy questionnaires but as integrated steps of an automated 'gateway system' which manages the implementation of new IT systems. This not only concerns data protection compliance, but also requirements under other laws, like export controls, financial regulations, etc. This may further entail that the PIA is not performed in one step, but in stages, and that parts that the DPA would consider part of the PIA are performed as part of other mandatory checks (for instance, as part of system security rather than in relation to just data security). The information on data protection may therefore not be available in a dedicated PIA in a central inventory but rather as part of a compliance dashboard combining all information on data protection, IT security, export controls, financial regulations, etc.

The example above illustrates how descriptions of the *means* by which multinationals should achieve data protection compliance are outdated the moment they are issued and stifle innovation as regards the most effective means to achieve data protection compliance in practice.[108] Rather than specifying the means, the three accountability requirements listed by the Working Party 29 (and as now also included in the Proposed Regulation) should be translated in a general framework requirement which imposes accountability on the multinational in achieving proper *outcomes*. In this case, for instance, the three requirements may be rephrased as a general obligation for multinationals 'to have readily available information on the compliance of their data processing operations and to have ongoing risk assessment and mitigation in place'.

Additional requirements identified by the Working Party 29 are:

(xi) being transparent on the internal complaints procedure (assuming such transparency concerns the number and nature of the complaints filed rather than only the existence of the complaints procedure itself) and on its data protection compliance also in its annual report;

(viii) setting up an internal procedure for the effective management and reporting of security breaches.

[108] See on the phenomenon of prescriptive requirements stifling legal innovation, Chapter 7, para 7.3.2.

Proposed Regulation These requirements are not (fully) reflected in the Proposed Regulation. Though earlier drafts of the Proposed Regulation contained a general publication requirement,[109] this requirement did not make it to the final version. Further, the Proposed Regulation provides for an obligation of the controller 'to document any personal data breaches, comprising the facts surrounding the breach, its effects and the remedial action taken',[110] but does not require him to implement a security breach notification procedure. Such requirement, however, would seem to follow from the general provision on accountability in the Proposed Regulation.[111]

Concerning the additional requirement (xi) on transparency, I indeed recommend that this be included in the BCR regime. As already indicated, the driving force for data protection compliance by multinationals is reputation and transparency requirements are therefore a key factor to capitalize on this driving force. This recommendation is also based on the evaluation of BCR as a form of TPR and CSR and applicable legitimacy requirements, which will be discussed in Chapters 10 and 11.

Concerning requirement (viii) on setting up internal procedures for the effective management and reporting of security breaches, the same comment applies that it concerns a specific element of compliance only and thereby misses the more overall obligation to ensure proper compliance procedures, which should be part of accountability of a multinational. Security breaches are only one of the causes that may lead to a data protection violation; other events may occur, data protection laws may change and require changes, an audit may be performed and disclose data protection violations that require correction or violations may be reported by means of a complaint by an individual. In all cases an effective management of the 'event' is indicated. Further, within a multinational a security breach of its IT systems may have far more implications than a breach of data protection. In case of a cyber crime attack, the financial systems of a company may be compromised, which may trigger disclosure obligations under laws regulating listed companies.[112] If health information is involved, this may lead to specific notification obligations under laws regulating medical and health information.[113] If confidential intellectual property or

[109] See n 78.

[110] Article 31(4) Proposed Regulation.

[111] Though Art 22(2) Proposed Regulation (the general provision on accountability) does not include a reference to Art 31. See further para 9.4.2.

[112] For instance, disclosure obligations under U.S. federal securities laws (including Sarbanes-Oxley and Security Exchange Act 1933 and 1934) are triggered if: the validity of financial statement information has been compromised; a material financial impact is to be expected; or the company has a disclosure obligation under foreign law. Separate disclosure obligations may be triggered depending whether a company is listed at the NYSE or Nasdaq. See for instance the disclosure requirements under s 2 of the NYSE Listing Manual. Specific data breach notification requirements apply to financial institutions: see the breach notification requirements issued by the federal banking agencies under the U.S. federal Gramm-Leach-Bliley Act (see Chapter 5, n 13).

[113] Such as the data breach notification requirements under the U.S. HIPPA and HITECH Act (see Chapter 5, n 12).

know-how of the multinational is stolen, this may lead to violation of export control laws.[114] Security breaches may further have consequences under labour law and telecommunications law.[115] Procedures relating to security breaches are therefore in most cases not specific to data protection breaches. If I include these obligations in an overall framework obligation for a multinational, this would be that the multinational has to have in place 'event management and complaint handling, i.e. procedures for responding to inquiries, complaints and data protection breaches'.

It is to be expected (and also advisable), that these additional requirements also be added to the BCR requirements. To be in control of its data processing operations, a multinational will have to have an inventory of its data processing operations as well as an ongoing risk assessment of data protection compliance. As to the requirement to have internal security breach management and notification procedures, most multinationals already have such policies in place in order to be able to comply with security breach notification laws.[116]

9.4.2 Proposed Regulation accountability requirements

The Proposed Regulation contains the following general accountability provision:[117]

> The controller shall adopt policies and implement appropriate measures to ensure and be able to demonstrate that the processing of personal data is performed in compliance with this Regulation, including the assignment of responsibilities, and the training of staff involved in the processing operations.

The Proposed Regulation subsequently provides a non-exhaustive list of accountability measures:[118]

(i) keeping the documentation pursuant to Article 28;
(ii) implementing the data security requirements laid down in Article 30;
(iii) performing a data protection impact assessment pursuant to Article 33;
(iv) complying with the requirements for prior authorization or prior consultation of the supervisory authority pursuant to Article 34(1) and (2);
(v) designating a data protection officer pursuant to Article 35(1); and

[114] For instance, U.S. export control laws require that a company obtains an export licence before certain technology is exported to specific countries. The U.S. also imposes trade sanctions and export embargoes against certain countries (currently Cuba, Iran, Syria, and Sudan) which are administered by the Office of Foreign Assets Controls (OFAC) of the U.S. Treasury Department.

[115] For instance, requiring that the works council be informed, or triggering security breach notification duties for telecommunication operators. See for the latter Art 2(4)(c) e-Privacy Directive, (Chapter 3, n 5). See also Kuner (Chapter 6, n 31), at 12.

[116] As discussed in Chapter 5, para 5.2.

[117] Article 22(1) Proposed Regulation.

[118] Article 22(2) Proposed Regulation.

(vi) if proportionate, implementing mechanisms to ensure the verification of the effectiveness of the above measures, which verification shall be carried out by independent internal or external auditors.[119]

The Proposed Regulation further empowers the Commission to adopt delegated acts for the purpose of specifying any further accountability criteria and measures.[120]

Before discussing whether the Proposed Regulation contains any additional accountability requirements, I have some general comments in respect of how the provision on accountability in the Proposed Regulation is set up. Apparently the Commission considered specific accountability measures so crucial that these became independent requirements in the Proposed Regulation. Examples are the requirement for controllers to keep certain documentation and the requirement to perform PIAs prior to introducing new processing operations that are likely to present specific risks.[121] Since these provisions are already included in the body of the Proposed Regulation it adds little to include these again in the list of accountability measures to be taken. Further, it is not easily understood why for instance the requirement for prior authorization or consultation of the DPA should specifically be included in the list of accountability measures.[122] This does not seem to be an accountability requirement in the sense that compliance with this requirement requires specific implementation measures. And if this requirement is referred to, why then not also refer to the notification obligation of a personal data breach to the DPA, which includes the obligation of the controller to document security breaches, facts surrounding the breach, and remedial actions taken.[123] Contrary to the requirement of prior consultation of the DPA, compliance with this requirement does in practice require implementation of data security breach incident procedures. In the overview in the accountability provision other provisions of the Proposed Regulation are also lacking, which in practice require accountability measures to ensure compliance, such as the newly introduced principle of data protection by design and by default. All in all the provision on accountability in the Proposed Regulation raises more questions than it answers. More clarity would have been achieved if the non-exhaustive list of accountability measures had been deleted altogether.

Looking in more detail at the accountability provision in the Proposed Regulation, there is one additional requirement not listed by the Working Party 29, which is the requirement to periodically verify the overall effectiveness of the totality of the controller's accountability programme.[124] This requirement encompasses an overall learning element and therefore provides for so-called 'double loop learning'.[125] This requirement is also one of the 'common fundamentals' of the accountability

[119] Article 22(3) Proposed Regulation.
[120] Article 22(4) Proposed Regulation.
[121] Articles 28 and 33 Proposed Regulation.
[122] Article 22(2)(d) Proposed Regulation.
[123] Article 31(4) Proposed Regulation.
[124] Article 22(3) Proposed Regulation.
[125] See n 34.

requirements as defined by the CIPL[126] and will be part of the recommendations to be made in Chapter 9, paragraph 9.4. Missing in the Proposed Regulation is how the Commission and the Working Party 29 may become engaged in this ongoing learning process of companies and the problems they are trying to manage in order for them to be able to improve their regulatory strategies accordingly (in order to achieve 'triple loop learning'). Under the Proposed Regulation, controllers have the obligation to maintain documentation with 'a *description* of the mechanisms to ensure the verification of the effectiveness of the accountability measures to be taken by the controller' and therefore not the actual *results* of the verifications of the compliance programmes.[127] The obligation of the controller to provide the prescribed documentation on request to the DPA therefore also does not apply to the actual results of the verifications.[128] This requirement was included in earlier drafts of the Proposed Regulation, but did not make it to the final version.[129] However, also this 'passive' information requirement would not have been sufficient to achieve the required 'triple loop learning'.[130] As discussed in paragraph 9.3.2, my recommendation is not to include this passive information requirement or the BCR requirements or to turn this into an active one, but to find other ways to engage EU legislators in the learning process of companies as to data protection compliance. This can be achieved for instance where the Proposed Regulation empowers the Commission to adopt delegated acts for the purpose of specifying any further accountability criteria and measures.[131] As part of the legislative process of adopting such acts, the Commission is required to 'carry out appropriate consultations during its preparatory work, including at expert level'.[132] By further periodically evaluating these delegated acts,[133] triple loop learning may be achieved.

9.4.3 Madrid accountability requirements

Besides the general accountability provision, the Madrid Draft Proposal for International Standards[134] also contains a list of compliance measures the application of which should be encouraged by the states. There is one additional requirement not

126 See para 9.4.4.
127 Article 28(2)(h) Proposed Regulation.
128 Article 28(3) Proposed Regulation.
129 See Art 25(2)(i) draft Proposed Regulation, Chapter 1, n 10.
130 See n 34.
131 Article 22(4) Proposed Regulation. The Commission is also empowered to adopt delegated acts in respect of the BCR requirements, see Art 40(3). EU regulators can delegate to the Commission the power to adopt acts in accordance with the recently introduced Arts 290 and 291 TFEU.
132 See also Recital 129 Proposed Regulation.
133 Pursuant to Art 90 Proposed Regulation, the Commission shall have to periodically submit reports on the evaluation and review of the Regulation to the European Parliament and the Council. The first report shall have to be submitted within four years after the entry into force of the Regulation.
134 See Art 22 Madrid draft proposal (Chapter 3, n 49) for an International Standard: 'States should encourage, through their domestic law, the implementation by those involved in any stage of the processing of measures to promote better compliance with applicable laws on the protection of privacy with regard to the processing of personal data. Such measures could include, among others:

listed by the Working Party 29 (and the Proposed Regulation): 'the implementation of a response plan that establishes guidelines for action in case of verifying a breach of applicable laws on the protection of privacy with regard to the processing of personal data, including at least the obligation to determine the cause and extent of the breach, to describe its harmful effects and to take the appropriate measures to avoid future breaches.'[135]

Though not listed by the Working Party 29 in its Opinion on accountability, the Working Party 29 does require in its WP Opinions that the BCR audit programme covers 'methods of ensuring that corrective actions have taken place'.[136] In respect of this Madrid requirement, the same comment applies as to the requirement to implement 'internal procedures for the effective management and reporting of security breaches'. A response plan as prescribed by the Madrid requirements is part of the follow-up of an 'event' (whether due to a security breach or other data protection violation discovered), and is covered by the overall framework obligation for a multinational as defined above to have in place 'event management and complaint handling, i.e. procedures for responding to inquiries, complaints and data protection breaches'.

(a) The implementation of procedures to prevent and detect breaches, which may be based on standardized models of information security governance and/or management.

(b) The appointment of one or more data protection or privacy officers, with adequate qualifications, resources and powers for exercising their supervisory functions adequately.

(c) The periodic implementation of training, education and awareness programs among the members of the organization aimed at better understanding of the applicable laws on the protection of privacy with regard to the processing of personal data, as well as the procedures established by the organization for that purpose.

(d) The periodic conduct of transparent audits by qualified and preferably independent parties to verify compliance with the applicable laws on the protection of privacy with regard to the processing of personal data, as well as with the procedures established by the organization for that purpose.

(e) The adaptation of information systems and/or technologies for the processing of personal data to the applicable laws on the protection of privacy with regard to the processing of personal data, particularly at the time of deciding on their technical specifications and on the development and implementation thereof.

(f) The implementation of privacy impact assessments prior to implementing new information systems and/or technologies for the processing of personal data, as well as prior to carrying out any new method of processing personal data or substantial modifications in existing processing.

(g) The adoption of codes of practice the observance of which are binding and that include elements that allow the measurement of efficiency as far as compliance and level of protection of personal data are concerned, and that set out effective measures in case of non-compliance.

(h) The implementation of a response plan that establishes guidelines for action in case of verifying a breach of applicable laws on the protection of privacy with regard to the processing of personal data, including at least the obligation to determine the cause and extent of the breach, to describe its harmful effects and to take the appropriate measures to avoid future breaches.'

135 See n 134, requirement sub (h).

136 See WP 108 (Chapter 6, n 7), para 6, at 7, requiring that the BCR audit programme covers 'methods of ensuring that corrective actions have taken place.'

9.4.4 Centre for Information Policy Leadership accountability requirements

In October 2010, the Centre for Information Policy Leadership[137] (*CIPL*) issued a discussion document 'Demonstrating and Measuring Accountability'[138] (*Accountability Discussion Document*), which identifies nine common fundamentals that an accountable organization should be prepared to implement and demonstrate to regulators.[139] As the Working Party 29 and Madrid requirements for accountability were already available at the time of drafting the Accountability Discussion Document, it is not surprising that the nine 'common fundamentals' identified by the CIPL show a near complete overlap therewith. The added value of the Accountability Discussion Document is that it sets out the collection of requirements (i) in a more logical grouping of requirements; (ii) as more general obligations, while still describing in the explanatory notes to the requirements what is understood under the relevant general heading; and this all (iii) in a terminology which is (more) familiar to companies. The nine common fundamentals identified by the CIPL are:

1. *Policies*: Existence of binding and enforceable written data privacy policies and procedures that reflect applicable laws, regulations and industry standards.
2. *Executive oversight*: Internal executive oversight and responsibility for data privacy and protection.
3. *Staffing and delegation*: Allocation of resources to ensure that the organization's privacy programme is appropriately staffed by adequately trained personnel.
4. *Education and awareness*: Existence of up-to-date education and awareness programmes to keep employees and on-site contractors aware of data protection obligations.
5. *Ongoing risk assessment and mitigation*: Implementation of a process to assist the organization in understanding the risks to privacy raised by new products, services, technologies, and business models, and to mitigate those risks.
6. *Programme risk assessment oversight and validation*: Periodic review of the totality of the accountability programme to determine whether modification is necessary.
7. *Event management and complaint handling*: Procedures for responding to inquiries, complaints, and data protection breaches.
8. *Internal enforcement*: Internal enforcement of the organization's policies and discipline for non-compliance.

[137] The CIPL acted as secretariat to a working group facilitated by various DPAs, which included 60 representatives of business, civil society, government, data protection and privacy enforcement agencies, and the European Data Protection Supervisor.

[138] The Centre for Information Policy Leadership, 'Demonstrating and Measuring Accountability, A Discussion Document, Accountability Phase II—The Paris Project,' October 2010, to be found at <http://www.informationpolicycentre.com/accountability-based_privacy_governance/> (Accountability Discussion Document). It is to be expected that the Accountability Discussion Document will prove a significant indicator of what privacy accountability will have to encompass.

[139] See Accountability Discussion Document (n 138), at 6.

9. *Redress*: The method by which an organisation provides remedies for those whose privacy has been put at risk.

An example where the fundamentals identified by the CIPL rightfully group certain Working Party 29 and Madrid accountability requirements together is the fifth fundamental 'Ongoing risk assessment and mitigation'. Here the Working Party 29 accountability requirements (i), (iii), and (ix) and the Madrid accountability requirement (h) are grouped under one heading. The explanatory notes to this fundamental explain this criterion by indicating that an organization should:

> be able to demonstrate the nature of their risk analysis. The organisation must show the rigor of the criteria against which analyses are carried out, and the suitability of those criteria to the nature of the data and data use. Further, the organisation should be able to demonstrate how decisions are made and steps are taken to mitigate risk. The organisation must also demonstrate that the decisions it takes to respond to identified risks are appropriate and effective.

This seems indeed a proper summary of how multinationals achieve compliance in practice. Most multinationals will have a data security policy setting the security requirements (both operational and technical) based on the privacy and other risks of different categories of data (for instance, the highest security classification will include not only sensitive data, but also critical financial data of a company and confidential IP of a company). The PIAs will subsequently show whether the data processed in a certain data processing system are properly classified in accordance with the classifications of this data security protocol. In case of data security or other data protection breaches, there will be a security breach response procedure which sets out the procedures to be followed and the decisions to be made. A proper response procedure will require that, if an actual data security or other data protection breach occurs, the various decisions and steps taken will be documented along the way (in meeting notes etc), in order to be able to assess the adequacy of the response made and to avoid future breaches.

The fifth fundamental further encompasses a learning element, ie experiences in the past are translated into actions both to avoid future breaches as well as improve the related response. The fundamentals as identified by the CIPL also provide a more overall learning element by requiring as the seventh fundamental that organizations provide for: programme risk assessment oversight and validation, where the totality of the accountability programme is periodically reviewed to determine whether modification is necessary. The fundamentals as defined by the CIPL therefore provide adequate 'double loop learning' and their coming into existence are further an example par excellence of 'triple loop learning' since the fundamentals have been drafted in a working group facilitated by various DPAs, which included 60 representatives of business, civil society, government, data protection and privacy enforcement agencies, and the European Data Protection Supervisor.[140] The ques-

[140] Paragraph 9.4.2.

tion is how can this triple loop learning be preserved also for the future? As indicated in paragraph 9.4.2, this can be achieved for instance where the Proposed Regulation empowers the Commission to adopt delegated acts for the purpose of specifying (i) any further accountability criteria and measures and (ii) BCR requirements.[141] The Commission is required to 'carry out appropriate consultations during its preparatory work, including at expert level'.[142] By further periodically evaluating these delegated acts,[143] triple loop learning may be achieved. My conclusion and recommendation is that EU legislators, when setting the main requirements for the BCR regime, should not add the additional accountability requirements as listed by the Working Party 29 and in the Madrid Draft Proposal for International Standards, as these are too specific and may prove even counterproductive to achieving optimal compliance. But instead set these requirements in more general obligations based on the common fundamentals as defined by the CIPL. An overall transparency requirement is missing from the common fundamentals. Again, also for reasons to be discussed as part of the evaluation of BCR as a form of TPR and CSR, my recommendation is to indeed make these transparency requirements part of the BCR regime. A final observation in respect of the common fundamentals identified in the Accountability Discussion Document is that these seem to be limited to accountability of a company in respect of *its own data processing operations*. Part of the business activities of any multinational is, however, that data are transferred to third parties outside the group of companies (which also constitutes processing of data). The Accountability Discussion Document does not identify common fundamentals in respect of accountability of companies in respect of such onward data transfers. The Proposed Regulation also provides that BCR have to specify the rules for onward data transfers[144] but does not provide any guidance on what these rules for onward transfers should look like. This element is further discussed in paragraph 9.5.1. A final recommendation is that the general accountability requirements should by preference not be included in the EU regulatory instrument itself (whether a revised directive or a regulation), but the defining of these requirements should be delegated to the Commission in accordance with Articles 290 and 291 TFEU.

Recommendation 12

To delegate the detailed norm-setting in respect of the BCR requirements to the Commission in accordance with Articles 290 and 291 TFEU, or as the next best alternative, to define the BCR requirements as general obligations of the multinational on the basis of the common fundamentals defined by the Centre for Information Policy Leadership, and add as requirements for BCR:

[141] Article 22(4) and 43(3) Proposed Regulation. EU regulators can delegate to the Commission the power to adopt acts in accordance with the recently introduced Art 290 TFEU.

[142] See Recital 129 Proposed Regulation and further Chapter 10, n 94.

[143] Pursuant to Art 90 Proposed Regulation, the Commission shall have to periodically submit reports on the evaluation and review of the Regulation to the European Parliament and the Council.

[144] Article 43(2)(e) Proposed Regulation.

- prescribe the reporting on BCR in the annual reports of company in a comparable format;
- the multinational should be transparent vis-à-vis the third-party beneficiaries as to the number of complaints received and the nature of these complaints under the internal complaints procedure.

9.5 Accountability for Onward Data Transfers in BCR?

As seen in Chapter 2, paragraph 2.2, there are systems which are based on a territorial approach for data transfers (based on 'adequacy' of protection in *countries*) and systems which have chosen the organizational approach (based on accountability of *organizations*). Accountability does not specifically restrict cross-border data flows, but imposes compliance obligations on parties that transfer personal data to a third party, regardless of where this third party is located. One example is the APEC Privacy Framework. Principle 26 APEC Privacy Framework requires that:

> When personal information is to be transferred to another person or organization, whether domestically or internationally, the personal information controller should obtain the consent of the individual or exercise due diligence and take reasonable steps to ensure that the recipient person or organization will protect the information consistently with these Principles.

Similarly, under the Canadian PIPED Act, companies are accountable for the measures that could be required of such company to provide a comparable level of protection taking, for instance, into account the adequacy level of the country of destiny.[145]

As an exception to the territory-based system of the EU, the EU introduced the BCR regime that reflects the organizational (ie the accountability) approach to regulate *intercompany* data transfers. As soon as the multinational with BCR transfers data outside the company group to a third party in a non-adequate country, however, the regular EU data transfer rules have to be complied with (ie the EU Standard Contractual Clauses, consent of data subjects, etc). The question is whether this system for *onward transfers* in the BCR regime should be replaced by a system based on accountability as well. As to the adequacy system in general it can be stated that more and more criticism can be heard that the EU adequacy approach to data transfers has proven inadequate. The main reason for this is that, even if data are transferred to an 'adequate country', enforcement of data protection violations may prove problematic even in such 'adequate countries' (see for examples Chapter 4, paragraph 4.3). Further, in practice the EU approach requires a full adequacy assessment of the data protection laws of each country

[145] See Chapter 2, n 54.

and proves insufficiently productive in achieving global data protection coverage.[146] Key trade partners of the EU like China, Japan, Brazil, India, and the US are not covered, which inevitably leads to non-compliance in practice.[147] The accountability approach to data transfers is clearly more flexible in tailoring to the transfers at hand and even facilitates some form of central enforcement against the data exporter who is often in the country where the data subject is domiciled (see Chapter 4, paragraph 4.4.4). However, the accountability approach also has its disadvantages, mainly being that it is too reactive and does not offer incentives to countries to adopt adequate data protection laws. Oddly enough, it does not matter which system is chosen as both systems can serve *as a starting point only*. Both systems in unadapted form are not attractive. As one author puts it: 'otherwise the first approach [the adequacy approach] will tend to be excessively bureaucratic and the second too reactive.'[148] For any of the two systems to be acceptable, additional measures are indicated.[149] As already indicated in Chapter 3, paragraph 3.1.5, it seems that the Commission intends to stick with the adequacy approach, but also intends to mitigate negative aspects of the adequacy system by for instance improving and streamlining BCR.[150] This approach seems to provide room to

[146] See Kuner (Chapter 2, n 55), at 263, stating that 'an examination of the current adequacy system shows that it is cumbersome, expensive, slow, and sends the wrong message to third countries'. He further calculates that with the present pace of approval of adequacy decisions, it will take 130 years to achieve some sort of global coverage. Taking into account that there are 192 member states of the United Nations only in total about 48 countries are considered adequate (27 Member States, 3 EFTA countries, eight countries with an adequacy ruling (see Chapter 2, n 18)) and 10 countries that have ratified Convention 108 and the Addendum to Convention 108 and are not already included in the foregoing countries (see Chapter 4, n 12). This leaves about 144 possible candidates. Kuner (Chapter 2, n 55), at 264 notes that 'half of these would never be found adequate for various reasons, such as they do not have a democratic system of government, a functioning legal system, or other basic requirements for adequacy.' It is clear that the adequacy solution will not lead to a global coverage (at least at any time in the foreseeable future). See also the findings of the Rand Report (Chapter 2, n 27), at 43: 'The study shows that the Directive's focus on adequacy assessments and the strategies to achieve this are inefficient and insufficiently productive in an increasingly globalised data market. (...) The promotion of alternatives—such as SCCs and BCR—should become a greater priority. The use of these alternatives should be facilitated for data controllers in any Member State, as was already noted above. In addition, it was noted by several interviewees that current adequacy assessments were not sufficiently effective, focusing mostly on a review of regulations and declared policy, rather than on the effectiveness of data protection. If the credibility of the adequacy assessment system is to be maintained, assessments should consider whether the principles put forward by the Directive are achieved in practice, which includes issues such as the actual independence of DPAs and court rulings on data protection issues, the availability of sufficient means to allow DPAs to operate in practice, and the existence of actual enforcement actions.' See also Kuner (Chapter 2, n 55), at 263.

[147] See the Rand Report (Chapter 2, n 27), at 43: 'Key economic trading partners are not covered by adequacy findings, which means that alternatives should play a crucial role in practice. When these are not easily available, non-compliance is de facto encouraged'. See also Kuner (n 8), at 29: 'The fact that some of the largest economies in the world (such as China and Japan) have not been the subject of a formal EU adequacy decision means that there must be substantial non-compliance at least with regard to data flows from the EU to those countries.'

[148] See citation Kuner in Chapter 2, n 55.

[149] See Kuner (Chapter 2, n 8), at 41, where he concludes that 'what is needed is for the two approaches to co-exist, whereby the solution selected by a country should be accompanied by measures to avoid its inherent disadvantages'.

[150] EC Communication on revision of the Directive, (Chapter 2, n 34), at 12. See also Arts 37–38 Draft Proposal.

keep the benefits of an adequacy approach (which stimulates third countries to adopt adequate data protection laws) while also providing for more flexible organizational measures (accountability approach) which may mitigate the downsides of the adequacy system. It is unclear, however, whether the new rules on BCR will adopt the accountability approach only as to *intercompany* transfers (as is currently the case) or will also extend to *onward data transfers*. Also the Proposed Regulation does not provide clarity. As to onward transfers, the Proposed Regulation just provides that the BCR will have to specify 'the requirements for onward transfers to organisations that are not bound by the policies'.[151] I take this as providing leeway for multinationals to include in BCR a regime for onward transfers based on accountability. What this regime should look like is, however, unclear. A regime for onward transfers based on accountability is much to be preferred to the current situation where a multinational with BCR has to comply with the regular EU data transfer rules if it transfers data outside the group to a third party in a non-adequate country. The present inflexible approach taken by the Commission vis-à-vis, for instance, the EU Standard Contractual Clauses, makes it unnecessarily burdensome for companies to comply. The following example may clarify this.

The EU Standard Contractual Clauses for Processors have been recently updated to cater for the situation where the controller involves a main processor, who in its turn involves sub-processors. This is by now a very common feature in large outsourcing arrangements.[152] Before the update of the Clauses, the controller had to enter into EU Standard Contractual Clauses with each of the non-EU entities of the supplier involved in the services. The aim of the updated Clauses was to simplify this situation where the multinational would have to enter into EU Standard Contractual Clauses with the main supplier only. The updated Clauses, however, now appear to apply only if the main processor is established outside the EU,[153] even though in most large outsourcing arrangements multinationals enter into the main outsourcing contract with the group company of a supplier in their own jurisdiction. This supplier entity will subsequently sub-contract with its group companies outside the EU. For those cases the EU Standard Contractual Clauses do not apply, which leaves these parties with the same situation as before the updated Clauses were issued, requiring the multinational to enter into multiple EU Standard Contractual Clauses with each of the non-EU entities of the supplier involved in the services.[154] The same applies when the multinational has more

[151] Article 43(2)(d) Proposed Regulation.

[152] Recitals 16 and 17 EU Standard Contractual Clauses for Processors (Chapter 3, n 79). See also Kuner (Chapter 3, n 79), at 5.

[153] Recital 23 EU Standard Contractual Clauses for Processors (Chapter 3, n 79); Kuner (Chapter 3, n 79), at 5 and 7; Opinion 3/2009 on the Draft Commission Decision on standard contractual clauses for the transfer of personal data to processors established in third countries under Directive 95/46/EC (data controller to data processor) (WP 161), 5 March 2009 (*WP Opinion on Standard Contractual Clauses for Processors*), at 3; and FAQs in order to address some issues raised by the entry into force of the EU Commission Decision 2010/87/EU of 5 February 2010 on standard contractual clauses for the transfer of personal data to processors established in third countries under Directive 95/46/EC, dated 12 July 2010 (WP 176) (*WP FAQs on Standard Contractual Clauses for Processors*), at 3.

[154] WP Opinion on Standard Contractual Clauses for Processors (n 153), at 3.

entities in the EU. The new EU Standard Contractual Clauses do not facilitate that these will be jointly signed by all EU group companies of the multinational.[155] Even if the multinational has BCR in place, each of the EU group companies of the multinational still has to enter into the EU Standard Contractual Clauses with each of the non-EU entities of the supplier involved in the services. If ever unnecessarily administrative burdens are created, these are examples. Multinationals and their multinational suppliers entering into an outsourcing arrangement on a global basis each have convincing reasons to ensure that their respective group companies are indeed bound by this arrangement. They achieve this by either entering into a global outsourcing arrangement between their respective parent companies, or if their counterparty is not the parent, requesting for instance a parent guarantee that all group companies will comply with their respective obligations. Why on earth the data protection obligations would not be able to follow that contractual structure but would require separate individual contracts between all group companies on either side is truly beyond me, especially if the multinational has BCR which are binding upon all group companies. What is relevant is that the multinational imposes binding obligations on the supplier and all its group companies involved. By setting as a requirement that for that purpose separate contracts have to be concluded, unnecessary administrative burdens are created without any added value as to material data protection, which is a recipe for non-compliance which in turn undermines the legitimacy of the material data processing principles which these norms aim to protect.[156] Such requirements should be avoided at all cost.

Proposed Regulation In Chapter 3, paragraph 3.1.5, I discussed the data transfer rules under the Proposed Regulation. What is relevant here is that the Proposed Regulation allows more 'organizational-based' data transfer solutions. In addition to the EU Standard Contractual Clauses 'appropriate safeguards' may also be adduced by (i) BCR; (ii) standard data protection clauses adopted by a DPA, provided these are declared generally valid by the Commission; and (iii) entering into of contractual clauses between controller or processor and the recipient of the

[155] WP FAQs on Standard Contractual Clauses for Processors (n 153), at 7 (FAQ 5).

[156] That an overly strict approach undermines the credibility of the Directive is acknowledged in the First Report on the Directive (Chapter 2, n 49), at 19: 'An overly lax attitude in Some Member States [as to data transfers] (...) risks weakening protection in the EU as a whole, because with the free movement guaranteed by the Directive, data flows are likely to switch to the "least burdensome" point of export. An overly strict approach, on the other hand, would fail to respect the legitimate needs of international trade and the reality of global telecommunications networks and risks creating a gap between law and practice which is damaging for the credibility of the Directive and for Community law in general.' A similar observation is made by Christopher Kuner, 'Internet Jurisdiction and Data Protection Law: An International Legal Analysis (Part 2)' [2010] *International Journal of Law and Information Technology*, vol 18; available at SSRN: <http://ssrn.com/abstract=1689495>, at 13, noting that 'when the jurisdictional scope of the law is much broader than the chance that the law will be enforced, there is a risk that respect for the law will be diminished', and at 15: 'a low chance of enforcement may cause controllers to regard data protection rules as a kind of bureaucratic nuisance rather than as "law" in the same category as tax laws, employment laws, etc.'

data, provided these contractual clauses obtained the prior authorization of the DPA.[157] However, if it remains a requirement that the EU Standard Contractual Clauses (or other data protection clauses) have to be signed or separately entered into by all group companies on all sides of the transaction, not much will be gained. New in the proposed regulation is that the data transfer rules are also directly applicable to processors.[158] As a result of this, the possibility of EU Standard Contractual Clauses will also be available to data processors when transferring data to a third party. Whether this is indeed an improvement of the current situation will depend on many factors. For instance, the question arises whether this will require yet additional EU Standard Contractual Clauses to be put in place. In the example where a controller in the EU contracts with a processor in the EU, who involves several sub-processors outside the EU, the controller has to enter into EU Standard Contractual Clauses with each of these sub-processors. However, the main processor in the EU is now also subject to the EU data transfer rules. Does this require the main processor also to enter into EU Standard Contractual Clauses with the sub-processors? This would be an additional administrative burden which does not increase the material data protection afforded to individuals. Improvements would be achieved, however, if it were possible for processors to put EU Standard Contractual Clauses in place with their non-EU group companies for all data transfers, after which it will no longer be required for EU controllers to enter into EU Standard Contractual Clauses with such non-EU processors. The same would apply if a controller and processor both have BCR. In that case no further contractual measures for data transfer would have to be complied with.

Given the inflexibility of the EU data transfer rules, I very much prefer that the new rules on BCR adopt the accountability approach for *onward data transfers* as well. An accountability approach to data transfers seems also to be favoured by the Rand Report[159] as well as by the CIPL in its New Approach to International Transfers.[160] The CIPL proposes that the revised Directive will authorize data transfers by a multinational to non-adequate countries if such a multinational has adopted a Binding Global Code providing that 'the data is processed, and continues

[157] Article 42(2) Proposed Regulation. See Art 43 Proposed Regulation for the requirements for transfers by way of BCR. See on these criteria in detail Chapter 6, n 69.

[158] See Art 40 Proposed Regulation.

[159] The position of the Rand Report (Chapter 2, n 27), is not completely clear as nowhere in the report is a clear choice made for the one or the other system. At 49, however, the Rand Report seems to implicitly recommend the accountability approach for data transfers, where it recommends recasting the Directive 'as an articulation of General Principles and Outcomes'. The Rand Report subsequently lists six General Principles (Legitimacy, Purpose restriction, Security and confidentiality, Transparency, Data subject participation and Accountability). The last requirement of accountability provides that those processing data are held accountable for the outcomes (of the first five principles). Note that the first five Principles *do not include data transfer requirements.* From this I derive that those processing data are accountable for compliance with these requirements regardless whether such third party is within or outside the EEA. This de facto amounts to adopting the accountability approach for onward data transfers as well.

[160] The CIPL New Approach to International Transfers (Chapter 6, n 61), at 2: 'We believe that a new framework for international data transfers, built on the experience with BCR and explicitly grounded on the Accountability principle, could be achieved with "Binding Global Codes (*BGC*)".'

to be processed, in accordance with the Code'. The proposal is however not clear on what the extent of accountability of the multinational is. I will discuss what this accountability approach for onward transfers might look like in the next paragraph.

9.5.1 Define the core principles only

I propose that EU legislators opt for an accountability approach, by limiting themselves to setting the core material data protection requirements that need to be put in place between multinationals and their external suppliers, without prescribing the *means and form* by which these requirements have to be achieved. Again, multinationals are well able to decide on the most optimal legal instrument to achieve the prescribed protection. My proposal deviates from the proposal made by the CIPL. The CIPL proposes that the revised Directive will authorize data transfers by a multinational to non-adequate countries if such a multinational has adopted a Binding Global Code providing that 'the data is processed, and continues to be processed, in accordance with the Code'.[161] This presupposes that the multinational transferring data to its external suppliers imposes the terms of its Global Code on its external suppliers. This will not always be necessary. It is possible that the external supplier has its own Binding Global Code (maybe even a BCR for processors). In that case the data may be transferred to such supplier without the multinational having to impose the terms of its Global Code on the external supplier. Suppliers processing data on behalf of many multinationals may be unable to apply a Binding Global Code from each of those multinationals. What is relevant is that the data obtain an adequate level of protection, not that the original Binding Global Code remains applicable to all other parties subsequently processing that data in the chain. The same may apply if the data processing by the external supplier is subject to the data protection law of a country that obtained an adequacy ruling.[162] My conclusion is that the accountability requirements of multinationals under the BCR regime for data transfers to third parties should not be to impose the BCR on such third parties, but should require a more thoughtful defining of the core data protection elements that have to be safeguarded.

9.5.2 Focus on alternative means of redress

EU legislators in setting these core requirements should focus not on traditional judicial legal rights and remedies of individuals covered by BCR, but concentrate on means of redress that actually achieve compliance in practice.[163] One example is provided as an illustration.

[161] See the CIPL New Approach on International Transfers (Chapter 6, n 61), at 9.

[162] See eg the draft Australian data protection law, which combines the adequacy approach and the accountability approach by providing that the multinational transferring data will remains accountable for the data even after transfer unless the data are transferred to an adequate country. See Chapter 31 of the Australian Law Reform Commission report at 1087–113.

[163] Kuner (Chapter 6, n 78), at 271.

In Chapter 7, paragraph 7.5, I explained that the EU Standard Contractual Clauses contain a third-party beneficiary clause, granting individuals rights against the data importer. The individuals obtain the right to address the data importer in case of a data protection breach by such data importer and, if this data importer goes bankrupt, the individual may address the data exporter instead. Given the practical obstacles for individuals bringing a claim against a data importer in, for instance, India, these rights may look good on paper, but have in practice no added value for individuals. Worse, as the rights are prescribed in detail in the EU Standard Contractual Clauses which may not be amended, multinationals contracting with the data importer have no interest in improving on these rights, even though they certainly would have the bargaining power to do so. Why not include in the 'core principles' for legally binding instruments that the instrument should provide for 'proper means of redress by individuals in case of onward transfers of their data' (as the BCR regime already requires in respect of data processing by the multinational itself). My expectation is that within a short period of time, outsourcing contracts will for instance provide that the data importer has to accept that individuals may file complaints via the complaints procedure of the multinational also against the data importer, that the data importer is required to respond to such complaints within certain time limits and to reimburse the multinational for any costs incurred in respect of facilitating the whole process. Alternatively, the parties to the outsourcing agreement may provide that complaints will be processed by the outsourcing supplier, being the party responsible for the factual processing and best placed to respond to complaints about security breaches. The outsourcing contract may subsequently provide that the multinational has to cooperate and respond to complaints relating to the data processed itself, etc. In other words, the requirement should be that appropriate redress is organized; the means how to achieve such redress should be left to the parties involved.

9.5.3 Conclusion and starting points for core principles

My conclusion is that the BCR requirements should provide for core principles as to what can be expected of a multinational when involving third parties in the processing of its personal data (whether within or outside the EU). As with the 'binding legal instruments' discussed above, these should be set in general accountability requirements and not be specified as mandatory contractual provisions to be included in each of the contracts between a multinational and third parties in the context of which data are transferred. It is beyond the scope of this book to list exhaustively the main core accountability requirements when controllers transfer data to third parties (whether a controller or a processor). I recommend that an inventory of these core requirements be made similar to the inventory made by the CIPL of the accountability requirements for *internal compliance* by the multinational. My recommendation to EU legislators is to delegate this task in the revised Directive to the Commission in order to ensure that these requirements remain adaptable to changing circumstances.[164] The Commission can then preferably organize a project similar to that undertaken by the CIPL (including periodic revision thereof) in order to ensure triple loop learning (see paragraph 9.2.2).

For this inventory some general starting points can be formulated.

One of these requirements should be that individuals will have 'proper means of redress'. I have already identified this as a requirement as part of the evaluation of proper supply chain management (see Chapter 7, paragraph 7.5).

Mandatory monitoring and auditing of all data processing operations of the data processor should not be one of the requirements (see Chapter 7, paragraph 7.5). It is sufficient that the multinational has a right to do so only. Whether it is indicated that a multinational exercises such rights will depend on the risk assessment of the relevant data processing.

A more general guideline for drafting the inventory is the realization that data processing is performed in networks rather than in neat one-to-one relationships.[165] Research in other areas of law shows an inherent weakness of a chain of contracts along the supply chain, replicating the required contractual clauses where regulatory obligations are passed on in the chain.[166] A straightforward requirement for multinationals to impose certain contractual obligations on its contract party may therefore not do the trick. The main objective of supply chain management is to minimize risks of non-compliance and to improve effectiveness and efficiency of control *at the source of such risk.*[167] Rather than imposing requirements on all parties in the network, a more productive exercise may be to first identify the risks, the source of these risks, and then allocate responsibilities accordingly. A factor in allocating responsibilities may also be which of the parties has the best contracting power to enforce compliance. Below is an illustrative example.

The Directive imposes obligations on the controller of data. At the time the first outsourcing transactions were concluded it was indeed the controller who was in the driving seat as to imposing all terms relating to the outsourcing, including security requirements and whether data were transferred to non-EU countries or not. Today, with more commoditized outsourcing services (like straightforward 'server management'), contractual terms on security and whether data transfers are taking place or not are (as much) dictated by the outsourcing supplier.[168] Looking

[164] On the possibility of delegation to the Commission, see Chapter 6, para 6.6.

[165] See Trudel (Chapter 7, n 39), Chapter 19, at 332–4; and Raab and Koops (Chapter 4, n 24), at 220, who have attempted to map the landscape of privacy actors in the online data protection arena 'showing a remarkable range of diverse and versatile actors with many potential interconnections and interrelationships'.

[166] Cafaggi (Chapter 7, n 32), at 9.

[167] In similar terms as to the management of risks in relation to food safety, see Cafaggi (Chapter 7, n 32), at 18.

[168] Teme (Chapter 2, n 27): 'An additional dichotomy in need of review is that between controllers and processors. Data protection law allocates responsibility and delineates duties according to a categorization of an organization as a "controller" or "processor." A controller, defined in the EU DPD as the party that "determines the purposes and means of the processing of personal data," is traditionally viewed as the owner of the database, the one who has a direct relationship with the individual and therefore locus of liability. The processor (or "mere processor") is traditionally perceived as a service provider, a servant to the master-controller, whose sole responsibility is keeping the data

at the relationship from a risk perspective, security breaches may occur at the data processing operations of the outsourcing supplier (especially when in transit to offshore group companies) rather than at the premises of the controller. Imposing an obligation on the controller to have proper security breach incident procedures in place and an obligation to impose a similar obligation on the outsourcing supplier may therefore not do the trick. The two security incident procedures will have to coincide, resulting in a joint handling of the relevant incident, each to the extent they have control over the relevant IT. The security incident issues will multiply the more sub-processors are involved. In this case, solutions will not be forthcoming by a contractual chain, but by allocating responsibilities where they are best placed. To reflect this, the BCR requirements should therefore not require a mandatory contractual provision that the processor should have data security procedures in place (as all will have these in standard form), but should require the multinational to allocate the relevant responsibilities as to data security breaches to the party in the network that is best placed and this in such a manner that accountability for the whole is achieved. The risk that by one-to-one contracting data protection obligations may be diluted and even prevent effective control is also recognized by the Working Party 29 in its Opinion on controller and processor:[169]

> The strategic issue here is that - with a plurality of actors involved in the process – the obligations and responsibilities stemming from data protection legislation should be clearly allocated and not dispersed along the chain of outsourcing/ subcontracting. In other words, one should avoid a chain of (sub-)processors that would dilute or even prevent effective control and clear responsibility for processing activities, unless the responsibilities of the various parties in the chain are clearly established.

Taking it one step further, even if the responsibilities of the parties may be clearly established in the network, rather than fragmented liability of the different parties accumulating to full liability, liability of each should be for the outcome of the network as a whole. In its Opinion on controller and processor, the Working Party 29 also seems to recognize the risk of fragmentation and to consider solving this by joint and several liability for all parties involved:[170]

> the multiplication of controllers may also lead to undesired complexities and to a possible lack of clarity in the allocation of responsibilities. This would risk making the entire processing unlawful due to a lack of transparency and violate the principle of fair

secure. Yet how far this description is from market reality today, where layer upon layer of service providers (processors?) undertake an increasing role in the clients' (controllers?) business processes, including providing consulting services, driving innovation, and managing change. Moreover, with the advent of cloud computing and its architecture as a stack of infrastructure, platform and software layers, the neat distinction between controllers and processors has muddled. This is a critical matter, since in the absence of a clearly identified controller the framework remains teetering without a focal point for responsibility/accountability.'

169 WP Opinion on controller and processor (Chapter 3, n 8), at 27.

170 WP Opinion on controller and processor (Chapter 3, n 8), at 24.

processing. (...) Against this background, it can be argued that joint and several liability for all parties involved should be considered as a means of eliminating uncertainties, and therefore assumed only in so far as an alternative, clear and equally effective allocation of obligations and responsibilities has not been established by the parties involved or does not clearly stem from factual circumstances.

Thought should be given to the question whether the present set-up of the Directive where the controller is the sole bearer of all data protection obligations is indeed the best *incentive* to achieve compliance in case of complex data processing operations. In light of the diminishing contracting power of multinationals vis-à-vis their multinational outsourcing suppliers, an obligation on *all parties* involved in a data processing (whether controller or data processor) to achieve accountability as to the end result, may ultimately prove the better stick. This may work as an incentive for all parties to come to a proper allocation of obligations in relation to the network. By separating the contractual form from the liability regime, it is left to the parties to allocate responsibilities where they are best placed.[171]

Proposed Regulation The Proposed Regulation delegates to the Commission the power to adopt detailed norms for BCR (and thus also for further norm-setting in respect of onward transfers by multinationals under BCR) in the form of delegated acts in accordance with Article 290 TFEU.[172] Main changes are that certain requirements will also be directly imposed on a processor of personal data,[173] and further that joint controllers may divide the controller responsibilities by an arrangement between them.[174] This concerns their internal liability. Each controller and processor involved in a processing remains jointly and severally liable for the entire amount of the damage.[175] As indicated before, I agree that the imposing of direct obligations on processors is a good way to ensure that processors in complex processing operations do not 'hide' behind their processorship in order to avoid liability. However, if the Proposed Regulation allows joint controllers to divide responsibilities between them, I do not see why this possibility would not also be extended to a division of responsibilities between joint processors (or between main and sub-processors) and further between (joint) controllers and such (joint or sub-) processors. If individuals keep their rights against any of them, there seems little to be said against such possibility to divide responsibilities. As indicated before, in complex processing operations, with more joint controllers and more joint processors, this may well result in an optimal allocation of the risks.

[171] Cafaggi (Chapter 7, n 32), at 25–6.
[172] Articles 43(3) and 86 Proposed Regulation.
[173] See for the direct obligations of a processor under the Proposed Regulation Chapter 6, para 6.3.3, n 39.
[174] Article 24 Proposed Regulation.
[175] Article 77(2) Proposed Regulation.

Recommendation 13

- To delegate the detailed norm-setting in respect of the core accountability principles for onward transfers under BCR by multinationals (see also Appendix 1) to third parties to the Commission in accordance with Articles 290 and 291 TFEU, or as the next best alternative, define these accountability principles taking into account the guidelines identified in this paragraph.
- To impose certain obligations direct on processors (such as in any event the data security obligations and data transfer obligations).
- To provide that (joint) controllers and (joint or sub-) processors may divide responsibilities between them.

9.6 Solution of Working Party 29 to Achieve Joint Responsibility of Controller and Processor

As a side issue, I note that the Working Party 29 in its Opinion on controller and processor[176] has taken a first step in the direction of achieving joint responsibility of controllers and processors in respect of a joint processing. Rather than a clear classification of a party as either a controller or a processor, it seems that in case of complex joint processing operations, the Working Party 29 has a preference to qualify all parties involved as to the different aspects of the processing as a (joint) controller rather than some as data processor only, to achieve maximum responsibility for the processing as a whole of all parties in order to avoid pointing fingers or gaps in liability:[177]

> The bottom line should be ensuring that even in complex data processing environments, where different controllers play a role in processing personal data, compliance with data protection rules and responsibilities for possible breach of these rules are clearly allocated, in order to avoid that the protection of personal data is reduced or that a 'negative conflict of competence' and loopholes arise whereby some obligations or rights stemming from the Directive are not ensured by any of the parties.

The Working Party 29 achieves this by (insofar as relevant here) three instructions on the concept of controller. The first is that the concept of controller should be considered as a *functional* one, in the sense that it is intended to allocate responsibilities where there is *factual* influence, and thus based on a factual rather than a formal analysis.[178] A telling example given by the Working Party 29 itself is the SWIFT example:[179]

[176] See Chapter 3, n 8.
[177] WP Opinion on controller and processor (Chapter 3, n 8), at 22.
[178] WP Opinion on controller and processor (Chapter 3, n 8), at 9.
[179] WP Opinion on controller and processor (Chapter 3, n 8), at 11.

> The fact itself that somebody determines how personal data are processed may entail the qualification of data controller, even though this qualification arises outside the scope of a contractual relation or is explicitly excluded by a contract. A clear example of this was the SWIFT case, whereby this company took the decision to make available certain personal data - which were originally processed for commercial purposes on behalf of financial institutions - also for the purpose of the fight against terrorism financing, as requested by subpoenas issued by the U.S. Treasury.

The Working Party 29 further introduces the concept of *pluralistic control.* According to the Directive it is possible that multiple parties may be responsible for a certain processing activity (and qualify as co-controllers). In its Opinion the Working Party 29 makes clear that this concept of pluralistic control refers not only to cases where the controllers *equally* determine purposes and means and are *equally* responsible for a single processing operation (ie the co-controllership as implied in the definition of controller).[180] According to the Working Party 29 many other forms and combinations of 'pluralistic control' are possible, where one party is controller for certain parts, aspects, or stages of the processing and another controller for other parts, aspects or stages.[181]

The third instruction of the Working Party 29 concerns the elements of the definition of controller: 'purpose and means'.[182] According to the Working Party 29 the determination of the 'purpose' of a processing activity is reserved to the controller. Whoever makes this decision is (de facto) controller. The determination of the 'means' of processing can be delegated by the controller, as far as *technical or organizational questions* are concerned. Means however, does—according to the Working Party 29—not only refer to the technical ways of processing personal data but also to the 'how' of processing, which includes questions like 'which data will be processed', 'which third parties will have access to these data', 'when will data be deleted', etc. Determination of the 'means' therefore includes both technical and organisational questions where the decision can be delegated to processors (eg 'which hardware or software will be used?') but also essential elements which are traditionally and inherently reserved to the determination of the controller, such as 'which data will be processed?', 'how long will they be processed?', 'who will have access to the data?'.[183] Delegation of these decisions to a processor may well have consequences for the qualification of the processor as a controller.

In line with the above, one would expect that security measures would fall under 'technical and organizational means', which traditionally can be delegated by the controller to the processor (without changing its qualification as a processor). The Working Party 29 confirms this but also highlights that in *some legal systems* decisions taken on security measures 'are particularly important, since security measures are explicitly considered as an essential characteristic to be defined by

[180] WP Opinion on controller and processor (Chapter 3, n 8), at 19.
[181] WP Opinion on controller and processor (Chapter 3, n 8), at 18.
[182] For the full definition of controller, see Art 2(d) Directive (Chapter 2, n 25).
[183] WP Opinion on controller and processor (Chapter 3, n 8), at 14.

the controller'.[184] The Working Party 29 itself indicates that this raises the issue of which decisions on security may entail the qualification of controller for a company to which processing has been outsourced, but does not answer this question.

The Working Party 29 gives a number of examples to illustrate how the instructions above work out in practice. The example that best illustrates how the Working Party 29 achieves joint controllership for the security measures is the example of an e-government portal, where certain public administration units outsource the servicing of requests of citizens for copies of public documents to a third-party service provider that will host such e-governmental portal. There is no question that the public administration units are the controllers in respect of the respective documents they issue. The party operating the e-governmental portal is instructed to perform the issuing of the copies on behalf of the relevant public administration units and is prohibited to use the documents for any other purposes. The fact pattern seems to indicate that the portal provider qualifies as a data processor as to the servicing of the requests of citizens on behalf of the public administration units. Based on the above instructions, the Working Party 29, however, concludes that the portal provider qualifies as a controller and is therefore responsible for the security of the transfer of the data from the user to the administration's system as this transfer is an essential part of the services provided for by the portal.[185]

> Example No. 11: E-Government portals
> E-Government portals act as intermediaries between the citizens and the public administration units: the portal transfers the requests of the citizens and deposits the documents of the public administration unit until these are recalled by the citizen. Each public administration unit remains controller of the data processed for its own purposes. Nevertheless, the portal itself may be also considered controller. Indeed, it processes (ie collects and transfers to the competent unit) the requests of the citizens as well as the public documents (ie stores them and regulates any access to them, such as the download by the citizens) for further purposes (facilitation of e-government services) than those for which the data are initially processed by each public administration unit. These controllers, among other obligations, will have to ensure that the system to transfer personal data from the user to the public administration's system is secure, since at a macro-level this transfer is an essential part of the set of processing operations carried out through the portal.

For a number of reasons I do not agree with this interpretation of the concept of controller. In the first place the interpretation is not in accordance with the legislative history of the Directive. It may be derived from the history that at the time it was contemplated that two parties could jointly decide on the purposes and means of the processing as a whole and as such be co-controllers[186] and further that

[184] WP Opinion on controller and processor (Chapter 3, n 8), at 15.

[185] WP Opinion on controller and processor (Chapter 3, n 8), at 21.

[186] See the opinion of the Commission on the amendments of the European Parliament to the draft Directive, accepting the amendment to Art 2(d) based on the possibility that in the context of one processing operation, 'a number of parties may *jointly determine the purpose and means of the processing* to be carried out'. The Commission subsequently states: 'It follows from this that, in such case, each of

different parties could be responsible for different *parts* of a data processing operation, each deciding for its part *the means and purposes of the processing* and as such being co-controllers.[187] What was not contemplated at the time was that a party could qualify as a controller based on the single fact that he would be tasked with one *aspect* of the processing (like decisions on security), without (also) determining the purpose and means of (part of) the processing itself. The history makes clear that a controller qualifies as the person who in the last instance is *responsible* for the decisions on the purposes and means, rather than the person who performs (parts of) the processing.[188]

In the example of the Working Party 29 on e-government portals, the third-party provider has no decision-making power as to the purposes of the processing of the data, who has access to the data, how long the data will be stored, etc. The public units remain (and should remain) in control. If the services had not been outsourced, the government would probably have set up its own portal for e-governmental services (as already done by numerous public units in many countries). The fact that the third-party provider probably decides on the security measures for the portal (and is probably best positioned to do so), does not change the fact that he does not have decision-making power as to the purposes and means of the processing. Though I agree with the Working Party 29 that it may be advisable to make data processors (in addition to controllers) responsible for data security, this should be achieved by making (also) the data processor directly responsible for the security of the processing in the revised Directive, rather than through a creative interpretation of the concept of controller.

the co-controllers must be constrained by the obligations imposed by the directive so as to persons about whom the data are processed'. See the Opinion of the Commission pursuant to Article 189 B (2) (d) EC Treaty, on the European Parliament's amendments to the Council's common position regarding the proposal for a European Parliament and Council Directive on the protection of individuals with regard to the processing of personal data and on the free movement of such data COM (95) 375 final, amending the Proposal of the Commission, at 3.

[187] See the leading commentary on the Data Protection by Ulrich Dammann and Spiros Simitis, *EG-Datenschutzrichtlinie* (Nomos Verlagsgesellschaft 1997), at 112–13. Simitris was one of the drafters of the Directive and is generally considered to have 'grandfathered' it. As this book is no longer generally available, here follows an unauthorized translation into English: 'The definition in the Directive is on purpose functional, so that when there are separate parts of a data processing complex, different parties determine the purposes and means of this data processing complex, and these are jointly responsible for the data processing. The Directive does not specify which controller obligation (eg information obligations, the obligation to keep data up to date, the obligation to secure the data), should be allocated to which party and this will have to be decided based on the meaning and purpose of the relevant provision of the Directive.'

[188] See the Explanatory Memorandum of the European Commission to the Amended proposal for a Council Directive on the protection of individuals with regard to the processing of personal data and on the free movement of such data, COM (92) 422 final—SYN 287, 15 October 1992, at 11: 'The controller is the person ultimately responsible for the choices governing the design and operation of the processing carried out (usually a chief executive of the company), rather than anyone who carries out processing in accordance with the controller's instructions. That is why the definition stipulates that the controller decides the objective of the processing. This is in line with Parliament's Amendment No. 17. The controller may process data himself, or have them processed by members of his staff or by an outside processor, a legally separate person acting on his behalf.' This Explanatory Memorandum is no longer available on the site of the European Commission. It can be retrieved from Archive of European Integration of the University of Pittsburg, at: <http://aei.pitt.edu/10375>.

Making the processor a controller has many consequences under the Directive that have unpredictable and undesired results. Many obligations are tied in with the qualification of a party as the controller, such as the provisions on applicable law as well as an obligation to comply with requests of individuals to access or correct their data. By making the processor a controller, the original controller no longer has decision-making power whether to comply with such request to access or correct data. This may seem a minor point, but by now there are court cases in Member States where abuse is made of access rights by individuals (by making repeated and unbridled requests or obtaining information for other purposes than to assess data protection compliance).[189]

Further, the instruction of the Working Party 29 that delegation of security measures may entail that a processor becomes a controller, this 'dependent on how important national law finds such security measures', is not workable in practice and is further contrary to EU law. Community concepts such as controller have their own autonomous meaning independent of the national laws of the Member States.[190]

Finally, situations such as the SWIFT case where processors change colour over time depending on incidental decisions of processors are unfit to base data compliance on. As indicated, issues of applicable law depend on the qualification of a party as a controller which should be a predictable concept. Again, the attempt of the Working Party 29 to impose joint obligations on data controllers and processors in joint processing situations is understandable and even commendable, but should not be achieved by an extensive interpretation of the concept of controller. Legal certainty requires that clarity is given by EU legislators on whether the distinction between controller and processors is still viable given the present network economy where joint processing operations are the rule rather than the exception and if so, whether this should lead to changes in imposing certain data protection obligations on processors (or jointly on controllers and processors) as well.

Proposed Regulation The Proposed Regulation follows the Working Party 29 by providing that if a processor processes data other than as instructed by the controller, the processor shall be considered to be a controller in respect of that processing and shall be subject to the rules on joint controllers.[191] As indicated above, I very much prefer the possibility to let parties involved in a joint-processing operation allocate the risks between them over the solution chosen by the Working Party 29 whereby processors are not subject to direct obligations but controllership

[189] See eg the case law in the Netherlands in respect of the refusal by a number of banks to (fully) comply with the mass requests by disappointed investors to access their personal data processed by these banks for use in their court cases against these banks. See on these court cases (from the perspective of the banks) W.A.K. Rank and A.J. Haasjes, 'Misbruik van de Wbp in civiele procedures tegen financiële instellingen' *Tijdschrift voor Financieel Recht* 2005–12, at 370–9 and (from the perspective of the investors) A.J.E. van den Bergen, 'De Wet bescherming persoonsgegevens in de financiële procespraktijk' *Tijdschrift voor Financieel Recht* 2005–10, at 296–306.

[190] This also according to the Working Party itself, see the WP Opinion on controller and processor (Chapter 3, n 8), at 8.

[191] Article 26(4) Proposed Regulation.

status is allocated to processors for certain aspects of the processing operation, through a creative interpretation of the concept of controller. As indicated, making the processor a controller has many consequences under EU data protection law, that have unpredictable and undesired results (see the example given above in respect of access rights of individuals). Further, the Proposed Regulation already provides that the processor may not process data except under the instruction of the controller. Processing of data against the instructions of the controller therefore already constitutes a violation of the obligations of the processor, which is punishable in its own right. The provision that a processor that processes data other than as instructed by the controller shall be considered a controller, seems therefore unnecessary (also in light of the other extensive direct obligations of processors under the Proposed Regulation), and more a manner to be able to enforce arbitrary violations of the Proposed Regulation against the processor (such as the lack of having performed a PIA in respect of a certain processing operation, while the original controller may well have done so). Again, making the processor a controller has many consequences under EU data protection law and should therefore be avoided.

Recommendation 14

Not to follow the recommendation by the Working Party 29 to include a provision in the revised Directive that processors that process data against the instructions of the controller shall be considered to be a controller.

9.7 Proposal of the Working Party 29 to Introduce Accountability for Onward Data Transfers

Another side issue, which merits discussion in this context, is the recommendation by Working Party 29 in its *Contribution to The Future of Privacy*, to include a general provision in the revised Directive 'that controllers remain accountable and responsible for the protection of data for which they are controllers, even if the data have been transferred to other controllers'.[192] This proposal is made by the Working Party 29 in the context of the section on BCR. According to the Working Party 29, the provision would fit in with introduction of the 'accountability principle' in the revised Directive (subsequently discussed by the Working Party 29 in Chapter 6). This seems mistaken. The accountability principle, as envisaged by the Working Party 29 and discussed in this chapter, entails that an independent obligation be included in the revised Directive that the controller has to have adequate measures in place to ensure compliance with the material data protection principles. This is also in line with the accountability principle as included in the

[192] WP Contribution on The Future of Privacy (Chapter 1, n 6), at para 39.

OECD Privacy Guidelines, the APEC Privacy Framework, the PIPED Act, the Madrid Draft Proposal for International Standards, and as now also reflected in the Proposed Regulation (see paragraphs 9.1 and 9.4.2). The additional provision, as proposed by the Working Party 29, that controllers remain accountable and responsible for the protection of data for which they are controller also after transfer, merely provides for external liability of the original controller for anything that happens with the data after the data have been transferred by him, this while these data are then outside his control.

The proposal by the Working Party 29 seems to be leading to an accumulation of the requirements of two different systems to regulate cross-border transfers. As an exception to the territory-based system of the EU, the EU introduced the BCR regime that reflects the organizational (ie the accountability) approach to regulate *inter-company data transfers*. As soon as the multinational with BCR transfers data outside the company group to a third party in a non-adequate country, however, the regular EU data transfer rules have to be complied with (ie the EC Model Clauses, consent of data subjects, etc). It is doubling requirements if companies with BCR have to comply both with the EU transfer rules (thus have to enter into the EU Standard Contractual Clauses with a third-party supplier) and on top of that be accountable for any data protection breach by such third party. This is not to say that I would prefer the EU data transfer rules above the accountability approach to data. This being said, accumulation of the requirements of both systems is not advisable.

In any event the provision proposed by the Working Party 29 seems more stringent than the accountability provision in respect of data transfers as included, for instance, in the APEC Privacy Framework. Principle 26 APEC Privacy Framework requires that:

> When personal information is to be transferred to another person or organization, whether domestically or internationally, the personal information controller should obtain the consent of the individual or exercise due diligence and take reasonable steps to ensure that the recipient person or organization will protect the information consistently with these Principles.

This provision therefore does not provide that the exporting organization is generally accountable for the data also after transfer. Similarly, under the Canadian PIPED Act, companies are not accountable per se for any breach after data transfer, but are accountable only for the *measures* that could be required of such company to provide a comparable level of protection taking, for instance, into account the adequacy level of the country of destiny.[193]

Finally, the provision proposed by the Working Party 29 is in such general terms ('controllers remain accountable and responsible for the protection of data for which they are controllers, even if the data have been transferred to other controllers'), that liability of the multinational may extend beyond its responsibilities under its BCR. The provision as proposed by the Working Party 29 does not refer

[193] See Chapter 2, n 54.

to the BCR regime and could therefore include any breach by the relevant third party of his respective national data protection laws (such as a breach of national notification obligations of such third party). I therefore recommend that EU legislators not follow the proposal of the Working Party 29.

Proposed Regulation The Commission, in its Proposed Regulation, does seem to follow the suggestion of the Working Party 29, where it provides that data transfers to a third country (or international organization) may only take place if the data transfer rules of the Proposed Regulation are complied with, 'including for onward transfers of personal data from the third country or an international organisation to another third country or to another international organisation'.[194] As this general principle for transfers precedes the other articles on data transfers, it would seem to apply in all cases irrespective of the legal basis for the data transfer (as provided for in the subsequent articles of the Proposed Regulation). This would entail that controllers and processors will be responsible not only to ensure that a valid ground is present when transferring data to a third party recipient, but also to regulate onward data transfers by such data recipient. It is unclear what this would require of controllers or processors if eg the relevant country has obtained an adequacy ruling, if the individual has consented to the transfer or one of the derogations apply such as that the transfer is necessary for the performance of a contract between the data subject and the controller. What additional measures would in those cases be required to ensure the protection of personal data also in case of onward transfers? As the Proposed Regulation does not provide that the Commission may adopt delegated acts to further specify this responsibility of controllers and processors 'for onward transfers by the third party recipient', no further detailed rules may be adopted by the Commission to clarify.

As with the proposal of the Working Party 29, it seems to lead to doubling requirements if companies have to ensure one of the legal grounds for transfer is available and on top of that have to regulate onward data transfers by such data recipient. Any requirements as to onward data transfers should be taken into account in the relevant legal grounds (eg be part of the EU Standard Contractual Clauses, other approved contractual clauses), rather than lead to additional requirements on top of these legal grounds. I therefore recommend deleting this provision from the Proposed Regulation.

Recommendation 15

Not to follow the recommendation by the Working Party 29 to include a provision in the revised Directive that controllers remain accountable and responsible for the protection of data for which they are controllers, even if the data have been transferred to other controllers.

[194] Article 40 Proposed Regulation, see also Recital 89 Proposed Regulation.

9.8 Conclusion as to Accountability

The conclusion is that the present requirements for BCR will not require substantive updating to be aligned with the accountability principle as envisaged by the Working Party 29, the Madrid Draft Proposal for International Standards, and the general literature on the accountability principle in other fields of law. Indeed, the conclusion seems to be justified that the BCR regime has served as a template for a model data compliance programme for all companies (also in case the relevant company does not transfer data across borders).[195] This is quite a step from the initial position by the Working Party 29 where BCR were grudgingly accepted as an alternative tool for data transfer compliance.[196] This being said, EU legislators are well advised to (i) introduce incentives for multinationals to implement BCR; (ii) introduce transparency requirements; (iii) update the BCR requirements in line with the generic accountability principles as defined by the CIPL; and (iv) list the core accountability requirements when multinationals transfer data to third parties outside their group of companies (whether a controller or a processor). An inventory of these last requirements should be made similar to the inventory made by the CIPL in respect of *internal compliance* by the multinational.

[195] See WP Opinion on the principle of accountability (Chapter 1, n 23), at 15. Obviously, the BCR requirements will have to be 'scaled' (ie depending on the size and nature of the data processing operations of a company. On scaling see the WP Opinion on the principle of accountability (-Chapter 1, n 23), at paras 43–8 and 51.

[196] WP 74 (Chapter 6, n 2), at 6.

10

BCR as a Form of Transnational Private Regulation

10.1 Rules for Rule-making

In Chapter 9, paragraph 9.1 on the principle of accountability, I mentioned that the regulatory initiatives to achieve accountability of organizations are often called 'meta-regulation', ie the regulation of internal self-regulation.[1] In paragraph 9.2, I discussed one aspect of meta-regulation, ie how regulators can provide companies with incentives and tools to use their own inherent 'regulatory capacities'. Another aspect of meta-regulation relates to the *optimal form* of meta-regulation to choose.[2] As Julia Black has put it, '[t]he "how" of regulation, or more particularly "how to do it better", is a burgeoning policy area and deserves separate consideration in its own right'.[3] The discipline of how to best regulate (the rules for rule-making, the search for meta-norms) has in the EU become known under the label 'Better Regulation' (*BR*),[4] which is the topic of this chapter. I note, however, that the two aspects of meta-regulation cannot be clearly divided into separate categories as these aspects to a certain extent overlap (ie some of the tools provided to companies to regulate have also to comply with the normative requirements for proper-self regulation).

The 'official' starting point for the rules of BR is the 2003 Inter-Institutional Agreement on Better Lawmaking, entered into between the European Parliament, the EU Council of Ministers, and the Commission.[5] This Inter-Institutional Agreement (together with other EU documents issued as part of the BR agenda)

[1] Many other terms are used in this context. One is the term 'horizontal supervision' (whereby actions are adjusted by the supervisory authority and the supervised entity in cooperation), as opposed to vertical supervision, which is the traditional *command and control* model whereby any actions of the supervised entity are corrected top down by the supervisory authority. See Ottow (Chapter 9, n 19), in particular para 2.1. On the expansion of regulation from government to governance, see Wessel and Wouters (Chapter 9, n 19), at 22–47.

[2] This paragraph draws on Bomhoff and Meuwese (Chapter 2, n 79).

[3] J. Black, *Legitimacy and the Competition for Regulatory Share*, LSE Working Paper 14/2009 (2009) at 15 and Bomhoff and Meuwese (Chapter 2, n 79), at 169 also citing Black.

[4] This term originated in the European Commission as a brand name for a strategy to improve EU law-making without making any explicit constitutional changes. See the 2003 Inter-Institutional Agreement on Better Lawmaking (Chapter 2, n 74). Recently, the Commission has made an effort to change the label into 'Smart Regulation': European Commission, Communication on 'Smart Regulation in the European Union' (COM/2010, 8 October 2010), at 543.

[5] Inter-Institutional Agreement on Better Lawmaking (Chapter 2, n 74).

(i) sets out the basic requirements for EU law-making, for instance as to requirements of consultation and transparency, and (ii) promotes co- and self-regulation when possible.[6] In accordance with requirements of BR, alternatives to legislation have to be considered. The Inter-Institutional Agreement marks the shift in European governance (with the turning point in 2001) 'ready to recognise, at times even promoting, non-state actors' activism (...), 'generating new informal alliances between European institutions (the Commission in particular) and private actors, both at European and the national level'.[7] The binding effects of the Inter-Institutional Agreement on the EU institutions are undisputed.[8] Looking at the definitions of self-regulation and co-regulation in the Inter-Institutional Agreement, the dividing line between the two seems to be that co-regulation implies legal measures while self-regulation does not.[9] The two aspects of the Inter-Institutional

[6] Inter-Institutional Agreement on Better Lawmaking (Chapter 2, n 74), in particular Article 16 and the White Paper on European Governance (Chapter 2, n 75), at 20, promoting especially co-regulation.

[7] See Fabrizio Cafaggi (Chapter 4, n 65), Chapter 10, at 203. The movement to BR was accelerated by the recommendations made by the Mandelkern Report and the following Communication by the European Commission. See Cafaggi (Chapter 4, n 65), at 211 and the Mandelkern Group on Better Regulation: Final Report (13 November 2001), available at <http://ec.europa.eu/governance/better_regulation/documents/mandelkern_report.pdf>;and 'Action Plan on Simplifying and Improving the Regulatory Environment,' COM (2002) 278 final. See further Colin Scott, *Regulatory Governance and the Challenge of Constitutionalism* EUI Working Paper RSCAS 2010/07, at 7.

[8] Cafaggi (Chapter 4, n 65), at 211, and literature therein referred to.

[9] Suzanne Nikoltchev, 'A European Perspective of Self-Regulation in the Media', in Fabrizio Cafaggi (ed.), *Reframing Self-Regulation in European Private Law*, at 277. The definitions of self-regulation and co-regulations provided for in the 2003 Inter-Institutional Agreement are generally not followed in the literature. The Inter-Institutional Agreement takes a top-down approach of the concept of self-regulation, where the assumption seems to be that 'self-regulation' is an alternative to legislation and is something that can be put in place, see Art 22: 'the possibility for economic operators, the social partners, non-governmental organisations or associations to adopt amongst themselves and for themselves common guidelines at European level (particularly codes of practice or sectoral agreements).' Many authors do not consider self-regulation as an alternative to regulation, but rather define self-regulation in substantive terms and not by reference to any legally authoritative source. See eg the definition provided by Zayènne D. Van Heesen-Laclé and Anne C.M. Meuwese, 'The legal framework for self-regulation in the Netherlands' *Utrecht Law Review*, 3(2) (December 2007), to be found at <http://ssrn.com/abstract=1083677> (citing: B. Morgan & K. Yeung, *An Introduction to Law and Regulation: Text and Materials* (Cambridge University Press 2007), at 92–3): 'We speak of self-regulation when an issue of public interest is addressed by standard-setting monitoring and/or enforcement carried out by private bodies vis-à-vis their members or affiliates who voluntarily subject themselves to this regulation. Self-regulatory arrangements may derive their authority from formal legal structures such as contract law, but they may also be primarily grounded in social consensus within a community.' A similar definition is given by Koops, Lips, Nouwt, Prins and Schellekens (Chapter 2, n 70), at 119–20. See further, Linda Senden, 'Soft Law, Self-Regulation and Co-Regulation in European Law: Where do they meet?' (January 2005) *Electronic Journal of Comparative Law* 9(1), at para 3.1, to be found at <http://www.ejcl.org>; and Fabrizio Cafaggi, preface, 'New Modes of Regulation in Europe: Critical Rethinking of the Recent European Paths', in Fabrizio Cafaggi (ed.), *Reframing Self-Regulation in European Private Law*, at xxiii. The same applies to the definition of co-regulation provided for in the Inter-Institutional Agreement. Article 18 defines co-regulation as: '[T]he mechanism whereby a Community legislative act entrusts the attainment of the objectives defined by the legislative authority to parties which are recognised in the field (such as economic operators, the social partners, non-governmental organisations, or associations).' In the literature a more informal definition of co-regulation is followed, qualifying co-regulation as any regulation that involves some form of engagement of government in stimulating, overseeing, or adopting what would otherwise be private or self-regulatory regimes. See Koops, Lips, Nouwt, Prins and Schellekens (Chapter 2, n 70), at 122 who

Agreement referred to above may be of relevance to BCR. The first element (the basic requirements as to EU law-making) may apply also to the norm-setting for BCR. The Inter-Institutional Agreement grandfathers the current European practice where private actors directly participate together with public officials in European policy-making in a formalized way. As a result 'the question has thus become: which combination of private and public actors is desirable in European policy design and implementation?'.[10] And as there is a growing number of autonomous legal orders: both public, private, and hybrid forms, the issue is not 'which system (ie public or private) will prevail, but rather how these systems can be coordinated so that they can "co-exist and co-evolve"'.[11] In this new setting there is a call for "one set of rules, common to public and private-law-making, including principles of delegation (degree and limits of delegatibility of law-making power) and more general coordination between public and private law-making".[12] This is especially relevant for BCR as BCR norm-setting is presently not undertaken by European legislators, but de facto by the Working Party 29.[13] The second element (promotion of co-regulation and self-regulation), is relevant as the Inter-Institute Agreement also provides that it does not consider co- and self-regulation to be appropriate instruments to regulate human rights.[14] Data protection qualifying as a human right, the question is whether this caveat applies to BCR.

As indicated in the introduction to this book, for BCR to be acceptable at the national and global level, they will have to 'build on the assumption of common reference points'.[15] The body of research and literature as to BR is potentially one of the sources for such common reference points or meta-norms.

10.2 Criteria for Evaluating Public Law

Before discussing potential meta-norms that can be distilled from the field of BR of transnational private regulation (*TPR*) (as opposed to BR of public law-making),[16] I note that a preliminary survey thereof shows many different opinions as to the

simply qualify as co-regulation any 'kind of regulation that is characterised by the cooperation between government and the private sector'. See extensively on co-regulation: Fabrizio Cafaggi, 'Rethinking Private Regulation', in Fabrizio Cafaggi (ed.), *Reframing Self-Regulation in European Private Law* (Kluwer Law International 2006), Chapter 1, at 27–34.

10 Cafaggi (Chapter 4, n 65), at 202.

11 Cafaggi (Chapter 4, n 65), at 204.

12 Cafaggi (Chapter 4, n 65), at 205.

13 As provided for under Art 29 Directive, among other things to promote a clear interpretation of the Directive.

14 The European Commission is also of that opinion. See White Paper on European Governance (Chapter 2, n 75), at 21; and the Inter-Institutional Agreement on Better Lawmaking (Chapter 2, n 74), at para 22.

15 Bomhoff and Meuwese (Chapter 2, n 79), at 165.

16 For an inventory of prior research see the 'Survey of Research Programmes', see Annex 2 to *The added value of private regulation in an international world? Towards a model of the legitimacy, effectiveness, enforcement and quality of private regulation*, HiiL 2007–2008, 1–21, to be found at <http://www.hiil.org>.

legitimacy and effectiveness of TPR to regulate corporate behaviour in a globalized society. Some conclude that TPR is not the answer to close the gap in the regulatory capacity of national states. Yet others suggest that, in comparison to public regulation, the new forms of TPR generate better behaviour of their actors in transnational settings, generate a higher degree of adherence, are more efficient and effective, are of higher quality, the norm-creating process is more transparent and democratic and thus more legitimate, and enforcement is less problematic.[17] Despite all these differences in opinion, there seems to be more or less consensus among all authors that *public* law-making should be evaluated based on four key criteria, which (adapted to the particulars of TPR) should also be taken as a starting point for evaluating TPR:[18]

- *Quality*. Quality of law tends to be measured in terms of traditional criteria applied to formal legislation. Qualitatively sound norms are inter alia: certain, predictable, unambiguous, while at the same time flexible, effective, and malleable. In most legal systems there is a formal quality control institutionalized through advisory bodies that also ensure alignment with existing regulatory regimes.
- *Legitimacy*. Legitimacy requirements concern the baseline demands placed on any form of decision-making. Are all those affected by a norm (ie the stakeholders) included in the process of its formulation? If so, how much weight is attached to their interests? If the process of norm creation has been fair and inclusive, dispute settlement can also systematically privilege certain interests over others, which undermines the legitimacy of the norms.
- *Effectiveness*. This concept refers to the degree to which norms succeed in regulating the conduct of a specific group of actors, whether by trust mechanisms, in realizing enforcements, or otherwise.
- *Enforcement*. Norms which cannot compel compliance or enforcement cannot be effective, legitimate, nor of sufficient quality.

It is clear that these evaluation criteria for public legislation at the national level: (i) cannot be simply transposed from the national to the international level; and (ii) cannot be simply applied one-to-one to TPR. These criteria first need to be 'transposed' (or as some label it 'privatized')[19] into criteria to apply to TPR. The

[17] Yesim Yilmaz, 'Private Regulation: a Real Alternative for Regulatory Reform,' Cato policy Analysis No 303 20 April 1998, available at <http://www.cato.org>. For a more nuanced view, whereby public regulation and TPR are complementary rather than substitutes, see Cafaggi (Chapter 2, n 70), at 16: 'The conventional view that associates legitimacy to the public sphere and effectiveness to the private sphere is deeply unsatisfactory. It is the nature of complementarily between the spheres and the relationship between legitimacy and effectiveness which varies at the transnational level.'

[18] See HiiL 2008, 'The added value of private regulation in an international world? Towards a model of the legitimacy, effectiveness, enforcement and quality of private regulation', at 5–7, to be found at <http://www.hiil.org>.

[19] See Bomhoff and Meuwese (Chapter 2, n 79), at 163. Or, as Cafaggi (Chapter 2, n 70) at 1, formulates it: '[TPR] still lacks a comprehensive and integrated set of common principles. The toolbox of regulatory instruments differs significantly form that developed in the domain of public

initial results of the HiiL Program show that despite the many difficulties in transposing these requirements to the TPR context, 'it does not seem impossible to turn public accountability of TPR into a reality'.[20] Before discussing these 'transposed' criteria, I will discuss some general guidelines or rules of thumbs as to how to 'privatize' the evaluation criteria of public law-making to TPR (see paragraph 10.4). To understand the issues in privatizing the evaluation criteria, it is essential to realize that other than with public law, the norm-setting for TPR often takes place at various levels as a result of which often more actors play a role than in public law-making. The criteria for evaluation of public law may therefore have to be divided over the various levels of norm-setting and this according to the involvement of the relevant actor in the overall norm-setting process. Further, to decide on the legitimacy of the norm-setting, it is relevant to identify who the stakeholders of the norms are (ie who are affected by the norms). As the next paragraphs are quite abstract, I will first summarize below the different levels of norm-setting for BCR, the actors involved, and the stakeholders that can be identified in the BCR norm-setting process.

10.3 Different Levels of Norm-setting for BCR

10.3.1 Actors involved in the BCR norm-setting process

The following actors are involved in the BCR norm-setting process:

- *European legislators.* European legislators enacted the Directive which sets the general framework for data protection in the EU. The Directive facilitates that Member States approve of data transfers if the controller 'adduces adequate safeguards with respect to the protection of personal data', which is the legal basis for approval of BCR.[21] The Directive does not provide for the material criteria for such adequate safeguards (ie for BCR), nor does any Commission decision. At present EU legislators are therefore not part of the norm-setting process for BCR, which is at present de facto undertaken by the Working Party 29. This may change if European legislators decide to include rules on BCR in the revised Directive (as per *Recommendation 1*). In that case also European legislators will qualify as one of the actors in the BCR norm-setting process.

international law.' Scott (n 7), at 7, addresses the issue from the other end, by labelling the phenomenon whereby private law is evaluated against public law criteria: the 'publicization of private law,' which 'involves the development of mechanisms and norms through which private actors are enrolled in the delivery of public functions'.

[20] See conclusions of Curtin and Senden (Chapter 2, n 70), at 18–19 and literature therein referred to.

[21] Article 26(2) Directive.

- *Working Party 29.* At present the general norm-setting process is undertaken by the Working Party 29 by issuing of Opinions setting out the requirements of the BCR regime.
- *Lead DPA.* The Lead DPAs are subsequently responsible for the approval procedure of individual BCR in the MRP. The DPAs therefore verify whether the BCR submitted by a multinational for approval meets the criteria set by the Working Party 29 in the WP Opinions.
- *Multinational applying BCR.* At the time the first BCR authorization applications to Lead DPAs were made, norm-setting was to a certain extent also performed by the multinational when it drafted its BCR in consultation with the Lead DPA. After the WP Opinions were issued, the norm-setting for BCR became more and more a top-down process by the Working Party 29 and the room to manoeuvre for the multinational became correspondingly smaller. At present the conclusion is that the multinational is no longer an actor in the BCR norm-setting process.

10.3.2 Stakeholders in the BCR norm-setting process

The following stakeholders can be identified in the BCR norm-setting process:

- *Multinationals.* The multinationals are the addressees of the Directive and the WP Opinions.
- *Beneficiaries.* The beneficiaries of the Directive and BCR are also stakeholders. In the case of BCR for employee data, these concern (former) employees and job applicants of the multinational. In the case of BCR for customer data, these concern the individual customers of the multinational (ie consumers) and all contact persons of its corporate customers, suppliers, and business partners.
- *Suppliers and business partners.* As supply chain management is part of the BCR regime, the third parties to which the multinational outsources data processing operations or otherwise transfers data are also stakeholders of BCR. They have an interest in how the data transfer regime in BCR norm-setting is set as this will also have an effect on their business model.

This book focuses on the present manner in which BCR norm-setting takes place. I will here concentrate on the norm-setting by the Working Party 29 and Lead DPAs rather than possible future norm-setting by European legislators. I have inserted additional text and footnotes in these chapters to reflect the changes as envisaged by the Commission in its Proposed Regulation. In any event, the public accountability of European legislators for their legislative acts in general is outside the scope of this book.

10.4 General Starting Points for 'Privatization' of Criteria for Evaluating Public Law

10.4.1 Enhanced accountability

In general many commentators[22] indicate that if norm-setting is done by 'de facto regulators', the four factors set out above in respect of public law-making should be applied in an enhanced manner (also labelled 'extended' accountability or 'aggregate' accountability).[23] The fact is that more and more non-governmental organizations are involved in the setting of norms in certain business sectors or areas of law. Some of the main features of such de facto regulators are: (i) they are governed by networks of state agencies acting not on behalf of the state but as independent actors; (ii) they lay down standards and general regulatory principles rather than strict rules; and (iii) they frequently contribute to the emergence of a system of decentralized enforcement or the regulation of self-regulation.[24] An example of a de facto regulator is the 'Basel Committee', in which the central bank directors of a limited number of countries harmonize their policies in such a way as to result in de facto regulation of the capital market.[25]

In anticipation of the evaluation of the BCR norm-setting procedure, I note that it is clear that the Working Party 29 qualifies as such a de facto regulator. The Working Party 29 (i) has been set up as the institutional body for cooperation among the DPAs;[26] (ii) has advisory status only[27] and issues Opinions to contribute to the uniform application of the Directive and advises on proposals for

[22] This paragraph draws on Wessel and Wouters (Chapter 9, n 19), para. 2.3 and Bärbel R. Dorbeck-Jung, 'Challenges to the Legitimacy of International Regulation: The Case of Pharmaceuticals Standardisation', in Andreas Follesdal, Ramses A. Wessel and Jan Wouters (eds.), *Multilevel regulation and the EU, The interplay between global, European and national normative processes* (Martinus Neijhof Publishers 2008), at para. 2.2, which gives a good summary of the literature available on this topic.

[23] Curtin and Senden (Chapter 2, n 70), at 6, in particular fn35. Cafaggi (Chapter 4, n 65), at 221. I note that the assumption that TPR is inherently less legitimate than public law may be valid for 'legitimate' states. However, the reality is that many states are not legitimate and in those cases TPR (for instance CSR codes regulating human rights) will be more legitimate than state laws violating those rights. Here I focus on the situation when state legislation does meet the four evaluation criteria for public law.

[24] See Wessel and Wouters (Chapter 9, n 19), at 28, under citation of K. Jayasuriya, 'Globalization, Law, and the Transformation of Sovereignty: the Emergence of Global Regulatory Governance' (1999) *Indiana Journal of Global Legal Studies*, vol 2, 453. Büthe and Mattli (Chapter 3, n 149), at Chapter 2, use a broader definition of de facto regulators and categorize four different types of de facto private regulators, of which the one described by Wessel and Wouters is one category only (though the first and the one with the longest history and most prominence). As the findings of Büthe and Mattli in respect of this category are of relevance for BCR, I will refrain from discussion of the other types distinguished by Büthe and Mattli.

[25] See Wessel and Wouters (Chapter 9, n 19), at 28 and 55–6. Another example provided there of a de facto regulator is the International Organisation of Securities Commissions (IOSCO), which deals with the transnationalization of securities markets and attempts to provide a regulatory framework for them.

[26] Pursuant to Art 29 Directive.

[27] See Art 29(1) Directive.

Community legislation having an impact on data protection rather than the issuing of strict rules;[28] and (iii) contributes to the emergence of self-regulation as promoted by the Directive. See on the norm-setting by the Working Party 29 in more detail paragraph 10.7.2 below.

Most commentators agree that if the norm-setting for TPR is done by a de facto regulator, the approach to the evaluation criterion legitimacy cannot merely reproduce the model of the public regulation process. Legitimacy must then be provided through a 'surrogate' legislative process that requires additional measures, such as stronger participation of the stakeholders in the regulation process, increased transparency of regulation, as well as increased accountability and control of de facto regulators.[29] Further, in the literature the question is raised whether TPR that regulate human rights should raise the bar as to legitimacy, and whether this depends also on the type of (human) right that is at stake.[30] The present findings of the HiiL Program indicate that further research is necessary in order to come to identify context-/area-/sector-specific elements which may contribute to enhancing legitimacy.[31]

A bit of a sidestep, but nevertheless highly interesting in this context, is that the requirements of 'stronger stakeholder participation' and 'increased transparency' are also indicated from the perspective of political science theory. Research reported in 2011 involved extensive empirical research into the norm-setting process by a number of global private regulators, by asking, 'Who gets to write the rules in these private bodies? What is the process of rule-writing? Who are the winners and losers in this process, and why?'.[32] The research shows that transnational norm-setting by de facto regulators is a highly political process, where stakes for multinationals are high and which results in winners and losers.[33] Particularly relevant is that the transnational rule-setting is rarely about reaching a compromise between the different regulatory models, but mostly involves making a choice for one model or approach over another.[34] Multinationals benefit from the transnational norms

[28] See Art 30 Directive and the Document 'Tasks of the Article 29 Data Protection Working Party', as published at <http://www.ec.europa.eu>. See further WP Contribution on the Future of Privacy (Chapter 1, n 6), para 7b about the functioning of the Working Party 29.

[29] Wessel and Wouters (Chapter 9, n 19), at para 2.2 and the literature cited therein; Cafaggi (n 9), at 38.

[30] Curtin and Senden (Chapter 2, n 70), at 6. Cafaggi (Chapter 2, n 70), at 15: 'The search for legitimacy for these various regulatory forms requires different answers depending on the origins and effects of the rule-making power. Regimes based on freedom of contract and association need different legitimacy responses from those based on the protection of fundamental rights or the environment.'

[31] As presently part of the HiiL Program, Chapter 1, n 21. See especially Curtin and Senden (Chapter 2, n 70), at 6.

[32] Büthe and Mattli (Chapter 3, n 149), at 214.

[33] Büthe and Mattli (Chapter 3, n 149), at 12.

[34] As Büthe and Mattli (Chapter 3, n 149), at 11 put it: 'standards do not embody some objective truth or undisputed scientific wisdom professed by experts (...) expertise is not a single correct set of beliefs about what works or what does not. A German accountant (...) who underwent eight years of studies, training, and examinations, is every bit an expert as an American Certified Public Accountant (CPA). Nevertheless, these experts are likely to vigorously disagree on how to best approach a wide range of financial reporting challenges, because any accounting tradition or school is deeply rooted in the business and legal cultures of a given country. As an official of the accounting Standards Board of

by increasing their export opportunities (previously foreclosed by cross-national differences in national rules).[35] Potential costs for multinationals are caused by having to redesign products and services to comply with transnational norms if these differentiate from their initial national norms.[36] Multinationals therefore have a strong incentive to seek to influence the process of transnational rule-making.[37] For those who succeed in pushing their domestic standards for adoption as international standards, switching cost will be minimal; for those who do not succeed, switching cost can be massive.[38] As a result, transnational rule making involves what game theorists call 'a co-ordination game with distributional conflict':[39] 'standardization implies the harmonization of different prior practices and therefore adjustment costs, at least for some. Consequently, it involves conflicts of interest over the distribution of those adjustment costs—even when the benefits of convergence on a single international standard clearly exceed the adjustment costs for each country or even each affected user.'[40] The research shows that the following factors determine which actors are likely to succeed in shaping the global norms: (i) technical expertise; (ii) financial means; (iii) timely information; and (iv) effective mechanisms of interest representation.[41] It is clear that multinationals are far more likely than employees, consumers, or civil society interest groups to have the required expertise and financial resources to participate in the transnational norm-setting. 'As a consequence representatives from industry in most cases vastly outnumber other stakeholders in international standard-setting, even when formal procedures, such as public notice-and-comment periods, create a nominally even playing field.'[42]

10.4.2 Empirical research

The only valid manner in which a full assessment may be made of BCR against the 'privatized' or 'transposed' criteria of evaluating public law is to perform empirical research. All of the evaluation criteria contain a perception element (ie are the

Japan (ASBJ) puts it: "there is no right or wrong answer.... It's like religion—Christianity or Buddhism". Global standardization is rarely about reaching a compromise among different regulatory models and approaches (a fusion between Christianity and Buddhism would be impossible to engineer) but instead about battles for pre-eminence of one approach or solution over another.'.

35 Büthe and Mattli (Chapter 3, n 149), at 6: 'The shift from domestic regulation to global private rule-making substantial gains, particularly to multinational and internationally competitive firms, for which it opens up commercial opportunities previously foreclosed by cross-national differences in standards and related measures.'

36 Büthe and Mattli (Chapter 3, n 149), at 8: 'At the same time the shift (...) also entails cost. To comply with international product standards, for example, firms may have to redesign their products, retool their production methods, or pay licensing fees to other firms whose proprietary technology may be needed to implement the international standard efficiently. These cost can be so massive, to the point where some feel forced to discontinue production of certain goods or even go out of business.'

37 Büthe and Mattli (Chapter 3, n 149), at 12.

38 See citation in n 36.

39 Büthe and Mattli (Chapter 3, n 149), at 5 (in particular fn 10) and at 42 (in particular fn 1).

40 Büthe and Mattli (Chapter 3, n 149), at 42.

41 Büthe and Mattli (Chapter 3, n 149), at 44–5.

42 Büthe and Mattli (Chapter 3, n 149), at 47–8, reffering to earlier research by the authors.

norms in BCR *perceived* as predictable and legitimate, to lead to compliance in practice, to be enforced in practice, etc). At the time this book was written, the empirical research is undertaken as part of the HiiL Program, where BCR are one of the forms of TPR which is evaluated against the transposed criteria.[43] The expectation is that based on these findings an informed assessment can be made as to (i) the extent to which the BCR norms, the creation process of BCR, the validation and implementation of BCR and the enforcement regime of BCR meet the 'transposed' criteria of Quality, Legitimacy, Effectiveness and Enforcement and (ii) the relative merits of BCR as compared with the data protection compliance of multinationals prior to implementation of their BCR. Proposals for improvement of the BCR regime will subsequently be made based on these assessments.

10.4.3 Normative criteria

This being said, there are some *normative elements* in the evaluation criteria of which it is known that these influence how norms are ultimately perceived and responded to in practice.[44] The pivotal factor for TPR in this respect is the question of legitimacy. The general assumption in the literature is that TPR provide a trade-off between a higher effectiveness and lower legitimacy (in particular the sub-component accountability).[45] To remedy possible gaps in terms of legitimacy, TPRs could introduce legitimacy-enhancing mechanisms, such as judicial control over the rule-making process. The existence of judicial review is one of the normative elements that do play a role in how legitimacy of TPR is perceived. Systems that limit or exclude judicial review of TPR decrease the chances that the relevant TPR are perceived as legitimate.[46]

10.4.4 Relative lack of legitimacy

An initial finding of the HiiL Program[47] is that 'today's global governance arena is not considered to be defined by unaccountable organisations, but rather by organisations that are either accountable to the wrong set of stakeholders or focus accountability on one set of stakeholders at the expense of others'.[48] An example of the latter is if a certain business community such as the cigarette industry (under the

[43] The final report of the HiiL Program is expected in December 2012.

[44] Linda Senden, *The OMC and its Patch in the European regulatory and constitutional landscape*, RSCAS 2010/61.

[45] See Cafaggi (Chapter 7, n 32), at 10.

[46] Aileen McHarg, 'The Constitutional Dimension of Self-Regulation,' in Fabrizio Cafaggi (ed.), *Reframing Self-Regulation in European Private Law* (Kluwer Law International 2006), at 93; Cafaggi (n 9), at xix.

[47] See Curtin and Senden's conclusions (Chapter 2, n 70), at 18–20 on which the following paragraphs draws.

[48] Curtin and Senden (Chapter 2, n 70), at 19 and Wessel and Wouters (Chapter 9, n 19), at 55–6. See also Communication from the Commission, 'Towards a reinforced culture of consultation and dialogue—General principles and minimum standards for consultation of interested parties,' 11 December 2002, COM(2002) 704 final, at 5: 'The Commission has underlined, in particular, *its intention to "reduce the risk of the policy-makers just listening to one side of the argument or of particular*

threat of public regulation) sets up a self-regulatory agency that issues a self-regulatory advertising code. The self-regulatory agency holds a consultation on the code and invites the government and all companies belonging to such business community (as addressees of the self-regulatory code), to submit comments, but overlooks to also consult other stakeholders of the code, such as consumer organizations, the anti-smoking associations, child advocacy groups, etc.

Below I first discuss whether, and if so which form of, TPR is suitable to regulate human rights (paragraph 10.5). I then elaborate on the concept of legitimacy from a normative perspective (paragraph 10.6) and finally evaluate the current BCR norm-setting regime against these normative criteria (paragraph 10.7).

10.5 TPR Regulating Human Rights

10.5.1 Introduction

Many consider TPR not to be suitable for regulating human rights. For instance the Commission in its White Paper on European Governance provided that co-regulation is 'only suited to cases where fundamental rights (...) are not called into question'.[49] Also the Inter-Institutional Agreement on Better Lawmaking which promotes co- and self-regulation when possible,[50] provides that 'these mechanisms are not available if fundamental rights or important political options are at stake'.[51] In the literature it is remarked that as to data protection 'this exception is questionable as the Directive itself explicitly asserts that codes of conduct must be promoted and it is quite clear that self-regulatory mechanisms including technological solutions will ensure the needed data protection more efficiently than certain legislative texts'.[52] Other authors just assume that the self-regulation promoted by the Directive fits in with the Inter-Institute Agreement on Better Lawmaking and promote the co-regulatory approach for inter alia BCR as the right approach in accordance with the Inter-Institute Agreement on Better Lawmaking. These authors give no consideration to the fact that data protection qualifies as a human right for which according to the Agreement on Better Lawmaking self- and co-regulation should not be available.[53] I fully agree with the conclusion (or the position) that as to data protection, self- and co-regulation as

groups getting privileged access [...]."' (citation from the White paper on European Governance (Chapter 2, n 75), at 17).

[49] See the White Paper on European Governance (Chapter 2, n 75), at 21.

[50] Inter-Institutional Agreement on Better Lawmaking (Chapter 2, n 74), in particular Art 16.

[51] White Paper on European Governance (Chapter 2, n 75) at 21. See Inter-Institutional Agreement on Better Lawmaking, Chapter 2, n 74), Art 17. The Dutch government is also of this opinion, see Koops, Lips, Nouwt, Prins, and Schellekens (Chapter 2, n 70), at 117, referring to Kamerstukken II, 1997–98, 25 880, at 180–1.

[52] Poullet (Chapter 4, n 65), at 253.

[53] See eg the Rand Report (Chapter 2, n 27), at 8 and 48. See further: Nikoltchev (n 9), Chapter 11, at 279, where the requirements for co-regulation are listed, including the negative requirement that co-regulation is not suitable if 'it involves human rights'. Further down, at 276 and at 282–3, various forms of self- and co-regulation of data protection in the online environment are

promoted and facilitated by the Directive[54] should be possible. This is however not because the Directive itself provides so, in the sense that the Directive would thereby overrule the exception formulated in the Inter-Institutional Agreement on Better Lawmaking. The reason is more fundamental, in the sense that the form of self-regulation promoted by the Directive is adequately embedded within public legislation as a result of which there are no valid arguments why this form of 'framework' legislation should not be appropriate. To the contrary, (as amplified hereafter) this form of framework regulation is considered in literature to be the appropriate form of TPR to choose if human rights are involved.

10.5.2 Rationale

The White Paper on Corporate Governance and the Inter-Institutional Agreement on Better Lawmaking do not clarify why they consider the caveat for human rights to be necessary. The first question is whether this caveat is still valid. The Inter-Institutional Agreement dates from 2003, at which time the rules of BR were starting to be developed. In January 2009, the Commission updated its 'Impact Assessment Guidelines',[55] that provide instructions for Commission staff when preparing Commission policy proposals. Part of the impact assessment that has to be performed is that the policy options have to be identified (non-EU policy action, regulation, directive, recommendation, communication, self-regulation, or co-regulation, or any combination of the foregoing).[56] Though the Impact Assessment Guidelines in the paragraphs where it discusses the various policy options contain many references to the 2003 Inter-Institutional Agreement,[57] the caveat that co- and self-regulation are not fit to regulate human rights is nowhere repeated. Instead of respecting all policy options (including if these include self-regulation and co-regulation), staff are expected to make an assessment of the social impact of the policy options (which includes making an assessment of the impact on human rights).[58] I take this as an indication that by now the thinking about BR of the EU institutions (or in any event the Commission) has been evaluated and that it is questionable whether the caveat (in its absolute form) is still valid.

The second question is whether the caveat (if still valid) is justified. One may infer that at the time the Inter-Institutional Agreement was entered into, the caveat reflected an implicit belief 'that fundamental rights should be only abridged through legislative acts of democratically elected bodies which are politically

discussed without also discussing whether data protection being a human right is suitable for self- and co-regulation at all.

[54] See Art 27 Directive and Chapter 3, para 3.1.9.

[55] European Commission Impact Assessment Guidelines of 15 January 2005, SEC(2009) 92, replacing the Commission Guidelines adopted in June 2005 and updated in March 2006, to be found at <http://ec.europa.eu/governance/impact/commission_guidelines/docs/iag_2009_en.pdf>.

[56] Impact Assessment Guidelines (n 55), at para 7 and Annex 7.

[57] Impact Assessment Guidelines (n 55), at Annex 7 at para 7.1 at 24. The Annex extensively discusses the different policy options and guidelines when which option is to be considered. These guidelines do not contain any reference to the caveat.

[58] Impact Assessment Guidelines (n 55), at para. 8 at 31 and Annex 8.1.

accountable and subject to constitutional review'.[59] The underlying assumption here seems to be that the fundamental rights expressed in the Constitution, being the expression of the state, only confer rights against the state (ie against public authority). In this view human rights do not have a horizontal effect, ie do not confer obligations on private parties.[60] The consequence would be that if private parties issue self-regulation these could tread on human rights without these human rights being enforceable against such private parties. In such cases the state has to intervene.[61] Hence, the requirement that any abridging of human rights should be through a legislative act, where a proper balancing of rights can be ensured.

The question is whether this is still a valid view. This view of human rights finds its basis in the origin of human rights, which were traditionally[62] crafted to protect individuals from abuse of power by the state, which at the time were the biggest aggregations of power in society.[63] Companies are in that tradition treated on the notion that they are private, not public, entities, ie are more like individuals than states. Accordingly, they are traditionally treated as *rights holders* of human rights, rather than duty holders.[64] The fact is, however, that many multinationals now

[59] See Fabrizio Cafaggi (n 9), at xviii, who assumes that this is the underlying rationale for the caveat. The view that fundamental rights should be only abridged through legislative acts of democratically elected bodies which are politically accountable and subject to constitutional review, is part of a broader constitutional discourse, which represents the idea that 'public power is or should be limited and subject to some higher form of control by reference to law. See Scott (n 7), at 1. The 'constitutionalists' critique has been voiced against any form of delegation of governmental power to regulatory agencies, as '[s]uch delegations may be quite extensive and arguably undermine the effectiveness of the limitations placed on legislative and executive power' (Scott (n 7), at 1). Scott, at 15, rejects this idea as 'orthodox constitutionalism, while it might once have been the most appropriate way to think about legitimating a governance centred on the nation state, is not capable of legitimating the diffuse governance patterns associated with contemporary regulation. An alternative narrative offered here seeks to match the variety of governance forms with varied forms of institutionalization which link processes and values of hierarchy, competition and community to appropriate governance forms.'

[60] On the horizontal effect of human rights, see Chapter 6, n 95 and Cafaggi (Chapter 2, n 70), at 28.

[61] Ziller (Chapter 6, n 95), at 154.

[62] Human rights arose out of the Enlightenment, see Amy Sinden, 'Addressing Corporate Environmental Wrongs', in McBarnet, Voiculescu, Campbell, *The New Corporate Accountability, Corporate Social Responsibility and the Law* (Cambridge University Press 2007), at 504 and 506.

[63] Sinden (n 62), at 505.

[64] The U.S. Supreme Court has held that corporations are 'persons' entitled to assert certain constitutional rights. For an overview of evolution of the doctrine of legal personhood and constitutional rights of corporations in the US see eg Elizabeth Pollman (31 December 2010), available at SSRN: <http://ssrn.com/abstract=1732910>. At 16, Pollman explains that the origins of the doctrine of legal personhood of corporations are found in *Santa Clara Co v Southern Pacific Railroad*, 118 U.S. 394 (1886). See, however, a recent decision of the US Supreme Court in *Federal Communications Commission v AT&T Inc.*, 562 U.S. (2011), that corporations do not enjoy the 'personal privacy' exemption under the Freedom of Information Act. It is noteworthy that in the context of the U.S. legal system one cannot make general statements on whether or not corporations do or do not enjoy a certain right regardless of a particular context. For instance, the right to privacy stems from the system of privacy law that does not have a single, hierarchical order of rules. Instead it consists of common law torts, constitutional, and statutory law, with various subjects of regulation and applicability. The complexity is further increased given that the U.S. is a federation where regulatory competence is divided between the federation and the states. See Paul M. Schwartz and Joel R. Reidenberg, *Data Privacy Law: A Study of United States Data Protection* (MICHIE Law Publishers 1996), at 102, as cited

wield as much or even more power than many states, and the conditions of individuals' lives are shaped as much by multinationals as by states, especially in the area of workers' rights (eg equal pay, working hours, etc).[65] Hence there now seems to be a broad consensus in the literature that as to certain human rights multinationals[66] should be (in addition to states) also *duty holders*.[67] In this view

in Purtova (Chapter 8, n 35), at 90. As a result, the decision not to grant a statutory privacy right to a corporate entity in *Federal Communications Commission v AT&T Inc*, is made for the purposes of application of the Freedom of Information Act and has no bearing for the scope of any constitutional privacy rights. The Court affirms that the Constitution's Fourth Amendment does protect a corporation against search and seizure, a recognized privacy interest (at 8). Simultaneously, the Restatement (Second) of Torts §6521, Comment c (1976) reads that a corporation has no privacy claim under the law of torts (cited in *Federal Communications Commission v AT&T Inc*, at 8).

In the EU, corporations possess (to a certain extent) rights to free speech and privacy. Article 1 of the First Protocol to the ECHR makes clear that both natural and legal persons have the right to the peaceful enjoyment of their possessions. Under the ECHR, corporations have been held to possess rights to free speech under Art 10 (for case law, see Karen Reid, *A Practitioner's Guide to the European Convention on Human Rights*, (Sweet & Maxwell 2007), at 344). Corporations further have a right to privacy under Art 8. In *Niemietz v Germany*, 72/1991/324/396, 16 December 1992, the European Court of Human Rights (*ECHR*) ruled that the words 'private life' and 'home' as mentioned in Art 8 ECHR, extend to professional or business activities or premises. See eg *Niemietz v Germany*, at 31: 'More generally, to interpret the words "private life" and "home" as including certain professional or business activities or premises would be consonant with the essential object and purpose of Article 8.' The ECJ, notably in competition cases, has followed the ECHR case law and also recognized that business activities (to a certain extent) fall within the protection of the 'home' as provided for by Art 8. See eg Case C-94/00 *Roquette Frères SA v Directeur général de la concurrence, de la consommation et de la répression des fraudes* (Commission of the European Communities, third party): 2002 E.C.R. I-9039: 'For the purposes of determining the scope of that principle in relation to the protection of business premises, regard must be had to the case-law of the European Court of Human Rights (...). According to that case-law, (...) first, the protection of the home provided for in Article 8 of the ECHR may in certain circumstances be extended to cover such premises (see, in particular, the judgment of 16 April 2002 in *Colas Est and Others v. France*, not yet published in the Reports of Judgments and Decisions, § 41)(...) and, second, the right of interference established by Article 8(2) of the ECHR "might well be more far-reaching where professional or business activities or premises were involved than would otherwise be the case" (*Niemietz v. Germany*, cited above, § 31).' See also Case C-238/99 *Limburgse Vinyl Maatschappij (LVM) v Commission and Others*, at para 245 et seq, etc) and Sinden (n 62), at 514.

[65] See John Ruggie, *Protect, Respect and Remedy: a Framework for Business and Human Rights*, 7 April 2008, A/HRC/8/5, to be found at <http://www.ohchr.org> (the 'Ruggie Report'), Addendum 2, which reports the results of research on the actual impact of multinationals on the various fundamental rights.

[66] Some human rights have clearly no relevance for multinationals. For instance, a multinational will not act as prosecutor and the criminal procedure rights of individuals are therefore of no relevance vis-à-vis multinationals. Other rights will require some creative adaption to apply in the context of multinationals. See for examples Chapter 11, para 11.2.1 below and in particular Chapter 11, n 17 below.

[67] See McBarnet (Chapter 4, n 24), at 56; McBarnet and Schmidt (Chapter 7, n 12), at 148–76; Andrew Clapham, *Human Rights Obligations of Non-State Actors* (Oxford University Press 2006), at Chapter 6; and Damian Chalmers, 'The Government and Citizenship of Self-Regulation', in F. Cafaggi (ed.), *Reframing Self-Regulation in European Private Law* (Kluwer Law International 2006), Chapter 6, at 187–8. Willem van Genugten, 'Handhaving van Wereldrecht, een kritische inspectie van valkuilen en dilemma's' [2010] *Nederlands Juristenblad-1*, at 12, more generally observes that the international legal order is transforming from being directed at the protection of state interests into the interests of the people (which he labels the 'humanitization' of the international legal order). He notes that this is visible in the effect of human rights on the key concepts of international law. In more detail, see Willem van Genugten, Kees Homan, Nico Schrijver, and Paul de Waart, *The United Nations of the Future; Globalization with a Human Face* (KIT Publishers 2006). See also Cafaggi

human rights do have 'horizontal effect'. The assumption that human rights have no horizontal effect is not only challenged in the literature, it is also challenged in positive law. Many national and international courts have applied human rights in private disputes.[68] In some countries the fundamental rights in the Constitution also equally apply to private and public relationships.[69] This being said, the caveat in the Inter-Institutional Agreement may remain relevant in case in a certain country human rights are not considered to have horizontal effect.[70]

The question is whether the above does necessarily mean that the EU institutions are right in their caveat that self- and co-regulation are not fit to regulate human rights. While the concerns of the Commission and EU institutions are understandable, a wholesale rejection of the possibility of using self- and co-regulation is contrary to current traditions and further without theoretical foundation.[71] There are many instances where fundamental rights are traditionally regulated by self-regulation.[72] Notable examples are the field of freedom of the press and the church,

(Chapter 2, n 70), at 28: 'The limited direct applicability of soft law to private parties derives from the more general principle of public international law which, conventionally, imposes primary responsibility on States. This view has been criticized and increasingly international law obligations are also applied directly to private parties.'

[68] Like in the U.S. and France, see Ziller (Chapter 6, n 95), at 155. See for other examples: Cafaggi (Chapter 2, n 70), at 28 especially fn 156, which includes Case 36/74, *Walrave v Association Union Cycliste Internationale*, 1974 ECR 1405, where the ECJ held that anti-discriminatory provisions of the Treaty of Rome also apply to private entities (employment discrimination).

[69] Like the Irish Constitution of 1937, see Ziller (Chapter 6, n 95), at 155. The issues discussed here relate to national constitutional law. There is also the question of whether human rights in the framework of the ECHR have horizontal effect. Here the fundamental rights are part of a treaty between sovereign states, and this justifies the question whether, and if so, to which extent, these are intended to confer obligations upon private parties against other private parties. In literature such *direct* horizontal effect of the ECHR provisions is generally rejected. See Harris, O'Boyle, and Warbrick, *Law of the European Convention on Human Rights* (2nd edn Oxford University Press 2009), at 20 in particular fn 177. However, in literature there is also general agreement that 'the human rights laid down in the Convention do (. . .) exercise (. . .) influence on the relationships between private parties'. See Arthur S. Hartkamp, 'Fundamental Rights, Fundamental Freedoms, and Contract Law', in Stefan Grundmann (ed.), *Constitutional values and European contract law* (Wolters Kluwer 2008), at 98; and Purtova (Chapter 8, n 35), at 224 as to horizontal effect of Art8 ECHR. Hartkamp, at 98, refers to the ECHR as having *indirect* horizontal effect. Other authors are hesitant to use horizontal effect terminology with regard to the 'obligations of the kind that exist under the Convention', see *Harris, O'Boyle &* Warbrick, fn 175 at 20. Leaving terminological disagreements aside, established case law under the ECHR recognizes that, if an article of the ECHR is found to impose positive state obligations, 'these obligations may involve the adoption of measures designed to secure respect for private life *even in the sphere of the relations of individuals between themselves*'. See eg ECHR 26 March 1985, *X and Y v The Netherlands*, Application no 8978/80, at para 23. This doctrine was upheld in further case law. See eg ECHR 17 July 2008, *I v Finland*, Application no 20511/03, and more recently, *Von Hannover v Germany* [2004] ECHR 294 (Application no 59320/00).

[70] Cafaggi (n 9), at xviii and Ziller (Chapter 6, n 95), at 153. The current trend in the EU is that horizontal effect of fundamental rights is rapidly emerging in doctrine. See B.J. De Vos, *Horizontale werking van grondrechten. Een kritiek* (Maklu Uitgevers, 2010), for a discussion of the doctrine under the main jurisdictions in Western Europe and case law thereon and (as the title promises) clear criticism as to the diffuseness of the concept and the (lack of sufficient) foundation of the concept itself. For the English summary see at 293 et seq.

[71] See Cafaggi (n 9), at xviii.

[72] McHarg (n 46), at 82 even observes that 'all constitutional systems are self-regulating to some degree: all rely to some extent on self-enforcing conventions and all face problems of balancing accountability and independence'.

where self-regulation is often constitutionally preferred to forms of public regulation and, to some extent, public regulation is even prohibited.[73] Based on the broad history of self-regulation in the area of human rights, one author concludes:

> it is, perhaps unsurprisingly, much easier to find constitutional supports for self-regulation than constitutional prohibitions. (...) thus as the attempts to find constitutional limits to privatisation has demonstrated, it is extremely difficult to identify a set of 'core' public functions which are irreducibly the state's responsibility. (...) This is not to say that some things are not more effectively done through public rather than private means. But the conclusion is inescapable that the lines drawn between public and private action are the result of political choices, conditioned by history, circumstance and tradition.[74]

Based on the foregoing it is difficult to maintain a blanket condemnation of the use of self- or co-regulation as a policy instrument for regulating human rights.[75] The key issue is more how concerns regarding human rights should influence the regulatory design for self-regulation and co-regulation, for instance by ensuring that the relevant rights and especially the outcome of any balancing of those rights against any other fundamental rights, are safeguarded by public framework legislation.[76] Indeed, this form of general framework legislation for TPR is in the literature considered to be the appropriate form to apply if fundamental rights are at stake.[77] As another author summarizes it:[78]

[73] Cafaggi (n 9), at xviii; Cafaggi (Chapter 4, n 64), at 213; and McHarg (n 46), at 80. McHarg lists examples and arguments why in certain cases self-regulation is not only permitted but actually required, in the sense that state regulation is prohibited in certain areas. Examples mentioned are self-regulation of the press and the church, both of which should operate separately and independently from government.

[74] McHarg (n 46), at 81, referring to T. Daintith and M. Sah, 'Privatisation and the Economic neutrality of the Constitution' [1993] *Public Law* 465 and D. Feldman and F. Campbell, 'Constitutional Limitations on Privatisation', in J.W. Bridge (ed.), *Comparative Law facing the 21st century* (UKNCCL, 2001).

[75] McHarg (n 46), at 93.

[76] McHarg (n 46), at 93, Cafaggi (Chapter 4, n 64), at xix. Scott (n 7), comes to a similar conclusion when discussing private law making from the perspective of 'constitutionalism.' See Scott at 1: 'Constitutionalism is a term which seeks to capture the idea that public power is or should be limited and subject to some higher form of control by reference to law.' The 'constitutionalists' critique has been voiced against delegation of governmental power to regulatory agencies, as '[s]uch delegations may be quite extensive and arguably undermine the effectiveness of the limitations placed on legislative and executive power'. Scott, at 1–2, notes that '[o]ne response to the diffusion of regulatory power is to seek the application of traditional modes of control and accountability, seeking their extension beyond state actors to those who were found to wield power'. Scott, at 2 (and at 15), however, suggests adopting a more comprehensive solution and to 'recognise diffusion not only in actors but also in modes of regulatory governance (...) by seeking to institutionalise broader modes of control and accountability which are best to match the governance powers which are targeted'.

[77] See Koops, Lips, Nouwt, Prins, and Schellekens (Chapter 2, n 70), at 143 and Cafaggi (Chapter 4, n 65), at 204: 'Common rules, often of constitutional relevance, should ensure that the private-law-making power is not exercised at the expense of other private groups.'

[78] Cafaggi (n 9), at xviii. See also Cafaggi (Chapter 4, n 65), at 214–15: 'Freedom of speech may also conflict with rights to privacy and data protection. Balancing different constitutional principles granting law-making-power to different private actors may translate into limitations and constraints for the exercise of PLM [Private Law Making]. These constraints can be considered organising principles of normative pluralism.'

> In the context of the discussion regarding fundamental rights, the key issue with co-regulation arises from the spectre of *conflicting* fundamental rights within the regulatory process, and the legitimacy of co-regulatory bodies and striking an appropriate balance between these rights. (...) For example, in the context of media regulation or press regulation there is a well-recognised conflict between the freedom of speech and the right to privacy. A biased selection favouring journalists or media firms over private organisations which represent the right to privacy may translate into an unacceptable balancing of those conflicting rights which may be constitutionally illegitimate. An initial response to this objection is to point out that the legislative act which defines the co-regulatory model is capable of identifying principles that ensure the right balance between competing rights and binds the private bodies to adhere to those enumerated principles.

Using framework legislation (and consultation of all relevant stakeholders) is not the sole device which can be used to encourage protection of fundamental rights in self- or co-regulation. Other elements can be used to enhance protection of fundamental rights, like judicial review.[79]

10.5.3 TPR of data protection

How does all the above apply to data protection? Different from most other human rights, data protection rights have from the outset also been directed at companies. Although the Directive applied from the outset also to data processing by the governments of the Member States, important areas of data processing by governments were initially excluded from the scope of the Directive (like processing for public safety, defence, state security, and for criminal law purposes).[80] These exceptions to the scope of the Directive have recently been 'remedied' by TFEU, that made Article 16 TFEU regulating data protection of general application (ie also applicable to all areas of data processing by governments).[81] The Directive (when implemented into national legislation) does therefore already impose direct data protection duties on multinationals (which thus have by definition horizontal effect).[82] To the extent that the Directive promotes self-regulation,[83] this is always

[79] See n 46 and Cafaggi (n 9), at 38, listing as mitigation measures for interest representation: '(a) by applying to private regulators' activities the participatory rules generally deployed by public regulators; (b) by designing a governance structure able to represent sufficiently diversified interests; and/or finally (c) by guaranteeing a system of liability able to protect those interests whose voice finds no representation within the organisation or which do not translate into participatory rights.'

[80] See Art 16 TFEU. See for details Chapter 3, n 3.

[81] The Proposed Regulation still has more or less the same scope as the Directive. Data processing by governments for purposes of public safety, defence, state security, and for criminal law purposes are governed by a separate proposal for a new directive issued by the European Commission at the same date as the Proposed Regulation; see Chapter 3, n 7.

[82] Under the Proposed Regulation, implementation in national legislation will no longer be necessary as a regulation has direct applicability in the Member States.

[83] Article 27 Directive reads as follows:

> 1. The Member States and the Commission shall encourage the drawing up of codes of conduct intended to contribute to the proper implementation of the national provisions adopted by the Member States pursuant to this Directive, taking account of the specific features of the various sectors.

under the umbrella of the Directive. This form of self-regulation is also labelled 'stipulated self-regulation', which is self-regulation accomplished within an existing general legal framework.[84] The general legal framework provides for minimum standards and conditions and is established by means of legislation and the framework promotes that further (technical) detailing is left to the relevant sector through a code of conduct.[85] Under the Directive, the organization that drafted an EU self-regulatory code can request the Working Party 29 to declare that the rules contained in its code properly implement the provisions of the Directive.[86] These 'conformity declarations' by the Working Party 29 are not binding. National courts having to decide on data protection violations will (have to) decide whether a certain data processing is legitimate based on applicable data protection law rather than based on the relevant self-regulatory code.[87] Conformity declarations can also be requested at the national level from the DPAs. Whether such decisions by the DPAs are binding or non-binding will depend on applicable national law. If the decision of the DPA is non-binding, the courts of the DPA will have to decide based on their national data protection law rather than based on the rules of the

2. Member States shall make provision for trade associations and other bodies representing other categories of controllers which have drawn up draft national codes or which have the intention of amending or extending existing national codes to be able to submit them to the opinion of the national authority.

   Member States shall make provision for this authority to ascertain, among other things, whether the drafts submitted to it are in accordance with the national provisions adopted pursuant to this Directive. If it sees fit, the authority shall seek the views of data subjects or their representatives.
3. Draft Community codes, and amendments or extensions to existing Community codes, may be submitted to the Working Party referred to in Article 29. This Working Party shall determine, among other things, whether the drafts submitted to it are in accordance with the national provisions adopted pursuant to this Directive. If it sees fit, the authority shall seek the views of data subjects or their representatives. The Commission may ensure appropriate publicity for the codes which have been approved by the Working Party.

[84] Koops, Lips, Nouwt, Prins, and Schellekens (Chapter 2, n 70), at 121.

[85] Koops, Lips, Nouwt, Prins, and Schellekens (Chapter 2, n 70), at 121 and 142; Poullet (Chapter 4, n 65), at 254.

[86] See Art 27(3) Directive.

[87] Although Art 27(3) Directive prescribes that 'Draft Community codes (...) may be submitted to the Working Party [and] this Working Party shall determine, among other things, whether the drafts submitted to it are in accordance with the national provisions adopted pursuant to this Directive', the Opinions that the Working Party may adopt on these matters do not go beyond the competences given to the Working Party pursuant to Art 30 of the Directive, and as such do not have binding effect. The publication by the Commission of the relevant opinion does not change this (see for publication by the Commission the last sentence of Art 27(3): 'The Commission may ensure appropriate publicity for the codes which have been approved by the Working Party.'). Kuner (Chapter 2, n 8), at 48 points out that also the practice of the Working Party when approving codes of conduct shows that the Working Party itself is of the opinion that its approvals are not meant to have a binding effect: 'The "uncertain legal status" of the codes approved by the Working Party is evident in the fact that while the Working Party has competence to determine whether "drafts submitted (...) are in accordance with the national provisions adopted pursuant to this Directive," (...) the Working Party has so far refused to approve or endorse any instrument that does not contain extensive disclaimers making it clear that application of the instrument is without prejudice to the provisions of national data protection law. This means that, notwithstanding approval of the Community code by the Working Party, its use is still subject to all the details of data protection law in the different Member States where it is used.' The consequence of the non-binding nature of Working Party Opinions is that they are not subject to review by the ECJ. The ECJ only reviews acts of the EU institutions and agencies 'which are intended to have legal effects', see Case 22/70 *Commission v Council* [1971] ECR 263, at para 42.

relevant self-regulatory code. If the decision of the DPA is binding, data protection violations will have to be decided based on the relevant code. However, in such case the conformity decision by the DPA will be subject to review by the courts.[88]

Based on the foregoing the conclusion is that self-regulation of data protection is regulated by the national laws of the Member States (ie is regulated by government legislation) and only when a self-regulatory code has obtained a conformity declaration by a DPA which is binding, is data protection regulated by the relevant self-regulatory code. However in that case, the decision of the DPA to issue the conformity declaration is subject to judicial review. By this procedure, it is ensured that self-regulation of data protection remains within the framework requirements of the Directive which is the appropriate form considered in literature to apply if fundamental rights are at stake.[89]

Proposed Regulation Under the Proposed Regulation self-regulatory codes are equally encouraged.[90] As to national codes of conduct the arrangement remains the same, with the difference that consultation of data subjects by the DPAs will be mandatory.[91] A notable difference is that Union codes of conduct may be submitted to the Commission.[92] The Commission can adopt an implementing act deciding that such European code has general validity.[93] The Commission has to consult stakeholders during the preparatory work.[94] The Commission further has to follow the examination procedure.[95] After adoption, the implementing act is

[88] As required by Art 28(3) Directive. For instance, Art 25(4) Dutch Data Protection Act provides that conformity declarations are 'equivalent to a decision (*besluit*) within the meaning of the Dutch General Administrative Regulations Act (*Algemene wet bestuursrecht*) and are therewith subject to administrative and judicial review. Article 25(4) further provides that the consultation procedure under the General Administrative Regulations Act applies to such decisions. This entails that the DPA has to make the request for a conformity declaration and the draft self-regulatory code available for consultation to the public for a period of four weeks, during which time interested parties may submit their comments. The possibility for consultation must be publicly announced. See the publication of the Dutch DPA *Gedragscodes, bescherming van persoonsgegevens door zelf-regulering*, at 15, available at <http://www.cbp.web.nl>.

[89] See Koops, Lips, Nouwt, Prins, and Schellekens (Chapter 2, n 70), at 143. For the sake of completeness, I note that some Member States 'within implementation have delegated rule-making power to private bodies'. See Cafaggi (Chapter 4, n 65), at 209. I will not further discuss the legitimacy of this form of delegation by Member States here.

[90] See on self-regulatory codes under the Proposed Regulation in detail Chapter 3, para 3.1.9.

[91] Article 38(2) Proposed Regulation.

[92] Article 38(3) Proposed Regulation.

[93] Article 38(4) Proposed Regulation.

[94] See Recital 129 Proposed Regulation which states in respect of delegated acts: 'It is of particular importance that the Commission carry out appropriate consultations during its preparatory work, including at expert level.' See further Communication from the Commission to the EP and the council—COM (2009) 673 final, at para 4.2. (Preparatory work for the adoption of delegated acts): 'In addition, and where necessary, the Commission will conduct any research, analysis, hearings and consultations required, in the form best suited to the fields in question and the time limits that have been laid down.'

[95] Article 38(4) Proposed Regulation. See for the examination procedure Art 87(2) Proposed Regulation and Art 5 of Regulation (EU) 182/2011 of the European Parliament and of the Council of 16 February 2011 laying down the rules and general principles concerning mechanisms for control by Member States of the Commission's exercise of implementing powers. The examination procedure should ensure that implementing acts cannot be adopted by the Commission if they are not in accordance with the opinion of a committee composed of representatives of the Member States and chaired by the Commission.

binding and data protection violations will have to be decided based on the Union code. The Commission act is subject to the general rules of review by the ECJ.[96] Also by these procedures, it is ensured that the relevant Union code will remain within the framework requirements of the Proposed Regulation.

10.5.4 BCR

The next question is whether the Directive also provides a 'sufficient general legal framework' for BCR. This question is justified as BCR are a different form of self-regulation than the self-regulatory codes promoted by the Directive. BCR are not submitted by multinationals for review to the Lead DPAs as to whether they comply with the *level of protection provided for by the Directive*, but are submitted for review to the DPAs whether they provide for an *adequate* level of protection as required for the transfer of data to non-adequate countries pursuant to Article 26(2) Directive. An adequate level is not necessarily the same level of protection as provided for by the Directive, which is generally assumed to be of a higher level. In Chapter 6, paragraph 6.6, I noted that the Directive does not (yet) explicitly recognize that BCR are an appropriate tool to provide adequate safeguards for the transfer of data and in any event does not define the main substantive requirements for the required adequate level to be provided by BCR. The Working Party 29 in the WP Opinions has recognized BCR as a valid tool for data transfers and defined these criteria, but these WP Opinions are not binding (ie do not qualify as government regulation). As a consequence, at present no proper formal legal framework exists for DPAs to review and authorize individual BCR, or for the national courts (and ultimately the ECJ) to be able to review BCR authorization decisions of the DPAs.[97] To ensure that BCR also have a formal legal basis as required for TPR regulating human rights, I therefore recommend that the revised Directive also provide a proper legal framework to recognize BCR as an appropriate tool to provide adequate safeguards for the transfer of data and to define the main substantive requirements for BCR to be set an adequate level. This is in line with the recommendation of the Working Party 29 itself, which recommendation the Commission intends to follow,[98] and is further incorporated in the Proposed Regulation (see Chapter 6, paragraph 6.6.1). This is further in line with *Recommendation 2* (made in Chapter 6, paragraph 6.6.6), and will therefore not lead to a separate recommendation here.

As a note of interest, I add that in Chapter 2, paragraph 2.1, I indicated that the introduction of corporate privacy policies by multinational companies has created a bottom-up pressure on national legal orders, which we saw reflected in the pressure on the DPAs to recognize these corporate privacy policies as a data transfer instrument. In respect of the regulation of self-regulation, in the literature a distinction is made between 'a bottom-up approach' and a 'top-down' approach. Though at the start the discussions about acceptance of BCR with the

[96] Article 263 TFEU.
[97] As required by Art 28(3) Directive.
[98] See Chapter 6, n 60.

various individual DPAs were bottom-up, the approach subsequently taken by the WP Opinions as to BCR (which in all probability will also be adopted in the revised Directive) is, however, very much the top-down approach. This is in conformity with the European approach to co-regulation which is also fundamentally top-down.[99]

10.6 The Concept of Legitimacy: The Normative Perspective

10.6.1 General introduction

In regulation theory 'legitimacy'[100] constitutes 'the acceptance that a person or organisation has a right to govern given by those it seeks to govern and those on whose behalf it purports to govern'.[101] For a regulatory norm to be legitimate, it must be accepted by those to whom it is addressed.[102] Rule-makers may claim legitimacy and may even engage in various strategies to enhance legitimacy. The extent to which they succeed, however, depends on the extent to which the rules are accepted by others. In that sense legitimacy is de facto more an objective empirical phenomenon rather than a normative abstraction.[103] There is no single answer to the question which regulatory norms ultimately become legitimate ('crystallize') and which do not. Factors which are known to play a role in the crystallization process are:

- *Distribution of the norm.* This concerns the extent to which the norms are known, accepted, and applied; training and education for those involved in applying the norm and information campaigns and notices may play a role;
- *Enforcement.* This concerns the rewards (and punishments) associated with (not) following the norm, the mechanisms and extent of enforcement.

[99] Yves Poullet, 'Selected comments on themes developed in this volume', in Bert-Jaap Koops et al (eds.), *Starting Points for ICT Regulation. Deconstructing Prevalent Policy One-Liners* (TCM Asser Press 2006), at 254. Senden (n 9), at para 3.1.

[100] This paragraph draws on the papers presented at the HiiL Annual Conference on Transnational Private Regulation, June 2010, Dublin, to be found at <http://www.privateregulation.eu>.

[101] For a discussion of the concept of legitimacy for example, see Robert Baldwin and Martin Cave, *Understanding Regulation: Theory, Strategy, and Practice* (Oxford University Press 1999), at Chapter 6 and Julia Black, 'Constructing and Contesting Legitimacy and Accountability in Polycentric Regulatory Regimes', in: [2008] 2 *Regulation & Governance*, at 137–64. For a discussion of legitimacy from an organisations theory perspective, see Marc Suchman, 'Managing Legitimacy: Strategic and Institutional Approaches' [1995] *Academy of Management Review* 20(3), at 571–610. Suchman notes at 573, that '[w]ithin contemporary organisations theory, legitimacy is more often invoked than described, and is more often described than defined'. Though Suchman adopts a very broad definition (legitimacy is a generalized perception or assumption that the actions of an entity are desirable, proper, or appropriate within some socially constructed system of norms, values, beliefs, and definitions), his insights are of (surprising) relevance for legitimacy from a legal perspective as well. In the footnotes I make some references to Suchman if a parallel with organizations theory may be made.

[102] Black (n 101), at 144.

[103] Donal K. Casey and Colin David Scott, 'The Crystallization of Regulatory Norms,' (22 February 2011), *Journal of Law and Society* 38(1), at 76–95. Available at SSRN: <http://ssrn.com/abstract=1772396> or doi:10.1111/j.1467-6478.2011.00535.x, at 87.

- *Transmission.* This concerns the extent to which the norm is transferred onto others which in its turn reinforces the legitimacy of the norm for the original actor (eg adoption of the norm may raise consumer expectations, which in its turn may legitimize the norm).[104]

10.6.2 Normative criteria

Although the legitimization or crystallization process is an empirical phenomenon, certain normative criteria do play a role in the way in which actors initially react to new regulatory norms (ie is this new rule a norm which is perceived as potentially 'legitimate'?).[105] Such perceived legitimacy will create a sense of obligation to act in accordance with such norms and even foster active support for such norms, which will ultimately lead to legitimacy.[106] In that sense the concept of legitimacy is not insulated from normative concerns of those actors to whom the norms are addressed, both as to how the norms are created and their substantive content.[107] The main normative sub-component of legitimacy is 'accountability'.[108] Accountability here is a different concept from the 'accountability principle' discussed in Chapter 9. In Chapter 9 'accountability' concerned the compliance measures that multinationals can take to achieve desired regulatory outcomes and to make these compliance measures verifiable to the regulators. These compliance measures often include the adoption by an organization of corporate self-regulatory codes. In this chapter 'accountability' concerns the question whether the regulatory process as to, in this case, such corporate self-regulatory codes meets the requirements of proper self-regulation (ie meets the requirements of BR). As I indicated in the beginning, the two concepts may to a certain extent overlap, for instance if a meta-regulator prescribes that companies have to introduce corporate self-regulation (ie implementation of the accountability principle) and further provides for procedural requirements how this self-regulation has to be established (ie provides for 'accountability' requirements in respect of the regulatory process).

As a sub-component of legitimacy, two conceptions of accountability can be distinguished:

- *Accountability as a virtue,* as a positive quality of organizations or officials (paragraph 10.6.3).
- *Accountability as a social mechanism,* as an institutional arrangement in which an actor can be held to account by a forum (paragraph 10.6.4).

I will discuss both concepts below. Before I do, I should note that the regulatory process can be divided in three phases: (a) the norm-setting phase; (b) the

[104] Casey and Scott (n 103), at 78 and 82.

[105] Casey and Scott (n 103), at 88.

[106] Casey and Scott (n 103), at 88 and 89.

[107] Casey and Scott (n 103), at 89.

[108] Alongside authorization and representation, see Curtin and Senden (Chapter 2, n 70), at 2, and references therein. Accountability is however the main sub-component, and will be concentrated upon here.

monitoring and evaluation phase (where application of the norms in practice is monitored and evaluated); and (c) the enforcement phase (where the norms are enforced).[109] For the regulatory process to be legitimate, all three phases have to meet accountability requirements. Accountability requirements relating to phase (a) are relevant to ensure *accountability ex ante* during the process of rule-making.[110] Accountability requirements relating to phase (b) and phase (c) are relevant when the process of rule-making is completed and seek to ensure *accountability ex post.* The two concepts of accountability to be discussed below provide for partly overlapping requirements in all three phases of the regulatory process. I will summarize the requirements to be derived from both concepts in paragraph 10.6.5, after which I will apply these requirements to the BCR regulatory process in paragraph 10.7.

10.6.3 Accountability as a virtue

The concept of accountability as a virtue is essentially seen as a normative concept, as a set of standards for the evaluation of the behaviour of actors. Accountability, or 'being accountable', is thus seen as a virtue, as a positive quality of organizations.[111] Studies into accountability as a virtue therefore often focus on the actual behaviour of organizations.[112] As there is no general consensus about standards that constitute accountable behaviour, the concept is contested.[113] However, some normative components have been identified which make an organization more accountable to its stakeholders. The Global Accountability Framework (*GAF*)[114] provides useful criteria for accountability as a virtue and identifies four core dimensions that make an organization more accountable to its stakeholders: (i) participation; (ii) transparency; (iii) evaluation; and (iv) complaints and response mechanisms.

(i) Participation

This describes the process through which an organization enables key stakeholders to play an active role in the decision-making processes and activities which affect them.[115]

[109] See Cafaggi (Chapter 4, n 65), at 215.

[110] Curtin and Senden (Chapter 2, 70), at 12.

[111] Curtin and Senden (Chapter 2, n 70), at 2. See Suchman (n 101), at 579 for a discussion of the concept of 'moral legitimacy' from an organizations theory which shows remarkable similarities with the concept of accountability as a virtue discussed in this paragraph. According to Suchman, moral legitimacy 'reflects a positive normative evaluation of the organization and its activities'. He discusses that moral legitimacy takes one of three forms: evaluations of outputs and consequences (consequential legitimacy); evaluation of techniques and procedures (procedural legitimacy); and evaluations of categories and structures (structural legitimacy). Suchman himself notes at 579 in fn 2 that 'consequential legitimacy and procedural legitimacy both reflect legal-rational authority'.

[112] Curtin and Senden (Chapter 2, n 70), at 2.

[113] Curtin and Senden (Chapter 2, n 70), at 2.

[114] As developed by One World Trust, a charity that conducts research on practical ways to make global organizations more responsive to the people they affect, and how the rule of law can be applied equally to all, see Monica Blagescu, Lucy de Las Casas, and Robert Lloyd, *Pathways to Accountability: The GAP Framework* (One World Trust 2005), to be found at <http://www.oneworldtrust.org>.

[115] Blasgescu, De Las Casas, and Lloyd (n 114), at 32–4. Suchman (n 101), discusses different types of legitimacy from an organization's policy perspective and indicates that granting participatory rights to constituents may enhance legitimacy. See at 578, where he discusses the type 'influence

(ii) Transparency

This concerns the provision of accessible and timely information to stakeholders and the opening up of organizational procedures, structures, and processes for their assessment.[116]

(iii) Evaluation

This encompasses the processes through which an organization, with involvement from key stakeholders, monitors and reviews its progress and results against goals and objectives; feeds learning from this back into the organization on an ongoing basis; and reports on the results of the process.[117]

(iv) Complaints and response mechanisms

These concern the mechanisms through which an organization enables stakeholders to address complaints against its decisions and actions, and through which it ensures that these complaints are properly reviewed and acted upon.[118]

I should note that requirements (i) transparency and (ii) participation concern phase (a) (norm-setting). Requirement (iii) evaluation concerns phase (b) (monitoring and evaluation). Requirement (iv) complaints and response procedure concerns phase (c) (enforcement).

The four normative criteria are not absolute; different legitimacy demands may be made by the different addressees of the regulatory norms (ie the stakeholders). In the case of BCR, different legitimacy demands may be made by the multinationals to which the rules are addressed and the beneficiaries of BCR, the employees and customers of the multinational. Such different legitimacy demands may lead to a 'legitimacy dilemma' for a regulatory regime.[119] A solution suggested in the literature[120] is to enhance legitimacy in such case by resorting to public

legitimacy' which 'arises when the organization incorporates constituents into its policy-making structures or adopts constituents' standards of performance as its own. In a world of ambiguous causality, the surest indicator of ongoing commitment to constituent well-being is the organization's willingness to relinquish some measure of authority to the affected audience (to be co-opted so to speak).' See further Suchman at 587–9 discussing strategies for gaining legitimacy: 'To achieve pragmatic legitimacy through conformity, an organization must either meet the substantive needs of various audiences or offer decision-making access, or both.' See finally Suchman at 580, where he discusses 'procedural legitimacy' (as one of the three forms of moral legitimacy, see n 111) and indicates that moral legitimacy can be enhanced 'by embracing socially accepted techniques and procedures'.

116 Blasgescu, De Las Casas, and Lloyd (n 114), at 30–2.

117 Blasgescu, De Las Casas, and Lloyd (n 114), at 34–6.

118 Blasgescu, De Las Casas, and Lloyd (n 114), at 37.

119 Cafaggi (Chapter 4, n 65), at 212.

120 Cafaggi (Chapter 4, n 65), at 222–3, lists in total four possible responses to conflict of interest situations. Two are mentioned in the text. The other two are: (i) competition (increasing the number of private law-makers and the degree of competition between them whereby full transparency as to the rules will force private law makers to disclose the features of the rule-making-process to the potential addressees); and (ii) regulatory networks (by adhesion to protocols or principles set by independent organizations).

oversight, either by issuing framework legislation[121] or by judicial oversight by making the regimes subject to judicial review. Another (overlapping) solution is to separate the functions of norm-setting, monitoring/evaluation, and enforcement into different organizations with independent governance bodies. TPR often lacks the so-called 'separation of powers', where the norm-setting, the implementation, and enforcement are in different hands. One measure is then to outsource compliance monitoring and dispute resolution to independent private bodies (or to the judiciary).[122] If it is simply not possible to have complete legitimacy from all aspects (ie the regime may not be perceived as legitimate by all stakeholders),[123] legitimacy may be enhanced by introducing greater participation and transparency as to the choices made.[124]

A separate normative legitimacy requirement identified in the literature is the requirement of the independence of regulators. This criterion relates to phase (a) (norm-setting).

(v) Independence

Independence of regulators is safeguarded through a prohibition on having any financial or other interest that could affect impartiality,[125] and can further be fostered by job rotation.[126]

10.6.4 Accountability as a mechanism

The concept of accountability as a mechanism concerns the question: can a regulator be held publicly[127] accountable *ex post* (ie who is accountable, to whom, and for what exactly and what institutional relation or arrangement(s) have been put into place for this?).[128]

[121] Cafaggi (Chapter 4, n 65), at 223, suggests that delegation is also possible provided that legitimacy requirements are imposed on the entity to which norm-setting is delegated at the same time. Cafaggi lists as legitimacy requirements: openness, transparency, representativeness, participation, and independence from vested interests.

[122] Cafaggi (Chapter 4, n 65), at 224.

[123] Julia Black (2008), *Constructing and Contesting Legitimacy and Accountability in Polycentric Regulatory Regimes'* LSE Law, Society and Economy Working Papers 2/2008 London School of Economics and Political Science Law Department, available at <http://www.lse.ac.uk/collections/law/wps/wps.htmm>, at 30.

[124] Casey and Scott (n 103), at 14. Cafaggi (Chapter 4, n 65), at 221: 'The solution of conflicts of interests increases accountability of PLM [Private Law Making].'

[125] Dorbeck-Jung (n 22), at 57.

[126] Dorbeck-Jung (n 22), at 57.

[127] Public accountability means that the account-giving process takes place in the public domain and not behind closed doors. Curtin and Senden (Chapter 2, n 70), at 7.

[128] Curtin and Senden (Chapter 2, n 70), at 14. According to Curtin and Senden (n 70), at 3, there are two different conceptions of accountability: accountability as a virtue, as a positive quality of organizations or officials; and (ii) accountability as a social mechanism, as an institutional arrangement in which an actor can be held to account by a forum. See for a justification of the choice to apply the concept of accountability as a mechanism, Curtin and Senden (n 70), at 18.

Accountability therefore refers to the mechanisms of oversight and control that render the exercise of the regulatory powers acceptable to those regulated (ie in this case the multinationals) and to those who will be affected positively or negatively by the conduct of the regulated parties (ie the beneficiaries of BCR). Other than with public regulators democratically empowered to enact public laws, with TPR it is mostly far more diffuse which actors participate in the norm-setting, and to which forums they should be accountable for their norm-setting. For a social relation to be subject to accountability, some authors require seven constituting elements: '(i) a relationship between an actor and a forum (ii) in which the actor has an obligation (iii) to explain and to justify (iv) his or her conduct (v) whereby the forum can pose questions (vi) and pass judgement and (vii) the actor may face consequences'.[129] The actors responsible for the outcome of the norm-setting can be an organization, including a public institution, companies involved in norm setting, standardization bodies, professional bodies, etc.[130] The accountability forum can also be an institution, including public authorities, but also the executives of a company, international organizations, audit offices, financiers, or the stakeholders (represented by interest groups, or otherwise).[131] As indicated, a key feature of TPR is that in the regulatory process of TPR both the actors and the accountability forums involved are often 'plural, partial and emergent'.[132] As a consequence two major complications can be identified as to the regulatory process of TPR: (i) the problem of the many hands (where it is difficult to identify the actors responsible for the outcome of regulation); and (ii) the problem of the many eyes (the risk that actors are accountable to a plethora of different accountability forums).[133] While the problem of the many hands might suggest that all the stakeholder communities should be made part of the rule-making process (to increase accountability of the actor), this would only exacerbate the problem of the many eyes. The conclusion of the HiiL Program is therefore that 'bringing the public back in should (...) be a balanced exercise'. To avoid situations of 'accountability paralysis' a prioritization has to take place both in respect of (i) the forums that are most significantly affected by the TPR regime and (ii) the most pressing issues on which the actor should be held accountable.

The constituting elements of accountability as a mechanism all concern ensuring *accountability ex post*.[134] The constituting elements can be grouped into three requirements:

[129] This is the definition introduced by M. Bovens, D. Curtin, and P. Hart (eds), *The Real World of EU Accountability: What Deficit?* (Oxford University Press 2010), at 37. This definition is also used by Curtin and Senden (Chapter 2, n 70), at 14.

[130] Curtin and Senden (Chapter 2, n 70), at 14.

[131] Curtin and Senden (Chapter 2, n 70), at 14.

[132] Curtin and Senden (Chapter 2, n 70), at 14.

[133] Curtin and Senden (Chapter 2, n 70), at 15.

[134] For these three criteria, see Curtin and Senden (Chapter 2, n 70), at 17. The breakdown of these three criteria into detailed questions is derived from the questionnaire used in the HiiL Program for the empirical research.

Information requirement

The actor is obliged to inform the forum about his or her conduct, by providing various types of data about the performance of tasks, outcomes, or procedures, which may also involve providing explanations and justifications. This requirement boils down to the following questions:

- Is there a formal obligation to explain and justify conduct and what is the nature—political, legal/judicial, administrative, professional, financial, otherwise—of this obligation (eg by public officials to supervisory agencies, courts, or audits)?
- Is there an informal—social, moral, professional, public—obligation to do so (eg press conferences, briefings, voluntary audits, public panels)?

Debate

There needs to be a possibility for the forum to interrogate the actor and to question the adequacy of the information or the legitimacy of the conduct.[135] This requirement leads to the following question:

- What are the possibilities for debate; can the forum interrogate the actor and question the adequacy of the information or the legitimacy of the conduct?

Pass judgment

The accountability forum may pass judgment which may take the form of approval of the annual accounts, denouncing a policy, publicly condemning behaviour, passing a negative judgement, or as a result thereof, the actor may face certain consequences like sanctions.[136] This requirement boils down to the following questions:

- What arrangements and policies have been put into place to enable the accountability forum to pass judgment?
- What evaluation process, both of regulatory outcomes and practices/policies, is provided for; what formal and informal complaint-and-response mechanisms have been put into place and how independent and credible are these?
- What consequences and/or sanctions may the actor(s) face for its conduct (eg (dis)approval of annual accounts, denouncement of a policy, public condemnation of behaviour)?
- What non-judicial means of dispute resolution are there and what formal judicial redress may be obtained?

[135] Curtin and Senden (Chapter 2, n 70), at 17.
[136] Curtin and Senden (Chapter 2, n 70), at 17.

Requirements (i) and (ii) apply to phase (b) monitoring and enforcement. Requirement (iii) is only relevant for phase (c) enforcement.

10.6.5 Cumulative overview accountability requirements

Taking together the evaluation criteria of accountability as a virtue and accountability as a mechanism, I come to the following overview.

Requirements to ensure accountability ex ante
Phase (a) norm-setting
(i) Participation
(ii) Transparency
(iii) Independence

Requirements to ensure accountability ex post
Phase (b) monitoring and evaluation
(iv) Evaluation
(v) Information requirement
(vi) Debate

Phase (c) enforcement
(vii) Complaints and response procedures
(viii) Information requirement
(ix) Debate
(x) Pass judgment

10.7 Are BCR Legitimate?: The Normative Perspective

10.7.1 Identifying the actors and accountability forums involved in the three phases

The accountability forums vary per actor involved in the BCR norm-setting process. To identify the main accountability relationships,[137] it has to be decided:

(i) Who are the most prominent actors that bear responsibility for the norm-setting?
(ii) What are the accountability forums; who are most significantly affected by the regime, both internally and externally?
(iii) What are the most pressing issues on which the actors should be held accountable?

[137] Because of the many hands and many eyes involved in the determination of the accountability relationship, prioritization is required in this regard in order to avoid accountability paralysis. These questions are also derived from the questionnaire drafted as part of the HiiL Program, for the purposes of performing the empirical research into the various forms of TPR.

Phase (a) BCR norm-setting process

The two main actors involved in the BCR norm-setting process and (in sequence of priority) their corresponding accountability forums are:

Working Party 29
For the Working Party 29 the following accountability forums may (in any event) be identified:

- the multinationals as addressees of the BCR regime;
- potential beneficiaries of BCR (ie employees, consumers, patients);
- suppliers and business partners of the multinational to which the multinational transfers data;
- the courts of the Member States, and ultimately the ECJ; and
- European legislators.

Lead DPAs
For the Lead DPAs the same accountability forums can be identified with the difference that now the specific employees and customers of the relevant multinational applying for BCR authorization will be the accountability forum.

Phase (b) monitoring and evaluation

The main actor involved in the monitoring and evaluation of BCR is the multinational and its accountability forums are:

- internal accountability forums: the board, the internal complaints committee
- external stakeholders (employees, consumers, patients)

Phase (c) enforcement

The main actor involved is the multinational and its accountability forums are:

- internal complaints committee;
- Lead DPA;
- national courts; and
- ECJ.

Below I will focus on the accountability of the actors in respect of their *specific part* in the BCR norm-setting process. For instance, the role of the Working Party 29 is mainly in the *ex ante* norm-setting process. The key role in the *ex post* accountability in relation to BCR is performed by the multinational. I will therefore evaluate whether the role of the Working Party 29 meets the *ex ante* accountability requirements. This is not to say that the Working Party 29 is, for instance, not also *accountable ex post* for its part in the BCR norm-setting. For instance, the

Working Party 29 will be accountable *ex post* to the Commission (being its advisory body). The same applies to the Lead DPA. The Lead DPA will be accountable *ex post* for the proper performance of its tasks to the public at large in its Member State. This general accountability *ex post* of the Working Party 29 and the Lead DPAs is outside the scope of this publication. I will review, however, to what extent decisions and Opinions of the Working Party 29 and the Lead DPA are subject to *judicial review*. This constitutes the accountability *ex post* of the Working Party and the Lead DPAs to the courts of the Member States and the ECJ. As indicated in paragraph 10.4.3, judicial review of norm-setting by de facto regulators may be a factor of relevance in deciding on the legitimacy of such norms.

10.7.2 Phase (a) BCR norm-setting by the Working Party 29

Introduction

The Working Party 29 is a de facto regulator. Pursuant to Article 29 Directive, the Working Party 29 has been set up as the institutional body for cooperation among the DPAs. The Working Party 29 has advisory status and acts independently.[138] Members are representatives of each of the DPAs, of the EDPS, and of the Commission. The tasks of the Working Party 29 are clearly formulated and are publicly available. It issues Opinions to contribute to the uniform application of the Directive and advises on proposals for EU legislation having an impact of data protection.[139] The Opinions of the Working Party 29 are non-binding but they are followed in practice by the DPAs and de facto set the rules for application of the Directive.

The Working Party 29 has issued Rules of Procedure of the Working Party,[140] pursuant to which the Working Party 29 is authorized to invite experts to attend meetings of the Working Party 29[141] and further to install sub-groups to prepare the position of the Working Party 29 on specific topics.[142] Members of the Working Party 29 may be further authorized to be assisted by experts 'in their confidence'.[143] The Rules of Procedure of the Working Party 29 do not include a requirement for the Working Party 29 to hold a public consultation or public hearing before issuing its opinions.

[138] Article 29(2) Directive.

[139] See the Document 'Tasks of the Working Party 29', as published at <http://www.ec.europa.eu>. See further WP Contribution on the Future of Privacy (Chapter 1, n 6), at para 7b about the functioning of the Working Party 29 and proposals of the Working Party 29 itself for improvement.

[140] The Rules of Procedure of the Working Party, Brussels, 15 February 2010, to be found at <http://www.ec.europa.eu> (*WP Rules of Procedure*).

[141] See Art 9 WP Rules of Procedure.

[142] Which the Working Party 29 is authorized to do pursuant to Art 16 WP Rules of Procedure (n 140).

[143] Which the Working Party 29 may authorize pursuant to Art 9 WP Rules of Procedure (n 140).

Norm-setting as to BCR

The Working Party 29 installed a sub-group on BCR,[144] which sub-group prepared the WP Opinions. The Working Party 29 held a consultation[145] and a public hearing[146] on the first of the WP Opinions, the input of which was taken into consideration into its subsequent WP Opinions. As part of the consultation a number of multinationals and industry groups were invited to submit their input, but no employee representatives or consumer interest groups.[147] At the public hearing about 30 representatives of the business community were present (which included both multinationals as addressees of the BCR regime and potential suppliers and business partners of those multinationals) and one consumer organization.[148] It is not known which members of the Working Party 29 participated in the BCR sub-group and whether any experts participated either in this sub-group or in the plenary meetings of the Working Party 29 or whether any of the members were assisted by an expert. The Working Party 29 draws up an annual report which is transmitted to the Commission, the European Parliament, and the Council and which is made public.[149]

Being a de facto regulator, any norm-setting by the Working Party 29 requires a strict (or even an enhanced) application of the legitimacy requirements.

10.7.3 Accountability *ex ante* Working Party 29

Re (i) Participation

It does not require much discussion that the BCR regime as developed by the Working Party 29 in the WP Opinions has *not* been inclusive in the sense that the

[144] This is based on oral information of DPAs. No public information is available on the existence of this sub-group (or other sub-groups for that matter), their mandates, their members, or meetings. According to the Dutch DPA, presently 15 DPAs are members of the BCR sub-group.

[145] A summary of the contributions can be found at: <http://ec.europa.eu/justice/policies/privacy/workinggroup/consultations/binding-rules_en.htm>.

[146] See the Official Summary of the Public Hearing on internal codes of conduct for multinationals drafted by the Dutch Data Protection Authority, to be found at <http://ec.europa.eu/justice/policies/privacy/docs/binding-rules/hearing_bcr_en.pdf>.

[147] Contributions were made by about 30 stakeholders from the business community, which included individual multinationals (eg ABNAMRO, Accenture, DaimlerChrysler, Citigroup, and Philips), but also international, regional, and national business organizations such as the International Chamber of Commerce (ICC), the American Chamber of Commerce to the European Union (AMCHAM), the Bundesverband der Deutschen Industrie (BDI), Gesellschaft für Datenschutz und Datensicherung (GDD), the Confederation of British Industry (CBI), the United States Council for International Business (USCIB), the European Banking Federation (FBE), and the Japan Business Council in Europe and further organizations such as an international US law firm, the International Communications Round Table (ICRT), the European Privacy Officers Forum (EPOF), and the Coalition on Global Information Flows. For their contributions, see: <http://ec.europa.eu/justice/policies/privacy/workinggroup/consultations/binding-rules_en.htm>.

[148] See n 146.

[149] Article 15 WP Rules of Procedure (n 140).

third-party beneficiaries (ie employee or consumer organizations[150] and civil society stakeholders) have been sufficiently included in the norm-setting process.[151] As business organizations (both as addressees of the BCR regime and as contracting parties) were amply represented in the norm-setting process, the risk even exists that the Working Party 29, while deciding on the WP Opinions, was subject to 'regulatory capture': if not all stakeholders are involved or heard, impartiality of the regulator is at risk.[152] This potential lack of legitimacy should be remedied in the future.[153] The opportune moment to remedy this shortcoming is the public consultation launched by the Commission as part of the review of the Directive, which was just finalized and resulted in publication of the Proposed Regulation (see Chapter 6, paragraph 6.6 above).[154] If *Recommendation 2* is followed and EU legislators delegate the further norm-setting in respect of BCR to the Commission pursuant to Articles 290 and 291 TFEU (as is currently reflected in the Proposed Regulation), a further consultation of the BCR stakeholders has to take place prior to such further norm-setting by the Commission.[155] In Chapter 6, paragraph 6.6.6, I discussed that as the Commission in its turn will not be able to specify all BCR requirements in full detail, the Working Party 29 will continue to play an important role in providing guidelines in respect of these requirements (for instance, the application of the BCR norms to certain industry sectors, such as the health industry or the telecoms sector). I further indicated that both the

[150] Participation of consumers will be effective only if their representatives can rely on the relevant expertise and financial sources, see Dorbeck-Jung (n 22), at 56.

[151] This is with the exception that apparently (next to 30 representatives of the business community) one consumer organization was represented at the public hearing held by the Working Party 29 on the first of seven WP Opinions. See the Official Summary of the Public Hearing on internal codes of conduct for multinationals drafted by the Dutch Data Protection Authority, at 1, to be found at <http://www.ec.europa.eu>. The Working Party 29 may seek the views of data subjects or their representatives pursuant to Art 27(3) Directive. Apparently the Working Party 29 (by now) also realizes that a broader consultation is indicated, where it announced in a WP Opinion on the principle of accountability (Chapter 1, n 23), at para 15, that it may develop a model data compliance programme for medium and large controllers in the future (which will be similar to the compliance programme of BCR) and then will consult 'all appropriate stakeholders.'

[152] See para 10.4.4 in particular n 48.

[153] See also Recommendation 5 of the Rand Report (Chapter 2, n 27) at 42:

> **Recommendation 5: Achieve broader liaison with stakeholders**
> The Article 29 Working Party should liaise more systematically with business representatives, third sector and NGO communities, and the perspectives of NGO representatives and citizen organisations should be more explicitly taken into account.

[154] This public consultation took place in two phases and involved all major stakeholders and lasted for more than two years. See for an overview the See the Explanatory Memorandum to the Proposed Regulation, Chapter 1, n 9, at 3–5.

[155] See para. 10.5.3, in particular n 94. See also the Report of the High Level Group of Company Law Experts on a Modern Regulatory Framework for Company Law in Europe, Brussels, 4 November 2002 (Chapter 4, n 31), at para 2: 'Many respondents commented that where primary regulation through a Directive would still be necessary, the Directive should be restricted to setting principles and general rules, leaving the detailed rules to secondary regulation. Where recourse is made to secondary regulation, democratic legitimacy must be ensured.'

Working Party 29 and the EDPS recommended that the Commission insist 'on a strong commitment by the members of the Working Party 29 to implement the views of the Working Party 29 into national practice'[156] and 'make the opinions [of the Working Party 29] more authorative' by including an obligation for the DPAs and the Commission 'to take utmost account of opinions'.[157] Based on these recommendations the expectation is justified that although no formal delegation of regulatory powers will take place to the Working Party 29, the Opinions of the Working Party 29 will (remain to) be more than just guidelines and will be policy rules de facto setting norms for DPAs and controllers.[158] Legitimacy demands require that also in respect of such de facto norm-setting, proper stakeholder consultation will take place. The suggestion by the EDPS, that as long as the opinions of the Working Party 29 are not given binding force, 'safeguards such as transparency and redress' do not come into play,[159] fails to recognize that legitimacy must also be ensured for de facto norm-setting.

Recommendation 16

- Hold a proper consultation of all stakeholders of BCR prior to enacting the norms for BCR in the revised Directive.
- Instruct the Commission to hold a consultation of all stakeholders of BCR prior to the further norm-setting on BCR by the Commission.

[156] WP Contribution on The Future of Privacy (Chapter 1, n 6), at para 99. See also Wugmeister, Retzer and Rich (Chapter 3, n 148), at 492.

[157] EDPS opinion on the revision of the Directive (Chapter 2, n 35), at 146: 'The EDPS recommends solutions which would make opinions of the Working Party more authoritative without modifying substantially its way of functioning.' The EDPS suggests including an obligation for the DPAs and the Commission to take utmost account of opinions and common positions adopted by the Working Party, based on the model adopted for the positions of the Body of European Regulators for Electronic Communications (BEREC). Furthermore, the new legal instrument could give the Working Party the explicit task to adopt 'interpretative recommendations'. These alternative solutions would give the positions of the Working Party 29 a stronger role, also before the Courts. For the position of the BEREC, see Regulation (EC) No 1211/2009 of the European Parliament and of the Council of 25 November 2009 establishing the Body of European Regulators for Electronic Communications (BEREC) and the Office, OJ L337, 9 18.12.200, p 1.

[158] Under the Proposed Regulation the Working Party 29 will be replaced by a European Data Protection Board (EDPB). See on the EDPS and its advisory powers, Chapter 3, para 3.1.8.

[159] EDPS Opinion on the revision of the Directive (Chapter 2, n 35), at 151: 'The EDPS would put a caveat against introducing stronger measures, such as giving binding force to WP29 positions. This would undermine the independent status of individual DPAs, which has to be guaranteed by the Member States under national law. If the Working Party decisions were to have a direct impact on third parties such as data controllers, new procedures should be foreseen including safeguards such as transparency and redress, including possibly appeal before the European Court of Justice.'

Re (ii) Transparency

It also does not require much discussion that the norm-setting procedure by the Working Party 29 is not sufficiently transparent. Transparency is provided effectively only if information is 'accessible, intelligible, all-embracing and objective'.[160] The Rules of Procedure of the Working Party 29 are publicly available,[161] but the minutes of the meetings of the Working Party 29 and any draft documents produced by the Working Party 29 are restricted, unless the Working Party 29 decides otherwise.[162] Further, though the Working Party 29 held a consultation on BCR of which the contributions are published[163] and a public hearing of which a (very) short summary of the discussions is published,[164] no information is available on:

- why the consultation was limited to certain companies and one consumer organization only;
- whether any experts were invited by the Working Party 29 to attend the relevant meetings of the Working Party 29;
- whether any sub-group was established to prepare the position of the Working Party 29 on the WP Opinions and if so, which members of the Working Party 29 participated in such sub-group, and what the mandate of such sub-group was;
- whether any members of the Working Party 29 were assisted by experts of their confidence; and
- if experts were involved, how they were selected, their competences, experiences, and dependencies, how any conflicts of interest were identified and dealt with, what their expert advice was, and the choices subsequently made based on this advice.[165]

[160] Dorbeck-Jung (n 22), at 56.

[161] To be found at <http://www.ec.europa.eu>.

[162] See Art 11(1) WP Rules of Procedure (n 140).

[163] For which a number of multinationals and industry groups were invited to submit their input. See for their contributions <http://www.ec.europa.eu>.

[164] See the Official Summary of the Public Hearing on internal codes of conduct for multinationals drafted by the Dutch Data Protection Authority, to be found at <http://www.ec.europa.eu>. The Public Hearing was attended by 30 representatives of the business community and one consumer organization.

[165] In response to a commitment made in the EC White Paper on European Governance (Chapter 2, n 75), at 19, the Commission issued guidelines on collection and use of expert advice in the Commission to provide for the accountability, plurality and integrity of the expertise used and expressed the intention that '[o]ver time these guidelines could form the basis for a common approach for all Institutions and Member States'. The guidelines were issued in 2002, see Communication from the Commission on the collection and use of expertise by the Commission: Principles and Guidelines, 11 December 2002, COM(2002) 713 final (*EC Communication on the use of experts*). The Guidelines at 9–10 provide for three core principles when seeking expert advice, the second of which is *'Openness.* The Commission should be open in seeking and acting on advice from experts. Transparency is a key precondition for more accountability for all involved. Transparency is required, particularly in relation to the way issues are framed, experts are selected, and results handled (...) Instead, the Commission must be capable of justifying and explaining the way expertise has been involved, and the choices it has made based on advice. In a similar way, accountability also extends to the experts themselves. They

This lack of transparency should be remedied in the future. This is also the recommendation of the First Report on the Directive[166] and the EDPS[167] and the intention of the Commission.[168] This is also reflected in the Proposed Regulation.[169]

Recommendation 17
Instruct the Working Party 29 to amend its Rules of Procedure to remedy the lack of transparency as to its decision-making process.

Re (iii) Independency

The next question is whether the Working Party 29 is sufficiently independent. The independence of the Working Party 29 is in principle ensured in the Directive.[170] The EDPS in its Opinion on revision of the Directive[171] rightfully notes that 'the strength of the [Working Party 29] is intrinsically linked with the independence and powers of its members'. The members of the Working Party 29 are representatives of the DPAs, the EDPS, and the Commission. The independence of the DPAs and the EDPS is in principle ensured in the Directive.[172] The ECJ (Case C-518/07 *Commission v Germany*)[173] ruled that the requirement of 'independence' of DPAs entails that the DPAs:

should, for example, be prepared to justify their advice by explaining the evidence and reasoning upon which it is based.' The first principle further includes the requirement of 'independency' which should aim at promoting practices 'to minimise the risk of vested interests distorting the advice proffered (. . .) by making dependencies explicit'.

166 First Report on the Directive (Chapter 2, n 26), at 23.

167 EDPS Opinion on the revision of the Directive (Chapter 2, n 35), at 144: 'Finally, reinforcing the powers for DPAs also requires stronger powers for the Working Party, with a structure including better rules and safeguards and more transparency. This will be developed for the advisory role as well as for the enforcement role of the Working Party.'

168 The lack of transparency of the Working Party 29 is implicitly acknowledged by the Commission in its Communication on the revision of the Directive (Chapter 2, n 34), at para 2, where it announces that the Working Party 29 should become a 'more transparent body'.

169 Article 68 Proposed Regulation sets out the EDPB's decision-making procedures, including the obligation to adopt rules of procedure and organize its own operational arrangements, including the establishment of sub-groups for specific issues or sectors.

170 This is also a requirement under Art 29(1) Directive.

171 EDPS Opinion on the revision of the Directive (Chapter 2, n 35), at para 142.

172 The independence of the DPAs is ensured by Recital 62 and Art 28(1) Directive and Art 8(3) TFEU. For the independence of the EDPS, see Art 41(1) Regulation (EC) No 45/2001 of the European Parliament and of the Council of 18 December 2000 on the protection of individuals with regard to the processing of personal data by the Community institutions and bodies and on the free movement of such data, [2000] OJ L8/1.

173 Case C-518/07, *Commission v Germany* [2010] OJ C 113, at 3–4. See at para. 30: 'the second subparagraph of Article 28(1) Directive 95/46 is to be interpreted as meaning that the supervisory authorities responsible for supervising the processing of personal data outside the public sector must enjoy an independence allowing them to perform their duties free from external influence. That independence precludes not only any influence exercised by the supervised bodies, but also any directions or any other external influence, whether direct or indirect, which could call into question

enjoy an independence allowing them to perform their duties free from external influence. That independence precludes not only any influence exercised by the supervised bodies, but also any directions or any other external influence, whether direct or indirect.

It is clear that in some Member States, the DPAs still lack sufficient independence, which should be remedied (see further paragraph 10.7.5).

However, also the Working Party 29 itself does not meet the test of independence as set by the ECJ. The EDPS[174] again rightfully notes that the Working Party 29 does not enjoy the required freedom of (indirect) external influence, as the Commission is 'at the same time member, secretariat and addressee of the Working Party's opinions', and concludes that the:

> autonomy of the Working Party should be ensured in the new legal framework, in accordance with the criteria developed for a complete independence of DPAs by the European Court of Justice in case C-518/07. The EDPS considers that the Working Party should also be provided with sufficient resources and budget and a reinforced secretariat, to support its contributions.

The Proposed Regulation will remedy these shortcomings.[175]

Finally, if experts are participating in the meetings of the Working Party 29, it is not clear whether they are representing any interest and as such their independence is not guaranteed.[176] This could be remedied for instance by a public declaration of interests by such experts.[177] Further, if sub-groups are installed for specific topics (as is apparently done for BCR), the risk of regulatory capture should be decreased by regular job rotation of the members of such sub-group.[178]

the performance by those authorities of their task consisting of establishing a fair balance between the protection of the right to private life and the free movement of personal data.'

174 EDPS Opinion on the revision of the Directive (Chapter 2, n 35) at para 142.

175 The Commission will no longer be a member of the (successor of the Working Party 29) the EDPB and the secretariat of the EDPB will be moved from the Commission to the EDPS, see Chapter 3, para 3.1.8.

176 Independence is safeguarded through a prohibition on having any financial or other interest that could affect impartiality. Dorbeck-Jung (n 22), at 57. See further the EC Communication on the use of experts (n 165) at 9: which provides for three core principles when seeking expert advice. The first is 'quality of advice', which has three determinants: 'excellence; the extent to which experts act in an independent manner; and pluralism.' As to 'independence' the Communication states: 'It is a truism that no one is entirely "independent": individuals can never entirely set aside all thoughts of their personal background—family, culture, employer, sponsor, etc. Nevertheless, as far as possible, experts should be expected to act in an independent manner. Experts can, of course, still bring to the table knowledge they hold by virtue of their affiliation, or nationality: indeed, experts may sometimes be selected for this very reason. Nevertheless, the aim is to minimise the risk of vested interests distorting the advice proffered by establishing practices that promote integrity, by making dependencies explicit, and by recognising that some dependencies—varying from issue to issue—could impinge on the policy process more than others.'

177 Dorbeck-Jung (n 22), at 57.

178 Dorbeck-Jung (n 22), at 57.

Recommendation 18

- Ensure the independence of the Working Party 29 in accordance with the criteria developed by the ECJ for independence of DPAs.
- Instruct the Working Party 29 to amend its Rules of Procedure to ensure its accountability as to independence by:
  - having any experts participating in its meetings issue a public declaration of interests;
  - introducing job rotation of the members of any sub-groups installed by the Working Party 29.

10.7.4 Accountability *ex post* Working Party 29

As set out before, the role of the Working Party 29 is mainly in the *ex ante* norm-setting process. The key role in the *ex post* accountability in relation to BCR is performed by the multinational, which role will be evaluated below. What remains relevant, however, is the *ex post* accountability of the Working Party 29 towards the courts of the Member States and the ECJ. This accountability can be reduced to the question of whether the norm-setting by the Working Party 29 is subject to judicial review. Opinions of the Working Party are not binding, and as a consequence are not subject to review by the ECJ.[179] However, the flip side is that the national courts of the Member States are not bound by these opinions either. National courts having to review decisions of their respective Lead DPA authorizing BCR will therefore (have to) apply their own national data protection law. In that process the courts may take the WP Opinions into account, but they are not bound by them. To that extent, the WP Opinions are subject to judicial review by the national courts (and ultimately the ECJ). There is, however, an important qualification. In Chapter 6, paragraph 6.5, I concluded that at present the Directive does not provide for the main substantive requirements for BCR to provide an adequate level of protection. Also for adequacy rulings, an 'adequate level' of protection is at present insufficiently defined.[180] As a consequence, if a national court (and ultimately the ECJ) has to review a decision by a Lead DPA on authorization for individual BCR, this court has very little guidance on the rules against which the relevant BCR should be evaluated. Any judicial review in this respect is therefore difficult. The above confirms the necessity of *Recommendation 2* to European legislators, ie to recognize BCR as an appropriate tool to provide

[179] The ECJ only reviews acts of the EU institutions and agencies 'which are intended to have legal effects', see Case 22/70 *Commission v Council* [1971] ECR 263, at para 42.

[180] See WP Contribution on the Future of Privacy (Chapter 1, n 6), at 11, where the Working Party 29 recommends to improve adequacy decisions, by '[d]efining more precisely the criteria for reaching the legal status of "adequacy", paying due attention to the approach of the WP29 and various other approaches to data protection around the world, and especially to the rights and principles laid down in the Joint proposal of International Standards on the Protection of Privacy'.

adequate safeguards for the transfer of data and to define the main substantive requirements for BCRs to be set at an adequate level. If this recommendation is indeed followed, the standard for judicial review of the WP Opinions becomes clear. This recommendation is followed in the Proposed Regulation.[181]

10.7.5 Phase (a) norm-setting by a Lead DPA in respect of individual BCR

For a description of the approval procedure of individual BCR applications by the Lead DPA as part of the Mutual Recognition Procedure (*MRP*), I refer to Chapter 6, paragraph 6.4. At the time the first BCR applications to DPAs were made, it was very much the relevant DPA that decided what the BCR should look like. When over time the WP Opinions were issued, the norm-setting for BCR became more and more a top-down process by the Working Party 29 and the room to manoeuvre for the DPAs became correspondingly smaller. For the DPAs that have joined the MRP, I would even claim that such DPAs are *applying* the BCR norms to the BCR application rather than *setting* norms for BCR applications. In these cases it may be maintained that the accountability requirements are no longer relevant. Insisting on participation of stakeholders in norm-setting is only relevant if actual influence can be exercised as to the outcome. At this time, however, not all DPAs have joined the MRP, and norm-setting still also takes place at the national DPA level. I will not discuss in detail whether this norm-setting by the DPAs meets requirements of participation of and transparency to stakeholders. Briefly put, these requirements are not met. The stakeholders in the BCR (customers and employees of the multinational) are not consulted in the individual BCR authorization procedures.[182] This would also not be advisable. The customers of the multinational are in most cases a diffuse group, spread out over numerous jurisdictions, and not represented in a specific body (other maybe than in general by international consumer organizations like BEUC or privacy interest organizations). Inclusion of these international organizations in the national approval process before a Lead DPA does not seem opportune. This would require *international* consumer organizations and civil society organizations to participate in each and every *national* BCR authorization procedure in the various Member States.[183] These international

[181] The Proposed Regulation recognizes BCR and codifies the main substantive requirements. Further detailed norm-setting is delegated to the Commission and will no longer be de facto delegated to the successor of the Working Party 29. See Chapter 6, para 6.6.2. Opinions of the successor of the Working Party 29 will remain non-binding; see Chapter 3, para 3.1.8.

[182] Though the employees are consulted on the BCR as part of the works council requirements, which have to be completed before BCR are formally adopted by the multinational and submitted to the Lead DPA for formal approval. See Chapter 6, para 6.4, in particular para 6.4.1.

[183] The solution here would also not be to organize the civil society and consumer organizations at the *national level* in order to support citizens in exercising their data protection rights (as recommended by some authors). Again, as BCR apply worldwide, the stakeholders are not national organizations but international organizations. See the Rand Report (Chapter 2, n 27), at x and 45:

> **Recommendation 7 – Strengthened support for exercise of rights**
> The DPAs, in conjunction with civil society stakeholders should work with consumer protection organisations (e.g. the European Consumers Association, BEUC) to institute a

stakeholder organizations should be consulted on the BCR norm-setting process (i) as part of revision of the Directive; (ii) prior to further detailed norm-setting on BCR by the Commission; and (iii) prior to the Working Party 29 issuing Opinions on BCR (as per *Recommendation 16*). If properly consulted at those times, legitimacy demands do not require that these organizations be (again) consulted on individual BCR applications. Here 'bringing the public back in' would be an example of 'too many eyes' and in any event a doubling of consultation of similar stakeholders on similar issues.[184]

The reason for not further elaborating on the legitimacy of current BCR norm-setting by individual DPAs is that such norm-setting should not take place at Member State level at all. In Chapter 6, paragraph 6.6, I discussed that norm-setting for data protection is the prerogative of EU legislators, where under the TFEU regime delegation of further detailed norm-setting can be to the Commission only. The role of the Working Party 29 should in principle be limited to providing further guidelines only. In this context there is no role for individual DPAs for norm-setting. If norm-setting does take place at the national level, this could entail that norm-setting can be influenced by national interests, while the BCR have to apply on an EU (even global) level. To avoid undue influences, norm-setting should take place at the level that corresponds with the scope of application of the relevant norms. In any event it is not advisable that the DPAs are concurrently involved in norm-setting and enforcement.[185] In the new constellation I therefore recommend that there will be no longer room for national policy guidelines as to authorization of BCR, such as currently issued by the DPAs in the UK and Austria.[186]

If my previous recommendations are followed, the role of the Lead DPAs will be limited to *applying* the BCR norms rather than *setting* norms in respect of BCR. This will be achieved by *Recommendation 2* (to recognize the BCR as an

> national network of grass-roots level 'accountability agents' to support citizens in the exercise of their fundamental rights. Although similar activities are currently undertaken by DPAs, resourcing constraints suggest that a more localized network would be a better approach, having a more widespread presence. These local accountability agents would act as another means for citizens to exercise their rights within existing arrangements.

Dorbeck-Jung (n 22), at 56 notes that participation of consumers will be effective only if their representatives can rely on the relevant expertise and financial sources. This is also a recommendation of Raab and Koops (Chapter 4, n 24), at 220.

[184] See Curtin and Senden (Chapter 2, n 70), at 15. An option that would be possible, but which I reject, is to prescribe in the revised Directive that the Lead DPA has to make the request for authorization and the draft BCR available to the public for consultation for a prescribed period. During this time, interested parties would then be able to submit their comments prior to the Lead DPA deciding on the authorization. This is, for instance, required by the Dutch Data Protection Act in respect of decisions of the Dutch DPA on conformity declarations in respect of self-regulatory codes (see n 88). However, these self-regulatory codes concern *national* self-regulatory codes specific for a certain industry sector. In those cases the relevant stakeholders are not yet consulted on such codes, and indeed if they are not consulted at that time, the stakeholders will not be consulted at all. Further, the national stakeholders for such codes are much better organized in the relevant Member State than at the EU level.

[185] Cafaggi (Chapter 4, n 65), at 222 and 224. See further Prins, Chapter 6, n 113.

[186] See Chapter 6, n 14.

appropriate tool to provide adequate safeguards for the transfer of data and define the main substantive requirements for BCRs to be set at an adequate level); *Recommendation 3* (to define and impose the MRP upon all Member States) and *Recommendations 16, 17,* and *18* (to ensure that further guidelines in respect of these norms as issued by the Working Party 29 would fully comply with the enhanced legitimacy requirements).

As BCR have EU-wide (even global) application, the most logical set-up would be to task the pan-EU Data Protection Supervisor (as per *Recommendation 4*) with central authorization of BCR applications. Though from a theoretical perspective this is optimal, I note that the EU headquarters of the multinational is in fact well placed to authorize, supervise, and enforce BCR. It seems more a matter to ensure that such Lead DPA applies EU norms rather than sets these and cannot be influenced by national interests. An acceptable in-between solution is reflected in the Proposed Regulation, which is discussed below.

Proposed Regulation Under the Proposed Regulation authorization of BCR will remain with the Lead DPA (as the DPA where the multinational has its main establishment). To ensure that the DPAs are aligned when acting as Lead DPA, the Lead DPA is required to submit its draft approval of BCR for opinion to the EDPB (the successor of the Working Party 29).[187] If the Lead DPA does not follow the opinion of the EDPB, the Commission may issue a further opinion[188] and ultimately adopt a decision requiring the Lead DPA to suspend the adoption of the draft authorization.[189] This assures that Lead DPAs *apply* BCR norms rather than *set* these norms. The Lead DPA will also be tasked with the enforcement of BCR.[190] The Proposed Regulation improves the coordination of enforcement in cross-border cases by requiring (in this case the Lead) DPA to invite other DPAs if individuals in the Member States of these DPAs are likely to be affected by a processing operation.[191] All in all the position of the EDPS is substantially strengthened under the Proposed Regulation by the 'back up' suspension power of the Commission and the delegation to the Commission to adopt implementing acts in relation to the matters to be submitted to the EDPS for opinion (which include draft BCR authorizations).[192]

Below I make some final remarks on the norm-setting by the Lead DPAs.

Re (ii) Transparency

At present the Lead DPAs do not publish their authorizations of BCR of a multinational. Also, the texts of these BCR are not publicly available. If multinationals rely on their authorizations in the course of business, their counterpart can therefore not verify whether this authorization is indeed granted and whether the relevant data processing is indeed covered by the BCR. Insofar as the

187 Articles 43(1) and 58(2)(f) Proposed Regulation.
188 Article 59(1) Proposed Regulation.
189 Article 60 Proposed Regulation.
190 See Chapter 6, para 6.6.1.
191 Article 56 Proposed Regulation.
192 Article 62 Proposed Regulation.

multinational itself publishes its BCR on its corporate website,[193] such counterpart cannot verify whether the published BCR indeed corresponds with the BCR as authorized. Though multinationals may not like the additional exposure of publication of the BCR authorization (including its text),[194] transparency requirements to stakeholders dictate that the BCR authorizations, including the text of the BCR itself, should be published. This recommendation is not reflected in the Proposed Regulation.

> **Recommendation 19**
> Require Lead DPAs to publish the BCR authorizations including the text of the BCR authorized.

Re (iii) Independence of Lead DPA

As to the requirement of independence, it is clear that the Lead DPAs should be independent from their stakeholders.[195] Insofar as individual Member States have not sufficiently ensured the independence of their DPA, this should be remedied.[196] As the Commission has announced it will remedy this in the upcoming revision of the Directive,[197] which is also reflected in the Proposed Regulation,[198] and has in the meantime already initiated enforcement action in this respect against

[193] BCR requirement (xiv) requires that the beneficiaries 'should have easy access to the BCR', which, where customers of multinationals are consumers, entails that the BCR for customer data are published on the corporate website of the multinational.

[194] The BCR regime does not require that BCR are published to the public at large. For instance BCR for employee data have to be made available to the employees only and not to the public at large. Additional exposure may be generated for the multinational if the BCR for employee data would be published (see Chapter 7, paragraph 7.3).

[195] Article 28(1) Directive. See for the requirements of independence as to DPAs: Case C-518/07, *Commission v Germany*, [2010] OJ C 113, at 3–4. On the role of DPAs, see Hustinx (Chapter 4, n 59), at 131. See more generally on the requirement of independence of national regulatory agencies Annetje Ottow and Saskia Lavrijssen, 'The legality of independent regulatory authorities', in: L. Besselink, F. Pennings, and A. Prechal (eds.), *The Eclipse of Legality* (Kluwer Law International 2010), Chapter 5, at 73–96.

[196] The independence of DPAs is not adequately ensured in all Member States, see Korff (-Chapter 2, n 27) for a review of the independence of the DPAs of the various Member States at 200–9.

[197] EC Communication on the revision of the Directive (Chapter 2, n 34), at para 2.5. See further the EDPS Opinion on the revision of the Directive (Chapter 2, n 35), at para 181: 'The EDPS fully supports the objective of the Commission to address the issue of the status of data protection authorities (DPAs), and to strengthen their independence, resources and enforcement powers. He recommends:

Codifying in the new legal instrument the essential notion of independence of DPAs, as specified by the ECJ;

Stating in the law that DPAs must be given sufficient resources;

Giving authorities harmonised investigation and sanctioning powers.'

[198] See on how the independence of DPAs is strengthened in the Proposed Regulation, Chapter 3, para 3.1.7.

certain Member States.[199] Since this is not of specific relevance to BCR only, no separate recommendation is included here.

Re (iv) Accountability ex post Lead DPA

The decision of a Lead DPA to authorize individual BCR is subject to judicial review by its national courts[200] (and ultimately by the ECJ).

But again, such judicial review is difficult owing to the fact that the BCR requirements are not included in the Directive. If *Recommendation 1* is followed and BCR are embedded in the revised Directive, this issue will be solved (see also in more detail Chapter 4, paragraph 4.4.3).

10.7.6 Accountability *ex post*: phase (b) monitoring and evaluation and phase (c) enforcement

The multinational is the actor involved in the monitoring and evaluation of BCR and the enforcement thereof. As the criteria for evaluation of phases (b) and (c) to a certain extent overlap, I will discuss them together.

Re (i) Monitoring and evaluation

No active monitoring takes place at the transnational (ie the Working Party 29) or the national level (by the Lead DPA). Given the extensiveness of the global compliance programmes of multinationals, a continuous monitoring by the Lead DPAs is unrealistic to say the least. The BCR regime currently provides that the multinational itself has to periodically audit its compliance, the results whereof have to be to the *internal accountability forums* of the multinational (ie its internal privacy function and its ultimate parent's board). The multinational has further to provide the results thereof to the Lead DPA at its request. Legitimacy demands, however, require the multinational also to implement to periodically review the totality of their BCR compliance programme to determine whether modification is necessary and to feed learning from this back into the organization on an ongoing basis. This is relevant as it is safe to say that data protection compliance programmes are still in development, where further innovations are possible and best practices have therefore not yet crystallized. My conclusion is that the chances of effectiveness of the BCR regime will be improved if companies would have to not only audit their compliance programmes and address any reported issues, but also evaluate their compliance programmes as a whole and incrementally improve them in light of this evaluation. Such incremental learning will also foster the

[199] See Case C-518/07, *Commission v Germany*, [2010] OJ C 113, at 3–4. On 6 April 2011, the Commission formally requested that Germany immediately comply with this judgment. See memo/11/220 on 11 April 2011, to be found on <http://europa.eu/rapid/pressReleasesAction.do?reference=MEMO/11/220&format=HTML&aged=0&language=EN&guiLanguage=en>.

[200] As required by Art 28(3) Directive.

self-regulatory capacity within the multinational and overcome (remaining) regulatory resistance.

As discussed in Chapter 9, paragraph 9.4.4, these criteria are also requirements under the accountability principle, see the 'common fundamental' sub 5 (ongoing risk assessment and mitigation) and 'common fundamental' sub 7 (programme risk assessment oversight and validation). I concluded there that these elements are not (sufficiently) part of the present BCR regime, and recommended adding these as requirements for BCR as per *Recommendation 12.*

Re (ii) Complaints and response procedures

A prerequisite for any form of redress is that BCR are enforceable. The requirement of enforceability is reflected in the first requirement of the BCR regime that the BCR should be 'externally binding' for the benefit of the beneficiaries of BCR (ie the employees and consumers whose data are processed under the BCR). BCR are in principle a unilateral undertaking by the multinational and not a contract. Many, but not all Member States take the view that rights may be granted to third parties by means of unilateral undertakings. If Lead DPAs in certain countries have doubts about whether the BCR are externally binding (ie legally enforceable) in their respective jurisdictions, a solution is to put a contract in place between the EU headquarters and, for instance, the group company in the jurisdiction of the DPA. In all Member States it is possible to grant third-party beneficiary rights in a contract. However, rather than having to resort to legal solutions to ensure that BCR are externally binding, it would simplify matters considerably if European legislators could provide in the revised Directive that BCR can be enforced as unilateral undertakings by the third-party beneficiaries (as was already *Recommendation 8*).

To ensure that individuals have sufficient possibility of redress the BCR regime requires that the multinational provides for an internal complaints and response procedure (BCR requirement (viii)). In Chapter 8, paragraph 8.1.3, it is described that individuals are provided with a central facility for complaints via the internal complaints procedure of the multinational, which overcomes many of the obstacles individuals encounter when enforcing their rights on a cross-border basis, even if damages of individuals are diffuse or too small to pursue through traditional judicial means and where jurisdictions have no (adequate) data protection laws or if insufficient enforcement (infrastructure) is available. If complaints are not adequately addressed, recourse is open to the Lead DPA and the courts of the Lead DPA (and ultimately the ECJ). At present certain DPAs lack certain enforcement rights (such as audit rights) and the fines the DPAs are authorized to impose are currently so low that these do not really pose a deterrent. It is therefore recommended to harmonize the enforcement and sanction powers of DPAs at the right level (as per *Recommendation 5*).

One of the requirements of the BCR regime is an internal complaints and response procedure (BCR requirement (viii)). If complaints are not adequately addressed, recourse is open to the Lead DPA and the courts of the Lead DPA (and ultimately the ECJ). This requirement is therefore adequately ensured.

Re (iii) Information

The information requirements of the BCR regime can be divided into *passive* information requirements (where the multinational has to provide information at request) and *active* information requirements (where the multinational has to provide information at its own initiative).

The *passive* information requirements are adequately safeguarded by the BCR regime:

- The multinational has an obligation to perform audits and has to provide the results of such audits to the Lead DPA[201] *upon its request* (see BCR requirement (xiii)).
- The Lead DPA has the right to perform audits itself (see BCR requirement (xii)).
- Compliance with the BCR is enforceable by the individuals via the Lead DPA and the court of the Lead DPA, as a part of which the multinational will have to provide information, explanations, and justifications (BCR requirement (ix)).
- The group companies have a duty to cooperate with the Lead DPA, to abide by its advice regarding the BCR, and to submit to its audits (BCR requirement (xii)).
- The burden of proof in respect of data protection breaches is on the multinational (BCR requirement (xi)).

As to *active* information requirements (ie mandatory periodical provision of information at the own initiative of the multinational) these are not adequately safeguarded in the current BCR regime. The active information obligations of the multinational are currently limited to reporting on privacy compliance to the *internal accountability forums* of the multinational:

- The results of the audit performed by the multinational have to be communicated to (i) its internal privacy function and (ii) its ultimate parent's board (BCR requirement (xiii)).
- Changes in the BCR must be reported to the Lead DPA (BCR requirement (xvi)).

[201] In Chapter 6, para 6.2, I discussed that the WP Opinions require that all DPAs obtain these rights, but that it has by now accepted that these rights may be concentrated with the Lead DPA; see Chapter 6, n 27.

- Group companies have to 'be transparent' if applicable law prevents them from complying with the BCR and, if in doubt what action to take, consult the Lead DPA (BCR requirement (xviii)).

The BCR regime does not prescribe any further active information duties of the multinational either to the Lead DPA or to the stakeholders. In light of the strong *passive* information requirements towards the Lead DPA, introduction of additional *active* information obligations towards the Lead DPA does not seem efficient. As already discussed in Chapter 9, paragraph 9.3.2, this will just increase administrative burdens on the multinationals, while leading to an information overload with the Lead DPA. This may lead to expectations of review of such information by the Lead DPA, which seems unrealistic and will therefore just work counterproductively. Further, many multinationals consider that actively providing auditing and evaluation reports to the Lead DPA may have a counterproductive effect by stifling the open manner in which internal audits and evaluations are performed if the participants are aware that the results will be reported to the Lead DPA. My recommendation is that other manners should be found to engage EU legislators in the learning process of the multinationals as to data protection compliance. This can be achieved for instance if the revised Directive were to empower the Commission to adopt delegated acts for the purpose of specifying the BCR requirements. As the Commission will be required to carry out appropriate consultations during its preparatory work, the experiences of the multinationals with their compliance programmes can be fed back. By further periodically evaluating these delegated acts, the learning cycle will be completed.

Insofar as stakeholders are concerned, multinationals do not currently have any *active* information requirements and the current *passive* information requirements (in case of complaints or litigation) seem to be insufficient. An active information requirement is therefore indicated. Such transparency towards stakeholders also follows from the introduction of the accountability principle discussed in Chapter 4, paragraph 4.3, which led to *Recommendation 12* (to prescribe the reporting on BCR in the annual reports of the company in a comparable format and further on the number of complaints received and the nature of these complaints under the internal complaints procedure). The Proposed Regulation does not contain a publication requirement.[202]

Re (v) Debate and re (vi) pass judgment

These requirements do not require much discussion as any decision of the multinational on complaints under the BCR are subject to review by the Lead DPA and the courts of the Lead DPA. Both instances traditionally incorporate the possibility to debate and pass judgment. As the Lead DPA and the courts of the EU

[202] The publication requirement included in earlier draft versions of the Proposed Regulation did not make it to the final version; see Chapter 9, n 78.

headquarters of the multinational have jurisdiction, sanctions can de facto be enforced on a global basis. There is currently no experience yet with the enforcement of the sanction powers by the Lead DPA. This has to be evaluated in due course. As to the enforcement powers of the individual Lead DPAs, there are concerns as to their harmonization and whether some of their sanctions are sufficient. This has already been discussed in Chapter 6, paragraph 6.5 and led to *Recommendation 4* (to provide for equal enforcement powers for DPAs and develop a common enforcement strategy for the DPAs to ensure equal enforcement).

10.8 Visualization Proposals

Figures 10.1, 10.2, and 10.3 visualize my proposals by comparing the current and future situation for the three phases of the regulatory process (a) norm-setting, (b) evaluation and monitoring, and (c) enforcement.[203]

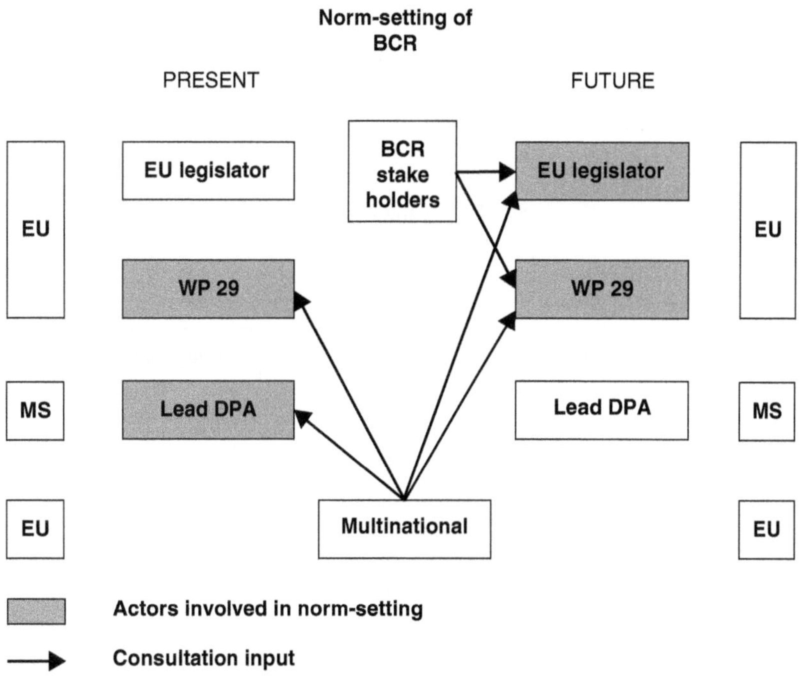

Figure 10.1 Norm-setting of BCR

[203] See Cafaggi (Chapter 4, n 65), at 215.

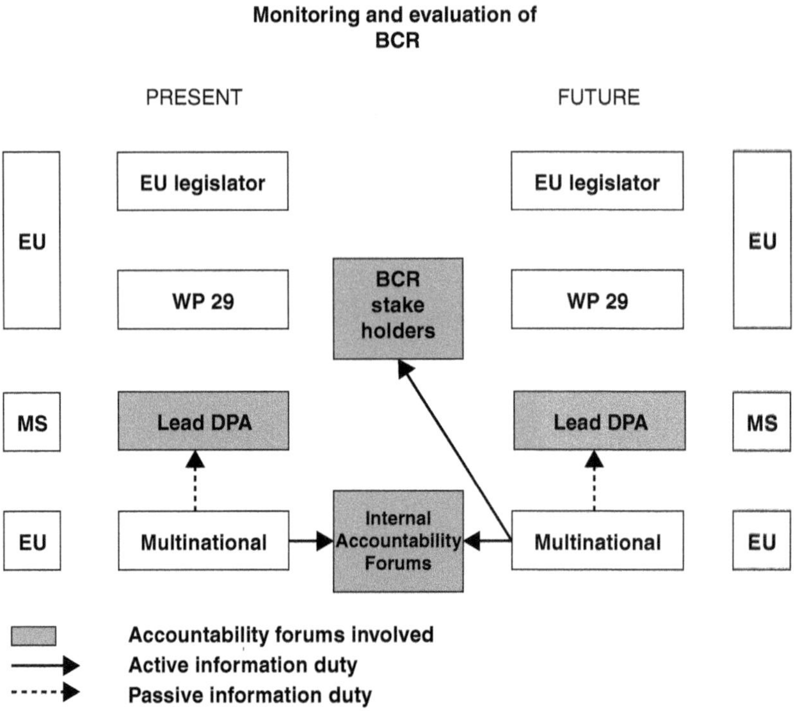

Figure 10.2 Monitoring and evaluation of BCR

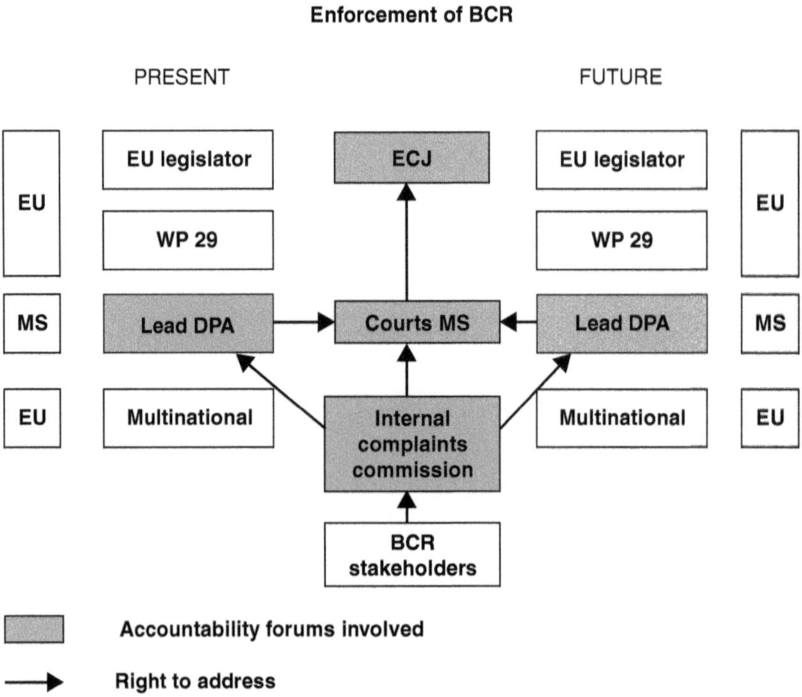

Figure 10.3 Enforcement of BCR

10.9 Conclusion as to Legitimacy of BCR as a Form of TPR

The conclusion is that the present requirements for BCR do require substantive updating to be aligned with legitimacy demands of TPR. This will not, however, lead to (many) new recommendations as these requirements also follow from an evaluation of the BCR regime against other disciplines (most notably the accountability perspective). Additional recommendations resulting from legitimacy demands to be made of BCR as a form of TPR are:

Recommendation 16

- Hold a proper consultation of all stakeholders of BCR prior to enacting the norms for BCR in the revised Directive.
- Instruct the Commission to hold a consultation of all stakeholders of BCR prior to further norm-setting on BCR by the Commission.

Recommendation 17

Instruct the Working Party 29 to amend its Rules of Procedure to remedy the lack of transparency as to its decision-making process.

Recommendation 18

- Ensure the independence of the Working Party 29 in accordance with the criteria developed by the ECJ for independence of DPAs.
- Instruct the Working Party 29 to amend its Rules of Procedure to ensure its accountability as to independence by:
  - having any experts participating in its meetings issue a public declaration of interests;
  - introducing job rotation of the members of any sub-groups installed by the Working Party 29.

Recommendation 19

Require Lead DPAs to publish BCR authorizations including the text of the BCR authorized.

11

BCR and Corporate Social Responsibility

Corporate Social Responsibility codes (*CSR codes*) typically involve a commitment by multinationals (usually in their Code of Ethics or Business Principles) to enhanced concern for human and civil rights, the environment, opposition to bribery and corruption, and fairness to their customers and suppliers. The number of multinationals adopting CSR codes has increased steadily over the years, and in the US all of the Fortune 500 companies have introduced CSR codes. The reporting on compliance with CSR codes has also steadily increased: 95 of the US top 100 companies produced a CSR report for 2005–06.[1] In December 2007 Vogel reported that approximately 300 CSR codes were issued governing 'most major global economic sectors, such as energy, minerals and mining, forestry, chemicals, textiles, apparel, footwear, sporting goods, project finance, and coffee and cocoa'.[2] The range of issues that multinationals include in their CSR codes is also constantly expanding and often now includes a commitment to protect the privacy of their employees and customers.[3] Many aspects of CSR codes have been discussed or referred to in previous paragraphs (and especially in the footnotes) as CSR codes (i) present similar issues under contract law (see Chapter 7); (ii) are based on the accountability principle (see Chapter 9); and (iii) are a form of TPR (see Chapter 10). As a consequence, I have already discussed how CSR codes being unilateral undertakings are enforced (see Chapter 7, paragraph 7.3), how CSR codes implement contractual supply chain management (see Chapter 7, paragraph 7.4), how legislators have introduced incentives to foster the introduction of CSR compliance programmes (see Chapter 9, paragraph 9.2), and whether self-regulatory CSR codes are a suitable tool to regulate human rights (see Chapter 10, paragraph 10.5). I have not yet discussed to what extent data protection is covered by *international instruments* setting guidelines for CSR codes, and if so, whether this has any repercussions for the BCR regime. This requires again a discussion of regulating human rights, not so much in the context of whether these may be regulated by self-regulation, but whether international instruments require that

[1] For an overview of the percentages over the last 10 years, see McBarnet (Chapter 4, n 24), at 10.

[2] David Vogel, 'Private Global Business Regulation' (2008) *Annual Review of Political Science* 11: 261–82, at 262.

[3] See Gus Hosein, 'Challenges in Privacy Advocacy', in Serge Gutwirth et al (eds.), *Reinventing Data Protection?* (Springer 2009), Chapter 15, at 254. See eg Art 1.5 of the General Business Principles of Royal Philips Electronics NV and its group companies, to be found at <http://www.philips.com/shared/assets/Investor_relations/pdf/businessprinciples/GeneralBusinessPrinciples.pdf>.

fundamental rights held by individuals should be viewed as imposing duties directly on multinationals even if these multinationals are active in countries *that do not recognize such human rights*. This is relevant for BCR as the current BCR regime allows multinationals to limit the scope of BCR to, for instance, EU-originated data only.[4] If international instruments on CSR require that the data of individuals in countries that do not provide for adequate data protection also be covered, these scope limitations would be in violation of these CSR instruments.

11.1 Norms Regulating CSR

Discussing *norms* regulating CSR seems a contradiction in terms. The adoption of CSR codes is routinely characterized as voluntary, companies going the extra mile to go beyond just compliance with law.[5] Though adoption of CSR codes is voluntary, there has been a firm push both from soft law (like international guidelines for CSR) and hard law (like disclosure and whistle-blowing requirements for CSR) that makes CSR codes much less voluntary than they may seem at first.[6] Further, once adopted, CSR codes are in most cases no longer voluntary.[7] However, also without explicit adoption of a CSR code, domestic and international courts have found avenues to grant binding effect to international soft law regarding CSR.[8]

What is relevant for BCR is to what extent any soft law concerning CSR also extends to data protection. And if so, whether such soft law actually requires (or is at least a strong driver for) multinationals to include data protection commitments in their CRS codes. In that case BCR would be more or less indispensible to ensure accountability in respect of these data protection commitments. Also, the question should be posed whether soft law in relation to CSR has by now become part of

[4] For other ways in which the scope of BCR may be limited see Chapter 6, para 6.2, in particular n 17 and n 18.

[5] The Commission in its Communication on CSR reported that there is large consensus that CSR is voluntary adopted behaviour by businesses over and above the legal requirement, see COM (2002) 347, at 8. In its subsequent 'Framework for Action,' the Commission made 'recognition of the voluntary nature of CSR' its first principle, see COM (2002) 347.

[6] McBarnet (Chapter 4, n 24), at 13.

[7] Cafaggi (Chapter 2, n 70), at 1 and 16; and Eijsbouts (Chapter 7, n 12), at 90 and fn 180 for further literature.

[8] Cafaggi (Chapter 2, n 70), at 28: 'While it is certainly true that the degree of "bindingness" is lower than (that of) hard law, it should be clearly acknowledged that domestic and international courts have granted binding effects to soft law through different avenues: international customary law, private law, mainly contract and civil liability', which various legal grounds are discussed at 27, with many examples in the footnotes see especially fn 154, at 28). See Clapham (Chapter 10, n 67). See for a comprehensive overview of the many (indirect) ways in which international CSR norms works through in the Dutch legal order and the various legal bases for enforcement thereof, A.J.A.J. Eijsbouts, 'Maatschappelijk (verantwoord) ondernemen: naast, in of met recht', in A.J.A.J. Eijsbouts et al, *Maatschappelijk Verantwoord Ondernemen en het Recht*, Preadviezen NJV 2010–1 (Kluwer 2010), at para 4, at 10 and Eijsbouts (Chapter 7, n 12), at paras 5, 6, and 7. See on enforcement of multilateral undertakings in general Chapter 7, para 7.3.

'good corporate governance' also labelled as 'corporate accountability' and as such part of the norms against which corporate conduct has to be evaluated.

11.2 CSR and International Law

11.2.1 Introduction

Discussing *international* norms regulating CSR also seems a contradiction in terms.[9] Multinationals are not subjects of international law as such.[10] Other than in specific EU regulations, etc, duties can only be imposed on them by national law, not by international law. As already discussed in Chapter 10, paragraph 10.5, human rights have also further traditionally been understood as rights that individuals enjoy against states. The fact is, however, that by now many multinationals wield as much or even more power than many states, and the conditions of individuals' lives are shaped as much by multinationals as by states, especially if such states are developing countries in need of revenues to repay their debts. As the CEO of Wal-Mart phrased it: 'Our size and scale means that even one small environmental change in our policy or our customers' habits has exponential impact around the world';[11] a phenomenon that has been labelled 'the Wal-Mart effect'. As rights are at bottom a response to the problem of power, the perspective on the role of multinationals has shifted over time. Multinationals in the context of CSR are nowadays considered more like states than individuals and thus should be located more on the public than the private side in assigning human rights and duties.[12] As Clapham in his classic work on human rights puts it: 'The definition of the public sphere (...) has to be adapted to include (...) new centres of power (...) such as (...) multinationals (...) [that] the individual now perceives [as sources] of authority, repression, and alienation.'[13] At the heart of these developments is the notion that companies owe obligations to the societies in which they operate, ie require a 'licence to operate', which licence has a number of dimensions. Besides the legal dimension, this licence also includes an economic and social dimension.[14] The social licence concept for instance includes the demands of the social environment, ie where a company's failure to meet social expectations can impair the company's reputation and trigger demands for stronger legal controls.[15] Due to these developments, there seems to be growing consensus in general terms that certain fundamental rights held by individuals may under circumstances be

[9] This paragraph draws on Muchlinski (Chapter 9, n 27), at 431–85 and Sinden (Chapter 10, n 62), at 501–26.

[10] Cafaggi (Chapter 2, n 70), at 28.

[11] As cited in McBarnet and Kurkchiyan (Chapter 5, n 41), at 61.

[12] Sinden (Chapter 10, n 62), at 506 and 515.

[13] Clapham, (Chapter 10, n 67), at 137.

[14] See for a good overview of the different dimensions of the licence to operate, Gunningham (Chapter 5, n 38), at 480–93. On licences to operate, see Eijsbouts (n 8), at para 3 at 8–10; and Eijsbouts (Chapter 7, n 12), at 61.

[15] Gunningham (Chapter 5, n 38), at 482.

viewed as imposing duties directly on multinationals even if these multinationals are active in countries that do not recognize such human rights.[16]

The question then arises as to what particular fundamental rights we are talking about. Clearly not all rights enforceable against states are relevant in the context of CSR of multinationals. For instance, a multinational will not act as prosecutor and the criminal procedure rights of individuals are therefore of no relevance vis-à-vis multinationals. Other rights will require some creative adaptation to apply in the context of multinationals.[17] Further, as indicated in Chapter 2, paragraph 2.3 there is a trend to bring increasingly more topics under the umbrella of CSR. At the moment consensus has not fully crystallized which fundamental rights should indeed lead to direct obligations for multinationals. I will argue below that (i) the right to data protection is included in the core human rights principles that are considered to impose direct duties on multinationals; and that (ii) the right to data protection does not require tailoring for application in this context.

11.2.2 Do the core CSR principles include data protection?

The following paragraphs will show that the right to privacy and data protection is one of the fundamental human rights covered by the international instruments of soft law on CSR. This is not surprising. Different from most human rights that traditionally are conceived of as norms primarily meant to shield individuals from repressive state action, data protection rights have from the outset been primarily directed at companies (see Chapter 10, paragraph 10.5.3). In the substantive literature on CSR, there is common ground on the international and intergovernmental human rights instruments that are leading in this respect, as evidenced by the consistent references thereto, such as the OECD Guidelines for Multinational Enterprises, the ILO's Tripartite Declaration of Principles concerning Multinational Enterprises and Social Policy, the UN Global Compact, and the Draft UN Norms 2003. Also relevant are the EU position on CSR and expected future

[16] See McBarnet (Chapter 4, n 24), at 56; McBarnet and Schmidt (Chapter 7, n 12), at 148–76; Clapham (Chapter 10, n 67), at Chapter 6 in particular para 6.11; and Chalmers (Chapter 10, n 67), Chapter 6, at 187–8. Willem van Genugten, 'Handhaving van Wereldrecht, een kritische inspectie van valkuilen en dilemma's,' 2010 *Nederlands Juristenblad* 1, at 12, as referred to in Chapter 10, n 67. See also in more detail Willem van Genugten, Kees Homan, Nico Schrijver, and Paul de Waart, *The United Nations of the Future; Globalization with a Human Face* (KIT Publishers, 2006). Also Cafaggi (Chapter 2, n 70), at 28: 'The limited direct applicability of soft law to private parties derives from the more general principle of public international law which, conventionally, imposes primary responsibility on States. This view has been criticized and increasingly international law obligations are also applied directly to private parties' referring to (see fn 156) 'Case 36/74, *Walrave v Association Union Cycliste Internationale*, 1974 E.C.R. 1405, where the ECJ held that anti-discriminatory provisions of the Treaty of Rome also apply to private entities (employment discrimination)'. However, see C.C. van Dam, *Onderneming en mensenrechten* (Boom Juridische Uitgevers 2008), at 29–30, who indicates that only a few international norms are directly applicable to multinationals (ie have horizontal effect), which includes the right to privacy. All other norms have indirect horizontal effect in the national legal orders, for instance via liability based on tort. See also Eijsbouts (Chapter 7, n 12), at 84 and 102.

[17] Sinden (Chapter 10, n 62), at 520.

developments based on the 'Ruggie Report'.[18] All these instruments include the right to privacy and data protection, as discussed below.

11.2.3 OECD Guidelines

In 1976, the first codification of CSR norms was undertaken by the OECD in the 'OECD Guidelines for Multinational Enterprises' (*OECD Guidelines*).[19] The OECD Guidelines were revised in 2000[20] and a further revision has been announced.[21] While the OECD Guidelines are non-binding, they benefit from the commitment of adhering governments to promote their actual observance by business. The OECD Guidelines are therefore relevant for multinationals whose corporate headquarters are established in one of the OECD member states (30 in total of which a number are EU Member States) and four additional states that have committed to the OECD Guidelines. The OECD Guidelines are further supported by the EU.[22] The OECD Guidelines have an international monitoring mechanism by means of National Contact Points (*NCP*). Parties that have complaints about a multinational's adherence to the OECD Guidelines can file complaints there. The relevant NCP subsequently performs fact-finding after which a mediation process begins. If this mediation process does not have the desired result (or the multinational does not cooperate), the NCP may draw up its own conclusions and publish these. This *naming and shaming* is a de facto sanction. Adherence to the OECD Guidelines is further often a requirement for the awarding of export credits and government subsidies. The character of the OECD Guidelines is therefore less voluntary than they may seem at face value.[23]

Pursuant to Principle 1 of the OECD Guidelines, multinationals should 'respect the human rights of those affected by their activities consistent with the host government's international obligations and commitments'. The human rights respected by the OECD host governments will include the right to privacy and data protection as these are recognized as such in the international conventions on human rights to which these host states are party.[24] Further, pursuant to Principle 5

[18] For a full overview, including how these instruments and initiatives relate to each other and their legal status, see the Report of the United Nations High Commissioner on Human Rights on the responsibilities of transnational corporations and related business enterprises with regard to human rights, UN Doc E/CN.4/2005/91, 15 February 2005, to be found at <http://ap.ohchr.org/documents/alldocs.aspx?doc_id=10900>.

[19] To be found at <http://www.oecd.org>.

[20] OECD Guidelines for multinational enterprises, Paris: OECD Publishing 2008, <http://www.oecd.org>.

[21] See OECD, Consultation on an update of the OECD Guidelines for Multinational Enterprises, Consultation Note, 8 December 2009, at <http://www.oecd.org>.

[22] For the list of adhering governments and the support of the EU, see the OECD Guidelines (n 20), at 6.

[23] Eijsbouts (n 8), at 17.

[24] See Art 12 Universal Declaration of Human Rights (1948); Art 17 International Covenant on Civil and Political Rights (1966); paras 5, 6(14), and 12(2b) ILO Code of Practice: Protection of Workers Personal Data (1997); Art 3(a) UN Guidelines for the Regulation of Computerized Personal Data Files (1990); and Art 9 OECD Guidelines: On the Protection of Privacy and Transborder Flows

Chapter VII of the OECD Guidelines, multinationals are required to 'respect consumer privacy and provide protection for personal data'. In the official commentary to this Principle, it is stated that 'enterprises could look to the OECD Guidelines Governing the Protection of Privacy and Transborder Flows of Personal Data as a helpful basis for protecting personal data'.[25]

11.2.4 UN Global Compact

The United Nations Global Compact (*UN Global Compact*)[26] is a voluntary initiative for multinationals that are committed to aligning their operations and strategies with human rights, labour conditions, the environment, and anti-corruption. Its 10 Principles find their origin in the Universal Declaration of Human Rights (among three other declarations).[27] The UN Global Compact was 'grandfathered' by UN Secretary-General Kofi Annan and launched on 26 July 2000. Currently about 6400 business and 2300 non-business participants in over 130 countries have engaged with the UN Global Compact. Pursuant to the first Principle, 'Businesses should support and respect the protection of internationally proclaimed human rights'. The commentary makes clear that this is understood to include the right to privacy and data protection of workers and consumers.[28]

11.2.5 Draft UN Norms 2003

At the level of the United Nations, there have been two initiatives to adopt instruments similar to the OECD Guidelines, but these have never passed the draft stage. The first is the Draft UN Code of Conduct for Transnational Corporations 1990[29] and the second is the Draft UN Norms on the Responsibilities of Transnational Corporations and Other Business Enterprises with regard to Human Rights 2003[30] (*Draft UN Norms 2003*). After various consultations and further

of Personal Data (1980). See further for the recognition of privacy and data protection as human rights in the EU, fn 3.

[25] See Part II of the OECD Guidelines (Chapter 2, n 40), at para 52.

[26] <http://www.unglobalcompact.org>.

[27] <http://www.unglobalcompact.org/AboutTheGC/TheTenPrinciples/index.html>.

[28] On Principle 1: 'Another approach some businesses find helpful is to start by looking at what the business is already doing to respect and support human rights, such as (...) respecting the privacy of customers and workers (...)', to be found at <http://www.unglobalcompact.org/AboutTheGC/TheTenPrinciples/principle1.html>. The self-assessment tool provided for the business participants to the UN Global Compact also contains a question on privacy compliance: 'Does the company respect the privacy of its employees whenever it gathers private information or monitors the workplace?' (Principle 1). The explanatory notes to this question say that: 'The question relates to the right to privacy. It is based on general principles contained in the following: Article 12 of the Universal Declaration of Human Rights (1948); Article 17 of the International Covenant on Civil and Political Rights (1966); paras. 5, 6 (14) and 12 (2b) of the ILO Code of Practice: Protection of Workers Personal Data (1997); Article 3(a) of the UN Guidelines for the Regulation of Computerized Personal Data Files (1990); and Article 9 of the OECD Guidelines: On the Protection of Privacy and Transborder Flows of Personal Data (1980).' See: <http://www.globalcompactselfassessment.org/humanrights/fairtreatment>.

[29] UN Doc E/1990/94.

[30] UN Doc E/CN.4/Sub.2/2003/12/Rev.2.

research it was determined that these Draft UN Norms 2003 would not become a legally binding instrument.

Pursuant to paragraph E, paragraph 12 of the Draft UN Norms 2003, multinationals have to 'observe standards that protect civil and political rights and are otherwise in accordance with the International Covenant on Civil and Political Rights and the relevant general comments adopted by the Human Rights Committee'.[31] The right to privacy qualifies as a civil right under Article 17 of the International Covenant on Civil and Political Rights.

11.2.6 ILO's Tripartite Declaration of Principles concerning Multinational Enterprises and Social Policy

In 1977, the International Labour Organization (*ILO*) adopted the Tripartite Declaration of Principles concerning Multinational Enterprises and Social Policy, which was subsequently amended in 2000 and 2006.[32] ILO's Governing Body includes representatives of governments and employers' and workers' organizations (ie it is tripartite). The principles laid down in this instrument offer guidelines to these social parties and multinationals in such areas as employment and conditions of work and life, which these parties are recommended to observe on a voluntary basis.

Pursuant to the first principle of the General Policy of the ILO Declaration, the social partners and multinationals should 'respect relevant international standards', and the preamble contains a specific reference to the activities of the OECD and the UN Commission on Transnational Corporations (which include the right to privacy and data protection). Pursuant to the first principle, the parties should further 'respect the Universal Declaration of Human Rights and the corresponding International Covenants adopted by the General Assembly of the United Nations' and 'should also honour commitments which they have freely entered into, in conformity with the national law and accepted international obligations.' The Universal Declaration of Human Rights and the International Covenant on Civil and Political Rights includes the right to privacy and data protection. In 1997, the ILO itself issued the ILO Code of Practice: Protection of Workers Personal Data.[33]

[31] Commentary on the Norms on the responsibilities of transnational corporations and other business enterprises with regard to human rights, at 14(e). To be found at: <http://www.unhchr.ch/Huridocda/Huridoca.nsf/0/293378ff2003ceb0c1256d7900310d90/$FILE/G0316018.pdf.>

[32] As adopted by the Governing Body of the International Labour Office at its 204th Session (Geneva, November 1977) as amended at its 279th (November 2000) and 295th Session (March 2006), to be found at <http://www.ilo.org>.

[33] Article 12 Universal Declaration of Human Rights (1948) and Art 17 International Covenant on Civil and Political Rights (1966). The ILO Code of Practice: Protection of Workers Personal Data, may be found at <http://www.ilo.org>.

11.2.7 EU position on CSR

The EU has opted to actively improve and promote the international instruments mentioned above, and therefore also encompasses the right to privacy and data protection.[34] So far, the EU approach to CSR has been based on voluntarism,[35] but the general expectation is that EU regulatory action on CSR is imminent.[36] Unlike the Commission, the European Parliament has consistently been in favour of a normative rather than a voluntary approach[37] and as early as 1998 called the Commission to bring out a European directive that would address all CSR issues, including making corporate reporting on CSR mandatory.[38] The EU further promotes CSR through the international development cooperation agreements it enters into with developing countries, by making human rights observance an essential element and a condition of trade terms and development aid.[39] This 'human rights clause' now applies to over 120 countries.[40]

However, even without regulatory action at the EU level, the initial Green Paper of the Commission on CSR is based on the premise that multinationals will observe both national and international legislation, in particular the human rights covenants.[41]

[34] This was made explicit for the first time in July 2001 in the European Commission, Green Paper, Promoting a European Framework for Corporate Social Responsibility, COM (2001) 366 final, at para 17. This approach was reinforced by subsequent communications from the Commission, the European Council, and the Parliament (European Commission, Communication Concerning Corporate Social Responsibility: A Business Contribution to Sustainable Development, COM (2002) 347 final, Council Resolution on Corporate Social Responsibility 2003 OJ C39/3). For an overview of activities of the EU to promote the international CSR instruments and further the debate thereon, see Voiculesco (Chapter 9, n 56), at 378–86; and L.F.H. Enneking, 'Crossing the Atlantic, The Political and Legal Feasibility of European Foreign Direct Liability Cases' 2009 *The George Washington International Law Review*, vol 40, at 907–10.

[35] The definition of CSR upon which the Green Paper is based is one of CSR: 'a concept whereby companies integrate social and environmental concerns in their business operations and in their interaction with their stakeholders on a voluntary basis'.

[36] Voiculesco (Chapter 9, n 56), at 395; Eijsbouts (n 8), at 15, and Enneking (n 34), at 912.

[37] As early as 1998, the European Parliament called for the establishment of a European framework setting a 'legal basis for multinationals operations all over the world', see European Parliament, Resolution on EU Standards for European Enterprises Operating in Developing Countries: Towards a European Code of Conduct, INI/1998/2075. See also A4-0508/98-Howitt and A4-0198/98-Fassa.

[38] European Parliament, Report on the Commission's Green Paper on Promoting a European Framework for Corporate Social Responsibility, A5-0159/2002 Final, at 18. The European Parliament has been part of the European CSR debate from the beginning. For an initial publication on this topic, see European Parliament, Resolution on EU Standards for European Enterprises Operating in Developing Countries: Towards a European Code of Conduct, INI/1998/2075. See also A4-0508/98-Howitt and A4-0198/98-Fassa.

[39] Such a clause has been defined and refined since the early 1990s. To ensure consistency in the text used and its application, a European Council Decision of May 1995 spelt out the modalities: Commission Communication on the Inclusion of Respect or Democratic Principles and Human Rights in Agreement Between the Community and Third Countries, COM(95) 216 of 23 May 1995 and Council Conclusions of 29 May 1995, EU Bulletin No 5 1995 at point 1.2.3. See on the impact of the human rights clause: Voiculescu (Chapter 9, n 56), at 384.

[40] Voiculesco (Chapter 9, n 56), at 385.

[41] See Green Paper (n 34), at para 52 and Voiculescu (Chapter 9, n 56), at 381 and 395.

Further, the relevant international norms have now found their way into many of the legal orders of the Member States, by means of a wide range of government initiatives, which in most cases combine a mix of hard and soft law (codes of conduct and reporting mechanisms being among the most common).[42] Authors researching the status of CSR norms in the international instruments therefore generally conclude that these norms are (to a certain extent) already part of the legal orders of the Member States and enforceable against multinationals.[43] This will *a fortiori* be the case if companies have adopted CSR codes containing a unilateral undertaking to abide by these CSR norms.[44] Authors even conclude that corporate self-regulation may be indispensable to avoid liability, for instance in industries with a high potential of violating particular rights.[45] An example given in this context is the situation where a parent company influences the production process of its products by issuing corporate guidelines. If a subsidiary causes damages following these instructions, the parent may be liable if the procedures issued were below the required standard of a reasonable operator.[46] Taking this one step further, a parent company may breach a duty of care to employees and customers if a parent is establishing subsidiaries in another country (known for instance not to have proper product safety requirements) without taking proper care of its production management by issuing corporate guidelines (including proper training and monitoring and auditing).[47] Regulatory action of European legislators on CSR will therefore to a certain extent be a codification of already existing and enforceable CSR norms.

11.2.8 The Ruggie Framework for future action

In 2005, the extensive discussions and fundamental differences of opinion on the Draft UN Norms 2003, and a call for making these Norms legally binding for

[42] Voiculescu (Chapter 9, n 56), at 394. See for an overview of the Dutch soft and hard law regulatory mix: Eijsbouts (Chapter 7, n 7), at 10.

[43] See McBarnet (Chapter 4, n 24), at 56; McBarnet and Schmidt, (Chapter 7, n 12), at 148–76; and Clapham (Chapter 10, n 67), at para 6.11. See further Stephen Bottomley and Anthony Forsyth, 'The New Corporate law: Employees' Interest', in McBarnet, Voiculescu, Campbell, *The New Corporate Accountability, Corporate Social Responsibility and the Law* (Cambridge University Press 2007), at 335, where it is recognized that 'in everyday corporate practice, the boundaries between the law and codes are not always felt so clearly. This idea builds on the argument developed elsewhere, that the category of law known as corporate law is being transformed into a broader category of law known as "corporate governance"': 'corporate law may in the past have been described as a one-dimensional body of law concerned with regulating the interests of investors, managers and directors. The impact of regulation has been to transform this body of law into an emerging law of corporate governance, which seeks to integrate the policies and concerns of broad areas of regulation into corporate law'. See for a similar conclusion in respect of the Dutch legal order, Eijsbouts (Chapter 7, n 12), at 82.

[44] See Chapter 7, para 7.3 for possibilities of enforcing such unilateral undertakings. For a comprehensive overview of common legal basis for enforcement of CSR codes in the various jurisdictions, see Glinski (n 10), at 119–47.

[45] See Glinski (Chapter 7, n 10), at 122 and 143.

[46] Glinski (Chapter 7, n 10), at 143.

[47] See for examples in a number of jurisdictions, Glinski (Chapter 7, n 10), at 143.

multinationals, led to the appointment of John Ruggie as UN Special Representative for Business and Human Rights and in 2008 to the 'Ruggie Report'.[48] The Ruggie Report presents a framework for further action on CSR and was adopted by the UN following extensive consultations with leading non-governmental organizations (*NGOs*) and large global business organizations (and was labelled the *UN Framework*).[49] The UN Framework lists the core human rights principles on which business has an impact and therefore must be respected, which include the right to privacy and data protection.[50]

The UN Framework subsequently comprises three core principles: (i) the duty of the state to protect against human rights abuses by third parties, including business; (ii) the corporate responsibility to respect human rights; (iii) and the need for more effective access of individuals to remedies. As to the first principle concerning the duty of states, the UN Framework is clear in the position that states should take action to help prevent human rights abuses *abroad* by corporations based within their territory, provided these actions meet an overall reasonableness test, which includes non-intervention in the internal affairs of other states and that states should be more creative in this respect than they are at present.[51]

As to the second principle, the UN Framework is clear that multinationals have a duty to observe human rights principles recognized by international law, even where national law does not provide so, and to have a system of 'due diligence' to ensure such compliance:

> 23. The corporate responsibility to respect human rights is the second principle. It is recognized in such soft law instruments as the [ILO] Tripartite Declaration of Principles Concerning Multinational Enterprises and Social Policy and the OECD Guidelines for Multinational Enterprises. It is invoked by the largest global business organizations in their submission to the mandate, which states that companies 'are expected to obey the law, even if it is not enforced, and to respect the principles of relevant international instruments where national law is absent'. It is one of the commitments companies undertake in joining the Global Compact. And the Special Representative's surveys document the fact that companies worldwide increasingly claim they respect human rights.
>
> 24. To respect rights essentially means not to infringe on the rights of others - put simply, to do no harm. Because companies can affect virtually all internationally recognized rights, they should consider the responsibility to respect in relation to all such rights, although some may require greater attention in particular contexts. There are situations

[48] See the Ruggie Report (Chapter 10, n 65).

[49] See the background paper on the UN Framework at 1, to be found at <http://198.170.85.29/Ruggie-protect-respect-remedy-framework.pdf>. The Human Rights Council of the UN has unanimously approved the Ruggie Framework and it is now referred to as the 'UN Framework'.

[50] See the Ruggie Report (Chapter 10, n 65), at 16. This can further be derived from the references to the international instruments made in the Ruggie Report (Chapter 10, n 65) (ie the OECD Guidelines, the ILO Declaration, and the UN Global Compact), which all include the right of privacy and data protection. For actual impact of multinationals on privacy, see Addendum 2 to the Ruggie Report, at 13, reporting that in 20–25 per cent of the cases reviewed an impact on privacy was reported.

[51] See Ruggie Report (Chapter 10, n 65), at para 17–22.

> in which companies may have additional responsibilities - for example, where they perform certain public functions, or because they have undertaken additional commitments voluntarily. But the responsibility to respect is the baseline expectation for all companies in all situations.
>
> 25. Yet how do companies know they respect human rights? Do they have systems in place enabling them to support the claim with any degree of confidence? Most do not. What is required is due diligence - a process whereby companies not only ensure compliance with national laws but also manage the risk of human rights harm with a view to avoiding it. The scope of human rights-related due diligence is determined by the context in which a company is operating, its activities, and the relationships associated with those activities.

The UN Framework further contains many suggestions for governments as to how to implement the UN Framework in both national and international jurisdictions.[52] The UN Framework is generally accepted as a milestone in the long-standing discussion on human rights obligations of multinationals.[53] Based on the Ruggie Report, the conclusion is justified that enforceable human rights obligations for multinationals are, or in any event will become, the norm rather than the exception.[54] This has consequences for the BCR regime as the BCR regime currently allows multinationals to limit the scope of BCR to for instance EU-originated data only.[55] I therefore recommend that EU legislators provide that the BCR regime be applicable to all data processed by a multinational.

Recommendation 20

Provide that the BCR regime applies to all personal data processed by the multinational adopting BCR.

11.2.9 Due diligence

The UN Framework requires that companies perform 'due diligence' in respect of their human rights compliance, which requires not only that they ensure compliance with national law, but also manage the risk of harming human rights with a view to avoiding harm. The scope of this due diligence is, according to the UN Framework, determined by the context in which a company operates, its activities, and the relationships associated with those activities. It is not surprising that the

[52] See also Ruggie Report (Chapter 10, n 65) at 16.

[53] Eijsbouts (n 8), at 15.

[54] Eijsbouts (Chapter 7, n 12), at 102 suggests introducing a global treaty imposing liability on the parent company for its group companies for violations of CSR norms by its group companies.

[55] See for other ways in which the scope of BCR may be limited Chapter 6, para 6.2, in particular n 17 and n 18.

'due diligence' as prescribed by the UN Framework to a large extent corresponds with the generally accepted accountability principles as discussed in Chapter 9. The due diligence requirement entails the implementation of a data protection compliance programme similar to that of BCR, with proper supply chain management, worldwide training, monitoring, auditing, and reporting.

> The Special Representative's research and consultations indicate that a basic human rights due diligence process should include the following:
>
> **Policies**
>
> 60. Companies need to adopt a human rights policy. Broad aspirational language may be used to describe respect for human rights, but more detailed guidance in specific functional areas is necessary to give those commitments meaning.
>
> **Impact assessments**
>
> 61. Many corporate human rights issues arise because companies fail to consider the potential implications of their activities before they begin. Companies must take proactive steps to understand how existing and proposed activities may affect human rights. The scale of human rights impact assessments will depend on the industry and national and local context. While these assessments can be linked with other processes like risk assessments or environmental and social impact assessments, they should include explicit references to internationally recognized human rights. Based on the information uncovered, companies should refine their plans to address and avoid potential negative human rights impacts on an ongoing basis.
>
> **Integration**
>
> 62. The integration of human rights policies throughout a company may be the biggest challenge in fulfilling the corporate responsibility to respect. As is true for States, human rights considerations are often isolated within a company. That can lead to inconsistent or contradictory actions: product developers may not consider human rights implications; sales or procurement teams may not know the risks of entering into relationships with certain parties; and company lobbying may contradict commitments to human rights. Leadership from the top is essential to embed respect for human rights throughout a company, as is training to ensure consistency, as well as capacity to respond appropriately when unforeseen situations arise.
>
> **Tracking performance**
>
> 63. Monitoring and auditing processes permit a company to track ongoing developments. The procedures may vary across sectors and even among company departments, but regular updates of human rights impact and performance are crucial. Tracking generates information needed to create appropriate incentives and disincentives for employees and ensure continuous improvement. Confidential means to report non-compliance, such as hotlines, can also provide useful feedback.

Evaluating these due diligence requirements, they do not lead to additional recommendations for BCR other than those already made based on evaluation of BCR against general accountability requirements (see *Recommendation 12*).

According to the UN Framework, companies further have to provide for *access to remedies*. In this respect the UN Framework explicitly notes that non-judicial mechanisms should be provided for by the company 'as enforcement by traditional judicial means is not adequate for enforcement of CSR'.[56]

> 84. For Non-judicial mechanisms play an important role alongside judicial processes. They may be particularly significant in a country where courts are unable, for whatever reason, to provide adequate and effective access to remedy. Yet they are also important in societies with well-functioning rule of law institutions, where they may provide a more immediate, accessible, affordable, and adaptable point of initial recourse.

The UN Framework further provides for criteria for such non-judicial mechanisms:

> 92. Non-judicial mechanisms to address alleged breaches of human rights standards should meet certain principles to be credible and effective. Based on a year of multi-stakeholder and bilateral consultations related to the mandate, the Special Representative believes that, at a minimum, such mechanisms must be:
>
> (a) Legitimate: a mechanism must have clear, transparent and sufficiently independent governance structures to ensure that no party to a particular grievance process can interfere with the fair conduct of that process;
> (b) Accessible: a mechanism must be publicized to those who may wish to access it and provide adequate assistance for aggrieved parties who may face barriers to access, including language, literacy, awareness, finance, distance, or fear of reprisal;
> (c) Predictable: a mechanism must provide a clear and known procedure with a time frame for each stage and clarity on the types of process and outcome it can (and cannot) offer, as well as a means of monitoring the implementation of any outcome;
> (d) Equitable: a mechanism must ensure that aggrieved parties have reasonable access to sources of information, advice and expertise necessary to engage in a grievance process on fair and equitable terms;
> (e) Rights-compatible: a mechanism must ensure that its outcomes and remedies accord with internationally recognized human rights standards;
> (f) Transparent: a mechanism must provide sufficient transparency of process and outcome to meet the public interest concerns at stake and should presume transparency wherever possible; non-State mechanisms in particular should be transparent about the receipt of complaints and the key elements of their outcomes.

Again, evaluating the dispute procedures of BCR, these seem to comply with the above criteria, but for the requirement of transparency of complaints made under these dispute procedures and their outcomes. The requirement on companies to report on their compliance with CSR was already part of the first publications of the European Parliament on CSR.[57] These transparency requirements already resulted

[56] Ruggie Report (Chapter 10, n 65), at para 84.

[57] European Parliament, Report on the Commission's Green Paper on Promoting a European Framework for Corporate Social Responsibility, A5-0159/2002 Final, at 18.

from the evaluation of BCR against general accountability requirements (Chapter 9, paragraph 9.4.3) and requirements of legitimacy (Chapter 10, paragraph 10.7.6) and will therefore not lead to a separate recommendation here.

Also, the UN Framework directs national governments (to the extent they have not done so yet) to ensure CSR norm-setting, enforcement, and adequate remedies for individuals. Multinationals are therefore well advised to embark in a timely fashion on their 'due diligence' in respect of data protection compliance as practice shows that implementation involves a time-intensive company-wide project, which requires the input and cooperation of nearly all business functions and suppliers of such company.[58] On the other hand, the BCR regime (as amended according to the *Recommendations*) may serve as a modern case study or even a template for the 'due diligence' as envisaged by the UN Framework.

11.2.10 CSR and the trust game

Taking a momentary sidestep, but nonetheless interesting in this context, the recommendation for transparency about compliance is indicated also from the perspective of economic theory, especially game theory. Research on CSR from this perspective shows that a crucial part of effective CSR is the 'reputation mechanism' which is the basis for the 'trust game':[59]

> Reputation is one of the most valuable, albeit intangible, of the firm's assets. It is reputation that induces the stakeholders to trust the firm and consequently to cooperate with it, so that transactions come about at low costs of control or bargaining.

For the trust game to work:

> principles and precautionary rules of behaviour must be communicated, given that reputation depends on them. The stakeholders base their judgements on the match among principles and rules announced ex ante, level of membership into the principles

[58] The implementation of BCR projects in most cases takes a period of at least two years.

[59] Sacconi (Chapter 2, n 86), at 317. For a comprehensive description of the trust game, see Sacconi at 319–21. Simply put, the trust game evolves around transactions between a stakeholder and a company. The stakeholder has to decide whether or not to place trust in the firm, entering or not entering into an exchange relationship with the firm. The firm then decides between abusing or not abusing the trust. If, after the stakeholder has entered, the firm does not abuse its trust, there will be a reasonably good outcome for both. However, if the stakeholder places trust in the firm, the latter has interest in abusing that trust, because in the short term (for the relevant transaction) this will create the most remuneration. Consequently for the subsequent transaction, the stakeholder will not grant its trust and the transaction will not take place. The underlying idea of the game of reputation is that there is an alternative solution which permits the transactions between the two parties to take place, if the basic game is infinitely iterated and an incentive is thus created for the firm to protect its reputation. In the overall game there are an infinite series of stakeholders (each a short-run player for just one game and deciding whether to enter or not) and the firm is the long-run player, lasting for all repetitions of the games. The firm's reputation is based on the probability assigned by each of the stakeholders that the firm will abuse or not abuse. The firm's reputation, whichever type it may be, increases as evidence is gathered that confirms it, but it diminishes dramatically if a single observation is made that falsifies the type. Short-run stakeholders will only decide to trust the firm after a series of non-abuses, as a result of which the expected utility of the entry decision is greater than non-entry. At this turning point, the firm may offset the cost of its initial series of non-entries against subsequent entries.

domain exhibited by any events [that] have occurred, and the behaviour adopted. Essential, therefore, is social accounting and reporting of the firm's performance in relation to the principles and norms announced.

This is not just a requirement for CSR codes to be effective. It may be elucidating for companies to realize that it is also in their interest to reap the benefits of this 'trust game'. To achieve this they will have to be transparent about their data protection compliance.

11.2.11 CSR of human rights

A final note is due on the topic of whether CSR codes are appropriate to regulate human rights. I have discussed TPR of human rights in Chapter 10, paragraph 10.5, where the conclusion was that TPR is not per se unsuitable to regulate human rights. Whether the relevant TPR is suitable will depend rather on how the TPR normative framework is set up. Given the general caveat for self- and co-regulation 'when human rights are at stake' made by the EU institutions,[60] it is not surprising that the view of the EU institutions on *CSR* also seems to be that these should not be based on voluntary guidelines and voluntary initiatives of multinationals.[61] Though the Commission at an earlier time reported a 'large consensus for voluntary CSR', this consensus already at the time did not include trade unions and civil society organizations that 'emphasised that voluntary initiatives are not sufficient to protect workers' and citizens rights'.[62] Also the Ruggie Report has made clear in many instances that 'compliance efforts cannot succeed unless we bring governments back in the equation'.[63] Based on the above, the general expectation is that EU regulatory action on CSR is imminent. If legislation on CSR is adopted, the question is whether this will make much difference for data protection obligations of multinationals and BCR. The answer is in all probability that this will make no difference. As indicated above, the Directive (and non-EU data protection laws for that matter) are at present already directed at multinationals. Further, if *Recommendation 2* is indeed followed, the Directive will provide for the required general framework legislation for BCR. Insofar as new CSR legislation were to be forthcoming containing obligations for multinationals in respect of CSR (including data protection), the expectation is that the BCR regime (as amended according to the *Recommendations*) will comply with any 'due diligence' or other requirements under such CSR legislation. Even, such amended BCR regime may serve as a modern case study or template for such 'due diligence' envisaged by the UN Framework.

[60] White Paper on European Governance (Chapter 2, n 75), at 2; and the Inter-Institutional Agreement on 'Better Lawmaking' (Chapter 2, n 75), in particular Art 16.

[61] The first to express this opinion was the European Parliament, in its Report on the Commission's Green Paper on Promoting a European Framework for Corporate Social Responsibility, A5-0159/2002 Final, at 18.

[62] Communication from the Commission concerning CSR, COM (2002) 347, at 4.

[63] See citation in McBarnet (Chapter 4, n 24), at 28.

12
Conclusion

BCR have come a long way. Initially multinationals put bottom-up pressure on the Working Party 29 and the individual DPAs to acknowledge their corporate privacy policies as an alternative legal tool for facilitating their intercompany transfers of personal data. Now the Working Party 29 is proposing to use BCR as a general template for corporate data protection compliance programmes per se. Further, the parallel with CSR codes is compelling. CSR codes are also based on accountability. Though in principle companies are free to choose the manner in which they achieve CSR compliance, in the absence of a CSR code and a compliance programme, non-compliance will in practice be a given. The same will apply if the accountability principle is also introduced for data protection. The conclusion is even justified that already at present international soft law instruments regulating CSR require multinationals to include data protection commitments in their CSR codes, as a consequence of which BCR are more or less indispensible to ensure accountability in this respect. This turns BCR from an alternative tool for data protection compliance into an indispensable tool for data protection for multinationals. In this light it is high time that the current uncertainties as to the validity and enforcement of BCR are solved (as per *Recommendations 2 and 9*), that the BCR authorization procedure is streamlined (as per *Recommendation 4*) and that the enforcement powers of DPAs are harmonized and a common enforcement strategy for the DPAs is developed to ensure equal enforcement (as per *Recommendation 5).* This should not be achieved by way of further opinions of the Working Party 29, but by a revision of the Directive, which should preferably take the form of an EU regulation (as per *Recommendation 6*). In both cases EU legislators are advised to delegate in such EU regulation or revised Directive, the detailed norm-setting to the Commission (as per *Recommendation 2*).

To ensure a wider uptake of BCR within the EU, European legislators are further advised to ensure that incentives are created for multinationals to adopt BCR (as per *Recommendation 13*). To further the recognition of BCR also in countries outside the EU for outbound data transfers from these countries, EU legislators are advised to engage with such countries to achieve mutual recognition and enforcement of BCR (as per *Recommendation 7*).

Multinationals introducing BCR have a strong interest in including a choice of law and forum clause in their BCR, as this will facilitate that all complaints under the BCR are ultimately dealt with by the Lead DPA and the courts of the Lead DPA, as the provisions of the BCR are negotiated with this DPA under the applicability of the Lead DPA's own law (this being the law under which the provisions of the BCR were drafted). This ensures for the multinational a consistent and predictable interpretation and application of the BCR. For the same reason the multinational has an interest in the Lead DPA having central supervision over the BCR. This is also in the interest of the beneficiaries of the BCR. Also based on my earlier research into the applicability and jurisdiction regime of the Directive, the conclusion of this book is that despite the fact that (i) the Directive has a broad scope of application; (ii) individuals have broad legal rights and remedies under the Directive; and (iii) DPAs have broad jurisdiction and enforcement powers, the current EU data protection regime does not lead to data protection compliance in practice or meaningful redress for individuals. Even if the applicability and jurisdiction regime of the Directive are properly harmonized and improved as per the recommendations in my earlier research,[1] this will not solve the cross-border enforcement issues encountered by individuals in this age of 'big data'. The BCR dispute procedure, as backed up by central government enforcement by the Lead DPA and courts of the Member State of origin of the multinational, provides individuals with a central facility for complaints which will address the many obstacles to cross-border enforcement of data protection by individuals. The individual will be able to file a complaint in his own language, with the group company with which he has a relationship and this regardless of where the breach occurred or which of the group companies was responsible for the breach. The group company that receives the complaint will be responsible for ensuring that the complaint is processed through the complaints procedure of the multinational and will ensure the required translations. If the complaints procedure does not lead to a satisfying result for the individual, the group company will facilitate the filing of the complaint with the Lead DPA or the courts of the Lead DPA. This procedure will lead to enforceable rights even if damages suffered by individuals are diffuse or too small to pursue through traditional judicial means, jurisdictions have no (adequate) data protection laws or if insufficient enforcement (infrastructure) is available. It further overcomes language issues and time zones and minimizes cost.

Given the uncertainties identified as to whether a valid choice of law and forum can be made in BCR for the laws and the courts of the Lead DPA, EU legislators are advised to ensure that such choices of law and forum may be made in BCR (as per *Recommendation 9*).

If European legislators were to introduce the country of origin principle also for data protection (as per *Recommendation 1*), it would seem that the possibility of a choice of law and forum in BCR would no longer be necessary, as in that case (i) the data processing operations of the multinational would already be governed by (just) the data protection law of the Member State of origin of the multinational; and (ii) the DPA and the courts of such Member State would already have central jurisdiction. Since the country of origin principle only applies to the extent that the data processing operations of the multinational are governed by EU data protection

[1] Moerel (Chapter 1, n 8, Chapters 2 and 3).

law, and since the BCR apply to the data processing operations of the multinational *worldwide*, the possibility of a choice of law and forum (and therefore *Recommendation 9*) remains relevant.

Having embraced the introduction of the country of origin and in its wake having accepted that in BCR a choice of law and forum may be made, I recommended stretching the imagination yet one step further. A multinational having BCR will then have to comply with the data protection law of its Member State of origin only. Multinationals, however, would ultimately be best served if they could apply one uniform data processing regime on *a global basis*. In other words, they would be best served if they could apply the BCR regime on a global basis, *including in the EU* (as per *Recommendation 10*). This will further reduce the administrative burdens of multinationals as they will be able to apply the BCR regime also in the EU without the necessity of introducing additional EU-specific requirements.

To foster the acceptability of BCR on a global scale, the search for common reference points with other disciplines and perspectives has resulted in a number of common requirements across disciplines. A striking example is the requirement of transparency of compliance results. This led to *Recommendation 12* to impose on multinationals a reporting obligation on their data protection compliance in their annual report in a comparable format. This transparency recommendation is based on the outcomes of an evaluation of the BCR regime from the:

(i) accountability perspective in general literature applicable to other fields of law;[2]
(ii) the introduction of the accountability principle for data protection;[3]
(iii) general policy research and literature in the area of consumer protection;[4]
(iv) general policy literature in the area of company law;[5]
(v) the law and economics approach;[6]
(vi) BCR as a form of TPR and legitimacy requirements in this respect;[7]
(vii) BCR as a form of CSR;[8] and
(viii) economic policy theory.[9]

It is also true for most other recommendations that each is based on the outcomes of the evaluation from at least two of these disciplines (see overview below). Many of the recommendations further overlap with those made by the Rand Report, the Working Party 29, the European Data Protection Supervisor (*EDPS*), the Centre for Information Policy Leadership (*CIPL*), and the Commission. The results thus combined may hopefully result in a better theoretical foundation for revision of the

[2] See Chapter 9, para 9.2.1.
[3] See Chapter 9, para 9.4.3.
[4] See Chapter 4, para 4.4.2.
[5] See Chapter 9, para 9.2.1.
[6] See Chapter 9, para 9.2.1.
[7] See Chapter 10, para 10.7.6.
[8] See Chapter 11, para 11.2.9.
[9] See Chapter 11, para 11.2.10.

Directive based on these recommendations of which many have already found their way into the Proposed Regulation.

12.1 Hypotheses

In paragraph 1.2.2, I discussed that while writing this book I had two hypotheses. The first being that BCR as an instance of TPR can do better than the present territory-based state regulation of data protection by the Directive. In summery my conclusion as to this hypothesis is that even if the applicability and jurisdiction regime of the Directive is harmonized and improved as per the recommendations in my earlier research,[10] BCR do indeed better than the present regulation of data protection in the Directive (i) in providing data protection to individuals; (ii) in providing enforcement to individuals; and (iii) in regulating transborder data flows.

12.2 Re (i) Avoiding Gaps in Data Protection

If BCR have indeed a global scope (as per *Recommendation 20*), data protection is also provided to data processed by the multinational in countries where no or less data protection is provided for by state laws. Thus gaps in data protection left by the regulation of nation states are no longer relevant.

12.3 Re (ii) Avoiding Gaps in Enforcement

If a choice of law and forum may indeed be validly made in BCR (as per *Recommendation 8*), and beneficiaries of BCR may indeed enforce their rights as unilateral undertakings under BCR (as per *Recommendation 9*) BCR will provide for better enforcement of data protection by individuals in practice. Individuals are provided with a central facility for complaints and the many obstacles to cross-border enforcement of data protection by individuals will be addressed. The individual will be able to file a complaint in his own language, with the group company with which he has a relationship and this regardless of where the breach occurred or which of the group companies was responsible for the breach. The group company that receives the complaint will be responsible for ensuring that the complaint is processed through the complaints procedure of the multinational and will ensure the required translations. If the complaints procedure does not lead to a satisfactory result for the individual, the group company will facilitate the filing of the complaint with the Lead DPA or the courts of the Lead DPA. This procedure will lead to enforceable rights even if damages of individuals are diffuse or too small to pursue through traditional judicial means, jurisdictions have no (adequate) data

[10] Moerel (Chapter 1, n 8, Chapters 2 and 3).

protection laws or if insufficient enforcement (infrastructure) is available. It further overcomes language issues and time zones and minimizes cost. These are all issues that presently constitute obstacles to the cross-border enforcement of data protection rights.

12.4 Re (iii) Improved Regulation of Transborder Data Flows

BCR result in lower administrative burdens for multinationals while at the same time providing more material data protection and redress in practice to individuals. This is a vast improvement to the situation where transborder data flows within multinationals are regulated by means of the EU Standard Contractual Clauses, which leads to high administrative burdens for multinationals, while at the same time the broad contractual data protection rights and remedies of individuals do not lead to meaningful data protection and redress in practice. If the BCR regime defines the core accountability principles for the situation when a multinational transfers personal data to third parties (as per *Recommendation 13*), the same will apply in the case of data transfers by the multinational to a third party outside its group of companies.

When writing this book, the second hypothesis was that the BCR regime is at present not sufficiently aligned with principles of PIL, best practices when implementing the principle of accountability, generally accepted legitimacy demands made of TPR, and best practices as to CSR. Here my conclusion is that this is indeed the case. If *Recommendations 12–20* are followed, BCR will be better positioned to be globally acceptable as a form of TPR to regulate global corporate conduct in the area of data protection.

APPENDIX 1

Overview of Recommendations to EU Legislators

Recommendations

1. Introduce the country of origin principle both for applicable law and jurisdiction and extend this principle also to countries having obtained an adequacy ruling under Article 25(6) Directive.
2. Recognize BCR as an appropriate tool to provide adequate safeguards for the transfer of data and define the main substantive requirements for BCR:
   - to be defined in general principles
   - to be set at an adequate level
   - taking into account the specific comments in Chapter 6, paragraph 6.6.6,

   and to delegate the further norm-setting to the Commission pursuant to Articles 290 and 291 TFEU.
3. Define the MRP and impose the MRP on all Member States.
4. Investigate whether it is indicated to establish a pan-European Data Protection Supervisory Authority to which certain decision-making and enforcement powers are delegated in case of data processing operations with an EU dimension.
5. Provide for equal enforcement powers for DPAs and develop a common enforcement strategy for the DPAs to ensure equal enforcement.
6. Replace the Directive by an EU regulation when revising the Directive.
7. Engage with non-EU countries in mutual recognition and enforcement of BCR as a tool for cross-border data transfers.
8. Provide that BCR can be enforced as unilateral undertakings by the beneficiaries of BCR.
9. Provide that in BCR a choice of law and forum may be made for the laws and courts of the Member State of the Lead DPA and further that the Lead DPA will have central supervision in respect of such BCR, and may involve other DPAs if so required for enforcement in the territories of the other Member States.
10. Provide that if multinationals adopt BCR, the BCR apply instead of the national data protection laws of the Member States.
11. Introduce incentives for multinationals to adopt BCR, such as:
    - risk-based sanctions for a violation of data protection by multinationals that have implemented BCR (whereby the implementation of a proper compliance program is a mitigating factor)
    - provide that if multinationals adopt BCR, the BCR apply instead of the national data protection laws of the Member States (as per *Recommendation 10*)
    - provide that in BCR a choice of law and forum may be made for the laws and courts of the Member State of the Lead DPA (see *Recommendation 9*)

- abolish the notification requirements, or, as next best alternative, provide for the possibility of central notification of all data processing of a multinational to the Lead DPA
- provide that multinationals having BCR do not have to have intra-group data processor agreements in place if group companies process personal data on behalf of other group companies
- provide that multinationals having BCR in place may in respect of onward data transfers to third parties have their EU (Delegated) Headquarters enter into EU Standard Contractual Clauses with such third party on behalf of all group companies
- exempt multinationals that have BCR in place from the *ex ante* consultation or authorization requirements as included in the Proposed Regulation.

12. To delegate the detailed norm-setting in respect of the BCR requirements to the Commission in accordance with Articles 290 and 291 TFEU, or as the next best alternative, to define the BCR requirements as general obligations of the multinational on the basis of the common fundamentals defined by the Centre for Information Policy Leadership, and add as requirements for BCR:
    - prescribe the reporting on BCR in the annual reports of company in a comparable format
    - the multinational should be transparent vis-à-vis the third-party beneficiaries as to the number of complaints received and the nature of these complaints under the internal complaints procedure.
13. To delegate the detailed norm-setting in respect of the core accountability principles for onward transfers under BCR by multinationals to third parties to the Commission in accordance with Article 290 and 291 TFEU, or as the next best alternative, define these accountability principles taking into account the guidelines identified in Chapter 9, paragraph 9.5.3.
    - To impose certain obligations direct on processors (such as in any event the data security obligations and data transfer obligations).
    - To provide that controllers and processors may divide responsibilities between them.
14. Not to follow the recommendation by the Working Party 29 to include a provision in the revised Directive that processors that process data against the instructions of the controller shall be considered to be a controller.
15. Not to follow the recommendation by the Working Party 29 to include a provision in the revised Directive that controllers remain accountable and responsible for the protection of data for which they are controllers, even if the data have been transferred to other controllers.
16. Hold a proper consultation of all stakeholders of BCR prior to enacting the norms for BCR in the revised Directive.
    - Instruct the Commission to hold a consultation of all stakeholders of BCR prior to the further norm-setting on BCR by the Commission.
    - Instruct the Working Party 29 to hold a consultation of relevant stakeholders prior to the Working Party 29 issuing opinions on BCR.
17. Instruct the Working Party 29 to amend its Rules of Procedure to remedy the lack of transparency as to its decision-making progress.

18.
    - Ensure the independence of the Working Party in accordance with the criteria developed by the ECJ for independence of DPAs.
    - Instruct the Working Party 29 to amend its Rules of Procedure to ensure its accountability as to independence by:
        - having any experts participating in its meetings issue a public declaration of interests
        - introducing job rotation of the members of any sub-groups installed by the Working Party 29.
19. Require Lead DPAs to publish the BCR authorizations including the text of the BCR authorized.
20. Provide that the BCR regime should apply to all personal data processed by the multinational adopting the BCR.

Overview of all recommendations

	Contract Law	PIL	Accountability	TPR	CSR	First Report	Rand Report	WP 29	EDPS	CIPL	EC
Recommendation											
1								•			
2			•	•	•	•	•	•	•	•	•
3							•	•	•	•	
4											•
5							•	•	•		•
6									•		•
7							•			•	•
8	•	•	•	•	•						
9		•									
10											
11	•		•		•		•	•	•	•	•
12			•	•	•						•
13	•		•								•
14											
15											
16				•			•				•
17				•		•			•		•
18				•					•		•
19			•	•	•						
20					•						

APPENDIX 2

BCR for Employee Data

[Company]
Privacy Code for Employee Data
Introduction

[Company] has committed itself to the protection of personal data of [Company] employees in the [Company] *[Code of Conduct]*.

This Privacy Code for Employee Data indicates how this principle shall be implemented. For the privacy code applicable to customer, supplier, and business partner data, refer to the *Privacy Code for Customer, Supplier, and Business Partner Data. [insert hyperlink to Code]*

Article 1—*Scope, Applicability, and Implementation*

Scope	1.1	This Code addresses the Processing of Personal Data of [Company] Employees (*Employee Data*) by [Company] or a Third Party on behalf of [Company].
Electronic and paper-based Processing	1.2	This Code applies to the Processing of Employee Data by electronic means and in systematically accessible paper-based filing systems.
Applicability of local law and Code	1.3	Employees keep any rights and remedies they may have under applicable local law. This Code shall apply only where it provides supplemental protection for Employee Data. Where applicable local law provides more protection than this Code, local law shall apply. Where this Code provides more protection than applicable local law or provides additional safeguards, rights, or remedies for Employees, this Code shall apply.
Sub-policies and notices	1.4	[Company] may supplement this Code through sub-policies or notices that are consistent with this Code.
Responsibility	1.5	The [*Responsible Executive*] shall be accountable for compliance with this Code.
Effective Date	1.6	This Code has been adopted by the *[Head of Legal or Head of Compliance]* of *[Company Holding]* and shall enter into force as of [] (*Effective Date*) and shall be published on the *[Company Intranet]* and be made available to Employees upon request.
Code supersedes prior policies	1.7	This Code supersedes all [Company] privacy policies and notices that exist on the Effective Date to the extent they address the same issues.
Implementation	1.8	This Code shall be implemented in the [Company] organization based on the time frames specified in Article 21.
Role of [Company EU Headquarters]	1.9	*[Company Holding]* has tasked *[Company EU Headquarters]* with the coordination and implementation of this Code.

Article 2—*Purposes for Processing Employee Data*

Legitimate Business Purposes	2.1	Employee Data shall be collected, used or otherwise Processed for one (or more) of the following purposes (*Business Purposes*): (i) *Human resources and personnel management.* This purpose includes Processing that is necessary for the performance of an employment or other contract with an Employee (or to take necessary steps at the request of an Employee prior to entering into a contract), or for managing the employment-at-will relationship, eg management and administration of recruiting and outplacement, compensation and benefits, payments, tax issues, career and talent development, performance evaluations, training, travel and expenses, and Employee communications (ii) *Business process execution and internal management.* This purpose addresses activities such as scheduling work, recording time, managing company assets, provision of central processing facilities for efficiency purposes, conducting internal audits and investigations, implementing business controls, and managing and using Employee directories (iii) *Health, safety, and security.* This purpose addresses activities such as those involving occupational safety and health, the protection of company and Employee assets, and the authentication of Employee status and access rights (iv) *Organizational analysis and development and management reporting.* This purpose addresses activities such as conducting Employee surveys, managing mergers, acquisitions, and divestitures, and Processing Employee Data for management reporting and analysis (v) *Compliance with legal obligations.* This purpose addresses the Processing of Employee Data as necessary for compliance with a legal obligation to which [Company] is subject or (vi) *Protecting the vital interests of Employees.* This is where Processing is necessary to protect the vital interests of an Employee. *[list all categories of business purposes]* Where there is a question whether a Processing of Employee Data can be based on a purpose listed above, it is necessary to seek the advice of the appropriate Privacy Officer before the Processing takes place.
Employee consent	2.2	Employee consent generally cannot be used as a legitimate basis for Processing Employee Data. One of the Business Purposes must exist for any Processing of Employee Data. If applicable local law so requires, in addition to having a Business Purpose for the relevant Processing, [Company] shall also seek Employee consent for the Processing. If none of the Business Purposes applies, [Company] may request Employee consent for Processing Employee Data, but only if the Processing has no foreseeable adverse consequences for the Employee. A request for Employee consent requires the authorization of the appropriate Privacy Officer prior to seeking consent.

Denial or withdrawal of Employee consent

2.3 The Employee may both deny consent and withdraw consent at any time without consequence to his employment relationship. Where Processing is undertaken at the Employee's request (eg he subscribes to a service or seeks a benefit), he is deemed to have provided consent to the Processing.
When seeking Employee consent, [Company] must inform the Employee:

(i) of the purposes of the Processing for which consent is requested;
(ii) of the possible consequences for the Employee of the Processing; and
(iii) that he is free to refuse and withdraw consent at any time without consequence to his employment relationship.

Limitations on Processing Data of Dependants of Employees

2.4 [Company] will Process Data of Dependants of an Employee if:
(i) the Data were provided with the consent of the Employee or the Dependant;

(ii) Processing of the Data is reasonably necessary for the performance of a contract with the Employee or for managing the employment-at-will relationship, or
(iii) the Processing is required or permitted by applicable local law.

Article 3—*Use for Other Purposes*

Use of Data for Secondary Purposes

3.1 Generally, Employee Data shall be used only for the Business Purposes for which they were originally collected (*Original Purpose*). Employee Data may be Processed for a legitimate Business Purpose of [Company] different from the Original Purpose (*Secondary Purpose*) only if the Original Purpose and Secondary Purpose are closely related. Depending on the sensitivity of the relevant Employee Data and whether use of the Data for the Secondary Purpose has potential negative consequences for the Employee, the secondary use may require additional measures such as:

(i) limiting access to the Data;
(ii) imposing additional confidentiality requirements;
(iii) taking additional security measures;
(iv) informing the Employee about the Secondary Purpose;
(v) providing an opt-out opportunity; or
(vi) obtaining Employee consent in accordance with Article 2.2.

Generally permitted uses of Data for Secondary Purposes

3.2 It is generally permissible to use Employee Data for the following Secondary Purposes provided appropriate additional measures are taken in accordance with Article 3.1:

(i) transfer of the Data to an Archive;
(ii) internal audits or investigations;
(iii) implementation of business controls;
(iv) statistical, historical, or scientific research;
(v) preparing for or engaging in dispute resolution;
(vi) legal or business consulting; or
(vii) insurance purposes.

Article 4—*Purposes for Processing Sensitive Data*

Specific purposes for Processing Sensitive Data	4.1	This Article sets forth specific rules for Processing Sensitive Data. [Company] shall Process Sensitive Data only to the extent necessary to serve the applicable Business Purpose. The following categories of Sensitive Data may be collected, used, or otherwise Processed only for one or more of the purposes specified below: [(i) *Racial or ethnic data*: (a) in some countries photos and video images of Employees qualify as racial or ethnic data. [Company] may process photos and video images for the protection of [Company] and Employee assets, site access, and security reasons and for inclusion in Employee directories; (b) providing preferential status to persons from particular ethnic or cultural minorities to remove or reduce inequality or to ensure diversity in staffing, provided that use of the relevant Sensitive Data allows an objective determination that an Employee belongs to a minority group and the Employee has not filed a written objection to the relevant Processing. (ii) *Physical or mental health data* (including any opinion of physical or mental health and data relating to disabilities and absence due to illness or pregnancy): (a) providing health services to an Employee provided that the relevant health data are processed by or under the supervision of a health professional who is subject to professional confidentiality requirements; (b) administering pensions, health and welfare benefit plans, maternity, paternity or family leave programmes, or collective agreements (or similar arrangements) that create rights depending on the state of health of the Employee; (c) reintegrating or providing support for Employees entitled to benefits in connection with illness or work incapacity; (d) assessing and making decisions on (continued) eligibility for positions, projects, or scope of responsibilities; (e) providing facilities in the workplace to accommodate health problems or disabilities. (iii) *Criminal data* (including data relating to criminal behaviour, criminal records, or proceedings regarding criminal or unlawful behaviour): (a) assessing an application by an Employee to make a decision about the Employee or provide a service to the Employee; (b) protecting the interests of [Company] with respect to criminal offences that have been or, given the relevant circumstances are suspected to have been, committed against [Company] or its Employees. (iv) *Sexual preference* (including data relating to partners of Employees): (a) administering Employee pensions and benefits programs; (b) administering Employee memberships. (v) *Religious or philosophical beliefs*: (a) accommodating religious or philosophical practices, dietary requirements, or religious holidays.]
General Purposes for Processing of Sensitive Data	4.2	In addition to the specific purposes listed in Article 4.1 above, all categories of Sensitive Data may be Processed for one (or more) of the following: (i) as required by or allowed under applicable local law;

(ii) for the establishment, exercise, or defence of a legal claim;
(iii) to protect a vital interest of an Employee, but only where it is impossible to obtain the Employee's consent first;
(iv) to the extent necessary to comply with an obligation of international public law (eg treaties); or
(v) [where the Sensitive Data have manifestly been made public by the Employee].

Employee consent for Processing Sensitive Data 4.3 Employee consent generally cannot be used as a legitimate basis for Processing Sensitive Data. One of the grounds listed in Article 4.1 or 4.2 must exist for any Processing of Sensitive Data. If applicable local law so requires, in addition to having one of the grounds listed in Article 4.1 or 4.2 for the relevant Processing, [Company] shall also seek Employee consent for the Processing. If none of the grounds listed in Article 4.1 or 4.2 applies, [Company] may request Employee consent for Processing Sensitive Data, but only if the Processing has no foreseeable adverse consequences for the Employee (eg Employee diversity programs or networks, research, product development, selection of candidates in hiring or management development processes). Article 2.3 applies to the granting, denial, or withdrawal of Employee consent.

Prior Authorization of Privacy Officer 4.4 Where Sensitive Data are Processed based on a requirement of law other than the local law applicable to the Processing, or based on the consent of the Employee, the Processing requires the prior authorization of the appropriate Privacy Officer.

Use of Sensitive Data for Secondary Purposes 4.5 Sensitive Data of Employees or Dependants may be Processed for Secondary Purposes in accordance with Article 3.

Article 5—*Quantity and Quality of Data*

No Excessive Data 5.1 [Company] shall restrict the Processing of Employee Data to those Data that are reasonably adequate for and relevant to the applicable Business Purpose. [Company] shall take reasonable steps to delete Employee Data that are not required for the applicable Business Purpose.

Storage period 5.2 [Company] generally shall retain Employee Data only for the period required to serve the applicable Business Purpose, to the extent reasonably necessary to comply with an applicable legal requirement or as advisable in light of an applicable statute of limitations. [Company] may specify (eg in a sub-policy, notice, or records retention schedule) a time period for which certain categories of Employee Data may be kept.
Promptly after the applicable storage period has ended, the Privacy Officer shall direct that the Data be:

(i) securely deleted or destroyed;
(ii) anonymized [alternative: de-identified]; or
(iii) transferred to an Archive (unless this is prohibited by law or an applicable records retention schedule).

Quality of Data 5.3 Employee Data should be accurate, complete, and kept up-to-date to the extent reasonably necessary for the applicable Business Purpose.

'Self-service' 5.4 Where [Company] requires an Employee to update his own Employee Data, [Company] shall remind him at least once a year to do so.

Article 6—*Employee Information Requirements*

Information requirements	6.1	[Company] shall inform Employees through a published privacy policy or notice about: (i) the Business Purposes for which their Data are Processed; (ii) which Group Company is responsible for the Processing; and (iii) other relevant information (eg the nature and categories of the Processed Data, the categories of Third Parties to which the Data are disclosed (if any), and how Employees can exercise their rights).

Article 7—*Employee Rights of Access and Rectification*

Rights of Employees	7.1	Every Employee has the right to request an overview of his Employee Data Processed by or on behalf of [Company]. Where reasonably possible, the overview shall contain information regarding the source, type, purpose, and categories of recipients of the relevant Employee Data. If the Employee Data are incorrect, incomplete, or not Processed in compliance with applicable law or this Code, the Employee has the right to have his Data rectified, deleted, or blocked (as appropriate). In addition, the Employee has the right to object to the Processing of his Data on the basis of compelling grounds related to his particular situation.
Procedure	7.2	The Employee should send his request to the appropriate Privacy Officer. Prior to fulfilling the request of the Employee, [Company] may require the Employee to: (i) specify the type of Employee Data to which he is seeking access; (ii) specify the data system in which the Employee Data are likely to be stored; (iii) specify the circumstances in which [Company] obtained the Employee Data; (iv) show proof of his identity; and (v) in the case of a request for rectification, deletion, or blockage, specify the reasons why the Employee Data are incorrect, incomplete, or not Processed in accordance with applicable law or the Code.
Response period	7.3	Within four weeks of [Company] receiving the request, the Privacy Officer shall inform the Employee in writing either (i) of [Company] position with regard to the request and any action [Company] has taken or will take in response or (ii) the ultimate date on which he will be informed of [Company's] position, which date shall be no later than [x] weeks thereafter.
Complaint	7.4	An Employee may file a complaint in accordance with Article 16.1 if: (i) the response to the request is unsatisfactory to the Employee (eg the request is denied); (ii) the Employee has not received a response as required by Article 7.3; or (iii) the time period provided to the Employee in accordance with Article 7.3 is, in light of the relevant circumstances, unreasonably long and the Employee has objected but has not been provided with a shorter, more reasonable time period in which he will receive a response.
Denial of requests	7.5	[Company] may deny an Employee request if: (i) the request does not meet the requirements of Articles 7.1 and 7.2; (ii) the request is not sufficiently specific; (iii) the identity of the relevant Employee cannot be established by reasonable means; (iv) the request is made within an unreasonable time interval of a prior request or otherwise constitutes an abuse of rights. A time interval between requests of six months or less shall generally be deemed to be an unreasonable time interval.

Article 8—*Security and Confidentiality Requirements*

Data security	8.1	[Company] shall take appropriate commercially reasonable technical, physical, and organizational measures to protect Employee Data from misuse or accidental, unlawful, or unauthorized destruction, loss, alteration, disclosure, acquisition, or access. To achieve this, [Company] has developed and implemented the [Company] [*list main ICT policies*] and other policies relating to the protection of Employee Data.
Staff access	8.2	Staff members shall be authorized to access Employee Data only to the extent necessary to serve the applicable Business Purpose and to perform their job.
Confidentiality obligations	8.3	Staff members who access Employee Data must meet their confidentiality obligations.

Article 9—*Automated Decision-making*

Automated decisions	9.1	Automated tools may be used to make decisions about Employees but decisions may not be based solely on the results provided by the automated tool. This restriction does not apply if: (i) the use of automated tools is required or authorized by law; (ii) the decision is made by [Company] for purposes of (a) entering into or performing a contract or (b) managing the employment-at-will relationship, provided the underlying request leading to a decision by [Company] was made by the Employee (eg where automated tools are used to filter job applications); or (iii) suitable measures are taken to safeguard the legitimate interests of the Employee, eg the Employee has been provided with an opportunity to express his point of view.

Article 10—*Transfer of Employee Data to Third Parties*

Transfer to Third Parties	10.1	This Article sets forth requirements concerning the transfer of Employee Data from [Company] to a Third Party. Note that a transfer of Employee Data includes situations in which [Company] discloses Employee Data to Third Parties (eg in the context of corporate due diligence) or where [Company] provides remote access to Employee Data to a Third Party.
Third Party Controllers and Third Party Processors	10.2	There are two categories of Third Parties: (i) *Third Party Processors*: these are Third Parties that Process Employee Data solely on behalf of [Company] and at its direction (eg Third Parties that Process Employee salaries on behalf of [Company]) (ii) *Third Party Controllers*: these are Third Parties that Process Employee Data and determine the purposes and means of the Processing (eg government authorities or service providers that provide services directly to Employees).
Transfer for applicable Business Purposes only	10.3	[Company] shall transfer Employee Data to a Third Party to the extent necessary to serve the applicable Business Purpose for which the Employee Data are Processed (including Secondary Purposes as

Article 10 (*cont.*)

per Article 3 or purposes for which the Employee has provided consent in accordance with Article 2).

Third Party Controller contracts

10.4 Third Party Controllers (other than government agencies) may Process Employee Data only if they have a written contract with [Company]. In the contract, [Company] shall seek to contractually protect the data protection interests of its Employees. All such contracts shall be drafted in consultation with the appropriate Privacy Officer.

Third Party Processor contracts

10.5 Third Party Processors may Process Employee Data only if they have a written contract with [Company]. The contract with a Third Party Processor must include the following provisions:

(i) the Processor shall Process Employee Data only in accordance with [Company]'s instructions and for the purposes authorized by [Company];
(ii) the Processor shall keep the Employee Data confidential;
(iii) the Processor shall take appropriate technical, physical, and organizational security measures to protect the Employee Data;
(iv) the Third Party Data Processor shall not permit sub-contractors to Process Personal Data in connection with its obligations to [Company] without the prior written consent of [Company];
(v) [Company] has the right to review the security measures taken by the Third Party Processor and the Third Party Processor shall submit its relevant data processing facilities to audits and inspections by [Company] or any relevant government authority;
(vi) the Third Party Processor shall promptly inform [Company] of any actual or suspected security breach involving Employee Data; and
(vii) the Third Party Processor shall take adequate remedial measures as soon as possible and shall promptly provide [Company] with all relevant information and assistance as requested by [Company] regarding the security breach.

Transfer of Data to a Non-Adequate Country

10.6 This Article sets forth additional rules for the transfer of Employee Data to a Third Party located in a country that is not considered to provide an 'adequate' level of protection for Employee Data (*Non-Adequate Country*).
Employee Data may be transferred to a Third Party located in a Non-Adequate Country only if:

(i) the transfer is necessary for the performance of a contract with the Employee, for managing the employment-at-will relationship, or to take necessary steps at the request of the Employee prior to entering into a contract or an employment-at-will relationship, eg for processing job applications;
(ii) a contract has been concluded between [Company] and the relevant Third Party that provides for safeguards at a similar level of protection as that provided by this Code; the contract shall conform to any model contract requirement under applicable local law (if any);
(iii) the transfer is necessary for the conclusion or performance of a contract concluded in the interest of the Employee between [Company] and a Third Party (eg in case of the booking of an airline ticket);

(iv) the Third Party has been certified under the United States Safe Harbor Program or any other similar program that is recognized as providing an 'adequate' level of data protection;
(v) the Third Party has implemented binding corporate rules or a similar transfer control mechanisms which provide adequate safeguards under applicable law;
(vi) the transfer is necessary to protect a vital interest of the Employee;
(vii) the transfer is necessary for the establishment, exercise, or defence of a legal claim;
(viii) the transfer is necessary to satisfy a pressing need to protect the public interests of a democratic society; or
(ix) the transfer is required by any law to which the relevant Group Company is subject.
Items (viii) and (ix) above require the prior approval of the Chief Privacy Officer.

Employee consent for transfer

10.7 [Company] generally shall not seek Employee consent for a transfer of Employee Data to a Third Party located in a Non-Adequate Country. One of the grounds for transfer listed in Article 10.6 must exist. If applicable local law so requires, in addition to having one of the grounds listed in Article 10.6, [Company] shall also seek Employee consent for the relevant transfer. If none of the grounds listed in Article 10.6 exists, [Company] may request Employee consent for a transfer to a Third Party located in a Non-Adequate Country, but only if

(i) the transfer has no foreseeable adverse consequences for the Employee; or
(ii) the consent is requested prior to the participation of the Employee in specific projects, assignments, or tasks that require the transfer of the Data.
Requesting Employee consent for a transfer requires the prior approval of the appropriate Privacy Officer. Prior to requesting Employee consent, the Employee shall be provided with the following information:
(i) the purpose of the transfer;
(ii) the identity of the transferring Group Company;
(iii) the identity or categories of Third Parties to which the Data will be transferred;
(iv) the categories of Data that will be transferred;
(v) the country to which the Data will be transferred; and
(vi) the fact that the Data will be transferred to a Non-Adequate Country.

Transfers between Non-Adequate Countries

10.8 This Article sets forth additional rules for transfers of Employee Data that were collected in connection with the activities of a Group Company located in a Non-Adequate Country to a Third Party also located in a Non-Adequate Country. In addition to the grounds listed in Article 10.6, these transfers are permitted if they are:

(i) necessary for compliance with a legal obligation to which the relevant Group Company is subject;
(ii) necessary to serve the public interest; or
(iii) necessary to satisfy a Business Purpose of [Company].

Article 11—*Overriding Interests*

Overriding Interests	11.1	Some of the obligations of [Company] or rights of Employees under this Code may be overridden if, under the specific circumstances at issue, a pressing need exists that outweighs the interest of the Employee (*Overriding Interest*). An Overriding Interest exists if there is a need to: (i) protect the legitimate business interests of [Company] including (a) the health, security, or safety of Employees; (b) [Company]'s intellectual property rights, trade secrets, or reputation; (c) the continuity of [Company]'s business operations; (d) the preservation of confidentiality in a proposed sale, merger, or acquisition of a business; or (e) the involvement of trusted advisors or consultants for business, legal, tax, or insurance purposes; (ii) prevent or investigate (including cooperating with law enforcement) suspected or actual violations of law, breaches of the terms of employment, or non-compliance with the [Company] Code of Ethics or other [Company] policies or procedures; or (iii) otherwise protect or defend the rights or freedoms of [Company], its Employees, or other persons.
Exceptions in the event of Overriding Interests	11.2	If an Overriding Interest exists, one or more of the following obligations of [Company] or rights of the Employee may be set aside: (i) Article 3.1 (the requirement to Process Employee Data for closely related purposes); (ii) Article 6.1 (information provided to Employees); (iii) Article 7.1 (rights of Employees); (iv) Articles 8.2 and 8.3 (Staff access limitations and confidentiality requirements); and (v) Articles 10.4, 10.5, and 10.6 (ii) (contracts with Third Parties).
Sensitive Data	11.3	The requirements of Articles 4.1 and 4.2 (Sensitive Data) may be set aside only for the Overriding Interests listed in Article 11.1 (i) (a), (c), and (e), (ii) and (iii).
Consultation with Chief Privacy Officer	11.4	Setting aside obligations of [Company] or rights of Employees based on an Overriding Interest, requires the prior consultation of the Chief Privacy Officer.
Information to Employee	11.5	Upon request of the Employee, [Company] shall inform the Employee of the Overriding Interest for which obligations of [Company] or rights of the Employee have been set aside, unless the particular Overriding Interest sets aside the requirements of Articles 6.1 or 7.1, in which case the request shall be denied.

Article 12—*Supervision and Compliance*

Chief Privacy Officer 12.1 *[Company EU Headquarters]* shall appoint a Chief Privacy Officer who is responsible for:

(i) establishing a Privacy Council as described in Article 12.2;
(ii) supervising compliance with this Code;
(iii) coordinating, communicating, and consulting with the Privacy Officers network on central data protection issues;
(iv) providing annual reports, as appropriate, to the [*Head of Legal/ Head of Compliance*] on data protection risks and compliance issues as described in Article 15.2;
(v) coordinating, in conjunction with the appropriate Privacy Officer, official investigations or inquiries into the Processing of Data by a government authority
(vi) dealing with conflicts between this Code and applicable law as described in Article 19.2;
(vii) approving transfers as described in Articles 19.1 and 10.6;
(viii) carrying out a privacy impact assessment (PIA) before a new system or a business process involving Processing of Personal Data is implemented;
(ix) deciding on complaints as described in Article 16;
(x) devising the data management processes, systems, and tools to implement the framework for data protection management as established by the Privacy Council, including to:
(a) maintain, update, and publish this Code and related sub-policies;
(b) collect, maintain, and update information regarding the structure and functioning of all systems that process personal data;
(c) provide data privacy training and awareness for Staff to comply with their responsibilities under this Code;
(d) implement appropriate internal audit systems to monitor, audit, and report compliance with this Code and ensure that [Company's internal audit department] can verify and certify such compliance in line with the [Yearly Company Assurance Process];
(e) establish procedures regarding data protection inquiries, concerns, and complaints; and
(f) determine and update appropriate sanctions for violations of this Code (eg disciplinary standards).

Privacy Council 12.2 The Chief Privacy Officer shall establish a Privacy Council. The Privacy Council shall create and maintain a framework for:

(i) the development, implementation, and updating of local individual data protection policies and procedures;
(ii) the maintaining, updating, and publishing of this Code and related sub-policies;
(iii) the creating, maintaining, and updating of information regarding the structure and functioning of all systems that process personal data (as required by Article 13);
(iv) the development, implementation, and updating of the data privacy training and awareness programs;
(v) the monitoring, auditing, and reporting on compliance with this Code;
(vi) the collecting, investigating, and resolving of privacy inquiries, concerns, and complaints; and
(vii) determining and updating appropriate sanctions for violations of this Code (eg, disciplinary standards).

Article 12 (*cont.*)

Privacy Officers 12.3 Each Group Company shall designate a Privacy Officer. [The Chief Privacy Officer shall act as the Privacy Officer for [Company Holding]], These Privacy Officers may, in turn, establish a network of Privacy Officers sufficient to direct compliance with this Code within their respective organizational unit.
The Privacy Officers shall:

(i) implement the data management processes, systems, and tools, devised by the Chief Privacy Officer to implement the framework for data protection management established by the Privacy Council in their respective organizational unit;
(ii) support and assess overall data protection management compliance within their organizational unit;
(iii) regularly advise their Responsible Executive and the Chief Privacy Officer on privacy risks and compliance issues;
(iv) maintain (or ensure access to) an inventory of the system information about the structure and functioning of all systems that process personal data (as required by Article 13.2);
(v) be available for requests for privacy approvals or advice as described in Article 7;(vi) provide information relevant to the annual privacy report of the Chief Privacy Officer (as required in Article 15);
(vii) assist the Chief Privacy Officer in the event of official investigations or inquiries by government authorities;
(viii) own and authorize all appropriate privacy sub-policies in their organizational unit;
(ix) direct that stored Employee Data be deleted or destroyed, anonymized, or transferred as required by Article 5.2;
(x) decide on and notify the Chief Privacy Officer of complaints as described in Article 16;
(xi) cooperate with the Chief Privacy Officer and the other Privacy Officers, and the *[[Company] Compliance Officers]* to:

• ensure that the instructions, tools, and training are in place to enable the organizational unit to comply with the this Code
• share and provide guidance on best practices for data protection management within their organizational unit
• ensure that data protection requirements are taken into account whenever new technology is implemented in their organizational unit;
• notify the Responsible Executive of the involvement of external service providers with Data Processing tasks for their organizational unit.

Responsible Executive 12.4 The Responsible Executive of each organizational unit [eg General Counsel/the head of finance of a business unit] is accountable that effective data protection management is implemented in his organizational unit, is integrated into business practices, and that adequate resources and budget are available.
Responsible Executives are accountable for:

(i) ensuring overall data protection management compliance within their organizational unit, also during and following organizational restructuring, outsourcing, mergers and acquisitions and divestures
(ii) implementing the data management processes, systems, and tools, devised by the Chief Privacy Officer to implement the framework for data protection management established by the Privacy Council in their respective organizational unit

(iii) ensuring that the data protection management processes and systems are maintained up-to-date against changing circumstances and legal and regulatory requirements;
(iv) ensuring and monitoring ongoing compliance of third parties with the requirements of this Code in case Employee Data are transferred by [Company] to a third party (including entering into a written contract with such third parties and obtaining a sign off of such contract from the legal department)
(v) ensuring that relevant individuals in their organizational unit follow the prescribed data protection training courses and
(vi) directing that stored Employee Data be deleted or destroyed, anonymized, or transferred as required by Article 5.2.

Responsible Executives are responsible for:

(i) appointing a Privacy Officer for their organizational unit
(ii) consulting with the Chief Privacy Officer in all cases where there is a conflict between applicable local law and this Code as described in Article 19.2 and
(iii) informing the Chief Privacy Officer of any new legal requirement that may interfere with [Company]'s ability to comply with this Code as required by Article 19.3.

Default Privacy Officer 12.5 If at any moment in time there is no Privacy Officer designated for a function or business, the designated *[compliance officer for the [Company] Code of Conduct]* for the relevant function or business is responsible for supervising compliance with this Code.

Privacy Officer with a statutory position 12.6 Where a Privacy Officer holds his position pursuant to law, he shall carry out his job responsibilities to the extent they do not conflict with his statutory position.

Article 13—*Policies and Procedures*

Policies and procedures 13.1 [Company] shall develop and implement policies and procedures to comply with this Code.

System information 13.2 [Company] shall maintain readily available information regarding the structure and functioning of all systems and processes that Process Employee Data (eg inventory of systems and processes, privacy impact assessments).

Article 14—*Training*

Staff training 14.1 [Company] shall provide training on this Code and related confidentiality obligations to Staff members who have access to Employee Data.

Article 15—*Monitoring and Auditing Compliance*

Audits	15.1	[Company] Internal Audit shall audit business processes and procedures that involve the Processing of Employee Data for compliance with this Code. The audits shall be carried out in the course of the regular activities of [Company] Internal Audit or at the request of the Chief Privacy Officer. The Chief Privacy Officer may request to have an audit as specified in this Article 15.1 conducted by an external auditor. Applicable professional standards of independence, integrity, and confidentiality shall be observed when conducting an audit. The Chief Privacy Officer and the appropriate Privacy Officers shall be informed of the results of the audits. Reported violations of the Code will be reported back to [*Responsible Executive/other?*] A copy of the audit results will be provided to the Dutch Data Protection Authority upon request.
Annual Report	15.2	The Chief Privacy Officer shall produce an annual Employee Data privacy report for the *[Head of Legal or Head of Compliance]* on compliance with this Code, data protection risks, and other relevant issues. Each Privacy Officer shall provide information relevant to the report to the Chief Privacy Officer.
Mitigation	15.3	[Company] shall, if so indicated, ensure that adequate steps are taken to address breaches of this Code identified during the monitoring or auditing of compliance pursuant to this Article 15.

Article 16—*Complaints Procedure*

Complaint to Privacy Officer	16.1	Employees may file a complaint regarding compliance with this Code or violations of their rights under applicable local law: (i) in accordance with the complaints procedure set forth in the [Company] Code of Conduct; or (ii) with the appropriate Privacy Officer. The appropriate Privacy Officer shall: (a) notify the Chief Privacy Officer; (b) initiate an investigation; and (c) when necessary, advise the business on the appropriate measures for compliance and monitor, through to completion, the steps designed to achieve compliance. The appropriate Privacy Officer may consult with any government authority having jurisdiction over a particular matter about the measures to be taken.
Reply to Employee	16.2	Within four weeks of [Company] receiving a complaint, the appropriate Privacy Officer shall inform the Employee in writing either (i) of [Company] position with regard to the complaint and any action [Company] has taken or will take in response or (ii) when he will be informed of [Company]'s position, which date shall be no later than [x] weeks thereafter. The appropriate Privacy Officer shall send a copy of the complaint and his written reply to the Chief Privacy Officer.

Complaint to Chief Privacy Officer	16.3	An Employee may file a complaint with the Chief Privacy Officer if: (i) the resolution of the complaint by the appropriate Privacy Officer is unsatisfactory to the Employee (eg the complaint is rejected); (ii) the Employee has not received a response as required by Article 16.2; (iii) the time period provided to the Employee pursuant to Article 16.2 is, in light of the relevant circumstances, unreasonably long and the Employee has objected but has not been provided with a shorter, more reasonable time period in which he will receive a response; or (iv) in the events listed in Article 7.4. The procedure described in Articles 16.1 to 16.2 shall apply to complaints filed with the Chief Privacy Officer.

Article 17—*Legal Issues*

Local law and jurisdiction	17.1	Any Processing by [Company] of Employee Data shall be governed by applicable local law. Employees keep their own rights and remedies as available in their local jurisdictions. Local government authorities having jurisdiction over the relevant matters shall maintain their authority.
Law applicable to Code; Code has supplemental character	17.2	This Code shall be governed by and interpreted in accordance with Dutch law. This Code shall apply only where it provides supplemental protection for Employee Data. Where applicable local law provides more protection than this Code, local law shall apply. Where this Code provides more protection than applicable local law or provides additional safeguards, rights, or remedies for Employees, this Code shall apply.
Lead Authority for supervision of Rules	17.3	Compliance with this Code shall be exclusively supervized by the Dutch Data Protection Authority in the Netherlands, which is also exclusively authorized to advise *[Company EU Headquarters]* on the application of this Code at all times. The Dutch Data Protection Authority shall have investigative powers based on the Dutch Data Protection Act. To the extent the Dutch Data Protection Authority has discretionary powers related to enforcement of the Dutch Data Protection Act, it shall have similar discretionary powers for enforcement of this Code.
Exclusive jurisdiction under Code	17.4	Any complaints or claims of an Employee concerning any supplemental right the Employee may have under this Code shall be directed to *[Company EU Headquarters]* only and shall be brought before the Dutch Data Protection Authority in the Netherlands or the competent court in Amsterdam, the

Article 17 (*cont.*)

		Netherlands. The Dutch Data Protection Authority and courts in Amsterdam, the Netherlands have exclusive jurisdiction over any supplemental rights provided by this Code. Complaints and claims shall be admissible only if the Employee has first followed the complaints procedure set forth in Article 16 of this Code.
Code enforceable against [Company EU Headquarters] only	17.5	Any additional safeguards, rights, or remedies granted to Employees under this Code are granted by and enforceable in the Netherlands against *[Company EU Headquarters]* only.
Available remedies, limitation of damages, burden of proof re damages	17.6	Employees shall only be entitled to remedies available to data subjects under the Dutch Data Protection Act, the Dutch Civil Code, and the Dutch Code on Civil Procedure. However, *[Company EU Headquarters]* shall be liable only for direct damages suffered by an Employee resulting from a violation of this Code. Provided an Employee can demonstrate that it has suffered damage and establish facts which show it is plausible that the damage has occurred because of a violation of the Code, it will be for *[Company EU Headquarters]* to prove that the damages suffered by the Employee due to a violation of the Code are not attributable to the relevant Group Company.
Mutual assistance and redress	17.7	All Group Companies shall cooperate and assist each other to the extent reasonably possible to handle: (i) a request, complaint, or claim made by an Employee; or (ii) a lawful investigation or inquiry by a competent government authority. The Group Company employing the Employee is responsible for handling any communication with the Employee regarding his request, complaint, or claim except where circumstances dictate otherwise. The Group Company that is responsible for the Processing to which the request, complaint, or claim relates, shall bear all costs involved and reimburse *[Company EU Headquarters]*.

Article 18—*Sanctions for non-compliance*

Non compliance	18.1	Non-compliance of Employees with this Code may result in disciplinary action up to and including termination of employment.

Article 19—*Conflicts between the Code and applicable local law*

Conflict of law when transferring Data	19.1	Where a legal requirement to transfer Employee Data conflicts with the laws of the Member States of the EEA or the law of Switzerland, the transfer requires the prior approval of the Chief Privacy Officer. The Chief Privacy Officer shall seek the advice of the *Head of Legal.* The Chief Privacy Officer may seek the advice of the Dutch Data Protection Authority or another competent government authority.
Conflict between Code and law	19.2	In all other cases, where there is a conflict between applicable local law and the Code, the relevant Responsible Executive shall consult with the Chief Privacy Officer to determine how to comply with this Code and resolve the conflict to the extent reasonably practicable given the legal requirements applicable to the relevant Group Company.
New conflicting legal requirements	19.3	The relevant Responsible Executive shall promptly inform the Chief Privacy Officer of any new legal requirement that may interfere with [Company]'s ability to comply with this Code.

Article 20—*Changes to the Code*

Prior approval	20.1	Any changes to this Code require the prior approval of the *[Head of Legal or Head of Compliance of [Company Holding]. [Company EU Headquarters]* shall notify the Dutch Data Protection Authority in case of significant changes to the Code on a yearly basis.
No employee consent	20.2	This Code may be changed without Employee consent even though an amendment may relate to a benefit conferred on Employees.
Entry into force	20.3	Any amendment shall enter into force after it has been approved and published on the *[Company Intranet].*
Relevant code	20.4	Any request, complaint, or claim of an Employee involving this Code shall be judged against this Code that is in force at the time the request, complaint, or claim is made.

Article 21—*Transition Periods*

General transition period	21.1	Except as indicated below, there shall be a two-year transition period for compliance with this Code. Accordingly, except as otherwise indicated, within two years of the Effective Date, all Processing of Employee Data shall be undertaken in compliance with the Code. During any transition period, [Company] shall strive to comply with the Code.
Transition period for new Group Companies	21.2	Any entity that becomes a Group Company after the Effective Date shall comply with the Code within two years of becoming a Group Company.
Transition period for Divested Entities	21.3	A Divested Entity may remain covered by this Code after its divestment for such period as may be required by [Company] to disentangle the Processing of Employee Data relating to such Divested Entity.

Article 21 (*cont.*)

Transition period for IT systems	21.4	Where implementation of this Code requires updates or changes to information technology systems (including replacement of systems), the transition period shall be four years from the Effective Date or from the date an entity becomes a Group Company, or any longer period as is reasonably necessary to complete the update, change, or replacement process.
Transition period for existing agreements	21.5	Where there are existing agreements with Third Parties that are affected by this Code, the provisions of the agreements will prevail until the agreements are renewed in the normal course of business.
Transitional period for local-for-local systems	21.6	Processing of Employee Data that were collected in connection with activities of a Group Company located in a Non-Adequate Country shall be brought into compliance with this Code within five years of the Effective Date.

Contact details	[Company] Privacy Office c/o [Company EU Headquarters] *[insert contact details]*

ANNEX 1 Definitions

Archive	ARCHIVE shall mean a collection of Employee Data that are no longer necessary to achieve the purposes for which the Data originally were collected or that are no longer used for general business activities, but are used only for historical, scientific, or statistical purposes, dispute resolution, investigations, or general archiving purposes. An archive includes any data set that can no longer be accessed by any Employee other than the system administrator.
Business Purpose	BUSINESS PURPOSE shall mean a purpose for Processing Employee Data as specified in Article 2 or 3 or for Processing Sensitive Data as specified in Article 4 or 3.
Chief Privacy Officer	CHIEF PRIVACY OFFICER shall mean the officer as referred to in Article 12.1.
Code	CODE shall mean this Privacy Code for Employee Data.
Company	[COMPANY] shall mean [Company Holding] and its Group Companies
[Company EU Headquarters]	[COMPANY EU HEADQUARTERS] shall mean [Company EU Headquarters] having its registered seat in [], the Netherlands.
[Company Holding]	[Company Holding] shall mean [Company Holding], having its registered seat in [].
Dependant	DEPENDANT shall mean the spouse, partner, or child belonging to the household of the Employee.
Divested Entity	DIVESTED ENTITY shall mean the divestment by [Company] of a Group Company or business by means of: (a) a sale of shares as a result whereof the Group Company so divested no longer qualifies as a Group Company; and/or (b) a demerger, sale of assets, or any other manner or form.

Effective Date	EFFECTIVE DATE shall mean the date on which this Code becomes effective as set forth in Article 1.6.
Employee	EMPLOYEE shall mean an employee, job applicant, or former employee of [Company]. This term does not include people working at [Company] as consultants or employees of Third Parties providing services to [Company].
Employee Data or Data	EMPLOYEE DATA or DATA shall mean any information relating to an identified or identifiable Employee (and his Dependants).
EEA	EEA or EUROPEAN ECONOMIC AREA shall mean all Member States of the European Union, plus Norway, Iceland, and Liechtenstein.
EU Data Protection Directive	EU DATA PROTECTION DIRECTIVE shall mean the Directive 95/46/EC of the European Parliament and of the Council on the protection of individuals with regard to the processing of and the free movement of such data.
Group Company	GROUP COMPANY shall mean [Company Holding] and any company or legal entity of which [Company Holding], directly or indirectly owns more than 50 per cent of the issued share capital, has 50 per cent or more of the voting power at general meetings of shareholders, has the power to appoint a majority of the directors, or otherwise directs the activities of such other legal entity; however, any such company or legal entity shall be deemed a Group Company only as long as a liaison and/or relationship exists, and that is covered by the [Company] Code of Conduct.
Head of Legal	HEAD OF LEGAL shall mean the Head of Legal of [Company Holding].
Head of Compliance	HEAD OF COMPLIANCE shall mean the Head of Compliance of [Company Holding].
Non-Adequate Country	NON-ADEQUATE COUNTRY shall mean a country that under applicable local law (such as Article 25 of the EU Data Protection Directive) is deemed not to provide an 'adequate' level of data protection.
Original Purpose	ORIGINAL PURPOSE shall mean the purpose for which Employee Data was originally collected.
Overriding Interest	OVERRIDING INTEREST shall mean the pressing interests set forth in Article 11.1 based on which the obligations of [Company] or rights of Employees set forth in Article 11.2 and 11.3 may, under specific circumstances, be overridden if this pressing interest outweighs the interest of the Employee.
Privacy Council	PRIVACY COUNCIL shall mean the council referred to in Article 12.2.
Privacy Officer	PRIVACY OFFICER shall mean a privacy officer appointed by the Chief Privacy Officer pursuant to Article 12.3.
Processing	PROCESSING shall mean any operation that is performed on Employee Data, whether or not by automatic means, such as collection, recording, storage, organization, alteration, use, disclosure (including the granting of remote access), transmission, or deletion of Employee Data.
Responsible Executive	RESPONSIBLE EXECUTIVE shall mean the executive as referred to in Article 12.4.
Secondary Purpose	SECONDARY PURPOSE shall mean any purpose other than the Original Purpose for which Employee Data is further Processed.
Sensitive Data	SENSITIVE DATA shall mean Employee Data that reveal an Employee's racial or ethnic origin, political opinions or membership of political parties or similar organizations, religious or philosophical beliefs, membership of a professional or trade organization or union, physical or mental health

ANNEX 1 (*cont.*)

	including any opinion thereof, disabilities, genetic code, addictions, sex life, criminal offences, criminal records, proceedings with regard to criminal or unlawful behaviour, or social security numbers issued by the government.
Staff	STAFF shall mean all Employees and other persons who Process Employee Data as part of their respective duties or responsibilities using [Company] information technology systems or working primarily from [Company]'s premises.
Third Party	THIRD PARTY shall mean any person, private organization, or government body outside [Company].
Third Party Controller	THIRD PARTY CONTROLLER shall mean a Third Party that Processes Employee Data and determines the purposes and means of the Processing.
Third Party Processor	THIRD PARTY PROCESSOR shall mean a Third Party that Processes Employee Data on behalf of [Company] that is not under the direct authority of [Company].

Interpretations
Interpretation of this code:

(i) Unless the context requires otherwise, all references to a particular Article or Annex are references to that Article or Annex in or to this document, as they may be amended from time to time.

(ii) Headings are included for convenience only and are not to be used in construing any provision of this Code.

(iii) If a word or phrase is defined, its other grammatical forms have a corresponding meaning.

(iv) The male form shall include the female form.

(v) The words 'include', 'includes', and 'including' and any words following them shall be construed without limitation to the generality of any preceding words or concepts and vice versa.

(vi) A reference to a document (including, without limitation, a reference to this Code) is to the document as amended, varied, supplemented, or replaced, except to the extent prohibited by this Code or that other document.

APPENDIX 3

BCR for Customer Data

[Company]
Privacy Code for Customer, Supplier, and Business Partner Data
Introduction

[Company] has committed itself to the protection of personal data of [Company] Customers, Suppliers, and Business Partners in the [Company] [Code of Conduct].

This Code indicates how this principle shall be implemented. For the rules applicable to Employee Data, refer to the *Privacy Code for Employee Data. [hyperlink]*

Article 1—*Scope, Applicability, and Implementation*

Scope	1.1	This Code addresses the Processing of Personal Data of Customers, Suppliers, and Business Partners by [Company] or a Third Party on behalf of [Company]. This Code does not address the Processing of Employee Data of [Company].
Electronic and paper-based Processing	1.2	This Code applies to the Processing of Personal Data by electronic means and in systematically accessible paper-based filing systems.
Applicability of local law and Code	1.3	Individuals keep any rights and remedies they may have under applicable local law. This Code shall apply only where it provides supplemental protection for Personal Data. Where applicable local law provides more protection than this Code, local law shall apply. Where this Code provides more protection than applicable local law or provides additional safeguards, rights, or remedies for Individuals, this Code shall apply.
Sub-policies and notices	1.4	[Company] may supplement this Code through sub-policies or notices that are consistent with this Code.
Responsibility	1.5	The [*Responsible Executive*] shall be accountable for compliance with this Code.
Effective Date	1.6	This Code has been adopted by the *[Head of Legal or Head of Compliance]* of *[Company Holding]* and shall enter into force as of [ ] (Effective Date) and shall be published on the *[Company website and Company Intranet]* and be made available to Individuals upon request.
Code supersedes prior policies	1.7	This Code supersedes all [Company] privacy policies and notices that exist on the Effective Date to the extent they address the same issues.
Implementation	1.8	This Code shall be implemented in the [Company] organization based on the time frames specified in Article 22.
Role of [Company EU Headquarters]	1.9	[Company Holding] has tasked *[Company EU Headquarters]* with the coordination and implementation of this Code.

Article 2—*Purposes for Processing Personal Data*

Legitimate Business Purposes	2.1	Personal Data shall be collected, used, or otherwise Processed for one (or more) of the following purposes (*Business Purposes*): [(i) *Development and improvement of products and/or services.* This purpose includes Processing that is necessary for the development and improvement of [Company] products and/or services, research, and development. (ii) *Conclusion and execution of agreements with Customers, Suppliers, and Business Partners.* This purpose addresses the Processing of Personal Data necessary to conclude and execute agreements with Customers, Suppliers, and Business Partners and to record and financially settle delivered services, products, and materials to and from [Company]. (iii) *Relationship management and marketing.* This purpose addresses activities such as maintaining and promoting contact with Customers, Suppliers, and Business Partners, account management, customer service, recalls and the development, execution, and analysis of market surveys and marketing strategies. (iv) *Business process execution, internal management, and management reporting.* This purpose addresses activities such as managing company assets, conducting internal audits and investigations, finance and accounting, implementing business controls, provision of central processing facilities for efficiency purposes, managing mergers, acquisitions, and divestitures, and Processing Personal Data for management reporting and analysis. (v) *Health, safety, and security.* This purpose addresses activities such as those involving safety and health, the protection of [Company] and Employee assets, and the authentication of Customer, Supplier, or Business Partner status and access rights (vi) *Compliance with legal obligations.* This purpose addresses the Processing of Personal Data necessary for compliance with a legal obligation to which [Company] is subject. (vii) *Protecting vital interests of Individuals.* This is where Processing is necessary to protect the vital interests of an Individual.] Where there is a question whether a Processing of Personal Data can be based on a purpose listed above, it is necessary to seek the advice of the appropriate Privacy Officer before the Processing takes place.
Consent	2.2	If a Business Purpose does not exist or if applicable local law so requires [Company] shall (also) seek consent from the Individual for the Processing. Where Processing is undertaken at the request of an Individual (eg he subscribes to a service or seeks a benefit), he is deemed to have provided consent to the Processing. When seeking consent, [Company] must inform the Individual: (i) of the purposes of the Processing for which consent is required; and (ii) other relevant information (eg the nature and categories of the Processed Data, the categories of Third Parties to which the Data are disclosed (if any), and how Individuals can exercise their rights).
Denial or withdrawal of consent	2.3	The Individual may both deny consent and withdraw consent at any time.

Article 3—*Use for Other Purposes*

Use of Data for Secondary Purposes	3.1	Generally, Personal Data shall be used only for the Business Purposes for which they were originally collected (*Original Purpose*). Personal Data may be Processed for a legitimate Business Purpose of [Company] different from the Original Purpose (*Secondary Purpose*) only if the Original Purpose and Secondary Purpose are closely related. Depending on the sensitivity of the relevant Personal Data and whether use of the Data for the Secondary Purpose has potential negative consequences for the Individual, the secondary use may require additional measures such as: (i) limiting access to the Data; (ii) imposing additional confidentiality requirements; (iii) taking additional security measures; (iv) informing the Individual about the Secondary Purpose; (v) providing an opt-out opportunity; or (vi) obtaining Individual consent in accordance with Article 2.2.
Generally permitted uses of Data for Secondary Purposes	3.2	It is generally permissible to use Personal Data for the following Secondary Purposes provided appropriate additional measures are taken in accordance with Article 3.1: (i) transfer of the Data to an Archive; (ii) internal audits or investigations; (iii) implementation of business controls; (iv) statistical, historical, or scientific research; (v) preparing for or engaging in dispute resolution; (vi) legal or business consulting; or (vii) insurance purposes.

Article 4—*Purposes for Processing Sensitive Data*

Specific purposes for Processing Sensitive Data	4.1	This Article sets forth specific rules for Processing Sensitive Data. [Company] shall Process Sensitive Data only to the extent necessary to serve the applicable Business Purpose. The following categories of Sensitive Data may be collected, used, or otherwise Processed only for one (or more) of the purposes specified below: [(i) *Racial or ethnic data*: in some countries photos and video images of Individuals qualify as racial or ethnic data. [Company] may process photos and video images for the protection of [Company] and Employee assets, site access, and security reasons, and the authentication of Customer, Supplier, or Business Partner status and access rights. (ii) *Criminal data* (including data relating to criminal behaviour, criminal records, or proceedings regarding criminal or unlawful behaviour) for protecting the interests of [Company] with respect to criminal offences that have been or, given the relevant circumstances are suspected to have been, committed against [Company] or its Employees.

Article 4 (*cont.*)

General Purposes for Processing of Sensitive Data	4.2	In addition to the specific purposes listed in Article 4.1 above, all categories of Sensitive Data may be Processed under (one or more of) the following circumstances: (i) the Individual has given his explicit consent to the Processing thereof; (ii) as required by or allowed under applicable local law; (iii) for the establishment, exercise, or defence of a legal claim; (iv) to protect a vital interest of an Individual, but only where it is impossible to obtain the Individual's consent first; (v) to the extent necessary to comply with an obligation of international public law (eg treaties); or (vi) [if the Sensitive Data have manifestly been made public by the Individual.]
Denial or withdrawal of consent	4.3	The information requirements of Article 2.2 and Article 2.3 apply to the granting, denial, or withdrawal of consent.
Prior Authorization of Privacy Officer	4.4	Where Sensitive Data are Processed based on a requirement of law other than the local law applicable to the Processing, the Processing requires the prior authorization of the appropriate Privacy Officer.
Use of Sensitive Data for Secondary Purposes	4.5	Sensitive Data of Individuals may be Processed for Secondary Purposes in accordance with Article 3.

Article 5—*Quantity and Quality of Data*

No Excessive Data	5.1	[Company] shall restrict the Processing of Personal Data to Data that are reasonably adequate for and relevant to the applicable Business Purpose. [Company] shall take reasonable steps to delete Personal Data that are not required for the applicable Business Purpose.
Storage period	5.2	[Company] generally shall retain Personal Data only for the period required to serve the applicable Business Purpose, to the extent reasonably necessary to comply with an applicable legal requirement or as advisable in light of an applicable statute of limitations. [Company] may specify (eg, in a sub-policy, notice, or records retention schedule) a time period for which certain categories of Personal Data may be kept. Promptly after the applicable storage period has ended, the Privacy Officer shall direct that the Data be: (i) securely deleted or destroyed; (ii) anonymized [alternative: de-identified]; or (iii) transferred to an Archive (unless this is prohibited by law or an applicable records retention schedule).
Quality of Data	5.3	Personal Data should be accurate, complete, and kept up-to-date to the extent reasonably necessary for the applicable Business Purpose.
Accurate, complete and up-to-date Data	5.4	It is the responsibility of the Individuals to keep his Personal Data accurate, complete, and up-to-date. Individuals shall inform [Company] regarding any changes in accordance with Article 7.

Article 6—*Individual Information Requirements*

Information requirements	6.1	[Company] shall inform Individuals through a privacy policy or notice about: (i) the Business Purposes for which their Data are Processed; (ii) which Group Company is responsible for the Processing; and (iii) other relevant information (eg, the nature and categories of the Processed Data, the categories of Third Parties to which the Data are disclosed (if any), and how Individuals can exercise their rights).
Personal Data not obtained from the Individual	6.2	If applicable local law so requires, where Personal Data have not been obtained directly from the Individual, [Company] shall provide the Individual with the information as set out in Article 6.1: (i) at the time that the Personal Data are recorded in a [Company] database; or (ii) at the time that the Personal Data are used for a mailing, provided that this mailing is done within six months after the Personal Data are recorded in a [Company] database.
Exceptions	6.3	The requirements of Article 6.2 may be set aside if: (i) it is impossible or would involve a disproportionate effort to provide the information to Individuals; or (ii) it results in disproportionate costs. These exceptions to the above requirements qualify as Overriding Interests.

Article 7—*Individual Rights of Access and Rectification*

Rights of Individuals	7.1	Every Individual has the right to request an overview of his Personal Data Processed by or on behalf of [Company]. Where reasonably possible, the overview shall contain information regarding the source, type, purpose, and categories of recipients of the relevant Personal Data. If the Personal Data are incorrect, incomplete, or not Processed in compliance with applicable law or this Code, the Individual has the right to have his Data rectified, deleted, or blocked (as appropriate). In addition, the Individual has the right to object to the Processing of his Data on the basis of compelling grounds related to his particular situation.
Procedure	7.2	The Individual should send his request to the contact person or contact point indicated in the relevant privacy policy. If no contact person or contact point is indicated, the Individual may send his request to [x]. Prior to fulfilling the request of the Individual, [Company] may require the Individual to:

Article 7 (*cont.*)

		(i) specify the type of Personal Data to which he is seeking access; (ii) specify, to the extent reasonably possible, the data system in which the Data are likely to be stored; (iii) specify the circumstances in which [Company] obtained the Personal Data; (iv) show proof of his identity; and (v) in the case of a request for rectification, deletion, or blockage, specify the reasons why the Personal Data are incorrect, incomplete, or not Processed in accordance with applicable law or the Code.
Response period	7.3	Within four weeks of [Company] receiving the request, the contact person, [contact point,] or Privacy Officer shall inform the Individual in writing either (i) of [Company] position with regard to the request and any action [Company] has taken or will take in response or (ii) the ultimate date on which he will be informed of [Company's] position, which date shall be no later than [x] weeks thereafter.
Complaint	7.4	An Individual may file a complaint in accordance with Article 17.1 if: (i) the response to the request is unsatisfactory to the Individual (eg the request is denied); (ii) the Individual has not received a response as required by Article 7.3; or (iii) the time period provided to the Individual in accordance with Article 7.3 is, in light of the relevant circumstances, unreasonably long and the Individual has objected but has not been provided with a shorter, more reasonable time period in which he will receive a response.
Denial of requests	7.5	[Company] may deny an Individual request if: (i) the request does not meet the requirements of Articles 7.1 and 7.2; (ii) the request is not sufficiently specific; (iii) the identity of the relevant Individual cannot be established by reasonable means; or (iv) the request is made within an unreasonable time interval of a prior request or otherwise constitutes an abuse of rights. A time interval between requests of six months or less shall generally be deemed to be an unreasonable time interval.

Article 8—*Security and Confidentiality Requirements*

Data security	8.1	[Company] shall take appropriate commercially reasonable technical, physical, and organizational measures to protect Personal Data from misuse or accidental, unlawful, or unauthorized destruction, loss, alteration, disclosure, acquisition, or access.
Staff access	8.2	Staff members shall be authorized to access Personal Data only to the extent necessary to serve the applicable Business Purpose and to perform their job.
Confidentiality obligations	8.3	Staff members who access Personal Data must meet their confidentiality obligations.

Article 9—*Direct Marketing*

Direct marketing	9.1	This Article sets forth requirements concerning the Processing of Personal Data for direct marketing purposes (eg contacting the Individual by e-mail, fax, phone, SMS, or otherwise, with a view of solicitation for commercial or charitable purposes).
Consent for direct marketing (opt-in)	9.2	If applicable law so requires, [Company] shall only send to Individuals unsolicited commercial communication by fax, e-mail, sms, and mms with the prior consent of the Individual ('opt-in'). If applicable law does not require prior consent of the Individual, [Company] shall in any event offer the Individual the opportunity to opt-out of such unsolicited commercial communication.
Exception (opt-out)	9.3	Prior consent of the Individual for sending unsolicited commercial communication by fax, e-mail, sms, and mms is not required if: (i) an Individual has provided his electronic contact details to a Group Company in the context of a sale of a product or service of such Group Company; and (ii) such contact details are used for direct marketing of such Group Company's own similar products or services; (iii) provided that an Individual clearly and distinctly has been given the opportunity to object free of charge, and in an easy manner, to such use of his electronic contact details when they are collected by the Group Company.
Information to be provided in each communication	9.4	In every direct marketing communication that is made to the Individual, the Individual shall be offered the opportunity to opt-out of further direct marketing communication.
Objection to direct marketing	9.5	If an Individual objects to receiving marketing communications from [Company], or withdraws her consent to receive such materials, [Company] will take steps to refrain from sending further marketing materials as specifically requested by the individual. [Company] will do so within the time period required by applicable law.
Third Parties and direct marketing	9.6	No Data shall be provided to, or used on behalf of, Third Parties for purposes of direct marketing without the prior consent of the Individual.
Personal Data of Children	9.7	[Company] shall not use any Personal Data of Individuals under the age of fourteen (14) years for direct marketing.
Direct marketing records	9.8	[Company] shall keep a record of Individuals that used their 'opt-in' or 'opt-out' right and will regularly check public opt-out registers.

Article 10—*Automated Decision-making*

Automated decisions	10.1	Automated tools may be used to make decisions about Individuals but decisions may not be based solely on the results provided by the automated tool. This restriction does not apply if: (i) the use of automated tools is required or authorized by law; (ii) the decision is made by [Company] for purposes of (a) entering into or performing a contract or (b) managing the contract, provided the underlying request leading to a decision by [Company] was made by the Individual (eg, where automated tools are used to filter promotional game submissions); or (iii) suitable measures are taken to safeguard the legitimate interests of the Individual, eg, the Individual has been provided with an opportunity to express his point of view.

Article 11—*Transfer of Personal Data to Third Parties*

Transfer to Third Parties

11.1 This Article sets forth requirements concerning the transfer of Personal Data from [Company] to a Third Party. Note that a transfer of Personal Data includes situations in which [Company] discloses Personal Data to Third Parties (eg, in the context of corporate due diligence) or where [Company] provides remote access to Personal Data to a Third Party

Third Party Controllers and Third Party Processors

11.2 There are two categories of Third Parties:

(i) *Third Party Processors*: these are Third Parties that Process Personal Data solely on behalf of [Company] and at its direction (eg, Third Parties that Process online registrations made by Customers)
(ii) *Third Party Controllers*: these are Third Parties that Process Personal Data and determine the purposes and means of the Processing (eg, [Company] Business Partners that provide their own goods or services directly to Customers).

Transfer for applicable Business Purposes only

11.3 [Company] shall transfer Personal Data to a Third Party to the extent necessary to serve the applicable Business Purpose (including Secondary Purposes as per Article 3 or purposes for which the Individual has provided consent in accordance with Article 2).

Third Party Controller contracts

11.4 Third Party Controllers (other than government agencies) may Process Personal Data only if they have a written contract with [Company]. In the contract, [Company] shall seek to contractually safeguard the data protection interests of its Individuals. All such contracts shall be drafted in consultation with the appropriate Privacy Officer. Individual Business Contact Data may be transferred to a Third Party Controller without a contract if it is reasonably expected that such Business Contact Data will be used by the Third Party Controller to contact the Individual for legitimate business purposes related to Individual's job responsibilities.

Third Party Processor contracts

11.5 Third Party Processors may Process Personal Data only if they have a written contract with [Company]. The contract with a Third Party Processor must include the following provisions:

(i) the Processor shall Process Personal Data only in accordance with [Company]'s instructions and for the purposes authorized by [Company];
(ii) the Processor shall keep the Personal Data confidential;
(iii) the Processor shall take appropriate technical, physical, and organizational security measures to protect the Personal Data;
(iv) the Third Party Data Processor shall not permit sub-contractors to Process Personal Data in connection with its obligations to [Company] without the prior written consent of [Company];
(v) [Company] has the right to review the security measures taken by the Third Party Processor and the Third Party Processor shall submit its relevant data processing facilities to audits and inspections by [Company] or any relevant government authority;
(vi) the Third Party Processor shall promptly inform [Company] of any actual or suspected security breach involving Personal Data; and

(vii) the Third Party Processor shall take adequate remedial measures as soon as possible and shall promptly provide [Company] with all relevant information and assistance as requested by [Company] regarding the security breach.

Transfer of Data to a Non-Adequate Country

11.6 This Article sets forth additional rules for the transfer of Personal Data to a Third Party located in a country that is not considered to provide an 'adequate' level of protection for Personal Data (*Non-Adequate Country*).

Personal Data may be transferred to a Third Party located in a Non-Adequate Country only if:

(i) the transfer is necessary for the performance of a contract with the Individual, for managing a contract with Individual, or to take necessary steps at the request of the Individual prior to entering into a contract, eg, for processing orders;
(ii) a contract has been concluded between [Company] and the relevant Third Party that provides for safeguards at a similar level of protection as that provided by this Code; the contract shall conform to any model contract requirement under applicable local law (if any);
(iii) the transfer is necessary for the conclusion or performance of a contract concluded in the interest of the Individual between [Company] and a Third Party (eg in case of recalls);
(iv) the Third Party has been certified under the United States Safe Harbor Program or any other similar program that is recognized as providing an 'adequate' level of data protection;
(v) the Third Party has implemented binding corporate rules or a similar transfer control mechanisms which provide adequate safeguards under applicable law;
(vi) the transfer is necessary to protect a vital interest of the Individual;
(vii) the transfer is necessary for the establishment, exercise, or defence of a legal claim;
(viii) the transfer is necessary to satisfy a pressing need to protect the public interests of a democratic society; or
(ix) the transfer is required by any law to which the relevant Group Company is subject.

Items (viii) and (ix) above require the prior approval of the Chief Privacy Officer.

Consent for transfer

11.7 If none of the grounds listed in Article 11.6 exist or if applicable local law so requires [Company] shall (also) seek consent from the Individual for the transfer to a Third Party located in a Non-Adequate Country.

Prior to requesting consent, the Individual shall be provided with the following information:

(i) the purpose of the transfer;
(ii) the identity of the transferring Group Company;
(iii) the identity or categories of Third Parties to which the Data will be transferred;
(iv) the categories of Data that will be transferred;
(v) the country to which the Data will be transferred; and
(vi) the fact that the Data will be transferred to a Non-Adequate Country.

Article 2.3 applies to denial or withdrawal of consent.

Article 11 (*cont.*)

Transfers between Non-Adequate Countries	11.8	This Article sets forth additional rules for transfers of Personal Data that were collected in connection with the activities of a Group Company located in a Non-Adequate Country to a Third Party also located in a Non-Adequate Country. In addition to the grounds listed in Article 11.6, these transfers are permitted if they are: (i) necessary for compliance with a legal obligation to which the relevant Group Company is subject; (ii) necessary to serve the public interest; or (iii) necessary to satisfy a Business Purpose of [Company].

Article 12—*Overriding Interests*

Overriding Interests	12.1	Some of the obligations of [Company] or rights of Individuals under this Code may be overridden if, under the specific circumstances at issue, a pressing need exists that outweighs the interest of the Individual (*Overriding Interest*). An Overriding Interest exists if there is a need to: (i) protect the legitimate business interests of [Company] including (a) the health, security, or safety of Employees or Individuals; (b) [Company]'s intellectual property rights, trade secrets, or reputation; (c) the continuity of [Company]'s business operations; (d) the preservation of confidentiality in a proposed sale, merger, or acquisition of a business; or (e) the involvement of trusted advisors or consultants for business, legal, tax, or insurance purposes; (ii) prevent or investigate (including cooperating with law enforcement) suspected or actual violations of law; or (iii) otherwise protect or defend the rights or freedoms of [Company], its Employees, or other persons.
Exceptions in the event of Overriding Interests	12.2	If an Overriding Interest exists, one or more of the following obligations of [Company] or rights of the Individual may be set aside: (i) Article 3.1 (the requirement to Process Personal Data for closely related purposes); (ii) Article 6.1 and 6.2 (information provided to Individuals, Personal Data not obtained from the Individuals); (iii) Article 7.1 (rights of Individuals); (iv) Articles 8.2 and 8.3 (Staff access limitations and confidentiality requirements); and (v) Articles 11.4, 11.5, and 11.6 (ii) (contracts with Third Parties).
Sensitive Data	12.3	The requirements of Articles 4.1 and 4.2 (Sensitive Data) may be set aside only for the Overriding Interests listed in Article 12.1 (i) (a), (c), and (e), (ii) and (iii).

Consultation with Chief Privacy Officer

12.4 Setting aside obligations of [Company] or rights of Individuals based on an Overriding Interest requires prior consultation of the Chief Privacy Officer.

Information to Individual

12.5 Upon request of the Individual, [Company] shall inform the Individual of the Overriding Interest for which obligations of [Company] or rights of the Individual have been set aside, unless the particular Overriding Interest sets aside the requirements of Articles 6.1 or 7.1, in which case the request shall be denied.

Article 13—*Supervision and Compliance*

Chief Privacy Officer

13.1 *[Company EU Headquarters]* shall appoint a Chief Privacy Officer who is responsible for:

(i) establishing a Privacy Council as described in Article 13.2;
(ii) supervising compliance with this Code
(iii) coordinating, communicating, and consulting with the Privacy Officers network on central data protection issues;
(iv) providing annual reports, as appropriate, to the [*Head of Legal/Head of Compliance*] on data protection risks and compliance issues as described in Article 16.2;
(v) coordinating, in conjunction with the appropriate Privacy Officer, official investigations or inquiries into the Processing of Data by a government authority;
(vi) dealing with conflicts between this Code and applicable law as described in Article 20.2;
(vii) approving transfers as described in Articles 20.1 and 11.6;
(viii) carrying out a privacy impact assessment (PIA) before a new system or a business process involving processing of personal data is implemented;
(ix) deciding on complaints as described in Article 17;
(x) devising the data management processes, systems, and tools to implement the framework for data protection management as established by the Privacy Council, including to:

- maintain, update, and publish this Code and related sub-policies;
- collect, maintain, and update information regarding the structure and functioning of all systems that process personal data;
- provide data privacy training and awareness for employees to comply with their responsibilities under this Code;
- implement appropriate internal audit systems to monitor, audit, and report compliance with this Code and ensure that [Company's internal audit department] can verify and certify such compliance in line with the [Yearly Company Assurance Process];
- establish procedures regarding data protection inquiries, concerns, and complaints; and
- determine and update appropriate sanctions for violations of this Code (eg disciplinary standards).

Article 13 (*cont.*)

Privacy Council	13.2	The Chief Privacy Officer shall establish a Privacy Council. The Privacy Council shall create and maintain a framework for: (i) the development, implementation, and updating of local individual data protection policies and procedures; (ii) the maintaining, updating, and publishing of this Code and related sub-policies; (iii) the creating, maintaining, and updating of information regarding the structure and functioning of all systems that process personal data (as required by Article 14); (iv) the development, implementation, and updating of the data privacy training and awareness programs; (v) the monitoring, auditing, and reporting on compliance with this Code; (vi) the collecting, investigating, and resolving of privacy inquiries, concerns, and complaints; and (vii) determining and updating appropriate sanctions for violations of this Code (eg, disciplinary standards).]
Privacy Officers	13.3	Each Group Company shall designate a Privacy Officer. [The Chief Privacy Officer shall act as the Privacy Officer for [Company Holding]]. These Privacy Officers may, in turn, establish a network of Privacy Officers sufficient to direct compliance with this Code within their respective organizational unit. The Privacy Officers shall: (i) implement the data management processes, systems, and tools, devised by the Chief Privacy Officer to implement the framework for data protection management established by the Privacy Council in their respective organizational unit; (ii) support and assess overall data protection management compliance within their organizational unit; (iii) regularly advise their Responsible Executive and the Chief Privacy Officer on privacy risks and compliance issues; (iv) maintain (or ensure access to) an inventory of the system information about the structure and functioning of all systems that process personal data (as required by Article 14.2); (v) be available for requests for privacy approvals or advice as described in Article 7; (vi) provide information relevant to the annual privacy report of the Chief Privacy Officer (as required in Article 16); (vii) assist the Chief Privacy Officer in the event of official investigations or inquiries by government authorities; (viii) own and authorize all appropriate privacy sub-policies in their organizational unit; (ix) direct that stored Personal Data be deleted or destroyed, anonymized or transferred as required by Article 5.2; (x) decide on and notify the Chief Privacy Officer of complaints as described in Article 17; (xi) cooperate with the Chief Privacy Officer and the other Privacy Officers, and the *[[Company] Compliance Officers]* to: • ensure that the instructions, tools, and training are in place to enable the organizational unit to comply with the this Code;

• share and provide guidance on best practices for data protection management within their organizational unit;
• ensure that data protection requirements are taken into account whenever new technology is implemented in their organizational unit;
• notify the Responsible Executive of the involvement of external service providers with Processing tasks for their organizational unit.

Responsible Executive 13.4 The Responsible Executive of each organizational unit [eg General Counsel/the head of finance of a business unit] is accountable that effective data protection management is implemented in his organizational unit, is integrated into business practices, and that adequate resources and budget are available.

Responsible Executives are accountable for:

(i) ensuring overall data protection management compliance within their organizational unit, also during and following organizational restructuring, outsourcing, mergers and acquisitions and divestures
(ii) implementing the data management processes, systems, and tools, devised by the Chief Privacy Officer to implement the framework for data protection management established by the Privacy Council in their respective organizational unit
(iii) ensuring that the data protection management processes and systems are maintained up-to-date against changing circumstances and legal and regulatory requirements;
(iv) ensuring and monitoring ongoing compliance of third parties with the requirements of this Code in case Personal Data are transferred by [Company] to a third party (including entering into a written contract with such third parties and obtaining a sign off of such contract from the legal department);
(v) ensuring that relevant individuals in their organizational unit follow the prescribed data protection training courses; and
(vi) directing that stored Personal Data be deleted or destroyed, anonymized, or transferred as required by Article 5.2.

Responsible Executives are responsible for:

(i) appointing a Privacy Officer for their organizational unit;
(ii) consulting with the Chief Privacy Officer in all cases where there is a conflict between applicable local law and this Code as described in Article 20.2; and
(iii) informing the Chief Privacy Officer of any new legal requirement that may interfere with [Company]'s ability to comply with this Code as required by Article 20.3.

Default Privacy Officer 13.5 If at any moment in time there is no Privacy Officer designated for a function or business, the designated *[compliance officer for the [Company] Code of Conduct]* for the relevant function or business is responsible for supervising compliance with this Code.

Privacy Officer with a statutory position 13.6 Where a Privacy Officer holds his position pursuant to law, he shall carry out his job responsibilities to the extent they do not conflict with his statutory position.

Article 14—*Policies and Procedures*

Policies and procedures	14.1	[Company] shall develop and implement policies and procedures to comply with this Code.
System information	14.2	[Company] shall maintain readily available information regarding the structure and functioning of all systems and processes that Process Personal Data (eg inventory of systems and processes, privacy impact assessments).

Article 15—*Training*

Staff training	15.1	[Company] shall provide training on this Code and related confidentiality obligations to Staff members who have access to Personal Data.

Article 16—*Monitoring and Auditing Compliance*

Audits	16.1	[Company] Internal Audit shall audit business processes and procedures that involve the Processing of Personal Data for compliance with this Code. The audits shall be carried out in the course of the regular activities of [Company] Internal Audit or at the request of the Chief Privacy Officer. The Chief Privacy Officer may request to have an audit as specified in this Article 16.1 conducted by an external auditor. Applicable professional standards of independence, integrity, and confidentiality shall be observed when conducting an audit. The Chief Privacy Officer and the appropriate Privacy Officers shall be informed of the results of the audits. Reported violations of the Code will be reported back to [*Responsible Executive/other?*] A copy of the audit results will be provided to the Dutch Data Protection Authority upon request.
Annual report	16.2	The Chief Privacy Officer shall produce an annual Personal Data privacy report for the *[Head of Legal or Head of Compliance?]* on compliance with this Code, data protection risks, and other relevant issues. Each Privacy Officer shall provide information relevant to the report to the Chief Privacy Officer.
Mitigation	16.3	[Company] shall, if so indicated, ensure that adequate steps are taken to address breaches of this Code identified during the monitoring or auditing of compliance pursuant to this Article 16.

Article 17—*Complaints Procedure*

Complaint	17.1	Individuals may file a complaint regarding compliance with this Code or violations of their rights under applicable local law in accordance with the complaints procedure set forth in the relevant privacy policy or contract. The complaint shall be forwarded to the appropriate Privacy Officer. The appropriate Privacy Officer shall: (a) notify the Chief Privacy Officer; (b) initiate an investigation; and (c) when necessary, advise the business on the appropriate measures for compliance and monitor, through to completion, the steps designed to achieve compliance. The appropriate Privacy Officer may consult with any government authority having jurisdiction over a particular matter about the measures to be taken.
Reply to Individual	17.2	Within four weeks of [Company] receiving a complaint, the appropriate Privacy Officer shall inform the Individual in writing either (i) of [Company] position with regard to the complaint and any action [Company] has taken or will take in response or (ii) when he will be informed of [Company]'s position, which date shall be no later than [x] weeks thereafter. The appropriate Privacy Officer shall send a copy of the complaint and his written reply to the Chief Privacy Officer.
Complaint to Chief Privacy Officer	17.3	An Individual may file a complaint with the Chief Privacy Officer if: (i) the resolution of the complaint by the appropriate Privacy Officer is unsatisfactory to the Individual (eg, the complaint is rejected); (ii) the Individual has not received a response as required by Article 17.2; (iii) the time period provided to the Individual pursuant to Article 17.2 is, in light of the relevant circumstances, unreasonably long and the Individual has objected but has not been provided with a shorter, more reasonable time period in which he will receive a response; or (iv) in one of the events listed in Article 7.4. The procedure described in Articles 17.1 to 17.2 shall apply to complaints filed with the Chief Privacy Officer.

Article 18—*Legal Issues*

Local law and jurisdiction	18.1	Any Processing by [Company] of Personal Data shall be governed by applicable local law. Individuals keep their own rights and remedies as available in their local jurisdictions. Local government authorities having jurisdiction over the relevant matters shall maintain their authority.
Law applicable to Code; Code has supplemental character	18.2	This Code shall be governed by and interpreted in accordance with Dutch law. This Code shall apply only where it provides supplemental protection for Personal Data. Where applicable local law provides more protection than this Code, local law shall apply. Where this Code provides more protection than applicable local law or provides additional safeguards, rights, or remedies for Individuals, this Code shall apply.
Lead authority for supervision of rules	18.3	Compliance with this Code shall be exclusively supervised by the Dutch Data Protection Authority in the Netherlands, which is also exclusively authorized to advise *[Company EU Headquarters]* on the application of this Code at all times. The Dutch Data Protection Authority shall have investigative powers based on the Dutch Data Protection Act. To the extent the Dutch Data Protection Authority has discretionary powers related to enforcement of the Dutch Data Protection Act, it shall have similar discretionary powers for enforcement of this Code.
Exclusive jurisdiction under Code	18.4	Any complaints or claims of an Individual concerning any supplemental right the Individual may have under this Code shall be directed to *[Company EU Headquarters]* only and shall be brought before the Dutch Data Protection Authority in the Netherlands or the competent court in Amsterdam, the Netherlands. The Dutch Data Protection Authority and courts in Amsterdam, the Netherlands have exclusive jurisdiction over any supplemental rights provided by this Code. Complaints and claims shall be admissible only if the Individual has first followed the complaints procedure set forth in Article 17 of this Code.
Code enforceable against [Company EU Headquarters] only	18.5	Any additional safeguards, rights, or remedies granted to Individuals under this Code are granted by and enforceable in the Netherlands against *[Company EU Headquarters]* only.
Available remedies and limitation of damages	18.6	Individuals shall only be entitled to remedies available to data subjects under the Dutch Data Protection Act, the Dutch Civil Code, and the Dutch Code on Civil Procedure. However, *[Company EU Headquarters]* shall be liable only for direct damages suffered by an Individual resulting from a violation of this Code. Where an Individual can demonstrate that it has suffered damage and establish facts which show it is plausible that the damage has occurred because of a violation of the Code, it will be for *[Company EU Headquarters]* to prove that the damages suffered by the Individual due to a violation of the Code are not attributable to the relevant Group Company.

Mutual assistance and redress	18.7	All Group Companies shall cooperate and assist each other to the extent reasonably possible to handle: (i) a request, complaint, or claim made by an Individual; or (ii) a lawful investigation or inquiry by a competent government authority. The Group Company who receives a request, complaint, or claim from an Individual is responsible for handling any communication with the Individual regarding his request, complaint, or claim except where circumstances dictate otherwise. The Group Company that is responsible for the Processing to which the request, complaint, or claim relates, shall bear all costs involved and reimburse *[Company EU Headquarters]*.

Article 19—*Sanctions for Non-compliance*

Non compliance	19.1	Non-compliance of Employees with this Code may result in disciplinary action up to and including termination of employment.

Article 20—*Conflicts between the Code and Applicable Local Law*

Conflict of law when transfer-ring Data	20.1	Where a legal requirement to transfer Personal Data conflicts with the laws of the Member States of the EEA or the law of Switzerland, the transfer requires the prior approval of the Chief Privacy Officer. The Chief Privacy Officer shall seek the advice of the Head of Legal. The Chief Privacy Officer may seek the advice of the Dutch Data Protection Authority or another competent government authority.
Conflict between Code and law	20.2	In all other cases, where there is a conflict between applicable local law and the Code, the relevant Responsible Executive shall consult with the Chief Privacy Officer to determine how to comply with this Code and resolve the conflict to the extent reasonably practicable given the legal requirements applicable to the relevant Group Company.
New conflicting legal requirements	20.3	The relevant Responsible Executive shall promptly inform the Chief Privacy Officer of any new legal requirement that may interfere with [Company]'s ability to comply with this Code.

Article 21—*Changes to the Code*

Prior approval	21.1	Any changes to this Code require the prior approval of the *[Head of Legal or Head of Compliance of [Company Holding]. [Company EU Headquarters]* shall notify the Dutch Data Protection Authority in case of significant changes to the Code on a yearly basis.
No employee consent	21.2	This Code may be changed without Individual's consent even though an amendment may relate to a benefit conferred on Individuals.
Entry into force	21.3	Any amendment shall enter into force after it has been approved and published on the *[Company website]*.
Relevant code	21.4	Any request, complaint, or claim of an Individual involving this Code shall be judged against this version of the Code as it is in force at the time the request, complaint, or claim is made.

Article 22—*Transition Periods*

General transition period	22.1	Except as indicated below, there shall be a two-year transition period for compliance with this Code. Accordingly, except as otherwise indicated, within two years of the Effective Date, all Processing of Personal Data shall be undertaken in compliance with the Code. During any transition period, [Company] shall strive to comply with the Code.
Transition period for new Group Companies	22.2	Any entity that becomes a Group Company after the Effective Date shall comply with the Code within two years of becoming a Group Company.
Transition period for Divested Entities	22.3	A Divested Entity may remain covered by this Code after its divestment for such period as may be required by [Company] to disentangle the Processing of Personal Data relating to such Divested Entity.
Transition period for IT systems	22.4	Where implementation of this Code requires updates or changes to information technology systems (including replacement of systems), the transition period shall be four years from the Effective Date or from the date an entity becomes a Group Company, or any longer period as is reasonably necessary to complete the update, change, or replacement process.
Transition period for existing agreements	22.5	Where there are existing agreements with Third Parties that are affected by this Code, the provisions of the agreements will prevail until the agreements are renewed in the normal course of business.
Transitional period for local-for-local systems	22.6	Processing of Personal Data that were collected in connection with activities of a Group Company located in a Non-Adequate Country shall be brought into compliance with this Code within five years of the Effective Date.

Contact details	[Company] Privacy Office c/o [Company EU Headquarters] *[insert contact details]*

ANNEX 1 *Definitions*

Archive	ARCHIVE shall mean a collection of Personal Data that are no longer necessary to achieve the purposes for which the Data originally were collected or that are no longer used for general business activities, but are used only for historical, scientific, or statistical purposes, dispute resolution, investigations, or general archiving purposes. An archive includes any data set that can no longer be accessed by any Employee other than the system administrator.
Article	ARTICLE shall mean an article in this Code.
Business Contact Data	BUSINESS CONTACT DATA shall mean any data typically found on a business card and used by the Individual in his contact with [Company].
Business Partner	BUSINESS PARTNER shall mean any Third Party, other than a Customer or Supplier, that has or had a business relationship or strategic alliance with [Company] (eg joint marketing partner, joint venture or joint development partner).
Business Purpose	BUSINESS PURPOSE shall mean a purpose for Processing Personal Data as specified in Article 2 or 3 or for Processing Sensitive Data as specified in Article 4 or 3.
Chief Privacy Officer	CHIEF PRIVACY OFFICER shall mean the officer as referred to in Article 13.1.
Code	CODE shall mean this Privacy Code for Customer, Supplier, and Business Partner Data.
[Company]	[Company] shall mean [COMPANY HOLDING] and its Group Companies.
[Company EU Headquarters]	[Company EU Headquarters] shall mean [Company EU Headquarters], having its registered seat in [], the Netherlands.
Company Holding	[COMPANY HOLDING] shall mean [Company Holding], having its registered seat in [].
Customer	CUSTOMER shall mean any Third Party that purchases, may purchase, or has purchased a [Company] product or service.
Divested Entity	DIVESTED ENTITY shall mean the divestment by [Company] of a Group Company or business by means of: (a) a sale of shares as a result whereof the Group Company so divested no longer qualifies as a Group Company; and/or (b) a demerger, sale of assets, or any other manner or form.
Effective Date	EFFECTIVE DATE shall mean the date on which this Code becomes effective as set forth in Article 1.6.

ANNEX 1 (*cont.*)

Employee	EMPLOYEE shall mean an employee, job applicant, or former employee of [Company]. This term does not include people working at [Company] as consultants or employees of Third Parties providing services to [Company].
Employee Data	EMPLOYEE DATA shall mean any information relating to an identified or identifiable Employee.
EEA	EEA or EUROPEAN ECONOMIC AREA shall mean all Member States of the European Union, plus Norway, Iceland, and Liechtenstein.
EU Data Protection Directive	EU DATA PROTECTION DIRECTIVE shall mean the Directive 95/46/EC of the European Parliament and of the Council on the protection of individuals with regard to the processing of and the free movement of such data.
Group Company	GROUP COMPANY shall mean [Company Holding] and any company or legal entity of which [Company Holding], directly or indirectly owns more than 50 per cent of the issued share capital, has 50 per cent or more of the voting power at general meetings of shareholders, has the power to appoint a majority of the directors, or otherwise directs the activities of such other legal entity; however, any such company or legal entity shall be deemed a Group Company only as long as a liaison and/or relationship exists, and that is covered by the [Company] Code of Conduct.
Head of Legal	HEAD OF LEGAL shall mean the Head of Legal of [Company Holding].
Head of Compliance	HEAD OF COMPLIANCE shall mean the Head of Compliance of [Company Holding].
Individual new line Non-Adequate Country	INDIVIDUAL shall mean any (employee of or any person working for) Customer, Supplier, or Business Partner. NON-ADEQUATE COUNTRY shall mean a country that under applicable local law (such as Article 25 EU Data Protection Directive) is deemed not to provide an 'adequate' level of data protection.
Original Purpose	ORIGINAL PURPOSE shall mean the purpose for which Personal Data was originally collected.
Overriding Interest	OVERRIDING INTEREST shall mean the pressing interests set forth in Article 12.1 based on which the obligations of [Company] or rights of Individuals set forth in Article 12.2 and 12.3 may, under specific circumstances, be overridden if this pressing interest outweighs the interest of the Individual.
Personal Data or Data Privacy Council	PERSONAL DATA shall mean any information relating to an identified or identifiable Individual. DATA PRIVACY COUNCIL shall mean the council referred to in Article 13.2.
Privacy Officer	PRIVACY OFFICER shall mean a privacy officer appointed by the Chief Privacy Officer pursuant to Article 13.3.
Processing	PROCESSING shall mean any operation that is performed on Personal Data, whether or not by automatic means, such as collection, recording, storage, organization, alteration, use, disclosure (including the granting of remote access), transmission, or deletion of Personal Data.
Responsible Executive	RESPONSIBLE EXECUTIVE shall mean the executive as referred to in Article 13.4.

Secondary Purpose	SECONDARY PURPOSE shall mean any purpose other than the Original Purpose for which Personal Data is further Processed.
Sensitive Data	SENSITIVE DATA shall mean Personal Data that reveal an Individual's racial or ethnic origin, political opinions or membership of political parties or similar organizations, religious or philosophical beliefs, membership of a professional or trade organization or union, physical or mental health including any opinion thereof, disabilities, genetic code, addictions, sex life, criminal offences, criminal records, proceedings with regard to criminal or unlawful behaviour, or social security numbers issued by the government.
Supplier	SUPPLIER shall mean any Third Party that provides goods or services to [Company] (eg an agent, consultant or vendor).
Staff	STAFF shall mean all Employees and other persons who Process Personal Data as part of their respective duties or responsibilities using [Company] information technology systems or working primarily from [Company]'s premises.
Third Party	THIRD PARTY shall mean any person, private organization, or government body outside [Company].
Third Party Controller	THIRD PARTY CONTROLLER shall mean a Third Party that Processes Personal Data and determines the purposes and means of the Processing.
Third Party Processor	THIRD PARTY PROCESSOR shall mean a Third Party that Processes Personal Data on behalf of [Company] that is not under the direct authority of [Company].

Interpretations
Interpretation of this code:

(i) Unless the context requires otherwise, all references to a particular Article or Annex are references to that Article or Annex in or to this document, as they may be amended from time to time.

(ii) Headings are included for convenience only and are not to be used in construing any provision of this Code.

(iii) If a word or phrase is defined, its other grammatical forms have a corresponding meaning.

(iv) The male form shall include the female form.

(v) The words 'include', 'includes', and 'including' and any words following them shall be construed without limitation to the generality of any preceding words or concepts and vice versa.

(vi) A reference to a document (including, without limitation, a reference to this Code) is to the document as amended, varied, supplemented, or replaced, except to the extent prohibited by this Code or that other document.

Index